MS	mean square
n	sample size, number of observations in a single group or condition
N	total number of observations
p	probability
q	Studentized range statistic
Q_1, Q_3	first and third quartiles
r	product moment correlation coefficient
R^2	proportion of variance accounted for by a model
s	sample standard deviation
s^2	sample variance
s_b	estimated standard error of regression coefficient
$s_{\overline{Y}}$	estimated standard error of the mean
$s_{\overline{Y}_1 - \overline{Y}_2}$	estimated standard error of the difference between two means
s_D	sample standard deviation of difference scores for matched pairs
$s_{\overline{D}}$	estimated standard error of the mean of difference scores for matched pairs
SP_{XY}	sum of products
SS	sum of squares
SS_e	sum of squares of residuals
t	Student's t statistic
w	half-width of confidence interval
$\overline{Y}$	sample mean
$\hat{Y}$	predicted or estimated value of Y
z	standard score

Introduction to

STATISTICS AND DATA ANALYSIS

for the Behavioral Sciences

Introduction to
STATISTICS
AND DATA ANALYSIS

for the Behavioral Sciences

Robert S. Lockhart
University of Toronto

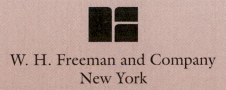

W. H. Freeman and Company
New York

For Joan and Carolyn

Acquisitions Editors:	Susan Finnemore Brennan
	Melissa Levine Wallerstein
Marketing Manager:	Kate Steinbacher
Project Editor:	Penelope Hull
Text Designer:	Cambraia Magalhaes
Text Illustrator:	Network Graphics
Cover Designer:	Cambraia Magalhaes
Cover Artist:	Janet Hamlin
Production Coordinator:	Julia de Rosa
Compositor:	Progressive Information Technologies
Manufacturer:	R R Donnelley & Sons Company

Library of Congress Cataloging-in-Publication Data

Lockhart, Robert S.
    Introduction to statistics and data analysis in the behavioral sciences / Robert S.
    Lockhart.
      p.   cm.
    Includes bibliographical references and index.
    ISBN 0-7167-2974-1
    1. Social sciences—Statistical methods.   I. Title.
HA29.L9354   1997   97-31126
519.5—dc21   CIP

Printed in the United States of America
First printing, 1997

W. H. Freeman and Company
41 Madison Avenue, New York, NY 10010
Houndmills, Basingstoke RG21 6XS, England

CONTENTS

PREFACE

TO THE INSTRUCTOR

This book differs from the standard introductory statistics text in several important ways. Although it covers the usual range of topics, it does so from a perspective that will increase students' understanding in a first course in statistical data analysis. The different methods of analysis are presented as minor variants of the single underlying strategy of fitting models, evaluating their goodness of fit, and deciding which model the data justify.

I have exploited this unifying theme by presenting the various methods as a gradually unfolding story, each step building on the previous one. A good sense of the story's plot line can be gained from the first section of Chapter 11. Intended as a retrospective summary for students, this section can serve instructors as a brief prospectus of the book's overall orientation. I urge instructors to read these few pages before anything else. The emphasis on unity also explains the book's preference for a smaller than usual number of chapters of greater than usual length.

One of the great virtues of the model-fitting approach is that, in a fairly obvious way, it embeds methods of data analysis in the broader scientific enterprise of discerning the underlying structure in noisy data. It is essential that students view data analysis from this perspective if they are to accept the importance of formal data analysis in the behavioral sciences.

One consequence of the model-fitting perspective is the view that confidence intervals and estimates of effect sizes offer information superior to that provided by the binary decision strategy of traditional hypothesis testing. Confidence intervals and effect size are given prominent roles in this text. Along the same lines, the text urges students to pay attention to the data—both before and after analysis—not just to the result of a statistical test.

I have taken seriously the concern that, compared to more traditional approaches, the present perspective may seem too abstract for an introductory level text. In fact, I think quite the opposite is true. A good case can be made that the model-fitting, model-evaluation approach is far more intuitive than the currently entrenched emphasis on statistical hypothesis testing. It makes it possible, for example, to introduce on a purely descriptive basis the concepts of models, residuals, accounting for variability as the reduction of residual variation, and measures of goodness of fit before tackling the more difficult concepts underlying statistical inference. Moreover, against this descriptive backdrop, the need for statistical inference becomes more compelling.

On the other hand, students need to understand the existing literature. No introductory text can ignore the reality that unless students have a good understanding of statistical hypothesis testing, much of the psychological literature becomes incomprehensible. This legacy turns out not to be a serious problem. Despite its orientation, students reading this text will end up covering the traditional methods. They will know about t-tests, analysis of variance, correlation and regression. They will learn about p-values and significance levels. The difference is that these concepts will have been presented in the broader context of model comparison. Interpreted as the evaluation of the residuals of a particular model, statistical significance is not rejected as a concept, but recast in terms of a choice between models.

I have adopted notation and terminology commonly used in many contemporary texts, although it occasionally differs from that found in some of the more traditional texts. For example, the terms *predictor* or *explanatory* variable are used in preference to *independent* variable, and *response* variable is used in preference to *dependent* variable. In line with the emphasis of the underlying unity of methods, Y rather than X is used throughout to denote the response variable and X is used for the predictor variable, even when the values of X are the labels of a categorical variable. In all cases, the model predicts values of Y as a function of values of X. Regression, analysis of variance, and even the simplest of *t*-tests are variations on a single principle.

Although the text is written so that it can be used without the assistance of computer analysis, the use of computers is encouraged in several ways. First, the model-fitting, model-evaluation orientation of the text is well-suited to the terminology used in packages such as SPSS or SAS. Indeed, this orientation seems essential to a full understanding of what these programs are doing. Moreover, it is the orientation that provides the foundation on which more advanced methods of analysis can be built. Second, students are not asked to complete laborious computations, and no computational formulas are given. Third, all the major data sets used in examples and exercises within the text are available in the form of an ASCII file. Finally, the accompanying *Student Guide and Computer Workbook* provides a detailed introduction to SAS and SPSS using data sets from the text as examples. The *Workbook* adds many examples and data sets of its own.

Not all computation by hand can or should be avoided. A strong emphasis throughout the book is the need to examine the raw data, and routine computer analysis without examination of the raw data is explicitly discouraged. In addition, step-by-step calculations with simple data are used in some exercises to illustrate basic concepts such as residuals and their sum of squares. However, in most exercises students are provided with the results of the intermediate computations needed to complete the analysis. Students with access to computer software will be able to use the results reported in the text to check their computer output.

TO THE STUDENT

The goal of this text is to introduce some of the basic methods used by behavioral scientists to extract from data answers to such questions as "Is the therapy effective?" or "Can one-day-old infants recognize their mother?" Answers are found by gathering data and subjecting them to appropriate analysis. Raw data do not speak for themselves; they need to be analyzed.

Texts such as this are often described as covering "introductory statistics," and, although this label is not inaccurate, it places the emphasis at the wrong point. For behavioral scientists the primary goal is to understand the data. Statistics is a tool that aids greatly in achieving this goal, but it is not an end in itself. The purpose of this text is not simply to teach statistics but to explain how statistical methods can serve the larger purpose of advancing scientific knowledge.

Whatever it is called, many students find a first course in data analysis difficult. There are many reasons for this common experience, but one that often remains unmentioned is the simple fact that some of the material *is* challenging. This point is not intended to raise your anxiety level. On the contrary, it is intended to reassure you that if you find some concepts difficult to grasp immediately, you are in good company. I have talked to many students who become frustrated when they cannot understand a concept on a first reading and mistakenly attribute the difficulty to their own inadequacies—their lack of aptitude, their poor math background, and so forth. Accept the fact that you may need to read some sections more than once.

SUPPLEMENTARY MATERIAL

1. Data Sets. Text files in ASCII format are available for all the designated data sets in the text as well as those used in the *Study Guide and Computer Workbook*. These data sets can be downloaded at the Lockhart website, located at www.whfreeman.com.

2. *Study Guide and Computer Workbook* by Robert S. Lockhart and Philip Groff. This supplement is in two parts. Part 1 provides chapter reviews, short-answer questions, additional problems, and a large number of more substantial exercises involving data sets of the kind that arise in real research. Part 2 provides an introduction to the use of SAS and SPSS statistical packages using data sets from the text as examples.

3. *Instructor's Manual* by Robert S. Lockhart. This supplement contains a general discussion of the underlying rationale for the present text and chapter by chapter suggestions.

4. *Test Bank.* This supplement contains 75 to 100 items per chapter.

ACKNOWLEDGMENTS

This book owes its existence to many people, especially the many students at the University of Kansas and Washington College who used a draft version of the text and provided valuable comments and recommendations for improvements. Students in my own course at the University of Toronto have worked through an even earlier version and they, along with my teaching assistants, have been an immense help. I am indebted to the Psychology Department at the University of California, Santa Barbara, where much of the book was written during a sabbatical leave.

I owe a great deal to the following reviewers, whose careful reading and constructive criticisms have done much to improve the final product: Frank M. Bagrash, California State University, Fullerton; Stephen L. Bieber, University of Wyoming; Richard W. Bowen, Loyola University, Chicago; Susan E. Dutch, Westfield State College; R. John Huber, Meredith College; James F. Juola, The University of Kansas; Roy S. Lilly, Kent State University; Geoffrey R. Loftus, University of Washington; John B. Pittenger, University of Arkansas at Little Rock; Joseph H. Porter, Virginia Commonwealth University; Catherine H. Renner, West Chester University; George J. Spilich, Washington College; Arnold D. Well, University of Massachusetts at Amherst. I also thank Norma D'Agostino at the University of Toronto who provided invaluable help with the exercises. My wife, Joan Grusec, read through each chapter as it emerged, and her detailed comments saved subsequent reviewers from battling many of the rough edges that plague first drafts. The task of bringing this book to print proceeded smoothly, thanks to the cheerful professionalism of the editorial staff at W. H. Freeman and Company. I am especially indebted to Susan Finnemore Brennan, Melissa Wallerstein, Penny Hull, and Jodi Simpson.

The orientation of this book reveals a general attitude towards statistics and data analysis acquired over many years in the close company of some the great practitioners of experimental behavioral science. I am especially indebted to Fergus Craik, Ben Murdock, Ian Spence, and Endel Tulving. If this book conveys anything of their commitment to the wise and honest use of data, it will have achieved its major purpose.

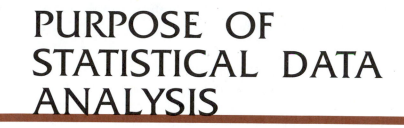

1 PURPOSE OF STATISTICAL DATA ANALYSIS

The first question many students ask when confronted with a course in statistical methods is "Why?" "Why do I need this course, and why do the behavioral sciences seem so preoccupied with statistics?" These questions are entirely justified. If you are going to devote the time and effort necessary to master the course, it is only fair that you should begin with a feeling that it might all be worthwhile. Contrary to a commonly held suspicion, the course is not a form of academic hazing. The best way to answer these questions is to describe the role of statistical data analysis in scientific discovery.

A major goal of science is to understand the forces that produce change and create variation. Planets move in their orbits, volcanoes erupt, new species arise as others go extinct. Atoms are split, genes spliced, and bacteria killed. In each case we observe or create change. The growth of scientific knowledge and power is very much the story of science's increasing capacity to understand variation and bring about change.

For the behavioral scientist, change and variation can be seen in the enormous diversity that marks all aspects of behavior. What controls variation in our moods? Why do some students become highly anxious during an exam while others remain relaxed? What causes some people to be in a state of chronic depression while others remain cheerful despite adversity? Why do some students have better memories than others? How can you lower test anxiety, relieve depression, or improve your memory?

All these questions are about differences and change; in brief, they are about variation. Statistical data analysis plays a decisive role in the quest to understand variation, and we will see that "accounting for variation" is a function that statistical data analysis performs in a literal sense. Data analysis is important because data cannot answer questions of any kind until they are analyzed. Contrary to a common claim, data do not "speak for themselves." They speak only through an interpreter, and that interpreter is data analysis. Seen in these terms, the mark of sound data analysis is its ability to clarify rather than distort the data's underlying message. For the behavioral scientist, statistical data analysis is a means to an end, not an end in itself.

Various forms of data analysis are based largely on a set of procedures that can be described loosely as "statistical," hence the use of the term statistics in the book's title. The term is doubly relevant because the terms *statistical* or *statistics* have a double

A major goal of science is to account for variation.

Data are the recorded set of observations from a scientific investigation. Each observation is a datum.

The term statistics has two meanings: as numbers and as an area of study and its methods.

meaning. On the one hand, the methods to be described make use of numbers—averages and proportions, for example—that provide summary descriptions of data, and such numbers are commonly referred to as *statistics*. This meaning of the term is conveyed in expressions such as "vital statistics," "crime statistics," or "unemployment statistics." A second, historically more recent meaning of the term refers to the branch of applied mathematics that has been largely responsible for the development of the various methods to be described in the following chapters. When you encounter a "course in statistics" or a university "department of statistics," the term *statistics* is being used in this second sense. A primary purpose of a course in statistics is not studying various numerical facts, such as unemployment rates, birth rates, and so forth, but studying the methods underlying the gathering of such statistics and how they are to be interpreted.

Chapter 1 introduces some elementary concepts that underlie the methods of data analysis developed in subsequent chapters. Section 1.1 explains the goal of data analysis as the description of the regularities in data. Such regularities are expressed in formal statements called models, and Section 1.1 explains the role of models in science's twin tasks of explaining and predicting. Sections 1.2 and 1.3 describe the major factors that determine the appropriate form of a model: the nature of the variables involved and features of the experimental design. It is these factors that determine the appropriate type of data analysis.

1.1 Overall Goal of Statistical Data Analysis

Rather than engaging in an abstract account of the purpose of statistical data analysis, consider a concrete example. The example is a simple one, but its principles are of great importance. The broad overview offered in this section is important because, in working through the material in this book, of the danger that the overall goal of data analysis will be lost in the details of the various procedures and their calculations. Think of this section as a quick sweep over the conceptual landscape. The remainder of the book adds rigor and detail to these basic concepts.

1.1.1 Prediction, Explanation, and "Accounting for the Data"

Differences in Test Anxiety

Suppose an investigator asks 14 students to rate their level of anxiety during an exam. They do so, using a seven-point scale ranging from 1 (totally relaxed) to 7 (near panic). The ratings the 14 students give are

Student	1	2	3	4	5	6	7	8	9	10	11	12	13	14
Rating	6	2	5	3	6	4	3	5	2	5	4	3	4	4

Note first that these ratings show considerable variation, the very thing science seeks to explain. The first and fifth students were highly anxious (they gave ratings of 6), whereas the second and ninth students were quite relaxed (ratings of 2). Other students gave ratings between these two extremes. The goal of the behavioral scientist is to explain this variability.

What would it mean to "explain" or "account for" the variability of these 14 ratings? For the scientist, explanation is closely tied to prediction. Although in science the term *explanation* encompasses a broader meaning, in the context of data analysis we equate explanation with ability to predict. If "accounted for" and "explained" are equated with predictability, then the variability among the 14 ratings would be fully explained or accounted for if we had a rule that would have enabled us to predict the exact value of each rating. The rule would tell us that student 1 would give a rating of 6, student 2 a rating of 2, and so on. Our next step is therefore to look more closely at the concept of prediction and how it is used in the context of data analysis.

But first, let's examine the nature of explanation and prediction and the term *accounting for variability* by making a short side trip. After we have described these concepts with simpler examples, we will return to the test anxiety data.

Accounting for Variability in Simple Data Sets

Examine the following set of 12 numbers, representing happiness ratings, in the row labeled **Y**. Each number appears under a label A or B in the row labeled **X**.

X	A	B	A	B	B	A	A	A	B	B	A	B
Y	5	10	5	10	10	5	5	5	10	10	5	10

For the sake of this example, we will refer to the numbers in the Y row as "the data," although these particular numbers were obviously manufactured for the sake of a clear example.

Note first that the data display variability: A number is either 5 or 10. What is the rule underlying the variability of these data? This is not a trick question, and the answer you have probably thought of is the one intended: "When the value in the X row is A, the number is 5; when the value in the X row is B, the number is 10." More briefly, A = 5, B = 10. This rule "explains" or "accounts for" the data in the following sense: *We can use the rule to "reproduce" the data, creating a perfect match between the original data and the numbers generated by the rule.*

In statistical data analysis, the rule that is used to account for the data is referred to as a *model.* We will adopt this terminology from now on. The model

$$A = 5$$

$$B = 10$$

explains or predicts when a number will be 5 and when it will be 10. If the numbers were all erased, the model alone would enable you to reproduce them. You would have no trouble filling in the empty row in the following table. In this sense, the model offers a perfect explanation of why the numbers change the way they do. It explains their variability.

X	A	B	A	B	B	A	A	A	B	B	A	B
Y												

Now consider another example, in which there are ten pairs of numbers, each pair consisting of an X-value and a Y-value. The first pair is (X = 6, Y = 12), the second pair is (X = 8, Y = 16), and so on.

X	6	8	3	1	9	4	6	5	4	2
Y	12	16	6	2	18	8	12	10	8	4

In the context of data analysis, explanation is equated with prediction.

In statistical data analysis, the rule that is used to account for the data is referred to as a model.

The correctness of a model is demonstrated by its capacity to reproduce the data.

The task is to predict the Y-values. If we did not know the X-values and had no other basis for predicting, such predictions would be very inaccurate, because the Y-values are highly variable. However, if the X-value is known, then a perfect prediction can be made. To obtain these predictions, we would use a model that states that the Y-value is twice the X-value. That is,

$$Y = 2X$$

It is important to understand the two principles involved in these examples.

■ The data themselves are used as the basis for formulating a model.

■ The appropriateness or correctness of the model lies in its capacity to reproduce or account for the variability in the data. The numbers generated by the model match the data as originally given.

Imagine next a second set of happiness ratings, this time with a slight complication.

X	A	B	A	B	B	A	A	A	B	B	A	B
Y	5.1	9.8	5.0	10.0	10.1	5.2	4.9	5.0	10.1	9.9	4.9	10.0

The previous model, A = 5, B = 10, no longer does a perfect job of reproducing the data. Many of the predictions are inaccurate—off by 0.1 or 0.2. The predicted values are nevertheless close to the original values.

Although imperfect, the match between the data and the model-generated values is close, and a plausible explanation is that the original model is basically correct but the data are a little "noisy." Later in this chapter, we will examine this intuitive explanation in greater detail.

Now, let's consider another data set in which the predictions made by the model A = 5, B = 10 are even more inaccurate. The prediction errors are given in the bottom row and were obtained by subtracting the predicted value from the datum value. Thus the negative sign for some of the errors indicates that the datum value was lower than the predicted value.

In statistical data analysis, the errors that a model makes in predicting the data are commonly referred to as *residuals*. A residual is the discrepancy between the datum value and the model's prediction. The residual for the first X is 0.4: The model predicts 5, but the actual observation was 5.4. The residual is that part of the observation "left over" after the model has made its prediction. Henceforth we will use the term *residual* rather than the term *error*.

> A residual is the discrepancy between the data value and the model's prediction.

X	A	B	A	B	B	A	A	A	B	B	A	B
Y	5.4	9.1	5.9	10.7	10.2	4.2	4.8	5.5	9.5	9.9	4.1	10.6
Prediction	5	10	5	10	10	5	5	5	10	10	5	10
Residual	.4	−.9	.9	.7	.2	−.8	−.2	.5	−.5	−.1	−.9	.6

One way of describing the inaccuracy of the model's predictions is to say that part of the original variability remains unpredicted by the model, or that some variability remains *unexplained*, or that it is *unaccounted for*. For example, the model does not explain why the first datum is 5.4 and not 5.

Not surprisingly, in the world of real data, such imperfect prediction, or unaccounted-for variability, is the usual state of affairs. With real data, the quest therefore changes from identifying the perfect model to finding the best model and evaluating just how good it is. One of the future tasks will be to define what is meant by "best" and to describe how good this best model really is. But so far we have established three characteristics of models and data:

- With real data, models make imperfect predictions.

- The discrepancy between a datum and the model's prediction is known as a residual.

- Residuals constitute unaccounted for or unexplained variability.

Residuals constitute unaccounted-for variability.

Accounting for Differences in Test Anxiety

Earlier we looked at the following anxiety ratings.

Student	1	2	3	4	5	6	7	8	9	10	11	12	13	14
Rating	6	2	5	3	6	4	3	5	2	5	4	3	4	4

An inspection of these ratings suggests no obvious model. Suppose, however, you were nevertheless challenged to devise a model that would predict the 14 values "as accurately as possible." To make this challenge more concrete, imagine the following task. Each of the 14 test anxiety ratings is written on a separate card, the 14 cards are shuffled, and one card is selected but hidden from your view. Your task is to predict the particular score on that card as accurately as possible. Having made your prediction and compared it with the number on the card, the card is returned to the deck, the deck reshuffled, and the process repeated.

What model should you adopt to minimize your residuals (prediction errors)? In the absence of a perfect model, your individual predictions will often be wrong, so some residuals are inevitable. These residuals reflect the fact that your model does not explain all the variability among the 14 ratings.

Although there is no perfect model, some prediction rules will be better than others. Predicting 3 or 4 is preferable to predicting 6, and predicting 7 or 10 would show very poor judgment indeed. However, several questions remain to be answered. Is there a single best prediction rule—a model that is guaranteed to minimize the residuals? What precisely do we mean by "minimizing the residuals"?

Such a model does exist and is quite simple: The best prediction is the average rating, and this prediction should be made on *every* trial. The average of the 14 ratings (the sum of the ratings divided by 14) is 4.0, so you should predict 4 on every trial. We will discuss the rationale for this model at greater length in Chapter 3. In the meantime, try playing the simple version of the game described in GameBox 1.1: Cut Your Losses.

Predicting an anxiety rating of 4 on every trial may be the best model, but it does a poor job of prediction. In this case, "best" is not very good. How can we improve our prediction and reduce our losses? The only way of improving these predictions is to use additional information. This need for additional information brings us to a more general aspect of scientific method.

Throughout science, the general strategy for improving prediction—for accounting for more of the data's variability—is to find factors that are related to the

Although there may be no perfect prediction rule, some rules will be better than others.

GameBox 1.1

Cut Your Losses

This is the first of several games that appear at various points in the book. These games are unlikely to compete with commercial board games for their entertainment value, but you may find that they make a point more effectively than several pages of verbal exposition. If nothing else, they provide an instructive diversion.

Many games such as Monopoly or the casino game craps involve rolling two dice and adding up the spots showing on the two dice. Cut Your Losses is a game in this tradition. It requires two or more players and two dice. Each player begins with 100 points and the goal is to avoid losing all 100 points. Once you have lost your 100 points, you are out of the game. The winner is the player who stays in the game the longest.

Each player takes a turn in rolling the dice. Before each roll, the player rolling the dice predicts the outcome. With two dice, the outcome can be any number from 2 (two ones) to 12 (two sixes). After the roll, the difference between the player's prediction and the actual outcome is calculated and then squared. The player subtracts this number of points from whatever points they currently possess. For example, suppose a player predicts eight and then rolls a two and a four for an outcome of six. Such an outcome would cost the player four (two squared) points.

The goal for each roll is therefore to minimize your loss by making the prediction as close to the outcome as possible. The player who predict most accurately will lose fewer points and stay in the game the longest.

What is the best strategy in this game? The answer is simple. The best strategy is to predict 7 for *every* roll. This claim may seem counterintuitive to some, but it will be justified in Chapter 3. In the meantime, play the game and test the "predict 7" strategy for yourself. You may not win on every occasion, but you will win more often than will an opponent who adopts a different strategy.

In science, the general strategy for improving predictions is to identify an additional related factor.

phenomenon under study. To account for why some species go extinct and others do not, an investigator might look at factors such as habitat loss, pollution, the adaptability of the species, and so forth. The investigator might also ask whether it is possible to reverse the process. Can change be created—species saved from extinction—by reducing pollution or preserving habitat?

To account for individual differences in test anxiety, a researcher might investigate possible relevant factors such as personality characteristics, study habits, and so forth. The investigator might also ask whether change can be created, say, through counseling or some form of therapy. We will use this possibility to continue the numerical example.

Imagine that we are given more information about the participants who contributed the 14 anxiety measures. We learn that seven of these participants have undergone a form of counseling therapy known as systematic desensitization, whereas the other seven participants have not. Ratings from those who had the therapy are designated T in the row labeled X; ratings from those who did not are designated C (control).

Student	1	2	3	4	5	6	7	8	9	10	11	12	13	14
Therapy (X)	C	T	C	T	C	C	T	C	T	C	T	T	C	T
Rating (Y)	6	2	5	3	6	4	3	5	2	5	4	3	4	4

We now repeat the previous prediction task with an important difference. Before making our prediction, we are given the value in the X row—we are told whether the selected rating belongs to a T (therapy) participant ($X = T$) or to a C (control, non-therapy) participant ($X = C$). Should this additional information lead us to change our prediction model and, if so, how? The answer to this question may not be obvious. However, if the ratings are rearranged and grouped according to their T and C labels, then the answer becomes more apparent.

Student	2	4	7	9	11	12	14	1	3	5	6	8	10	13
Therapy (X)	T	T	T	T	T	T	T	C	C	C	C	C	C	C
Rating (Y)	2	3	3	2	4	3	4	6	5	6	4	5	5	4

Inspecting the data in this form suggests that, if we know that the score comes from a T participant ($X = T$), then the appropriate prediction would be a relatively small number, such as 3. On the other hand, if the score is from a C participant ($X = C$), then the appropriate prediction would seem to be a larger number, such as 5. Suppose we apply the model

$$\text{predict } 3 \text{ if } X = T$$

$$\text{predict } 5 \text{ if } X = C$$

The values 3 and 5 were obtained by using the principle of predicting the average rating. The average rating for the seven T participants is 3; for the seven C participants, it is 5. Notice that now the worst outcome is to be off by 1. Using the information about whether the rating came from a T or C participant makes our predictions more accurate than they were when this information was unavailable.

Another way of describing this increased accuracy is to say that the second model accounts for more of the variability of the ratings than does the original model. Much (but not all) of the original variability of the anxiety ratings is accounted for by the fact that some of the participants have undergone therapy and some have not. Notice that the variability among the ratings of the T participants is smaller than the variability displayed by the mixture of all 14 ratings. Without knowledge of whether the participant was T or C, the possible value of the rating ranged from 2 to 6. The variability of the ratings for the C participants is similarly smaller than that of all the students. Again, this reduced variability underlies the increased accuracy in predicting the ratings for C participants.

This example illustrates four general principles of data analysis.

■ Data analysis seeks a model that will account for the variability in the data.

■ With real data, the model's predictions will be imperfect, some of the variability will remain unpredictable or unaccounted for. Unaccounted-for variability is the enemy of accurate prediction.

Unaccounted-for variability is the enemy of accurate prediction.

■ Although all models may be imperfect, some models will be better than others. One model is better than another if its predictions are more accurate—if it accounts for more of the variability.

■ Science improves its models by discovering relevant factors that, when taken into account, enable the model to account for more of the variability.

These general points form the underlying structure of the remainder of this book, and there is a great deal more to be said about each of them. Basic concepts such as variability and accuracy of predictions will need more formal definitions, and a number of technical terms will have to be introduced. Before proceeding, however, one aspect of our various examples needs comment.

The General and the Particular

It may have occurred to you that finding a model that will predict the data is a pointless exercise and that the term *predict* is being used in an odd way. After all, the data already exist, and we know their values. So what is the purpose, or even the meaning, of trying to *predict* them?

The answer to this question lies in an important characteristic of science. Science is concerned with the general rather than the particular. A student, once having undergone counseling, may no longer be troubled by test anxiety, a fact that may be of great interest to the counselor as well as to the student. However, this anecdote is of scientific interest only insofar as it offers a clue to what might be true generally. Is there something to be learned from this particular student's experience about the counseling procedure *in general*?

This broader interest of the scientist is both theoretical and practical. On the theoretical side, the scientist seeks general laws, not merely descriptive anecdotes. In this sense, each number in the data set—each anxiety rating, for example—can be thought of as an anecdote. The behavioral scientist would like to formulate a general law that applies, not only to the students who contributed the data, but also to students in general.

The same principle applies throughout science. A chemist measuring the boiling point of a liquid is not interested in a particular thermometer reading as an end in itself, but only as a means of finding the boiling point of the liquid in general. A cancer drug that proves effective for one patient may be of little scientific interest until it can be established that this anecdotal evidence is a result that is true more generally.

The concern science has with the general rather than the particular explains the real purpose of a model constructed and evaluated on a specific set of data. *The purpose in formulating a model is not merely to account for the data at hand, but to use these data as a means to formulate a model that is true more generally.* The assumption is that, if a model works well for the existing data, then it can be used to predict outcomes that have not yet been observed. This assumption is not one that can be taken for granted, and one of our major concerns will be to establish criteria for such generalizations.

In the test anxiety example, the data indicate that those students who had undergone counseling had lower anxiety ratings than those who did not, and this difference was reflected in the revised model. Both the original and the revised models were formulated and justified in terms of the 14 ratings actually obtained. The matter of interest to the scientist, however, is whether the revised model will apply to other students. Is it true *generally* that this form of counseling reduces test anxiety, or is the model true only for the particular 14 students actually observed? You might think of the results from these students as 14 separate anecdotes. One of the questions to be addressed throughout the book is essentially "How many anecdotes does it take to establish a general truth?"

In statistical data analysis, the distinction between the particular and the general is often made in terms of a distinction between the sample and the population. An experiment produces *sample* data: the ratings of 14 individuals on a particular occasion. However, the investigator is interested in what might be true more generally—true for a much larger set of individuals and occasions. This larger set is referred to as the *population*. The actual data are then referred to as a sample from this population. In these terms, the goal of data analysis is to use the sample data to discover what is true in the population. We will have more to say about this distinction in later chapters.

A sample is a subset of a larger population.

1.1.2 Signal and Noise: A Useful Metaphor

In Section 1.1.1, we considered the following happiness rating data.

X	A	B	A	B	B	A	A	A	B	B	A	B
Y	5.1	9.8	5.0	10.0	10.1	5.2	4.9	5.0	10.1	9.9	4.9	10.0

The model A = 5, B = 10 provides good but imperfect predictions of these data; it accounts for most but not all of the variability in the data. The data were described as a "noisy" version of the previous example in which the same model gave perfect predictions.

This metaphorical use of the term *noise* contains an important insight. The idea behind this metaphor is that observational data are made up of two basic components. On the one hand, the data contain regularities described by the underlying model, but on the other hand, we rarely see the model manifested in pure form. Instead, the action of the model is masked by influences that produce discrepancies between what the model dictates and what is actually observed. The model may predict that when X = A then Y = 5, but what we observe is Y = 5.1. If we think of the model as a signal and the disturbing influences as noise, then data can be thought of as signal embedded in noise, and the task of data analysis as distinguishing the signal from its noisy background.

The auditory system performs a type of data analysis that literally separates signal from noise. Suppose you are listening to an audiotape of 10 seconds of a flute playing a single note. Along with this tone is steady background sound: *ssshhhh* . . .—the sound of a noisy tape. The auditory system has no difficulty in separating the two sounds, and the compelling perception is that of a pure tone against a noisy background. Indeed, the perception is so compelling that it is tempting to think that two physically separate sound waves are reaching your eardrum, one from the flute, the other from the tape noise. In fact, there is only one sound wave. The remarkable accomplishment of the auditory system is to take this sound wave and analyze its two separate components: the pure tone from the flute and the background noise.

The task facing statistical data analysis is essentially the same as that accomplished by the auditory system. The "signals" in data often show themselves as regularities. Noise, on the other hand, reveals itself in irregular, haphazard features of the data. If the regularity is strong relative to the noise, then a simple graph may be sufficient to demonstrate the distinction. Although data do not always give up their secrets so

The regularity in data is the signal. The haphazard features are the noise.

easily, the following graphical examples offer a compelling demonstration of the signal and noise metaphor in the context of an important scientific discovery.

Dark Adaptation

We have all had the experience of walking from bright light into a darkened room and noticing that after a brief period of time our eyes grow accustomed to the dark. We are soon able to see around us, even in very dim light. What mechanisms in the visual system underlie this adaptation?

Consider this simplified version of an experimental procedure to measure the eye's sensitivity to light. A light is flashed on and off and observers must state whether or not they have seen the flash. By varying the intensity of the light, the experimenters can measure the minimum light intensity that the observer can detect. Such a measurement is known as the *absolute threshold*. In the present experiment, the absolute threshold is measured after different periods of dark adaptation. At the start of the experiment (0 minutes in the dark), the observer is accustomed to ordinary daylight. The observer is then placed in a totally dark room and the absolute threshold measured at 1-minute intervals over a 30-minute period. The graph in Figure 1.1a shows the threshold after various adaptation times from 0 to 30 minutes.

In Figure 1.1a, the absolute threshold (light intensity) is plotted on the vertical axis, or *y*-axis, and the duration of dark adaptation on the *x*-axis. The height of each dot (data point) on the graph corresponds to the absolute thresholds as measured at each of the time intervals. When we look at all the data points in Figure 1.1a, it is not difficult to see them as part of a smooth curve—in fact, *two* smooth curves, as shown in Figure 1.1b. These are the well-known dark adaptation curves found in textbooks

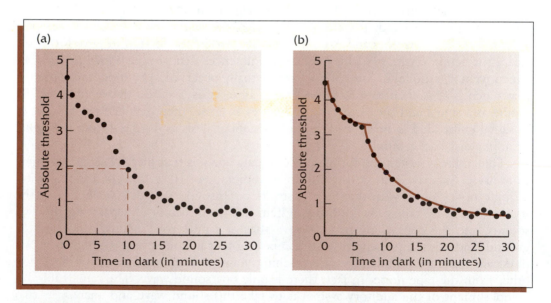

Figure 1.1

(a) Hypothetical dark adaptation data showing how the eye's sensitivity to light increases as the length of time in the dark increases. Each dot represents the minimum amount of light that the eye needs to detect a brief flash of light at a specific time. For example, after 10 minutes in the dark, the observer can detect a flash that is just under 2 intensity units. (b) Smooth curves drawn through the dark adaptation data. These curves can be thought of as the signal in the data and the scatter of the points about the curve as the noise.

of visual perception. The curves can be thought of as the signal part of these data, capturing their underlying regularity. The curves constitute the rule or model that would be used to predict the absolute threshold after some specified time in the dark.

Most of the dots do not lie exactly on the curve, discrepancies indicating that the model is an imperfect predictor. These prediction errors, or residuals, illustrate what is often metaphorically described as noise; the errors appear to be scattered about the smooth curve in a haphazard fashion. In this example, there is so little noise that the smooth curves—the general form of the model—are apparent from a simple visual inspection of the graph.

The basic idea is that the data can be interpreted as a slightly noisy version of the underlying regularity described by the smooth curves. In terms of the metaphor, the original data are a blend of signal and noise, and data analysis (which, in this example, consisted simply of drawing the smooth curves by eye) separates the blend into its component parts. In the direct language of data analysis, the data have been broken down into the predictions of a model (the smooth curves) and residuals. That is,

$$\text{data} = \text{model prediction (curves)} + \text{residual}$$

Mental Rotation

In 1971, Roger Shepard and Jacqueline Metzler reported results from an experiment in which participants were shown pairs of patterns representing three-dimensional objects (Figure 1.2). Participants in the experiment were asked to decide whether or not two figures represented different orientations of the same three-dimensional object. In Figure 1.2, the two figures labeled **A** represent the same object, because one picture can be rotated so that it becomes the same as the other. The two figures labeled **B** represent different objects, because there is no rotation that allows one picture to become the same as the other.

Shepard and Metzler had participants view pairs of figures such as these. For those pairs in which one figure was a rotated version of the other, the angle of rotation was varied from 0 degrees (both figures in the same orientation) to 180 degrees of rotation. Shepard and Metzler recorded the time each participant took to make a "same" judgment for each pair. Figure 1.3 is a graph of these times for the various angles of rotation. The graph gives the strong impression that the observation points lie on a straight line. By drawing the straight line, the investigators separated the original data into model (the line) plus residual. As in the dark adaptation example,

$$\text{data} = \text{model prediction (line)} + \text{residual}$$

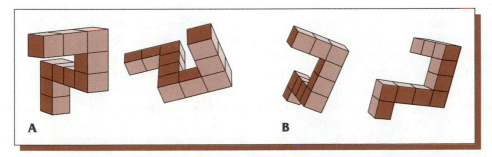

Figure 1.2
Figures used in the Shepard and Metzler (1971) experiment. The two figures labeled **A** represent the same object. The two figures labeled **B** represent different objects. (Adapted with permission from R. N. Shepherd and J. Metzler, Mental rotation of three-dimensional objects, *Science, 171* (February 19), 701–703. Copyright 1971 American Association for the Advancement of Science.)

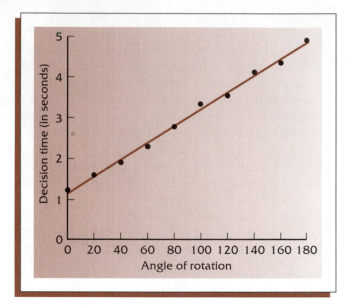

Figure 1.3

Plot of the time taken to judge that one figure is a rotated version of the other as a function of angle of rotation. (Adapted with permission from R. N. Shepherd and J. Metzler, Mental rotation of three-dimensional objects, *Science, 171* (February 19), 701–703. Copyright 1971 American Association for the Advancement of Science.)

Sex and Social Interaction

In the two previous examples, the regularities indicating the signal take the form of a smooth curve or a straight line. However, in the behavioral sciences, the signal often takes a simpler form. Rather than a curve or a straight line, regularities might consist of a simple difference that indicates the impact of some systematic influence. The following example is from child psychology and is based on results from an experimental study of social interaction among toddlers by Jacklin and Maccoby (1978).

Are infants as young as 33 months sensitive to the sex of a same-age playmate? You may think that infants under the age of 3 are too young to respond to sex differences, but are they? To answer this question, Jacklin and Maccoby placed pairs of 33-month old infants in a playroom. Some pairs were the same sex, some pairs were different. They observed the level of interaction between the members of each pair.

Hypothetical (and idealized) data from such an experiment are listed in Table 1.1 and plotted in Figure 1.4. The plot shows the amount of social interaction for each pair of the 20 pairs of toddlers. In this case, the underlying regularity appears to consist of two horizontal lines, one for same-sex pairs and one for different-sex pairs.

The horizontal lines drawn through the two sets of points represent a simple model consisting of a constant for each condition. For the same-sex pairs, this constant (the height of the line) is around 30 interactions; for the different-sex pairs, it is around 20. In other words, the model suggested by the graph is "predict 30 interactions for same-sex pairs, predict 20 interactions for different-sex pairs." Once again, this model, and the values of 30 and 20, are the result of an informal analysis. Formal methods will come later. Notice that this model has the same general form as the one used for the test anxiety example.

As in previous examples, the data values themselves are discrepant from the model's predictions: The data are a noisy version of the underlying regularity described by the model. In this case, the regularity is a constant—a fixed value, although a different value for each condition:

data = model prediction (condition constant) + residual

Table 1.1 Number of social interactions (Y) between pairs of infants

Pair	X	Y
1	S	31
2	S	28
3	S	32
4	D	20
5	S	31
6	S	29
7	D	23
8	S	27
9	D	19
10	D	20
11	D	18
12	D	21
13	D	20
14	S	33
15	S	29
16	S	30
17	S	30
18	D	17
19	D	19
20	D	21

Twenty pairs were observed. Ten of these pairs were of the same sex (X = S), ten were of different sexes (X = D).

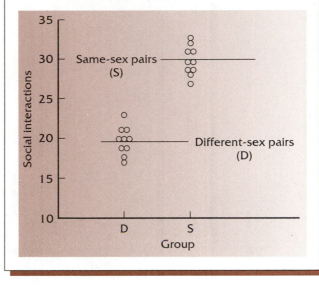

Figure 1.4
Plot of the data in Table 1.1. Each dot represents the number of social interactions for a pair of infants.

Signal-to-Noise Ratio

Another aspect of the signal and noise metaphor is helpful in understanding the challenge facing data analysis. Imagine that you are driving out of a large town with your car radio turned to a local talk show. At the start, the voices are clear, but as you get farther away, they become increasingly faint and the background noise begins to dominate, until finally there is nothing but noise. An engineer would describe this process as a steady reduction in the signal-to-noise ratio.

The stronger the background noise relative to the signal, the more difficult it is to understand the signal or even to be sure that there is any signal at all. Recall the example at the beginning of this section. If the sound of the flute is very faint and the tape noise very loud, the flute may be inaudible.

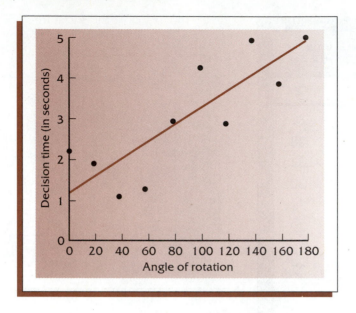

Figure 1.5
Much noisier version of data from a repetition of the experiment plotted in Figure 1.3.

A similar relationship holds in statistical data analysis. The noisier the data, the more difficult it is to discern the signal—to discover the appropriate underlying model—and the less accurate the predictions will be. As an example, suppose we have data from a less carefully conducted repetition of the mental rotation experiment. These new data, plotted in Figure 1.5, are much noisier. The points are more widely scattered, and it is no longer obvious that the regularity underlying these data points is a straight line. Moreover, even if the straight-line model is accepted, the model's predictions will be much less accurate than those in the original example (Figure 1.3). The model predicts that the data points should fall on the line, but most of them are far from it.

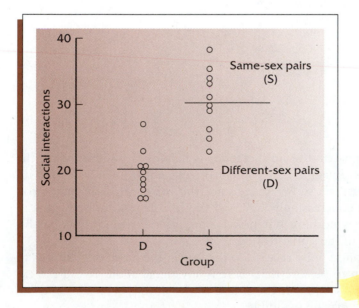

Figure 1.6
Noisier version of the data shown in Figure 1.4.

Figure 1.6 shows a graph of data from an imaginary repetition of the social inter-action study described earlier. In this version of the study, the data are much noisier. In the original graph (Figure 1.4), the points clustered tightly around one of two dis-tinct values: one value for same-sex pairs and one for different-sex pairs. With the noisy data, this relationship is less obvious. Moreover, if we were to use the previously derived model "predict 30 interactions for same-sex pairs and 20 interactions for dif-ferent-sex pairs," the predictions would be less accurate than those in the original ex-ample. Graphically, these less accurate predictions (larger residuals) are represented by the distances of the data points from their respective horizontal lines. For the same-sex pairs, it is the distance from the line at 30 interactions; for the different-sex pairs, it is the distance from the line at 20 interactions.

Sources of Noise

What makes data more or less noisy? Why might one pair of same-sex infants in-teract 35 times and another pair of same-sex infants interact only 25 times and a third pair 30 times? In matters of measurement and controlled observation, the behavioral sciences face difficulties greater than those that confront the physical sciences. Living organisms are continuously changing and no two are exactly the same. Consider something as apparently straightforward as measuring reaction time to a flash of light and contrast this measurement situation with something equally as simple in the phys-ical sciences—measuring the boiling point of water. In obtaining stable measure-ments, a more formidable challenge faces the behavioral scientist. Unlike the water in the beaker, there are countless ways in which a participant can change states from one measurement occasion to the next.

These difficulties are by no means fatal to sound scientific method. They do mean, however, that experimental control is a much more difficult problem in the be-havioral sciences than in the physical sciences—hence, the emphasis placed on experi-mental design and statistical analysis in the behavioral sciences.

1.1.3 From Regularity to Mechanism

The basic aim of science is to construct models that identify underlying causes of phenomena and thereby support predictions. How does identifying the signal in data advance our understanding of underlying causes? What is gained by pointing out that the pattern of dark adaptation follows two distinct smooth curves, that decision time in the mental rotation experiment follows a straight line, or that the social interaction data fall into two distinct clusters? Is the purpose merely to provide an elegant de-scription of the data?

To answer these questions, consider first the case of the dark adaptation curves. Look carefully at Figure 1.1a and notice the sharp break at around 7 minutes, indicat-ing the need for two curves. Such a sudden change suggests that a second influence has entered to disrupt the hitherto smooth curve. In this example, the suggestion is that two mechanisms are involved in dark adaptation. One mechanism, reflected in the short top curve, adapts quickly (in the first 7 minutes) but not very much, in that it flattens out at a relatively high threshold level. The lower (longer) curve drops more gradually, over a period of 30 minutes, but it drops a lot further, showing a much higher degree of adaptation.

A mechanism is an underlying causal influence.

Physiologists have determined exactly what the two mechanisms are. The two distinct curves correspond to the differential adaptation of rods and cones in the retina. The cones are light-sensitive cells, most of which are tightly packed around an area near the center of the retina known as the fovea. Insofar as they adapt at all, these cells adapt very rapidly to light, producing the upper curve in Figure 1.1b. Rods, a different type of light-sensitive cells, are found more in the periphery of the retina. They adapt more slowly than cones but actually are much more sensitive to light. It is rods that are responsible for the lower curve.

Consider the mental rotation experiment as a second example (Figure 1.7). What does the straight line tell us about underlying processes? It tells us two things:

■ When the two figures are both in the same orientation (zero rotation), the decision time is about 1.13 seconds. This value is the point at which the straight line crosses the *y*-axis.

■ Every degree of rotation adds a *constant* interval of time (about 0.021 seconds) to the decision time needed to make the same/different judgment. For example, a rotation through 20 degrees adds an extra $20 \times 0.021 = 0.42$ seconds to the decision time. So for this amount of rotation, the total decision time would be $1.13 + 0.42 = 1.55$ seconds. Similarly, the increase in decision time for a figure rotated through 110 degrees would be 110×0.021 or 2.31 seconds, giving a total decision time of $1.13 + 2.31 = 3.44$ seconds.

Shepard and Metzler suggested that this finding is compatible with the following hypothesis: Participants make their judgments by mentally rotating one figure until it is in the same orientation as the other. This mental rotation occurs at a constant rate of about 0.021 seconds (21 milliseconds) for every degree of rotation.

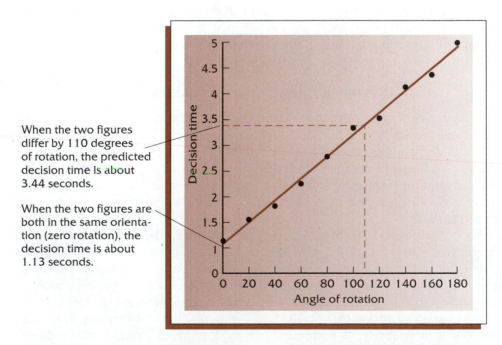

When the two figures differ by 110 degrees of rotation, the predicted decision time is about 3.44 seconds.

When the two figures are both in the same orientation (zero rotation), the decision time is about 1.13 seconds.

Figure 1.7
Explanation of the slope and intercept of the straight-line model for the mental rotation experiment. (After Shepard & Metzler, 1971)

The social interaction experiment has a simpler result, but even its simple model indicates the existence of an underlying mechanism. Why else would the model need to specify a different value for the number of social interactions depending on whether the pair is composed of same-sex or different-sex individuals? This single study gives few clues about the nature of the mechanism. We know from this single result that, whatever the mechanism, it is one that operates in infants as young as 33 months and that it influences the amount of social interaction in a sex-dependent way. Further studies would be needed to specify the mechanism more precisely.

These examples demonstrate how casual mechanisms can be revealed in the models that capture the regularities in data. In these cases, the regularities appeared in simple graphical plots. Unfortunately, the process of identifying the appropriate model is not always as simple as plotting a graph. The noisy versions of two of the examples made this point. Moreover, scientists usually seek to describe the hidden regularities in data with the aid of mathematical equations. Such equations specify the exact details of the model. The goal of data analysis is to discover just what equations will do the job of accurately describing the regularities.

The history of science provides many demonstrations of this endeavor, but perhaps the best example of a discovery with revolutionary consequences is that of Johannes Kepler some 400 years ago. The equations that state Kepler's three laws are essentially models fitted to a vast quantity of astronomical observations. The models provide a very elegant explanation of the data and account for virtually all the variability. The first law, for example, states that planets follow an elliptical orbit, with the sun at one focus. But the real significance of the laws goes well beyond their elegance and good fit. The laws are important clues to the pattern of gravitational forces operating on planets, and some 60 years later they formed the foundation for Isaac Newton's formulation of general laws of gravitation.

Replicability and Predictability

Science assumes that the forces that create change are themselves stable, not fickle. Valid models are revealed not only through the regularities in a single set of data, such as the dark adaptation study or the social interaction study, but also through the fact that these regularities are reproducible. A term commonly used in scientific discourse is *replicable*. Replicability is a basic tenet of science and amounts to the claim that identical conditions will always yield identical results; the observations will remain constant as long as the conditions remain constant. We will refer to this tenet as the *principle of replicability*.

Notice that the principle of replicability is really a special case of the concern science has with the general rather than the particular. In this case, the particular refers to an observation made on a single occasion or in a single experiment. Replicability implies that the result can be obtained, not just on that occasion or from that one experiment, but generally—whenever the appropriate observation is made or the same experiment conducted. Replicability therefore implies predictability. If the conditions are identical, then the outcome is perfectly predictable: It will be exactly the same as last time.

Models, then, describe the regular and replicable components in data—the signals. Noise, on the other hand, is precisely the opposite. It corresponds to the aspects of data that are irregular, unstable, and thus unpredictable. Such instability, if it exists, is assumed to be the result of a multitude of small but uncontrolled influences. In the

The principle of replicability in science asserts that identical conditions yield identical results.

Replicability implies predictability of results.

Signals are the regular, replicable components in data.

dark adaptation curves of Figure 1.1, this instability is reflected in the discrepancy between the data points (the dots) and the smooth curve. The smooth curves themselves—the signal—would appear and reappear in the same general form whenever the observational procedure was repeated. This aspect of the data would be totally predictable. But the small distance between each data point and the curve would not be predictable. A dot that is slightly above the curve on one measurement occasion might be slightly below it on the next, it might be closer to the curve, or it might be farther away. Which of these many possible outcomes would actually occur is quite unpredictable.

Similarly, if further observations were made in the mental rotation experiment, we would not expect a precise replication of the exact location of each data point. We would, however, predict that observations would fluctuate about a similar straight line. In the social interaction study, we would not expect to replicate the exact location of each data point, but we would expect to observe a similar separation of the two clusters corresponding to same- versus different-sex conditions.

The preceding paragraphs contain some obvious hedges. We claimed that the dark adaptation curves would appear and reappear in the same *general form;* for the mental rotation experiment, we claimed that further observations would fluctuate about a *similar* straight line; in the social interaction study, the claim was to expect a *similar* separation. These italicized hedges reflect a major challenge that the next few chapters will face head on.

The challenge is this: If we were to repeat these experiments, we would not expect to obtain exactly the same results. In the dark adaptation experiment (Figure 1.1), we would not expect to obtain exactly the same location of the curves; in the mental rotation experiment (Figure 1.3), we would not expect exactly the same straight line; we would not expect precisely the same location of the horizontal lines in the social interaction study (Figure 1.4). Why these failures to obtain exact replication?

The problem is that the true location of the curves, line, and points are unknown. In this respect, the situation is not like measuring the boiling point of water. In that case, noise could be thought of as fluctuation about a known true value of 100 degrees Celsius. But in our examples, *the location of the curves, line, and points was based on the data from that particular experiment;* as we have taken some pains to point out, these data points are subject to noise. For this reason, the particular locations for curves, lines, and points are only *estimates* of the true locations—the best we can do on the basis of the data available. If the experiment were repeated, slightly different estimates might be obtained.

What we *would* expect, however, is that the signal should take the same general form from one repetition of the experiment to another. In a repetition of the dark adaptation experiment, for example, we should always see two descending curves; in the mental rotation experiment, we should always obtain a straight line; for the social interaction experiment, we should observe the separation of the scores for the two conditions. In brief, we expect to replicate the *form* of the signal, if not its detailed specifications.

There is a distinction between strict and general replicability.

This discussion suggests that it is worthwhile to distinguish *strict replicability* from what might be termed *general replicability.* Strict replicability demands that precisely the same measurement be obtained on each repetition of an observation under a given set of conditions. General replicability makes more lenient demands. It concedes the point that the inevitable intrusions of noise will result in a violation of strict replicability, and therefore it requires only that a repetition of an investigation should lead to the same general conclusion but not necessarily the identical numerical values.

1.1.4 Economy in Explanations: The Principle of Parsimony

Analogy from Jurisprudence

We are all familiar with the legal principle that an accused person is presumed innocent until proved guilty beyond a reasonable doubt. The burden of proof rests with the prosecution. If the prosecution cannot establish its case beyond a reasonable doubt, then the accused has a right to acquittal, despite the fact that the jury may feel that the person was guilty. There is a common belief that acquitting a guilty person is less of an injustice than finding an innocent person guilty. Thus, when an accused person is acquitted, the person's innocence may still be in doubt.

In science, a similar principle operates. For example, if an investigator claims that a particular drug reduces depression or that a novel method of instruction improves classroom performance, then the burden of proof rests with the investigator. The scientific community, acting like a jury, demands that the effectiveness of the drug or the method of instruction be established beyond any reasonable doubt. Otherwise, the scientific community would consider that the claim was "not established." In other words,

> *Potential influences on behavior such as drugs or training methods are assumed to be innocent (to have no effect) until the evidence establishes their guilt (that they do have an effect) beyond reasonable doubt.*

Science differs from the legal process in three important ways:

■ If the evidence is inconclusive, there is no need for science to make a firm decision one way or the other. Instead, science can settle for a statement that merely describes the relative strength of the evidence. Unlike the usual legal process, science makes it possible to remain noncommittal on an issue for whatever period of time it takes to accumulate further evidence. The period may last for years or even decades.

■ Unlike courtroom trials, science can repeat the "trial" over and over again, and previous "verdicts" can be changed. In science, the "acquittal" does not preclude the possibility of a later retrial as it does in some legal systems. In science, the investigator can always gather further evidence and retry the case.

■ Science demands that the criterion "beyond a reasonable doubt" be spelled out more clearly than it is in the legal realm. As we will see, one way of achieving greater clarity is to enlist the aid of probability theory.

Why should science demand evidence "beyond a reasonable doubt" before accepting a claim? The answer lies in the principle of *parsimony*. This principle is a policy of not making explanations more complicated than the data demand. For example, do not invoke explanatory concepts such as drugs, therapy, or instructional methods, unless the data demand them—unless their need has been established beyond a reasonable doubt.

Where the analogy breaks down

In science, explanations should not be more complicated than they need to be to account for the variability in the data.

Parsimony is not a claim that nature is uncomplicated, or that the correct explanation will necessarily turn out to be the simplest. Such a claim would be quite misleading. Rather, it is a pragmatic rule urging that explanations be kept as simple as the evidence permits.

Applying the Principle of Parsimony to Drug Testing

As an example, consider an experiment designed to test a new drug treatment for depression. The results show that, after the treatment, the level of depression among those receiving the treatment is no different from that of a control group who did not receive the drug. How should this result be explained? One researcher claims that the drug is ineffective, that it has no effect on depression. A second researcher offers a different explanation, claiming that the situation is rather more complicated. This alternative claim is that the drug does in fact lower depression, but it also produces side effects, such as sleep loss, that in turn *increase* depression. Thus the direct beneficial effects of the drug are canceled out by these negative side effects.

Notice that both explanations account for the actual results. The second explanation, however, violates the principle of parsimony because it includes more explanatory entities than the data warrant. The first explanation accounts for the data just as well and needs to invoke neither drug effects nor side effects. Thus the scientific community would interpret the results of this experiment by saying, "Case unproved: Until there is stronger evidence—evidence that establishes the effectiveness of the drug beyond a reasonable doubt—we will assume that the drug has no effect." Notice that this interpretation does not rule out the possibility that the more complicated explanation might actually be correct. The results of the experiment do not rule it out. However, as matters stand, the burden of proof rests with the advocates of the more complicated explanation. The drug is assumed innocent (ineffective) until proved guilty beyond a reasonable doubt. Advocates of the drug's effectiveness would need to conduct further experiments that could separate the alleged counteracting influences of drug and side effect.

1.1.5 Statistical Data Analysis in Everyday Problems

Although our major concern will be the formal analysis of scientific data, the basic concepts underlying these methods are relevant to a wide range of everyday problems. We have already encountered one such concept, the idea that unaccounted for variability is the enemy of accurate prediction. Although it may not be immediately obvious, this concept is one you already possess. Consider the following problems, taken from an experiment reported by Nisbett, Krantz, Jepson, and Kunda (1983).

Imagine that you are exploring a hitherto undiscovered island and encounter new objects, animals, and people. You observe their features and wish to predict whether these features would be true of other examples:

■ Suppose the physicist on your expedition discovers a rare element he calls floridium. When heated to a high temperature, the physicist's sample of floridium burns with a green flame. What is the probability that a second sample of floridium will burn with a green flame when heated to a high temperature?

■ Suppose you encounter a male member of an island tribe called the Barrotos. He is obese. What is the probability that a second male member of the Barrotos tribe will also be obese?

■ Suppose the Barrotos man is brown in color. What is the probability that a second male member of the Barrotos tribe will also be brown in color (as opposed, say, to red, yellow, black, or white)?

Most participants in the Nisbett et al. experiment expressed much more confidence in their prediction that another sample of floridium would burn with a green flame than that another Barrotos man would be obese, and much more confidence in their prediction that another Barrotos man would be brown in color than that another Barrotos man would be obese. Underlying this difference is the idea that the basic attributes of physical elements are not subject to variability, nor, within a tribal group, are physical features such as skin color. On the other hand, everyday experience tells us that an attribute such as body weight is quite variable. This variability results in a less confident prediction. In other words, we already have an intuitive knowledge of the inverse relationship between variability and prediction.

The fact that everyday prediction is sensitive to perceived variability has been demonstrated in a study by Quattrone and Jones (1980). They showed that people's willingness to generalize from the behavior of a specific group member to the group as a whole depended on the observer's perception of the group's variability. The more homogeneous or stereotypical the perception, the greater the willingness to generalize. Because people are more aware of the variability within their own group and view other groups as more homogeneous (more stereotypical) than their own, people are more willing to generalize from observations of the behavior of an out-group member than for a member of their own group.

Comprehension Check 1.1

Important Concepts

1. The overall goal of statistical analysis is to account for variability. This goal is achieved by formulating a model that describes the regularities in data.

2. A model is a prediction rule that reproduces the data. In practice, the model's prediction will be imperfect: It will not account for all the variability. Data analysis seeks a model that minimizes these prediction errors, which we call residuals.

3. The metaphor of signal and noise helps us understand the goal of statistical data analysis. We can think of data as consisting of a signal (the regularity described by the model) embedded in noise (represented by the residuals). Thus the relationship *data = signal + noise* becomes, in the language of statistical data analysis, *data = model prediction + residual.*

4. Models provide more than an elegant description of the data; they are an important clue to underlying mechanisms. Kepler's laws of planetary motion and the dark adaptation curves are classic examples of regularities that provide a foundation for inferring causal mechanisms.

5. If a model captures regularities that stem from underlying causal mechanisms, then the model should be replicable. If the experiment is repeated, then the same model should be appropriate, at least a model of the same general form (general replicability), if not one that is numerically identical (strict replicability).

6. The principle of parsimony, commonly accepted throughout science, asserts that the model should be the simplest that the data will allow. The model should be made more complex only if the need for such increased complexity has been established beyond a reasonable doubt.

7. The concepts underlying statistical data analysis are relevant to a wide range of everyday situations.

Problems

Problem 1

Ten participants, five female (F), five male (M), rated a movie on a seven-point scale ranging from 1 (bad) to 7 (good):

Sex	F	M	F	M	M	F	F	F	M	M
Rating (R)	6	4	6	5	4	5	6	7	4	3

Compare the following models (prediction rules) for these data.

Model 1 $R = 5$ (This model ignores sex.)

Model 2 $R = 6$ for Females; $R = 4$ for Males

Model 3 $R = 7$ for Females; $R = 3$ for Males

Calculate the residuals for each observation for each model. Use these residuals to judge which model does the best job of predicting the observations.

Sex	F	M	F	M	M	F	F	F	M	M
Rating (R)	6	4	6	5	4	5	6	7	4	3
Model 1 residuals										
Model 2 residuals										
Model 3 residuals										

Problem 2

The graphs in Figure 1.8 show the results from two experiments testing short-term memory. The proportion of items recalled is measured under retention intervals ranging from 0 (immediate recall) to 24 seconds. Describe (either graphically by drawing a curve, straight line, etc., or verbally) what you consider to be the "signal"—the regularity underlying the data points—in each of these graphs. Which of the two graphs contains the noisier data?

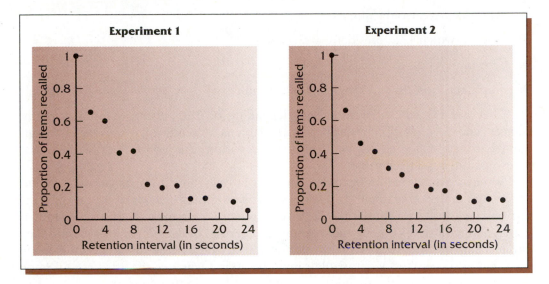

Figure 1.8
Plots of the proportion of items recalled as a function of time after viewing (Problem 2).

Problem 3

As part of a study of driver safety, an investigator wants to know how long it takes for a driver's foot to reach the brake pedal following the sudden appearance of an object 50 meters in front of the car. Using a simulator that mimics this driving condition, the investigator measures the reaction time for one participant on ten different occasions over the span of a 1-hour session in the simulator. The investigator notes that these ten times are quite variable and describes this variability as "noise." List factors that you think might have contributed to the noise in these data.

Problem 4

In continuing the exploration of the imaginary island described in Section 1.1.5, you discover an example of a new species of bird, which the islanders call a *frake*. The frake has webbed feet and is tending a nest with four chicks. If you were to encounter a second example of a nesting frake, in which of the following two predictions would you be more confident? (a) It will have webbed feet. (b) The nest will have exactly four chicks. Give the reason for your answer.

1.2 Variables

As noted in Section 1.1, the form in which regularities are expressed depends on the nature of the variables involved. The model that captures the regularities underlying the dark adaptation data will have a different form from that needed to describe the social interaction data. Thus we need to identify the various distinctions among types of variables.

A *variable* is any attribute of objects, people, or events that, within the context of a particular investigation, can take on different values. All the following attributes are variables:

- height of 3-year-old children

- states in which U.S. presidents were born

- GPA of psychology majors

- simple reaction time to the onset of a stimulus

They can take on different values, depending on the person, occasion, circumstances, and so forth. The opposite of a variable is a constant. A *constant* is any attribute of objects, people, or events that, within the context of a particular investigation, has a fixed value.

Some attributes can be treated as variables in one context but as constants in another. Age is a good example. In a study investigating the behavior of 3-year-olds, the attribute age may be a constant—all the children are the same age. But if the study is concerned with development and investigates children of ages 2, 3, and 4 years, then age is a variable. In any given context, you can decide whether an attribute is being regarded as a constant or a variable simply by asking whether the attribute takes on different values. If it does, then it is a variable—at least in that context.

The opposite of a variable is a constant.

Context sometimes determines whether an attribute is a variable or a constant.

1.2.1 Quantitative and Categorical Variables

There are a number of different types of variables, but one of the more common distinctions is between quantitative and categorical variables. This distinction plays an important role in determining how data are displayed and analyzed.

Quantitative variables are variables such as height, decision time, or proportion of items answered correctly. Values of these variables are numbers; and because the numbers represent quantities, the numbers can be added or subtracted. It makes sense to speak of increasing 2 inches in height, adding 1.2 seconds to a decision time, or reducing the number of correct items from 75% to 60%.

Conversely, variables such as sex, occupation, or country of birth are *categorical*, or *nominal, variables*. The value of a categorical variable is simply the name, or other symbol, that designates the category to which a particular object, person, or event belongs. Unlike the arithmetic treatment of a quantitative variable, addition or subtraction of the values of a categorical variable makes no numerical sense. You cannot add (in the arithmetic sense) a lawyer and a psychologist to obtain some third occupation in the way you can add 5 seconds to 10 seconds to obtain a third value of time (15 seconds). With categorical variables, the only possible kind of arithmetic is counting the frequency with which each category is observed. In a group of people, it is possible to count the number of lawyers, psychologists, and so forth.

A potential source of confusion arises when numbers are used simply as convenient symbols to label categories, as distinct from being used to indicate quantity. There is nothing wrong with this nominal use of numbers, but when numbers *are* used in this way, you must resist the temptation to believe that if you add, subtract, or perform any other arithmetic operation on them you will get a meaningful arithmetic result. For example, numbers are used to designate field positions in baseball. A pitcher is designated 1, the catcher 2, and the first baseman 3, and so on. As category labels, these numerical designations are perfectly clear, but they are just that—labels. It makes no sense to perform arithmetic on the numbers: You cannot add the pitcher to the catcher and get a first baseman, just because in ordinary arithmetic 1 plus 2 equals 3.

The values of quantitative variables are numbers.

The values of categorical variables are the category labels.

Beware of numbers used purely for labeling.

1.2.2 Discrete and Continuous Quantitative Variables

Quantitative variables can be broken down into two types, *discrete* and *continuous*.

Discrete (Quantitative) Variables

A discrete variable has a finite number of distinct (discrete) quantitative values. Examples of discrete variables are the number of children in a family, the number of courses a student has completed, and the number of heads in three tosses of a coin.

There are two essential features of discrete variables as they will be used in this text:

■ The number of possible values of the variable is limited. For different variables, the number of possible values might vary, but it is always a finite number. The range of possible values for the variable "number of heads in three tosses of a coin" will be smaller than for the variable "number of children in a family," but neither can be infinitely large.

■ Between each of the numerical values of the discrete variable, there are gaps—numerical values that are not included in the set of possible quantitative values. In the case of a variable such as the number of children in a family, the values 1.5 or 2.3 are impossible; only integers are permissible. Similarly, three tosses of a coin cannot result in 1.5 or 0.8 heads.

Continuous (Quantitative) Variables

A continuous variable is a variable such as time, weight, or height that has a continuous range of values; within this range, the variable can take on an infinite number of possible values. Furthermore, within this range, there are no gaps. In other words, for any two values of the variable, *no matter how close the values may be,* it is always possible, in principle, to obtain a value intermediate between the two. For example, time is a continuous variable in that for any two values, say 3.754 seconds and 3.755 seconds, there is a third possible value (such as 3.7545 seconds) that is intermediate between the two. The same would be true, no matter how many decimal places the two initial measures were taken to; you could always obtain an intermediate value by taking it to one further decimal place. Unlike the discrete variable that had a finite number of possible values, the number of possible values is unlimited for a continuous variable.

In practice, of course, the accuracy of the measuring instrument imposes limits on the number of possible values of the continuous variable that can actually be measured. If the variable is the time taken to answer a simple question, measuring this response time to six decimal places (to the nearest millionth of a second) would be quite impractical, given the equipment typically used in such experiments. Nor would such extreme accuracy serve any useful purpose; in this example, measurement to the nearest tenth of a second would be sufficient.

Measurements taken with typical laboratory equipment and many psychological tests only approximate the ideal of a continuous variable. Consider a measurement of 2.3 seconds for the time to answer a simple question. This value is an approximation of the exact (but unknown) time. This exact time might have been 2.336512 . . . seconds or 2.3462091 . . . seconds. The value of 2.3 seconds is taken as an approximation of all times that fall in the interval of 2.25 to 2.35 seconds. The values of 2.25 and 2.35 are sometimes referred to as the *real* or *exact* limits of the interval. In many experiments, decision time is measured to the nearest millisecond (thousandths of a second). A simple reaction time measured as 452 milliseconds, for example, has a real interval of 451.5 and 452.5.

1.2.3 Response Variables and Predictor or Explanatory Variables

In scientific studies, it is important to distinguish between predictor and response variables. As the name suggests, a *predictor variable* is the variable that serves as the basis on which predictions are made. Predictor variables are also referred to as *explanatory variables*. The *response variable*, on the other hand, is the variable whose value we want to predict and whose variance we want to explain or account for.

In some texts, the term *independent variable* is used to refer to predictor variables and the term *dependent variable* to refer to response variables. Unfortunately, the terms *independent* and *dependent* are used with a different meaning in the context of probability theory. The less ambiguous terms *predictor* (or *explanatory*) and *response* are therefore preferable. Not only are these terms less ambiguous, they also convey more accurately the role that each type of variable plays in statistical data analysis.

> **A predictor variable serves as the basis for predicting values of the response variable.**

Throughout this book, we will adopt the usual convention of using X to denote the predictor variable and Y to denote the response variable. This convention is reflected in the traditional graph in which values of the predictor variable are shown on the horizontal axis or *x*-axis, and values of the response variable on the vertical axis, or *y*-axis.

> **X denotes the predictor variable; Y denotes the response variable.**

Consider the example of the test anxiety ratings with which this chapter began. The ratings themselves were the response, or Y, variable. In this case, Y was a quantitative variable, and the goal was to predict its values or, equivalently, to explain the variability of the ratings. The variable that was used in an effort to accomplish this goal was whether or not the rating came from a person who had undergone counseling therapy. This variable was the predictor variable, the X variable. It is a categorical variable with just two possible values: therapy or no therapy. In the original description of the example, these values were labeled T(herapy) and C(ontrol). Knowing the value of the predictor variable (X = T or X = C) improved our ability to predict the value of the response variable: the participant's anxiety rating.

In the dark adaptation experiment, the predictor variable was time in the dark, measured in minutes. The response variable was the absolute threshold: how much light was needed to see the flash. Both variables were quantitative. We wish to predict the value of the response variable (the absolute threshold) on the basis of the value of the predictor variable (time in the dark). Equivalently, we could say that time in the dark is the explanatory variable that explains much of the variability of the response variable. Notice that the graph follows the custom of plotting the predictor variable on the horizontal (*x*-) axis and the response variable on the vertical (*y*-) axis.

In the mental rotation example, the predictor variable was the angle of rotation of the comparison figure; the response variable was the time taken to make a judgment of sameness. Both variables were quantitative. In the social interaction study, the predictor variable was the sex of the toddler pairs (same versus different) and the response variable was the amount of social interaction. In this case, the predictor variable was categorical, the response variable quantitative.

The distinction between categorical and quantitative variables can sometimes become confusing when applied to predictor variables. Drug studies provide a good example. Suppose an experiment consists of just two conditions. In one condition, participants receive 1.5 mL of an antidepressant drug, participants in the second, control condition receive 0 mL. The response variable is a measure of depression. In this example, this predictor variable seems quantitative with values of 1.5 and 0 mL. However, the experiment is not designed to develop a quantitative rule that would enable us to predict depression for various drug dosage levels. We could, of course, redesign the experiment with this purpose in mind, administering doses of, say, 0, 0.5, 1.0, 1.5, and 2.0 mL to different participants. In this case, the predictor variable would appropriately be considered quantitative. However, as originally designed with just 0 and 1.5 mL, the experiment had the purpose of answering a simpler, categorical question: Does the presence or the absence of the drug make a difference?

This example illustrates the point that the difference between categorical and quantitative predictor variables is not only a matter of the nature of the variables themselves. It is also a matter of the design and purpose of an experiment; and, in particular, it is a matter of the type of prediction rule (model) that the investigator plans to derive from the data.

With a categorical predictor, *the investigator aims to produce a model that predicts values of the response variable only for those values of the predictor variable actually included in the experiment.* With a quantitative predictor variable, the investigator wants to produce a model that will predict the response variable for *all* values of the predictor variable within the range covered by the experiment. In the dark adaptation experiment, for example, the threshold was not measured at 10.5 minutes. However, the model (represented by the continuous curve) enables us to predict a value for the threshold that would be expected at 10.5 minutes.

The difference in the models for categorical and quantitative predictor variables can be seen in a very elementary way in two of the examples used in Section 1.1.

Recall the happiness rating data.

Predictor variable (X)	A	B	A	B	B	A	A	A	B	B	A	B
Response variable (Y)	5	10	5	10	10	5	5	5	10	10	5	10

We can now apply our newly acquired terms to this example. The labels A and B are the two values of a categorical predictor variable (X), and the values 5 and 10 are values of the response variable (Y). The model for these data was for X = A, Y = 5, for X = B, Y = 10.

Recall the algebraic example.

Predictor variable (X)	6	8	3	1	9	4	6	5	4	2
Response variable (Y)	12	16	6	2	18	8	12	10	8	4

In this case, the predictor variable (X) is quantitative, with values ranging from 1 to 9. The model for these data was Y = 2X.

Notice the important difference between these two models. With a quantitative predictor variable, a single statement, Y = 2X, is sufficient for all predictions. In fact, the single model statement covers all values of X not included in the original set. For

A given predictor variable may be categorical or quantitative, depending on the purpose of the investigation.

example, X = 7 is not in the data set, but the model can nevertheless be applied to yield a prediction of 14. With a categorical predictor variable, however, each value of the predictor variable requires a separate prediction: one for X = A and one for X = B. If there were additional values of the categorical predictor variable (C, D, and so on, representing added conditions in an experiment), then we would have to extend the model by making additional statements, one for each added value.

One clue that an experiment has been designed with the intention of treating the predictor variable as quantitative is that the experiment includes at least three values (and usually more) of the predictor variable. Moreover, the particular values will have been chosen to span meaningful intervals of the predictor variable. These properties clearly apply to the dark adaptation study and the mental rotation experiment.

Consider other typical examples of a predictor variable being treated as quantitative. In a study of forgetting, the investigator chooses intervals of 0, 1, 10, 24, and 48 hours between the time of study and the time of the memory test. The goal is to establish a forgetting curve over the range 0 to 48 hours. Another example would be a drug experiment in which the investigator includes four different dosage levels, the particular levels chosen depending on the nature of the drug. In this case, the goal is to establish a dose–response curve over the range of dosage levels included in the experiment.

In summary, the values of a predictor variable may be defined in terms of numbers, but the numbers may serve merely as category labels and the predictor variable may be treated as categorical.

- If the predictor variable is treated as categorical, then the model provides a prediction rule that applies only to those values of the predictor variable actually included in the experiment.

- If the predictor variable is treated as quantitative, then the model provides a prediction rule that can be used to make predictions of responses for all values of the predictor variable, not just those values actually included in the experiment.

Response variables may also be either categorical or quantitative. Response variables may also be either categorical or quantitative, although we have yet to consider an example of a categorical response variable. With categorical response variables, the response is not quantified but simply assigned to a category; and this classification constitutes the value of the response variable for that observation. Response variables such as "preferred presidential candidate" or "approval of capital punishment (yes or no)" would be examples of categorical response variables.

Another example of a categorical response variable might appear in a study of social compliance. In this study, participants are asked to comply with a relatively innocuous request: They are asked to sign a petition promoting a clean environment. The purpose of the experiment is to find out whether this initial compliance will increase the likelihood that the participant will comply with a *later* request to do something they would not really want to do. In this example, the response variable is compliance or noncompliance to this later request. It is a categorical variable because responses are scored simply yes or no; the participant did or did not comply. There is no attempt to quantify the degree of compliance.

The distinctions between categorical and quantitative variables and between response and predictor variables yield four possible combinations: categorical predictor and categorical response variables, quantitative predictor and quantitative response variables, and so forth. Let's consider various examples of these possible combinations. The dark adaptation and the mental rotation experiments are examples of studies in which both predictor and response variables are quantitative. The social interaction experiment, however, has a categorical predictor variable and a quantitative response variable.

Study of Attitude Change

This study is a second example of a categorical predictor variable combined with a quantitative response variable. It was designed to examine the effect of threat of punishment on children's attitudes. Does forbidding a child to play with a toy make the toy more desirable to the child, or less? This experiment begins with children rating the desirability of a set of toys. The experimenter then designates one of the well-liked toys as a "forbidden" toy, telling the child that he or she is not to play with this particular toy when left alone with the toys. The experiment has two conditions. Half the children receive a threat of very mild disapproval should they play with the forbidden toy; the other half receive a threat of very severe disapproval. Each child then has a period in which he or she is left alone with the toys. After this "temptation period," the children are asked to rate the desirability of each of the toys, including the forbidden toy. The response variable is the change in rating of the forbidden toy from its initial rating. The predictor variable is whether the threat of punishment was mild or severe.

Study of the Facial Expressions of Emotion

In this study, both predictor and response variables are categorical. The investigators wanted to know whether different emotions are accompanied by distinct facial expressions. Is there, for example, a distinctive facial expression for fear? For disgust? To study this question, investigators showed participants a set of photographs of facial expressions. Actors had been used to produce the photographs, and each photograph depicted one of six different emotions: fear, happiness, disgust, surprise, sadness, and anger. Participants were given these names, shown the set of photographs, and then asked to judge which of the six emotions each expression depicted. As noted earlier, the predictor variable is categorical, with six possible values: the six emotions depicted in the facial expression. The response variable is also categorical: Which of the six emotions did the participant choose when asked to judge the expression portrayed?

Study of Infant Imitation

Investigators wanted to know whether infants as young as 3 weeks show any capability to imitate gestures such as (1) protruding the lips, (2) protruding the tongue, (3) opening the mouth, or (4) moving their fingers in a simple sequence of movements. To answer this question, investigators place 14- to 21-day-old infants in a darkened room with nothing to look at besides the well-lit face of the model, who is a person the infant has not seen before. The model performs one of the experimental gestures, and the infant's response is recorded. The responses to each of the four gestures are classified into one of seven gestural categories. Again, the predictor variable is categorical: the gesture made by the model. The response variable is also categorical: the gesture the infant responded with.

Thus far, we have not considered an example of a quantitative predictor variable combined with a categorical response variable, but such combinations are not uncommon. One example is clinical diagnosis. The response variable is a diagnostic category such as "obsessive compulsive disorder," "frontal lobe damage," or "dyslexia." The predictor variable (or variables), however, might be quantitative, such as a test score.

		Predictor variable	
		Categorical	Quantitative
Response variable	Categorical	Infant imitation Facial expression	Clinical diagnosis Career counseling
	Quantitative	Social interaction Attitude change	Dark adaptation Mental rotation

Table 1.2 Two types of predictor variable combined with two types of response variable

A similar example is career counseling. The response variable might be categorical: a particular career. The predictor variable (or variables) might again be scores on aptitude or personality tests. The two types of predictor variables, when combined with the two types of response variables, result in the four possible combinations, which can be summarized in a table such as Table 1.2.

Behavioral and other social scientists often conduct studies in which the distinction between predictor and response variables breaks down altogether. A common example is in the domain of ability and personality testing. A psychologist may be interested in whether there is a relationship between verbal ability and spatial reasoning, or between measures of anxiety and depression. Do anxious people also tend to be depressed? These are interesting and legitimate questions; but notice that either measure—anxiety or depression—might be considered the predictor variable or the response variable. It makes as much sense to predict depression on the basis of anxiety as to use depression to predict anxiety. This situation, termed *correlational*, will be considered in Chapter 9.

In some cases, the distinction between response and predictor variables breaks down.

1.2.4 Manipulated and Natural Predictor Variables

In most sciences, it is possible to study variability in one of two ways. One way is to observe variability as it occurs naturally. The second way is to create variability through experimental manipulation.

Research into the causes of cancer provides an example of this two-pronged approach. Studies contrasting the characteristics of people who acquire cancer with those who do not have yielded valuable insights into possible causes and provided bases for predicting the risk of acquiring cancer. Hereditary background, diet, and smoking are well-known examples. At the same time, laboratory and controlled clinical studies attempt both to create cancer cells (using carcinogens and animals) or destroy them (using drugs or radiation). Whether the purpose is to create or destroy, the general goal is to bring about change in order to understand what causes it.

Studies in the behavioral sciences follow a similar two-pronged approach. An investigation of test anxiety might identify students who report high test anxiety and compare them with students who remain relaxed. What differences between these two groups might account for their different reactions to the testing situation? Another investigator might conduct an experiment to find out whether a special form of counseling reduces test anxiety. The former approach examines differences in anxiety as they exist; the latter endeavors to *create* a difference through a therapeutic intervention. Both investigators share a common aim: They both seek to understand factors that might produce differences in levels of test anxiety. Their common goal is to account for variation.

In most of the examples we have considered so far, the predictor variables have been the creation of the researcher, and it is the researcher who has decided on their values. In the attitude change experiment, for example, the instructions to each child about the forbidden toy are conditions created by the researcher, and the particular levels of disapproval were chosen by the researcher. Moreover, the researcher can ensure that the two conditions differ only with respect to the degree of threatened disapproval and in no other way. This exertion of control by the researcher is not always the case. Predictor variables are often measured attributes that reflect naturally occurring properties of the participants or of the environment rather than the creations of the researcher. This possibility holds for both categorical or quantitative predictor variables. Consider the following examples.

- The predictor variable is age; the response variable is vocabulary size.

- The predictor variable is IQ; the response variable is annual income.

- The predictor variable is father's employment status; the response variable is child abuse.

- The predictor variable is height; the response variable is running speed.

- The predictor variable is ethnic group; the response variable is family size.

- The predictor variable is occupation; the response variable is rating of job satisfaction.

- The predictor variable is sex; the response variable is religious affiliation.

- The predictor variable is hours of sunshine in a given week; the response variable is score on a depression scale at the end of that week.

- The predictor variable is degree of marital conflict within a family; the response variable is the degree of maladjustment of children in that family.

In each of these examples, the value of the predictor variable is determined by some naturally occurring—as opposed to experimenter-created—attribute of the participants or of the environment. We will refer to such variables as natural variables. A *natural predictor variable* may be a measurement reflecting a quantitative variable such as IQ, height, and hours of sunshine, or it may be a classification of individuals or events according to the values of a categorical variable such as ethnic group, sex, or day of the week.

Predictor variables that are under the control of the researcher will be termed *manipulated predictor variables*. In a dark adaptation experiment, a researcher can arrange for any participant to be in a dark room for 15 minutes, or any other appropriate time period. The researcher also can ensure that the period is exactly 15 minutes and that the room is completely dark. In the attitude change study, the investigator determined exactly what wordings constituted "mild" and "severe." In brief, the researcher can manipulate the value of the predictor variable at will to create the desired value.

A natural predictor variable is one whose values reflect some naturally occurring attribute.

A manipulated predictor variable is one whose values can be set by the experimenter.

The experimenter also has complete control over which participant takes part in which condition. In the attitude change study, the researcher can exert tight control, not only over the instructions, but also over which child participates in which condition. For example, the researcher can decide whether to assign a participant to the mild or severe disapproval condition by tossing a coin. This random assignment is sound because it eliminates any bias that might systematically favor one condition over the other.

With natural predictor variables, the situation is different. A researcher cannot manipulate a participant's age, IQ, height, ethnic group, or the hours of sunshine in a day. A researcher cannot decide by the toss of a coin whether a participant should be assigned to the male or to the female group. The only control that a researcher has over a natural predictor variable is through selection. Participants can be chosen because they are a certain age or because they belong to a particular ethnic group; days can be selected because they had a certain amount of sunshine, fathers can be selected because they are unemployed, and so forth. In this way, groups can be formed, defined by some common characteristic of interest, and response measurements taken.

In some cases, a variable may be manipulated in one context and natural in another. Suppose an investigator is interested in the effect of a tranquilizer on problem-solving ability. One possibility would be to form two groups: an experimental group that receives the tranquilizer and a control group that does not. A second possibility is to have one group made up of volunteers who have been using the tranquilizer (by their own choice for reasons that have nothing to do with the experiment) and another group of volunteers who have not used the tranquilizer. In the former example, the predictor variable is manipulated; in the latter, it is a natural variable.

Comprehension Check 1.2

Important Concepts

1. The type of model, and the way in which data are analyzed and interpreted, depends on a number of distinctions between different kinds of variables. A variable is an attribute that can take on different values whereas a constant has a single fixed value.

2. There is an important distinction between quantitative and categorical variables. Quantitative variables assume values that represent the amount of some attribute such as time, intelligence, aggression, or family size. Ordinary arithmetic operations such as addition and multiplication can be applied to these numbers. Quantitative variables may be continuous or discrete. The values of categorical variables, on the other hand, consist of labels denoting discrete categories. A categorical variable such as country of birth can have different values for different people (United States, Canada, Mexico, etc.), but such values cannot be added or subtracted; the only permissible operation is counting the number of times each category is represented.

3. There is another important distinction between predictor, or explanatory, variables and response variables. A major goal of science is to predict the value of response variables or to explain the variability of the response measure on the basis of a given value of the predictor/explanatory variable. Predictor variables are the basis from which predictions are made, whereas the value of the response variable is the value we seek to predict. Both predictor and response variables may be either quantitative or categorical. Thus there are four possible combinations of types of predictor variables with types of response variables, all four of which can be found in behavioral sciences studies. A closely related alternative terminology refers to the predictor variable as the independent variable and the response variable as the dependent variable.

4. Predictor variables may be natural or manipulated. Natural variables such as age and country of birth refer to existing attributes, and their values cannot be manipulated by an investigator. With manipulated predictor variables such as drug dosage or the amount of reward, the investigator can determine which value of the predictor variable (amount of drug or level of reward) an experimental participant receives.

Problems

Problem 1

Would each of the following normally be considered a variable or a constant?

a. your heart rate

b. final grades of students in this course

c. distance between London and Paris

d. number of inches in a meter

e. number of minutes in an hour

f. height of adult Canadians

g. speed of light

h. weight of 4-year-old children

Problem 2

Imagine research studies using the following predictor variables. In each case, decide whether the variable is a manipulated or a natural variable.

a. in a study of academic achievement, SAT score

b. in a study of visual acuity, the exposure duration of a visual stimulus

c. in a study of behavioral problems in children, single- versus two-parent families

d. in a study of personality attributes, birth order (first-born, second-born, etc.)

e. in a study of pain sensitivity, drug versus placebo

f. in a memory study, retention interval

g. in a study of job satisfaction, years of post-secondary education

h. in a study of brain function in rats, the location of an implanted electrode

i. in a study of brain function in stroke patients, location of brain damage

j. in a study of infant development, premature versus full-term infants

Problem 3

Table 1.3 contains eight empty cells corresponding to possible combinations of types of predictor variables with types of response variables. Although similar to Table 1.2 it is expanded to include the distinction between manipulated and natural predictor variables. Following this table is the description of eight studies, representing one example of each of the eight cells. Assign each of these studies to its appropriate cell.

Study 1 How effective are different psychotherapies? A large-scale study compared the effectiveness of four major forms of therapy in the treatment of anxiety with a fifth control condition: psychodynamic; humanistic; cognitive; behavioral; no treatment (control condition). Volunteer patients were assigned by the investigator to one of the five conditions. The anxiety level of each patient after 6 months was measured, using an evaluation scale that measures anxiety level on a 100-point scale.

Study 2 Does psychological distress increase the likelihood of developing a cold? Although colds are caused by a virus, it has been argued that through their effects on the immune system, stress and negative emotional states lower the body's resistance to this virus. To investigate the matter, researchers used questionnaires to evaluate the degree of recent stress and negative emotions experienced by a large group of volunteers. This questionnaire was used to obtain a distress score (on a 10-point scale) for each of the volunteers. The volunteers were then exposed to a cold virus. The investi-

Table 1.3 Data for Problem 3

		Response variable	
		Categorical	Quantitative
Manipulated predictor variable	Categorical	_____	_____
	Quantitative	_____	_____
Natural predictor variable	Categorical	_____	_____
	Quantitative	_____	_____

gators monitored the volunteers over the following 6 days and recorded whether or not they developed a cold. This experiment is based on one conducted by Cohen et al. (1991).

Study 3 It is known that people use another's facial expression to judge which emotion that person is feeling. But are such judgments influenced by the emotional state of the person making the judgment? As part of a larger study, the investigator asked whether participant's classification of facial expressions would be influenced by how sad the participant was. To answer this question, the investigator had different groups of volunteers undergo a mood induction procedure (watching a sad movie) for different lengths of time: 0, 15, 30, or 60 minutes. After this induction procedure, each volunteer looked at a series of photographs of faces, classifying each facial expression as expressing one of six possible emotions.

Study 4 As part of a study of driver safety, an investigator wants to know the effect of blood-alcohol level on the length of time it takes for a driver's foot to reach the brake pedal following the sudden appearance of an object 50 meters in front of the car. Using a simulator that mimics this driving condition, the investigator measures this reaction time for volunteers under five different conditions: after consuming either 0, 0.5, 1.0, 1.5, 2.0, or 2.5 ounces of alcohol, administered as pure (tasteless) alcohol mixed with orange juice so that, apart from the effects of the alcohol, the volunteers are unaware of which condition they are in.

Study 5 An instructor in a course called Introductory Research Methods in the Behavioral Sciences is curious to know whether aptitude in mathematics might help predict the final grades in the course. To investigate this question, the instructor, at the beginning of the course, administers a test of mathematical aptitude to each student and compares this score with the student's final numerical course grade expressed as percentage. (Suppose the instructor found that mathematical aptitude *did* relate to final course mark. What conclusions could you draw from this finding?)

Study 6 In a study of ethnic career aspirations among adolescents, participants from five ethnic groups (Black, non-Hispanic White, Hispanic, Asian, American Indian) chose from a list of ten alternatives the occupational category they planned to pursue.

Study 7 Does the persuasive power of an argument depend on the source (as opposed to the strength) of the argument? To answer this question, an investigator presented volunteer college students with arguments in favor of requiring students to pass a set of comprehensive exams in order to graduate. Volunteers in one group were told that the arguments had been prepared by high school students; volunteers in another group heard the same arguments but were told they had been prepared by a Commission on Higher Education. After hearing the arguments, the volunteers recorded whether they agreed or disagreed with the proposal. This experiment is based on one reported by Petty, Cacioppo, and Goldman (1981).

Study 8 Are there cultural differences in self-concepts? A study designed to address this question asked American and Japanese students to take a test of self-concept in which they circled the ten statements that they considered revealed most about themselves. Some of these statements were personal attributes (*I am ambitious, I am friendly*), others were statements that served as social identifiers (*I am a student, I am the eldest son in my family*). The responses of each of the students were scored for the percentage of their responses that were statements of personal attributes.

1.3 Aspects of Experimental Design

Sound data analysis presupposes sound experimental design.

Effective data analysis presupposes sound experimental design. Before gathering data, a careful investigator gives a great deal of thought to the conditions under which observations will be made, and how subjects will be assigned to these conditions. Poor judgment in matters of design can seriously undermine the value of data, and even render it worthless.

Moreover, statistical data analysis can rarely rescue data from a badly designed experiment. In this section, we consider two concepts that are fundamental to experimental design.

1.3.1 Bias and Precision

Methods of experimental design have two broad goals:

■ to eliminate *bias*

■ to ensure adequate *precision*

Bias

Bias is the tendency for observations to differ systematically from their true value.

Suppose our goal is to estimate a person's simple reaction time. We know measurements will vary from one occasion to another, sometimes larger than the true value, sometimes smaller. Bias would exist if, as a result of some unwanted influence, the observations tended to be systematically larger (or smaller) than the true value. An estimate is unbiased if each measurement is just as likely to be greater than the true value as it is to be less, in the same way that a coin is called unbiased if it is as likely to land heads as tails.

Precision

Precision is the amount of variability in measurements. The less variability, the greater the precision.

Precision is the amount of the measurements' variability about the true value. The less variability, the greater the precision. Precision is thus the opposite of noise. Measurements of reaction time that did not stray outside the range 440 to 450 milliseconds would be more precise (less noisy) than measurements fluctuating between 400 and 500. The data in Figure 1.3 and 1.4 reflect greater precision than their noisier counterparts in Figures 1.5 and 1.6.

Relationship between Bias and Precision

Bias and precision are analogous to properties of a sharpshooter's rifle. Moore and McCabe (1993) use the metaphor of archery to make the same point, along with a figure similar to Figure 1.9. A rifle that is unbiased and precise will consistently hit close to the point that is aligned in the rifle's sight (Target A in Figure 1.9). A rifle that is unbiased but lacking precision will scatter bullets around the target, with the aligned target at the center of the scatter (Target B). A rifle that is biased but precise will consistently hit the same location (there will be little scatter), but this location will not correspond to the point aligned in the rifle's sight (Target C). A rifle that is both biased and lacking in precision will scatter bullets around a point that does not correspond to the point aligned in the rifle's sights (Target D). These figures illustrate that bias and precision are independent of each other. Measurements can be unbiased but lack precision, or be precise but biased.

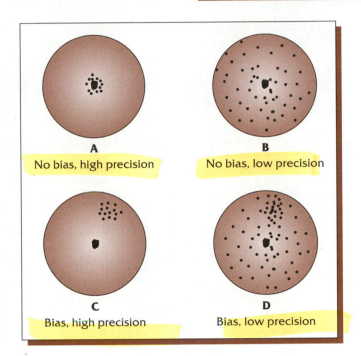

Figure 1.9
Graphical illustration of the difference between bias and precision. The center block dot is analogous to the true but unknown value of a measurement. The smaller dots represent attempts to estimate this value (After Moore & McCabe, 1993, p. 263).

1.3.2 Eliminating Bias

There are two basic techniques for handling bias:

■ experimental control

■ randomization

Experiments with Flawed Designs

Let's look at two experiments with designs that could introduce bias. We will pinpoint the design flaws and then consider how experimental control and randomization might be used to correct them.

■ *Experiment 1. Treating depression*   This experiment aims to evaluate the effectiveness of a drug designed to treat depression. The investigator plans to use a group of depressives and compare their levels of depression before and after using the drug.

■ *Experiment 2. Treating a phobia*   This experiment was designed to evaluate the effectiveness of systematic desensitization (a form of behavioral therapy) in treating a simple phobia such as fear of flying. The participants in the experiment were volunteer clients, all of whom suffered from fear of flying. The experiment has two conditions, an experimental condition and a control condition. From the total of 36 participants, the investigator asks for volunteers to be in the experimental group and accepts the first 18 who volunteer. The remaining 18 participants are assigned to the control condition.

The aim of both these experiments is to evaluate the difference between the two conditions. The data will provide an estimate of this difference for each experiment. We want this estimate to be unbiased: There should be no *systematic* influence on the difference between the two conditions other than the presence or absence of the drug

(Experiment 1) or the therapy (Experiment 2). Uncontrolled factors will inevitably introduce noise into the data and influence the observed difference, but

> *The design of the experiment must ensure that such uncontrolled influences do not tend to favor, in any systematic way, one condition over the other.*

Consider the drug example first. Comparing depression before and after the participants had undertaken the drug regimen is not an ideal procedure. If the participants did show improvement, the drug is not the only possible influence to which the improvement might be attributed. There may have been spontaneous remission over the time interval of the treatment, a phenomenon that is not at all uncommon. In this case, the observed difference between before and after is a biased estimate of the effectiveness of the drug.

In the phobia treatment experiment, the investigator invited volunteers to take part in the experimental condition and accepted the first 18 who volunteered. This form of self-selection is likely to result in a systematic difference between the participants in the two conditions. Differences are likely to exist in their personalities, in the severity of symptoms, or in any number of unknown factors, all of which might lead to an eagerness or reluctance to volunteer. For example, the more severely phobic volunteers may be more eager to try the therapy; less severely phobic volunteers may be more hesitant. It is also possible that the more severely phobic participants may believe the therapy will be ineffective in their case and therefore be *less* keen to volunteer for the experimental group. The important point is that, in either case, there would be a bias that the experimental design must eliminate, either through experimental control or randomization.

Eliminating Bias through Experimental Control

Experimental control is perhaps the most obvious method of eliminating a source of bias. It corresponds to the commonsense idea that the two conditions being compared should differ only with respect to the factor under investigation (the presence or absence of therapy, for example). Then,

> *If a difference between the two conditions is observed, the factor under investigation is the only possible cause of that difference; all other potential extraneous causes have been held constant.*

Such extraneous factors may influence the response measure; but if they do, their effect is the same for both conditions and therefore cannot create a difference.

Consider the experiment designed to evaluate the drug treatment of depression. Rather than test the same participants before and after treatment, a better design would be to have an experimental group that receives the drug and a control group of different participants who do not receive the drug. This experimental procedure eliminates spontaneous remission as a source of difference, because, if it occurs at all, it should occur equally in both groups.

However, other factors in this experiment remain uncontrolled. For example, the expectations of the participants and of the investigator can influence response measures.

Use of a double-blind technique can eliminate these potential sources of bias. This control is commonly achieved by ensuring that neither the participant nor the observer knows whether the participant was in the experimental condition receiving the drug or in the control condition.

This "blindness" is usually established by using a *placebo* for the control participants. A placebo could take the form of a look-alike pill containing no active substance. Volunteers in both groups follow identical procedures and receive exactly the same instructions. The only difference is the presence or absence of the active drug ingredient inside an identical pill casing.

When a possible source of influence (such as the participants' expectations, or spontaneous recovery) has been left uncontrolled, the results of an experiment are ambiguous because the outcome has more than one possible cause. In such cases, the possible causes are said to be confounded.

For example, if the groups differ with respect to both the therapeutic procedure and participants' expectations, then therapeutic procedure is confounded with participants' expectations.

The double-blind technique is just one example of the many strategies that investigators have at their disposal as a means of improving experimental control. Although the general need for experimental control may be intuitively obvious,

Designing an experiment with adequate experimental control depends on knowledge of the content area.

Investigators acquire a knowledge base of potential biases that may be quite unfamiliar to an expert in another area. Experts in the area of child behavior are sensitive to the biases that can arise when studying young children; social psychologists know the biases that can result from the interaction between a participant and an investigator. Every domain of study has its own minefield of potential biases. However familiar a researcher may be with the theory and principles of experimental design, conducting research in an unfamiliar area is a hazardous undertaking.

Eliminating Bias through Randomization

The original design of the phobia treatment experiment was criticized on the grounds that assigning the first volunteers to the experimental condition introduced a bias attributable to systematic differences among participants in the two conditions. There are many other differences among participants that constitute a potential source of bias. Examples are age, sex, and severity of phobia, attitude toward therapy, motivation, and personality variables. You can probably think of many more. The challenge is to ensure that the influences exerted by such factors do not bias the estimate of the difference between the two conditions.

In theory, these factors could be subject to experimental control by equating the two groups with respect to age, sex, and every other conceivable influence. In practice, it may be possible to equate one or two of these factors—say, age and sex—but

Randomization can supplement or replace experimental control as a means of removing bias.

matching on more than a few such factors is usually impossibly complex and expensive. Moreover, no matter how many factors are equated, it can never be assumed that every relevant source of bias has been covered. The practical solution to this problem is to supplement or replace the strategy of experimental control with that of randomization. Whether a particular participant is assigned to the experimental group or the control group is determined by chance. We will refer to this process as random assignment.

Random assignment is a process in which all possible assignments of participants to conditions are equally likely. Imagine that you are required to assign the 36 participants randomly to the two groups of the phobia experiment, placing 18 in each group. One way of doing this would be to have each participant choose a card from a well-shuffled deck of 36 cards, 18 of which are designated Experimental and 18 designated Control. In practice, random assignment is achieved by using a computer to simulate this process. Before the availability of computers, researchers typically used published tables of random numbers to achieve this end. Whatever method is used to achieve randomization, it should be objective. One device that is especially poor at randomizing is human intuition. Attempts at informal, intuitive random assignment of participants to conditions (for example, "The last two were in the experimental condition, so I think it's about time to have someone in the control condition") guarantees that the assignment will *not* be random.

Whatever method is used to achieve randomization, the method should be objective.

Random assignment ensures that any differences between conditions cannot be attributed to a bias in the way in which participants were assigned to conditions. Any difference between conditions that results from individual differences among participants is governed purely by chance.

Control and Randomization Compared

It is important to be clear on the distinction between these two techniques, because they are based on quite different principles. Experimental control eliminates bias by creating a level playing field. It equates or holds constant potential sources of bias. Randomization, on the other hand, does not guarantee such equality. Rather, it ensures that the effects of any inequality between the conditions are chance-governed and therefore unsystematic. Experimental control ensures equality; randomization ensures only equal opportunity.

There is a further difference between experimental control and randomization. Experimental control provides a means of *eliminating* the effects of the unwanted influence, whereas randomization *distributes* these effects in a random (and thus unbiased) fashion across the conditions.

1.3.3 Studies with Natural Predictor Variables

Section 1.2.4 distinguished between natural and manipulated predictor variables. Natural variables are variables such as age, country of birth, sex, and the like. Such variables refer to existing attributes, so, for a given individual, the investigator cannot manipulate their values.

A direct consequence of using natural predictor variables is that random assignment of participants to conditions is impossible.

No random process can assign a child to a 10-year-old group if he or she happens to be 12 years old.

In experiments that do not use randomization, great care must be taken to avoid drawing unwarranted conclusions about causes. There are two kinds of causal ambiguity. The first kind concerns the direction of causality—a confusion between cause and effect. Suppose a researcher finds that behavioral problems are more prevalent among children in families with high levels of spousal conflict. A natural interpretation of such a result is that spousal conflict caused the behavior problems in the children of that family. But it is possible that causality could also operate in the opposite direction, that the children's behavioral problems caused spousal conflict—heated arguments, for example, over how children should be disciplined.

Directional ambiguity can sometimes be resolved on logical grounds. An investigation might find that 10-year-olds learn a task more rapidly than 8-year-olds. Clearly, learning speed cannot cause a change in age. In other cases, one direction of causation is far more plausible than the other. Suppose child abuse is found to be higher in families in which the father is unemployed. It is logically possible that child abuse could cause unemployment—for example, if the parent were fired as a consequence of a criminal conviction for child abuse. But a more plausible interpretation is that unemployment status has causal links to the abusive behavior—the father is at home all day, suffers from a sense of frustration and low self-esteem, and so forth.

Care needs to be taken when appealing to plausiblity as a means of deciding the direction of causality. Sometimes the less plausible direction turns out to be the correct one. A good example is the relation between reading skill and the frequency of regressive eye movements. Regressive eye movements occur during reading when the eye fixates back on a point in the text that has already been read. It is known that poor readers have more regressive eye movements than do good readers. One interpretation is that regressive eye movements are a bad reading habit that causes slow reading, and that reading could therefore be improved by eliminating these movements. Is there an alternative interpretation? There is, and it turns out to be the correct one. Rather than being the cause of bad reading, regressive eye movements are *caused by* poor reading. They usually reflect a comprehension failure that requires a regressive movement to fill in missed information. Thus direct attempts to eliminate regressive eye movements are not likely to be effective.

There is a second source of ambiguity that is more pervasive and often more subtle than the confusion between the direction of cause and effect. This possibility is that the only causal link between the predictor and the response variable is through some third extraneous factor. One possible cause for a higher rate of child abuse in families in which the father is unemployed is that a third factor—perhaps a highly aggressive personality—has led to both unemployment and abusive behavior.

Causal ambiguity arises from the fact that when groups are formed on the basis of some naturally occurring attribute, the groups will differ, not only with respect to *that* attribute, but also with respect to all other related attributes. Families that differ with respect to the employment status of the father are likely also to differ with respect to family income and a host of other variables. Unlike manipulated predictor variables, the researcher cannot ensure that the specified basis of natural predictor variables is the only basis on which groups might differ.

The problems associated with natural predictor variables should not be taken to mean that such studies have no value. They can suggest causal relationships, even if they do not establish them unambiguously. These suggested hypotheses can then be followed up with further studies. Moreover, the use of natural predictor variables is

One kind of causal ambiguity is in the direction of causality: between cause and effect.

A second kind of causal ambiguity is the possible role of a third extraneous factor.

sometimes the only way of investigating certain questions. Manipulated predictor variables frequently pose insurmountable practical or ethical problems; often both. Quite apart from the practical obstacles, it is difficult to imagine obtaining ethical approval to manipulate employment status or family size. Because the understanding to be gained is important, sophisticated methodologies for studies using natural predictor variables have been developed in an effort to investigate possible causal relations. Such methodologies (termed causal modeling) are well beyond the scope of this book, but you should be aware that such methods exist.

Comprehension Check 1.3

Important Concepts

1. The goal of experimental design is to eliminate bias and ensure adequate precision.

2. Bias is an effect that systematically influences one condition differently from another.

3. Precision refers to the amount of the measurements' variability about the true value.

4. One method of controlling bias is through experimental control. The goal of experimental control is to ensure that potentially biasing influences are held constant across the conditions of an experiment.

5. Randomization is a second method of eliminating bias. Randomization does not eliminate the effect of uncontrolled and unwanted influences. Rather it ensures that such influences are determined by chance and thus do not exert a systematic biasing effect.

6. Studies with natural predictor variables cannot use randomization to assign participants to conditions. The causal interpretation of the results from such studies can be ambiguous.

Chapter 1 Exercises

Exercise 1   "Foot-in-the-door" phenomenon

Suppose your task is to persuade people to place large antipollution signs on their front lawns. What processes might influence a person's willingness to comply with such a request? One possibility (in which some salespeople obviously believe) is often referred to as the "foot-in-the-door" effect. Compliance, so the claim goes, is more likely if you have already persuaded the person to agree to a much more innocuous request. Attribution theory provides some plausibility for this prediction. According to one interpretation of attribution theory, the initial compliance to the innocuous request changes the participant's disposition and attitude toward such actions. Given that very mild pressure was all that was needed to obtain compliance to this request, the tendency is for the participant to attribute compliance to internal (dispositional) causes rather than to external causes such as the persuasiveness of the interviewer. This change in self-perception then encourages compliance to the second, larger request. The validity of this hypothesis is examined in the following experiment. It is modeled after the original study reported by Freedman and Fraser (1966).

In this experiment, each of 80 households is to be asked to mount a large anti-pollution sign. An interviewer visits a randomly selected half of these households just once and asks them to mount the large sign. The interviewer records whether they agree or refuse to mount the sign. The other 40 households are visited twice. On the first visit, the interviewer makes a relatively innocuous request—to sign a petition promoting a clean environment. Then, a week later, the same interviewer returns with the more substantial request to mount the sign. The interviewer again records whether they agree or refuse to mount the sign. Will households in this second, two-visit group be more willing to mount the sign than those in the one-visit group?

a. What is the predictor variable in this experiment?

b. Is the predictor variable quantitative or categorical?

c. Is the predictor variable natural or manipulated?

d. What values of the predictor variable are used in the study? Note that for categorical predictor variables, the values are the names of the categories.

e. What is the response variable in this experiment?

f. Is the response variable quantitative or categorical?

g. What are the possible values of the response variable in the study?

Exercise 2   Undermining intrinsic motivation

Attributional analyses have also been used to understand children's behavior. The participants in this study are nursery school children, all of whom have displayed at least a moderate interest in drawing as a voluntary activity. All children are asked to make some drawings and are given 6 minutes to do so. Before this period of drawing begins, half of the participants are told that they will receive a "Good Player Award" as a reward for their participation. The other half are told nothing about a reward and receive none.

One week later, all the children take part in a 1-hour free-play session. Drawing is one of the activities they can choose. An observer measures the amount of time each child spends drawing during this 1-hour period. Will the two groups differ in this measure? One obvious prediction is that children in the previously rewarded condition will spend more time drawing. However, an attributional analysis suggests exactly the opposite. This experiment is modeled after experiments reported by Lepper, Greene, and Nisbett (1973).

There were 38 participants in this experiment. They were assigned randomly to the two conditions, 19 participants in each.

a. What is the predictor variable in this experiment?

b. Is the predictor variable quantitative or categorical?

c. Is the predictor variable natural or manipulated?

d. What values of the predictor variable are used in the study?

e. What is the response variable in this experiment?

f. Is the response variable quantitative or categorical?

Exercise 3   Imitation of gestures in 3-week-old infants

In this previously mentioned study, we ask whether infants as young as 3 weeks show any capacity to imitate gestures such as protruding the lips or tongue, opening the mouth, or moving their fingers in a simple sequence of movements. To answer this question, investigators place 14- to 21-day-old infants in a darkened room with nothing to look at except the well-lit face of the model, who is a person the infant has not seen before. The model performs one of the experimental gestures, and the infant's response is recorded. To avoid the biasing influence of expectation, the person who classifies the infant's response is unaware of the model's gesture, a safeguard known as "blind" scoring. The responses to each of the four gestures are classified into one of seven categories of gestures, and the number of responses in each category is tallied. In Table 1.4, the numbers in bold type correspond to imitative responses (e.g., responding with a lip protrusion to a lip protrusion gesture). The study and the results are modeled after a number of studies described in Rosenblith (1992, p. 366).

a. What is the predictor variable in this experiment?

b. Is the predictor variable quantitative or categorical?

c. Is the predictor variable natural or manipulated?

d. What values of the predictor variable are used in the study?

e. What is the response variable in this experiment?

f. Is the response variable quantitative or categorical?

g. What are the possible values of the response variable in the study?

h. Examine the data in the table. Do you see any meaning in these numbers in terms of an answer to the question: Is there any evidence that infants imitate gestures?

Table 1.4 Data for Exercise 3

| | Gesture shown to infant | | | |
Responses	Lip protrusion	Mouth opening	Tongue protrusion	Finger movements
Lip protrusion	**29**	18	16	20
Mouth opening	12	**27**	18	19
Tongue protrusion	22	21	**31**	26
Finger movements	15	14	17	**28**
Hand opening	23	23	29	24
Finger protrusion	20	20	10	10
Passive hand	19	17	19	13

Exercise 4 Intermodal matching in 1-month-old infants

Imagine being blindfolded and asked to explore a novel object by touch. The blindfold is then removed and you are asked to pick out this object from a larger set of similarly (but not identically) shaped objects. This task in *intermodal matching* is easily accomplished by experienced children or adults, but what of 1-month-old infants? One possibility is that, at the beginning of life, sense modalities are independent and the ability to correlate visual with tactual sense impressions requires experience in the simultaneous visual and tactual exploration of shapes. Another possibility is that such matching can occur without direct experience.

In this experiment, modeled after results reported by Meltzoff and Borton (1979), 40 infants ranging in age from 26 to 33 days were given 90 seconds of tactual (oral) familiarization with (less technically, they were allowed to suck) one of two objects resembling a pacifier. Care was taken to ensure that the infant could not see the object. For one of these objects, the section that the infant sucked was a smooth sphere; for the other, it was a smooth sphere to which had been attached a number of small nubs, thus making it both tactually and visually distinct. After the 90-second period of familiarization, infants were shown both shapes side by side for a period of 20 seconds. One shape was tactually familiar, the other was not. The response variable was a measure of visual preference, that is, the proportion of total looking time the infant spends looking at the tactually familiar object. Preference is indicated by the extent to which this proportion is greater than 50%. To show a preference, of course, the infant must be able to discriminate visually between the two objects.

   a. What is the predictor variable in this experiment?

   b. Is the predictor variable quantitative or categorical?

   c. Is the predictor variable natural or manipulated?

   d. What values of the predictor variable are used in the study?

   e. What is the response variable in this experiment?

   f. Is the response variable quantitative or categorical?

   g. A model for the results of this experiment might take the following form:

$$\text{proportion of looking time} = 50\% + A$$

How, verbally, would you describe the quantity A?

Exercise 5 Short-term forgetting

In this short-term memory experiment, participants were shown three consonants, for example, **P-S-K.** Immediately upon reading the three letters, a three-digit number appears, for example, **708.** Participants were instructed that upon seeing the number they are to begin immediately counting backward by threes: "705, 702, . . ." as rapidly as possible until a tone sounds, at which point they are to recall the initial three consonants. Participants were given a long sequence of these trials. The tone occurred after either 3, 6, 9, 12, 15, or 18 seconds of backward counting. These were the six different retention intervals. The short-term memory of each of the 35 participants is the proportion of correctly remembered items at each retention interval.

a. What is the predictor variable in this experiment?

b. Is the predictor variable quantitative or categorical?

c. Is the predictor variable natural or manipulated?

d. What values of the predictor variable are used in the study?

e. What is the response variable in this experiment?

f. Is the response variable quantitative or categorical?

g. A retention interval of 10 seconds is not one of the values of the predictor variable included in this experiment. However, the data might be used to make a prediction about the probability of remembering after 10 seconds. Explain in general terms how such a prediction might be possible.

Exercise 6   The peg word mnemonic

A commonly used mnemonic technique is known as the "peg word" method. The first step in mastering this technique is to learn a set of ten words that serve as pegs on which to "hang" the items to be remembered. The most common peg list is the following rhyme.

one is a bun	*six is a stick*
two is a shoe	*seven is a heaven*
three is a tree	*eight is a gate*
four is a door	*nine is a line*
five is a hive	*ten is a hen*

Researchers designed an experiment to evaluate this technique. In one condition (normal instructions), participants were given 20 words and instructed simply to "try to remember" each so that they could later recall the words. In the other condition (mnemonic instructions), participants studied the same 20 words but were instructed in the peg method. They first learned the list of ten peg words and were then instructed to associate (using imagery) two words with each peg. One day later, participants were asked to recall the list of 20 items.

The experimenter recorded the number of words correctly recalled out of 20.

a. What is the predictor variable in this experiment?

b. Is the predictor variable quantitative or categorical?

c. Is the predictor variable natural or manipulated?

d. What values of the predictor variable are used in the study?

e. What is the response variable in this experiment?

f. Is the response variable quantitative or categorical?

Chapter 1 Review

Terms

You should know the meaning of the following terms.

bias
discrete and continuous quantitative variables
experimental control
manipulated and natural variables
model
parsimony
precision
quantitative and categorical variables
randomization
residual
response and predictor or explanatory variables
statistics (two meanings)
strict and general replicability

Quiz

Complete each sentence with a term from the following list. The same term may be used more than once.

2%	5%	bias	categorical
confounding	continuous	discrete	explanatory variable
general replicability	manipulated	model	natural
parsimonious	predictor	quantitative	randomly
residual	response	strict replicability	

A statement that predicts (explains) the value of a response variable for a given value of the predictor variable is called a _____. If the values of the predictor variable are attributes of the participants (such as their height), then it is called a _____ predictor variable. If the attribute was age, then it is a _____ natural predictor variable, whereas if it was country of birth, it would be a _____ natural predictor variable. A term equivalent to predictor variable is _____.

An experiment comparing the effectiveness of three different instructional methods (labeled A, B, and C) for teaching arithmetic assigned 20 different students to each method. The labels A, B, and C constitute the values of a _____ _____ _____ variable. The effectiveness of the methods was evaluated, using a standard test of arithmetic. Students' scores on this test are values of a _____ _____ variable.

The investigator claims that method A improved performance by 10% more than did methods B and C and that there was no difference between B and C. More precisely, the investigator's _____ predicts a test score of 75% for students from method A and 65% for students from methods B and C. Betty was a student in method A who scored 80% on the test. This score has a _____ of 5%. Alex studied under method B and scored 67%. This score has a _____ of _____%.

A critic of this study claims that all three teaching methods are equally effective and that the apparent benefit of method A was a fluke. Whether or not it is correct, the critic's claim is more _____ than that of the investigator.

Prompted by this criticism, the investigator repeats the experiment, finding this time that method A improves performance by 8% more than did methods B and C, and that again there is no difference between B and C. This second result is an example of _____ although a failure of _____.

The investigator reveals that each of the three instructional methods was taught by a different teacher and that participants were allowed to sign up for whichever teacher they preferred. This method of assigning the participants to conditions is likely to intro-duce _____ into estimates of the differences between conditions, _____ the effects of the instructional methods with teacher ability, and differences among the students. A better method would have been to assign the participants _____.

In a study of social development, the predictor variable was age. In a second study, the predictor variable was number of siblings. Both these variables are natural and quan-titative, but age is a _____ quantitative variable whereas number of siblings is a _____ quantitative variable.

Chapter 2 Preview

Chapter 1 describes the broad goals of statistical data analysis and introduces some of the basic terminology that distinguishes different kinds of variables.

In Chapter 2, we begin to examine actual data. Data provide the basis on which models are fitted and evaluated; but before proceeding with these steps, we first need to explore the data. We need to ensure that there are no abnormalities that would make model fitting or evaluation problematic. We also need to calculate basic numerical summaries that capture important properties of the data. Having completed this task in Chapter 2, in Chapter 3 we will begin to combine the general concepts of Chapter 1 with the specific numbers of Chapter 2.

2 GRAPHICAL AND NUMERICAL DESCRIPTIONS OF DATA

In Chapter 1, we set out the broad goals of statistical data analysis. In this chapter, we begin a detailed treatment of actual data. The ultimate goal is to use data to construct and evaluate models; but before we can achieve this objective, we need to be able to display data and provide a numerical description of their basic features. As always, it is reasonable to ask why. There are three reasons: to communicate, to estimate, and to check data fitness.

Communication The first reason for displaying and describing data is communication. It is often desirable to display data in a way that makes their important features readily comprehensible to the reader. Both graphs and numerical descriptors can serve this purpose, and both are commonplace in magazines, news reports, and scientific publications. The reporting of unemployment rates, family income, baseball standings, results of opinion polls, or the national debt are everyday examples. The use of graphs and numbers to capture the basic features of a set of data is often referred to as *descriptive statistics*, and as noted in the introduction to Chapter 1, the numerical descriptors themselves are referred to simply as *statistics*. It is customary to distinguish descriptive statistics from *inferential statistics*, procedures through which the data are used to make inferences—inferences about the components of a model, for example.

Estimation The concept of inferential statistics leads to the second reason for descriptive statistics: They provide the basic numerical building blocks of the models to be described in Chapter 3. In this context, statistics are more than simple descriptions of data. They serve as estimates of what might be true more generally, what might be true in the population.

How accurate are these estimates? If an experiment leads to the claim that an increase in blood-alcohol level from 0 to 0.05% increases reaction time by 0.2 seconds, how accurate is the value 0.2? Might the true value be 0.3 seconds, or even 0? An opinion poll may claim that 34% of voters favor one presidential candidate and 30% a rival candidate. These are descriptive statistics. But are these percentages accurate enough to ensure that the apparent lead of the first candidate is real and not just an

Descriptive statistical procedures use graphs and numbers to capture the basic features of a data set.

Inferential statistical procedures use data to make inferences.

artifact of the particular sample of voters polled? The major role of inferential statistics is to answer such questions, and although it might seem paradoxical, we will see as the story unfolds that the basis of such answers is a bootstrap operation through which the statistics themselves provide the answer.

Health Check The third reason for representing data with graphs and numerical descriptors is to ensure that our data are "healthy." Data are healthy if there are no features that would make it misleading to use a particular descriptive statistic or that would undermine our ability to obtain sound answers to the inferential questions posed in the preceding paragraph. A symptom of ill health that we will look for is the presence of *outliers:* rogue data points that are way out of line with the rest of the data. Graphical methods of displaying data are particularly useful in detecting such symptoms. If the data do have features that undermine accurate communication or the soundness of a planned method of analysis, then appropriate steps must be taken. Either we must somehow treat the symptoms or, if that proves to be impossible, switch to less misleading descriptors or a more appropriate method of analysis.

Data points that are way out of line with the rest of the data are called outliers.

We begin the diagnostic process by examining various methods of arranging data into tables and graphs so that important features become obvious under simple inspection. We then consider various numerical descriptors that also capture basic features and, as we pursue our efforts to explain the data, will serve as the building blocks for the fitting and evaluation of models.

2.1 Displaying Data as Distributions of Frequencies

There are several methods of tabulating and graphing data. We will first consider categorical variables and then quantitative variables.

2.1.1 Frequency Distributions for Categorical Variables

Categorical variables, you will recall, are variables that consist of a set of categories such as country of birth, occupation, gender, or species. With categorical variables, data will be a record of which category each observation belongs to.

The values of categorical variables are simply names or some other symbol serving as a label for each category. Consider the data in Data Set 2.1, which are based on a study of 26 infants' imitations of adult gestures. In this study, the infant is seated in front of the adult who, when she has the infant's attention, makes a gesture such as opening her mouth or poking out her tongue. The table records which of five

Data Set 2.1   Gestures of 26 infants in response to seeing tongue protrusion
(Response code: LP, lip protrusion; MO, mouth opening; TP, tongue protrusion; FM, finger movements; HO, hand opening.)

Infant	1	2	3	4	5	6	7	8	9	10	11	12	13
Response	TP	FM	MO	HO	TP	MO	HO	TP	LP	TP	MO	FM	TP

Infant	14	15	16	17	18	19	20	21	22	23	24	25	26
Response	HO	LP	FM	TP	MO	HO	LP	HO	TP	MO	LP	HO	TP

Table 2.1 Frequency distribution for the data in Data Set 2.1

Response	Frequency
Lip protrusion (LP)	4
Mouth opening (MO)	5
Tongue protrusion (TP)	8
Finger movements (FM)	3
Hand opening (HO)	6

possible responses each infant gave after seeing an adult model poke out her tongue (tongue protrusion).

Just looking over Data Set 2.1 does not tell us much. However, if we count up the number of times each response was given, we get the results given in Table 2.1, and this tabulation enables us to see the pattern of results more clearly. Such a table is called a *table of frequencies.* It tells us, for example, that four infants responded with the gesture of protruding their lips and five with opening their mouth. Because categorical data consist simply of counting up the frequency for each category (rather than an observation that is the quantity of some attribute), such data are often referred to as "count data."

2.1.2 Graphs of Frequency Distributions for Categorical Variables

The most common graphical representation of frequency distributions of categorical variables is the *bar chart.* A bar chart of the frequencies in Table 2.1 is shown in Figure 2.1. The height of each bar indicates the frequency of occurrence of one

Bar charts are used to display frequencies of categorical variables.

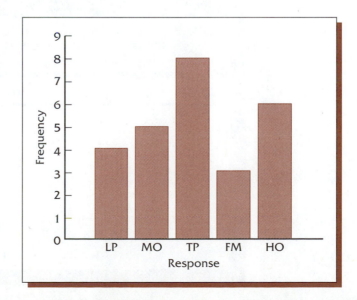

Figure 2.1
Bar chart of the frequency distribution in Table 2.1. Response abbreviations are defined in Table 2.1.

category. Notice that a space is left between each bar. This is a customary way of indicating that each category is distinct or separate. (As we will see in Section 2.1.4, if the variable is quantitative, then no space is left between the bars.) Notice, too, that the order of the five response categories along the horizontal axis is quite arbitrary. Any other ordering would have been equally acceptable.

Now consider the data in Data Set 2.2, which represent the brand choice of 50 consumers who were asked to choose between five brands, labeled A through E. The frequency distribution for this data set is shown in Table 2.2. The appropriate bar chart is shown in Figure 2.2.

Data Set 2.2 Brand choice of 50 consumers

C	B	F	C	C	E	A	A	C	D
C	C	B	D	C	E	A	D	C	C
D	A	C	D	B	C	B	C	D	C
B	D	C	B	F	A	C	B	F	C
B	D	A	D	B	B	C	D	B	C

It is often more meaningful to convert the raw frequencies into proportions of the total number of observations. Instead of reporting that 6 out of the 50 consumers preferred brand A, we report that .12, or 12%, of the consumers preferred that brand. The resulting distribution is called a *proportional frequency distribution.* Notice that when plotted as a bar chart, this proportional frequency distribution will look exactly the same as that for the simple frequencies; the only change is in the scale on the vertical axis.

Table 2.2 Distribution of frequencies (f) and proportions of brand preferences of 50 consumers

Brand	f	Proportion
A	6	.12
B	11	.22
C	18	.36
D	10	.20
E	2	.04
F	3	.06
Total	50	1.00

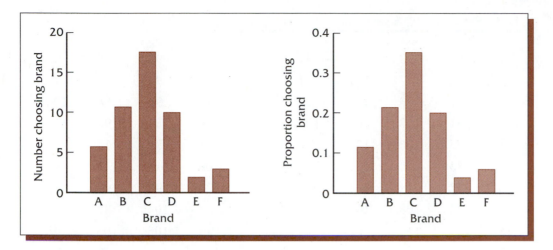

Figure 2.2
Bar chart of frequencies and of proportions for the brand preferences given in Table 2.2.

2.1.3 Frequency Distributions for Quantitative Variables

With quantitative variables, numbers replace category labels as the basis for tallying frequencies. The switch to quantitative variables requires a few modifications that will be introduced through examples. Consider the study (also described in Problem 3 of Section 1.2) exploring cultural differences in self-concepts. American and Japanese students were asked to take a test of self-concept in which they circled the ten statements that revealed most about themselves. Some of these statements were personal attributes *(I am ambitious, I am friendly);* others were statements that served as social identifiers *(I am a student, I am the eldest son in my family).* The following data are for the American students only. Each score is the number of responses (out of a maximum of ten) that were statements of personal attributes.

4	6	7	7	6	4	8	6	9	8
8	5	6	7	6	6	5	8	3	6

Even with such a small number of single-digit scores, it is not easy to extract information from such a listing. An effective way of describing these ratings would be to tally the frequency with which each occurs. The resulting table of frequencies is shown in Table 2.3, in which ratings are denoted by the letter Y. The column headed f indicates the frequency with which that score occurred. Thus a rating of $Y = 9$ occurred once, a rating of $Y = 8$, four times, and so on. Notice that the column of frequencies (the numbers in the f column) must sum to the total number of scores in the sample, namely, 20. We will denote this total by n.

In this example, there are only seven different scores (3 through 9), so it is easy to list each score individually and tally its frequency. However, when scores span a much wider range, it is unreasonable to list every score individually. Why? Consider Data Set 2.3, which gives intelligence test (IQ) scores taken from a sample of 100 participants. These scores range from 69 to 142. We could tally the frequency of occurrence for each of the 74 scores that span this range, but because there are only 100 scores in all, most of these tallies would be either 1 or 0.

Table 2.3
Frequency distribution of number of personal-attribute statements circled by American students

Y	f
9	1
8	4
7	3
6	6
5	3
4	2
3	1
	$n = 20$

f denotes frequency.

n denotes the total number of observations in a sample.

Data Set 2.3   IQ scores for 100 participants

98	80	93	69	109	81	123	97	87	88
74	102	127	111	104	137	79	98	96	97
113	122	100	107	88	123	113	96	88	106
137	91	103	100	109	75	96	101	95	118
96	123	106	133	79	120	91	88	114	80
96	83	102	101	97	142	100	114	113	89
108	82	95	104	121	96	71	93	93	84
97	92	108	104	91	93	84	104	82	96
85	124	114	92	93	119	96	105	103	108
117	111	124	97	135	92	114	103	92	97

Class Intervals

When scores cover a wide range, they can be grouped into class intervals.

There is a simple solution to the problem posed by the wide range of individual scores. It is to group the scores into intervals and then tally the frequency of scores that fall within each of these intervals. For example, rather than tallying the frequency of an IQ of 107, we treat a score of 107 as a member of the interval 100–109. These intervals are called *class intervals*, and frequencies correspond to the number of scores belonging to each of the class intervals. Table 2.4 shows a distribution using class intervals.

Table 2.4 Frequency distribution of IQ scores for 100 participants

Class interval	f
140–149	1
130–139	4
120–129	9
110–119	12
100–109	23
90–99	30
80–89	15
70–79	5
60–69	1
	Total f = 100

Deciding on the Number of Class Intervals

There are a number of practical considerations that enter into the construction of a frequency distribution using class intervals. How many intervals should there be? What should their width be? There are no hard and fast answers to these questions, but there are guidelines. Remember that the purpose of forming frequency distributions is to convey information—to display the data in a way that shows its salient features and reveals any abnormalities. The guidelines, then, are intended to be used, along with good sense, to strike a balance between showing too much detail and showing too little detail.

As a rule of thumb, the number of class intervals should be somewhere between 5 and 15. Within this range, the larger the number of scores (n), the larger the number of class intervals that are justified. It is inappropriate to have 15 different class intervals if there are only 20 scores; but if $n = 200$, the larger number of class intervals may be justified. It is customary to make the width of the class interval a convenient number such as 2, 5, 10, or some multiple of 10. Intervals should all be the same width. Putting these guidelines together leads to the following procedure for deciding on the number and width of class intervals.

> **Class intervals should all be the same width.**

Step 1 Find the difference between largest and smallest score to determine the range.

Step 2 Divide the range by a possible class interval width, such as 2, 5, or 10. The quotient gives the approximate number of class intervals, so you are looking for a width that yields a quotient between 5 and 15. If the division yields a fraction, as it usually will, round up to the next whole number.

In the IQ example, the highest of the 100 scores was 142 and the lowest 69. Thus the range is $142 - 69 = 73$. A class interval width of 5 would yield approximately 15 class intervals ($73/5 = 14.6$), whereas a width of 10 yields approximately 8 class intervals. These estimates may be off by 1 or 2, depending on the exact values of the highest and lowest scores relative to the boundaries of the class intervals, but the approximation is good enough to make the necessary decision. In this example, a class interval width of 10 requires the lowest interval to be 60–69 and the highest interval to be 140–149, resulting in a total of nine intervals. With a class interval width of 5, the lowest and highest intervals would be 65–69 and 140–144, respectively, yielding a total of sixteen intervals. A width of 2 would obviously yield too many intervals. A width of either 5 or 10 would be acceptable, although the width of 5 gives 16 class intervals, which is just above our guideline maximum of 15. The relatively large number of scores (100) might be used to justify this departure from the guidelines. Neither width is wrong, and the choice is largely a matter of taste. In Table 2.4, for example, we opted for the wider class interval and fewer intervals.

2.1.4 Graphs of Frequency Distributions for Quantitative Variables

There are three forms of graphs commonly used to represent frequency distributions for quantitative variables. One such graph, known as a histogram, is a close relative of the bar chart. The second is the frequency polygon, and the third is known as a stemplot.

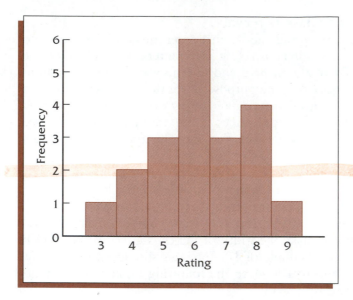

Figure 2.3
Frequency histogram of the ratings from Table 2.3.

Histograms

A histogram uses adjoining bars to depict class frequencies.

A histogram of the data in Table 2.3 is shown in Figure 2.3. Notice that, unlike the bar chart, a histogram has no gaps between the bars. Such gaps would be inappropriate, because the intervals are not discrete categories as they were with categorical variables, but sections of a quantitative continuum.

The histogram for the distribution of IQ scores with a class interval width of 10 is shown in Figure 2.4. What would this histogram have looked like if we had elected the narrower class interval of 5? The graph of such a distribution is shown in Figure 2.5.

Frequency Polygons

The frequency polygon is essentially the same graph as a histogram. The only difference is that instead of representing the frequency of each class interval with a bar,

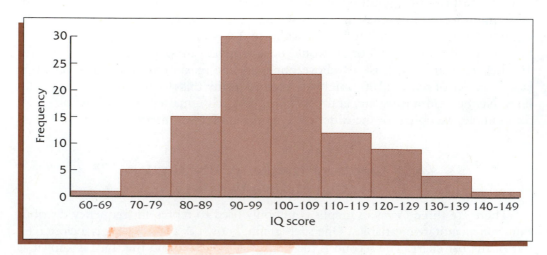

Figure 2.4
Frequency histogram of the IQ scores from Table 2.4.

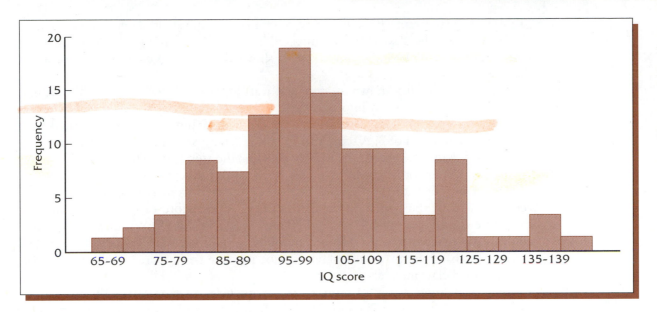

Figure 2.5
Frequency histogram of the IQ scores with class intervals of width 5.

in a polygon the frequency is represented by a point located above the midpoint of the class interval (Figure 2.6).

The height of the point corresponds to the frequency of that class interval. The polygon is then formed by joining these points with straight lines. At each end of the distribution, a line is drawn down to the *x*-axis, representing 0 frequency for the class intervals below the bottom and above the top class intervals.

A frequency polygon uses points to depict class frequencies.

Stemplots

When frequencies are tabulated in class intervals, information is lost about the particular value of each score within the interval. In the distribution of IQ scores

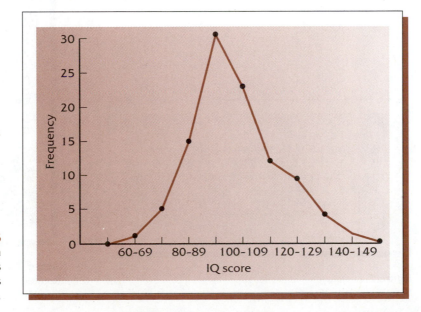

Figure 2.6
Frequency polygon of the IQ scores with class intervals of width 10.

(Table 2.4), a score of 101 and 108 were treated as equivalent. They counted simply as two scores in the class 100–109 interval. The tabulation in Figure 2.7, known as a *stemplot,* avoids this loss of information. It shows the same IQ data used to construct Table 2.4.

Stemplots are also known as stem-and-leaf displays. To construct such a display, each score is broken down into two parts: a *leaf,* which is the last digit of the score, and a *stem,* which is all the digits before the last digit. Thus a score of 87 would have a stem of 8 and a leaf of 7. A score of 121 would have a stem of 12 and a leaf of 1.

The left-hand column of the display contains the stems, usually ordered from low to high, although ordering from high to low is also acceptable. The leaf is the sequence of numbers to the right of each stem, ordered from low to high. Thus the very first row in the display indicates that there is one score of 69, the second row that there is one score of 71, 74, and 75 and two scores of 79. With a stemplot, you could reconstruct the entire data set, number by number, without any loss of information. Such an exact reconstruction is not possible from a frequency distribution with grouped class intervals.

Stemplots are also known as stem-and-leaf displays.

Stemplots offer a way of representing frequencies that preserves the identity of each number. They also offer some of the advantages of a frequency distribution, and even some of the graphical features of a histogram. If each digit in the leaf is typed such that each digit occupies a constant width on the page, then the length of the leaf is a graphical representation of frequency. Turn the stemplot on its side and each leaf corresponds to the column of a histogram, the stem indicating the class interval (Figure 2.8). Note that this technique works only if the original stem values were ordered from low (top of plot) to high (bottom of plot).

Notice that the stem numbers in Figure 2.7 correspond to a frequency distribution with a class interval width of 10. Just as it is possible to form shorter class intervals in an ordinary frequency distribution, it is possible to split a stem into two or

Figure 2.8
Rotated version of the stemplot from Figure 2.7.

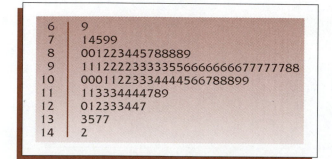

Figure 2.7
Stemplot of the IQ data.

```
 6 |  9
 7 |  14
 7 |  599
 8 |  00122344
 8 |  5788889
 9 |  111222233333
 9 |  5566666666677777788
10 |  00011223334444
10 |  566788899
11 |  113334444
11 |  789
12 |  01233344
12 |  7
13 |  3
13 |  577
14 |  2
```

Figure 2.9
Stemplot of the IQ data with a stem width of 5 rather than 10.

more parts. For example, the stem value of 7 in Figure 2.7 supports a leaf for all values of 70 through 79. We can split this stem into one part that supports a leaf for values 70 through 74, and a second part that supports values 75 through 79. Figure 2.9 shows a stemplot for the same data, with each stem value corresponding to a class interval width of 5.

Two distributions—say, from two conditions of an experiment—can be represented in *back-to-back stemplots*. The data from a study comparing verbal ability for two age groups illustrate this graphical technique (Data Set 2.4). The study compared the scores for a vocabulary test in which children were asked the meanings of words. Children in one group were 6 years old; children in the other were 8 years old. The response variable was the proportion of words correctly defined.

Back-to-back stemplots are used to represent two distributions.

Data Set 2.4   Vocabulary test scores

6-year-old-group

.75	.71	.34	.54	.51	.67	.57	.93	.95	.63
.63	.55	.40	.28	.82	.54	.83	.49	.52	.89
.72	.62	.36	.61	.43	.79	.88	.59	.66	.34
.78	.61	.56	.53	.57	.69	.48	.69	.33	.67
.51	.63	.27	.58	.55	.55	.58	.62	.42	.88

8-year-old-group

.76	.66	.57	.80	.93	.42	.91	.96	.85	.48
.74	.90	.85	.64	.74	.78	.98	.66	.77	.81
.88	.70	.53	.80	.83	.75	.67	.95	.81	.67
.69	.86	.86	.83	.71	.59	.87	.82	.80	.95
.45	.80	.63	.94	.75	.94	.88	.42	.78	.98

6-year-old group		8-year-old group
87	.2	
443	.3	
6	.3	
320	.4	23
98	.4	58
443211	.5	3
988776555	.5	79
3332211	.6	34
99776	.6	66779
21	.7	0144
985	.7	556788
32	.8	000011233
988	.8	5566788
3	.9	01344
5	.9	55688

Figure 2.10

Back-to-back stemplots of the vocabulary test data.

Figure 2.10 shows a back-to-back stemplot. The common stem is the center column, and the leaves on each side represent the scores in the two groups, one group on the left, the other on the right.

Figure 2.10 also illustrates how a stemplot can be formed when the data are decimal fractions rather than whole numbers. Proportions pose no special problem. Once it has been decided how many decimal places should be retained, the same rules can be applied for breaking each score into its stem and leaf components. Notice also that each stem has been split into two. For example, the stem value .5 appears twice, once for scores .50 to .54 and once for scores .55 to .59. Stems should be split according to the same general steps that were used to decide on the number of class intervals for ordinary frequency distributions.

Back-to-back stemplots enable the viewer to make a very direct comparison between the scores of the two groups. For example, it is readily apparent from this stemplot that 8-year-olds tend to have higher scores than 6-year-olds, although there is substantial overlap between the two groups.

2.1.5 Features of Distributions

We now have at our disposal a number of techniques for conveying to a reader the basic features of a set of data. The obvious next question is this: What features should we look for, and why? Remember, in moving beyond the purely descriptive goal of communication, our main purpose is to check the fitness of the data for further analysis, where "further analysis" might be something as simple as providing a numerical summary. In evaluating a frequency distribution, three basic features are important:

■ symmetry versus asymmetry

■ presence of more than one peak in the distribution

■ presence of outliers

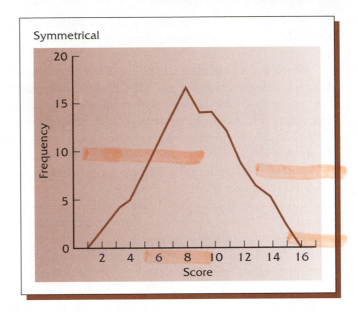

Figure 2.11
Symmetrical frequency
distribution.

Skewed (Asymmetrical) Distributions

Compare the three distributions that appear in Figures 2.11 and 2.12 in the form of frequency polygons. In the distribution in Figure 2.11, the frequencies are spread approximately symmetrically around the center point of the distribution. This symmetry does not hold for the two distributions in Figure 2.12. Such asymmetrical frequency distributions are described as being *skewed*. Skew may be either positive or negative. Figure 2.12a shows *positive skew*, the scores being heaped toward the low end of the scale and stretched out at the high end. Figure 2.12b shows the opposite symmetry, *negative skew*, with the scores heaped at the high end and stretched out at the low end. An effective mnemonic for keeping straight which is positive and which is negative is to focus on the elongated tails of the asymmetric distributions,

In positively skewed distributions the scores are heaped toward the low end and stretched out at the high end.

In negatively skewed distributions the scores are heaped toward the high end and stretched out at the low end.

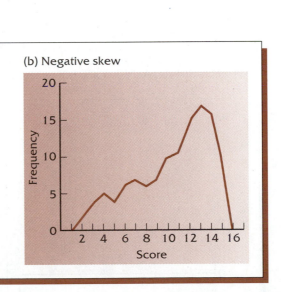

Figure 2.12
Skewed frequency distributions.

and associate high with positive and low with negative. Thus, if the stretched tail is at the high end of the scale, then the skew is positive; if it is at the low end, it is negative.*

What causes a distribution to be skewed and why does it matter? The major cause of skewed distributions is the fact that measurements are often constrained to fall within certain limits. There are many reasons for such constraints. For example, a student taking a test consisting of true/false items cannot get more than 100% correct or fewer than 0%. If the test is so easy that most students score near 100%, then the distribution is likely to be negatively skewed. Such a cause of skew is sometimes termed a *ceiling effect*—there is no headroom for brilliant students to show off.

A corresponding situation can arise in a memory experiment. If the task is too easy, most participants may obtain a near-perfect score, again producing a negatively skewed distribution. Conversely, an extremely difficult task may result in positively skewed distributions with scores bunched at the bottom end of the scale, a situation commonly termed a *floor effect*. Skew is sometimes the result of social or economic constraints operating at one end of a measurement scale. For example, distributions of annual income or house prices are usually positively skewed, with dollar values compressed at the low end, but with virtually no ceiling at the high end.

Skewing is readily apparent in either a histogram, a frequency polygon, or a stemplot. There are two reasons why it is important to find out about skew. First, badly skewed distributions pose difficulties for some of the statistical methods that we will cover in later chapters. In such cases, it might be desirable to apply certain corrective methods that will transform the scores into a more symmetrical form. (These methods are beyond the scope of this introductory book, but you should be aware that they exist.) Second, skew may indicate problems with the measuring instrument. For example, it may indicate that a test or some other task is too easy or too difficult. The following example is rather extreme, but it makes an important point. Suppose a teacher wants to evaluate the spelling ability of a class of 14-year-old students and sets as a test the following five words for students to spell: *ball, pot, hat, top, sit*. When the scores on this test (number correct out of 5) are tabulated, the resulting distribution would probably look something like Figure 2.13.

* The designations *positive* and *negative* for the two forms of skew are not as arbitrary as they may seem. There is, in fact, a numerical index—a statistic—that quantifies the degree of skew; and, although we will not use it, this statistic often appears in the output from computer packages. The formula for calculating the statistic is such that a negative skew results in a negative value, and a positive skew a positive value. The descriptive labels *positive* and *negative* derive from this property of the statistic.

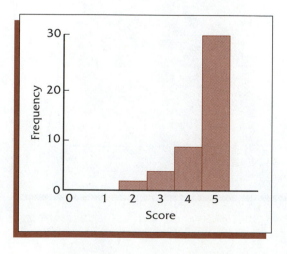

Figure 2.13
Strong negative skew reflecting a ceiling effect.

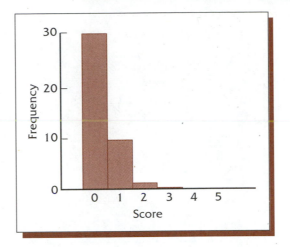

Figure 2.14
Strong positive skew reflecting a floor effect.

This distribution shows strong *negative* skew, most students scoring either 4 or 5. The problem that this skew points to is that the test is not doing a very good job at discriminating good spellers from mediocre or even poor spellers. The test is so easy that both good and mediocre spellers perform at or near the ceiling. The test does not give good spellers a chance to show just how good they are.

Similarly, if the test items were *rhinoceros, pterodactyl, psoriasis, lucubrate, staphylococci,* the likely result would be a distribution like that shown in Figure 2.14. This distribution is strongly *positively* skewed, most students scoring either 0 or 1. Again, this floor effect reflects the test's poor ability to discriminate. This version of the test will not discriminate poor from mediocre spellers, because only the very best spellers will score more than 0 or 1. In brief, a test that is too difficult, or too easy, will not do a good job of evaluating the full range of ability that the test was intended to assess.

Examining distributions for skew may suggest certain test or experimental modifications that will allow genuine differences to show themselves.

Bimodal Distributions

The distributions shown in Figures 2.11 and 2.12, although differing in skew, have one important feature in common. They can all be described as *single-peaked*. They appear to have a single point of maximum frequency, the frequencies of other scores falling off on either side. Compare those distributions with the distribution shown in Figure 2.15. This distribution appears to have two peaks, one at 5 and another at 12 and is described as *bimodal,* meaning "two modes." Single-peaked distributions are commonly called *unimodal*.

> *The term mode refers to a score of maximum frequency—a peak in the distribution (see Section 2.2.1). A bimodal distribution is one with two modes or peaks.*

A frequency distribution that is strongly bimodal suggests that there is something amiss in the way the participants were selected, or in the way the measuring instrument was designed, or, most commonly, in the combination of the two. Bimodality usually indicates that the measuring instrument is dividing the participants into two distinct subgroups. For example, suppose an experimenter gives a test of French

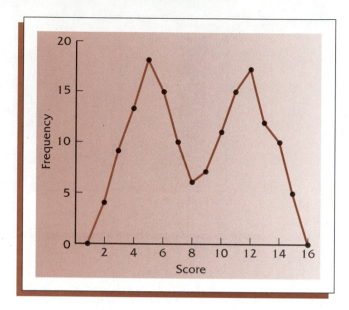

Figure 2.15
Bimodal frequency distribution.

language proficiency to a group of participants consisting partly of native French speakers and partly of subjects with only a rudimentary knowledge of French. If a single frequency distribution of the scores is then plotted, a bimodal distribution is the likely outcome. Why? Because, if you were to subdivide the group into native and nonnative French speakers, and plot separate frequency distributions for each of these subgroups, you would probably find two distinct distributions that only partially overlap. Put simply, the scores tend to fall at one end of the scale or the other, with relatively few scores in the middle.

Outliers

Outliers are extreme scores at either end of a distribution that seem separate from the main distribution of scores. Suppose the scores from a 16-item spelling test resulted in the frequency histogram shown in Figure 2.16. The graph shows two scores

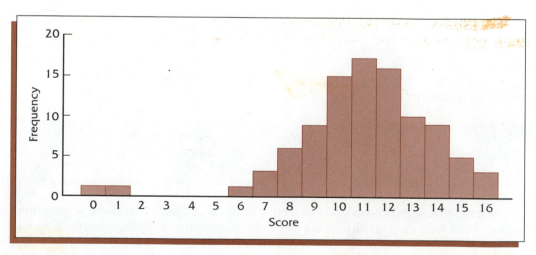

Figure 2.16
Frequency distribution with two outliers at the low end.

that appear to be outliers; one student scored 1 and another scored 0. Such extreme scores suggest that there is some cause that separates the performance of these two students from that of the rest of the group. One possible cause is dyslexia or a related learning disability. A simpler explanation is that these students did not take the test seriously. Of course, the graph itself cannot give any clue as to which, if either, of these explanations is correct. What it can do is indicate to the investigator the existence of outliers and suggest that something unusual has happened that needs further examination.

Consider a second example of how outliers might occur. Suppose a participant in an experiment is viewing a long sequence of stimuli, each consisting of a short string of letters. Instructions to the participant are to press a key labeled Y if the letters spell and English word and to press N if they do not.* In a lexical decision task, responses rarely take more than 1 second. But the task is scarcely exciting, and occasionally the subject's attention might waiver: The stimulus appears and a full 5 or 6 seconds elapse before the subject presses the response key. The recording equipment, accurate to the nearest millisecond, dutifully records a response time of 5.762 seconds. Apart from a few other lapses of attention that also have response times of around 5 seconds, all other response times are near 1 second.

Outliers, then, are data points that are so extreme relative to other scores in the distribution that it is reasonable to assume they result from some unintended circumstance.

There are many causes of outliers in addition to the ones mentioned so far. Poorly worded instructions might lead one or two subjects to misunderstand what was required of them, their misunderstanding resulting in a few low scores, that is, scores at chance level. Perhaps equipment problems resulted in stimuli being improperly presented or responses wrongly recorded. Even something as simple as human error in entering data via a computer keyboard (a misplaced decimal point, for example) can show up as an outlier. Any of these situations can result in numbers that are very distant from what might reasonably be expected. Whatever the cause, the detection of outliers is important to sound data analysis. The detection of outliers can also serve a more fundamental purpose of pointing to the need for improved experimental procedures: better instructions, for example, or more frequent rest periods, or more reliable computer software.

A wise researcher does not submit data to further analysis until the data have been examined for outliers, and if found, suitably treated.

Most important, however, is the fact that if they are undetected or ignored, outliers can have a serious distorting effect on numerical descriptors of data and subsequent statistical analyses. We will return to this last point after we have discussed numerical descriptions in Section 2.2.

---

* This task is known as a *lexical decision task* and is an important technique used in the study of reading processes.

Dangers of Automated Data Analysis

Graphs of frequency distributions (including stemplots) are useful in detecting features of data that could pose difficulties for the data's subsequent interpretation. It is important that an investigator be aware of these features so that suitable corrective measures can be taken, or interpretations appropriately qualified. This "health check" was the third justification for prior examination of data mentioned at the beginning of the chapter. The need for such an examination underlines the danger of performing a computer analysis of data without first examining the raw data themselves. Experienced investigators usually examine their data for unusual features before subjecting them to routine statistical analysis. However, given the high level of automation in both the gathering and analysis of data, it is all too easy to move from subjects' responses to the final results of a statistical analysis without ever having seen the actual numbers that constitute the data. Graphs of data provide an effective form for such an examination.

Comprehension Check 2.1

Important Concepts

1. The basic graphical and numerical methods used to describe sets of data serve three purposes:

■ They communicate the salient features of data.

■ They are the building blocks for inferences that take us beyond a mere description of the data to statements about what might be true in the population.

■ They allow a check on the data for features that might compromise either accurate communication (purpose 1) or the subsequent use of the data to fit and evaluate models.

2. Data can be tallied into frequency distributions in various ways:

■ If the response variable is categorical, then the frequency distribution records the number of instances falling within each category. Such data can be displayed graphically in the form of a bar chart.

■ If the response variable is quantitative, then the frequency distribution records the number of each score. Typically scores will be grouped into class intervals, and frequencies are the number of observations falling within each interval. Such data can be displayed graphically in the form of a histogram or a frequency polygon.

3. Stemplots (also termed stem-and-leaf displays) combine a graphical form of presentation with the preservation of complete numerical information.

4. Important features of distributions are skewness (asymmetrical frequency distributions), bimodality, and the presence of outliers. These features are relevant to the choice and interpretation of numerical descriptions of frequency distributions.

Problems

Problem 1   Facial expressions and emotions (Data Set 2.5)

Are facial expressions a reliable indicator of emotion? This question was posed in Section 1.2.3. As part of an experimental study of this question, 50 participants were shown a photograph and asked to judge which of six emotions the facial expression portrayed. The six possible emotions along with their scoring code were happiness, H; surprise, Su; sadness, Sa; anger, A; disgust, D; fear, F. The 50 responses are shown in Data Set 2.5.

Data Set 2.5   Facial expression responses (Problem 1)

H	Su	Su	Sa	H	A	H	A	Su	Su
Su	F	F	Su	F	Su	F	Su	F	D
F	H	Su	H	F	Su	Sa	Su	H	A
Su	D	Su	F	Su	F	F	H	A	D
D	Su	A	Su	H	Su	Su	F	Su	Su

Tabulate a frequency distribution for these responses and then construct an appropriate graphical representation of the distribution.

Problem 2   Social interactions among toddlers (Data Set 2.6)

This exercise uses a new version of the social interaction study with toddlers that was described in Chapter 1. The study asked whether toddlers as young as 33 months were sensitive to whether their same-age playmate is of the same or a different sex. Pairs of toddlers were placed together in a playroom setting and given a desirable toy to play with. The question of interest is whether the amount of social interaction between the two is different, depending on whether they are the same sex or different sexes. This question might be answered by observing paired infants and recording how often they interact with each other.

Hypothetical data from such a study are given in Data Set 2.6 for each of two conditions. In one condition, the 30 pairs of toddlers are the same sex; in the second condition, there are another 30 different-sex pairs. The response variable is the number of social interactions that occurred in a 30-minute time period.

Data Set 2.6   Amount of interaction in pairs of toddlers (Problem 2)

Same-sex pairs

29	25	37	37	34	28	29	35	35	30	28	32	29	30	27
33	35	30	28	31	28	27	22	33	32	36	32	27	32	39

Different-sex pairs

24	21	28	22	20	20	24	15	26	13	27	29	22	22	26
26	26	21	22	19	22	18	17	16	20	29	24	23	19	19

a. Tabulate a separate frequency distribution for the data in each of these conditions.

b. Draw a histogram of the frequencies for each condition.

c. Set up a back-to-back stemplot for the data from these two conditions

Problem 3   **Course grades (Data Set 2.7)**

The final numerical grades of 135 students enrolled in a course entitled *Introductory Research Methods in the Behavioral Sciences* are listed in Data Set 2.7.

Data Set 2.7   Final numerical grades for statistics class (Problem 3)

83	94	92	64	63	55	62	60	58	61	47	68	64	66	79
49	77	76	75	77	67	68	69	69	88	72	76	69	72	75
63	44	87	72	62	72	82	75	98	90	89	63	69	64	58
82	43	75	76	80	56	71	57	72	71	76	77	83	57	60
65	56	76	83	73	81	59	84	60	81	70	78	53	73	56
82	95	88	69	64	67	70	48	66	54	70	72	51	89	57
68	56	58	65	67	82	48	71	64	66	43	64	78	86	52
71	56	75	62	91	70	65	58	92	70	54	41	57	79	56
66	69	75	78	57	80	69	76	73	77	69	79	91	72	77

a. Set out the stem you would use in constructing a stemplot for these grades. Choose any one number in the stem and construct its leaf. The stemplot in Figure 2.17 is for these data, using a stem width of 5. Compare your answer to the corresponding leaf in this display. A student from this course obtained a mark of 81. How many students obtained a mark higher than 81? Another student from this course obtained a mark of 56. How many students obtained a mark lower than 56?

b. Use the stemplot to set out the numerical values of a corresponding frequency distribution for these grades. If you were to graph this distribution, what form of graph would you use? Locate the class interval that contains the student's mark of 81.

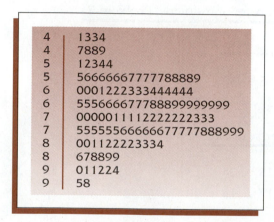

4	1334
4	7889
5	12344
5	56666667777788889
6	0001222333444444
6	5556666777888999999999
7	000001111222222222333
7	55555566666677777888999
8	001122223334
8	678899
9	011224
9	58

Figure 2.17
Stemplot for numerical grades of 135 students (Problem 3).

Notice that although the interval can be located, the exact value of 81 is lost and it is no longer possible to say exactly how many students obtained a mark higher than 81. It is, however, possible to approximate this number by counting how many grades fell in class intervals higher than the class interval containing 81. Count the number of such grades.

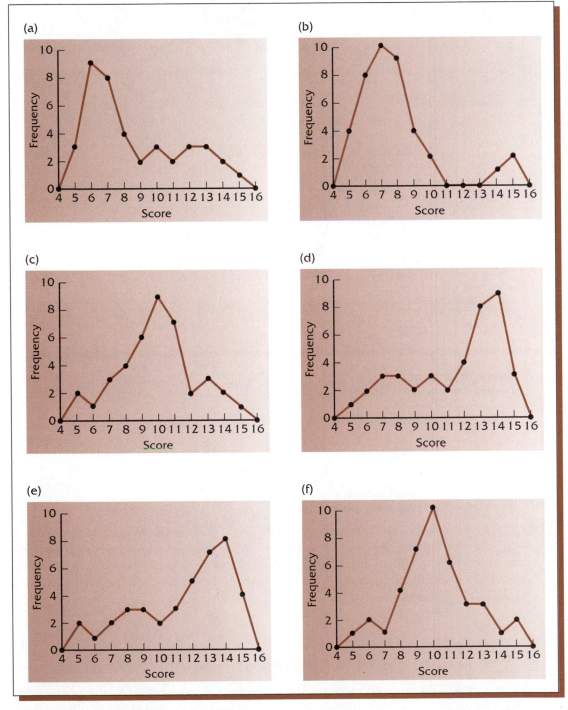

Figure 2.18
Nine frequency polygons for Problem 4.

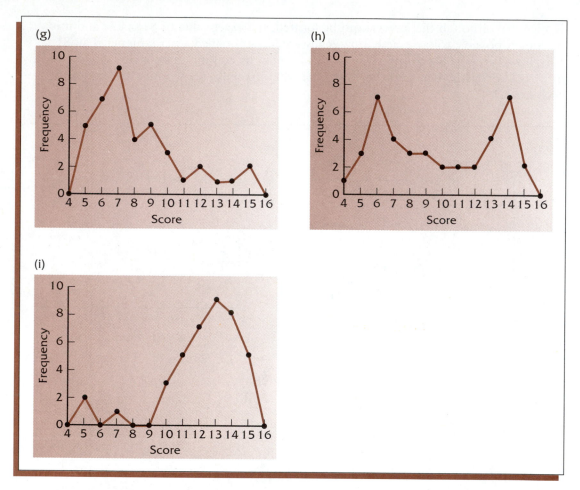

Figure 2.18 (continued)
Nine frequency polygons (Problem 4).

Problem 4   **Frequency polygons**

The nine frequency polygons in Figure 2.18, each with 40 observations, represent the distribution of scores on a 15-item math test for nine different groups. Examine each frequency polygon, noting features such as skew, bimodality, or values you suspect might be outliers. (A formal criterion for outliers will be given in Section 2.2.3.)

2.2   Numerical Descriptions of Frequency Distributions

Graphical representations can tell us a great deal about data, but important features of data can also be captured by numerical indices. As noted previously, such indices—for example, the mean or the median—are called statistics.

2.2.1 Statistics Describing the Center or Location of a Distribution

The most commonly used description of distribution is one that conveys information about what is normal or typical. Even without any formal knowledge of statistics, people have a strong intuitive understanding of what is typical, usual, or normal—a sense of what is to be expected. Among adult males, a height of 5′11″ seems typical, a height of 6′5″ seems atypical but not extraordinarily so; but a height of 7′ would seem very unusual. Similarly, most people would describe an annual income of $400,000 as very rare, one of $100,000 as unusual, and one of $40,000 as common. In some sense, part of our knowledge of our world consists of informal frequency distributions of various attributes that enable us to evaluate just how unusual a given value is. An income of $40,000 seems in some sense to be in the middle of our mental distribution of incomes, whereas an income of $400,000 seems very distant from this midpoint. The concepts of typicality and the range of normality can be formalized and used as the basis for the scientific description of data.

When using categorical variables, it is useful to know which category is typical, in the sense of occurring with the highest frequency. The category with the highest frequency is known as the *mode,* sometimes abbreviated Mo. Consider, for example, the data showing the response gestures of infants who have seen a model poke out her tongue. The data were graphed as a bar chart in Figure 2.1 which, for convenience, is reproduced as Figure 2.19. The mode of this distribution is tongue protrusion (TP), the same gesture they have just seen. That is, the data indicate that the modal or typical response of infants to a gesture is to imitate the gesture.

Describing the Center of Scores for Quantitative Variables: Mode, Mean, and Median

Mode Although the concept of the mode as the most frequent score is commonly used with categorical variables, it can also be applied to distributions of quantitative variables. Again the mode will be the most frequently occurring

> **The mode is the most frequently occurring score or class interval.**

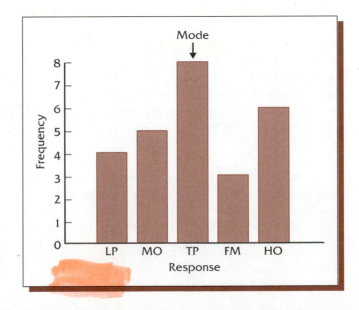

Figure 2.19
Bar chart of gestural responses of infants. The mode is TP.

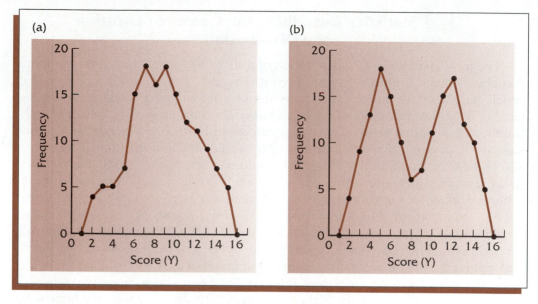

Figure 2.20

Two frequency distributions. Only the distribution on the right would be judged bimodal.

score, or for grouped data, the midpoint of the most frequently occurring class interval. If you think in terms of a frequency polygon, the mode is the peak of the distribution.

However, a difficulty arises in identifying the mode when the distribution shows two peaks—two scores tied, or approximately tied, for maximum frequency. For bimodal distributions, there are two options, and the choice between them is largely a matter of judgment. If the two peaks are close together and not much higher than the frequencies of the scores between them, then a common convention is to take as the mode the midpoint between the two peaks (see Figure 2.20a). For these data, the mode could be reported as 8, midway between 7 and 9.

If the two peaks in a distribution are far apart and the drop in frequencies between them quite marked, as they are in Figure 2.20b, then it is likely that the distribution is genuinely bimodal (see Section 2.1.5). The distribution in Figure 2.20b would be judged bimodal despite the fact that one of the peaks is slightly higher than the other. In this case, it is appropriate to report *both* modes, 5 and 12. If in doubt about which of these two situations applies, it is safest to report both modes. Remember the purpose in reporting the mode is to convey information about the distribution, so the guiding principal is not to conceal features that might signify something of importance.

$\overline{Y}$ denotes mean.

The mean of a set of scores is the sum of those scores divided by the number of scores.

Mean, $\overline{Y}$ The mean of a set of scores is simply the sum of those scores divided by the number of scores. The mean of the four scores 1, 8, 5, and 6 is $(1 + 8 + 5 + 6)$ divided by 4, yielding a value of 5. If the letter Y denotes the scores and $\overline{Y}$ (pronounced "Y-bar") is used to denote the mean of those scores, then this definition of the mean can be expressed with the following formula

$$\overline{Y} = \frac{\Sigma Y}{n}$$

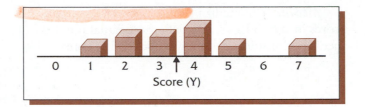

Figure 2.21
The mean, indicated by the arrow, is the balance point of the scores.

The symbol Σ (capital Greek letter sigma) is used to denote the operation of addition. Thus ΣY is simply shorthand for saying "add up all the values of Y." The letter *n* denotes the number of scores.

Consider a second example, in which the values of Y are set out in a row.

Y   2   1   4   3   4   5   7   2   3   4

The sum of the ten Y values is 35, so

$$\overline{Y} = \frac{\Sigma Y}{n} = \frac{35}{10} = 3.5$$

There is another way of describing the mean that offers a slightly different perspective on the same value. The mean is the balance point of the scores, as illustrated in Figure 2.21. The scores are represented by disks of equal weight, placed on a balance bar at a point corresponding to their value. The point about which these disks would balance is the mean and is indicated by the arrow.

Yet another way of stating this relationship is in terms of the distance of each disk from the balance point. The sum of the distances to the left of the balance point is the same as the sum of the distances of the disks to the right. If points to the left are treated as negative distances and those to the right as positive distances, then all these positive and negative distances will sum to 0: The negative distances will exactly balance the positive distances.

Zero-Sum Principle Translating the balance metaphor back into scores leads to a general result that we will refer to as the *zero-sum principle:* If each score is expressed as a distance from the mean, then the sum of these distances is 0. This relationship is shown in Table 2.5, in which the distance between each score and the mean (the balance point) is shown in the right-hand column and is denoted by $Y - \overline{Y}$. More formally, the values $Y - \overline{Y}$ are known as *deviations from the mean.* Expressing a score in these terms is rather like expressing a person's IQ as 10 points above average (the average IQ is 100) rather than as 110, or describing the temperature as 3 degrees below normal. The idea of expressing each score as a deviation from its mean is one that will occur time and again throughout the remainder of this book. For the present, it is sufficient to take note of the concept deviation from the mean and of the simple but important zero-sum principle:

If scores are expressed as deviations from their mean, then the sum of the deviations from the mean is always 0.

Σ denotes addition operation.

n denotes number of units.

The mean is the balance point of the scores.

Table 2.5
Each score (Y) is expressed as a deviation from the mean $\overline{Y} = 3.5$

Y	$Y - \overline{Y}$
2	−1.5
1	−2.5
4	+0.5
3	−0.5
4	+0.5
5	+1.5
7	+3.5
2	−1.5
3	−0.5
4	+0.5
Sum	
35	0

The median is the value that divides a set of scores into two halves.

Median The median (sometimes abbreviated Md) is the value that divides a set of scores into two halves. By definition, equal numbers of scores lie above and below the median. Consider the following set of 11 scores:

3   5   9   8   1   7   4   9   7   4   6

If we order these scores from lowest to highest, we see that the median is 6: Five scores are below 6 and five are above:

1   3   4   4   5   6   7   7   8   9   9

If the number of scores is even, then the median may fall between two scores. Such is the case with the ten values in Table 2.5 Ordered from smallest to largest, they are

1   2   2   3   3   4   4   4   5   7

The median need not be an actual score from the distribution.

For these scores, the median falls between the fifth and sixth scores, that is, between 3 and 4. In such cases, the median is taken as the midpoint between the two, that is, 3.5. Notice that the median need not be an actual score from the distribution, just as the mean need not be an actual score.

The stemplot provides a convenient basis for calculating the median because it sets out the scores in rank order, with the lowest score at the beginning of the top leaf. It is a simple matter to count scores until the median is reached, using the aforementioned guidelines to deal with odd or even numbers of scores.

Consider the back-to-back stemplots for the vocabulary test scores (Figure 2.10), which are reproduced in Figure 2.22. There are 50 scores in each of the two data sets, so the median for each set will lie midway between the twenty-fifth and twenty-sixth scores. For the 6-year-old vocabulary test data, this point is between .58 and .59 (indicated by the vertical bar in the stemplot), so the median is 0.585. For the 8-year-

6-year-old group		8-year-old group
87	.2	
443	.3	
6	.3	
320	.4	23
98	.4	58
443211	.5	3
9|88776555	.5	79
3332211	.6	34
99776	.6	66779
21	.7	0144
985	.7	556788
32	.8	0|00011233
988	.8	5566788
3	.9	01344
5	.9	55688

Figure 2.22
Back-to-back stemplots from Figure 2.10 with the location of the medians indicated by the vertical bars.

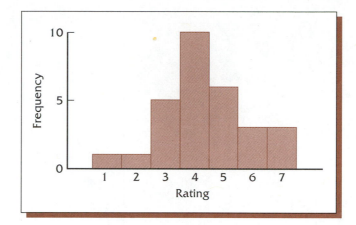

Figure 2.23
Histogram of ratings from 25 respondents. The modal rating is 4.

old vocabulary test data, this point is between two scores with the same value (.80), so the median is .80.

Comparing the Mean, Median, and Mode

Which of the three possible measures of location should be used?

First, note that if the variable is categorical, there is no choice. Among the three measures we have considered, the mode is the only appropriate statistic.

Second, if the distribution has no outliers and is symmetrical, then the mode, mean, and median will all have the same value. The mean is the statistic most commonly reported. One circumstance in which the mode might be preferred arises when the response variable, although regarded as quantitative, is really a set of ordered discrete categories, such as letter grades derived from percentages.

Another example of data sets with ordered discrete categories is ratings. A participant might be asked to rate the attractiveness of a photograph on a seven-point scale, 1 through 7. The ratings from 25 participants are shown in the histogram in Figure 2.23. The mean of this distribution is 4.2 and the mode is 4. It would be perfectly legitimate to report the mean of 4.2 as the "average rating." The distribution is approximately symmetrical and the difference between the mean and the mode is therefore small. On the other hand, 4.2 is not a score value that a participant in an experiment could actually give; ratings were confined to whole numbers. If the investigator wanted to convey the information that a rating of 4 was the most commonly chosen, then the mode might be preferred. A point worth stressing is that, in situations such as this, the choice is not a matter of right and wrong; rather, it is a matter of what property of the data the investigator wants to convey. Moreover, there is no rule against reporting both statistics, if each conveys a different perspective on the data.

> There is no rule against reporting two statistics, if each conveys a different perspective on the data.

Other Location Statistics: Quartiles, Deciles, and Percentiles

The concept behind the median can be extended to a more detailed breakdown of score locations. Whereas the median divides the score distribution into two halves, *quartiles* divide the distribution into quarters. To divide a distribution into quartiles, we need three values. The first value, known as the *first quartile*, is the value that divides the lower 25% of scores from the upper 75%. The second value is the median, which can also be thought of as the *second quartile*. The *third quartile* is the score

> Quartiles divide the distribution into quarters.

```
 6  | 9
 7  | 14
 7  | 599
 8  | 00122344
 8  | 5788889
 9  | 1112|22233333
 9  | 5566666666777777778|8
10  | 00011223334444
10  | 566788899
11  | 1|13334444
11  | 789
12  | 01233344
12  | 7
13  | 3
13  | 577
14  | 2
```

Figure 2.24
Stemplot of the IQ scores (Figure 2.9) showing location of median and quartiles (vertical bars).

Q denotes quartile.

that divides the lower 75% of scores from the upper 25%. The first and third quartiles are denoted by Q_1 and Q_3, respectively.

We can illustrate the calculation of the quartiles by using the distribution of IQ scores in Figure 2.9, reproduced here as Figure 2.24. We begin by locating the median. There is an even number of scores (100); so, using the stemplot and counting down from the low end of the distribution, the median will fall between the fiftieth and the fifty-first score. This dividing point will place 50 scores on each side. These values can be located in the stemplot in Figure 2.24. Counting down from the top of the stemplot, the fiftieth score we come to is 98, and so too is the fifty-first. So the median is 98.

To obtain Q_1, we consider the 50 scores below the median. Q_1 is essentially the midpoint of this lower half of the distribution, the point that divides *it* into two halves of 25 scores each. Thus calculating Q_1 is equivalent to calculating the median for the bottom half of the scores. The score that divides these 50 scores into two halves is midway between the twenty-fifth and the twenty-sixth scores. Counting from the median of the stemplot toward the low end (up in the stemplot), we find that the twenty-fifth score is 92, as is the twenty-sixth; so Q_1 is 92. The third quartile is calculated similarly. It will be the midscore of the top 50 scores and therefore located between the twenty-fifth and the twenty-sixth scores above the median. Counting from the median in the stemplot toward the high end (down in the stemplot), we find that the twenty-fifth and the twenty-sixth scores are both 111; so $Q_3 = 111$.

Deciles divide a data set into ten equal parts.

Deciles divide the score distribution even more finely into ten equal parts, 10% of the scores occurring in each part. Such a division requires nine decile values. The first decile will separate the bottom 10% from the top 90%, the second decile the bottom 20% from the top 80%, and so on. The median corresponds to the fifth decile.

Percentiles divide a data set into 100 parts.

Percentiles provide a still finer division, dividing the distribution into 100 parts, with 1% of the scores falling into each. There are 99 percentile values, and the median corresponds to the fiftieth percentile. The first and third quartiles correspond to the twenty-fifth and the seventy-fifth percentiles, respectively. The use of so fine a division as percentiles makes sense only if the number of scores is quite large. For this reason, percentiles are most commonly used in connection with large-scale testing programs such as the SAT or the GRE. If a student score in such a test is quoted as being at the eighty-seventh percentile, it indicates that the score is at a point that marks off the bottom 87% from the top 13%. Because percentiles indicate where a score falls relative to other scores, they are sometimes referred to as *percentile ranks.*

> **Percentile values are sometimes called percentile ranks.**

2.2.2 Dispersion Statistics: Describing the Spread of Scores

Compare the two frequency polygons in Figure 2.25. Each polygon reports the results of a different 20-item spelling test (Tests A and B) given to 25 students. Both distributions have the same mean, median, and mode—a value of 10. However, the distributions are quite different in a way that is not reflected in any of these three measures of location. The difference is one of *spread,* or *dispersion.* In the Test A distribution, the scores are tightly grouped around the center value of 10, whereas in the Test B distribution, they are widely dispersed about the center. We need a numerical index—a statistic—that will capture this quality of dispersion. There are several candidates: range, interquartile range, variance, and standard deviation.

> **Dispersion is the spread of scores about their central location.**

Range

The simplest measure of dispersion is the *range,* the distance between the lowest and the highest scores. For Test A, the minimum score is 8 and the maximum score is 12. (In reading minimum and maximum scores from the graph, do not be misled into thinking the lowest score is 7 or that the highest score is 13. Although these values are marked, they occur with zero frequency—that is, they do not occur at all.) The range is therefore $(12 - 8) = 4$. For Test B, it is $(16 - 5) = 11$.

> **Range is the difference between the highest and the lowest scores.**

The range has the advantage of being easily calculated and readily understood, so it is commonly used in everyday reporting. However, as an all-purpose descriptor, it has serious disadvantages. The major disadvantage is that, because it is based on just two scores from the entire distribution (the highest and lowest), it is extremely unstable and very vulnerable to outliers. In Test A, for example, the addition of a single score of 3 would more than double the range. Giving the test to a new sample of students would probably result in a very different value for the range. Moreover, because the range is determined by just two scores, it tends to increase as the number of observations increases. Every additional score is an opportunity for a lower minimum or a higher maximum score.

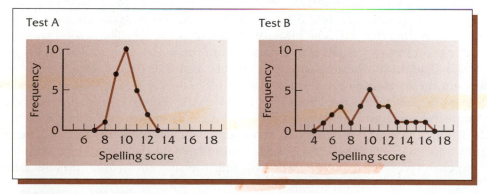

Figure 2.25
Frequency distributions with markedly different variances.

Interquartile Range (IQR)

The *interquartile range* (abbreviated *IQR*) is the distance between the values of the first and third quartiles ($Q_3 - Q_1$).

$$IQR = Q_3 - Q_1$$

In the distribution of Test A scores, $Q_1 = 9$ and $Q_3 = 11$, so $IQR = 2$. By contrast, in Test B, $Q_1 = 8$ and $Q_3 = 12$, giving $IQR = 4$.

We can also think of the interquartile range as the range that covers the middle 50% of the scores. Thus the *IQR* is sometimes referred to as the *midrange* of a distribution.

Variance and Standard Deviation

Another way of thinking about the spread of scores is in terms of the extent to which scores are dispersed about the center of the distribution. The variance is a statistic that measures the degree of dispersion about the mean. Consider again the two distributions of spelling scores shown in Figure 2.25.

In both distributions of spelling scores, the mean is 10. But when we compare Test A with Test B, we see a marked increase in the spread of the scores *around* this mean. How might this increase in spread be captured numerically? The method to be described is based on a concept discussed previously in Section 2.2.1. The basic idea is to express each score as a deviation from the mean and to measure dispersion in terms of the size of these deviations. The greater these deviations are from the mean, the greater the dispersion.

One way to capture this dispersion in a single number would be to calculate the average deviation by taking the *absolute* distance between each score and the mean, and then averaging all these absolute distances. Note that if we took the sign of the difference into account rather than taking absolute differences, the sum would always be 0 (recall the zero-sum principle; Section 2.2.1). Although this statistic, sometimes termed the *mean absolute deviation*, would provide a perfectly valid measure of dispersion, it is not a statistic that is much used. A statistic that captures this same idea of dispersion about the mean and that *is* widely used is the variance. Closely related to the variance is the *standard deviation*, which is simply the square root of the variance. We will use the symbol s^2 to denote the variance of a set of observations and s to denote the standard deviation.

Instead of using the *absolute* deviations, the variance uses the *squared* deviations from the mean. Note that squaring a deviation has the effect of making all values positive and, in this sense, has the same effect on the direction of the difference as taking the absolute difference. Table 2.6 gives the same ten scores that were used to illustrate the mean in Table 2.5. The mean of the ten scores is 3.5. The second column in this table expresses each score as a deviation from the mean, $Y - \overline{Y}$, also copied from Table 2.5. The third column is simply the square of this deviation (e.g., $1.5^2 = 2.25$). If we sum these values in the third column, we obtain the *sum of the squared deviations from the mean*. This total is an important quantity and is usually referred to by a less cumbersome term. It is known simply as the *sum of squares* and symbolized SS. If there is any ambiguity about which scores are being referred to, then a subscript might be added. Thus SS_Y indicates the sum of squares for the scores designated by Y.

We can express the sum of squares (in full, the sum of squared deviations from the mean) in terms of the following formula

$$SS = \sum (Y - \overline{Y})^2$$

Table 2.6 Deviations and squared deviations from the mean used in Table 2.5, $\overline{Y} = 3.5$

Y	$Y - \overline{Y}$	$(Y - \overline{Y})^2$
2	−1.5	2.25
1	−2.5	6.25
4	+0.5	0.25
3	−0.5	0.25
4	+0.5	0.25
5	+1.5	2.25
7	+3.5	12.25
2	−1.5	2.25
3	−0.5	.25
4	+0.5	.25
Column sums 35	0	26.5

If we sum the numbers in the third column of our example, we get $SS_Y = 26.5$.

The *variance* is defined as the average (mean) of the sum of squares. In later chapters, the variance will sometimes be referred to as a *mean square*, capturing this concept of the average sum of squares. Averaging the sum of squares is accomplished by dividing the sum of squares, not by the number of scores, n, as you would have every right to expect, but instead by $n - 1$. The reason for using $n - 1$ rather than n will be discussed shortly under the heading degrees of freedom. Dividing by $n - 1$ gives the following formula for the variance.

$$s^2 = \frac{SS}{n - 1}$$

In our example, the variance is

$$s^2 = \frac{26.5}{9} = 2.9$$

If we replace SS with its explicit formula, we obtain the complete formula for the variance:

$$s^2 = \frac{\sum (Y - \overline{Y})^2}{n - 1}$$

Standard Deviation

The *standard deviation* is the square root of the variance:

$$s = \sqrt{\frac{SS}{n - 1}} = \sqrt{\frac{\sum (Y - \overline{Y})^2}{n - 1}}$$

The variance is the average of the sum of squares and is sometimes called the mean square.

s^2 denotes variance.

The standard deviation is the square root of the variance.

s denotes standard deviation.

The unit of measurement of the standard deviation is the same as that of the scores themselves.

The variance is a dimensionless number.

The major goal of statistical data analysis is to understand the sources of variance.

In our example, the standard deviation is $s = \sqrt{2.94} = 1.7$.

It is important to note that the unit of measurement of the standard deviation is the same as that of the scores themselves. For example, if the measures are centimeters and the distribution has a standard deviation of 5.0, then it is entirely appropriate to refer to the standard deviation as 5.0 centimeters. To make this point in a different way, if the mean of this distribution is 10, then a score of 15 is 5 centimeters, or *one standard deviation* above the mean. A score of 12.5 would be 2.5 centimeters or 0.5 standard deviations above the mean. This property is not true of the variance. The unit of measurement of the variance is not the same as the scores themselves. You would be wrong if you described the variance of this distribution as 25.0 centimeters (or even 25.0 square centimeters).

The variance, defined as the average sum of squares, is a concept of immense importance. It, along with the standard deviation, will enter into almost every statistical procedure that we will use. The reason for this importance lies in the simple fact that the variance is a statistic that provides an overall description of the extent to which scores differ. In Chapter 1, we used the general term *variability* to describe this concept. The variance provides a clearly defined measure of variability. Chapter 1 also described the goal of data analysis as "accounting for variability" or "explaining variability." We can now replace the intuitive term *variability* with *variance*. In brief, the major goal of statistical data analysis is to account for, or explain, variance.

Degrees of Freedom

There remains the question of why the averaging processes uses $n - 1$ rather than n. There are two perspectives from which we can view the reason for the use of $n - 1$. The first has to do with the previous discussion about science being concerned with the general rather than the particular, and the corresponding distinction between samples and populations. Recall from Section 1.1.1 that one of the three purposes in calculating statistics was to estimate what might be true in the population, not just of the sample. That is to say, our interest in the variance, s^2, is that it serves as an estimate of the variance in the population. It turns out that using $n - 1$ as a divisor provides a better estimate than using n does. It is better in the sense that if n is used, the value of s^2 tends to underestimate the actual population value. The use of $n - 1$ corrects this bias.

If our interest were only in describing the variance of the sample data and not in using it as an estimate, then the use of n as a divisor would be justified. In fact, some textbooks distinguish the sample variance (calculated by using n) from the sample-based estimate of the population variance (calculated by using $n - 1$). However, because our use of the variance will always be as an estimate, it is simpler to think of the sample variance as the value obtained by dividing $n - 1$.

The second perspective on this use of $n - 1$ rather than n leads us to a new concept, that of *degrees of freedom*. Although the sum of squares is obtained by summing n numbers, there are only $n - 1$ *independent* numbers. What does this mean? Consider the ten numbers in the second column of Table 2.6. Notice that they sum to 0, an instance of the zero-sum principle. One consequence of this constraint is that if we know the value of any nine of these ten deviations, it is easy to work out the missing tenth value. It would be the value needed to bring the total back to 0. For example, suppose that the deviation for the tenth score were missing. The sum of the remaining nine deviations is -0.5. Because all ten deviations must sum to 0, it follows that the missing tenth deviation is $+0.5$. Furthermore, because the values in column 3 are simply the squares of those in column 2, it follows that, once nine of the squared deviations are known, the tenth missing value can be derived.

In summary, although there are n squared deviations, the nth value can always be derived from the other $n - 1$. Of the n scores, $n - 1$ are free to vary; but once they are fixed, so too is the nth score. The technical term *degrees of freedom*, usually abbreviated to *df*, is used to capture this concept. The concept of degrees of freedom is an important one that will be developed further in subsequent chapters. For present purposes, it is sufficient to note that, when calculating the variance (or the standard deviation), the divisor we will use is not n, but $n - 1$.

These considerations lead to a general definition of the variance (or mean square):
The variance or mean square is the sum of squares divided by the degrees of freedom.

df denotes degrees of freedom.

The variance or mean square is the sum of squares divided by the degrees of freedom.

2.2.3 Effects of Skew, Outliers, and Bimodality on Measures of Location and Spread

Defining an Outlier

Before proceeding, we can use the statistics described in the preceding section to offer a more explicit definition of an outlier. The following definition makes use of the interquartile range, *IQR*. According to this criterion, an outlier is any observation that lies more than $1.5 \times IQR$ above the third quartile or more than $1.5 \times IQR$ below the first quartile. That is, an observation is an outlier if it

■ falls below the criterion value of $Q_1 - 1.5 \times IQR$

■ falls above the criterion value of $Q_3 + 1.5 \times IQR$

IQR denotes interquartile range.

Consider the spelling test data described in Section 2.3 and graphed in Figure 2.25. In the distribution of Test A scores, $Q_1 = 9$ and $Q_3 = 11$, so $IQR = 2$. Given these values, $1.5 \times IQR = 1.5 \times 2 = 3$. Thus a score greater than 14 or less than 6 would be classified as an outlier. For Test B, $Q_1 = 8$ and $Q_3 = 12$, giving $IQR = 4$, so $1.5 \times IQR = 1.5 \times 4 = 6$. For this distribution, a score greater than 18 or less than 2 would be classified as an outlier. You will note that, according to this criterion, neither distribution has an outlier.

Skew and Outlier Effects

The effect of skew and outliers on measures of location and spread can be summarized briefly. Outliers and skew can have a strong influence on the mean, the variance, and the standard deviation. Both have little effect on the median or the quartiles, and thus little effect on the interquartile range. Positive skew, or outliers at the high end, will cause the mean to be greater than the median; negative skew, or outliers at the low end, will have the reverse effect, that is, the mean will be less than the median. In both cases, the variance and the standard deviation will be greater than they would be if the outliers, or the extended tail, were somehow removed.

Outliers and skew can have a strong influence on the mean, the variance, and the standard deviation, but little effect on the median or the quartiles.

The effect of skew on the mean and the median can be seen in the distributions shown in Figures 2.11 and 2.12, reproduced in Figure 2.26 with the mean and median indicated. For the symmetrical distribution, the mean and median are virtually identical; for the positively skewed distribution, the mean is greater than the median; but for the negatively skewed distribution, the median is greater than the mean. These differences reflect the greater impact of extreme scores on the mean. Note also that, although the range of scores is the same in all three distributions, the variance is greater for the two skewed distributions.

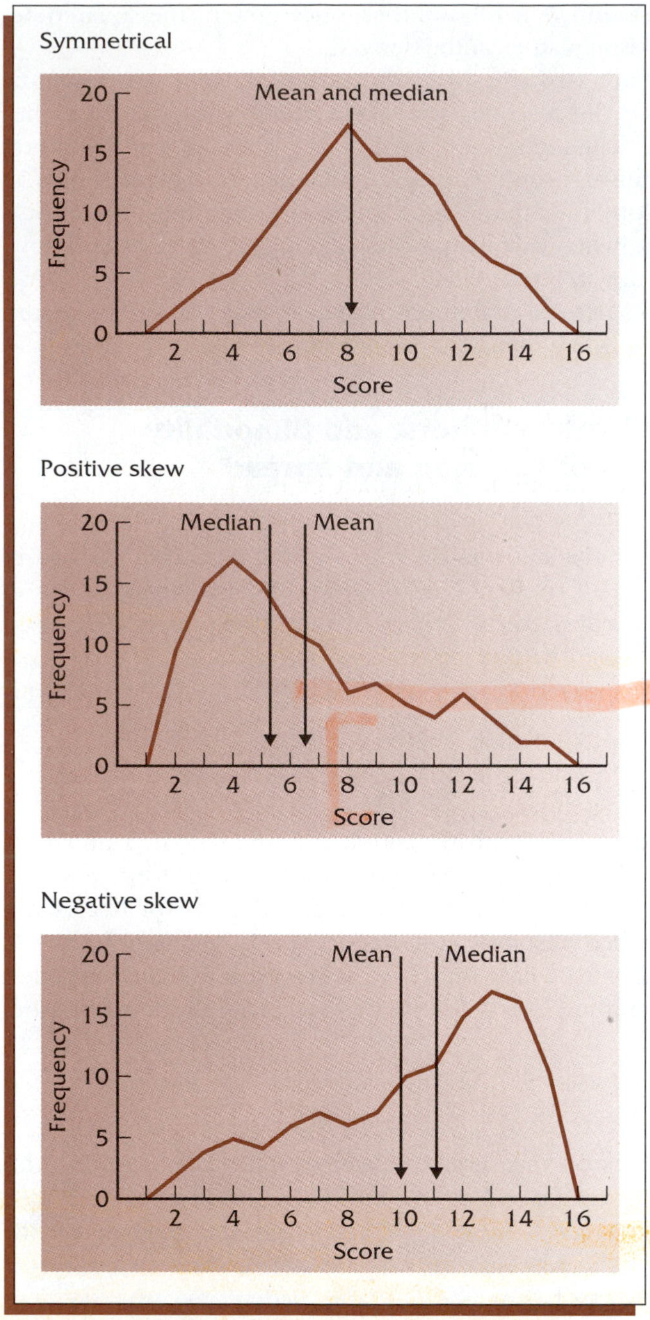

Figure 2.26
Relationship between the mean and median in symmetrical and skewed frequency distributions.

These points make sense when you remember that the mean and the variance take into account the *magnitude* of differences in a way that the median and quartiles do not. Both the extended tail of a skewed distribution and the presence of outliers imply scores that are distant from the mean. It is even possible to think of outliers at the high end of a distribution as an extreme form of positive skew, the only difference being that in a skewed distribution the extreme scores extend smoothly from the central distribution, whereas outliers are typically a separate cluster. Medians and quartiles are determined by the *ordering* of scores, not the size of differences as such. For example, if a score is above the median, doubling its value would leave the median unchanged; the score is still in the top 50%. That is the only fact that matters to the median. On the other hand, doubling the score will increase the mean, because it will result in an increase in the total of the scores. It will increase the standard deviation because, by doubling the score, the difference between this score and the new mean is increased.

A simple numerical example is sufficient to illustrate this point. Consider a distribution consisting of just five scores: 1, 4, 5, 7, and 8. For these scores, the mean and the median are both 5. The standard deviation is 2.74. Suppose one of these scores, the score of 8, is changed to 80 because of a typographical error in entering the data into a computer. The mean increases from 5 to 19.4, and the standard deviation jumps from 2.74 to 33.95! The median, however, is unchanged at 5.

In summary, extreme scores have a strong impact on the mean and standard deviation, but relatively little impact on the median, quartiles, and, by extension of the same line of reasoning, deciles and percentiles. For this reason, statistics such as the median, quartiles, deciles, and so on, are sometimes described as *resistant* statistics.

In the simple matter of communication, the median or mode and the midrange may do a better job when distributions are highly skewed. However, when the goal is model fitting, the mean and the variance are the statistics of interest. These are precisely the statistics that are most sensitive to skew and outliers. Consequently, examining and graphing data are very important and blind automation of data analysis is dangerous.

Resistant statistics are those on which extreme scores and skewness have little influence.

Bimodality

Bimodality causes a different problem. With strongly bimodal distributions, the mean and the median no longer represent a score that is common or typical. Both statistics are located at the center of the distribution, but it is the essence of bimodality that the center contains very few scores. In extreme cases, the numerical value of both statistics may represent something that is nonexistent.

Suppose a group of people were asked to rate on a 10-point scale the extent to which they agreed with someone who had just given a talk advocating capital punishment. The mean and median rating might be around 5 or 6; but, if the distribution had the form shown in Figure 2.27, both statistics would be meaningless or, even worse, seriously misleading. They suggest that the "typical person" is neither strongly for nor against the issue, when, as Figure 2.27 shows, exactly the opposite is true.

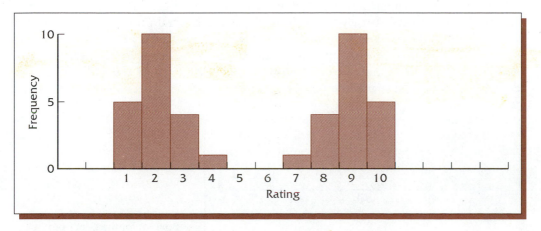

Figure 2.27
Bimodal distribution produced by ratings on an issue upon which people hold extreme opinions.

For strongly bimodal distributions, report the fact of bimodality and the values of both modes.

As a final example, suppose that you tally the number of legs and tails of a sample of dogs and their owners. You would find that the average number of legs is three and the average number of tails is 0.5. Such is the misleading nature of averages when taken over strongly bimodal distributions.

For strongly bimodal distributions, it is inappropriate to report either the mean or the median. Instead, report the fact of bimodality; and, if it is informative, report both modes.

2.2.4 Boxplots

Boxplots provide a simple graphical representation of data that captures features of both the location and spread of a distribution. In its simplest form, a boxplot uses five statistics. In order, these statistics are

$$\text{minimum}-Q_1-\text{median}-Q_3-\text{maximum}$$

Boxplots are sometimes called box-and-whisker plots.

The "box" of the boxplot consists of a rectangle bounded by the first and third quartiles. Within this rectangle, the median is indicated by an internal dividing line. Extending from each end of the rectangle are "whiskers" (the plots are sometimes called box-and-whisker plots), one whisker ending at the minimum, the other at the maximum score. Thus the entire length of the plot indicates the range of the scores. (The height of the boxes is arbitrary.)

Figure 2.28 shows a boxplot for the data from Test B shown in Figure 2.25. As noted previously, this distribution has a median of 10, $Q_1 = 8$, and $Q_3 = 12$. The range of scores was 5 to 16. All this information is conveyed in the boxplot.

Drawing a boxplot for a single distribution is informative, but not a great deal is gained over simply listing the five critical statistics. Boxplots are particularly useful in comparing distributions. Figure 2.29 shows boxplots for both versions of the spelling test. The plots have been turned sideways to provide a more compact presentation. The side-by-side boxplots make it clear, even at a glance, that (1) both tests have the same center point as measured by the median, (2) there is a marked difference between the ranges for Test A and Test B, and (3) Tests A and B have different interquartile ranges. The difference in spread between these two tests is shown in the length of the whiskers—the spread of scores beyond the *IQR*—and in the greater *IQR* for Test B.

There are several variants of the basic boxplot just described, but we will consider just one. Often the minimum and/or the maximum scores are sufficiently extreme to be considered outliers, so they tell us little about the general properties of the distribution. If the maximum score is an outlier, then the whisker is not extended all the way to the maximum score. Similarly, if the minimum score is an outlier, then the other whisker is not extended to that score. Instead, the ends of the whiskers are extended to a point that marks the border between acceptable scores and outliers. What

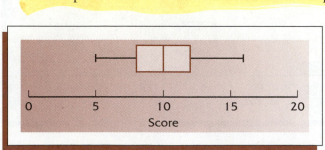

Figure 2.28
Boxplot for the data from Test B.

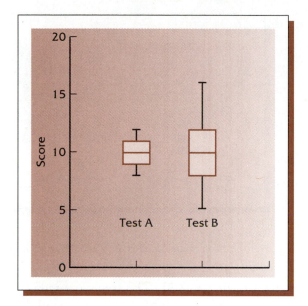

Figure 2.29
Side-by-side boxplots for the spelling test results.

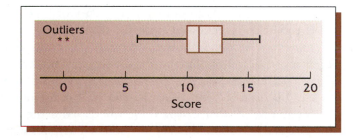

Figure 2.30
Boxplots for the data graphed as a histogram in Figure 2.16.

defines this border? When the data contain outliers, it is usual to extend the whiskers a distance of 1.5 times the interquartile range beyond the boundaries of the box. This distance corresponds to the previously mentioned demarcation rule for outliers. The outliers themselves are represented in the boxplot as dots or asterisks beyond the whiskers' extremities.

Figure 2.30 is a boxplot for the data that were used to illustrate outliers in Section 2.1.5 and were shown in histogram form in Figure 2.16. From this boxplot, we can read off values of 10, 11, and 13 for Q_1, median, and Q_3 respectively; and, ignoring the outliers at the low end, note that the scores range from 6 to 16.

2.2.5 Location and Dispersion Statistics in Everyday Problems

Consider the following problem.

Located in a small city, the manufacturing firm of Avex has 31 employees. Salary data show that the average salary for Avex employees is $45,000, an average that is higher than for any other comparably sized firm in the manufacturing sector in that city. What additional information might you request before deciding that Avex is generous to its employees?

The additional information you should request is the dispersion of the salaries or, better still, the complete distribution of the salaries. Consider the three possibilities

Case A		Case B		Case C	
1	4	1	46	1	5
1	57	2	0011246	2	357
2	2233	3	02235578	3	134778
2	5566788	4	256	4	0022455679
3	0011233	5	0	5	2345669
3	5677	6	368	6	258
4	001	7	34788	7	5
4	67	8	5		
•••	•••	9	4		
49	5				

Figure 2.31
Stemplots of annual salaries in three different cases.

shown in Figure 2.31. The stemplots record annual salaries in thousands of dollars. All three distributions have the same mean: $45,000. However, these means are from very different distributions.

In Case A, there is an outlier—the salary of $495,000 for the chief executive officer. If this salary is removed from the distribution, the mean salary of the remaining 30 employees is only $30,000. Although it is arithmetically correct to claim an average salary of $45,000, this statistic gives a very misleading impression of the "typical" salary. The median salary of all 31 employees is $30,000. Notice that if the salary of the CEO is doubled, but other salaries held constant, the mean salary for all 31 employees jumps to almost $61,000, whereas the median salary remains at $30,000. This insensitivity of the median to outliers illustrates why the median is sometimes described as a resistant statistic.

Case B shows a distribution that is distinctly bimodal. This bimodality reflects the fact that the Avex company has two types of employees: about ten highly skilled scientists and engineers, who command high annual salaries averaging around $75,000, and a larger number of less skilled positions, with an average salary closer to $30,000. Although, for all employees, the mean salary is $45,000 and the median salary is $37,000, neither of these statistics gives an accurate impression of the "typical" salary.

Case C shows a distribution in which the mean provides a reasonable index of typicality. The distribution is roughly symmetrical, and both the mean and the median are $45,000. Even here, however, the mean (or the median) does not convey information about the variance of the salary distribution. Compare the case C distribution with that of case D (Figure 2.32). Again, the mean is $45,000, but in this case there is much less variability.

Consider a second problem.

A student at a small university must choose between enrolling in an introductory course in psychology and one in sociology. Both courses are equally attractive and potentially useful with respect to the student's career plans. She therefore decides to take whichever course is likely to result in her obtaining a higher grade. She reads a report that states that the average grade in introductory sociology was 68%, whereas the average in psychology was only 58%. The student suspects that it will be more difficult to obtain a high grade in psychology and is therefore inclined to enroll in sociology. What additional information should the student request before deciding?

```
Case D

3 | 4
3 | 68
4 | 0011122223333444
4 | 5556677889
5 | 34
5 | 6
```

Figure 2.32
Stemplot of annual salaries for Case D.

As in the previous example, the additional information needed is information about the distribution. Assuming "average" refers to the mean, she should ask for the value of the medians. Suppose that the medians for the two courses were 65%. This statistic suggests that there is something odd about the distribution of the psychology course grades. The fact that the median is higher than the mean indicates either that the grade distribution has a strong negative skew or that it contains some low-end outliers. It is possible, for example, that the psychology distribution contains the grades of some students who missed the final exam and who were assigned an exam grade of 0. If these outliers were removed, the mean might jump to a value near the median.

Information about the variance would also be useful. If the variance of the psychology grades is much greater than those for sociology, it could be that there were more grades of A in psychology than in sociology, despite the higher mean of the latter. If such were the case, then it might be easier for our imaginary student to obtain an A in psychology than in sociology.

There are many other possibilities that might lie behind the difference in grade averages for the two courses. The lesson is obvious: Important decisions should not be based purely on the means of distributions. The interesting information is often contained in other details of the distribution.

Whenever you read an "average" in a magazine article or news report, before drawing conclusions, you should ask yourself several questions.

■ What statistic does "average" actually refer to? It will usually be the mean, but not always. It could be the median.

■ Is the distribution skewed? If so, in what direction?

■ Are there outliers?

■ Even if the distribution is unimodal, symmetrical, and without outliers, it may be important to know the variance. Miami, Florida and Death Valley, California both have annual average temperatures of 24°C (76°F), but you would be wise to investigate the variance before deciding which warm climate you would like to enjoy year-round.

Comprehension Check 2.2

Important Concepts

1. Numerical summaries of frequency distributions are termed statistics. Statistics covered in this chapter fall into two broad classes: those that describe the center or location of the distribution and those that describe the dispersion or spread of the observations.

2. The mode, median, and mean are the statistics commonly used to describe the center of a distribution. With categorical data, the mode is the only appropriate statistic. With quantitative data, all three are permissible, although the median and mean are more commonly used than the mode.

3. The zero-sum principle states that, if scores are expressed as deviations from their mean, then the sum of the deviations from the mean is always 0.

4. Other location statistics are quartiles, deciles, and percentiles. For these statistics, a certain proportion of the distribution lies above and a certain proportion lies below the statistic's value. The first quartile (Q_1), for example, is a value below which 25% of the distribution falls and above which 75% of the distribution falls.

5. Dispersion statistics include the range, the interquartile range *(IQR)*, the variance, s^2, and the standard deviation, *s*. The variance is the average of the squared deviation of each score from the mean. The average is obtained by using the degrees of freedom ($n - 1$) as the divisor. The standard deviation is the square root of the variance. The term sum of squares is short for "sum of the squared deviations from the mean." A variance is therefore an average sum of squares and is often referred to as a mean square.

6. Skewness and outliers have a strong influence on the mean, the variance, and the standard deviation. The median, the quartiles (and thus the *IQR*) remain relatively unaffected by these distribution features and are therefore sometimes referred to as resistant statistics.

7. Boxplots combine a simple graphical summary of resistant location and dispersion properties of a distribution.

Problems

Note: Some students find that this section contains more problems than necessary to grasp the concept. Others find the extra problems useful practice. You should judge for yourself when further problems are no longer serving a useful purpose.

Problem 1   Modal brand choice

Table 2.2 gave the distribution of frequencies for the brand choice of 50 consumers. What is the mode of this distribution?

Problem 2   Means and medians for social interaction data (Data Set 2.6)

Repeated here is Data Set 2.6 from the study of social interaction among same-sex and different-sex pairs of toddlers. The same data were used in Problem 2 of Section 2.1.

Data Set 2.6   Amount of interaction between pairs of toddlers (Problem 2)

Same-sex pairs

29	25	37	37	34	28	29	35	35	30	28	32	29	30	27
33	35	30	28	31	28	27	22	33	32	36	32	27	32	39

Different-sex pairs

24	21	28	22	20	20	24	15	26	13	27	29	22	22	26
26	26	21	22	19	22	18	17	16	20	29	24	23	19	19

Calculate the mean and median for both sets.

Problem 3   Expressing scores as deviations

For the same-sex pairs data in Problem 2, express each of the 30 scores as a deviation from the mean. Do the same for the different-sex pairs data. Check that in each case the sum of the deviations is 0.

Problems 4 and 5 involve intuitive estimation of statistics. The purpose of these exercises is to increase your sensitivity to some of the properties of data that can be noticed by careful inspection. For many students, descriptive statistics such as means and medians remain abstract concepts unrelated to actual data. There is also a practical value in being able to "eyeball" data and gain a sense of statistics such as the mean. Such a sense can be useful in detecting obvious errors in computation. Even when a computer package is used, such errors can arise. The cause is not usually the computer program itself, but errors in data entry or in the instructions to the program. A misplaced decimal point, for example, might result in a mean that can be detected as suspect and corrected, because its value is out of line with the value estimated through visual inspection.

Problem 4   Intuitive judgments of means

Look back at the nine data sets you examined in Problem 4 of Comprehension Check 2.1. By inspecting the frequency polygon for each of these sets (Figure 2.18), form an intuitive estimate of the mean in each case. *Note:* Do not perform actual computations until after you have made your intuitive estimate; premature computations would defeat the purpose of the exercise. You should check each answer as you go, not wait until you have completed the set. In this way, you can provide yourself with feedback that will serve to bring your intuitive estimates gradually into line with the actual values.

Problem 5   Checking calculations of the mean (Data Set 2.8)

Means for each of the ten data sets in Data Set 2.8 are reported at the bottom of the sets. Two of these mean values are obviously incorrect. Circle any incorrect values. Do not calculate the means; the incorrect values are incorrect to such a degree that they will be obvious upon careful inspection.

Data Set 2.8   Ten data sets for Problem 5

	1	2	3	4	5	6	7	8	9	10
	22	45	18	34	15	54	16	32	13	34
	20	51	9	38	18	43	13	37	9	34
	33	38	14	36	13	33	16	14	6	35
	31	50	15	43	11	44	15	27	14	36
	31	57	12	36	13	42	13	15	15	47
	23	51	18	45	15	45	16	25	10	42
	24	54	13	33	14	53	16	28	12	37
	28	34	13	36	18	51	16	17	7	37
	27	42	11	37	15	50	15	29	13	34
	18	57	8	31	17	38	17	26	13	43
	17	44	5	43	16	52	13	16	9	34
	15	55	18	37	17	54	18	26	17	28
	29	46	9	41	15	43	14	27	8	27
	24	49	10	31	17	57	14	27	11	35
	21	53	13	33	13	43	17	28	14	38
	33	41	10	31	12	44	14	32	15	34
	29	44	12	41	13	59	14	33	15	40
	23	51	16	37	12	37	17	19	8	47
	35	43	10	33	18	55	19	20	13	31
	24	53	13	40	12	46	12	26	10	36
	24	59	12	39	16	65	13	24	14	30
	30	67	11	42	15	52	12	19	7	42
	13	44	12	34	17	53	12	20	17	44
	21	49	12	38	19	40	13	34	11	42
	29	49	12	32	15	42	14	21	13	38
	27	50	9	32	16	53	17	32	11	34
	33	28	13	36	14	47	20	20	17	34
	33	53	12	29	15	67	14	21	15	43
	14	48	8	52	17	39	16	25	13	37
	19	33	14	42	13	41	14	31	11	36
Mean	25	48	12	42	15	48	15	25	12	32

Problem 6   **Calculating the *IQR***

Refer to the stemplot in Figure 2.24. What is the interquartile range of this distribution?

Problem 7 Obtaining the sums of squares

Table 2.7 contains the 25 observations for each of the two versions of the spelling test (A and B) graphed in Figure 2.25. In both cases, the mean is 10.0.

a. Express each score as a deviation from its mean. Notice that the absolute value of these deviations is generally larger for Test B.

b. Square each of these deviations and sum them to get the sum of squares (SS) for each test.

Table 2.7 Spelling test statistics, $\overline{Y}_A = \overline{Y}_B = 10$ (Problem 7)

Y_A	$Y_A - \overline{Y}_A$	Y_B	$Y_B - \overline{Y}_B$
11		16	
10		10	
8		7	
10		8	
9		13	
10		5	
9		11	
10		12	
9		10	
10		7	
12		14	
11		6	
9		11	
11		9	
10		12	
9		10	
10		11	
9		9	
10		15	
11		10	
10		9	
9		12	
12		7	
10		10	
11		6	

c. Using these SS values, calculate the variance and the standard deviation for each test.

Intuitive judgments of the variance (Data Set 2.9)

This exercise involves intuitive estimation of relative values of the variance, using the eight data sets in Data Set 2.9. The purpose of this exercise is similar to that of Problem 5 in Comprehension Check 2.2, namely, to increase your sensitivity to general properties of data that can be noticed by careful inspection. Inspect the relevant data sets in Data Set 2.9 and compare the variability of the data for the following eight pairs of data sets. For each pair of data sets, decide which one has the larger variance. *Note:* Do not perform actual computations until after you have made your intuitive estimate.

1	Sets 3 and 5	*5*	Sets 2 and 8
2	Sets 1 and 7	*6*	Sets 4 and 5
3	Sets 4 and 6	*7*	Sets 6 and 7
4	Sets 1 and 2	*8*	Sets 3 and 8

Data Set 2.9 Eight data sets for Problem 8

1	2	3	4	5	6	7	8
43	102	37	123	73	72	111	49
46	76	37	100	61	70	101	42
67	98	39	113	90	69	96	34
56	79	37	102	105	67	106	36
83	93	37	116	63	68	102	46
22	107	38	131	84	72	93	61
71	99	49	106	65	66	105	49
78	93	43	124	101	70	101	42
51	72	35	113	94	70	99	50
64	112	43	102	77	74	106	54
55	114	37	91	79	69	114	58
77	89	47	120	83	73	103	64
58	95	45	103	91	71	103	42
93	88	40	120	65	70	98	59
66	92	40	110	69	71	94	43
56	81	41	109	83	69	108	51
42	97	42	111	64	72	105	42
55	97	47	96	86	70	117	49
44	85	46	108	48	67	99	56
53	71	41	99	77	73	102	52

Compared with the mean, it is rather more difficult to judge the numerical value of the variance or standard deviation. However, a rough rule of thumb is that, provided there are no outliers, the standard deviation should be somewhere between one-fourth and one-third of the range. (The range is the difference between the largest and smallest score.) For small samples, such as the eight data sets in this problem, it is likely to be closer to one-third; for larger samples (more than, say, 50), it is closer to one-fourth. This rule of thumb yields only a very rough approximation, but it is often close enough to detect a gross error in computation or data entry. It should *never* be used as a substitute for the formal calculation. Using this rule of thumb, estimate the standard deviation for the eight data sets.

Problem 9 **Checking calculations of the mean and standard deviation (Data Set 2.10)**

The mean and standard deviation are given at the bottom of each of the five data sets in Data Set 2.10. Some of these values are obviously wrong. Which?

Data Set 2.10 Five data sets for Problem 9

1	2	3	4	5
54	16	32	13	34
43	13	37	9	34
33	16	14	6	35
44	15	27	14	36
42	13	15	15	47
45	16	25	10	42
53	16	28	12	37
51	16	17	7	37
50	15	29	13	34
38	17	26	13	43
52	13	16	9	34
54	18	26	17	28
43	14	27	8	27
57	14	27	11	35
43	17	28	14	38
44	14	32	15	34
59	14	33	15	40
37	17	19	8	47
55	19	20	13	31
46	12	26	10	36
65	13	24	14	30
52	12	19	7	42

(continued on next page)

Data Set 2.10   Five data sets for Problem 9 *(continued)*

	1	2	3	4	5
	53	12	20	17	44
	40	13	34	11	42
	42	14	21	13	38
	53	17	32	11	34
	47	20	20	17	34
	67	14	21	15	43
	39	16	25	13	37
	41	14	31	11	36
Mean	48	15	25	12	32
Standard deviation	2	6	12	3	5

Problem 10   **Using stemplots to evaluate distributions**

This problem (and Problem 11) involves consideration of the five data sets, shown in Figure 2.33 and represented as stemplots ($n = 30$ for each set). Answer the questions by using features of the stemplots rather than by performing explicit calculations.

a. List any of the data sets (if there are any) for which both the mean and the median would be a poor (i.e., misleading) measure of central tendency.

Data set 1	Data set 2	Data set 3	Data set 4	Data set 5
3 | 47	3 | 57	3 | 5	4 | 48	4 | 7
4 |	4 | 02234	4 |	5 | 0255569	5 | 44
5 | 557	4 | 56679	5 | 44	6 | 335	5 |
6 | 2468	5 | 1344	5 |	7 | 7	6 | 24
7 | 022789	5 | 5667	6 |	8 | 6	6 | 68
8 | 0155668	6 | 1	6 | 6	9 | 277	7 | 013
9 | 1468	6 | 557	7 | 3	10 | 33579	7 | 577
10 | 37	7 |	7 | 7	11 | 0355579	8 | 012
11 | 5	7 |	8 |	12 | 0	8 | 588
12 | 2	8 | 1	8 | 6		9 | 4
	8 | 8	9 | 0		9 | 57
	9 |	9 | 557		10 | 024
	9 | 5	10 | 112		10 | 9
		10 | 5579		11 |
	11 | 37	11 | 02444		11 | 6
	12 | 2	11 | 557899		
		12 | 3		15 | 6
				16 | 9
				21 | 4

Figure 2.33
Stemplots of five data sets for Problems 10, 11, and 12.

b. List any of the data sets (if there are any) for which you would expect the mean to be substantially *greater* than the median.

c. List any of the data sets (if there are any) for which you would expect the mean to be substantially *less* than the median.

Problem 11   Identifying outliers

Using the criterion that an outlier is any observation that lies more than $1.5 \times IQR$ above the third quartile, or more than $1.5 \times IQR$ below the first quartile, identify any outliers in the five data sets in Figure 2.33. (Use the stemplots to locate Q_1 and Q_3.)

Problem 12   Drawing boxplots

Draw boxplots for the five data sets shown in Figure 2.33. For those data sets with outliers, extend the whiskers only to the $1.5 \times IQR$ criterion for outliers, plotting the outliers themselves as dots outside the whiskers.

Problem 13   Describing average height

The following values are the heights (in centimeters) of 20 members of a school basketball squad. If you wanted to impress another team with the overall height of your squad, which statistic would you use, the mean or the median?

| 180 | 181 | 178 | 185 | 183 | 181 | 178 | 160 | 182 | 179 |
| 184 | 161 | 180 | 183 | 164 | 181 | 180 | 162 | 183 | 182 |

Problem 14   Describing average house price

The average (mean) house price in a large city is $295,000, but the median house price is only $210,000. What is the most likely cause of this difference between the two statistics?

Problem 15   A case of changing means

Will Rogers, a comedian and social commentator of the 1920s and 30s, once claimed that when people from Oklahoma migrated to California, they thereby raised the average intelligence of both states. Although the comment was intended as a joke, explain how such an outcome is arithmetically possible.

2.3   Linear Transformations of Scale and *z*-Scores

2.3.1   Rescaling Scores

It is sometimes necessary to rescale scores: Measurements taken in inches may have to be rescaled to centimeters, or measurements taken in degrees Fahrenheit may have to be rescaled to degrees Celsius. Measurements made in inches could be rescaled into centimeters by multiplying each score by 2.54 because 1 inch = 2.54 centimeters. Thus 1 yard (36 inches) is $2.54 \times 36 = 91.5$ cm. If the original measures were made in degrees Fahrenheit, then, to rescale them into degrees Celsius, we would subtract 32 from each score and multiply the resulting difference by 5/9. Thus the boiling point of water (212°F) becomes (212 − 32 × (5/9) = 100°C.

Each of these transformations is accomplished by multiplying each score by a constant and/or adding or subtracting a constant. Scale transformations that involve multiplication by and/or addition of constants are known as *linear transformations.*

Effect of Linear Transformation on Mean, Median, and Mode

Linear transformations are some combination of (1) multiplication of each score by a constant and (2) addition of a constant to each score. We can look at the effect of each of these operations separately.

Multiplication by a Constant If each score is multiplied by a constant, then the mean, the median, and the mode are multiplied by that constant. If reaction time scores have a mean of 0.786 seconds and each score is transformed into milliseconds (thousandths of a second) by multiplying by 1000, then the mean of the new scores would be 786 milliseconds. A median of 0.715 seconds would become 715 milliseconds. Division is really just another form of multiplication; so if scores are divided by a constant, then the mean, the median, and the mode are divided by that constant. Thus if we converted distance measures from centimeters to inches by dividing each score by 2.54, then a mean of 56 centimeters becomes a mean of 22 inches.

Addition of a Constant If a constant is added to each score then the mean, the median, and the mode are increased by that constant. Suppose a class instructor judges that a term test was unfairly difficult because it produced a class mean of 60, a median of 58, and a mode of 56. The remedy might be to add 10 points to every student's score. The new class mean would be 70, the new median 68, and the new mode 66.

Effect of Linear Transformation on Variance and Standard Deviation

Addition of a Constant Adding a constant to each score will have no effect on the variance. This noneffect becomes apparent by noting that adding a constant to each score will not change the difference between any two scores. It cannot make the scores more variable. Moreover, as we have just seen, the same constant is added to the mean, so the deviation of any score from the mean will also be unchanged, the sum of squared deviations (SS) will be unchanged, and the sum of these deviations will still be 0.

Multiplication by a Constant However, multiplying (or dividing) each score by a constant will influence the variance, because this transformation will change the difference between any two scores. Scores 10 and 6 have a differences of 4. If each is multiplied by 2 the difference becomes 20 − 12 = 8. That is, the difference between any two scores is multiplied by the same constant. Multiply each score by 2 and a difference of 4 becomes a difference of 8. Divide each score by 2 and the difference becomes 5 − 3 = 2, which is half the original difference.

Similarly, if each score is multiplied by a constant, then the deviation of each score from the transformed mean will also be multiplied by that constant. Consider a distribution with a mean of 10. If all scores are multiplied by 5, this mean becomes 50 and a score of 14 becomes 70. The original deviation of 14 − 10 = 4 becomes 70 − 50 = 20, which is the original deviation of 4 multiplied by 5. Note that the sum of these deviations for the transformed scores will still be 0.

Scale transformations that involve multiplication by and/or addition of constants are known as linear transformations.

If each score is multiplied by a constant, then the mean, the median, and the mode are multiplied by that constant.

If a constant is added to each score, then the mean, the median, and the mode are increased by that constant.

Adding a constant to each score will have no effect on the variance or the standard deviation.

The consequence of this multiplicative effect is the following rule: If scores are multiplied by a constant, then the standard deviation is multiplied by this constant, and the variance is multiplied by the *square* of the constant.

As an example, consider transforming scores from inches to centimeters by multiplying each score by 2.54. If the standard deviation of the distribution of distances measured in inches is 3.70 (variance = 13.69), then the standard deviation of the transformed measures in centimeters is $3.70 \times 2.54 = 9.40$. The *variance* of these transformed scores is $13.69 \times 2.54^2 = 88.32$. Note that, within rounding error, 88.32 is 9.40^2, so, for the transformed scores, the variance is, as always, the square of the standard deviation.

Effect of Linear Transformation on Form of Distribution

No combination of addition or multiplication by a constant—no linear transformation—will alter the form or overall shape of a frequency distribution: Skewed distributions will still be skewed exactly as they were before the transformation, bimodal distributions will remain bimodal, symmetrical distributions will remain symmetrical, and so forth.

Nonlinear Transformations

This text will use only linear transformations. However, contrasting a linear transformation with one that is nonlinear may help you understand the nature of the distinction. Furthermore, if the transformation is not linear, no simple relationship holds between the original mean, variance, and so on and the corresponding statistics for the transformed scores. The only way to calculate such statistics for the transformed scores is to perform a complete recalculation, using the transformed scores.

An example of a *nonlinear* transformation is the *reciprocal* transformation. Suppose we wish to convert time measures to speed measures. An animal is timed as taking 8.4 seconds to run the full length of an alleyway that is 90 centimeters in length. This time measure can be converted into a speed measure by taking its reciprocal. That is, a time of 8.4 seconds to travel 90 centimeters becomes a speed of $(1/84)(90) = 10.7$ centimeters per second. If all the time scores are transformed in this way, what is the effect on the mean and standard deviation? As pointed out in the previous paragraph, there is no simple answer to this question; the only thing to do is to perform the transformation on each score and recalculate whatever statistics are needed. In particular, note that the new mean will not be the reciprocal of the original mean, nor will the new standard deviation be the reciprocal of the old standard deviation. Such relationships hold only for linear transformations—those involving the addition and multiplication of constants.

A second example of a nonlinear transformation might arise in a study of animal behavior. Suppose that the territory marked out by each male of the species is approximately circular. The size of each animal's territory is measured as an area (*A*) in square meters. The investigator decides that it makes more sense to transform this measure into the length of the area's perimeter—the circumference of the circle. This transformation is accomplished by transforming each measure according to the formula

$$\text{perimeter} = 2\sqrt{\pi A}$$

We could call this a square-root transformation because it involves taking the square root of the original area measure, *A*. As with the reciprocal transformation,

---

If scores are multiplied by a constant, then the standard deviation is multiplied by this constant, and the variance is multiplied by the *square* of the constant.

Linear transformations will not alter the shape of a distribution.

The reciprocal transformation is a nonlinear transformation.

Table 2.8 Effect of addition or multiplication by a constant on various properties of a distribution

Statistic or feature	Effect of addition of a constant, c	Effect of multiplication by a constant, k
Mean	Increased by c	Multiplied by k
Median	Increased by c	Multiplied by k
Mode	Increased by c	Multiplied by k
Sum of squares	No effect	Multiplied by k^2
Variance	No effect	Multiplied by k^2
Standard deviation	No effect	Multiplied by k
IQR	No effect	Multiplied by k
Form of distribution	No effect	No effect

there is no simple relationship between the original and transformed mean and standard deviation. For example, if the mean area measure had been $\overline{A}$, you could *not* calculate the mean perimeter ($\overline{P}$) measure by applying the formula $\overline{P} = 2\sqrt{\pi\overline{A}}$.

The effects of addition or multiplication by a constant are summarized in Table 2.8. This table includes the interquartile range and the sum of squares, neither of which was discussed. You should confirm for yourself that the entries in the table are correct.

2.3.2 Standard Scores or *z*-Scores

Consider the following questions. Which is longer, 5 inches or 12 centimeters? Which is warmer, 90°F or 30°C? To answer questions such as these, we must bring the measures to a common scale. As we apply the appropriate linear transformation, we note that 5 inches is 12.7 centimeters and that 90°F is 32°C, so we know that 5 inches is longer than 12 centimeters and that 90°F is warmer than 30°C.

For psychological measurement, the situation is not quite so straightforward, because in any given application there is often no agreed upon scale of measurement analogous to centimeters or °C. Suppose Jane obtains 15 out of 20 in one midterm test and 35 out of 50 in a second midterm. On which midterm did she do better? A simple way to answer this might be to convert each to a percentage. In this comparison, Jane's performance is better on the first test (75%) than on the second (70%). However, such a comparison might be misleading. Suppose the first test was quite easy, the class average being 16 out of 20 or 80%, whereas the second was more difficult, yielding a class average of only 33 out of 50 or 66%. Thus in the first test, Jane scored below the class average, whereas in the second test she was above average. Relative to the mean, then, Jane has done better on the second test than on the first. To make this type of comparison, we need to transform Jane's test scores into common units relative to the mean. One way of doing this is to transform each of the test score distributions so that they have the same mean and standard deviation. Our previous discussion of linear transformations tells us exactly how to do this.

z denotes standard score.

In transforming each of the test scores so that they have the same mean and standard deviation, we could decide to use whatever mean and standard deviation was convenient—so long as they were the same for both distributions. However, a common convention is to transform the scores so that they have a *mean of 0* and a *standard deviation of 1*. Scores transformed in this way are referred to as *standard scores* and, by convention, are denoted by the letter z. Standard scores are therefore often referred to as *z-scores*.

Standard scores have a mean of 0 and a standard deviation of 1.

How can scores be transformed so that they have a mean of 0 and a standard deviation of 1? If Y denotes a score from a distribution with a mean of $\overline{Y}$, then Y can be converted to a standard score according to the formula

$$z = \frac{Y - \overline{Y}}{s}$$

Where does this formula come from? It can be derived by using our account of linear transformations. The derivation has two steps. First, the mean can be changed by adding or subtracting a constant. If $\overline{Y}$ is subtracted from each score, then the mean of $\overline{Y}$ would be reduced by the value $\overline{Y}$. This results in a new mean of 0. Note that this operation of subtracting $\overline{Y}$ from each score leaves the standard deviation unchanged.

The second step is dividing by s. We know that dividing each score by a constant divides the standard deviation by that constant. If a distribution has a standard deviation s, then we can transform it into one with a standard deviation of 1.0 if we divide each score by s. If each score is divided by s, then the new standard deviation is $s/s = 1.0$. Note that the mean of 0 will not be influenced by this division by s; 0 divided by s remains 0.

Step 1 gives the numerator of the score transformation $(Y - \overline{Y})$. Step 2 gives the denominator.

Returning to our example of Jane's test scores, suppose that the first midterm had a standard deviation of 4 and the second midterm had a standard deviation of 7. Then Jane's standard score, or z-score, for the first midterm is

$$z = \frac{15 - 16}{4} = \frac{-1}{4} = -0.25$$

Her standard score for the second midterm is

$$z = \frac{35 - 33}{7} = \frac{2}{7} = +0.29$$

We can express these results in words by saying that, in the first midterm test, Jane's score was 0.25 of a standard deviation (or .25 standard deviation units) *below* the mean (below being reflected in the negative value), whereas in the second midterm test, her score was 0.29 standard deviation units *above* the mean. More generally, z-scores can be thought of as scores that have been rescaled into standard deviation units above (positive scores) or below (negative scores) the mean. For standard scores, the unit of measurement is the standard deviation.

For standard scores, the unit of measurement is the standard deviation.

The general form of the standard scores will appear in various guises throughout this book, so it is worth noting what we might call the "generic" standard score. This general form is

$$\text{standard score} = \frac{\text{score} - \text{mean of scores}}{\text{standard deviation of scores}}$$

2.3.3 Transforming a Distribution to a Specified Mean and Standard Deviation

Transforming scores into z-scores may be the most common transformation, but a mean of 0 and a standard deviation of 1 is not always what is needed. For example, IQ scores are derived from test scores that have been rescaled to have a mean of 100 and a standard deviation of 15. These particular values for the mean and standard deviation are not naturally occurring phenomena but are values agreed upon by convention. They are achieved by rescaling test scores.

Suppose that an instructor has given an exam that resulted in a mean mark of 62.4 and a standard deviation of 12.3. She wants to rescale the scores to achieve a mean of 70 and a standard deviation of 10. It is simplest to perform this rescaling in two steps. The first is to transform the original scores into standard scores. The second is to transform the standard scores into scores with the desired mean and standard deviation. The second step is essentially the same operation in reverse order.

Step 1 The original scores are converted to standard scores by using the formula

$$z = \frac{Y - 62.4}{12.3}$$

Step 2 To transform the z-scores from a mean of 0 to a mean of 70, and from a standard deviation of 1 to a standard deviation of 10, first multiply each z-score by the desired standard deviation—in this case, 10. The result will be new scores with a standard deviation of 10 and a mean of 0. Next add the desired mean—in this case, 70—to each of these new scores. This operation results in a new mean of 70 but leaves the standard deviation unchanged at 10.

Suppose that a student had an original mark of 74. The z-score equivalent of this score is $(74 - 62.4)/12.3 = 0.943$. The new score is obtained by multiplying this z-score by 10 and adding 70. This operation yields a new score of $9.43 + 70 = 79.43$.

In summary the two steps for transforming a distribution to a specified mean and standard deviation are

Step 1 Subtract the original mean from each score and then divide by the old standard deviation.

Step 2 Perform these two operations in reverse (and in reverse order), using the desired mean and standard deviation: Multiply by the new standard deviation and then add the desired mean.

Comprehension Check 2.3

Important Concepts

1. A linear rescaling or transformation of scores involves multiplying each score by a constant and/or adding a constant to each score. Stated symbolically, a transformation of a score from one scale (X) to a new scale (Y) is linear if it has the general form $Y = kX + c$.

2. Multiplying each score by a constant multiplies both the mean and the standard deviation by that constant, and the variance by the square of that constant.

3. Adding a constant adds the same constant to the mean but leaves the standard deviation and the variance unchanged.

4. A linear transformation of special interest is one that converts scores to standard scores: scores that have a mean of 0 and a standard deviation of 1. Standard scores are denoted by the letter z and are commonly called z-scores.

5. Scores can be transformed to any specified mean and standard deviation.

Problems

Problem 1   Linear and nonlinear transformations

Which of the following transformations are linear?

a. Ounces are converted to grams.

b. In a decision-making study, response times are measured in seconds. This measure is converted to a speed measure by taking the reciprocal of each time. Thus a response time of 0.5 sec becomes a speed of 2 responses per second.

c. In a memory experiment, the response measure is number of items correctly recognized in a list of 120 items. This frequency score is converted to a proportion of correct answers by dividing each score by 120.

Problem 2   Transforming scores

Table 2.9 gives actual scores from each of the experiments in Problem 1 plus the animal behavior (territorial marking) example in Section 2.3.1. Complete each of the four tables by filling in the missing transformed scores. Some of the transformations have already been done to show you how to perform the transformations correctly. Check the correctness of your answers to Problem 1 by plotting the relationship

		Time		**Frequency**		**Area**	**Circumference**
Ounces	**Grams**	**(s)**	**Speed**	**($n = 120$)**	**Proportion**	**(A)**	**(C)**
1.4	39.7	1.4	.71	84	.70	30	19.4
1.2	34.0	2.2	.45	96	.80	50	25.1
0.8	22.7	1.0	1.0	110	.92	42	23.0
1.7	_____	1.9	_____	93	_____	55	_____
1.4	_____	1.6	_____	104	_____	38	_____
1.3	_____	2.8	_____	76	_____	25	_____
0.9	_____	0.9	_____	88	_____	48	_____
2.1	_____	2.3	_____	95	_____	45	_____
0.7	_____	1.7	_____	80	_____	30	_____

Table 2.9 Transformations for Problem 2

between the original scores (on the x-axis) and the transformed scores (on the y-axis). If the transformation is linear, your graph should be a straight line. *Note:* 1 ounce = 28.35 grams and the circumference of a circle is $C = 2\sqrt{\pi A}$, where A is the area and $\pi = 3.14$.

Problem 3   Traansforming scores

a. An investigator measuring reaction time reports a mean and standard deviation of 0.658 and 0.284 seconds, respectively. The editor of the journal to which the report was submitted asks that the measures be converted from seconds to milliseconds (thousandths of a second). What are the values of the mean and standard deviation of these transformed times?

b. A personality scale measuring depression has 50 items, and the score is the number of items (out of 50) for which the participant has selected the depression-indicative alternative. The mean and standard deviation of scores on this scale were found to be 28 and 8.3, respectively. If the scores were transformed to proportions (by dividing each by 50), what would the values of the mean and standard deviation of these transformed scores be?

Problem 4   Calculating z-scores

The mean of the following ten scores is 8.0, and their standard deviation (using $n - 1 = 9$ as the divisor) is 2.0. Under each score, write the corresponding z-score. Check your answers by calculating the mean and the standard deviation of these z-scores, remembering to use 9 as the divisor for the standard deviation. You should get 0 and 1.0, respectively.

Y	5	8	7	10	9	11	6	10	6	8
z	___	___	___	___	___	___	___	___	___	___

Problem 5   Converting to proportions

a. A vocabulary test has 40 items, and a person's score on the test is the number of correctly answered items. The mean performance on this test is 25, and the standard deviation of the test scores is 4.5. Three people score 36, 20, and 16, respectively. Convert each of these obtained scores to a standard score.

b. All the scores in the vocabulary test are converted to proportions by dividing each score by 40. What are the mean and variance of this new set of scores?

c. The scores of 36, 20, and 16, when converted to proportions, become 0.9, 0.5, and 0.4. Convert each of these to a standard score. These scores should be the same as the standard scores you obtained in a. Why?

Problem 6   Using z-scores to compare performance levels

John scores 26/50 in a math test and 60/100 in a chemistry test. The math test scores had a mean of 28 and a standard deviation of 7. The chemistry test scores had a mean of 70 and a standard deviation of 12. By converting each of John's scores to z-scores, decide which test John did better on, relative to others in the class.

Problem 7   Rescaling to T-scores

Some psychological tests rescale the score to have a mean of 50 and a standard deviation of $s = 10$. Such scores are conventionally termed T-scores. Convert the ten z-scores in Problem 4 to T-scores. Check your answers by calculating the mean and the standard deviation of these T-scores, remembering to use 9 as the divisor for the standard deviation. You should get 50 and 10.0, respectively.

Problem 8   Converting a score to a T-score

Suppose you have a set of test scores that you now want to convert to T-scores (scores with a mean of 50 and a standard deviation of 10). If the mean of the original test scores is 72 and the standard deviation is 14, what is the T-score for an original score of 60?

Chapter 2 Exercises

For most of these exercises, you will play the role of data-physician, using either a stemplot, histogram, or frequency polygon to check the set for symptoms such as skew (positive or negative), outliers, or bimodality.

Exercise 1   "Foot-in-the-door" phenomenon (Data Set 2.11)

Recall that each of 80 households in this experiment is to be asked to mount a large antipollution sign. An interviewer visits a randomly selected half of these households just once and asks them to mount the large sign. The other 40 households are visited twice. On the first visit, the interviewer makes a relatively innocuous request to sign a petition promoting a clean environment. Then, a week later, the same interviewer returns with the more substantial request to mount the sign. The question to be answered is whether households in this second, two-visit, group will be more willing to mount the sign than those in the one-visit group. Data Set 2.11 lists the response of each household to the request to mount the large antipollution sign.

Data Set 2.11   Results of visits for Exercise 1
(P, participant; R, refused; A, agreed)

ONE-visit group

P	1	2	3	4	5	6	7	8	9	10
Response	R	A	R	R	A	R	A	R	R	R

P	11	12	13	14	15	16	17	18	19	20
Response	R	A	R	R	R	R	R	R	R	R

P	21	22	23	24	25	26	27	28	29	30
Response	A	R	R	R	R	A	R	R	R	R

P	31	32	33	34	35	36	37	38	39	40
Response	R	R	A	A	R	A	R	R	R	R

TWO-visit group

P	Response				P	Response			P	Response			P	Response		
P	1	2	3	4	5	6	7	8	9	10
Response	R	A	A	R	A	A	A	R	A	A
P	11	12	13	14	15	16	17	18	19	20
Response	R	A	A	R	A	A	A	R	A	A
P	21	22	23	24	25	26	27	28	29	30
Response	A	R	R	R	R	A	R	A	A	R
P	31	32	33	34	35	36	37	38	39	40
Response	A	R	R	R	R	A	R	A	R	R

a. For each condition, tally the frequency of "refused" and "agreed" responses.

b. Draw a graph appropriate for these kinds of data, using as the response measure the proportion (out of 40) of households agreeing.

c. What would you look for in the graph to gain some sense of whether the results support the prediction of attribution theory? Review the answer you gave to the corresponding question in Exercise 1, Chapter 1.

Exercise 2 Opinion change (Data Set 2.12)

A possible basis for predicting compliance in the foot-in-the-door study is that the initial act (signing the petition, for example) changes the participant's disposition toward such actions. Given the very little pressure needed to obtain compliance to the initial request, the tendency is for the participant to attribute compliance to internal (dispositional) causes rather than to external causes. Briefly, the participant's answer to the question "Why did I agree to sign the petition?" is, in effect, "Because I'm that kind of person." This change in self-perception and the desire to maintain self-consistency makes the person more likely to comply with the more demanding request.

If this analysis is correct, it has a number of important implications. Consider the following situation. Participants have just completed a long, boring, and seemingly worthless task. To add insult to injury, they are now required to persuade others that the task is actually enjoyable and worth doing, although, of course, none of the participants actually believes this. Suppose half of these participants each receives $100 for this attempt to persuade, whereas the other half each receives only $1. Having done their best and received their respective payments, each participant is then required to rate the original (long, boring) task for how enjoyable it was, using a scale that runs from 0 (extremely unpleasant) to 10 (extremely pleasant). Would you predict any difference in the ratings between the generously and the minimally rewarded participants? If there is a difference, which of the two would find the task retrospectively more pleasant (or less unpleasant). A reasonable guess might be that it would be participants receiving the $100 payment on the grounds that such a reward may make the whole experience seem more worthwhile.

However, there is another line of argument that predicts otherwise. The participants receiving the $100 payment have a strong external justification for having done something they didn't actually believe in. The discrepancy between what they did and what they believe can be resolved by pointing to the reward. The participants receiving the $1 payment have no such justification. In an effort to explain their behavior, the participants in this condition will resort to an explanation in terms of their own attitudes and motivations. Their effort to persuade will seem less inconsistent with their beliefs if they convince themselves that the original task was not so unpleasant after all. Thus, according to an attributional analysis, those receiving the $1 payment should give the higher ratings. Which prediction, if either, is correct?

This experiment is modeled after Festinger and Carlsmith (1959). There were 48 participants, assigned randomly to the two conditions, 24 participants in each (Data Set 2.12).

Data Set 2.12   Ratings by participants for Exercise 2

Condition 1 ($1 payment)

7	7	2	4	4	3	6	6
6	6	5	5	7	6	5	4
6	5	9	3	3	7	3	1

Condition 2 ($100 payment)

5	5	9	4	6	5	6	8
6	8	6	7	4	9	4	7
5	3	7	7	5	5	7	6

a. This question reviews concepts from Chapter 1.

■ What is the predictor variable in this experiment?

■ Is the predictor variable quantitative or categorical?

■ Is the predictor variable natural or manipulated?

■ What values of the predictor variable are included in the study?

■ What is the response variable in this experiment?

■ Is the response variable quantitative or categorical?

b. For each condition, plot a frequency distribution and check data for

■ *Skewness.* Skewness might result from participants tending to use one extreme of the scale.

■ *Bimodality.* Bimodality could occur if participants tended to choose one extreme or the other—some loved it, others hated it, but few were indifferent.

■ *Outliers.* Outliers might arise if a participant misunderstood the rating scale.

c. Calculate the mean for each condition.

d. Locate the median and the mode of each distribution.

e. The sum of squares for one of these conditions is SS = 82; for the other, it is SS = 58. Calculate the variance corresponding to each of these sums of squares. By inspecting the graphs, judge which distribution has the larger variance.

Exercise 3   Undermining intrinsic motivation (Data Set 2.13)

The data for this experiment consist of the time, in minutes, each child spent drawing during the 1-hour period (Data Set 2.13a). Details of the experiment were given in Exercise 2, Chapter 1.

Data Set 2.13a   Drawing time for Exercise 3

After reward

| 5.2 | 8.5 | 1.9 | 6.5 | 8.8 | 5.5 | 2.3 | 3.7 | 16.0 | 7.9 |
| 1.9 | 6.0 | 5.2 | 7.2 | 0.0 | 7.8 | 2.4 | 4.7 | 7.8 | |

After no reward

| 8.4 | 10.8 | 8.2 | 9.6 | 2.5 | 7.5 | 12.6 | 10.8 | 13.8 | 11.3 |
| 8.9 | 9.8 | 10.1 | 10.6 | 11.3 | 9.7 | 9.4 | 10.5 | 11.5 | |

a. For each condition, construct a stemplot. Check data for skew, bimodality, and possible outliers.

b. Table 2.10 gives the median (Md) and the two quartiles for each condition. What is the *IQR* for each condition?

c. Using the criterion that an outlier is any observation that lies more than $1.5 \times IQR$ above the third quartile or more than $1.5 \times IQR$ below the first quartile, confirm that the suspicious-looking observations in the stemplot really are outliers.

d. Construct boxplots for each condition. Include the outliers in your plot.

e. The variance for one of these conditions is $s^2 = 12.75$; for the other, it is $s^2 = 5.5$. By inspecting the boxplot, judge which distribution has the larger variance.

Table 2.10 Statistics for Exercise 3

Condition	Q_1	Md	Q_3
Reward	2.4	5.5	7.8
No reward	8.9	10.1	11.3

Table 2.11 Statistics for Exercise 3

Condition	Q_1	Md	Q_3	Mean	Variance	Standard deviation
Reward	(2.40)[a]	(5.50)	(7.80)	(5.75)	(12.75)	(3.57)
	2.38	5.35	7.80	5.18	6.98	2.64
No reward	(8.90)	(10.10)	(11.30)	(9.86)	(5.47)	(2.34)
	9.28	10.30	11.30	10.27	2.43	1.56

a. Original data in parentheses, revised data without outliers below.

In Data Set 2.13b, the outliers have been removed. Now $n = 18$ for each condition. Table 2.11 gives various statistics for the original data (in parentheses) and for the reduced set with the outliers removed.

Data Set 2.13b Drawing time for Exercise 3 with outliers removed

After reward

5.2	8.5	1.9	6.5	8.8	5.5	2.3	3.7	7.9
1.9	6.0	5.2	7.2	0.0	7.8	2.4	4.7	7.8

After no reward

8.4	10.8	8.2	9.6		7.5	12.6	10.8	13.8	1.3
8.9	9.8	10.1	10.6	11.3	9.7	9.4	10.5	11.5

f. Calculate the new *IQR* for each condition and compare these values with the original. Why is the effect of removing outliers on the standard deviation greater than its effect on the *IQR*?

g. Compare the effect of dropping the outliers on the means with its effect on the medians. Why is the effect greater for the means?

Exercise 4 Imitation of gestures in 3-month-old infants

The responses to each of the four gestures were classified into one of seven categories and the number of responses in each category tallied (Table 2.12).

a. Plot an appropriate graph for each of the four conditions.

b. What statistic would you use to describe the center of each of these four distributions?

c. Do these statistics provide any support for the hypothesis of imitation?

Table 2.12 Imitation of gestures in 3-month-old infants (Exercise 4)

Responses	Gesture shown to infant			
	Lip protrusion	Mouth opening	Tongue protrusion	Finger movements
Lip protrusion	**29**	18	16	20
Mouth opening	12	**27**	18	19
Tongue protrusion	22	21	**31**	26
Finger movements	15	14	17	**28**
Hand opening	23	23	29	24
Finger protrusion	20	20	10	10
Passive hand	19	17	19	13

Exercise 5   Intermodal matching in 1-month-old infants (Data Set 2.14)

This purpose of this experiment was described in detail in Exercise 4, Chapter 1. The response variable was a measure of visual preference—the proportion of total looking time the infant spends looking at the tactually familiar object (Data Set 2.14). Preference is indicated by the extent to which this proportion is greater than 50%.

Data Set 2.14   Visual preferences for Exercise 5

44	75	63	95	94	41	47	92	37	39
94	60	66	59	85	96	57	73	87	48
90	87	53	62	81	96	42	86	81	77
63	45	46	93	85	45	74	84	96	33

a. Construct a stemplot and check data for skewness, bimodality, and possible outliers.

b. By examining the scores and the stemplot, form a rough estimate of the mean and standard deviation of these scores.

c. Would you expect the median of this distribution to be greater than, less than, or approximately equal to the mean? The actual mean is 69.3. Use the stemplot to locate the median, thereby checking your answer to the first part of this question.

d. The sums of squares for these data is 16,434. What is the standard deviation? Compare this value with your rough estimate. It is common for people's rough estimates in this distribution to be lower than the actual value. Suggest a reason why this might be so.

Exercise 6   Face recognition in newborn infants (Data Set 2.15)

Can newborn infants distinguish their mother's face from that of a stranger. To answer this question, we use the viewing-preference technique employed in the intermodal matching experiment. In this study, modeled after the work reported by Bushnell, Sai, and Mullin (1989), 48 newborns (neonates) were exposed simultaneously to the face of their mother and the face of another woman (a stranger) of similar complexion and hair color. The infants ranged in age from 13 to 100 hours, with a mean age of 50 hours. The two women stood behind a screen so that only their well-lit faces were visible to the baby. The 48 scores in Data Set 2.15 represent the percentage of total looking time spent by each infant looking at his or her mother's face. Thus the extent to which the score is above 50 is a measure of the degree of preference for mother's face over that of the stranger.

Data Set 2.15   Percentage of looking time for Exercise 6

64	68	28	59	41	59	59	72	46	58
67	58	78	75	48	82	66	21	73	55
62	56	61	93	86	87	55	84	86	92
49	92	51	63	38	28	18	76	65	29
51	87	67	76	48	53	89	57		

a. This question reviews concepts from Chapter 1.

■ What is the predictor variable in this experiment?

■ Is the predictor variable quantitative or categorical?

■ Is the predictor variable natural or manipulated?

■ What values of the predictor variable are included in the study?

■ What is the response variable in this experiment?

■ Is the response variable quantitative or categorical?

b. Construct a stemplot and check data for skewness, bimodality, and possible outliers.

c. Use the stemplot to calculate the median and both quartiles.

d. What is the interquartile range of this distribution?

e. Draw a boxplot for the data.

Exercise 7   Infant perception of partly occluded stationary objects
(Data Set 2.16)

This experiment uses the habituation technique to answer an interesting question about object perception in 4-month-old infants. It is modeled after experiments reported by Kellman and Spelke (1983).

Imagine a vertical rod, the center section of which cannot be seen because it is occluded by a rectangular strip of plywood; only the top and bottom thirds can be seen (Figure 2.34a). Thus what we *actually* see is not a single rod, but two separate sections of the rod aligned vertically. As adults we *infer* from this alignment that we are viewing a single rod, but in fact it *could* be two different short rods that just happen to be lined up on either side of the rectangular strip. That is, the stimulus in Figure 2.34a is compatible with both the rod depicted in Figure 2.34b, and the two

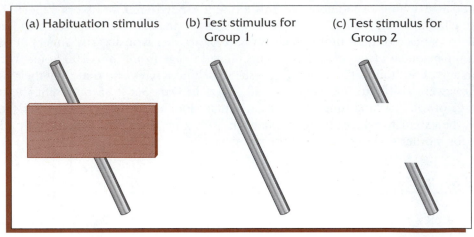

Figure 2.34
Stimuli used in the study of infant perception of partly occluded objects (Exercise 7).

sections of rod depicted in Figure 2.34c. What will 4-month-olds perceive: a single rod partly occluded, or two distinct rods, one on either side of the rectangle?

To answer this question, investigators habituated 48 infants ranging in age from 14 to 18 weeks to the stationary occluded rod (Figure 2.34a) through repeated exposure. Following this habituation was a test of novelty preference. For this test, half of the infants (Group 1) were shown the single nonoccluded rod (Figure 2.34b). If infants perceived the initial habituating stimulus as a single rod, then infants in this group should show no novelty preference; they are not seeing anything different from what they *perceived* during the habituation trials. The other 24 infants (Group 2) were shown the two short, separated, aligned rods, again without any occluding rectangle (Figure 2.34c). If infants perceived the initial habituating stimulus as a single rod, then infants in this group should show a novelty preference. The response measure is the length of time spent looking at the test stimulus (Data Set 2.16). Remember that the longer the looking time, the greater the novelty preference.

There were 48 participants in the experiment. They were assigned randomly to the two conditions, 24 in each.

Data Set 2.16a   Original data set of looking times (Exercise 6)

Group 1: Shown nonoccluded rod

26	34	21	32	31	11	21	16	28	79	18	41
40	36	8	13	40	13	19	0	20	23	25	22

Group 2: Shown separated, aligned sections

18	13	18	16	22	25	29	19	28	35	14	24
27	20	33	3	9	8	70	36	12	34	26	13

Data Set 2.16b Reduced data set of looking times (Exercise 6)

Looking time for Group 1: Shown nonoccluded rod

26	34	21	32	31	11	21	16	28		18	41
40	36	8	13	40	13	19	0	20	23	25	22

Looking time for Group 2: Shown separated aligned sections

18	13	18	16	22	25	29	19	28	35	14	24
27	20	33	3	9	8		36	12	34	26	13

a. For the two conditions, and using the original data set, construct back-to-back stemplots and check data for skew, bimodality, and possible outliers.

The original data set contains two outliers, one in each condition. The reduced data set has $n = 23$; the outliers have been removed.

b. Draw side-by-side boxplots for these data.

c. The means for the original ($n = 24$) data set were 25.7 and 23.0 for Groups 1 and 2, respectively. What are the corresponding means for the revised data ($n = 23$)? *Hint:* You do not need to redo the addition of 23 numbers; make use of the original mean based on $n = 24$.

d. The sum of squares for the revised data ($n = 23$) were 2,577 and 1,877 for Groups 1 and 2, respectively. What are the variances and standard deviations for each of these groups? What would be your rough estimate of the variances and standard deviations of the original ($n = 24$) data set?

Exercise 8   IQ scores of identical twins (Data Set 2.17)

Data Set 2.17 gives the data of IQ scores for 100 pairs of monozygotic (identical) twins reared apart. This data set will be used for an exercise in a later chapter, but prior to that analysis the data need to be checked for any anomalies, such as outliers.

a. What class interval width would you use to construct a stemplot for each set of 100 IQ scores?

Data Set 2.17 IQ scores for A and B twins for Exercise 8

Pair	1	2	3	4	5	6	7	8	9	10
Twin A	128	107	116	89	123	110	97	109	90	96
Twin B	136	105	107	73	128	113	100	117	88	95

Pair	11	12	13	14	15	16	17	18	19	20
Twin A	102	109	116	99	105	107	106	117	117	101
Twin B	99	104	99	90	92	105	107	92	120	73

Pair	21	22	23	24	25	26	27	28	29	30
Twin A	94	85	108	103	131	97	75	105	101	99
Twin B	95	88	96	90	112	92	90	88	99	106

(continued on next page)

Data Set 2.17   IQ scores for A and B twins for Exercise 8 *(continued)*

Pair	31	32	33	34	35	36	37	38	39	40
Twin A	104	79	109	97	107	98	85	82	108	83
Twin B	104	94	111	93	90	95	111	75	103	83
Pair	41	42	43	44	45	46	47	48	49	50
Twin A	113	101	120	79	109	93	95	77	114	102
Twin B	120	108	92	91	108	80	83	85	131	88
Pair	51	52	53	54	55	56	57	58	59	60
Twin A	109	136	102	100	82	91	105	96	93	105
Twin B	93	132	113	87	97	71	112	96	96	118
Pair	61	62	63	64	65	66	67	68	69	70
Twin A	133	93	73	121	89	102	106	123	108	74
Twin B	125	106	93	103	90	111	107	110	97	66
Pair	71	72	73	74	75	76	77	78	79	80
Twin A	108	108	94	123	129	82	113	121	94	83
Twin B	125	101	113	122	111	88	107	122	93	104
Pair	81	82	83	84	85	86	87	88	89	90
Twin A	80	110	80	118	92	106	109	85	88	105
Twin B	77	120	100	111	101	126	142	90	85	86
Pair	91	92	93	94	95	96	97	98	99	100
Twin A	93	90	102	118	129	126	85	84	89	136
Twin B	89	92	99	125	131	127	87	81	114	124

A twins

```
 7 | 34
 7 | 5799
 8 | 00222334
 8 | 55558999
 9 | 00123333444
 9 | 566777899
10 | 01112222234
10 | 5555566677788888999999
11 | 00334
11 | 667788
12 | 011333
12 | 6899
13 | 13
13 | 66
```

B twins

```
 6 | 6
 7 | 133
 7 | 57
 8 | 0133
 8 | 55677888889
 9 | 00000012222233334
 9 | 555666779999
10 | 001133444
10 | 5566777788
11 | 011111223334
11 | 78
12 | 000224
12 | 555678
13 | 112
13 | 6
14 | 2
```

Figure 2.35
Stemplots of IQ scores
for A and B twins in
Exercise 8.

b. The stemplots shown in Figure 2.35 represent the data in Data Set 2.17. Use the stemplots to check the following results, which have been rounded to the nearest whole numbers.

A twins: $Q_1 = 91$, Md = 102, $Q_3 = 110$
B twins: $Q_1 = 90$, Md = 100, $Q_3 = 112$

What is the *IQR* of each of these distributions?

c. Using the $1.5 \times IQR$ criterion, establish that there are no outliers in either distribution.

Exercise 9   Scores on the WAIS (Data Set 2.18)

Data Set 2.18 gives total scores for the five Performance and six Verbal subtests of the Wechsler Adult Intelligence Scale (WAIS) for 104 participants aged 17–18 referred for testing because of their extremely poor academic performance. For details about the WAIS and its subtests, see Matarazzo (1972).

Data Set 2.18   WAIS Verbal and Performance scores for Exercise 9
(P, participant; Verb, verbal score; Perf, performance score)

P	1	2	3	4	5	6	7	8	9	10
Verb	30	35	34	37	26	31	27	37	27	19
Perf	28	27	29	40	27	32	32	33	26	31

P	11	12	13	14	15	16	17	18	19	20
Verb	38	35	27	35	35	23	30	17	39	32
Perf	27	32	29	33	37	29	31	33	27	33

P	21	22	23	24	25	26	27	28	29	30
Verb	42	31	24	29	37	27	27	22	38	25
Perf	28	21	34	36	38	24	33	33	35	33

P	31	32	33	34	35	36	37	38	39	40
Verb	39	36	32	9	37	30	33	35	36	28
Perf	28	28	22	24	38	28	30	34	31	24

P	41	42	43	44	45	46	47	48	49	50
Verb	20	28	30	26	31	31	33	28	30	30
Perf	33	30	35	30	23	27	33	25	20	32

P	51	52	53	54	55	56	57	58	59	60
Verb	31	34	29	33	30	39	33	34	29	19
Perf	69	66	33	18	22	39	25	32	31	22

P	61	62	63	64	65	66	67	68	69	70
Verb	33	36	23	17	32	38	39	22	13	29
Perf	34	27	36	26	27	33	33	28	17	30

(continued on next page)

Data Set 2.18 WAIS Verbal and Performance scores for Exercise 9 (P, participant; Verb, verbal score; Perf, performance score) *(continued)*

P	71	72	73	74	75	76	77	78	79	80
Verb	31	34	33	32	32	35	39	29	35	32
Perf	23	24	30	21	19	33	21	28	36	30

P	81	82	83	84	85	86	87	88	89	90
Verb	26	30	29	30	28	31	31	34	22	40
Perf	26	32	33	23	26	28	33	33	28	31

P	91	92	93	94	95	96	97	98	99	100
Verb	25	32	29	22	39	33	30	31	38	36
Perf	33	28	27	23	36	27	33	36	26	26

P	101	102	103	104
Verb	33	28	33	45
Perf	61	64	30	38

a. What class interval width would you use to construct a stemplot for each set of scores?

b. The stemplots representing these data are shown in Figure 2.36. Use them to check the following results:

Verbal Scores: $Q_1 = 28$, Md $= 31$, $Q_3 = 35$
Performance Scores: $Q_1 = 26$, Md $= 30$, $Q_3 = 33$

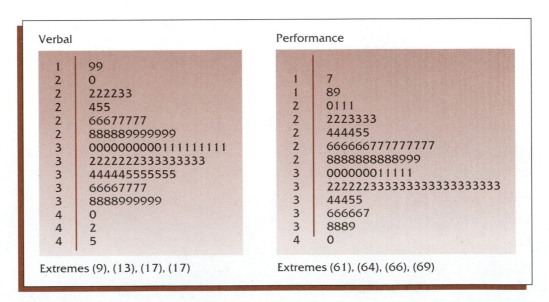

Figure 2.36
Stemplots of WAIS Verbal and Performance scores for Exercise 9.

What is the *IQR* of each of these distributions?

c. The computer package used to produce the stemplots (SPSS) refers to outliers as "extremes." Using the $1.5 \times IQR$ criterion, check that the outliers have been appropriately identified.

Chapter 2 Review

Terms

bar chart
bimodal
boxplot (box-and-whisker plot)
degrees of freedom
frequency distribution
frequency polygon
histogram
interquartile range *(IQR)*
linear transformation
mean
mean square
median (Md)
mode (Mo)
outlier
quartiles (Q)
resistant statistics
skew (positive and negative)
standard deviation
standard score
stemplot (stem-and-leaf plot)
sum of squares
variance
z-scores

Formulas

Mean: $\overline{Y} = \dfrac{\sum Y}{n}$

Interquartile range: $IQR = Q_3 - Q_1$

Sum of squares: $SS = \sum (Y - \overline{Y})^2$

Sample variance of *n* scores: $s^2 = \dfrac{SS}{n - 1}$

Sample standard deviation of *n* scores: $s = \sqrt{\dfrac{SS}{n - 1}}$

Standard score: $z = \dfrac{Y - \overline{Y}}{s}$

Quiz

Complete each sentence with a term from the following list. The same term may be used more than once.

linear transformation	mean	mean square	median
negatively skewed	outliers	third quartile	resistant statistic
positively skewed	first quartile	standard deviation	standard scores
degrees of freedom	sum of squares	variance	interquartile range

The interval that marks off the middle 50% of the scores in a distribution, leaving 25% in each tail, is known as the _____. The value that marks off the bottom 75% of scores from the top 25% is called the _____.

Because the median is not strongly influenced by a few _____, it is described as a _____. The _____, another location statistic, would not be described in this way. A distribution in which the mean is greater than the median is asymmetrical; more precisely, it is _____.

Converting temperature readings from degrees Fahrenheit to degrees Celsius is an example of a _____. A special case of a _____ is rescaling the scores to have a _____ of 0 and a _____ of 1. These rescaled scores are called _____.

Another name for a variance is a _____. Both are obtained by dividing the _____ by the _____.

Chapter 3 Preview

The next step is to combine the general concepts introduced in Chapter 1 with the specific numerical properties of distributions described in Chapter 2. In Chapter 3, we will develop further the concept of a model and show how statistics such as the mean and the variance can be used to estimate components of the model and to describe how well the data fit the model. Such a measure of goodness of fit provides a descriptive index that can provide a basis for comparing competing models.

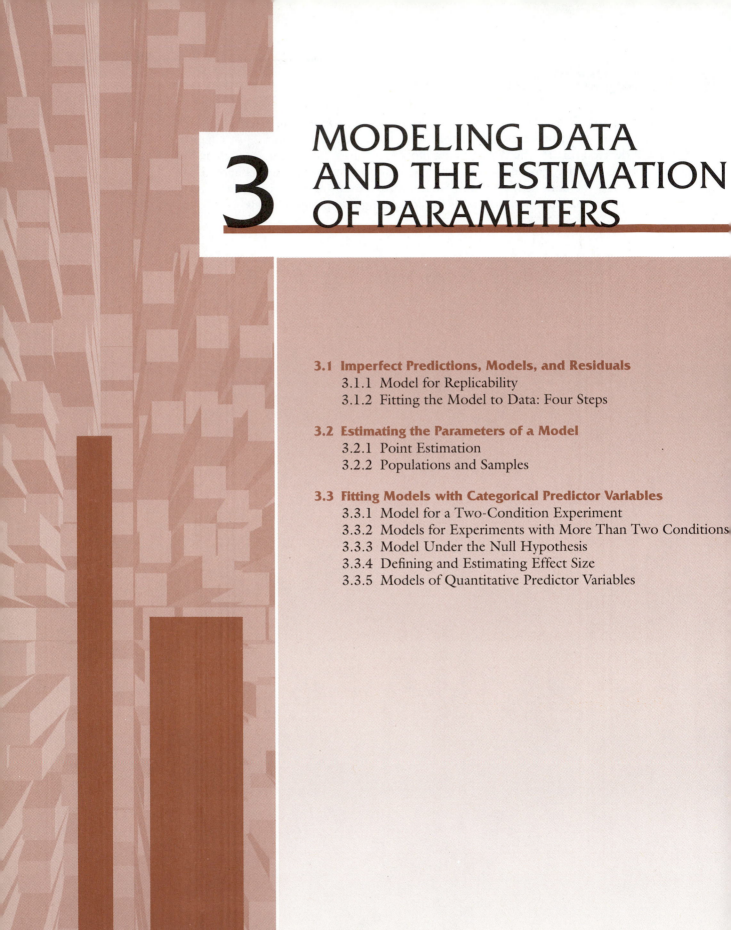

3 MODELING DATA AND THE ESTIMATION OF PARAMETERS

We begin Chapter 3 by making more explicit the general concept of a model, following up the ideas introduced in the first part of Chapter 1. Using the material from Chapter 2, the informal ideas of Chapter 1 can be rigorously defined. The exposition begins with the simplest of examples—measuring a single response variable under a single condition. The desired measurement could be the boiling point of water, the speed of a person's reaction to a warning signal, the visual threshold after 10 minutes in a dark room, or the amount of social interaction between two toddlers of the same sex. According to the principle of replicability, repeated measurements under such fixed conditions should yield identical measurements, but, as illustrated in Chapter 1, real research rarely achieves this ideal. In practice, control is imperfect and data are noisy. The challenge is to model such noisy data.

A model specifies a rule that will predict or reproduce the data. The term *parameter* is introduced to designate the components of the rule. The values of such parameters are usually unknown. After all, if the investigator knew these parameter values, the research would probably be unnecessary. In statistical data analysis, the solution to the problem of specifying the values of these unknown parameters is to *estimate* their values from the data themselves. It is this process of estimation that draws heavily on the material of Chapter 2, especially the concepts of the mean and the variance.

Modeling data by estimating values of parameters is termed "fitting the model to the data." The goal is to obtain estimates that provide the best possible fit. But what constitutes a "good fit"? How is goodness of fit measured? Chapter 3 answers these questions, again using simple examples of measuring a response variable under a single set of conditions.

Most experiments investigate more than one condition. The usual goal is to compare two or more different conditions. For example, by how much does the consumption of 1 ounce of alcohol change the time it takes to react to a warning signal from the reaction time of a participant with a zero level of blood alcohol? How does the visual threshold change with increasing lengths of time in the dark? Is there more

A parameter is a component of the rule that constitutes the model.

social interaction between pairs of toddlers of the same sex than there is between tod-dlers in different-sex pairs? The second half of Chapter 3 will describe how to model data from simple experiments in which the aim is to compare two or more different conditions. These models provide the foundation for answering such questions.

3.1 Imperfect Predictions, Models, and Residuals

3.1.1 Model for Replicability

Chapter 1 introduced the concept of replicability, the principle that the same con-ditions will yield the same observation. In its strict form, replicability implies that the same conditions will yield precisely the same measurement. If we use Y to denote this measurement, the concept of replicability predicts that the value of Y should always be the same. This prediction can be expressed in the statement

$$\hat{Y} = \text{constant}$$

The "hat" (^) above Y is the conventional symbol for "predicted value of." In a specific example, Y might refer to the boiling point of water, the reaction time to the onset of a stimulus, or the number of social interactions between infants in different-sex pairs. For these examples, the statement claims nothing more than that, for a fixed condition, the measurement should always be the same. For reasons that will soon be-come apparent, the symbol μ (the Greek letter mu) is conventionally used to denote this constant. So the statement becomes

$$\hat{Y} = \mu$$

You can think of this statement as a model for the principle of replicability. As such it is the simplest and most basic model in all of science. Nevertheless, it has the essential feature of all models in that it is the statement of a rule for predicting the value of an observation, even though this particular model does nothing more than claim that, for the same set of conditions, every observation should have the same value, μ. In Chapter 1, we used an informal version of this model when we adopted the rule "predict 30 social interactions for same-sex pairs, predict 20 social interac-tions for different-sex pairs." In this example, we took values of $\mu = 30$ and $\mu = 20$ for same-sex and different-sex pairs, respectively.

Parameters of a Model

The constant μ is termed a *parameter* of the model. Parameters are the constants within a model that are the basis for predicting the observations. Knowing that, for water, $\mu = 100°C$ enables us to predict that whenever the boiling point of water is measured, the reading should be 100°C.

A parameter is constant, of course, only for specified conditions. For different phenomena or different conditions, the parameter μ may have different values. The planets Earth and Mars might both be modeled as a sphere, but they have different radii. The radius is the parameter needed to define a sphere uniquely; and without knowing its value, we could not make quantitative predictions.

Recall the signal and noise analogy used in Chapter 1. A model such as $\hat{Y} = \mu$ can be thought of as a statement that describes the *signal* component of data. The model makes claims about that component of the data that is predictable—claims about the structure or regularity in the data. The model for the dark adaptation data graphed in

^ denotes predicted value of.

Parameters may take on different values for different conditions.

Figure 1.1a would consist of equations defining the smooth curves drawn in Figure 1.1b. The model for the mental rotation data in Figure 1.3 would be the equation of the straight line drawn in that figure.

Including Residuals (Noise) in the Model

In much of science, and especially in the behavioral sciences, reproducing precisely the same conditions is a difficult and often impossible task. Observations vary from one occasion to another—from one sample to another. As noted in Chapter 1, observations are inevitably noisy, and the model's predictions therefore are imperfect. In brief, the model does not account for all of the variability in the data.

How can science deal with measurements that present imperfect pictures of their underlying model, measurements that ought to be constant (because they are measuring a single condition) but vary from one measurement to the next? Statistical data analysis addresses this question, and the remainder of this chapter, along with Chapter 4, will set out the fundamental principles of the answer. These basic principles are simple and elegant, and represent one of the great achievements in scientific method.

Measuring Behavior under a Single Condition

Suppose that an investigator wishes to measure a person's simple reaction time to a flash of light. Five attempts to measure the reaction time yield the following five measurements expressed in milliseconds.

Measurement attempt	1	2	3	4	5
Measure (Y)	487	531	410	444	478

Notice first that the measured reaction time is variable. Because these observations are made under a single condition, the model $\hat{Y} = \mu$ should apply. However, despite every effort to hold the conditions constant, this model does not predict the data with perfect accuracy. Our observations (Y) do not conform to the model's prediction ($\hat{Y} = \mu$). In Chapter 1, the term *residual* was introduced to describe such errors. Recall that a residual is simply the difference between the observed measure (Y) and the model's prediction ($\hat{Y} = \mu$). If we use e to denote the residual, then, writing this relation as a simple equation, we have

$$e = Y - \hat{Y} = Y - \mu$$

This relationship can be expressed in a slightly different way by rearranging the terms of this equation and writing it as

$$Y = \mu + e$$

In this form, the model states that the reaction times have two components. One is a constant, the parameter μ, the true reaction time. The other component is the residual, the discrepancy between our actual observation and this true value. This model has the general form introduced in Chapter 1:

$$\text{observation} = \text{model prediction} + \text{residual}$$

Expressing the model in this way reveals the double challenge facing statistical data analysis. The first challenge is the familiar problem that each measurement of the

The residual is the difference between the observed value (Y) and the model's prediction.

e denotes residual.

reaction time yields a different measurement; so even if we knew the value of μ, our predictions for individual reaction times would be imperfect. The second challenge is that we do not know the value of μ. If all we have is a set of variable observations, we have no way of knowing which, if any, of these measurements is the true value.

The idea that an observation can be modeled as true value plus a residual is an old one; it dates back to the beginning of the nineteenth century. However, such a formulation is of little value by itself. It does little to advance our understanding to say that each of our measurements of simple reaction time is a mixture of true and residual components unless we can use the measures to say something useful about the true value, μ.

3.1.2 Fitting the Model to Data: Four Steps

We are confronted with a model $(Y = \mu + e)$ that has an unknown parameter, μ. In tackling this problem, the only information at our disposal is the sample data—in this case, five observations. How do we use these data to address the problem of the unknown parameter, μ? In such a situation, data analysis typically proceeds through the following steps:

Step 1 Use the data to *estimate* the values of any unknown parameters.

Step 2 Use the estimate(s) to obtain a *fit* between model and data.

Step 3 Using this fitted model, *calculate residuals*.

Step 4 Use the residuals to measure *the goodness of the fit* of the model.

Notice that these four steps are essentially those described in the informal analysis in Chapter 1. Let us work through the four steps, using the reaction time example.

Step 1   Estimating μ

The first step involves obtaining an *estimated* value of μ. The estimate we will use is the mean of the five observed measures, $\overline{Y}$, calculated according to the procedures described in Chapter 2. A good question to ask is, Why *this* particular estimate rather than some other? Why not the median, for example? The short answer is that we should use as the best estimate the one that provides the best fit between model and data. Goodness of the fit is measured in terms of the size of the residuals. The smaller the residuals, the better the fit. The reason for using the mean as an estimate of μ is that it produces smaller residuals than any other estimate.

> **Goodness of fit is measured in terms of the size of the residuals.**

Step 2   Fitting the Model

This step entails nothing more than substituting our estimated value of the unknown parameter into the model equation. The original model statement $(Y = \mu + e)$ then becomes

$$Y = \overline{Y} + e$$

In words, we might express this relationship as

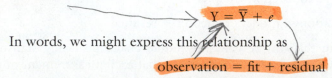

observation = fit + residual

The value of $\overline{Y}$ for the data in Table 3.1 is 470.0, so we have as our fitted model

$$Y = 470.0 + e$$

Step 3   Calculating the Residuals

This step involves finding the residuals by calculating the difference between each measure and the mean of 470.0. We can then express our observed measure Y as the sum of two components: the observed mean (fit) and a residual.

Applying these three steps to the data set yields the numbers in Table 3.1. If you add up the five residuals, you will discover that they sum to 0, so the mean of the residuals is also 0. In fact, quite apart from the rationale developed in this chapter, you will see that these residual values are nothing more than the deviations from the mean. They are the same deviations that would be obtained as the first step in calculating the variance. Compare the second column in Table 2.7 with the column headed "Residual" in Table 3.1. The values are obtained in exactly the same way, by subtracting the mean from each score. The fact that the residuals sum to 0 is therefore no coincidence but another example of the zero-sum principle that was stated in Chapter 2 in the context of calculating the variance: When scores are expressed as deviations from their mean, the sum of the deviations is 0.

The residual values are precisely the same deviations from the mean that form the basis of the variance. This fact provides an interesting new insight into the variance itself. If the model $Y = \mu + e$ is fitted to a single set of scores, then the sum of squares (SS) of the scores (as described in Chapter 2) is also the sum of the squared residuals. It follows that, because the variance of the scores is simply SS divided by the degrees of freedom $(n - 1)$, the variance of the scores is also the variance of the residuals. In brief, for the fitted model $Y = \overline{Y} + e$, the variance of scores and the variance of residuals are one and the same thing.

It is helpful to step back from these arithmetic details and consider this perspective on the variance from a greater distance. The claim is that the variance of the scores is also the variance of the residuals and that the variance therefore provides an index of the overall magnitude of the residuals. If observations are being made under

> Residuals are the deviations from the mean used to calculate the variance.

Table 3.1 Measurements from Data Set 3.1 expressed as their mean plus residual

Replication Attempt	Measure (Y)	Mean	Residual (e)
1	487	470	+17
2	531	470	+61
3	410	470	−60
4	444	470	−26
5	478	470	+8
Sum	2350		0

The sum of squares of the residuals is a measure of the unpredictability of the data.

conditions that ought to be constant, and ought therefore to yield constant measurements, then the appearance of *any* variability in the measurements is a reflection of incomplete control. It is variance that the model $\hat{Y} = \mu$ cannot explain, an inability to predict scores precisely. The variance therefore serves as an index of the extent to which control has been lost, resulting in variance that cannot be accounted for. The sum of squares (or the variance) therefore provides a measure of goodness of fit for the model $\hat{Y} = \mu$. It reflects the fact that the larger the variance, the poorer the fit.

SS_e denotes the sum of squares of the residuals.

When the sum of squares refers to residuals, we will usually denote it as SS_e. The subscript e indicates that the sum of squares is being thought of in relation to the fitted model. When this sum of squares is divided by the degrees of freedom ($n - 1$), the resulting variance, or mean square, will be written MS_e.

$$MS_e = \frac{SS_e}{n - 1}$$

MS_e denotes the mean square of the residuals.

Although the mean square of the residuals corresponds to the variance of the observations, not every example of a variance should be thought of as measuring the overall size of residuals. This way of thinking of the variance is appropriate only when the model $Y = \mu + e$ is appropriate, that is, when Y is a response measure for a single condition that *ought* to obey the strict principle of replicability. In other circumstances, the variance may be a measure of "legitimate" differences rather than being regarded as the unwanted effects of imperfect control. If an investigator is interested in individual differences in a variable such as IQ, mechanical aptitude, or extroversion, then there is no sense in which measurements across individuals should be constant. In this case, the model $Y = \mu + e$ is quite inappropriate, and so too is the idea that the variance is a measure of residuals. Variance in this example is a measure of the degree to which individuals differ and may be the investigator's primary interest. The situation is quite different from an experimental condition in which variation is seen as a failure to hold conditions constant.

Comprehension Check 3.1

Important Concepts

1. A model that expresses the principle of replicability is $\hat{Y} = \mu$, where $\hat{Y}$ is the predicted value of observation and μ is a constant.

2. The constant μ is called the parameter of the model. The relationship between the model's prediction ($\hat{Y} = \mu$) and data can be summarized in the statement

observation = model prediction + residual

3. The residual associated with any particular observation is the difference between this prediction and the observation, and reflects the breakdown of strict replicability.

4. In terms of the analogy used in Chapter 1, the model's prediction rule is the signal in the data, and the residuals are the noise.

5. Because the parameters of the model are unknown, their values must be estimated from the data. These estimates can be used to fit the model to the data. The relationship between data and the model can then be stated as

$$\text{observation} = \text{model fit} + \text{residual}$$

6. Once residuals have been calculated, a measure of the goodness of fit of the model can be calculated as their sum of squares, SS_e. Dividing SS_e by its degrees of freedom $(n - 1)$ gives the mean square of the residuals, MS_e.

Problems

Problem 1   Lexical decision task

A procedure commonly used in the study of reading is a task known as "lexical decision." Observers are shown a string of letters, which may or may not spell an English word. For example, the observer might be shown HERMIT on one trial and PONDEG on another. The observer's task on each trial is to decide as quickly as possible whether or not the letters form an English word. The response measure is decision time measured in milliseconds. For the moment, we will be concerned only with those trials on which the letter string was actually a word. The following data set gives the decision times for ten of these trials.

Trial	1	2	3	4	5	6	7	8	9	10
Decision time (Y)	455	501	483	470	487	461	523	512	490	478

a. The mean of these ten observations is $\overline{Y} = 486$ milliseconds. Calculate the residual for each of the ten observations. You can check your answers by adding up the ten residuals. They should sum to 0. What are the variance and standard deviation of these ten observations?

b. The observation for trial 4 is 470 milliseconds. The model for these observations is taken to be

$$Y = \overline{Y} + e$$

Write out the numerical values of the components of this model for the trial 4 observation.

c. Ignoring sign, which observation in this data set has the smallest residual? Which has the largest?

3.2 Estimating the Parameters of a Model

Section 3.2 begins by offering a more detailed explanation of why, in fitting the model $Y = \mu + e$, the mean $(\overline{Y})$ is the statistic of choice for estimating μ. The intuitive answer given in Section 3.1 was that the best estimate is the one that provides the best fit between model and data, and that the goodness of the fit is reflected in the size of the residuals—the smaller the residuals, the better the fit. We are now in a position to say exactly what these claims mean. In Section 3.2, we will also clarify the nature of parameters by offering a concrete interpretation of the relationship between statistics such as $\overline{Y}$ and the parameters they estimate.

3.2.1 Point Estimation

A point estimate consists of a single number.

This section discusses the role of $\overline{Y}$ as a point estimate of μ. Why the term *point*? An estimate is termed a *point estimate* to indicate that it consists of a single number, a single point in the measurement scale. Later we will discuss a different form of estimation, called *interval estimation*, that consists of a range of values. Whereas a point estimate will claim that a single point—a number such as 10.3, for example—is the best estimate of μ, an interval estimate will claim that an interval of values—the interval 9.7 to 10.9, for example—contains the true value, μ.

Begin by imagining a range of possible candidate estimates for μ. We could use any values you care to think of. The mean, $\overline{Y}$, is just one of these possibilities. Each of these imagined estimates could be used to fit the model $Y = \mu + e$ by substituting its value for μ and then calculating e for each of the five scores.

The results of such an exercise are recorded in Table 3.2. This table takes various values as potential estimates for μ, starting at the low end, with 460 milliseconds and working up to a value of 480 milliseconds. Steps 2 and 3 of the model fitting procedure are then completed, using each potential estimate to replace μ and calculating the resulting residuals for each of the five measurements. For example, if we take 460 as our estimate, then the residual for the first measurement (487) would be

$$487 - 460 = +27$$

Different estimates produce different residuals.

Notice that as the estimate of μ varies from 460 to 480, the residuals change. They seem larger for 460 than for 465, for example. Intuitively, 465 seems a better estimate than 460. We expect that the value 470, the mean of the five observations, will turn out to be the best of all—but on what grounds? Casual perusal of the residuals

Table 3.2 Residuals for each of the five measures associated with different possible estimates of μ

Obtained measure	Possible estimates of μ				
	460	465	470	475	480
487	+27	+22	+17	+12	+7
531	+71	+66	+61	+56	+51
410	−50	−55	−60	−65	−70
444	−16	−21	−26	−31	−36
478	+18	+13	+8	+3	−2
Sum of squares	8850	8475	8350	8475	8850

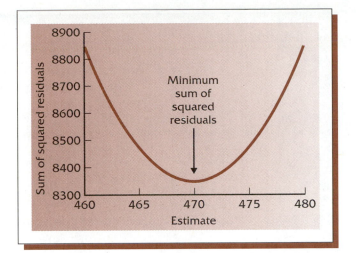

Figure 3.1
The sum of squared residuals varies in size, depending on the value used to estimate the parameter μ. The sum of squares is a minimum when the mean of the data is used as the estimate.

is too intuitive. What we need is (1) an objective index that will measure the overall size of the residuals and (2) an unambiguous rule for finding the estimate that makes this index as small as possible.

Throughout data analysis, the commonly used index of the overall magnitude of the residuals is either their sum of squares or their mean square. The bottom row of Table 3.2 gives the sum of the squares for each of the estimates. Notice that these values for the sum of the squares vary from one estimate to another and that 465 results in a smaller sum of squares than 460 does. This result corresponds to our previous intuition that the mean (470) produces the smallest sum of squares of any of the candidate estimates. But what of all the other possible candidates? Table 3.2 gives sums of squares for just five selected values; of these five values, the estimate of 470 yields the smallest sum of squares. But is it better than 471, or 469?

Figure 3.1 plots the values of the sums of squares for a continuous set of estimates ranging from 460 to 480. The graph shows that, indeed, the minimum sum of squares is obtained when 470 is used as the estimate. As the estimates increase or decrease from this value, the sum of squares increases.

Figure 3.1 is a graphical demonstration of the fact that $\overline{Y}$ is the best estimate of μ. What makes this estimate the best of all possible estimates is that it yields the *minimum sum of the squared residuals* or, more briefly, the *minimum sum of squares.* Because it produces the smallest possible sum of squares, the same mean ($\overline{Y}$) is referred to as a *least squares estimate* of μ.

This property of $\overline{Y}$ can be established rigorously by using elementary differential calculus, and the proof is outlined in MathBox 3.1. It will interest those who have taken a course in calculus. However, understanding this proof is by no means necessary for an understanding of the concept of least squares.

The solution to the problem of the best estimate is the solution you were led to expect. The estimate that minimizes the sum of the squared residuals is the mean of the observed values. The conclusion to all this discussion, then, is that the mean of the observations is the least squares estimate of the parameter μ. Another common way of stating this is to describe the mean as the best estimate "in the least squares sense."

There are other desirable properties of estimates besides satisfying the least squares criterion, but with one notable exception they are beyond the scope of an introductory text. The exception is the important requirement that an estimate be *unbiased,* a concept introduced in Chapter 1 and treated more formally in Chapter 4.

SS_e provides an index of the overall size of the residuals.

The criterion for the minimum sum of squares is called least squares.

The mean of the observations is the least squares estimate of the parameter μ.

MathBox 3.1

Proof That the Sample Mean Is the Least Squares Estimate of μ

To show that the sample mean is the least squares estimate of the population mean involves only very elementary differential calculus. First we set out the formula for the sum of squares, expand it, then differentiate this expanded formula with respect to the estimate (denoted by M), set this derivative to 0, and finally solve for M.

We need to find the value of M that yields the minimum sum of the squared residuals, SS.

The sum of squares if given by the expression

$$SS = \Sigma(Y - M)^2$$

Expanding the right-hand side, we have

$$SS = \Sigma(Y^2 - 2YM + M)^2$$
$$= \Sigma Y^2 - 2M\Sigma Y - \Sigma M^2$$

We now differentiate with respect to M:

$$\frac{\partial SS}{\partial M} = -2\Sigma Y + 2\Sigma M$$

Because the desired value of M is a constant, $\Sigma M = n$M (M is added to itself n times). Thus

$$\frac{\partial SS}{\partial M} = -2\Sigma Y + 2n M$$

Setting this derivative to 0 gives

$$-2\Sigma Y + 2n M = 0$$

This relation gives us

$$M = \frac{\Sigma Y}{n}$$

which is the sample mean, $\overline{Y}$.

3.2.2 Populations and Samples

An investigation is made up of *n* observations, where *n* is the sample size.

As noted previously, the observations made in a particular investigation are usually called a *sample*. Five measurements of simple reaction time would be referred to as a sample. The letter *n* is used to indicate the number of such observations, or the *sample size*.

The word *sample* is also commonly used as an adjective to describe a statistic such as the mean or the variance when these statistics have been calculated on the basis of sample data. Thus $\overline{Y}$, the mean of the observations, is called the *sample* mean and s^2 the sample variance. Such statistics are referred to generally as *sample* statistics.

Underlying the concept of a sample is the idea that the particular observations made are a subset of a much larger set of potential observations, namely, all the obser-

GameBox 3.1

Cut Your Losses Revisited

Cut Your Losses was a game described in Chapter 1. We are now in a position to describe how to cut your losses to a minimum.

Recall that each player takes a turn in predicting the outcome from rolling two dice. After the roll, the difference between the predicted and actual outcome is calculated, squared, and the player who rolled and predicted the outcome loses this number of points. A player is out of the game upon losing all of the 100 starting points.

The material in Section 3.2.1 indicates the optimal strategy for playing this game. Notice first that the amount lost on each trial is the squared residual: the square of the difference between the outcome and the prediction. The total amount lost at any point in the game is therefore the sum of the squared residuals to that point. Thus the optimal strategy in playing this game is one that minimizes the sum of the squared residuals. Section 3.2.1 tells us that the mean is the value that achieves this goal.

The best strategy is therefore to predict the mean on every trial. The mean outcome from the roll of two dice is 7 (midway between 1 and 12, the two extreme outcomes). Notice that this strategy corresponds to using the model $Y = \mu$, where $\mu = 7$. If the game were played by rolling four dice, the same model ($Y = \mu$) would apply, but with a different parameter value of $\mu = 14$.

It may seem counterintuitive to guess the same outcome on every trial, and it is certainly unexciting. However, if the goal is to win, then there is no better strategy. If in doubt, play the game using this strategy. You may not win every time, but you will win more often than opponents who adopt a different strategy.

vations that might have been made. Practical difficulties aside, there is no limit, in principle, to the number of measurements of the boiling point of water that might have been made or to the number of measurements of simple reaction time. The term *population* is used to refer to this larger unlimited set. The observations actually made can then be referred to as a sample from this population.

If observations are regarded as a sample from a much larger—perhaps infinitely large—population, then it makes sense to think of this population of measures as also having a distribution with a mean, variance, median, quartiles, and all the other statistics covered in Chapter 2. When referring to these population counterparts of sample statistics, we use the term *parameters*, terminology that is consistent with our previous use of parameter when referring to μ as a component of our basic model. Thus a distinction is made between the mean as a sample statistic (denoted by $\bar{Y}$) and the mean as a population parameter (denoted by μ). It is for this reason that the symbol μ was used in the original statement of the model for replicability.

In summary, the *sample mean* is the mean of the observations actually sampled, and μ, the parameter of our model, is interpreted as the *population mean*: the mean of the population of observations from which the sample was drawn.

Similarly, the variance s^2 of a sample of n observations can be thought of as the sample variance, and its population counterpart as the population variance. It is customary to denote the population values with the Greek letter counterparts of the

> A population is the entire set of potential observations from which the sample has been selected.

> Parameters are the population counterparts of sample statistics such as the mean or the variance.

Roman letters used for sample statistics. Thus for the population variance, the lowercase s is replaced by its Greek equivalent σ (lowercase sigma); so population variance is denoted by σ^2 and population standard deviation by σ.

What does this distinction between population and sample have to do with modeling and estimation? The answer to this question is quite important. It offers a new perspective on what is meant by the parameters of a model: The parameters of a model are the population counterparts of sample statistics. According to this view, the parameter μ in the model for simple reaction time is interpreted as the mean of the population of reaction times. The sample mean, $\overline{Y}$, of the five observations is thus interpreted as an estimate of the mean of the population of reaction times: $\overline{Y}$ is an estimate of μ. According to this view, a model is a statement about what is true in the population.

> **The parameters of a model are the population counterparts of sample statistics; a model is a statement about what is true in the population.**

Identifying the parameter μ with the mean of the population gives a more concrete meaning to the idea expressed in Section 3.1.1 that μ is the *true* value of the variable being measured. The true value is simply the value that would be obtained if the sample were expanded to include the entire population. This interpretation has the advantage of neatly sidestepping an endless discussion about the meaning of "true," but it has its own difficulties. In any particular context, exactly what is the population? What, for example, is the population of measurements of the boiling point of water, or of the reaction time to a warning signal?

A straightforward but somewhat misleading answer to this question is to identify a population with a large group of people or animals. This definition might be called the literal or demographic interpretation of the term *population*. We can speak of the population of the United States or of the state of California, or the population of polar bears in the Arctic. It is the definition of a population that would be used appropriately by those conducting surveys and opinion polls. However, in the world of research data, such a simple interpretation of population is not always appropriate.

Strictly speaking, a population or a sample refers not to individuals but to measurements.

Strictly speaking, a population or a sample refers not to individuals but to measurements: a sample of reaction times selected from a population of reaction times, or a sample of IQ scores from a population of IQ scores. Often the basis for choosing these measurements is the selection of individuals. A sample of 20 IQ scores is obtained by selecting 20 individuals to provide the IQ scores. In such cases, it is reasonable and harmless, if not strictly correct, to think of the sample in terms of individuals. Suppose, however, that the sample consists of measurements such as the boiling point of water or five reaction times taken from the same individual. What is the population in these cases? These examples indicate the need for a more general concept of population than the literal demographic one.

Populations will be assumed to be infinitely large.

The broader definition of population is more abstract. It refers to a conceptual rather than a physical population. If we think of a sample as a set of observations taken under specified conditions, then, in relation to this sample, the population is the set of all possible observations that might have been taken under these same conditions.

How big is the population? All the methods discussed in this book assume that this conceptual population is very large—so large that, for all practical purposes, it can be regarded as infinite. Sample sizes are therefore limited only by practical considerations; in principle, their size (n) is unlimited.

As an example of the distinction between sample and population, consider again the five reaction times reported on page 123. These reaction times, measured under specified conditions, constitute a sample of $n = 5$. According to the present definition of a population, this sample is one drawn from the set of all conceivable measurements taken under these conditions. With this definition, it becomes possible to think of samples and populations in much broader terms. Rather than a selection of individuals, the sample might be a selection of occasions for a single individual. In a language experiment, it might be a selection of words. In a study of animal behavior, it might be a selection of locations *and* occasions.

In fact, most studies in the behavioral sciences sample from a population that ranges over many attributes. (Attributes over which a population ranges are those attributes that are not held constant across repeated observations.) In measuring simple reaction time, for example, different measurements might involve different participants, different times of the day, and different stimuli, all of which are likely to influence reaction time. The particular participants, times, and stimuli constitute a sample from the population of possible participants, times, and stimuli. The goal of research is to establish what is true in this population, not merely what is true of the sample. Science, remember, is concerned with the particular (the sample) only as a means of discovering what is true more generally (true in the population). The aim of selecting a sample, then, is to provide some basis for generalizing beyond the particularities of the sample to the population from which the sample was selected. Just how this generalization is achieved provides the subject matter of following chapters. It should be stressed at the outset, however, that the grounds on which generalization can be justified are critically dependent on how the sample was selected.

Comprehension Check 3.2

Important Concepts

1. Usually the values of the parameters of a model are unknown and must be estimated from the data. Once the parameters have been estimated, the model can be fitted to the data.

2. The prediction rule generates fitted values, so we can describe the data as

$$\text{observation} = \text{model fit} + \text{residual}$$

3. A goal in fitting the model is to make the residuals as small as possible. The sum of squares of the residuals (SS) provides a measure of goodness of fit. The larger the sum of squares, the poorer the fit. A desirable estimate of a parameter is one that yields the smallest possible SS. Such an estimate is said to satisfy the criterion of least squares.

4. If data are thought of as a sample from a larger population of potential observations, then each parameter of the model can be thought of as the population counterpart of the sample statistic. Thus the parameter μ is interpreted as the population mean—the population counterpart of the sample mean, $\overline{Y}$. According to this view, a model is a statement about what is true in the population.

Problems

Problem 1   Lexical decision task

In Problem 1 of Comprehension Check 3.1, you calculated the sum of squares of the residuals for the ten decision times of the lexical decision task.

Trial	1	2	3	4	5	6	7	8	9	10
Decision time (Y)	455	501	483	470	487	461	523	512	490	478

These residuals were calculated as the differences between each score and the sample mean of 486 milliseconds. This sample mean was taken as the estimate of μ.

Suppose that, instead of using the sample mean, we use the sample median to estimate μ. The median is 485. Convince yourself that using the sample mean as an estimate of μ results in a smaller sum of squares than does using the median. To do this, first substitute the median for the mean and then recalculate the residuals as the difference between each score and the median. Then calculate the sum of squares of these new residuals. (This sum will be larger than that obtained by using the mean of 486 milliseconds.)

Problem 2   Coin toss

A coin is tossed 20 times and the proportion of times it lands heads is recorded. This value turns out to be 8 out of 20, or a proportion of .4.

a. How would you describe the population of which this set of 20 tosses is considered a sample?

b. The proportion of heads in the sample of 20 was .4. Given your definition of population, what would you say was the *population* proportion of heads?

3.3 Fitting Models with Categorical Predictor Variables

Thus far we have limited the discussion to situations in which observations are made under a single condition. Now we will extend the idea of model fitting to studies in which there are two or more conditions.

3.3.1 Model for a Two-Condition Experiment

Investigators designed an experiment to evaluate the effectiveness of a form of therapy known as systematic desensitization in treating a simple phobia, such as fear of flying. The therapy begins by training clients in muscle relaxation. After this training, they are asked (over a number of sessions) to imagine increasingly frightening scenes, each time engaging in the relaxation procedure learned initially.

The participants in this experiment were volunteer clients, all of whom suffered from fear of flying. A randomly chosen half of the volunteers were assigned to a control condition and received only general counseling. The other half were assigned to an experimental condition that received desensitization therapy.

The two conditions constitute the two values of a categorical predictor variable (X). If we use subscripts to distinguish the two conditions, then the values of the predictor variable are no therapy (X_1) and therapy (X_2). After counseling or therapy, each volunteer was confronted with a potentially frightening scene involving flight. The response measure, a measure of fear, was each volunteer's increase in heart rate (measured in beats per minute) following the presentation of the scene.

For the no-therapy control condition (X_1), we will denote the measured increase in heart rate by Y_1, and for the experimental therapy condition (X_2), by Y_2. The actual data are shown in Data Set 3.1. In this example, there is an equal number of observations in each condition, which we can denote by n. However, we should allow for the possibility in other experiments of unequal sample sizes across the conditions. In such cases, we can use $n_1, n_2, \ldots, n_i$ to denote respectively the number of observations in the first, second, . . . , and ith conditions. In Data Set 3.1, $n_1 = n_2 (= n) = 18$.

> n_1, n_2, etc. denote the number of observations in each condition.

Data Set 3.1 Responses for the two conditions in the phobia treatment experiment (Increase in heart rate (beats per minute) following the presentation of a potentially frightening scene; P, participant)

Control condition X_1 ($\bar{Y}_1 = 10.2$)

P	1	2	3	4	5	6	7	8	9
Y_1	8.4	10.8	8.2	9.6	5.5	12.6	10.8	14.0	11.3

P	10	11	12	13	14	15	16	17	18
Y_1	8.9	9.8	10.1	10.6	11.3	9.7	9.4	10.5	12.1

Experimental condition X_2 ($\bar{Y}_2 = 5.2$)

P	19	20	21	22	23	24	25	26	27
Y_2	5.2	8.5	1.9	6.5	8.8	5.5	2.3	3.7	7.9

P	28	29	30	31	32	33	34	35	36
Y_2	1.9	6.0	5.2	7.2	0.0	7.8	2.4	4.7	8.1

There is one further point about notation. We will use N to indicate the total number of observations in a study. That is,

$$N = n_1 + n_2 + \ldots$$

In Data Set 3.1, $N = 18 + 18 = 36$. When there is only one condition, then N and n are equivalent. In these cases, we choose to use n, as we have in previous examples.

A model for this two-condition experiment is a very simple extension of the model for a single condition. We will model each of the two conditions separately, each condition with its own distinct parameter. We will use subscripts to distinguish the parameters: The parameter associated with the first condition will be denoted by μ_1, and the parameter associated with the second condition will be denoted by μ_2. Using the distinction between sample and population, we could describe μ_1 as the population mean for increase in heart rate for volunteers in the control condition and

> N denotes the total number of observations in a study.

μ_2 as the population mean for increase in heart rate for volunteers in the experimental condition. Using this notation, we can write the model for the two conditions as

$$Y_1 = \mu_1 + e \quad \text{(control condition)}$$

$$Y_2 = \mu_2 + e \quad \text{(experimental condition)}$$

To fit this model to the data in Data Set 3.1, we follow the first three steps given in Section 3.1.2.

Step 1 Use the data to estimate the unknown parameter.

We take $\overline{Y}_1\ (=\ 10.2)$ as our estimate of μ_1 and $\overline{Y}_2\ (=\ 5.2)$ as our estimate of μ_2.

Step 2 Use the estimate to obtain a fit between model and data.

We substitute our estimates into our original model statement. This substitution gives us

$$Y_1 = \overline{Y}_1 + e$$
$$= 10.2 + e$$

and

$$Y_2 = \overline{Y}_2 + e$$
$$= 5.2 + e$$

Step 3 Using this fitted model, calculate residuals.

To obtain the residuals note that $e = Y - \overline{Y}$. Thus the first residual for the control condition (Y_1) is $8.4 - 10.2 = -1.8$. Table 3.3 gives the residuals for each measurement.

Step 4 Measure the goodness of fit of the model.

As in the single-condition case, it will prove useful to have an index of the overall size of the residuals. In the single-condition case, this index was the sum of the squared residuals (SS_e). The same measure can be obtained separately for each of the two conditions in the therapy evaluation experiment. For the control condition, we will use SS_1 to denote the sum of squares:

$$SS_1 = (-1.8)^2 + 0.6^2 + \ldots + 1.9^2 = 59.6$$

For the experimental condition, we will use SS_2 to denote the sum of squares:

$$SS_2 = 0.0^2 + 3.3^2 + \ldots + 2.9^2 = 120.3$$

It is useful to obtain a single measure of residuals by adding these two sums of squares. We can write this addition as

$$SS_e = SS_1 + SS_2 = 179.9$$

The value of SS_e can be converted to a mean square, MS_e. This averaging results in a single value for MS_e that measures the average variability of the residuals within the two conditions. Such averaging is justified, provided it is assumed that the true or population variances within each condition (σ_1^2 and σ_2^2) are the same (that $\sigma_1^2 = \sigma_2^2$) and that s_1^2 and s_2^2 are therefore both estimating the same value.

The assumption that the population variances are the same for both conditions is known as *the assumption of homogeneity of variance*. This assumption is important for two reasons. First, if the assumption of homogeneity of variance is false, then the av-

The assumption of homogeneity of variance is that the population variances for the conditions are equal.

Table 3.3 Residuals for each volunteer in each of the conditions of the phobia treatment experiment

	Control condition				Experimental condition		
P	Y_1	$\overline{Y}_1$	e	P	Y_2	$\overline{Y}_2$	e
1	8.4 =	10.2	−1.8	19	5.2 =	5.2	+0.0
2	10.8 =	10.2	+.6	20	8.5 =	5.2	+3.3
3	8.2 =	10.2	−2.0	21	1.9 =	5.2	−3.3
4	9.6 =	10.2	−0.6	22	6.5 =	5.2	+1.3
5	5.5 =	10.2	−4.7	23	8.8 =	5.2	+3.6
6	12.6 =	10.2	+2.4	24	5.5 =	5.2	+0.3
7	10.8 =	10.2	+0.6	25	2.3 =	5.2	−2.9
8	14.0 =	10.2	+3.8	26	3.7 =	5.2	−1.5
9	11.3 =	10.2	+1.1	27	7.9 =	5.2	+2.7
10	8.9 =	10.2	−1.3	28	1.9 =	5.2	−3.3
11	9.8 =	10.2	−0.4	29	6.0 =	5.2	+0.8
12	10.1 =	10.2	−0.1	30	5.2 =	5.2	+0.0
13	10.6 =	10.2	+0.4	31	7.2 =	5.2	+2.0
14	11.3 =	10.2	+1.1	32	0.0 =	5.2	−5.2
15	9.7 =	10.2	−0.5	33	7.8 =	5.2	+2.6
16	9.4 =	10.2	−0.8	34	2.4 =	5.2	−2.8
17	10.5 =	10.2	+0.3	35	4.7 =	5.2	−0.5
18	12.1 =	10.2	+1.9	36	8.1 =	5.2	+2.9

erage misrepresents the size of the residuals in each of the conditions. For one condition, the average value will exaggerate the true size of the residuals, whereas, for the other, it will underestimate the true value. The second reason is that many of the methods we will be using in later chapters are based on this assumption.

If the assumption of homogeneity of variance is accepted, then we can drop the subscripts and use σ^2 to denote this common value. Averaging is accomplished by adding the two sums of squares and dividing by the combined (total) degrees of freedom. The combined degrees of freedom are obtained by simply adding up the degrees of freedom for each condition. In our phobia treatment example, there are $n - 1 = 17$ degrees of freedom for each of the two conditions, so the total degrees of freedom is $17 + 17 = 34$. Thus the single variance estimate for our example is

$$\text{MS}_e = \frac{\text{SS}_e}{df} = \frac{179.9}{17 + 17} = 5.3$$

MS$_e$ is the estimate of the common population variance.

This mean square is a single estimate of σ^2, the variance of the observations (also of the residuals) in each condition. You may have noted that the sum of squares for Y_2

is twice the size of that for Y_1 (120.3 versus 59.6) and wondered whether this ratio casts doubt on the assumption that $\sigma_1^2 = \sigma_2^2$, because s_2^2 is actually twice as large as s_1^2. This concern is reasonable, and formal methods exist for evaluating the assumption that $\sigma_1^2 = \sigma_2^2$, although they will not be discussed in this text. In this particular case, the difference is not large enough to be a serious worry.

A general formula for the common variance estimate allows for the possibility that there may be a different number of observations in each condition. This general formula is

$$MS_e = \frac{SS_1 + SS_2}{(n_1 - 1) + (n_2 - 1)}$$

where n_1 is the number of scores in the first condition and n_2 is the number of scores in the second condition.

If there is an equal number of observations in each condition (n), then this formula simplifies to

$$MS_e = \frac{SS_1 + SS_2}{2(n - 1)}$$

3.3.2 Models for Experiments with More Than Two Conditions

Fitting models for experiments with more than two conditions is a straightforward extension of the two-condition case. For three conditions, for example, the model could be set out as

$$Y_1 = \mu_1 + e$$
$$Y_2 = \mu_2 + e$$
$$Y_3 = \mu_3 + e$$

Assuming n observations in each condition, the value of MS_e would be

$$MS_e = \frac{SS_1 + SS_2 + SS_3}{3(n - 1)}$$

Fitting models for experiments with more than two conditions is a straightforward extension of the two-condition case.

The degrees of freedom for MS_e are $N - k$.

If we consider the general case of an experiment with k conditions, then the degrees of freedom for calculating MS_e would be $k(n - 1)$. If we expand this expression, we have $k(n - 1) = kn - k = N - k$. In other words, the degrees of freedom for MS_e is the total number of observations less the number of conditions.

This result applies also to the case in which the conditions have unequal numbers of observations. In that case, the degrees of freedom would be $(n_1 - 1) + (n_2 - 1) + (n_2 - 1) + \ldots + (n_k - 1) = N - k$.

The formula $N - k$ for the degrees of freedom for MS_e is an example of a very general principle governing degrees of freedom. Note that in calculating the sum of squares for each condition, we first need to calculate an estimate of the mean of that condition. If there is a total of k conditions, then we need to estimate k means to obtain the value of SS_e. One degree of freedom is lost in each condition for each of these estimates. Thus the total of N observations is reduced to $N - k$ degrees of freedom.

A very general principle governing degrees of freedom is

> *The number of degrees of freedom associated with a sum of squares is the total number of observations less the number of independent parameters that were estimated in forming the sum of squares.*

3.3.3 The Model Under the Null Hypothesis

Full Model and Null Model

The preceding example used the data from the phobia treatment experiment to fit a model with two parameters, μ_1 and μ_2. For the control condition, we had

$$Y_1 = \mu_1 + e$$

and for the experimental condition,

$$Y_2 = \mu_2 + e$$

It will be convenient to refer to this model as the "full" model because we want to compare it with an even simpler model for the same data, a model that asserts that $\mu_1 = \mu_2$. For this model, we can drop the subscripts and replace μ_1 and μ_2 with the single value μ. The hypothesis that $\mu_1 = \mu_2 = \mu$ is known as the *null hypothesis,* a term that captures the claim that the experimental conditions make no difference to the observations—that their effect is null. The null hypothesis is often written as

$$H_0: \quad \mu_1 = \mu_2 = \mu.$$

The null hypothesis is that $\mu_1 = \mu_2 = \mu$.

This hypothesis can be contrasted with the hypothesis underlying the full model, which claims instead that

$$H_1: \quad \mu_1 \neq \mu_2.$$

H_0 denotes null hypothesis.

Under the null hypothesis $\mu_1 = \mu_2 = \mu$, so we have a model with just one parameter, μ. We will refer to this model as the *null model.* With just one parameter, the null model takes on a simpler form. For the control condition,

$$Y_1 = \mu + e$$

and for the experimental condition, the model is exactly the same:

$$Y_2 = \mu + e$$

The null model is $Y_1 = Y_2 = \mu + e$.

The estimate of μ is the overall mean: the mean of all observations, denoted by $\overline{Y}$. In our example, this would be the mean of all 36 observations, which is 7.70. A shortcut method of obtaining the overall mean is to calculate the average of $\overline{Y}_1$ and $\overline{Y}_2$. That is,

$$\overline{Y} = \tfrac{1}{2}(\overline{Y}_1 + \overline{Y}_2)$$

The estimate of μ is $\overline{Y}$, the overall mean.

For the data in our example,

$$\overline{Y} = \tfrac{1}{2}(10.2 + 5.2) = 7.7$$

Fitting the Null Model

Now we can use this value of the overall mean to fit the null model to the data. If we replace μ with 7.7, the null model becomes $Y = 7.7 + e$. The residual for each score is therefore $e = Y - 7.7$. The results are shown in Table 3.4. The first score is

Table 3.4 Residuals for the data from the phobia treatment experiment under the null hypothesis model

Y_1		$\overline{Y}$	e	Y_2		$\overline{Y}$	e
8.4	=	7.7	+0.7	5.2	=	7.7	−2.5
10.8	=	7.7	+3.1	8.5	=	7.7	+0.8
8.2	=	7.7	+0.5	1.9	=	7.7	−5.8
9.6	=	7.7	+1.9	6.5	=	7.7	−1.2
5.5	=	7.7	−2.2	8.8	=	7.7	+1.1
12.6	=	7.7	+4.9	5.5	=	7.7	−2.2
10.8	=	7.7	+3.1	2.3	=	7.7	−5.4
14.0	=	7.7	+6.3	3.7	=	7.7	−4.0
11.3	=	7.7	+3.6	7.9	=	7.7	+0.2
8.9	=	7.7	+1.2	1.9	=	7.7	−5.8
9.8	=	7.7	+2.1	6.0	=	7.7	−1.7
10.1	=	7.7	+2.4	5.2	=	7.7	−2.5
10.6	=	7.7	+2.9	7.2	=	7.7	−0.5
11.3	=	7.7	+3.6	0.0	=	7.7	−7.7
9.7	=	7.7	+2.0	7.8	=	7.7	+0.1
9.4	=	7.7	+1.7	2.4	=	7.7	−5.3
10.5	=	7.7	+2.8	4.7	=	7.7	−3.0
12.1	=	7.7	+4.4	8.1	=	7.7	+0.4

The total sum of squares is the sum of squares under the null model.

SS_{total} denotes total sum of squares.

8.4, so its residual is $8.4 - 7.7 = 0.7$. Notice that the sum of squares of these residuals is simply the sum of squares of the entire sample of 36 scores considered as a single set. The predictor variable X, denoting the particular condition each score came from, is ignored. For this reason, the sum of squares under the null model is usually referred to as the *total sum of squares* and denoted by SS_{total}. If we sum the squared residuals for all 36 observations in Table 3.4, the result is a total sum of squares of $SS_{total} = 404.9$.

It is interesting to compare the residuals for the null model with those obtained for the full model in which μ_1 and μ_2 were not assumed to be equal. Such a comparison between residuals is the basis on which the goodness of fit of the two models can be compared.

The sum of squares for the full model was calculated as Step 4 in fitting the model:

$$SS_e = SS_1 + SS_2 = 59.6 + 120.3 = 179.9$$

The difference between SS_{total} (= 404.9) and SS_e (= 179.9) represents how much better the fit of the full model is than that of the null model. Recall that the smaller the sum of squared residuals, the better the fit. The difference between these two values quantifies this superiority and provides a formal measure of the concept of "accounting for the variability" introduced informally in Chapter 1.

The difference between SS_{total} and SS_e quantifies the variability accounted for by the full model, and this difference can be written as SS_{model}. We therefore have the simple relationship:

$$SS_{model} = SS_{total} - SS_e$$

For our example, $SS_{model} = 404.9 - 179.9 = 225.0$.

The size of SS_{model} is a direct reflection of the differences among the means of the conditions, and its value can be calculated directly from the values of the condition means. Rather than derive the formula, we will simply state it for an experiment with just two conditions and n participants in each:

$$SS_{model} = \tfrac{1}{2}n(\overline{Y}_1 - \overline{Y}_2)^2$$

For the phobia treatment experiment, this formula gives

$$SS_{model} = \tfrac{1}{2}n(\overline{Y}_1 - \overline{Y}_2)^2 = \tfrac{1}{2} \times 18 \times 5.0^2 = 225.0$$

This is the value obtained previously as the difference between SS_{total} and SS_e.

This relationship between SS_{model} and the difference between $\overline{Y}_1$ and $\overline{Y}_2$ should not be surprising. The greater the difference between $\overline{Y}_1$ and $\overline{Y}_2$, the strong the evidence that the null model is inadequate and that a full model is required to account for the variability. More generally, SS_{model} is a measure of the variability (differences) among the means of the conditions.

Comparing the Residuals for Full and Null Models

It is common to express the value of SS_{model} as a proportion of SS_{total} and to describe it as the proportion of the total variance that the full model accounts for. For our example, this proportion is $225.0/404.9 = .56$ or 56%; so we can say that, for these data, the full model accounts for 56% of the total variability.

This index of improved fit is a valuable piece of information and is symbolized R^2. In symbols, we can write

$$R^2 = \frac{SS_{model}}{SS_{total}}$$

R^2 denotes the proportional reduction in the sum of the squared residuals achieved by the full model.

The value of $R^2 = .56$ confirms what is suggested by even a casual inspection of the data for our example. The residuals associated with the full model are, on the whole, much smaller than those for the null model. That is, the full model provides a better fit to the data than does the null model.

This comparison suggests that we should choose the full model in preference to the null model. Chapter 1 claimed that one of the overall goals of statistical data analysis was to find the model that provided the best fit. However, Chapter 1 also claimed that we should apply the principle of parsimony and choose the simplest possible model. Because it has only one parameter (μ), the null model is more parsimonious than the full model, which has two parameters (μ_1 and μ_2). Thus parsimony suggests the null model, whereas goodness of fit suggests the full model. The resolution of this conflict requires an answer to the question (also posed in Section 1.1.4), Does the evidence establish the need for the full model "beyond a reasonable doubt"? Is the drop in the size of the sum of squared residuals from 404.9 to 179.9, a 56% reduction, substantial enough to justify the less parsimonious model?

Answering this question requires considerably more background than has been covered thus far. It is valuable, however, to pose the question in purely descriptive terms before embarking on the details of how such descriptive measures of goodness of fit form the basis for making principled decisions between models.

The various sums of squares introduced in Section 3.3.3 are fundamentally important and will reappear throughout the book. MathBox 3.2 provides a convenient review of what they mean.

3.3.4 Defining and Estimating Effect Size

In our phobia treatment experiment, the difference between the means of the two conditions was

$$\overline{Y}_1 - \overline{Y}_2 = 10.2 - 5.2 = 5.0 \text{ beats per minute}$$

This value of 5.0 beats per minute is a *point estimate* of the true or population difference $\mu - \mu_2$. The difference between the means of conditions is often referred to as *effect size*. It reflects the extent to which the conditions of the experiment are "having an effect on" or "making a difference in" the observations. How big an effect is 5.0? This is a difficult question to answer because there is no obvious standard with which to compare it. Moreover, it would be difficult to compare the difference of 5 beats per minute with the results from a comparable experiment that used a different response variable—for example, one that had volunteers rate their fear level on a seven-point scale, or one that measured change in skin temperature. A difference of 5 beats per minute cannot be compared directly with a difference of 2 on a rating scale or a change of 0.5°C in skin temperature any more than a length of 1 meter can be compared with a weight of 75 grams.

This problem is similar to the one discussed in Section 2.3.2. In that section, we wanted to find a method of comparing scores on different scales—a student's scores on different midterm tests, for example. The solution was to express the scores in units of the standard deviation; and we called them standard scores.

There are several methods of measuring effect size, but the simplest, and the one presented in this section, adopts a rationale that is essentially the same as the one behind the standard score. Expressed in terms of population parameters, the effect size (d) is defined as

$$d = \frac{\mu_1 - \mu_2}{\sigma}$$

This index is sometimes referred to as "Cohen's d" after Jacob Cohen, who has done much to promote the use of the index. In this formula, σ is the standard deviation of the scores (or, equivalently, the residuals) for each condition, which we again assume to be the same for both conditions.

We will usually not know the values of the population means μ_1 and μ_2, or of the standard deviation, σ. However, an estimate of d ($\hat{d}$) can be obtained by replacing these parameter values with their corresponding sample-based estimates. The estimate of σ is taken to be $\sqrt{MS_e}$, the square root of the common variance estimate, MS_e.

This substitution gives us

$$\hat{d} = \frac{\overline{Y}_1 - \overline{Y}_2}{\sqrt{MS_e}}$$

Effect size refers to the difference between the means of conditions.

The index measures effect size in units of the standard deviation.

d denotes index of effect size.

$\hat{d}$ denotes estimate of effect size.

MathBox 3.2

Sums of Squares

1. All sums of squares are measures of variability. Sums of squares, when divided by the appropriate degrees of freedom, are called mean squares.

2. Consider an experiment with two conditions. Suppose we assume that the null hypothesis is true—that the conditions have the same population mean. We can therefore calculate a single mean for the total set of observations and obtain the sum of the squared deviation of each score from this mean. The result is called the *total sum of squares* and is denoted SS_{total}. The total sum of squares is the sum of squares under the null model.

3. Suppose we assume that the null hypothesis is false, assuming instead that the conditions have different means. That is, we assume that a full model is necessary. Separate sums of squares can be obtained for each condition by summing the squared deviation of each score from the mean of its condition. When these two sums of squares are added together, we have the *sum of squares of the residuals* for the full model. This sum of squares is denoted by SS_e.

4. The difference between SS_{total} and SS_e is a direct measure of how much better the fit of the full model is than that of the null model. Think of SS_{total} as all the variability in the data and SS_e as the variability remaining after the full model has been fitted. The larger the reduction, the more variability the full model has accounted for. For this reason, the difference between SS_{total} and SS_e is referred to as SS_{model}. This statement can be expressed as the relation

$$SS_{model} = SS_{total} - SS_e$$

If all sums of squares are measures of variability, it is reasonable to ask what variability S_{model} measures. The answer to this question is that SS_{model} measures the variability (differences) among the means of the conditions.

5. It is informative to rearrange the terms of the above equation as

$$SS_{total} = SS_{model} + SS_e$$

In this form the equation expresses the idea that fitting the full model takes the total variability in the data and partitions it into two components. One component is the variability accounted for by the full model, the other is the unaccounted for variability remaining after the full model has been fitted.

6. A useful index of the effectiveness of the full model in accounting for variability is to express SS_{model} as a proportion of the original total sum of squares. This ratio is denoted by the symbol R^2.

$$R^2 = \frac{SS_{model}}{SS_{total}}$$

For the phobia treatment experiment, $MS_e = 5.3$ (see Section 3.3.1), so the estimated effect size would be

$$\hat{\mathbf{d}} = \frac{10.2 - 5.2}{\sqrt{5.3}} = 2.2$$

Conventional Descriptions of Effect Size

Is $\mathbf{d} = 2.2$ a big effect? Cohen (1988) suggests some conventions for describing effect sizes. According to Cohen, a $\mathbf{d}$ value of 0.8 or more is a *large* effect. So, although we have only an estimate of $\mathbf{d}$ rather than the true value, it is safe to conclude that the effect size for this experiment is very large indeed. A $\mathbf{d}$ value of 0.5 is considered a medium effect; a value of 0.2 is considered small.

We will make further use of the concept of effect size in later chapters. For the present, effect size can be thought of as a descriptive statistic that provides an index that can be compared across different experiments and even across different response variables.

3.3.5 Models of Quantitative Predictor Variables

So far, we have described models of categorical predictor variables. Models of quantitative predictor variables will be described in Chapter 9. However, a brief comparison of these two kinds of models is instructive.

A quantitative predictor variable is the length of time in the dark in a study of dark adaptation (Figure 1.1) or the angle of rotation in the mental rotation study (Figure 1.3). The goal of studies with quantitative predictor variables is to provide a rule that predicts values of the response variable (visual threshold, decision time) across a continuous range of values of the predictor variable.

Predicting from Continuous Functions

Imagine a study of drug effectiveness in treating depression. The quantitative predictor variable is drug dosage level. In this case, the prediction rule might be a con-

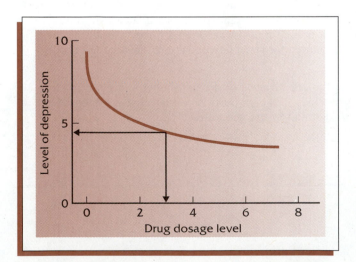

Figure 3.2

Hypothetical function for predicting level of depression for values of the quantitative variable, drug dosage, over the range 0 to 8.

tinuous function such as the curve shown in Figure 3.2. The experiment itself included five conditions: 0, 2, 4, 6, and 8 units of the drug. However, the curve enables us to predict depression level for not only these five values, but intermediate values as well. For example, the arrows in the figure show that with a dosage level of 3 units, the predicted level of depression is just under 5. The curve makes this prediction even though a dosage level of 3 was not included in the experiment.

Categorical variables, however, predict values of the response variables only for the values of the predictor variable actually included in the experiment. Thus, in the phobia treatment experiment, predictions are possible for only the two conditions actually used in the experiment. Hence the results for this experiment would be graphed as a bar chart with no line connecting the two values (Figure 3.3).

The difference between categorical and quantitative predictor variables is reflected in the different forms of the model for each. Models for both types of predictor variables have the general form

$$observation = model\ prediction + residual$$

or, if fitted from sample data,

$$observation = fit + residual$$

With categorical variables, "model prediction" consists of predictions based on just those conditions included in the experiment. For the two-condition phobia treatment experiment, the fitted full model was

$$Y_1 = 10.2 + e$$

$$Y_2 = 5.2 + e$$

If the experiment were to be expanded by a third condition, the model would change only by the addition of another specific prediction for that condition.

With models for quantitative predictor variables, however, the prediction takes the form of a mathematical function that captures the form of a curve, or the location and orientation of a straight line. A simple example of a straight-line function is the one fitted to the mental rotation data shown in Figure 1.3. That figure plotted the time volunteers took to judge "same" for two figures differing in degree of rotation. The graph of these data points reproduced in Figure 3.4 suggests that they would be well modeled by a straight line.

Models for categorical predictor variables make predictions for just those conditions included in the experiment.

With models for quantitative predictor variables, predictions take the form of a mathematical function.

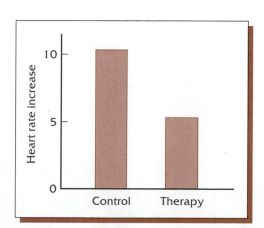

Figure 3.3
Hypothetical prediction rule for increase in heart rate, based on the categorical variable control versus therapy. Prediction is possible only for the values of the predictor variable actually included in the experiment.

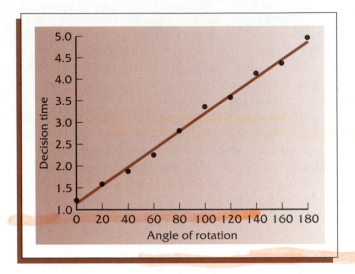

Figure 3.4
Graphical representation of the linear prediction rule for the mental rotation data.

Comprehension Check 3.3

Important Concepts

1. Models for studies with a categorical predictor variable that has two or more conditions are simple extensions of the model for replicability of a single condition.

2. A full model for such experiments has one parameter for each condition. Each such parameter corresponds to the population mean for that condition. Under the full model, the sum of squares of the residuals is SS_e and the corresponding mean square obtained by dividing this sum of squares by degrees of freedom is MS_e.

3. The calculation of a single value of MS_e to represent both conditions is based on the assumption that the population variances are the same for both conditions: the assumption of homogeneity of variance.

4. A simpler model, the null model, is one based on the null hypothesis that these parameters are all equal. Under the null model, the sum of squares of the residuals is simply the sum of squares for all the scores and is denoted by SS_{total}.

5. The difference between SS_{total} and SS_e quantifies the variability accounted for by the full model. This difference is denoted SS_{model}.

6. The variability accounted for by the full model can be expressed as a proportion of SS_{total} to give a measure of the proportion of variance accounted for by the model. This proportion is denoted by R^2.

$$R^2 = \frac{SS_{model}}{SS_{total}}$$

7. A commonly used measure of effect size is an estimate of Cohen's **d**:

$$\hat{d} = \frac{\overline{Y}_1 - \overline{Y}_2}{\sqrt{MS_e}}$$

This measure is especially useful in comparing effect sizes across different experiments.

8. Models for categorical predictor variables differ from those for quantitative predictor variables. They predict values of the response variable only for values of the predictor variable included in the experiment. Models for quantitative predictor variables, on the other hand, consist of a rule that predicts values of the response variable for any value of the predictor variable within a specified range, whether or not that value was a condition in the experiment. Models are to be found whenever data are used to formulate a predictive rule. As Box 3.1 illustrates, their use is not limited to formal science.

Problems

Problem 1   Social interactions between toddlers (Data Set 2.6)

In Problem 2 of Comprehension Check 2.2, you calculated the mean for social interaction between pairs of same-sex and different-sex toddlers. The means were 31.0 (same-sex pairs) and 22.0 (different-sex pairs). Use the values in Data Set 2.6 (page 69) to work through the first three steps of fitting the model:

$$Y_1 = \mu_1 + e$$
$$Y_2 = \mu_2 + e$$

Note: You calculated the residuals for these data in answering Problem 3 of Comprehension Check 2.2, so start with those results.

Problem 2

What is the null model for this experiment? Work through the three steps of fitting the null model for the data in Problem 1.

Problem 3

The sums of squares for the same-sex and different-sex pair conditions are 446 and 484, respectively.

a What is the value of MS_e for these data?

b. What is the estimate of the effect size, **d**, for this experiment?

Problem 4

For each of the following experiments, identify the predictor and response variables, and then identify whether or not the experiment would be appropriately modeled by using a categorical or quantitative predictor variable.

a. How well does the Scholastic Aptitude Test (SAT) predict students' grade point average (GPA) at the end of their first year in college? To answer this question, the SAT scores of 100 college-bound students are obtained at the end of their senior high school year, then their GPAs are obtained at the end of their freshman year.

Box 3.1

Models in the Wider World of Science and Beyond

Models are common in virtually every branch of science. They range from very simple models, such as those considered in this chapter, to models so complex that they cannot be stated explicitly as equations but exist only in the form of a computer program. However, no matter how simple or how complex, all models share a common rationale. The rational underlying the simple model $Y = \mu + e$ is no different from that for a complex model of the economy or the world's weather. The rationale is to construct a formal description of the regularities in data (finding a model that fits the data), evaluating the fit, and, if the fit is satisfactory, using that description to predict further outcomes.

Constructing models is not limited to science. Consider the following model.*

$$G = \left(\frac{H + BB + HP}{AB + BB + HP} \right) + \left(\frac{3(TB - H)}{4AB} \right) + \left(\frac{R}{H + BB + HP} \right) -$$
$$\left(\frac{H}{AB} + \frac{BB + HP}{AB + BB + HP} + \frac{ER}{H + BB + HB} - \right.$$
$$\left. \frac{SO}{8(AB + BB + HP)} - F \right)$$

The model seems complex enough to belong to an advanced physics text, but it comes from a different source altogether. It is taken from a 1954 photograph in *Life Magazine*. In the photograph, there is a person seen pointing at the blackboard on which the model was written. This person is not Albert Einstein, however, but Branch Rickey, the legendary baseball manager of the Brooklyn Dodgers. The use of modeling in baseball may seem unlikely to some people, but not to aficionados of the game.

Branch Rickey's model becomes less awesome once the various terms are explained. The model predicts the response variable of winning efficiency (G) on the basis of a number of predictor variables: number of hits (H), bases on balls (BB), bases on being hit by the pitcher (HP), at bats (AB), total bases (TB), earned runs (ER), strikeouts (SO), and fielding (F). Thus the first line of the model is an overall index of offense, and the bottom line is a measure of concessions through defense. The model expresses winning percentage as the difference between offense and defense. Baseball experts will recognize the meaning of each component in this model. The first element in the top line, for example, is on-base average, the second is extra-base power, and so forth.

The model proved quite accurate, although, as with all models, its predictions were not perfect. To be consistent with our own notation, we should either place a hat ($^\wedge$) above the G in Branch Rickey's model, or add a residual component (e).

* This description is based on the account given in Gigerenzer et al. (1989), a book enthusiastically recommended to anyone interested in the history and social impact of probability and statistical methods.

b. An experiment is designed to evaluate two programs designed to treat hyperactive children. One program consists of weekly sessions of behavior therapy over a 10-week period; the other uses a drug treatment over the same time period. Four conditions are used: The first is a control group that receives no treatment; the second is a group that receives only the weekly behavior therapy; the third is a group that receives only the drug treatment; the fourth is a group that receives both the weekly behavior therapy and the drug treatment. The level of hyperactivity of each child is measured at the end of the 10-week period.

c. How rapidly does the size of a child's vocabulary increase with age? To answer this question, vocabulary size was estimated (using a verbal comprehension test) for children of six different ages: 2, 3, 4, 6, 8, and 10 years.

Chapter 3 Exercises

Many of the exercises for this chapter will make use of values of statistics obtained in the exercises at the end of Chapter 2. Deciding *which* values are relevant is part of the current set of exercises and therefore will not be noted explicitly. However, most of the calculations have been done, and relevant results can be obtained from the answers to the problems for Chapter 2.

Exercise 1   Opinion change

The results for this experiment consist of simple whole numbers and thus lend themselves to a full analysis without the aid of anything more than a hand calculator. Details of the experiment were described in Exercise 2, Chapter 2 (Data Set 2.12).

Take as the full model for this experiment

$$Y_1 = \mu_1 + e$$

$$Y_2 = \mu_2 + e$$

a. Complete Table 3.5 by obtaining estimates of μ_1 and μ_2, and calculating the residuals for each of the scores in both conditions. Check that they sum to 0 for each condition.

b. Calculate the sum of squares of these residuals.

c. Compare your answers with the values obtained in Chapter 2, Exercise 2, using this same data set. The sums of squares were $SS_1 = 82.0$ and $SS_2 = 58.0$.

d. Calculate the common sum of squares (SS_e) and then the mean square (MS_e) of these residuals across the two conditions.

e. Write a model for this experiment under the null hypothesis that $\mu_1 = \mu_2$.

f. Recalculate residuals under this simpler null hypothesis model.

g. Calculate the sum of squares of the residuals under this null hypothesis model.

h. Calculate an estimate of Cohen's **d** statistic for the difference between the two conditions of this experiment.

$$\hat{d} = \frac{\overline{Y}_1 - \overline{Y}_2}{\sqrt{MS_e}}$$

Table 3.5 Responses in opinion change study					
Condition 1: $1 payment			**Condition 2: $100 payment**		
Y_1	$\overline{Y}_1$	e	Y_2	$\overline{Y}_2$	e
7	_____	_____	5	_____	_____
7	_____	_____	5	_____	_____
2	_____	_____	9	_____	_____
4	_____	_____	4	_____	_____
4	_____	_____	6	_____	_____
3	_____	_____	5	_____	_____
6	_____	_____	6	_____	_____
6	_____	_____	8	_____	_____
6	_____	_____	6	_____	_____
6	_____	_____	8	_____	_____
5	_____	_____	6	_____	_____
5	_____	_____	7	_____	_____
7	_____	_____	4	_____	_____
6	_____	_____	9	_____	_____
5	_____	_____	4	_____	_____
4	_____	_____	7	_____	_____
6	_____	_____	5	_____	_____
5	_____	_____	3	_____	_____
9	_____	_____	7	_____	_____
3	_____	_____	7	_____	_____
3	_____	_____	5	_____	_____
7	_____	_____	5	_____	_____
3	_____	_____	7	_____	_____
1	_____	_____	6	_____	_____

Exercise 2 Undermining intrinsic motivation in children

Exercise 3 in Chapter 2 (Data Set 2.13) gave the mean and the variance (Table 3.6) for the two conditions for the reduced data ($n = 18$) of this experiment. The response measure was the amount of time, in minutes, that each child spent drawing.

a. Using these results, what is the sum of squares of the residuals for each of the two conditions?

b. What is the mean square of the residuals, MS_e, for the two? Why might you be suspicious of the appropriateness of forming this single estimate?

Table 3.6 Statistics for motivation experiment (Exercise 3.2)

Condition	Mean	Variance
Reward	5.18	6.98
No reward	10.27	2.43

c. Using estimates of Cohen's **d** statistic as defined in Exercise 1, decide which experiment, the opinion change experiment of Exercise 1 or this experiment, has the larger effect.

Exercise 3 Effect of threat level on desirability

In this experiment, 7-year-old children play with a set of toys and are then asked to rank them by choosing their favorite toy, their next favorite, and so on. The experimenter then designates the child's second preference as a *forbidden* toy, telling the child that he or she is not to play with this particular toy when left alone with the toys. There are two conditions. Half the children receive a threat of mild disapproval should they play with the forbidden toy; the other half receive a threat of very severe disapproval. Each child then has a period in which he or she is left alone with the toys. During this period, none of the children actually plays with the forbidden toy, but this conformity is not itself the observation of major interest; in fact, we are interested in whether this conformity has produced any change in the perceived desirability of the forbidden toy. After this "temptation period," the children are asked to rate, on a ten-point scale, the desirability of each of the toys, including the forbidden toy. The forbidden toy, you will remember, was their original second preference.

Will the desirability of the forbidden toy differ for the two groups? According to attribution theory, children in the mild threat condition should be more likely to attribute their conformity to internal rather than external forces. That is, they attribute their conformity to properties of the forbidden toy: "It wasn't such a great toy after all." On the other hand, children in the severe threat condition should be more likely to attribute their conformity to external forces. That is, they attribute their conformity to the threat of punishment, leaving the perceived desirability of the forbidden toy unchanged. This experiment is modeled after experiments reported by Lepper (1973).

There were 40 participants in this experiment. They were assigned randomly to the two conditions, 20 participants in each (Data Set 3.2).

Data Set 3.2 Ratings for Exercise 3

After mild threat

4	6	7	7	5	4	8	5	9	9
8	5	4	7	6	6	5	8	7	6

After severe threat

8	10	9	4	6	9	5	6	9	10
8	7	9	10	6	10	7	6	8	9

a. This question reviews concepts from Chapter 1.

■ What is the predictor variable in this experiment?

■ Is the predictor variable quantitative or categorical?

■ Is the predictor variable natural or manipulated?

■ What values of the predictor variable are included in the study?

■ What is the response variable in this experiment?

■ Is the response variable quantitative or categorical?

b. This question reviews concepts from Chapter 2. For each condition, plot a frequency distribution and check data for

■ *Skewness.* Skewness might reflect the fact that participants were tending to use one extreme of the scale.

■ *Bimodality.* Bimodality might occur if participants tended to choose one extreme or the other. Some thought the toy extremely desirable, others hated it, but few were indifferent.

■ *Outliers.* Perhaps there is a child who misunderstood the rating scale, or perhaps there is just an unusual individual in the sample.

c. Write out a full model for the results of this experiment and obtain estimates of the parameters. (These data have simple numbers, so calculation by hand is not burdensome.)

d. Write out a null hypothesis model for the results of this experiment and obtain an estimate of its parameter.

e. For each of the two models (full and null), calculate the residual associated with (1) a score of 5 in the mild threat condition and (2) a score of 9 in the severe threat condition.

f. The sum of squares (SS) for the mild threat condition is $SS_1 = 48.2$; for the severe threat condition, $SS_2 = 63.2$. What is the value of MS_e?

g. Calculate an estimate of Cohen's **d** statistic for the difference between the two conditions of this experiment. Based on this statistic, how would you describe the "influence of threat level"? Do these results appear to support the prediction based on attribution theory?

Chapter 3 Review

Terms

Cohen's **d**
full model
goodness of fit
homogeneity of variance
least squares criterion and estimate
mean square
MS_e
null hypothesis
null model
parameter (of a model)
point estimate
population
R^2
sample
SS_e
SS_{model}
SS_{total}

Formulas

For two independent conditions:

$$SS_e = SS_1 + SS_2$$

$$MS_e = \frac{SS_e}{df}$$

$$df = 2(n - 1) \quad \text{for groups of equal size}$$

$$df = (n_1 - 1) + (n_2 - 1) = N - 2 \quad \text{for groups of unequal size}$$

For k independent conditions:

$$SS_e = SS_1 + SS_2 + \ldots + SS_k$$

$$MS_e = \frac{SS_e}{df}$$

$$df = k(n - 1) \quad \text{for groups of equal size}$$

$$df = N - k \quad \text{for groups of unequal size}$$

$$SS_{model} = SS_{total} - SS_e$$

Proportion of variance accounted for by the model: $R^2 = \dfrac{SS_{model}}{SS_{total}}$

Estimated Cohen's **d**: $\hat{d} = \dfrac{\overline{Y}_1 - \overline{Y}_2}{\sqrt{MS_e}}$

Quiz

Complete each sentence with a term from the following list. The same term may be used more than once.

parameters	degrees of freedom	full model	SS_e
goodness of fit	homogeneity of variance	sample	SS_{model}
least squares	mean square	null model	SS_{total}
MS_e	point estimates	population	R^2

Science uses data to construct general laws. In statistical terms, this statement means that observations from a _____ are used to derive a model stating what might be true in the _____. The data are used to estimate the _____ of the model. These estimates are chosen to satisfy the _____ criterion. They each consist of a single number and are therefore called _____.

In evaluating a model, the sum of squares of the residuals (symbolized by _____) reflects the _____ of the model. By dividing this sum of squares by the appropriate _____, we obtain the _____ (symbolized by _____). When there are two or more conditions, this value assumes that the population variance of the residuals is the same for each condition. This assumption is called _____.

A model that does not include the predictor variable (claiming that it has no effect) is called the _____. The sum of squares of the residuals for this model is symbolized by _____. The model that *does* include the predictor variable is called the _____. The sum of squares of the residuals for this model is symbolized by _____. The difference between these two sums of squares is symbolized by _____ and is an index of the effectiveness of the model. When this difference is divided by _____, we obtain _____, the proportion of variance accounted for by the model.

Chapter 4 Preview

Chapter 3 leaves us with a criterion (least squares) for obtaining point estimates of the parameters of a model, a method of fitting a model, and a way of measuring the goodness of fit of the model in terms of the sum of squares of the residuals.

The next step is to move beyond this purely descriptive stage into one that enables us to make inferences. Having obtained the best point estimate and the best fit of the model, we need to know just how good "best" is. For example, the sample mean may be the best estimate of μ, but just how close is $\overline{Y}$ to the true value, μ? What can we say about the size of the difference $\overline{Y} - \mu$? Also needed is a method for deciding between competing models of the same data and resolving the conflict between parsimony and improved goodness of fit.

Answers to these questions are based on a conceptual leap of immense importance, first made in 1809 by the great German mathematician, Carl Friedrich Gauss. In modern terminology, Gauss's great insight was that residuals could be treated as *random variables*. That is, he applied probability theory to the interpretation of residuals. Therefore, it is to the topic of probability and random variables that we must turn.

4 PROBABILITY DISTRIBUTIONS

Chapter 3 ended with a description of a method for fitting a model to data and measuring goodness of fit as the sum of squared residuals. The method gave a best-fitting model in the sense that the model used estimates of the parameters that produced the minimum sum of squared residuals. Although this least squares fit is an important achievement, it leaves one basic question unanswered: How close is $\overline{Y}$ to μ? What can we say about the value of $\overline{Y} - \mu$? All we know at this stage is that $\overline{Y}$ is the best *point* estimate of μ; but an investigator will want to know something about the accuracy of this estimate. A least squares estimate may simply be the best of a bad bunch. The first step in addressing the question, and the topic of this chapter, is to understand the apparently chaotic behavior of residuals. Chapter 5 then uses these results to obtain a more informative estimate of $\overline{Y}$.

4.1 Law of Large Numbers and the Meaning of Probability

It should now be clear that the discrepancy between $\overline{Y}$ and μ is a direct consequence of noise. We also know that in a world of imperfect experimental control, noisy data are inevitable: Estimates differ from their true values, models fit imperfectly, residuals abound, and strict replication is an unattainable goal. The inevitability of noise means that uncertainty cannot be *eliminated* from statistical data analysis any more than it can be eliminated from the outcome of a baseball game or tomorrow's stock prices. Uncertainty cannot be eliminated, but its behavior can be understood. Although it may seem a contradiction in terms, the chaotic fluctuations we have called noise actually behave in very lawlike ways, and this lawful behavior enables uncertainty to be quantified. As is so often the case in science, quantification is the key to understanding and control. The task of quantifying uncertainty and understanding its lawful behavior is the field of *probability theory*.

The task of probability theory is to quantify uncertainty and understand its lawful behavior.

4.1.1 Models of Residuals

Probability theory can be applied to the behavior of residuals and can be used to quantify the uncertainty residuals bring with them. The degree of uncertainty reflected in the size of the residuals is the major determinant of the degree of uncertainty that surrounds the unknown difference between $\overline{Y}$ and μ.

Measuring Reaction Time

An investigator asks the question, "How long does it take for a driver's foot to reach the brake pedal following the sudden appearance of an object 50 meters in front of the vehicle?" The investigator makes ten measurements with the following results. The response measure is time in milliseconds.

661	605	642	704	662	770	741	626	713	636

The sample mean of these ten observations is $\overline{Y} = 676$ milliseconds. This value provides the best (in the least squares sense) single-value estimate, or point estimate, of the "true" time, μ, that it takes for a driver's foot to reach the brake pedal. The parameter μ can also be thought of as the population value, the mean of an infinitely large number of observations from which these particular ten observations were drawn.

The fitted model for these data would be

$$Y = \overline{Y} + e$$

where e is the residual associated with each observation, that is, the discrepancy between the fitted value ($\overline{Y}$) and the observation, Y.

The fitted model to our ten reaction times is $Y = 676 + e$. The residual for each of the ten measures is given in Table 4.1.

Mechanical Models of Residuals

Each of the residuals in the data for a driver's reaction time to apply the brakes can be thought of as the result of the many small influences that are beyond the control of the investigator, for example, momentary fluctuations in attention or the precise location of the right foot. To gain a sense of what it means to consider residuals as the result of the many small influences, consider the following metaphor. Imagine a well-shaken urn containing a very large number of balls, some red, some blue. Think of each ball as representing the effect on reaction time of some uncontrolled influence: The red balls represent influences that *increase* reaction time, whereas the blue balls represent the various influences that *decrease* reaction time. The residual is determined by selecting a number of balls—100, say—from the urn and counting the number of red and blue balls and returning them to the urn ready for the next measurement. Suppose that each red ball adds 1 millisecond to the reaction time, each blue ball subtracts 1 millisecond. The net result of summing these positive and negative influences constitutes the residual, e, which is then added to (or subtracted from) the true value, μ, to yield the observed measure, Y.

Another mechanical model of the processes underlying residuals is a device that is often found in science museums. It was invented by Francis Galton in the early 1870s to illustrate the cumulative effects on observations of what Galton termed "distur-

Table 4.1 Observations and residuals for the fitted model $Y = \overline{Y} + e$

Y	$e(= Y - \overline{Y})$
661	−15
605	−71
642	−34
704	28
662	−14
770	94
741	65
626	−50
713	37
636	−40
$\overline{Y} = 676$	SS = 25932

bances." Galton called the device the *quincunx,* a rather odd name chosen because of the pin arrangement. The word *quincunx* means "five points arranged with one point at each of the four corners of a rectangle and the fifth point at the center." A simple five-row version of the quincunx is illustrated in Figure 4.1.

Francis Galton invented a mechanical model of residuals: the quincunx.

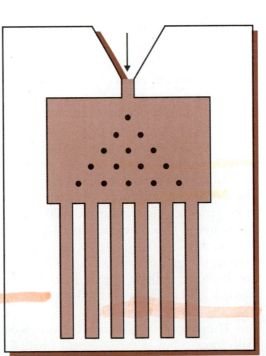

Figure 4.1
Diagrammatic sketch of a small quincunx. Balls are fed through the top funnel, strike a pin in each row (the black dots), and end up in one of the bottom bins.

The quincunx consists of a glass-faced panel with a funnel at the top through which lead shot or small ball bearings can fall. Immediately below the funnel are horizontal rows of pins. As each ball drops through the funnel, it strikes a pin in the top row and falls either left or right into the second row, where it strikes a second pin and again falls left or right to the row below. The ball continues bouncing its way to the bottom row, where it is collected in a bin that marks the point along the bottom row at which the ball's journey ends.

Categories are mutually exclusive if belonging to one category precludes belonging to any other.

Note that a ball cannot end up in more than one bin. The bins at the bottom of the quincunx are therefore said to be a set of *mutually exclusive* categories. The general meaning of the term *mutually exclusive* is "cannot occur together." In other words, categories are mutually exclusive if belonging to one category precludes belonging to any other. Two events are mutually exclusive if they cannot occur together. In a single toss of a coin, landing heads and landing tails are mutually exclusive events.

The idea behind the quincunx was that the ball striking the pin mimicked the effect of a small influence. If the ball fell to the right, the influence could be thought of as positive (analogous to a red ball in the urn example). If the ball fell to the left, it could be thought of as negative (analogous to a blue ball in the urn example). The complete fall of each ball from the top row to the bottom row modeled the cumulative effect of a set of these small influences. A well-designed quincunx is one in which the ball, when it strikes a pin, falls equally often to the left or to the right. The pin acts like a traffic director who tosses a coin and points either right for heads or left for tails.

Balls falling through the quincunx show an emergent regularity as the number of balls increases.

The passage of each ball is quite chaotic as it descends row by row, deflecting haphazardly left or right until it reaches its final resting place somewhere in the bottom row of bins. However, the quincunx demonstrates a dramatic result. If a large number of balls are allowed to fall, the accumulation of balls in the bottom bins takes on a regular form. Figure 4.2 shows typical results from a quincunx with ten rows of pins through which 100 balls have fallen. The height of the resulting stack of balls in each column represents the frequency with which balls ended up in that bin.

The quincunx is a mechanical model that approximates the process assumed to be underlying the noisiness of data, and the emergent regularity of the distribution of the balls in the bottom bins is a key to the orderly behavior of the residuals. As such, it is a mechanical model of a process that is fundamental to statistical data analysis. It is therefore appropriate that we examine the theory behind the emergent regularity that the quincunx displays. How can order emerge from such chaotic elements? The answer to this question brings us directly to the heart of probability theory.

Two principles underlie the regularity of the quincunx: the law of large numbers and the central limit theorem.

There are two fundamental principles that underlie the emergent regularity displayed by the quincunx. They are as fundamental to probability theory as Newton's laws of motion are to physics. One is known as the *law of large numbers;* the other is the *central limit theorem*. We will examine each, using the quincunx as a demonstration device just as Galton did 120 years ago. We will vary our experiments with the quincunx in two different ways. One way is to vary the number of balls fed through the funnel. The second way is to vary the number of rows of pins in the quincunx. Of course, the number of rows of pins will also determine the number of bins needed at the bottom. If there are 19 rows of pins, then 20 bins are needed to record every possible end position for the balls. In general, the number of bins needed is one more than the number of rows.

The law of large numbers is an account of what happens to the proportion of balls in each bin as the number of balls fed through the funnel increases from a small

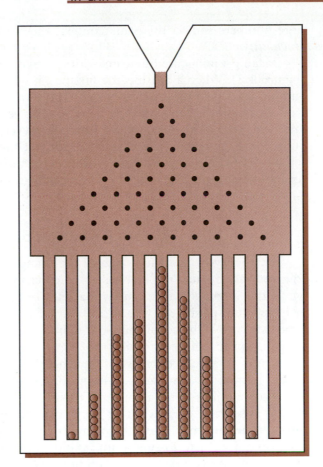

Figure 4.2
Quincunx with ten rows of pins through which 100 balls have fallen. The height of each stack at the bottom represents the number of balls that ended up in that bin.

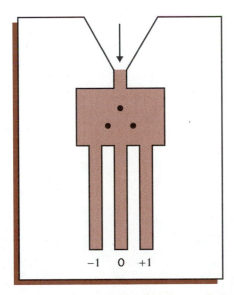

Figure 4.3
Miniature quincunx with just two rows of pins.

to an infinitely large number. The central limit theorem (see Section 4.3) is an account of what happens when both the number of balls *and* the number of rows of pins are increased to an infinitely large number. We consider first the law of large numbers and, in this same context, the sense in which we are using the term *probability*.

Imagine a miniature quincunx with just two rows of pins and three receiving bins (Figure 4.3). When a ball hits the first pin, it deflects left or right. It then hits a second pin and again deflects left or right and into the appropriate receiving bin. There are four possible routes that the ball can take: left both times, left then right, right then left, and right both times. Notice however, that both the left-then-right sequence and the right-then-left sequence deliver the ball to the same center bin. What can we predict about the behavior of balls fed through the funnel of this very simple version of the quincunx? The answer forms the subject matter of Section 4.1.2.

4.1.2 A Definition of Probability

The theory behind the design of the quincunx is that each of the four routes is equally likely because the ball has an equal chance of deflecting left or right at each pin. If this is true, then we can say that each of the four routes has one chance in four of happening, equivalent to a probability of $p = .25$. Two of these routes yield the same outcome—the center bin—so there are two out of four chances of ending in this bin, a probability of $p = .50$.

A moment's reflection reveals that the quincunx is equivalent to tossing a coin a certain number of times and counting the number of heads or tails. The number of tosses corresponds to the number of rows of pins and the bins record the number of heads (Figure 4.4). Each set of these coin tosses corresponds to one ball falling through the quincunx. Thus the path of one ball falling through our miniature quincunx is equivalent to tossing a single coin twice. In two tosses of the coin, there are four possible outcomes: head both times, head then tail, tail then head, and tail both times. The fact that in the quincunx the left-then-right sequence and the right-then-left sequence delivered the ball to the same bin corresponds to the fact that the head-then-tail and the tail-then-head sequences both yield the same outcome: one head. Thus, in two tosses of a coin, the probability of two heads is .25; of one head, .5; and of no heads, .25.

Probabilities are denoted by the symbol *p*.

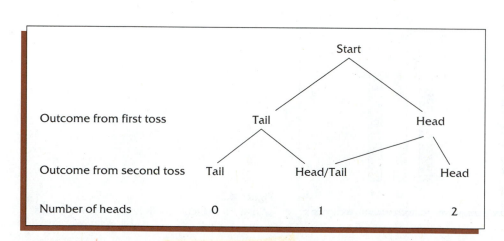

Figure 4.4
The four possibilities from two tosses of a coin. This figure is logically equivalent to Figure 4.3.

The reasoning behind these probabilities is simple enough. In each case, it is possible to specify a set of equally likely alternative outcomes. These equally likely alternative outcomes are often referred to as *elementary events.* In the case of the miniature quincunx and the two coin tosses, there are four such alternatives.

> *Probability is then defined as the number of (equally probable) ways that the event can occur divided by the total number of equally probable events.*

For landing in the leftmost bin of the miniature quincunx, there is just one way this outcome (elementary event) can occur out of the four possible ways, so the probability is a ratio of 1 to 4, or .25. There are two ways to land in the center bin, so the probability of landing in the center bin is a ratio of 2 to 4, or .5.

Notice that the elementary event is the route that the ball follows, not the bin in which the ball finally lands. Because different routes can lead to the same bin, final outcomes are not equiprobable. Similarly, the elementary events in tossing a coin are the particular sequences of heads and tails, not the number of heads. The same number of heads can result from different sequences of heads and tails. The elementary events HT and TH both lead to the same final outcome of one head.

The fact that some equiprobable elementary events lead to the same final outcome is the key to understanding why the probabilities (and the balls) tend to pile up in the center. In general, there are more pathways through a quincunx that lead to the center bins than to the end bins. In the two-row version, there are two paths that lead to the center but only one path to each of the end bins. In a four-row quincunx, there is, again, just one path to the extreme left (or extreme right). To land in the leftmost bin, for example, the ball must deflect left *every* time. By contrast, there are six different paths to the centermost bin. A ball is therefore six times more likely to end up in the center bin than in the extreme left bin.

4.1.3 Relation Between Probabilities and Sample Proportions

In Section 4.1.2, the definition of probability was purely rational or theoretical in the sense that the probabilities were obtained without any reference to how the balls in the quincunx or coins actually behave. If the conception of probability contained in this definition has any merit, then it ought to predict the distribution of outcomes that actually occurs when coins are tossed or balls rolled through the funnel of the quincunx. The claim that there is a probability of .25 that a ball will land in the leftmost bin of the quincunx ought to be related to the proportion, or relative frequency, of balls that actually land in that bin. Moreover, if we can establish a valid theory of the quincunx, we also have a theory for the behavior of residuals. The crucial link between these theoretically derived probabilities and observed proportions is the law of large numbers.

Origins of the Law of Large Numbers

The idea that theoretical probabilities could be related to observed relative frequencies is much older than Galton's quincunx. It originated in the work of Jacob Bernoulli at the end of the seventeenth century. Jacob is the best-known member of quite an extended family of Bernoullis, as many as 12 of whom contributed to various branches of mathematics and physics (Stigler, 1986, p. 63). Jacob Bernoulli died in

1705, leaving behind unpublished manuscripts that were assembled by his nephew Nicholas Bernoulli and subsequently published in 1713 under the title of *Ars Conjectandi (The Art of Conjecture)*. In this groundbreaking work, Bernoulli presented theorems that formed the basis of what, a century later, was to be known as the law of large numbers. In its simplest and most basic form, Bernoulli's theorem states that

> *As the number of observations increases [more balls in the quincunx, more coins tossed, for example], the observed proportion provides an increasingly stable estimate of the corresponding probability.*

n denotes sample size.

Suppose 40 balls are rolled through the miniature two-row quincunx and 12 of them end up in the leftmost bin. Following the discussion in Chapter 3, we can refer to the total number of observations (balls) as the sample size, *n*. The observed proportion of balls in the leftmost bin is then 12/40, or .30. As we have seen, the theoretical probability of landing in the leftmost bin is .25. But, in our thought experiment, there is a difference between observation and the theoretical value. The difference is .30 − .25 = .05. Bernoulli's theorem states that, *as the sample size increases, such differences tend to become smaller and smaller.*

The key concept underlying the law of large numbers is that of stability: Large samples make it unlikely that any particular sample proportion will stray far from the theoretical probability of which it is an estimate. Insurance companies and gambling casinos rely heavily on the law of large numbers to ensure stable profits. Slot machines and roulette wheels, for example, are set such that the probability of the house winning is greater than .5, the probability of the player winning less than .5. (Casinos are profit-making institutions, not charities!) Consider the following question: Who is more likely to end up making a profit, someone who plays for 15 minutes or someone who plays for 3 hours?

The law of large numbers implies that the 15-minute player is more likely to come out ahead than the 3-hour player. The outcome for the 3-hour player is based on a much larger sample than the outcome for the 15-minute player. The 3-hour player's success rate is therefore more likely to be close to the theoretical probability of winning (which is less than .5) than is the success rate of the 15-minute player. The lesson from the law of large numbers for gambling in such situations is that the longer you play, the more likely it is that you will end up with a net loss.

MathBox 4.1 gives a more detailed and formal statement of the law of large numbers. However, the law's core concept can be stated briefly:

> *The effect of increasing sample size is to increase the probability that a sample-based estimate will be close to the parameter it is estimating.*

Probability is interpreted as long-run relative frequency.

The law of large numbers is based on an interpretation of probability as a *long-run relative frequency,* or a population proportion. For a single flip of a coin, stating that the probability of its landing heads is .5 can be understood only in relation to a large number of tosses. The value of .5 means that, in the long run (as *n* becomes infinite), the relative frequency of heads becomes 50%. Another way of expressing this same meaning would be to say that the population proportion is .5. When *n* becomes infinite, the sample proportion corresponds to the population proportion.

MathBox 4.1

Law of Large Numbers

The law of large numbers states that as the sample size increases, differences between the observed proportion and the theoretical probability tend to become smaller and smaller. Such differences can be thought of as residuals in that they are the difference between an observation and a theoretical prediction.

Suppose we specify a particular residual size; any small value will do, but we will take .03 as our example. Then the simplest form of Bernoulli's theorem (and of the law of large numbers) states that as the number of observations increases, it becomes increasingly likely that the observed residual will be less than .03. We could have chosen .02, .007, or any other number, instead of .03 and still made the corresponding claim. For example, as the number of observations increases, it becomes increasingly likely that the observed residual will be less than .02, or be less than .007 — less, in fact, than any number you care to designate. Equivalently, we can say that the larger the number of observations, the less likely it is that residuals will exceed a specified value such as .02, .03, or .007. It is in this sense that, with an increasing sample size, the observed proportion becomes an increasingly stable estimate of the theoretical probability.

We can express all this symbolically. As in Chapter 3, we denote the value of the observed residual by e. Let k denote any designated value of a residual (.03, for example). As usual, n denotes the number of observations, the sample size. Then Bernoulli's theorem states that the probability that e is less than k approaches certainty (a probability of 1) as n becomes infinitely large. Symbolically, then, we have

$$P(e < k) \rightarrow 1 \text{ as } n \rightarrow \infty$$

where the symbol P is read as "the probability that." We can make the value of k as small as we please, smaller than .03 or .007. Even if we designate it to be as minuscule as, say .00001, the theorem still holds. *Eventually,* with a large enough value of n (and n may need to be very large indeed), it becomes virtually certain that the observed proportion will differ from the theoretical probability (.5 in the case of a fair coin) by no more than .00001.

There have been a number of attempts to demonstrate the validity of the law of large numbers by actually tossing coins large numbers of times. Moore and McCabe (1993, p. 281) tell us that around 1900, Karl Pearson, an English statistician whose name we will encounter again in Chapter 9, tossed a coin 24,000 times. The result? 12,012 heads, a proportion of .5005. Modern computers make such heroic achievements in persistence unnecessary. The accompanying boxplots illustrate a modern-day version of Pearson's effort.

Each boxplot is based on the distribution of 100 estimates of a true probability value of .5 — for example, the probability of obtaining a head in the toss of a fair coin. The estimates for each of the five plots are based on using a different number of coin tosses ranging from $n = 10$ to $n = 10,000$. Thus the first boxplot is the result of tossing the coin ten times and recording the proportion of heads. This operation is repeated 100

(continued on next page)

MathBox 4.1 (*continued*)

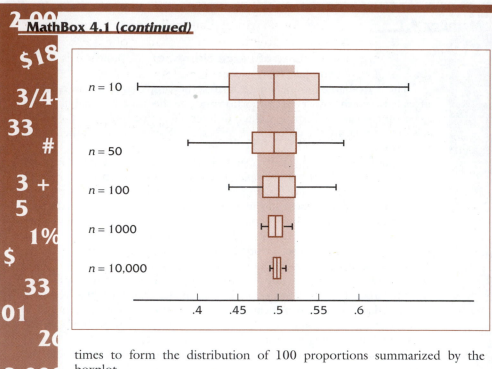

times to form the distribution of 100 proportions summarized by the boxplot.

For this example, the value of k in the statement of the law has been taken as .02. The shaded band down the center represents the values of $.5 \pm k$, that is, .48 to .52. Thus sections of the boxplot inside this band represent estimates that differ from the true value by less than .02 (that is, $e < k$). These estimates have residuals with values that are less than .02.

Notice that, as n increases, there is a dramatic decrease in the number of estimates falling outside the $\pm .02$ band. Remember that the center rectangle (box) of a boxplot contains 50% of the observations. Thus, when estimates are based on a few observation ($n = 10$), most estimates fall outside the band; when $n = 100$, on the other hand, the box is entirely within the band, a result indicating that more than half the estimates had residuals less than .02. When $n = 10,000$, the entire plot is within the band, a result indicating that none of the 100 estimates had residuals larger than .02.

Taking a different value of k would not have altered matters. A smaller value (a narrower band) merely means that a larger n would be needed to ensure that estimates will fall within the band.

In summary, as n becomes large, it approaches certainty that e will be less than k. That is, $P(e < k) \rightarrow 1$ as $n \rightarrow \infty$.

The distinction between populations and samples was introduced in Chapter 1 and discussed further in Section 3.2.2. The relation between a sample proportion and its corresponding probability is another example of a relation between a sample statistic and a parameter, similar in nature to the relation between $\overline{Y}$ and μ. It will be helpful to review the distinction between population and sample in this new context of sample proportions and probabilities.

In Section 3.2.2, we pointed out that the concept of a population could not be limited to population in the demographic sense of a population of individuals. The interpretation of probability as a "population proportion" reinforces the need for the broader and more abstract concept of population. For the quincunx, the population would refer to an infinite number of imaginary balls rolled through the device. For coin tossing, the population is the hypothetical infinite number of tosses.

These examples should not be taken to mean that *every* population is hypothetical. In other cases, the concept takes on a meaning close to the demographic one. Consider the probability that a person has blood type B, or that a high school senior has an SAT score above 600, or that a child will be born with Down syndrome. In these cases, the probability can be identified with actual outcomes or attributes of existing individuals, and it becomes more natural to think of probability as equivalent to a population proportion. The claim that the probability of a person has blood type B is .21 is readily seen as equivalent to claiming that 21% of the population has that blood type. Similarly, the claim that the probability that a high school senior has an SAT score above 600 is .16 is readily seen as equivalent to claiming that 16% of the population has an SAT score above 600.

When populations of measures can be identified with attributes of existing individuals or events (such as a population consisting of SAT scores of high school seniors), the size of the population is clearly not literally infinite. This matter is not a cause for concern. In such cases, the population, although finite in size, is sufficiently large that, for all practical purposes, it can be treated as infinite. Throughout this book, it will always be assumed that populations are, for all practical purposes, infinite in size.

4.1.4 Concept of Random Selection and Random Samples

The rational definition of probability described in Section 4.1.2 was built on the idea of equally likely elementary events. A process of selection that ensures that each element or elementary event has an equal chance of being selected is called *random:* A single selection from a set of elements is random if all elements have an equal probability of being selected. For example, each of the possible routes of a ball through a perfectly engineered quincunx has an equal chance of happening, so the particular route that a ball follows can be thought of as a random selection of one route from all possible routes.

Actions such as balls deflecting through the pins of a quincunx, tossing coins, rolling dice, shuffling decks of cards, and spinning a roulette wheel or a wheel of fortune are simple mechanical techniques aimed at ensuring that the selection is random. They are designed to ensure that each elementary outcome has an equal chance of happening or being selected.

Randomizing devices such as those seen on television to select winning lottery numbers may seem like an impressive display of the Rube Goldberg school of modern technology, but randomizing devices of one sort or another have a very long history. The forerunner of the modern die, for example, was the heel bone of a small animal such as a sheep called the astragalus. Astragali are known to have been used in board games at the time of the First Dynasty in Egypt (c. 3500 B.C.) (David, 1962, p. 4). Modern technology has also introduced electronic versions of these mechanical devices, and many computer programs include a random number generator that can be used to simulate the behavior of dice, roulette wheels, and shuffled decks of cards.

The concept of random selection makes it possible to be more precise about what it means to interpret probability as a population proportion. Consider the claim that the probability of a high school senior having an SAT score above 600 is .16. This probability is equivalent to claiming that 16% of the population has an SAT score

Selection is random if all elements have an equal probability of being selected.

above 600. A more precise way of stating the probability would be to say, "the probability of *a randomly selected* high school senior having an SAT score above 600 is .16." Similarly, the claim that the probability of a person belonging to blood group B is .21 is more precisely stated as, "the probability of a person selected at random from the population belonging to blood group B is .21."

Random Sample

The idea of randomly selecting a single element can be extended to selecting a set of *n* elements. Such a set is called a sample of size *n*. Just as in a single random selection each *element* has an equal chance of being selected, in random sampling each potential *sample* has an equal chance of being selected. A more formal definition of random sampling is

> *A random sample of size n is a sample chosen from the set of all possible samples of size* n *such that each of these samples has an equal probability of being selected.*

Random sampling defined in this way is often referred to as "simple random sampling" to distinguish it from more complex sampling methods often employed in professional surveys. Such advanced sampling methods are beyond the scope of this introductory text. The practical and theoretical aspects of random sampling, along with the wider use of randomization in designing experiments, will be discussed in Chapter 6.

Independence

There is a slightly different way of describing a random sample. We can say a sample is random if each of the *n* selections is (a) random and (b) independent of any other selection. The term *independent* was used informally in Chapter 3, and it is a concept that will reappear at various other points throughout the book. Here is a more formal definition of independence:

> *Two events (call them A and B) are independent if the probability of one of them happening is the same regardless of the outcome of the other.*

That is, the probability that A occurs is unaffected by whether or not B happpens. In a sampling process, independence means that the selection of one case does not change the probability that any other case will be selected.

Tossing coins and rolling dice provide clear examples of independence. If two coins are tossed, the probability of one coin landing heads remains at .5 regardless of the outcome of the other. If a die is rolled twice, the chances of obtaining a 4 on the second roll are 1 in 6 regardless of how the die landed on the first roll.

Under some everyday circumstances, the concept of independence may seem counterintuitive. Consider the following example.

Susan and Bob have three children, all boys. They had hoped for a daughter but had planned to have only three children. They decide to have a fourth child, having read that among families with four children, the probability of having all four boys is small—just 1 chance in 16. They figure that the probability that their next child will be a girl is therefore 15/16. Evaluate this argument.

Susan and Bob have fallen prey to some very poor reasoning. It is true that among four-child families only 1 family in 16 has all boys. But if a family already has three boys, then the probability that a fourth child will be a girl is .5. It would be .5 regardless of the outcome of the first three births, because each birth is an independent event. The probabilities associated with the fourth birth are uninfluenced by the outcomes from the first three.

The fallacy underlying Susan and Bob's reasoning is a common one. The mistaken idea is that the process underlying sex of offspring, or outcomes from coin tosses, have a built-in self-correcting propensity. Thus, after a sequence of boys, the probability of a girl is judged to be greater than .5 so that the existing imbalance can be corrected. This belief is often referred to as the gambler's fallacy. If, in a sequence of coin tosses, there have been four heads in a row, it is tempting (but mistaken) to believe that for the next toss it is better to bet on a tail than a head. The outcomes are independent, and the probability of a tail remains .5.

Mistaken thinking about independence sometimes takes a form opposite that of Susan and Bob. In this case, the outcome of an event is mistakenly assumed to increase the likelihood of it happening again. Consider the following example.

Bill goes to a casino to play the slot machines. After only 5 minutes, he hits a jackpot and wins $200, having spent only $10. Bill decides to continue playing the machine, arguing either that this is his lucky night or that he has stumbled onto a lucky machine. Either way, he argues, this is his chance to win a lot of money.

Bill is assuming that the outcome during the first 5 minutes is predictive of what the machine will do in the future. But if the outcomes are independent of one another, the probability of Bill winning in the future is uninfluenced by whether or not he has already won. If Bill were familiar with the law of large numbers as well as the concept of independence, then he would realize that his best course of action is to quit while he is ahead. The law of large numbers tells him that the longer he plays (the larger the sample of outcomes), the more likely it is that his total payback from the machine will be close to what the machine is engineered to return—a loss for Bill and a profit for the casino. His short-term winning was a chance discrepancy (a positive residual) that becomes less probable as the sample size increases.

Comprehension Check 4.1

Important Concepts

1. The "noisiness" of data as reflected in variability of the residuals can be modeled by a simple mechanical device such as Francis Galton's quincunx.

2. Despite the chaotic behavior of single elements (balls in the quincunx), the cumulative behavior of many elements is orderly and becomes increasingly stable as the number of elements increases.

3. This increasing stability is described by the law of large numbers, which states that as the number of observations increases, the difference between a sample proportion and the theoretical probability (or population proportion) becomes smaller. According to this view, probability is interpreted as long-run relative frequency.

4. A random selection is a selection for which each potential element has an equal chance of being selected. A random sample is a sample chosen such that each potential sample has an equal chance of being selected.

5. Two events (A and B) are independent if the probability that A occurs is unaffected by whether or not B occurs.

Worked Examples

Example 1   Three-row quincunx

Imagine (or sketch) a quincunx with three rows of pins.

a. How many bins are needed at the bottom to record the final location of the ball?

b. List all the possible paths that a ball might follow in falling through the quincunx. Use L to indicate a left deflection and R to indicate a right deflection. Thus one possible path would be LLL, another LLR.

c. For each of the final bins, calculate the probability that a ball will land in that bin.

d. Explain why more balls end up in the center bins than in either of the bins at the ends.

Answer

a. Four bins are needed.

b. There are eight possible paths: LLL, LLR, LRL, LRR, RLL, RLR, RRL, RRR.

c. The four possible final locations correspond to 0, 1, 2, or 3 right deflections. The probability of each of these outcomes is 1/8, 3/8, 3/8, 1/8, respectively. The probability of zero right deflections is 1/8 because just one of these eight elementary events (LLL) results in this outcome. Three of the eight elementary events yield a final outcome of one right deflection (LLR, LRL, RLL). Similarly, three of the eight elementary events yield a final outcome of two right deflections (LRR, RRL, RLR), and just one of the eight elementary events (RRR) results in three right deflections.

d. More balls end up in the center bins than in either of the bins at the ends because there are more elementary events that lead to those bins. Because each of these elementary events is equiprobable, there are more chances (a higher probability) of ending in a central bin.

Example 2   Coin tosses

John tosses a fair coin 40 times and counts the number of heads. Jane tosses the coin 60 times. Who is more likely to obtain more than 55% heads, John or Jane?

Answer John. The question asks which person is more likely to obtain a residual larger than .05. In this case, the residual is the difference between the sample proportion of .55 and the theoretical probability of .50. The law of large numbers states that larger residuals are more likely with smaller samples.

Example 3   Hospital problem

The law of large numbers has some simple practical applications. Consider the following problem taken from Kahneman and Tversky (1972).

A certain town is served by two hospitals. In the larger hospital, about 45 babies are born each day; in the smaller hospital, about 15 babies are born each day. In 1 year, an average of .5 (50%) of the babies are girls and .5 are boys, but the exact percentage varies from day to day.

For a period of 1 year, each hospital recorded the number of days on which more than .6 (60%) of the babies were girls.

Which hospital do you think recorded more such days?

a. larger

b. smaller

c. about the same

Answer This question asks the relative likelihood of the two hospitals obtaining a residual as large as .1 (10%). This .1 residual is the difference between the theoretical value of .5 and the specified value of .6. The question could therefore be rephrased to ask, In which hospital, the larger or the smaller, are residuals as big as .1 more likely to occur? The law of large numbers is precisely the claim that smaller samples (characteristic of the small hospital) are more likely than large samples to produce large residuals, that is, residuals larger than a specified size. The correct answer is therefore b.

Example 4   Random selection

A teacher of a class of 30 students is asked to choose one of the students "at random." What does this mean? Offer a suggestion as to how this random selection might be accomplished.

Answer Random selection means that each of the 30 students would have an equal chance of being selected. This selection might be accomplished by writing each student's name on a card, *thoroughly* shuffling the resulting deck of 30 cards, and selecting one card from the deck. If the teacher has computing skills, then another way would be to assign a number (1 through 30) to each student and have the computer generate a random number between 1 and 30 (inclusive). A *nonrandom method* would be to take an alphabetical class list, close your eyes and stick a pin in the list. One suspects that, under this procedure, someone in the middle of the list (Jane Miller) is more likely to be selected than someone at the alphabetical extremes (Fred Abbot or Betty Zygler). The point is that the procedure should *guarantee* that each student has an equal probability of being selected. Informal, intuitive methods such as the pin-sticking procedure may or may not be random in this sense, but a skeptic would have good grounds for doubting it.

Problems

Problem 1   Guessing in a multiple-device test

A student estimates that she knows most of the material for an upcoming multiple-choice term test; therefore she feels confident of passing. Given that her major goal is to pass the exam (the actual passing grade is less important), should the student prefer a 50-item test or a 10-item test? Explain to the student the reason for preferring one over the other.

Problem 2   Opinion poll

An opinion poll has established that just prior to a local election, candidate A leads candidate B by 5% of the popular vote. Assume that the opinion poll is accurate and that there is no last-minute issue to change the 5% lead for candidate A. Which candidate should be more hopeful of a large voter turnout on the election day?

Problem 3   Coin tosses

a. John tosses a fair coin 30 times and counts the number of heads. Jane tosses the coin 60 times and also counts the number of heads. Who is more likely to obtain more than 40% heads, John or Jane?

b. John and Jane toss different coins. One of these two coins is biased, the other is fair. John tosses his coin 30 times, Jane tosses hers 60 times. Suppose that they both obtain 40% heads. Which of the two coins would you more strongly suspect of being biased?

Problem 4   Dice outcomes

In the game Cut Your Losses, two dice are thrown and the score is the sum of the two. This total can range from 2 (1 on both dice) to 12 (6 on both dice). Are the scores over this range equally probable? Explain your answer.

Problem 5   Demonstrating random selection

In planning a TV quiz show, contestants can be asked questions from any of five content areas. Before each question is asked, the content area is to be determined randomly. The show producers not only want the selection to be random, they also want the audience to be convinced that the selection was random. If "Sports" is one of the areas, what is the probability that this will be the randomly selected area? Suggest a device suitable for TV that would assure the viewing audience that the selection was truly random.

4.2   Discrete Probability Distributions

A probability distribution specifies the probabilities for all possible outcomes.

The theoretical probabilities for the miniature quincunx can be represented by a histogram in which the height of each bar represents the probability of each outcome. Such a specification of probabilities across the entire set of possible outcomes is known as a *probability distribution*. For the miniature quincunx, there are just three possible final outcomes, so the distribution takes on the very simple form shown in Figure 4.5.

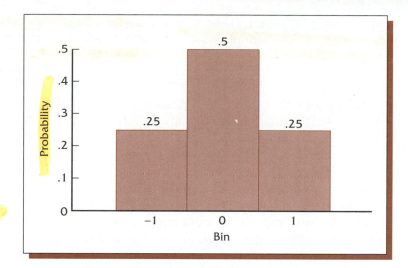

Figure 4.5
Distribution of
probabilities for the
miniature quincunx.

For convenience, the three bins of the miniature quincunx have been labeled -1, 0, and $+1$. These would be the numbers we would get if we used a scoring scheme that scored $-\frac{1}{2}$ each time the ball deflects left and $+\frac{1}{2}$ each time the ball deflects right. Another possible scoring scheme would be to score 0 for a left deflection and 1 for a right deflection. The effect of this 0-and-1 scoring scheme is simply to count the number of deflects to the right. The leftmost bin would then score 0, because to land in this bin, both deflections must be left. The center bin would score 1, because to land in this bin, one of the deflections must be left and one right. The rightmost bin would score 2, because to land in this bin, both the deflections must be right. This scoring would record the outcome from tossing a coin twice, where 0, 1, and 2 correspond to the number of heads rather than the number of right deflections. Either scoring system leads to the same distribution; only the scores under the bars are different.

Notice that the three probabilities sum to 1. In *any* probability distribution, the probabilities will sum to 1 because the distribution gives the probabilities for all possible outcomes—100% of outcomes corresponds to a probability of 1. It is certain (a probability of 1) that the outcome will be one of the events labeled on the horizontal axis.

The probabilities of a probability distribution always sum to 1.

4.2.1 Discrete Random Variables

The variable defined by these three final outcomes of the miniature quincunx is a *discrete* variable in the sense defined in Section 1.2.2. Recall that a discrete variable was one with a finite number of distinct (discrete) quantitative values. A discrete variable was contrasted to a continuous variable, such as time or height, which varies over a continuous range of values and thus has an infinite number of possible values.

The final outcome of the miniature quincunx is a *discrete* variable with three possible values. An added feature of this variable compared with those considered in Chapter 1 is that there is a probability distribution defined over its values. When a variable has an associated probability distribution, it is termed a *random variable*. We will use this term extensively in the remainder of this book.

Thus the values on the horizontal axis of Figure 4.5 (-1, 0, $+1$) are values of a random variable. This variable is discrete, so it can be described more precisely as a discrete random variable. Continuous variables can also be treated as random

A random variable is any variable that has a probability distribution defined over the range of its values.

variables (see Section 4.3). In principle, *any* variable—categorical or quantiative—can be treated as a random variable; the only requirement is that there be a probability distribution defined over all possible values of the variable.

Why the need for this special term? It would be possible to get by without it, and many introductory textbooks do. However, the term *random* is useful because it marks an important distinction. It indicates that, in addition to being a measurement scale, the variable can have probability statements applied to its values. The three outcomes from the miniature quincunx define the three possible values of a discrete variable. This discrete variable becomes a discrete *random* variable when a probability value is assigned to each of these outcomes, as shown in Figure 4.5.

Random variables can be continuous or discrete.

Random variables can be continuous as well as discrete. Reaction time is a variable; but, if we refer to reaction time as a *random* variable, we mean that we intend to make probability statements about reaction time—statements like "the probability is .7 that the reaction time will be longer than 300 milliseconds," or "the probability is .5 that the reaction time will be between 300 and 400 milliseconds." Once again the term *random* conveys useful information about how the variable is to be used. Notice that a variable may be treated as a random variable in one situation and a nonrandom variable in another. In some circumstances, there may be an interest in making probability statements about reaction time, but not in other circumstances. Being a random variable is not an intrinsic property of the variable.

Everyday Variables as Random Variables

The following situations pose questions that could be answered by taking everyday variables and treating them as random variables, although precise answers would require additional information.

What is the probability that the score on the SAT of a randomly chosen high school senior will be below 400? Usually we might consider SAT score as an ordinary quantitative variable. Values of the variable are the scores of students taking the test. To answer this question, however, the variable must be treated as a random variable. The probability distribution would specify probabilities over the range of possible SAT scores.

A certain 5-mile stretch of highway averages five accidents per year; some years it is higher than five, in other years lower. What is the probability that in any given year there will be more than eight accidents? To answer this question, the variable "number of accidents per year" needs to be treated as a random variable. The probability distribution would then specify probabilities for different numbers of accidents.

A restaurant owner advertises fresh oysters on the dinner menu. The owner knows that, when oysters appear on the menu, the average number ordered in one evening is 10 dozen. Some evenings, it is higher than 10; in others, it is lower. If the owner buys too many oysters, there is the risk of expensive waste; if too few are bought, there is the risk of running out and having dissatisfied customers. The owner decides to buy sufficient oysters such that there is only a .10 probability that the number of oysters ordered by the customers will exceed the number available. How many oysters should the owner buy? Here the random variable is "the number of oysters ordered by the customers." The probability distribution would specify probabilities for different numbers of oysters ordered. This distribution would enable the owner to specify the number that must be ordered to ensure that the probability is only .10 that customers will order more than this number.

The average rainfall in a certain region is 20 inches per year. If in any given year the rainfall is below 10 inches, crops will be lost. What is the probability that the rainfall will be less than 10 inches in any given year? Here the random variable is "annual rainfall." The probability distribution would specify probabilities across the complete range of possible annual rainfalls and, in particular, the probability that the value of the random variable will be less than 10.

Blood type is a categorical variable with four possible values: O, A, B, and AB. What is the probability that a randomly chosen person has blood type AB? Blood type is being treated as a categorical random variable when there is a known probability for all four possible blood types.

4.2.2 Binomial Distribution

Figure 4.5 shows the probability distribution for the miniature quincunx with two rows and therefore just three possible outcomes. Distributions for a quincunx with 5, 10, and 20 rows are shown in Figure 4.6. The calculation of the probabilities for these distributions follows the same rationale we used for the miniature two-row quincunx. However, as soon as the number of rows is more than five or so, calculating the probabilities becomes a major arithmetic undertaking not to be attempted without a computer or an appropriate set of tables.

The probability distributions shown in Figure 4.6 belong to a class of probability distributions known as the *binomial distribution*. Binomial distributions are of great practical importance; they specify the probabilities, not only for mechanical processes such as a ball moving through the quincunx or the tosses of a coin, but also for many everyday situations and natural phenomena. To understand why the binomial distribution has such wide application, it is necessary to understand in slightly more abstract terms the nature of the process that results in a binomial distribution.

Defining Features of a Binomial Distribution

The binomial distribution specifies the probabilities for final outcomes that are governed by processes having the following two features.

■ **There is a set of n elementary events, or "trials."** For the quincunx, each row (each deflection) constitutes a trial; in coin tossing, each toss is a trial. (The fact that the symbol n was used previously to refer to the number of balls in the quincunx should not be confusing. In any particular context, it will be perfectly clear to what value n refers.)

■ **Each trial has exactly two possible outcomes, which occur with a fixed probability.** We will use p to denote the probability of one of these outcomes. Because there are just two possible outcomes, the probability of the other outcome is $1 - p$. For the quincunx, the two possible outcomes are left deflection or right deflection; in coin tossing, it is heads or tails. In both these cases, $p = 1 - p = .5$. Note, however, that a binomial distribution is not limited to probabilities of .5. The important point is that, whatever the value of the

p denotes probability of an outcome.

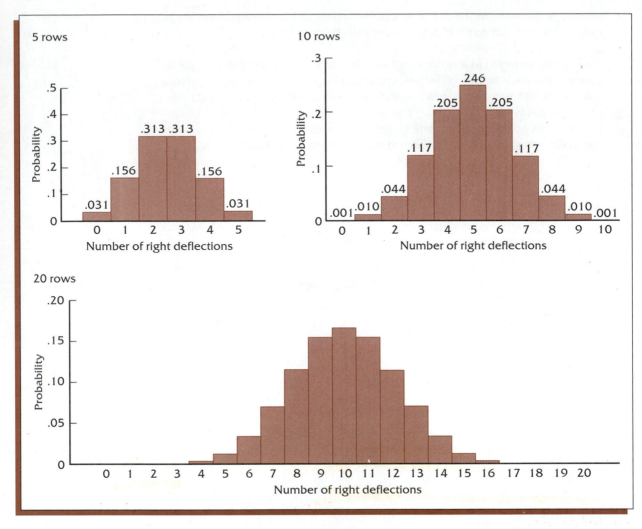

Figure 4.6
Probability distributions for three quincunx with different numbers of rows of pins: 5, 10, and 20.

probability, it must be *constant*. We could imagine a quincunx engineered so that the probability was $p = .4$ of deflecting left and $1 - p = .6$ of deflecting right. Outcomes from this right-biased device would still be described by a version of the binomial distribution, but only if the bias of $p = .4$ of deflecting left and .6 probability of deflecting right was true for *every* pin.

The term *binomial* means literally "two names" or "two categories," and it captures the defining feature of the distribution, namely, that each trial has just two possible outcomes: left/right; head/tail; male/female, etc.

Situations Described by the Binomial Distribution

To illustrate the practical relevance of this distribution, here are some everyday questions that the binomial distribution could answer.

What is the probability that families with five children will have three girls and two boys? In this example, a "trial" is the birth of a child and the two possible outcomes are girl/boy. Here $p = .5$, the probability that a newborn will be a girl. The relevant binomial distribution is one with $n = 5$ and $p = .5$. This distribution is the top distribution shown in Figure 4.6. We can read off the answer from the graph as .313. The probability that the family will have three girls is the same as a five-row quincunx having three right deflections or of getting three heads in five tosses of a coin.

In a term test, a student encounters four questions on a topic he has not studied. The questions are multiple choice, with three alternative answers. He decides to guess the answer to each of the four questions, so, for each question, he has one chance in three of being correct. What is the probability that he will get all four answers correct? Here the relevant binomial distribution is one with $n = 4$ and $p = \frac{1}{3}$.

An investigator is studying the learning abilities of 3-year-old children. The 3-year-old's task is to decide which of two locations contains a prize. The correct location is governed by a rule. Learning this rule would enable the child to predict the correct location. If no learning has occurred, the child's choices will be no better than chance. After a training session, the investigator evaluates learning by presenting the child with ten test trials, in each of which the child must choose between the two alternative locations. The child chooses correctly on seven of the ten test trials. What is the probability that the child could perform at this level, answering seven or more correctly, if in fact no learning has occurred? Here the relevant binomial distribution is one with $n = 10$ and $p = .5$.

Figure 4.7 graphs binomial distributions for three different values of p and two values of n. Notice that binomial distributions are symmetrical only in the case of $p = (1 - p) = .5$. The symmetry is obvious in the top row of Figure 4.7, but notice that figures in the second row have a distinct negative skew and that figures in the third row have a distinct positive skew. In general, the binomial distribution will be positively skewed when $p < .5$ and negatively skewed when $p > .5$. This relationship is not surprising. For example, if there is only a small probability (p) of guessing the correct answer of each multiple-choice test question, then correct answers are relatively infrequent and total test scores tend to the low end. The distribution in Figure 4.7 for $n = 5$ and $p = .25$, which corresponds to the score of someone who guessed the answers to five four-alternative questions, shows that there is a probability of .237 of getting none correct, but only .001 of getting all correct.

4.2.3 Obtaining Probabilities for Binomial Distributions

The calculation of probabilities for the binomial distribution is quite cumbersome; therefore, probabilities are obtained from tables or computer programs. The tables provided in this book give probabilities for only a small number of distributions, but they are sufficient to become familiar with the principles underlying their use.

The binomial distribution is defined in terms of two parameters, n and p. As we have seen, the probabilities for possible outcomes vary, depending on the values of these parameters. Table 4.2 gives binomial probabilities for distributions with $n = 5$ for various values of p ranging from $\frac{1}{4}$ to $\frac{3}{4}$. Statistical Table 2 in Appendix C gives

Binomial probabilities depend on the values of n and p.

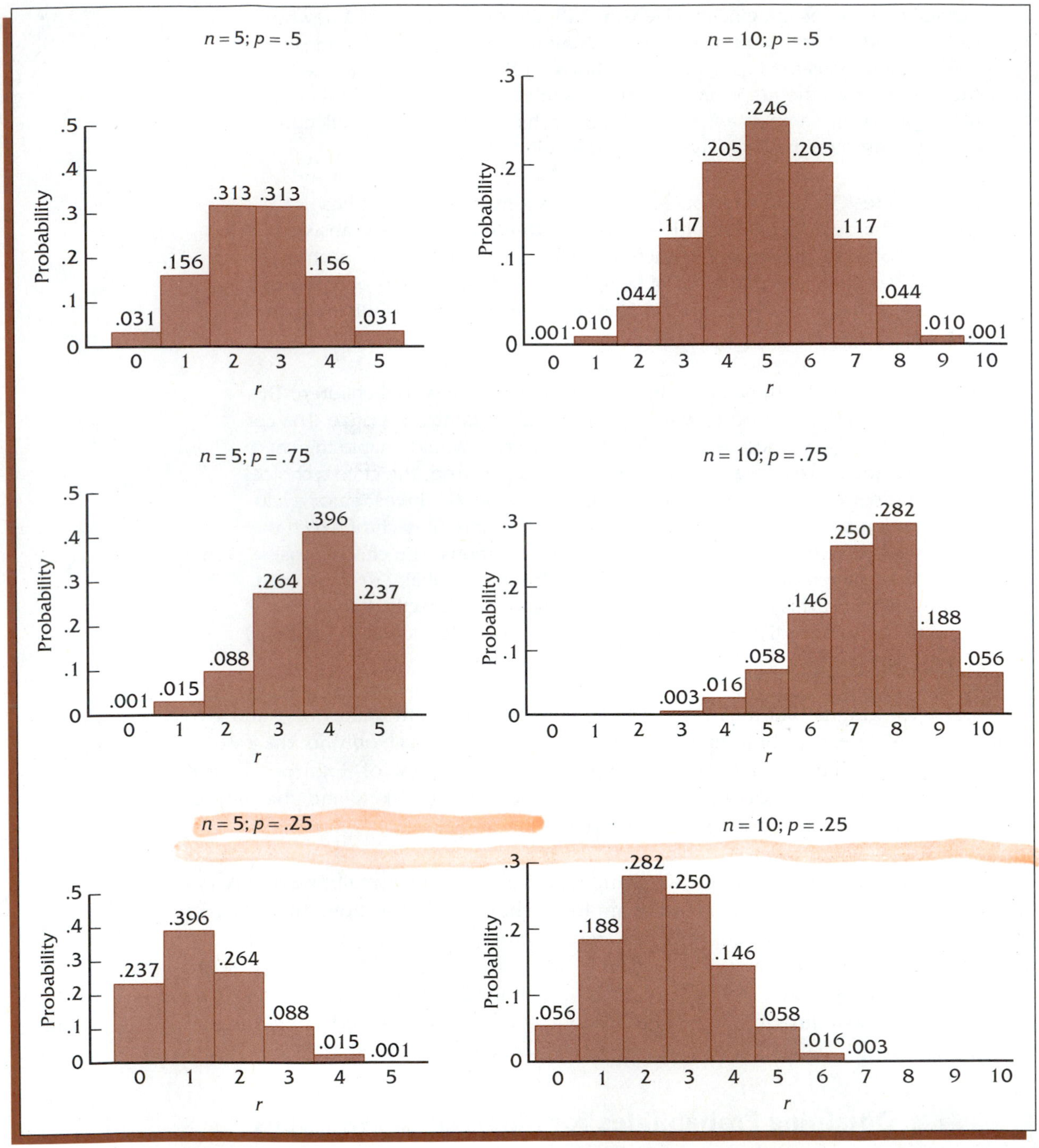

Figure 4.7
Binomial distributions for different values of *p* and *n*. Because the probabilities above each bar have been rounded to three decimal places, the sum of these probabilities may be .999 or 1.001.

r denotes index of possible outcomes.

probabilities for these same values of *p* for values of *n* from 5 to 10. It is helpful to think of each distribution in concrete terms. Think of *n* as the number of tosses of a coin. The values of *r* in the left column represent each of the possible outcomes—the number of heads. Because there are five tosses, *r* can range from 0 to 5. The columns to the right give probabilities for different values of *p*. Thus the column headed ¼

r	$\frac{1}{4}$	$\frac{1}{3}$	$\frac{1}{2}$	$\frac{2}{3}$	$\frac{3}{4}$
0	.237	.132	.031	.004	.001
1	.396	.329	.156	.041	.015
2	.264	.329	.313	.165	.088
3	.088	.165	.313	.329	.264
4	.015	.041	.156	.329	.396
5	.001	.004	.031	.132	.237

Table 4.2 Binomial probabilities when $n = 5$, with column heading p.

gives probabilities for a badly biased coin for which the probability of landing heads is $\frac{1}{4}$. Notice that the columns for $p = \frac{1}{4}, \frac{1}{2},$ and $\frac{3}{4}$ contain the probabilities used to plot the graphs in the left-hand side of Figure 4.7.

n is the number of trials (for example, number of tosses of the coin).

p is the probability of one of the two possible outcomes (for example, the probability of the coin landing head).

r is an index of the number of times this outcome occurs (for example, the number of heads in n tosses).

Obtaining Probabilities of Single Outcomes

Obtaining probabilities for a given outcome is simply a matter of consulting Table 4.2 or one in the Appendix for the relevant value of n, then locating the appropriate values of r and p. Suppose, for example, we want the probability that a family of five will have exactly one girl. For this problem, $n = 5$, $r = 1$, and $p = .5$. To obtain the probability from the table, we locate the row for $r = 1$ and follow it across until we reach the column for $p = .5$. This column gives us the probability of .156. Thus the probability of the family having one girl (and therefore four boys) is .156. Note that this is the same probability as the family having four girls and one boy. This result follows from the symmetry of the binomial distribution when $p = .5$.

Consider another problem. A student answers five three-alternative multiple-choice questions by guessing. What is the probability that the student will get exactly three of the questions correct? For this question, $n = 5$, $r = 3$, and $p = \frac{1}{3}$. The value of $p = \frac{1}{3}$ comes from the assumption that, with three alternatives, there is one chance in three of guessing correctly. Consulting the table, we find that the intersection of the row for $r = 3$ and the column for $p = \frac{1}{3}$ gives the value .165.

Obtaining Probabilities for Ranges of Outcomes

For some problems, the required probability corresponds to a range of outcomes rather than a single outcome. For example, we might want to know the probability of the student in the previous problem getting three or more items correct by guessing.

Probabilities for ranges of outcomes such as this are obtained by adding up the probabilities for all the events within the range.

Thus we can find the probability of the student getting three or more items correct by adding up the probabilities for getting 3, 4, and 5 correct. From Table 4.2, we find that the probability is .165 + .041 + .004 = .210.

The probability of the 3-year-old guessing which of two locations is correct on seven or more of ten trials can be obtained from the top right distribution in Figure 4.7 because, for this example, $n = 10$ and $p = .5$. We add up the probabilities for the columns with values of 7 or more. This operation gives a probability of .117 + .044 + .010 + .001 = .172.

Comprehension Check 4.2

Important Concepts

1. A probability distribution is a distribution that specifies the probability of different values of a variable.

2. A variable with an associated probability distribution is called a random variable. Therefore a random variable is a variable about which probability statements will be made.

3. Random variables may be categorical or quantitative; and, if quantitative, they may be either discrete or continuous.

4. A commonly used example of a discrete probability distribution is the binomial distribution. This distribution specifies a probability for every possible outcome of a process that consists of n trials on each of which one of two possible outcomes can occur with a constant probability. A prototypical example is tossing a coin n times and counting the number of heads. The binomial distribution specifies a probability for every possible number of heads. Many everyday situations are equivalent to this prototypical example.

5. Probabilities for single outcomes or a range of outcomes for the binomial distribution can be obtained from tables once n and p are known, and the relevant outcomes (values of r) have been specified.

Worked Examples

Example 1   Probability distribution for a single die

When an ordinary six-sided die is rolled, there are six possible outcomes and, assuming the die to be fair, each outcome is equally probable. Draw a histogram of the probability distribution for a single roll of a fair die. Is the random variable in this case continuous or discrete?

Answer There are six possible outcomes, so our task is to specify the probability of each of these outcomes. Each of the six faces of the die is equally likely to appear: The probability of each outcome is 1/6 or .167. Figure 4.8 is a geometrical representation of this claim in the form of a histogram. The vertical axis measures probability. The horizontal axis represents the outcome variable with its six possible

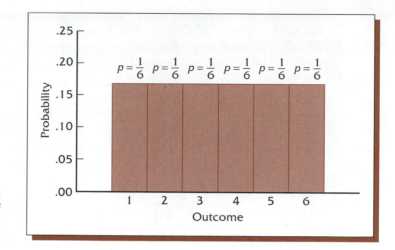

Figure 4.8
Probability distribution of the six possible outcomes from the toss of a fair die.

values. Associated with each of these values is a bar, the height of which indicates the probability of that value of the outcome variable. Because each event is equally likely, the height of each bar is the same and equal to .167. Note that, because the distribution includes all possible outcomes, the sum of the probabilities must be 1. When, as in this example, every possible outcome is equally probable, the probabilities are distributed uniformly, and the overall shape of the probability distribution will be rectangular. Not surprisingly, such distributions are termed *uniform*, or *rectangular*, distributions. In this case, the random variable is discrete. There are just six possible outcomes, and intermediate values such as 2.5 cannot occur.

Example 2   Number of homicides

A criminologist defines a variable as "number of homicides in a calendar year." Explain what it would mean to consider this variable as a *random* variable.

Answer The number of homicides in a calendar year is a variable because the value varies from one year to another. The variable becomes a random variable if we can assign a probability to each possible value of the variable. It would then be possible to answer questions such as, "What is the probability that the number of homicides in a calendar year will be greater than 25?" The most likely purpose of treating this variable as a random variable would be to answer such questions.

Example 3   Guessing in a term test

In a term test, a student encounters six three-alternative multiple-choice questions on a topic she has not studied. She decides to guess the answer to each of the six questions.

   a. What is the probability that the student will get no answers correct?

   b. What is the probability that the student will get exactly two answers correct?

   c. What is the probability that the student will get three or more answers correct?

Answer The relevant binomial distribution is one with $n = 6$ and $p = \frac{1}{3}$. The relevant table of probabilities is in Statistical Table 2 in Appendix C and is reproduced in Table 4.3 for convenience. The relevant column ($p = \frac{1}{3}$) is shaded.

Table 4.3 Binomial probabilities for $n = 6$

	p				
r	$\frac{1}{4}$	$\frac{1}{3}$	$\frac{1}{2}$	$\frac{2}{3}$	$\frac{3}{4}$
0	.178	.088	.016	.001	.000
1	.356	.263	.094	.016	.004
2	.297	.329	.234	.082	.033
3	.132	.219	.312	.219	.132
4	.033	.082	.234	.329	.297
5	.004	.016	.094	.263	.356
6	.000	.001	.016	.088	.178

a. The probability that the student will get no answers correct is found by consulting the row for $r = 0$. The value in the shaded column ($p = \frac{1}{3}$) is .088.

b. The probability that the student will get exactly two answers correct is found by consulting the row for $r = 2$. The value in the shaded column ($p = \frac{1}{3}$) is .329.

c. The probability that the student will get three or more answers correct is found by consulting the rows for $r = 3$, 4, 5, and 6 (the outcomes corresponding to getting three or more answers correct) and adding up the probabilities. These values, found in the shaded column, are

$$.219 + .082 + .016 + .001 = .318$$

Thus the probability that the student will get three or more answers correct (get a passing grade) is .318.

Problems

Problem 1 Suicide rate

The suicide rate in a large town averages 10 per year, although the exact number varies from one year to another. A clinical counselor is alarmed to find that there were 15 reported suicides in the past year and asks whether this increase is a normal fluctuation or indicative of some unusual circumstance. Explain how the counselor's question might be addressed by treating the number of suicides as a random variable.

Problem 2 Locating binomial probabilities

The purpose of this exercise is to ensure that you understand the relationship between the tabulated values and the corresponding geometrical representation of the probability distribution. Complete as much of this exercise as you think useful.

Figure 4.7 shows binomial distributions for various values of p and n. Consult Statistical Table 2 and locate the probabilities corresponding to the outcomes represented in the graphs. The probability for that outcome is given at the top of each bar in Figure 4.7. You should be able to locate that number in the table.

Problem 3   Committee selection

A class consists of 60 students, 20 of whom favor an essay exam and 40 of whom favor a multiple-choice exam. There is therefore a probability of $\frac{1}{3}$ that a randomly chosen student from this class will favor an essay exam and a probability of $\frac{2}{3}$ that the selected student will favor a multiple-choice exam. A committee of 10 students is formed by randomly selecting 10 of the 60 students.

a. What is the probability that exactly 5 committee members will be students who favor an essay exam and 5 will be students who favor a multiple-choice exam?

b. What is the probability that a majority of committee members (6 or more) will be students who favor an essay exam?

c. What is the probability that a majority of committee members (6 or more) will be students who favor a multiple-choice exam?

4.3   Central Limit Theorem and the Normal Distribution

The law of large numbers describes what happens when the number of balls in the quincunx is increased until they become infinitely many. We now turn to the question of what happens when the number of rows of pins also becomes infinite. Of course, with this change, not only must the infinite number of balls be imaginary, so too must the quincunx itself.

4.3.1   Continuous Variables and Smooth Curves

The number of bins needed at the bottom of the quincunx to record the possible outcomes is one more than the number of rows. Recall that one way of thinking of the bins is that they record the number of right deflections. This number can range all the way from 0 (every deflection was to the left, shunting the ball into the leftmost bin) to n, the number of rows (every deflection was to the right, shunting the ball into the rightmost bin). As the number of rows becomes infinitely large, so too does the number of bins. The effect of such an increase is that the measurement scale, represented by the row of bins, changes from a discrete to a continuous variable. If the scale is taken to represent the number of right deflections, then the outcomes are no longer limited to a set of discrete possibilities; the number of possible outcomes is infinitely large.

If we are to model the residuals for continuous variables, such as reaction time, then our mechanical version of the model, the quincunx, will also need to model outcomes that can be considered a continuous variable. For this reason, the imaginary quincunx with an infinitely large number of rows is exactly what we need.

The theoretical probabilities for the ordinary quincunx were specified by the binomial distribution. To specify probabilities when the number of rows in the quincunx becomes infinite, we need to know what happens to the binomial distribution as n becomes infinite. The mathematician Abraham de Moivre first formulated the answer to this question in 1733. It is interesting that de Moivre's motivation was the

As the number of rows in the quincunx becomes infinite, the outcome variable changes from continuous to discrete.

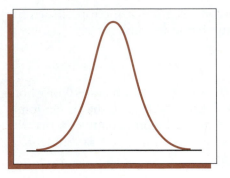

Figure 4.9
The smooth curve resulting from a binomial distribution when *n* becomes infinite.

need to find a way of avoiding the excessive arithmetic involved in calculating binomial probabilities. The situation prompted de Moivre to derive a distribution that could be used to approximate binomial probabilities for large values of *n*. The distribution de Moivre devised for this purpose would later prove to be even more important than the binomial distribution itself.

The shape of the distribution that de Moivre derived is shown in Figure 4.9. It is a symmetrical bell-shaped distribution with a single peak. The left and right extremes of the distribution are referred to as the tails. Although the tails appear to touch the horizontal axis, in fact, they never quite do. In theory, the tails extend infinitely in both directions, the distribution spanning the range $-\infty$ to $+\infty$. In practice, the height of the tails above the horizontal axis becomes negligible within a relatively short distance from the center.

Notice that the histogram bars of the binomial distribution have become a smooth curve now that the variable is continuous rather than discrete. The histogram bars become lines of zero width, and the smooth curve is formed by the points representing the tops of these lines moving smoothly across the horizontal axis over the range of the variable.

In 1812, the French mathematician Pierre Laplace independently derived de Moivre's distribution. Both Laplace and Carl Friedrich Gauss interpreted this distribution as the *law of errors*, using it to describe variation in astronomical observations as well as a number of other applications, including gambling and artillery fire.

In the concluding paragraph of Chapter 3, we mentioned Gauss's insight that probability theory could be helpful in understanding the nature of variability in scientific data. The work of Laplace and Gauss in the early nineteenth century is the first application of the concept of a probability distribution to the understanding of errors (or, in our preferred terminology, residuals) in scientific observations. However, this extension by Laplace and Gauss of de Moivre's early numerical application proved to be just the beginning of much bigger things. Throughout the nineteenth century, an increasing number of biological variables were discovered that displayed the distinctive bell shape, and eventually, as a result of the curve's widening range of applicability, the distribution became known as the *normal distribution*. Prior to achieving this status as something of a natural law, the distribution was called the Laplace-Gaussian distribution, or simply the *Gaussian distribution*, a terminology that remains current in many areas, especially in the physical sciences, engineering, and the study of sensory processes such as vision and acoustics.

The early champion of the normal distribution was the Belgian astronomer Adolphe Quetelet (1796–1874), who developed the idea of the average as nature's ideal. The ideal height, for example, was the average height, and departures from average constituted nature's "error." It was the normal distribution that described this

As *n* becomes infinite, the binomial distribution becomes a smooth curve.

Gauss and Laplace described the curve as the law of errors.

Nineteenth-century researchers found that many natural variables (such as height) followed the normal distribution.

pattern of errors as they distributed themselves around the mean. To demonstrate that attributes such as height followed the normal distribution, Quetelet developed a goodness-of-fit procedure that compared an observed proportional frequency distribution with the proportions predicted by a normal distribution. It is interesting to note that, to calculate these predicted proportions, Quetelet actually calculated probabilities from a binomial distribution with $n = 999$. This value of n may seem odd unless you recall that with $n = 999$ there are 1000 possible outcomes, making this value of n computationally convenient. Thus, a century after de Moivre derived the normal curve as an approximation to the binomial, we find Quetelet reversing the process.

The fact that the normal distribution seemed to describe so many phenomena was not the only reason for its importance. Throughout the nineteenth century, statistics was thought of largely in the descriptive sense of gathering measurements and presenting them in a way that described natural phenomena, both biological and social. Increasingly, however, statistics also became a branch of applied mathematics; and in this development of the mathematical basis of statistical data analysis, the normal distribution again proved to be of central importance. Although subsequent chapters will introduce distributions in addition to the normal, these distributions are all related in one way or another to the normal distribution.

4.3.2 Central Limit Theorem

The various threads that make up the history of the normal distribution are more interrelated than is immediately apparent. Its use as an approximation to the binomial distribution, its ability to capture the structure of so many natural phenomena, and its pivotal role in the development of statistical theory, are all related to a single general principle known as the *central limit theorem.* Laplace first formulated it in 1810. Stated informally, the principle makes the following claim: A variable (for example, height, weight, residuals) that is the net result of adding together a large number of contributing independent outcomes will have an approximately normal distribution. The approximation improves as the number of contributing outcomes increases. The theorem is a *limit* theorem because it describes what happens in the limit, as the number of contributing elements becomes infinite. The adjective *central* conveys the sense that this particular limit theorem (there are others) is basic or fundamental.

We have already described the best-known example of the central limit theorem in action: the normal distribution emerging from the binomial distribution. The final location of the ball in the quincunx or the number of heads from n tosses of a coin is precisely the situation to which the central limit theorem applies. The final location of the ball in the quincunx is the additive result of a large number of contributing outcomes, each outcome being a left or right deflection. In the case of coin tossing, each outcome is head or tail. If the outcome head is scored 1 and tail scored 0, then the sum of these outcomes is simply the number of heads. Thus any process that is analogous to the action of the quincunx or to coin tossing, and therefore appropriately modeled by the binomial distribution, will obey the central limit theorem. It will produce a normal distribution as n becomes large.

A More General Application of the Central Limit Theorem

The central limit theorem is more general and more powerful than the example of the binomial distribution would suggest. The binomial distribution is essentially the end product of adding a sequence of zeros and ones, although the entities being

A variable that is the net result of adding together many independent components will have a normal distribution.

added need not be literally 1 and 0; they could be -1 and $+1$, or $-\frac{1}{2}$ and $+\frac{1}{2}$. Nevertheless, there must be just two possible values, and it must be the same two values for each trial. However, the central limit theorem does not insist on such a limitation. As an example of this added power of the central limit theorem, consider the six possible outcomes from rolling a die. The score can range from 1 to 6. Suppose we roll two dice, as players do in many board games such as Monopoly or the game Cut Your Losses described in Chapters 1 and 3. The recorded outcome is the sum of the two dice, a score that can range from 2 (two ones) to 12 (two sixes), a total of 11 possible outcomes. Each outcome is the sum of contributing elements, each of which can range from 1 to 6. What is the probability of obtaining each of these 11 possible outcomes? What, for example, is the probability of obtaining a total of 8 from the roll of two dice? The relevant probability distribution is shown in Figure 4.10a. The impressive result is that this distribution shows early signs of becoming bell-shaped (in fact, it is triangular) even though the variable is the sum of just two outputs.

Figure 4.10a is a distribution of probabilities. These probabilities can be thought of as proportions based on an infinitely large number of rolls of the two dice. Making the distribution in Figure 4.10a more bell-shaped is therefore not a matter of making more rolls but of having more dice.

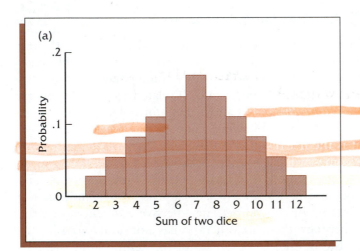

Figure 4.10
(a) Probability distribution for the possible outcomes from rolling two dice. (b) Probability distribution for the possible outcomes from rolling five dice.

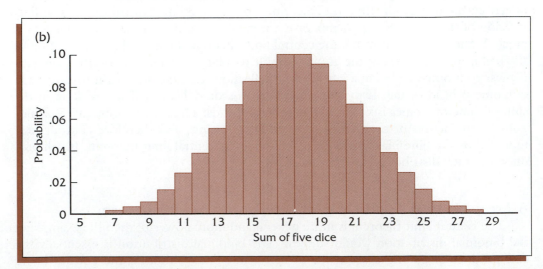

Suppose that five dice are tossed. The variable is the sum of each of the five outcomes, so the scores range from 5 to 30. The force of the central limit theorem is now readily apparent. The probability distribution for this scenario is shown in Figure 4.10b, and the emerging bell shape is quite clear.

This impact of the central limit theorem helps explain why so many natural phenomena appear to be normally distributed. If attributes such as height and weight are influenced by a number of independent contributing factors that add to determine the final measurement, then it follows from the central limit theorem that the attribute will be normally distributed. Thus the rationale that has been developed in this chapter to explain why the normal distribution is an appropriate model for residuals also explains why investigators in the nineteenth century, such as Quetelet, were so impressed by the number of natural variables they found to be normally distributed.

This powerful impact of the central limit theorem has one further important implication for the practical aspects of data analysis. The theorem states that a variable formed by the sum of independent elements will be well approximated by a normal distribution. One variable that matches this characterization perfectly is the sample mean. By definition, the sample mean is the sum of independent elements: the scores that are added together and divided by n. If you are worried about the division by n, remember that division by a constant will do nothing to alter the shape of the distribution. The implications for statistical data analysis of this particular application of the central limit theorem are enormous and form the subject matter of Chapter 5.

> **The impact of the central limit theorem helps explain why so many natural phenomena appear to be normally distributed.**

4.3.3 Properties of Distributions of Continuous Random Variables

In discussing properties of distributions of continuous random variables, we will use the normal distribution as an example, but these general properties apply to any distribution of a continuous variable. We have already seen the general shape of the normal distribution (Figure 4.9), although, as you may have noted, the graph left both axes unlabeled. As in a discrete probability distribution, the horizontal axis represents values of a random variable, although the variable is now continuous rather than discrete. The appropriate labeling of the vertical axis, however, requires the introduction of a new concept.

Probability Density

For discrete random variables, the bars of the probability distribution designate the probability for each discrete value of the variable—the probability of obtaining exactly two heads in four tosses of a coin, for example. For continuous random variables such as reaction time, height, and body weight, the probability distribution designates probabilities over a continuous range of values. Within this range, there are no gaps. Unlike the discrete variable that had a finite number of possible values, a continuous random variable has an unlimited number of possible values.

The unlimited number of possible values has an important implication for the terminology used for probability distributions of continuous variables. Unlike the situation for discrete random variables, in the case of continuous random variables, it is inappropriate to ask the probability that the random variable *equals* some particular value. The only possible answer to this question would be 0. For example, the probability that a randomly selected person will be 170 pounds in weight means, strictly speaking, *exactly* 170 pounds; not 170.0000001, nor 169.9999999 pounds, but

> **With continuous variables, statements of probability are always about ranges of values, not single values.**

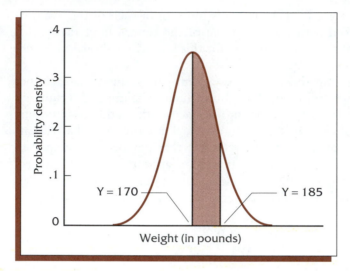

Figure 4.11
Probability distribution for a continuous variable such as weight of adult males. The probability density (height of the curve) is greater at Y = 170 pounds than at Y = 185 pounds.

170.0000000 . . . , the zeros extending to infinity. The number of possible values is infinitely large for a continuous variable, so it makes no sense to assign a probability to any such single number. The question becomes meaningful if it is rephrased and expressed instead as the probability of the person's weight being in the interval 169.5 to 170.5 pounds. *With continuous variables, statements of probability are always about ranges of values, not single values.*

The resolution of this problem is to refer to the height of the continuous probability distribution at a particular point, not as probability, but as *probability density*. Figure 4.11 shows a probability distribution for a continuous variable such as adult male weight. The probability density (height of the distribution) is greater at Y = 170 pounds than at Y = 185 pounds.

The height of the continuous probability distribution at a particular point is known as probability density.

Probability density at a particular value can be thought of as the concentration of probability at that point. It is helpful to draw an analogy between probability density and speed of travel. Imagine one car traveling at 50 miles per hour. In such a case, it makes no sense to ask how far the car travels at a *point* in time. The question "How far did the car travel at 12 noon?" is the same as asking the probability that the decision time will be *exactly* 354 milliseconds. Both values are points on a continuum and span a zero time interval. In both cases, however, it does make sense to ask about *intervals* of time. How far does the car travel between 12 noon and 12:05 P.M.? What is the probability that the decision time will be between 300 milliseconds and 400 milliseconds? Both these questions are sensible and, with sufficient information, answerable. The speed of the car at a single point in time (instantaneous velocity) is analogous to the probability density of the decision time at a single point. Just as speed determines the distance traveled for a fixed interval of traveling time, probability density determines the probability associated with a fixed interval of decision time.

Because they are smooth curves, distributions of continuous variables can usually be defined with an equation that gives the height of the curve for any value of the random variable. Because this height specifies probability density rather than simple probability, such distributions and their defining equations are more accurately termed *probability density functions* rather than simply probability distributions. However, no great harm is done by using the expression *probability distribution* as a generic term to cover all cases, even for the probability density function of a continuous random variable.

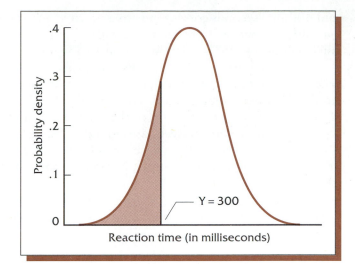

Figure 4.12
Probability density function for reaction time. The shaded area corresponds to the probability that reaction time (Y) will be less than 300 milliseconds.

Probability as Area under the Curve

With continuous variables, probabilities can be represented by areas under the curve. Remember that with continuous distributions, probability statements are always about ranges of values—the probability that reaction time will be less than 300 milliseconds or that it will be between 300 and 400 milliseconds, for example. The area representation means that probabilities correspond to the area under the distribution curve within this range. Figure 4.12 illustrates this point; the shaded area represents the probability that the reaction time (Y) will be less than 300 milliseconds. In Figure 4.13, the shaded area represents the probability that the reaction time (Y) will be between 300 and 400 milliseconds. For purposes of this example, reaction time is assumed to be normally distributed, although for real data this is not always the case.

High probability density means that quite small intervals of the random variable correspond to a relatively large area under the curve, and thus to an interval of relatively high probability. Similarly, high speed means that quite small time intervals correspond to large distances. For this reason, the 100-millisecond interval between 300

With continuous variables, probabilities can be represented by areas under the curve.

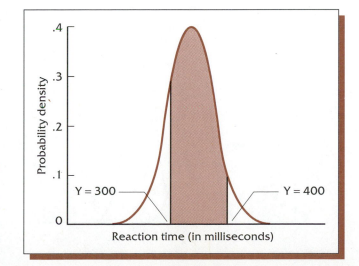

Figure 4.13
Probability density function for reaction time. The shaded area corresponds to the probability that reaction time (Y) will be between 300 and 400 milliseconds.

and 400 milliseconds corresponds to a much larger area than would the 100-millisecond interval between 200 and 300 milliseconds. Both represent an interval of 100 milliseconds, but the former interval spans a region of higher probability density.

The total area under a continuous probability distribution is 1.0.

Just as the probabilities in a discrete probability distribution must sum to 1, the total area under a continuous probability distribution is 1. This requirement reflects nothing more profound than the fact that the distribution covers all possible values of the variable Y. One implication of the total area being 1 is that if the area (probability) to the left of 300 milliseconds is found to be .2, for example, then the area (probability) to the right of 300 milliseconds is .8. This relationship makes obvious sense. If the probability that Y < 300 is .2, then the probability that Y > 300 must be 1 − .2 = .8.

Remember that the value 300 is a point on the continuum and therefore spans no area under the curve, just as a point in time spans no distance for a moving car. It thus makes no sense to ask about the probability that Y = 300.

4.3.4 Parameters of the Normal Distribution

The normal distribution is a family of curves, each member defined by the value of μ and σ.

Recall that the binomial distribution was actually a family of distributions, the exact form of the distribution depending on the values of n and p. The normal distribution is also a family of curves. In this case, the exact form of each distribution depends on two values with which we are quite familiar: the mean, μ, and the standard deviation, σ (or, equivalently, the variance, σ^2). Once μ and σ are specified, so too is the exact shape and location of the normal distribution. Figure 4.14 shows three normal distributions with the same standard deviation but different means. Figure 4.15 shows three normal distributions with the same mean but different standard deviations.

μ denotes population mean.

σ denotes standard deviation of the population.

The values of μ and σ define a unique normal distribution from among the family of normal distributions in the same way that the radius defines a unique circle from the family of circles, or the length and height define a unique rectangle. In all these cases, there is a mathematically defined form that requires a certain number of parameters to specify the family member uniquely. The normal curve and the rectangle require two parameters to make this unique specification. A circle or a square would require just one parameter.

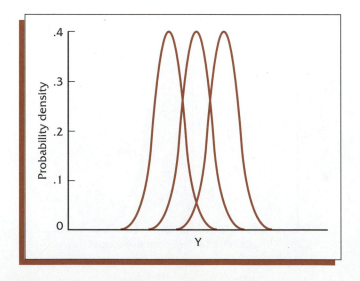

Figure 4.14
Three normal distributions, each with the same variance, but different means.

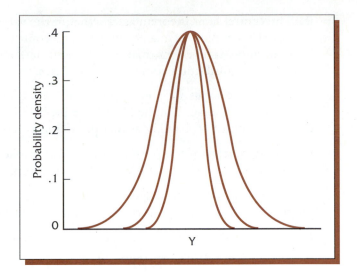

Figure 4.15
Three normal distributions, each with the same mean, but different variances.

No matter what the value of μ and σ, the normal distribution preserves its perfectly symmetrical bell-shaped form. Because of its symmetry, the mean, median, and mode of a normal distribution all have the same value (Figure 4.16), and this value is the point of maximum probability density. In fact, for a continuous distribution, the mode is defined as the point of maximum probability density—the peak of the distribution. Symmetry also implies that 50% of the area falls on either side of the mean.

Because of its symmetry, the mean, median, and mode of a normal distribution all have the same value.

Comprehension Check 4.3

Important Concepts

1. As n increases infinitely, the binomial distribution becomes a continuous variable with a symmetrical bell-shaped distribution. Known originally as the law of errors, its more familiar name is the normal distribution. Thus the probability distribution for a quincunx with infinitely many rows of pins is the normal distribution.

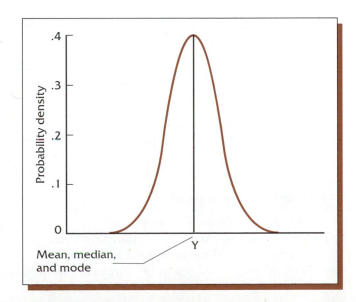

Figure 4.16
Normal distribution, showing the mean, median, and mode. Because the distribution is symmetrical, they all have the same value.

2. The central limit theorem asserts that, if the values of a variable are the net result of the addition of many independent contributions, then that variable will have an approximately normal distribution. The approximation improves as the number of contributing components increases.

3. For a continuous variable, a probability always refers to an interval of values, not to a point value. The height of the probability curve at a given point is the concentration of probability at that point and is referred to as probability density.

4. The symmetry of the normal distribution implies that the mean, median, and mode have the same value. The mode is the point of highest probability density.

5. The probability of a range of values is the area of the curve covered by that range. Thus $P(a < Y < b)$ is the area under the curve between a and b.

6. The normal distribution is a family of distributions. A distribution is defined uniquely by specifying the values of two parameters: the mean, μ, and the standard deviation, σ.

Worked Examples

Example 1   Driving time

Driving to work takes John an average of 25 minutes, although the time varies from one day to another. The number of traffic lights that John has to stop at determines this variation. The 20 traffic lights on the route are uncoordinated; they are red or green independently of one another.

a. Why would you expect the probability distribution of driving time to be a normal distribution?

b. What driving time has the highest probability density?

Answer

a. The variation in driving time is made up of the sum of 20 independent additive components, so the central limit theorem tells us that the resulting distribution will be normal. Whether a traffic light is green or red can be thought of as equivalent to tossing a coin: head there is no delay; tail adds 30 seconds to the trip.

b. The mean of this distribution is 25 minutes, and in the normal distribution the mean (which is also the median and mode) has the highest probability density.

Example 2   Arrival time

Suppose John (from Example 1) sets out to work 30 minutes before he needs to arrive. He would like to know the probability that he will arrive on or before the time he needs to arrive. What additional information would he need to know about the normal distribution that describes his travel time to answer this question?

Answer He needs to know the variance (or the standard deviation) for the normal distribution to be specified exactly.

Problems

Problem 1 Arrival time

Why does it make no sense to ask John (from Examples 1 and 2) to specify the probability that it will take him exactly 24.0 minutes to drive to work?

Problem 2 Examples of the central limit theorem

Try to think of another everyday example such as John's driving time that would result in a normal distribution through the operation of the central limit theorem. Identify the properties needed for the central limit theorem to be appropriate.

Problem 3 Distributions of height

For the height of adult men, $\mu = 69.0$ inches. Assuming that the distribution of height is symmetrical, what is the mode of this distribution? Which of the following 2-inch intervals would include the height of the greater number of men?

a. 68.0 to 70.0 inches
b. 64.0 to 66.0 inches

4.4 Obtaining Probabilities for Normally Distributed Variables

Section 4.3 introduced the general concept of probabilities as areas under a curve. This concept can be used to obtain the numerical values of probabilities for normally distributed random variables. The methods involve extensive use of the area representation of probability.

4.4.1 Areas Under the Normal Curve

If probabilities are represented by areas under the curve, then obtaining probabilities is a matter of finding the area that corresponds to the specified values of the random variable. For example, suppose Y represents the height of adult males in inches and is normally distributed with a mean of 69.0 inches and that we want to obtain the probability that a randomly chosen height will be greater than some designated value—say, 71.0 inches. This probability can be written P(Y > 71.0), where P is shorthand for the expression "the probability that." The probability can be represented graphically as all the area to the right of the value Y = 71.0. This representation of P(Y > 71.0) is shown in Figure 4.17.

P denotes "the probability that."

Similarly, the probability of the randomly selected height falling within the interval 66.0 to 71.0 inches, P(66.0 < Y < 71.0), is represented by the area of the shaded portion in Figure 4.18.

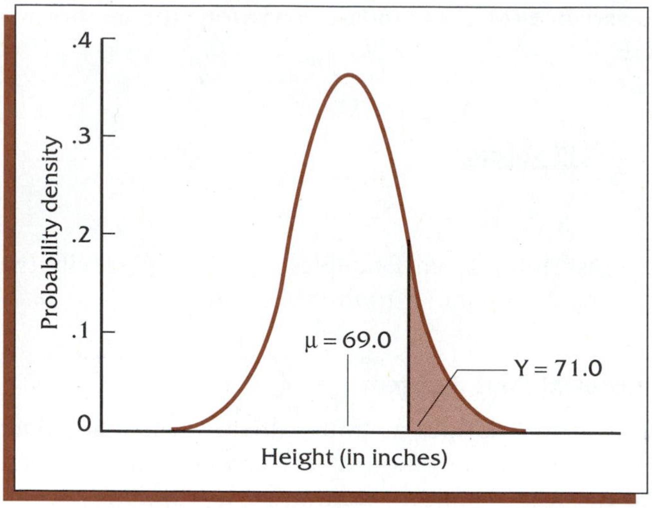

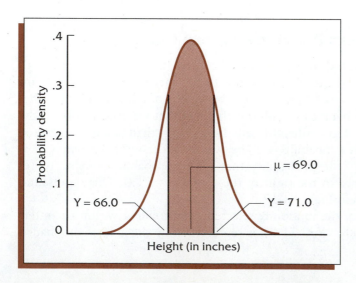

Figure 4.17
Normal distribution with a mean $\mu = 69.0$. The shaded area corresponds to the probability that the random variable, Y, is greater than 71.0.

Having given a graphical representation of probabilities for normally distributed random variables, the remaining task is to obtain these probabilities in precise numerical form. Our task is to calculate areas within a normal density curve such as the shaded portions of Figures 4.17 and 4.18. If you have completed a course in basic calculus, you might recognize this problem of calculating the area under a curve as a standard problem in the integral calculus. For those interested, the problem is set out in these terms in MathBox 4.2. However, even those expert in calculus would not use their skill to calculate the desired areas. The calculations are complex, and answers can be more easily obtained either from published tables or from computer packages. We will use a table of areas under the normal curve.

When publishing tables of the normal distribution, an obvious difficulty arises. Although normal distributions share a common general form, the exact form and location depends on the particular values of the standard deviation and the mean. Hence the possible number of distributions is infinite. The resolution of this difficulty is to publish tables for just one particular normal distribution: a distribution defined by particular values of the mean and standard deviation. These chosen values are a mean of 0 and a standard deviation of 1.0. You will recall from Section 2.3.2 that

The table of the normal distribution gives probabilities for a distribution with $\mu = 0$ and $\sigma = 1$.

Figure 4.18
Normal distribution with a mean $\mu = 69.0$. The shaded area corresponds to the probability that the random variable, Y, falls between 66.0 and 71.0.

MathBox 4.2

Areas Under the Normal Distribution

Students familiar with the integral calculus will know that, for continuous functions, areas are obtained by solving a definite integral. Areas between two values, a and b, of a continuous function $F(Y)$ are found by integrating the function between these two values.

$$A = \int_a^b F(Y)dY$$

Areas under the normal distribution are found in exactly this way. The function for the normal distribution expresses probability density $F(Y)$ for all values of Y over the range $-\infty$ to $+\infty$. The formula is

$$F(Y) = \frac{1}{\sigma\sqrt{2\pi}} e^{-\frac{1}{2}\left(\frac{Y-\mu}{\sigma}\right)^2}$$

where π and e are mathematical constants ($\pi = 3.1416\ldots$, $e = 2.7183\ldots$) and μ and σ are the mean and standard deviation, respectively.

For the standardized normal curve, $\mu = 0$ and $\sigma = 1$, so the function simplifies to

$$F(z) = \frac{1}{\sqrt{2\pi}} e^{\frac{-z^2}{2}}$$

If we wish to obtain the area under the normal curve between the two z-score values of z_1 and z_2, we would integrate this function between these two values. That is,

$$A = \int_{z_1}^{z_2} \frac{1}{\sqrt{2\pi}} e^{\frac{-z^2}{2}}$$

The solution to this definite integral is represented geometrically by the shaded portion in the figure.

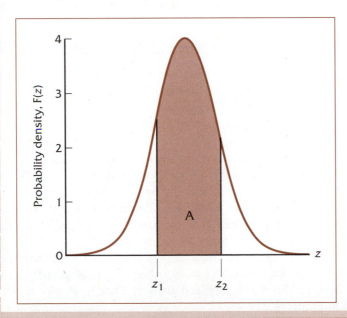

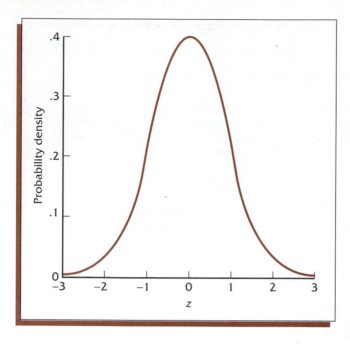

Figure 4.19
Standardized normal distribution. The random variable is designated z and has a mean $\mu = 0$ and a standard deviation $\sigma = 1$.

values of a variable that has a mean of 0 and a standard deviation of 1.0 are called standard scores and are usually designated by the letter z. Thus tables of the normal distribution give areas (probabilities) for normally distributed z-scores. The general strategy for obtaining areas under normal distributions of variables with various means and standard deviations is to convert these variables to standard score form, using the methods described in Section 2.3.2. Details of this strategy will be described after we have examined the normal distribution of standard scores.

Figure 4.19 shows a normal distribution of z-scores. Notice that the mean at the center of the distribution is 0. The values on the horizontal axis are standard scores. A score of $z = +1$, for example, represents a score one standard deviation above the mean; a score of $z = -1$ represents a score one standard deviation below the mean.

4.4.2 Using the Table of the Normal Curve: Standard Scores

We can use the table of the normal distribution to find areas (probabilities) for a specified range of z-scores. Tables of the normal distribution appear in a number of different formats in different textbooks. However, they all convey exactly the same information. The table in this book gives probabilities (areas) on each side of the particular value of z. Table 4.4 gives these values for a subset of z-values taken from the complete table in the Appendix and rounded to three decimal places. For example, a z-value of 1.0 has an area of .841 to the left of $z = 1$ and an area of .159 to the right (Figure 4.20). Notice that these two areas must sum to 1, the area under the entire distribution. Consequently, only one of the two columns is strictly needed, because the second column could be obtained by subtracting the value in the first column from 1. Both columns are provided simply as a convenience.

Table 4.4 enables us to obtain the probabilities associated with ranges of z-scores. For example, if we need to know the $P(z > .5)$, the table tells us that the area to the right of $z = .5$ is .309, so this is the required answer. That is, $P(z > .5) = .309$. This result is illustrated in Figure 4.21.

Table 4.4 Portion of the table of the normal distribution, showing probabilities (areas) to the left and right of various z-scores

z	Area to the left of z	Area to the right of z
0.00	.500	.500
0.10	.540	.460
0.20	.579	.421
0.30	.618	.382
0.40	.655	.345
0.50	.691	.309
0.60	.726	.274
0.70	.758	.242
0.80	.788	.212
0.90	.816	.184
1.00	.841	.159
1.10	.864	.136
1.20	.885	.115
1.30	.903	.097
1.40	.919	.081
1.50	.933	.067
1.60	.945	.055
1.70	.955	.045
1.80	.964	.036
1.90	.971	.029
2.00	.977	.023

The shaded row indicates that a z-score of 1.0 has an area of .841 to the left and .159 to the right.

Notice that Table 4.4 gives only positive values of z. Because of the symmetry of the distribution, probabilities associated with negative values of z can easily be obtained by using their positive counterparts. First, ignoring the minus sign, consult the table. Then reverse the two columns: for negative values of z, the value in the "area to the right" column is, in fact, the area to the left; the value in the "area to the left" column is, in fact, the area to the right. As an example, the probability that $z > -.5$ is .691. This relationship between positive and negative values of z is illustrated in Figures 4.21 and 4.22.

Consider next probabilities associated with an interval of z-scores—for example, $P(.5 < z < 1.5)$. The diagram for this problem is shown in Figure 4.23. The method of obtaining the area in the shaded portion consists of three simple steps:

Probabilities for negative values of z can be obtained by reversing the columns.

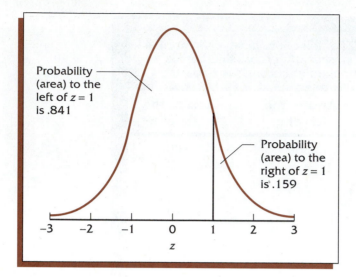

Probability (area) to the left of $z = 1$ is .841

Probability (area) to the right of $z = 1$ is .159

Figure 4.20
Standardized normal distribution, showing probabilities (areas) to the left and right of a z-score of 1.0. Note the values in row for $z = 1$ in Table 4.4.

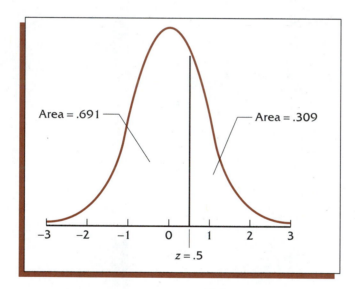

Area = .691

Area = .309

$z = .5$

Figure 4.21
Normal z-score distribution, showing areas to the left of $z = +.5$ [$P(z < +.5)$] and to the right of $z = +.5$ [$P(z > +.5)$].

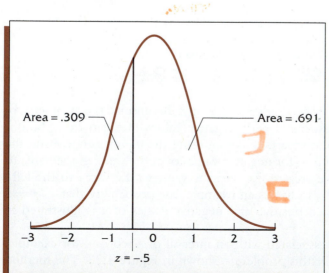

Area = .309

Area = .691

$z = -.5$

Figure 4.22
Normal z-score distribution, showing areas to the left of $z = -.5$ [$P(z < -.5)$] and to the right of $z = -.5$ [$P(z > -.5)$].

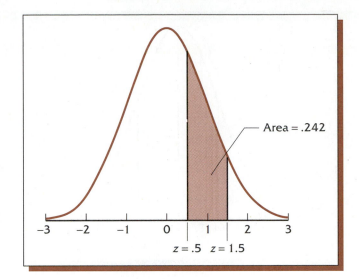

Figure 4.23
Normal z-score distribution,
showing the area
corresponding to
P(.5 < z < 1.5).

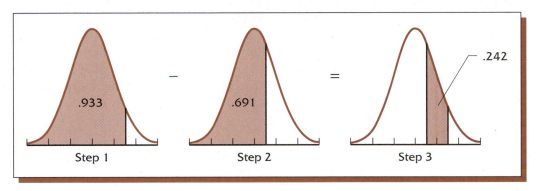

Figure 4.24
Obtaining the area between two values by subtracting the area below the lower value from the
area below the higher value.

Step 1 From the table, read off the area to the left of z = 1.5. This gives a value
of .933.

Step 2 Read off the area to the left of 0.5. This gives a value of .691.

Step 3 The difference between these two values corresponds to the shaded area
and the required answer. That is,

$$P(.5 < z < 1.5) = .933 - .691 = .242$$

These steps are illustrated in Figure 4.24.

Example
Obtain the following probabilities in a normal distribution of z-scores.

$$P(0 < z < +1.0) \qquad P(-1.0 < z < 0)$$
$$P(1.0 < z < 2.0) \qquad P(-2.0 < z < -1.0)$$
$$P(z > +2.0) \qquad P(z < -2.0)$$

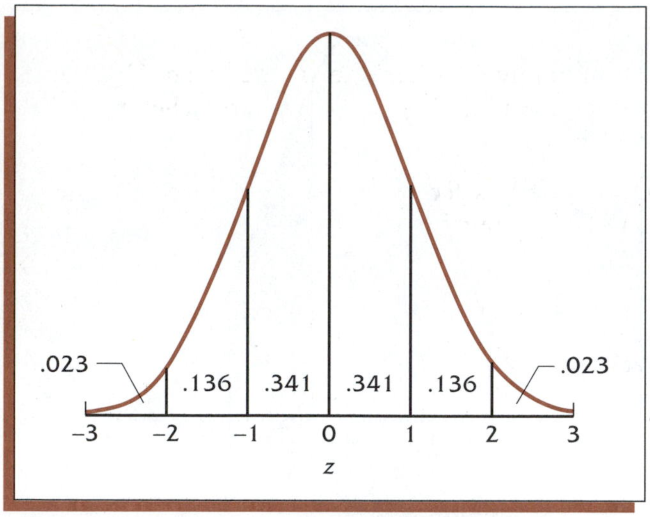

Figure 4.25
Standardized normal distribution marked off in standard deviation units.

The question can be diagrammed as shown in Figure 4.25. The question asks for the area of each panel of this figure. Note that because of symmetry, we need to calculate areas on only one side of the distribution.

The area between $z = 0$ and $z = +1.0$ is found by subtracting the total area to the left of the mean from the area to the left of $z = 1$. The area to the left of the mean is .5, and the area to the left of $z = +1.0$ is .841. This gives the desired area of $.841 - .500 = .341$. By symmetry, the area between $z = 0$ and $z = -1.0$ is also .341.

The area between $z = +1.0$ and $z = +2.0$ is found by subtracting the area to the left of $z = +1.0$ from the area left of $z = +2.0$. This operation gives an area of $.977 - .841 = .136$. By symmetry, the area between $z = -1.0$ and $z = -2.0$ is also .136.

Finally, the area to the right of $z = +2$ can be read directly from the table, a value of .023. Alternatively, it can be calculated by subtracting the area to the left of $z = 2.0$ from the distribution's total area of 1.0. By symmetry, the area to the left of $z = -2.0$ is also .023.

As a check on these calculations, note that the three areas sum to .500 (.341 + .136 + .023). In summary, we can claim the following about all normal distributions.

■ Approximately 68% of cases fall within a standard deviation on either side of the mean (34% on each side).

■ A further 27% of cases fall between one and two standard deviations from the mean (13.6% on each side).

■ Approximately 5% fall in the extreme tails beyond two standard deviations from the mean.

4.4.3 Using the Table of the Normal Curve: Non-Standard Scores

Now let's consider the general case of normally distributed variables that are not expressed as standard scores. Consider height of adult men as an example. Assume that the height of adult men is normally distributed, with a mean of $\mu = 69.0$ inches and a standard deviation of $\sigma = 3.0$ inches.

We would like to answer questions such as

■ What is the probability that a randomly selected man is taller than 72.0 inches? Equivalently, what proportion of men in the population are taller than 72.0 inches?

■ What is the probability that a randomly selected man is taller than 65.0 inches? Equivalently, what proportion of men are taller than 65.0 inches?

■ What is the probability that a randomly selected man is shorter than 68.0 inches? Equivalently, what proportion of men are shorter than 68.0 inches?

■ What is the probability that a randomly selected man is between 67.0 and 71.0 inches tall? Stated more precisely, what is $P(67.0 \leq \text{height} \leq 71.0)$? Equivalently, what proportion of men are between 67.0 and 71.0 inches tall?

Each of these four questions is answered by converting the relevant heights from inches to standard scores and then using the full table of the normal distribution (Statistical Table 1) to obtain the appropriate area. Thus a height of 72.0 inches becomes

$$z = \frac{72.0 - 69.0}{3.0} = \frac{3.0}{3.0} = 1.0$$

(handwritten annotation: *mean* pointing to 69.0)

Consulting Statistical Table 1 of the normal distribution for $z = 1.0$, we find that $P(z > 1.0) = .1587$. Rounding to two decimal places, we find that the proportion of heights greater than 72.0 inches is .16. That is, the probability is .16 that a randomly chosen man will be taller than 72.0 inches. Equivalently, we could say that approximately 16% of men are taller than 72.0 inches.

Similarly, the proportion of men who are taller than 65.0 inches is found by converting this height to a z-score.

$$z = \frac{65.0 - 69.0}{3.0} = \frac{-4.0}{3.0} = -1.33$$

Consulting Statistical Table 1, we find $P(z > -1.33) = .9082$. That is, approximately 91% of men are taller than 65.0 inches.

To find the probability that a randomly selected man is shorter than 68.0 inches, we obtain

$$z = \frac{68.0 - 69.0}{3.0} = \frac{-1.0}{3.0} = -0.33$$

Consulting Statistical Table 1, we find $P(z < -0.33) = .3707$; so this value is the probability that a randomly selected man is shorter than 68 inches. In other words, approximately 37% of men are shorter than 68 inches.

To find $P(67.0 < \text{height} < 71.0)$, we need to convert both heights to z-scores. In any of these problems, but especially with those involving intervals, it is helpful to sketch a rough diagram of the required interval (Figure 4.26). Converting first the lower value of 67.0 inches, we have

$$z = \frac{67.0 - 69.0}{3.0} = \frac{-2.0}{3.0} = -0.67$$

Probabilities for non–z-scores are found by converting the scores to standardized form.

It is helpful to sketch a rough diagram of the required interval.

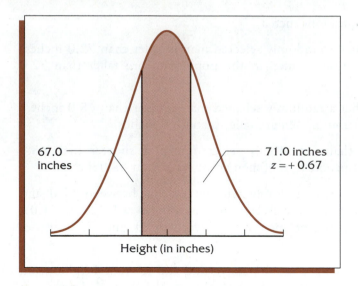

Height (in inches)

Figure 4.26
Normal distribution for height. The shaded area represents P(67.0 < height < 71.0).

Then the upper value is

$$z = \frac{71.0 - 69.0}{3.0} = \frac{2.0}{3.0} = +0.67$$

From Statistical Table 1 we find that the area to the left of $z = +0.67$ is .7486. The area to the left of $z = -0.67$ is .2514. The shaded area is the difference between these two values. That is,

$$P(-.67 < z < +.67) = .7486 - .2514 = .4972$$

Another way of making this calculation is to note that the required area is the total area of the curve (1.0) less the combined nonshaded area in the two tails. This calculation gives the required area as $1.0 - (2)(.2514) = .4972$. We can conclude that approximately 50% of men are between 67.0 and 71.0 inches tall.

4.4.4 Obtaining Scores That Mark Off Designated Probabilities

Suppose we wish to answer the following questions.

■ How tall does a man need to be in order to be among the tallest 10% of men in the population?

■ A clothing store claims to cater to "unusually tall" and "unusually short" men. If "unusual" is defined as heights in the top and bottom 5% of the distribution, what range of heights would be classified as "usual"?

These questions differ from those previously considered in that they provide a probability and ask for a score that marks off that area. Previous questions have been the exact reverse, providing a score and asking a question about probability. Not surprisingly, then, answering this new form of question is a matter of following the same steps in the reverse order.

Step 1 Use the table of the normal distribution to find the z-score corresponding to the probability or proportion specified in the problem.

Step 2 Transform the z-score into the scale defined in the problem—height in inches, for example.

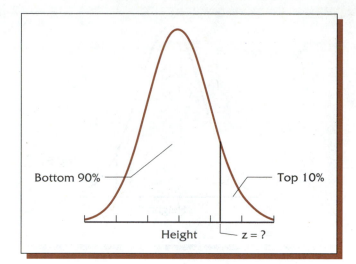

Figure 4.27
Normal distribution divided into top 10% and bottom 90%.

Consider the question of how tall a man needs to be in order to be among the tallest 10% of all men. For this question and others, it is helpful to sketch a diagram of the problem (Figure 4.27). To find the required value of z that marks off the top 10%, we consult the table of the normal distribution (Statistical Table 1). Instead of starting with the column of z-scores, as we did before, we start with the column areas. The required z-score marks off an area 90% to the left and 10% to the right. We find this value by scanning down the area columns until we reach the area closest to the .90/.10 split and then reading off the corresponding z-score. In this case, the z-value is 1.28. This is the z-score that marks off 90% to its left and 10% to its right.

The final step is to convert the z-score of 1.28 to height in inches. The method is to reverse the steps involved in calculating a z-score. Recall that

$$z = \frac{Y - \mu}{\sigma}$$

This equation states that, to convert a raw score to a z-score, we subtract the mean ($\mu = 69.0$ inches) and divide by the standard deviation ($\sigma = 3.0$ inches).

Rearranging the terms of this equation gives

$$z \times \sigma = Y - \mu$$

and thus

$$Y = \mu + (z \times \sigma)$$ *z-score to scale*

Now we *first multiply* by the standard deviation and *then add* the mean. Thus a z-score of 1.28 becomes a height score of $(1.28 \times 3.0) + 69.0 = 72.84$. The answer to the original question is that a man must be taller than 72.84 inches to be among the top 10%.

Rather than attempting to memorize this equation as an abstract formula, think of the preceding operation in the following terms. The z-value of 1.28 tells us that the required height is 1.28 standard deviations above the mean of 69.0 inches. Each standard deviation unit is 3.0 inches, so 1.28 standard deviation units is 1.28 times 3.0, or 3.84 inches. Thus the required height is 3.84 inches above the mean, which is $69 + 3.84$, or 72.84 inches. In brief, the formula says, to obtain the score, simply add (or subtract if z is negative) z standard deviation units to the mean.

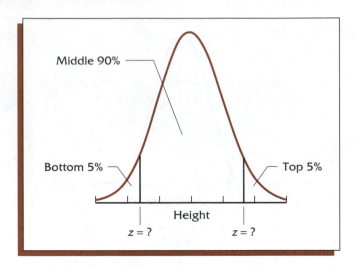

Figure 4.28
Normal distribution divided into a middle area of 90%, with 5% in each tail.

The second problem asks for the range of heights that marks off usual from unusual heights, where unusual is taken to mean those heights falling into the top and bottom 5% of the distribution. The problem is sketched in Figure 4.28.

What z-score marks off the top 5%? Consulting the table in the Appendix and scanning the area columns, we find that the exact value .95 is not listed. We find that a z-value of 1.64 marks off 94.9% to the left and 5.1% to the right, and the next z-value in the table, 1.65, marks off 95.1% to the left and 4.9% to the right. In short, our required value is somewhere between 1.64 and 1.65. In such cases, where both z-values are equally close, either 1.64 or 1.65 can be used. Alternatively, an interpolated value of 1.645 could be used. We will use a value of $z = 1.64$ for the present example.

We now know that the height that marks off the top 5% is 1.64 standard deviation units above the mean. By symmetry, the score that marks off the *bottom* 5% is 1.64 standard deviation units *below* the mean ($z = -1.64$). Because $\sigma = 3.0$, a z-score of 1.64 corresponds to $3.0 \times 1.64 = 4.92$ inches. Thus the upper cutoff value is 4.92 inches above the mean of 69.0 and the lower cutoff is 4.92 inches below the mean. In other words, a range of 69.0 ± 4.92 (the interval 64.08 inches to 73.92 inches) is the "usual" range, with heights outside this interval deemed "unusual" (Figure 4.29). The interval of usual height is a height within 4.92 inches of the mean.

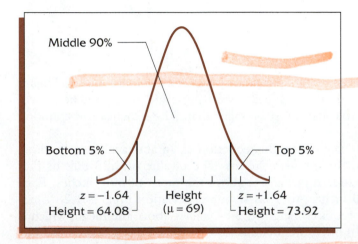

Figure 4.29
Normal distribution of height, showing the interval that defines the middle 90% of the distribution and the extremes of height defined as the top and bottom 5% of heights.

Comprehension Check 4.4

Important Concepts

1. Tables of the normal distribution give areas (probabilities) for a distribution with a mean of 0 and a standard deviation of 1.0. As noted previously, such scores are termed z-scores.

2. Probabilities for distributions not expressed as z-scores can be obtained by converting the original scores to z-scores.

3. Scores that mark off designated probabilities in a normal distribution can be obtained by reversing the order of the steps used to calculate probabilities for designated scores.

Worked Examples

Example 1 **Probabilities for normally distributed z-scores**

A table of the normal distribution gives values for scores with a mean of 0 and a standard deviation of 1.0. Example 1 involves the direct use of the tabulated values for such z-scores. Except for example (a), use the table of the normal distribution in the Appendix to find the requested probabilities. Why can (a) be answered without reference to the tables?

a. $P(z > 0.0)$ **e.** $P(-1.0 < z < 1.0)$
b. $P(z < 1.0)$ **f.** $P(-1.5 < z < 1.5)$
c. $P(z > 1.0)$ **g.** $P(0.0 < z < 1.0)$
d. $P(z > 0.5)$ **h.** $P(1.0 < z < 2.0)$

Answers If any of the following answers and their brief explanations are unclear, consult Section 4.4.2. In many of these problems, there is more than one way of arriving at the correct answer. For example, in calculating the shaded area in Figure 4.26, two equivalent methods were shown.

a. $P(z > 0.0) = .5$ (no table is needed because 0.0 is the mean and the normal distribution is symmetrical)

b. $P(z < 1.0) = .8413$ (obtained directly from table)

c. $P(z > 1.0) = .1587$ (obtained directly from table)

d. $P(z > 0.5) = .3085$ (obtained directly from table)

e. $P(-1.0 < z < 1.0) = .6826$ [$1.00 - (2 \times .1587)$, or equivalently, $.8413 - .1587$]

f. $P(-1.5 < z < 1.5) = .8664$ [$1.00 - (2 \times .0668)$, or equivalently, $.9332 - .0668$]

g. $P(0.0 < z < 1.0) = .3413$ ($.8413 - .5$)

h. $P(1.0 < z < 2.0) = .1359$ ($.9772 - .8413$)

Example 2   **Probabilities for a normally distributed variable, Y**

a. A variable, Y, has a normal distribution, a mean $\mu = 12.4$, and a standard deviation $\sigma = 3.8$. Find $P(Y > 7.0)$.

b. A variable, Y, has a normal distribution, a mean $\mu = 100$, and a standard deviation $\sigma = 14$. Find $P(90.0 < Y < 110.0)$.

Answer Both these problems are answered by converting the values of Y to z-scores.

a.

$$z = \frac{7.0 - 12.4}{3.8} = -1.42$$

From the table of the normal distribution, $P(z > -1.42) = .9222$.

b. Note that this question asks for the probability that Y is within 10 units on either side of the mean. For $Y = 90$,

$$z = \frac{90.0 - 100.0}{14.0} = -0.71$$

From the table of the normal distribution, $P(z < -0.71) = .2389$. For $Y = 110$,

$$z = \frac{110.0 - 100.0}{14.0} = +0.71.$$

From the table of the normal distribution, $P(z > +0.71) = .2389$.
The $P(90.0 < Y < 110.0) = 1.00 - .2389 - .2389 = .5222$ (Figure 4.30).

Example 3   **Quartiles of the normal distribution**

Suppose that, in a given population, the height of adult males is normally distributed with a mean of 69.0 inches and a standard deviation of 3.0 inches.

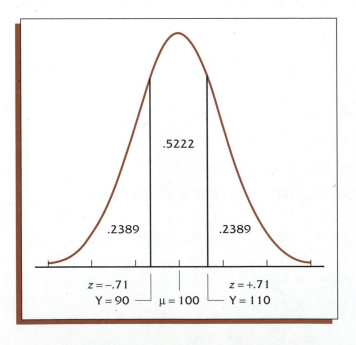

Figure 4.30
Normal distribution of the variable Y showing the interval between Y = 90 and Y = 110.

a. What are the first and third quartiles of this distribution of height?

b. What is the interquartile range of this distribution?

Answer

a. Recall that the first and third quartiles of the distribution are scores that leave 25% of the area in each tail. The first step is to establish the z-scores that correspond to the two quartiles. The third quartile marks off .75 below its value and .25 above. We therefore need a z-score corresponding to $P(z) = .75$ and $1 - P(z) = .25$. The closest tabled z-score is 0.67. By symmetry, the first quartile is a z-score of -0.67. The next step is to convert these z-scores to height measured in inches. To convert from z scores to inches with a standard deviation of 3.0, we multiply by 3.0. Thus .67 z-score unit corresponds to .67 × 3.0 = 2.0 inches. The third quartile is 2.0 inches above the mean of 69.0 and the first quartile is 2.0 inches below the mean. Hence, $Q_1 = 67.0$ inches and $Q_3 = 71.0$ inches.

b. $IQR = Q_3 - Q_1 = 71.0 - 67.0 = 4.0$ inches

Problems

Problem 1 Probabilities for normally distributed z-scores

The variable z has a normal distribution with $\mu = 0$ and $\sigma = 1.0$. Work out the requested probabilities.

a. $P(z < -1.0)$ **g.** $P(-1.5 < z < -0.5)$

b. $P(z < 0.5)$ **h.** $P(-.67 < z < .67)$

c. $P(z < -1.5)$ **i.** $P(-1.65 < z < 1.65)$

d. $P(z > -0.5)$ **j.** $P(-2.0 < z < 2.0)$

e. $P(z < -0.7)$ **k.** $P(-.25 < z < .25)$

f. $P(z < 1.96)$ **l.** $P(-1.96 < z < 1.96)$

Problem 2 Probability for a normally distributed variable, Y

Work out the values of the requested probabilities for the following normally distributed variables, which have different means (μ_Y) and standard deviations σ_Y.

a. $\mu_Y = 5.0,$ $\sigma_Y = 2.0,$ $P(Y > 7.0)$

b. $\mu_Y = 2.0,$ $\sigma_Y = 1.5,$ $P(Y > 5.0)$

c. $\mu_Y = 20.0,$ $\sigma_Y = 4.0,$ $P(Y < 16.0)$

d. $\mu_Y = 12.0,$ $\sigma_Y = 3.0,$ $P(Y > 9.0)$

e. $\mu_Y = 6.0,$ $\sigma_Y = 2.5,$ $P(Y > 10.0)$

f. $\mu_Y = -2.0,$ $\sigma_Y = 4.0,$ $P(Y > 0.0)$

g. $\mu_Y = 42.0,$ $\sigma_Y = 10.0,$ $P(Y > 50.0)$

h. $\mu_Y = 11.0$, $\sigma_Y = 2.5$, $P(Y < 6.1)$

i. $\mu_Y = 17.3$, $\sigma_Y = 2.7$, $P(Y > 20.0)$

j. $\mu_Y = 18.4$, $\sigma_Y = 2.7$, $P(16.8 < Y < 20.0)$

k. $\mu_Y = 10.0$, $\sigma_Y = 4.0$, $P(8.0 < Y < 12.0)$

l. $\mu_Y = 4.0$, $\sigma_Y = 0.5$, $P(3.5 < Y < 4.5)$

m. $\mu_Y = 6.7$, $\sigma_Y = 1.3$, $P(4.7 < Y < 8.7)$

n. $\mu_Y = 87.0$, $\sigma_Y = 12.2$, $P(74.0 < Y < 100.0)$

o. $\mu_Y = 14.3$, $\sigma_Y = 2.4$, $P(9.6 < Y < 19.0)$

p. $\mu_Y = 50.0$, $\sigma_Y = 9.0$, $P(44.0 < Y < 56.0)$

q. $\mu_Y = 30.0$, $\sigma_Y = 3.9$, $P(25.0 < Y < 35.0)$

r. $\mu_Y = 45.0$, $\sigma_Y = 6.3$, $P(40.0 < Y < 50.0)$

Problem 3 **Deciles of a normal distribution**

A training program has developed an aptitude test to help with the award of admission scholarships. Scores on this test have a normal distribution with a mean of $\mu = 50.0$ and a standard deviation of $\sigma = 8.0$. The test is used in the following way. Applicants who score in the bottom 60% are not considered further. Applicants who score in the top 10% (above the ninth decile) are offered a scholarship automatically. Students in the top 20% (above the eighth decile) but not in the top 10% are placed on a waiting list and will receive a scholarship if a sufficient number of first offers are declined. Applicants in the top 40% (above the sixth decile) but not in the top 20% are given an interview to determine whether their names might be added to the waiting list. What are the aptitude test scores that define the criterion points corresponding to the sixth, eighth, and ninth deciles? Deciles were defined in Section 2.2.1.

4.5 Normal Distribution as a Model for Residuals

This chapter began with the promise of bringing a measure of understanding and order to the chaotic behavior that characterizes residuals. This understanding and order is based on two assumptions.

Residuals are assumed to be normally and independently distributed.

■ The residuals are independent of one another. This assumption implies that the size of a residual for one observation is uninfluenced by the size of any other method.

■ The residuals have a normal distribution.

A succinct way of stating these assumptions is to say that the residuals are assumed to be normally and independently distributed.

We have described how the normal distribution provides a plausible model of the behavior of residuals—and many natural phenomena as well. Residuals have been tamed in the sense that by modeling them as a normally distributed random variable, we can make probability statements about their effects. However, to obtain probabilities for a normal distribution, it is necessary to know its mean and variance.

4.5.1 Parameters of the Distribution of Residuals

The population variance of the distribution of residuals, σ_e^2, will usually be unknown. The way around this difficulty is to estimate its value from the data. As shown in Chapter 3, this estimate of a population variance for a single sample of scores is s^2, the sum of squared residuals divided by $n - 1$. To have a complete model of the residuals, we also need to specify the mean of the distribution. On this matter, we make the following important assumption: The mean of the distribution of residuals is assumed to be 0.

This assumption is not an obscure theoretical nicety, but one of great practical importance. The assumption amounts to the claim that the residuals are *unbiased*. The term *unbiased* was introduced in Chapter 1. In the present context, unbiased means that the residuals have no *systematic* tendency to increase or decrease the value of each observation—that their long-run influence is neutral or even-handed. For the quincunx, the absence of bias corresponds to the balls deflecting left or right with equal probability; hence, in the long run, the number of left deflections is balanced by the number of right deflections.

A situation in which this assumption of zero mean was violated would be one in which the net impact of the residuals was not neutral. Consider the example of a driver's reaction time to apply the brakes. Bias implies that the uncontrolled influences that make up the residuals constitute a systematic influence that tends either to increase or decrease the measured reaction time relative to its true value. If, for example, the bias is on the plus side, then the observed values will tend to be larger than they should be and the mean residual would be more likely to be a positive number than a negative one. It would be as if balls in the quincunx were more likely to deflect right than left.

As a concrete example of how bias might enter into an experiment, consider again the measurement of reaction time to apply a car's brakes. An important condition of this experiment is that the driver does not know when to expect the appearance of the object that signals the need to apply the brakes. Suppose, however, that the equipment is constructed in such a fashion that the appearance of the object is preceded by the sound of a mechanical switch that starts the mechanism to display the object. Observers will quickly learn to use this sound as a warning signal that the object is about to appear. The effect of this signal will be to exert a bias that will shorten the average reaction time relative to that obtained with equipment that produced no such signal.

How does an investigator ensure that the residuals are unbiased—that their true mean is zero? Eliminating bias from observations is a task for sound experimental design, something that must be done as part of the data-gathering process. Once the data have been gathered, it is extremely difficult—and usually impossible—to eliminate bias through methods of statistical data analysis. This point is a further example of the more general principle that statistical data analysis is not a remedy for bad experimental design.

The treatment of residuals as a random variable leads to a final comment about our previously used metaphor of signal and noise. For the methods we will discuss, noise can now be defined quite rigorously. Noise is a random variable with a normal distribution, a mean of 0, and a variance that is usually unknown but can be estimated from the data. An important goal in designing an experiment is to ensure that uncontrolled influences behave like noise in this sense. The sinister property of bias is that, because it exerts a steady, systematic influence, it is an unwanted influence that has assumed the guise of a signal. In fact, its disguise is so effective that in most cases statistical data analysis cannot even detect its presence, let alone eliminate it.

The mean distribution is assumed to be 0.

The impact of residuals is unbiased if the population mean of the residuals is 0.

Eliminating bias is a matter of sound experimental method.

4.5.2 Distribution of Response Measures

For measures of a single variable, the distributions of e and Y can be treated as the same.

The basic model with which the chapter began was $Y = \mu + e$ and its fitted counterpart, $Y = \overline{Y} + e$. We now know that the residual portion of these models, e, will be assumed to have a normal distribution with a mean of 0 and a variance σ_e^2, which can be estimated from the data.

As pointed out in Section 3.1.2, the variance of the residuals is also the variance of the scores. Another way of expressing this relationship is to say that the variability of the response measures (Y) is attributable entirely to the uncontrolled influences reflected in the residuals. As the model states, Y is simply e with an added constant, and adding a constant does not change the variance. Similarly, adding a constant does not change the shape of a distribution, so if e has a normal distribution, then Y will also have a normal distribution.

The important consequence of these relationships is that we can refer to the distributions of e and Y interchangeably. And, as just mentioned, we can also refer to their variances interchangeably. This interchangeability is convenient, because it is usually more straightforward to refer to the distribution and variance of the observations themselves (Y) than to those of the residuals. Furthermore, we can use the same terminology for measures of attributes (such as height or ability measures) that we may not wish to model in terms of residuals. To repeat a point made previously, the difference between a response variable such as reaction time and a measured attribute such as height is merely in how we interpret the source of variability. In the case of reaction time, the source of variability is viewed as uncontrolled influences. In the case of height, the source of variability is viewed as naturally occurring individual differences. But in both cases, the net outcome is a normally distributed random variable.

Comprehension Check 4.5

Important Concepts

1. Residuals are assumed to be normally and independently distributed.

2. To be able to make probability statements, we will need to know the mean and standard deviation of the normal distribution.

3. The standard deviation will usually be unknown. The way around this difficulty will be to estimate its value from the data.

4. The mean of the residuals will be assumed to be 0. This assumption is of great practical importance; it is equivalent to the assumption that the residuals are unbiased. Ensuring the absence of bias is a matter of sound experimental design.

5. For a single set of observations, the distribution of the response measures and the distribution of the residuals, are distributions with the same shape and variance.

Chapter 4 Exercises

Exercise 1 Percentile ranks of SAT scores

Scores on the Scholastic Aptitude Test (SAT) are scaled to have a mean of $\mu = 500$ and a standard deviation $\sigma = 100$. They are assumed to have a normal distribution.

a. Convert the following student scores to percentile ranks. That is, find the percentage of cases that fall below each of the scores. The first score is worked out as an example.

640   550   480   370   680

Sample Answer A score of 640 converts to a z-score of $(640 - 500)/100 = 1.40$. Consulting the table of the normal distribution shows a z-score of 1.40 has a value $P(z)$ of .9192. Multiplying by 100 and rounding to the nearest whole number, we get a percentile rank of 92; 92% of scores are lower than 640, 8% are higher.

b. Which SAT scores mark the first and third quartiles of the distribution? What is the interquartile range *(IQR)* for SAT scores?

c. What are the nine SAT scores that mark the nine decile ranks of the SAT distribution? The first decile is worked out as an example.

Sample Answer The first decile marks off the bottom 10% from the top 90% of scores. The z-score that achieves this can be found from the tables of the normal distribution. Take $P(z) = .9$ and note that z is negative. It gives $z = -1.28$. That is, the first decile is 1.28 standard deviations below the mean, or $1.28 \times 100 = 128$ SAT score units below the mean. Thus $d_1 = 500 - 128 = 372$.

Exercise 2   IQ scores

IQ scores have a mean of $\mu = 100$ and a standard deviation of $\sigma = 15$. Note that these values of μ and σ are not some curious natural phenomenon; these values are conventions, and intelligence tests are intentionally scaled to these values by applying the methods described in Section 2.3.3.

a. A school board decides to identify students in the top 5% of the IQ range for a special program. What is the minimum IQ score needed to be classified in the top 5%?

b. What is the interquartile range *(IQR)* for IQ scores?

7	34	
7	5799	
8	00222334	
8	55558999	$Q_1 = 91.50$
9	00123333444	
9	566777899	$Md = 102.00$
10	01112222234	
10	555556667778888899999	$Q_3 = 109.50$
11	00334	
11	667788	
12	011333	
12	6899	
13	13	
13	89	

Figure 4.31
Stemplot for Exercise 3.

c. An investigator seeking to evaluate the difficulty level of some new software decides to evaluate it by using students "in the normal IQ range." This range is defined as IQ scores of 90 to 110. What percentage of students fall in this range? Consider scores of 90 and 110 to be within this range.

Exercise 3 Sample and theoretical quartiles

Figure 4.31 shows the stemplot for the IQ scores for A-twins from the IQ scores for 100 pairs of monozygotic (identical) twins reared apart (Data Set 2.17). In Exercise 2, you established the theoretical (population) value of Q_1 and Q_3 for a distribution of IQ scores. Use the stemplot for the A-twins of this data set to check the given values of Q_1 and Q_3. Compare these sample values with the theoretical values and comment on any differences.

Chapter 4 Review

Terms

- binomial distribution
- central limit theorem
- continuous random variable
- discrete random variable
- elementary event
- independence
- law of large numbers
- mutually exclusive
- normal distribution
- parameters of normal distribution
- probability as long-run relative frequency
- probability density
- probability distribution
- random sample
- random selection
- random variable
- unbiased

Formulas

Obtaining a score that marks off a designated probability: $Y = \mu + (z \times \sigma)$

Quiz

Question 1

Complete each sentence with a term from the following list. The same term may be used more than once.

discrete random	continuous random	binomial
law of large numbers	long-run relative frequency	probability density
normal distribution	parameters	

A variable is defined as the number of heads obtained when a coin is tossed ten times. This variable is an example of a _____ variable. The probability distribution of this variable is a _____ distribution. Even if the coin is fair, the ten tosses will not always result in exactly 50% heads and 50% tails. The _____ tells us that obtaining 60% or more heads is less likely for 100 tosses than for 10 tosses. This result is based on an interpretation of probability as _____.

Probability distributions can be defined for variables such as height, weight, and IQ. These variables are examples of _____ variables and, like many natural attributes, their probability distribution has the form of a _____. Such a distribution is uniquely specified by two _____: the mean and the variance. The height of the distribution at any point is known as the _____ at that value of the variable.

Question 2

Decide whether each of the following statements is true or false.

a. In a normal distribution, the mean and median are always the same.

b. In a normal distribution, the probability density is greater at $z = +1.0$ than at $z = +0.2$.

c. In a normal distribution, the probability that $z > .2$ is greater than the probability that $z < -.2$.

d. The total area under a probability distribution is always 1.0.

e. The binomial distribution is always symmetrical.

Chapter 5 Preview

The task of Chapter 5 is to take the normal distribution model of residuals and use it to obtain more information about the value of the unknown mean, μ. We need to move beyond a simple point estimate such as $\overline{Y}$, and be able to say something about just how close this estimate is to μ. Statements such as

> *It is almost certain that the estimate of 650 milliseconds is within 50 milliseconds of the true value.*

are more informative than statements such as

> *The best estimate is 650 milliseconds, but how close it might be to the true value is unknown.*

The payoff from our normal distribution model of the residuals is that it will enable us to make this more informative kind of statement about the difference between $\overline{Y}$ and μ.

5 SAMPLING DISTRIBUTIONS AND INTERVAL ESTIMATION

Chapter 4 described how residuals can be treated as a normally distributed random variable and how other variables such as height or test scores might also be normally distributed. In Chapter 5, we will use this result to obtain a new kind of estimate of the parameter μ, an estimate that is more informative than the point estimate $\overline{Y}$. This new form of estimate, known as an interval estimate, will be expressed in probabilistic terms. The interval that provides this estimate is called a confidence interval.

Unlike the point estimate, which consists of a single value, the interval estimate consists of a *range* of values. This range is one that we can claim "probably" includes the value of μ. Informal versions of confidence intervals are used in everyday discussions to express estimates of various quantities. If asked to estimate the age of an instructor, you might guess 40, but not being sure that she is exactly 40, you might reply, "somewhere between 38 and 42 years" or "40, give or take 2 years," and feel quite confident that this range includes the true value. A formal version of this confidence interval adds an explicit level of confidence expressed as a probability. The formal version of our age estimate might take the form, "The probability is .95 that the interval 40 ± 2 (or 38 to 42) years contains the instructor's true age."

The goal, then, is to calculate such interval estimates for μ. Before we can do this, there is one important conceptual step that must be taken: We must be able to make probability statements about possible values of $\overline{Y}$.

5.1 Sampling Distribution of the Mean

The following set of data will be used in our exposition of the sampling distribution of the mean.

Braking Reaction Time

Data for the braking reaction time was presented at the beginning of Chapter 4. These data were used as a prototypical example of an investigator attempting to obtain measurements under carefully controlled conditions. The investigator made ten observations:

| 661 | 605 | 642 | 704 | 662 | 770 | 741 | 626 | 713 | 636 |

The response measure is time measured in milliseconds. These observations have a mean $\overline{Y} = 676$ milliseconds. The sum of squares of the residuals was 25,932, so the variance of the residuals (or of Y) is $25,932/9 = 2881.3$.

In this example, we would like to know how close the value of 676 milliseconds is to the true value of the reaction time, the population mean. The first step in obtaining a confidence interval is to be able to make probability statements about $\overline{Y}$. This step requires that we treat $\overline{Y}$ as a random variable. In making this important step, it is first necessary to understand how $\overline{Y}$ can be thought of as a variable at all.

5.1.1 Sample Mean as One Value of a Random Variable

$\overline{Y}$ can be treated as a variable.

In what sense is $\overline{Y}$ a variable? The answer is not obvious. The observed sample mean $\overline{Y}$ is a single number, whereas a variable, by definition, takes on different values. For the braking reaction time data, the sample mean was 676 milliseconds. It is easy to see that residuals or reaction time itself constitute a variable; the different values are apparent in the data; reaction time varies from one measurement to the next.

Understanding how $\overline{Y}$ can be considered to be a variable involves understanding how $\overline{Y}$ can take on different values. First imagine a particular $\overline{Y}$ (such as 676 milliseconds) as just one value from a larger set of possible values, *even though the experiment itself yields just the single value of 676*. This larger set of other possible values consists of the values of $\overline{Y}$ that would be obtained from different samples of observations. The value of 676 is but one of many possible values; it is the value peculiar to this set of ten observations. The absence of strict replication implies that a different set of ten observations would yield a different value of $\overline{Y}$. In other words, $\overline{Y}$ is a variable because it can take on different values, the different values being the means of different samples. The fact that we have just one sample, and therefore just one value for $\overline{Y}$, should not conceal the fact that other values are possible.

If we treat $\overline{Y}$ as a random variable, then the probability distribution of $\overline{Y}$ is the normal distribution.

$\overline{Y}$ can be thought of as one observation from a population of means: the means of all possible samples of size n.

Having grasped the concept that $\overline{Y}$ is a variable, the next step is to understand how to make probability statements about possible values of $\overline{Y}$, that is, how it can be treated as a *random* variable. As we learned in Chapter 4, all that is required to achieve this goal is a probability distribution. What probability distribution (more properly, what probability density function, because $\overline{Y}$ is a continuous variable) is appropriate? The answer is not surprising. The probability density function for $\overline{Y}$ is the normal distribution.

The formal proof of this result rests on the assumption that Y itself is normally distributed. As explained in Chapter 4, this assumption is usually a plausible one. However, thanks to the central limit theorem, the distribution of $\overline{Y}$ is well approximated by the normal distribution even if the distribution of Y is not exactly normal. The central limit theorem is relevant because, as pointed out in Chapter 4, the mean is based on the sum of independent elements—the observed values of Y—and this condition, you will remember, is precisely the condition under which the central limit theorem applies.

The practical upshot of the central limit theorem is that the distribution of $\overline{Y}$ is very well approximated by a normal distribution, even if the original variable, Y, is not normally distributed. For this reason, most investigators do not engage in elaborate procedures to check on the validity of the normality assumption. A visual check using the methods suggested in Chapter 2 is sufficient. Only distributions that are clearly bimodal or severely skewed need cause concern. Moreover, the larger the sample size, n, on which $\overline{Y}$ is based, the less the cause for concern. As n increases, greater departures from normality of the Y distribution can be tolerated.

> Because of the central limit theorem, the distribution of $\overline{Y}$ is well approximated by the normal distribution.

5.1.2 Sampling Distribution of the Mean

We now introduce an important point of terminology. When a random variable is a sample statistic (as $\overline{Y}$ is), then its probability distribution is known as a *sampling distribution*. Because in this case the statistic is the mean, the distribution is known as the *sampling distribution of the mean.*

One way of thinking about the sampling distribution of $\overline{Y}$ for the sample of ten reaction times is to imagine repeating, over and over, the process of gathering ten measures, calculating a sample mean for each repetition, and then plotting these means as a proportional frequency distribution. If the number of repetitions became infinitely large (and if our measuring instrument became infinitely fine), then the distribution of these sample means would be a normal distribution. The single value of $\overline{Y}$ that we actually obtain can be thought of as a single observation, a single value of $\overline{Y}$ drawn at random from this distribution of $\overline{Y}$ values. That is, we think of 676 as a sample of size 1, a single observation from a normal distribution.

> The distribution of $\overline{Y}$ is known as the sampling distribution of the mean.

Given that the form of the sampling distribution of $\overline{Y}$ is the normal distribution, the next question concerns its mean and its variance. We consider the mean first. The mean of the sampling distribution of $\overline{Y}$ is μ. Note, however, that this result holds only if the residuals have a mean of 0; if the residuals are biased, then $\overline{Y}$ will give a biased estimate of μ. In fact, the usual definition of an *unbiased estimate* is that the mean of the estimate's sampling distribution equals the parameter that it estimates. This definition of an unbiased estimate makes intuitive sense. If you imagine many samples being drawn, the various sample means would vary, some would be greater than μ, some would be less; but there would be no systematic trend in either direction. If these sample means were themselves averaged, the resulting "mean of the means" would stabilize at the true value (μ) as more and more sample means were averaged.

Biased residuals were discussed in Section 4.5.1. If, for example, the residuals are biased on the positive side, then $\overline{Y}$ will tend to overestimate the true value of μ; if

> The mean of the sampling distribution of $\overline{Y}$ is μ, the population mean.

> An estimate is unbiased if the mean of the estimate's sampling distribution equals the parameter that it estimates.

they are biased on the negative side, then $\overline{Y}$ will tend to underestimate the true value of μ. This potential source of bias in estimating $\overline{Y}$ is the reason for the stress placed on sound experimental methods.

Thus far we know that the sampling distribution of the sample mean is a normal distribution with a mean μ. But to specify a unique normal distribution, we need also to know the variance. We will denote the variance of the sampling distribution of the mean by $\sigma_{\overline{Y}}^2$. This variance has a very simple relationship to the variance of the response measures themselves. It is the variance of the response measures σ_Y^2 divided by n. That is, the variance of the distribution of $\overline{Y}$ is

$$\sigma_{\overline{Y}}^2 = \frac{\sigma_Y^2}{n}$$

where n is the number of observations on which $\overline{Y}$ was based. The standard deviation of the sampling distribution of the mean is known as the *standard error of the mean* and is denoted by $\sigma_{\overline{Y}}$:

$$\sigma_{\overline{Y}} = \frac{\sigma_Y}{\sqrt{n}}$$

It is important to maintain a clear distinction between the variance of the scores themselves (σ_Y^2) and the variance of the sampling distribution of means ($\sigma_{\overline{Y}}^2$). As the subscripts indicate, for the variance of the scores themselves, the variable is Y, whereas for the variance of the sampling distribution of means, the variable is $\overline{Y}$.

It may seem unreasonable that we can know the variance or the standard error of the probability distribution for $\overline{Y}$ when the data provide only a single value of $\overline{Y}$. It is as if we could know the variability of infant birth weight from a measurement of weight taken from a single newborn. If the goal were to estimate the variance weight of newborn infants, a single measured birth weight of 7.5 pounds provides no basis for inferring the variance of the entire distribution of birth weights. It seems reasonable to insist that at least two (and preferably more) measures are needed to provide any clue to variability.

The situation with respect to $\overline{Y}$ is, however, different from such single-observation examples in one very important way. The observed value of $\overline{Y}$ may itself be just a single observation from the sampling distribution of $\overline{Y}$, but this single value is based on a total of n observations, not just one. The inferential link—the step that seems almost to gain us something for nothing—is that, for a given sample size, the variability of the sampling distribution is completely determined by the variability of the response measures themselves. Although the formal proof that $\sigma_{\overline{Y}}^2 = \sigma_Y^2/n$ is beyond the scope of this text, it is important to grasp the basic implications of this formula.

The important concept is that the size of the standard error is determined by just two factors:

■ The variability of the scores themselves, σ_Y^2. The larger σ_Y^2 is (the noisier the data), the less sure we can be that $\overline{Y}$ will be close to μ.

■ The sample size, n. The larger the number of observations, the closer $\overline{Y}$ is likely to be to μ. Large samples provide better estimates.

In brief, the less noisy the data and the larger the sample size on which $\overline{Y}$ is based, the smaller the standard error is, and thus the closer to μ $\overline{Y}$ is likely to be.

Margin notes:

$\sigma_{\overline{Y}}^2$ denotes variance of the distribution of $\overline{Y}$.

σ_Y^2 denotes variance of Y, the response measures.

The standard error of the mean is the standard deviation of the sampling distribution of the mean.

$\sigma_{\overline{Y}}$ denotes standard error of the mean.

5.1.3 Simple Use for the Sampling Distribution of the Mean

We have established that $\overline{Y}$ can be considered to be a random variable that has a normal distribution with a mean of μ and a standard deviation (standard error) of $\sigma_{\overline{Y}} = \sigma_Y/\sqrt{n}$. If we knew the values of μ and $\sigma_{\overline{Y}}$, we could apply the methods described in Chapter 4 and answer questions about the probability of obtaining a value of $\overline{Y}$ greater or less than a designated value, or being within a designated interval of values.

IQ Scores

IQ scores have a mean of $\mu = 100$ and a standard deviation of $\sigma = 15$. Suppose an investigator plans to select a random sample of $n = 25$ participants from the general population and obtain IQ scores for each. What is the probability that the mean IQ of this sample ($\overline{Y}$) will be

greater than 105.0?
less than 97.0?
between 95.0 and 105.0?

We can use the sampling distribution of $\overline{Y}$ to obtain probabilities.

These questions are answered in exactly the same way as those in Section 4.4. The only difference is that now the random variable is the sample mean rather than ordinary scores. The problem is diagrammed in Figure 5.1. The shaded area indicates the required probability.

To find $P(\overline{Y} > 105.0)$, we convert the value 105.0 to a z-score and then consult the table of the normal curve. To do this, we first need the standard deviation, $\sigma_{\overline{Y}}$, of the distribution of $\overline{Y}$.

$$\sigma_{\overline{Y}} = \frac{\sigma_Y}{\sqrt{n}} = \frac{15.0}{\sqrt{25}} = 3.0$$

Then

$$z = \frac{\overline{Y} - \mu}{\sigma_{\overline{Y}}} = \frac{105.0 - 100.0}{3} = 1.67$$

From the tables of the normal curve (Statistical Table 1 in Appendix C) we find that the area to the right of $z = 1.67$ is .0475, which is the required probability. Thus

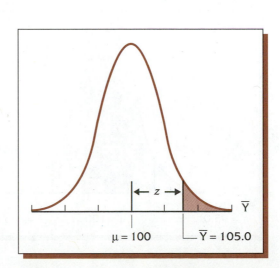

Figure 5.1
Sampling distribution of $\overline{Y}$, with a mean of 100 and a standard error of 3.0. The shaded area indicates the probability of obtaining a sample mean greater than 105.0.

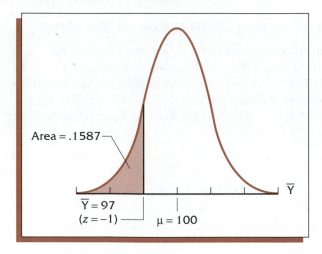

Figure 5.2
Sampling distribution of $\overline{Y}$, with a mean of 100 and a standard error of 3.0. The area in the left tail indicates the probability of obtaining a sample mean less than 97.0.

the probability that a sample of 25 will have a mean greater than 105 is quite small—less than 5%.

To calculate $P(\overline{Y} < 97.0)$, the appropriate z-score is

$$z = \frac{\overline{Y} - \mu}{\sigma_{\overline{Y}}} = \frac{97.0 - 100.0}{3} = -1.0$$

The required probability is the area to the left of $z = -1.0$, as shown in Figure 5.2. From Statistical Table 1, we find that this area is .1587.

To find $P(95.0 < \overline{Y} < 105.0)$, we need to find the area indicated in Figure 5.3. The simplest way to find the area of the center portion is to find the combined area in the two tails and subtract it from 1.0. We know from the first question that the area in the right-hand tail is .0475. By symmetry, this is also the area in the left-hand tail. The combined area in the two tails is therefore .0950, so the area in the central portion is $1.0 - .0950 = .9050$. The answer is

$$P(95.0 < \overline{Y} < 105.0) = .9050$$

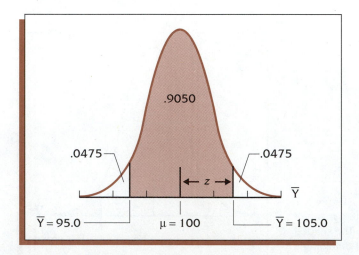

Figure 5.3
Sampling distribution of $\overline{Y}$, with a mean of 100 and a standard error of 3.0. The central area indicates the probability of obtaining a sample mean between 95.0 and 105.0.

Comprehension Check 5.1

Important Concepts

1. The most important concept in this section is the idea that the sample mean can be considered to be a variable. Although only one value of $\overline{Y}$ may be obtained, this value can be thought of as a single observation from a population of $\overline{Y}$ values made up of the means of all possible samples of the same size.

2. The next step is to treat the sample mean as one value of a random variable. The probability distribution that is defined on the variable $\overline{Y}$ is termed the sampling distribution of the mean.

3. The sampling distribution of the mean is a normal distribution with mean μ and standard deviation $\sigma_{\overline{Y}} = \sigma_Y / \sqrt{n}$. The distribution of $\overline{Y}$ will be well approximated by the normal distribution even if the distribution of Y itself is not normal. This result is an example of the force of the central limit theorem.

4. The standard deviation of the sampling distribution of the mean, $\sigma_{\overline{Y}}$, is termed the standard error of the mean. The size of the standard error of the mean is determined by two factors: the standard deviation of Y (σ_Y) and the sample size (n).

5. If the mean and standard error are known, the sampling distribution of the mean can be used to answer simple questions about the probability of obtaining a sample mean within a designated range of values.

Worked Examples

Example 1 **Height of adult males**

In a certain population, the mean height of adult males is $\mu = 68.2$ inches. Two random samples are drawn, one of size $n = 10$, the other of size $n = 50$. Assuming height (Y) is normally distributed, answer the following questions.

a. For which sample is it more likely that the mean, $\overline{Y}$, is greater than 69.0 inches?

b. For which sample is it more likely that the mean, $\overline{Y}$, is less than 67.5 inches?

c. For which sample is it more likely that the mean, $\overline{Y}$, is within $\frac{1}{2}$ inch(es) of the population value of $\mu = 68.2$ inches?

d. If the standard deviation of height is 2.8 inches, check each of the answers to (a) through (c) by calculating the exact probabilities referred to in the questions.

Answer

a–c. The answers to these questions are based on the insight that the larger the sample size n, the smaller the variance (and standard deviation) of the distribution of $\overline{Y}$. A smaller variance implies a smaller likelihood of extreme observations. In this case, the observations are values of $\overline{Y}$. Thus the answer to the first two questions is the smaller sample and the answer to the third question is the larger sample. For example, the first question asks essentially for the probability that $\overline{Y}$ is more distant from μ than 0.8 inch. The second question asks for the probability that $\overline{Y}$ is more distant from μ than 0.7 inch. The third question can be rephrased as, "For which sample is the mean less likely to be distant from the mean by more than $\frac{1}{2}$ inch?"

d. Because we know the mean and the standard deviation (the standard error) of the distribution of $\overline{Y}$, we can convert values of $\overline{Y}$ to standard (z) form and use tables of the normal distribution to obtain the required probabilities. The problem therefore is essentially the same as those of Section 4.4. The present problem is a special case of those in Section 4.4. Now the random variable is $\overline{Y}$ and the relevant standard deviation is therefore the standard deviation of *that* random variable, namely, $\sigma_{\overline{Y}}$, the standard error.

We know that $\sigma_Y = 2.8$; so, for the sample of size 10, the standard error is

$$\sigma_{\overline{Y}} = \frac{\sigma_Y}{\sqrt{n}} = \frac{2.8}{\sqrt{10}} = 0.885$$

For the sample of size 50, the standard error is $2.8/\sqrt{50} = 0.396$. In summary, for samples of size 10, sample means are normally distributed with a mean of 68.2 inches and a standard deviation (standard error) of 0.885 inch. For samples of size 50, sample means are normally distributed with a mean of 68.2 inches and a standard deviation (standard error) of 0.396 inch.

For (a), we need to know $P(\overline{Y} > 69.0)$. To obtain this value, we convert 69.0 to its z-score equivalent. For $n = 10$ samples,

$$z = \frac{\overline{Y} - \mu}{\sigma_{\overline{Y}}} = \frac{69.0 - 68.2}{0.885} = \frac{0.8}{0.885} = 0.90$$

For $n = 50$ samples,

$$z = \frac{\overline{Y} - \mu}{\sigma_{\overline{Y}}} = \frac{69.0 - 68.2}{0.396} = \frac{0.8}{0.396} = 2.02$$

Consulting the normal curve tables, we find that the probability that $z > 0.90$ is .1841 and that the probability that $z > 2.02$ is .0217. These results confirm the previous answer that the small sample is more likely to have a mean that is greater than 69.0 inches. (*Note:* If you are unclear about the basic procedures for obtaining probabilities under the normal curve by converting to z-scores and then using the normal curve table, review the material in Section 4.4.)

For (b), we need to know $P(\overline{Y} < 67.5)$. To obtain this value, we convert 67.5 to its z-score equivalent. For $n = 10$ samples,

$$z = \frac{\overline{Y} - \mu}{\sigma_{\overline{Y}}} = \frac{67.5 - 68.2}{0.885} = \frac{-0.7}{0.885} = -0.79$$

For $n = 50$ samples,

$$z = \frac{\overline{Y} - \mu}{\sigma_{\overline{Y}}} = \frac{67.5 - 68.2}{0.396} = \frac{-0.7}{0.396} = -1.77$$

Consulting the normal curve tables, we find that the probability that $z < -0.79$ is .2148 and that the probability that $z < -1.77$ is .0384. These results confirm the previous answer that the small sample is more likely to have a mean that is less than 67.5 inches.

For (c), we need to know $P(67.7 < \overline{Y} < 68.7)$. To obtain this value, note first, that 67.7 and 68.7 are equidistant from the mean; thus, because of symmetry, we need to convert just one of these scores to z-score form. One z-score will be the negative of the other. We will convert 68.7 to its z-score equivalent. For $n = 10$ samples,

$$z = \frac{\overline{Y} - \mu}{\sigma_{\overline{Y}}} = \frac{68.7 - 68.2}{0.885} = \frac{0.5}{0.885} = 0.56$$

For $n = 50$ samples,

$$z = \frac{\overline{Y} - \mu}{\sigma_{\overline{Y}}} = \frac{68.7 - 68.2}{0.396} = \frac{0.5}{0.396} = 1.26$$

Thus, for the $n = 10$ sample, we need the area between $z = \pm 0.56$, and for the $n = 50$ sample, we need the area between $z = \pm 1.26$. Consulting the normal curve tables, we find that the probability that $(-0.56 < z < 0.56)$ is .4246 and the probability that $(-1.26 < z < 1.26)$ is .7924. These results confirm the previous answer that the larger sample is more likely to have a mean within $\frac{1}{2}$ inch of the population mean.

Problems

Problem 1 Probabilities for values of the sample mean

This problem is of the boot camp variety—routine drill—intended to impress on you that $\overline{Y}$ can be treated as a random variable, just as Y can, and that the standard deviation of $\overline{Y}$ (the sampling distribution) can be inferred from the standard deviation of Y. You may find that there are more exercises here than it is worthwhile for you to complete. Complete as many as are needed to ensure that you understand the procedure. For each set of parameters, μ and σ_Y, calculate $\sigma_{\overline{Y}}$ (the standard error of the mean) and probability for the given value of n.

a. $\mu = 5.0$, $\sigma_Y = 2.0$, $n = 16$, $P(\overline{Y} > 5.5)$

b. $\mu = 2.0$, $\sigma_Y = 1.5$, $n = 25$, $P(\overline{Y} > 1.7)$

c. $\mu = 20.0$, $\sigma_Y = 4.0$, $n = 9$, $P(\overline{Y} < 18.0)$

d. $\mu = 12.0$, $\sigma_Y = 3.0$, $n = 36$, $P(\overline{Y} > 11.0)$

e. $\mu = 6.0$, $\sigma_Y = 2.5$, $n = 20$, $P(\overline{Y} > 7.0)$

f. $\mu = -1.0$, $\sigma_Y = 4.0$, $n = 40$, $P(\overline{Y} > 0.0)$

g. $\mu = 42.0$, $\sigma_Y = 10.0$, $n = 35$, $P(\overline{Y} > 44.0)$

h. $\mu = 11.0$, $\sigma_Y = 2.5$, $n = 45$, $P(\overline{Y} < 11.5)$

i. $\mu = 17.3$, $\sigma_Y = 2.7$, $n = 22$, $P(\overline{Y} > 17.0)$

j. $\mu = 12.4$, $\sigma_Y = 3.8$, $n = 50$, $P(\overline{Y} > 12.0)$

k. $\mu = 10.0$, $\sigma_Y = 4.0$, $n = 37$, $P(9.0 < \overline{Y} < 11.0)$

l. $\mu = 4.0$, $\sigma_Y = 0.5$, $n = 15$, $P(3.8 < \overline{Y} < 4.2)$

m. $\mu = 6.7$, $\sigma_Y = 1.3$, $n = 42$, $P(6.4 < \overline{Y} < 7.0)$

n. $\mu = 87.0$, $\sigma_Y = 12.2$, $n = 60$, $P(84.0 < \overline{Y} < 90.0)$

o. $\mu = 14.3$, $\sigma_Y = 2.4$, $n = 34$, $P(13.8 < \overline{Y} < 14.8)$

p. $\mu = 50.0$, $\sigma_Y = 9.0$, $n = 20$, $P(49.0 < \overline{Y} < 51.0)$

q. $\mu = 30.0$, $\sigma_Y = 3.9$, $n = 44$, $P(29.0 < \overline{Y} < 31.0)$

r. $\mu = 45.0$, $\sigma_Y = 6.3$, $n = 30$, $P(45.0 < \overline{Y} < 46.0)$

s. $\mu = 18.4$, $\sigma_Y = 2.7$, $n = 32$, $P(18.0 < \overline{Y} < 19.0)$

t. $\mu = 100.0$, $\sigma_Y = 14.0$, $n = 27$, $P(95.0 < \overline{Y} < 100.0)$

Problem 2   **Mean SAT-V scores**

A random sample of 50 high school students from a certain school district will take the verbal component of the Scholastic Aptitude Test (SAT-V). From a different school district, a smaller random sample of 20 students will also take the SAT-V. Scores on the (SAT-V) are scaled to have a mean of $\mu = 500$. Assuming that the samples from both schools can be considered to be random samples from the general population of students on which the SAT-V was scaled, answer the following questions without doing any computations.

a. Is one sample more likely than the other to have the higher mean? If so, which sample?

b. Which sample is more likely to have a mean greater than 510?

c. Which sample is more likely to have a mean less than 485?

d. Which sample is more likely to have a mean within the range 500 ± 10?

e. Scores on the SAT-V are scaled to have a standard deviation of $\sigma = 100$. What is the standard error of the mean for (i) samples of size $n = 20$, and (ii) samples of size $n = 50$?

f. Calculate the first and third quartiles and then the interquartile range *(IQR)* of the sampling distribution of mean SAT-V scores for (i) samples of size $n = 20$ and (ii) samples of size $n = 50$. Explain in ordinary English why one of these *IQR*s is smaller than the other.

g. Support your answers to (b), (c), and (d) by calculating exact probabilities.

5.2 Calculating Confidence Intervals

An interval estimate is a range of values that "probably" includes the true value.

Using the normal distribution model of the residuals, we described in Section 5.1 the method for calculating probabilities for possible values of $\overline{Y}$ when μ and σ_Y were known. How can we use this method to calculate confidence intervals when μ is *unknown*? Before beginning a detailed account of these calculations, it is valuable to have a clear understanding of the general concept of a confidence interval and the sense in which it provides an interval estimate. Although the calculations are quite straightforward, such an understanding helps avoid losing sight of the purpose of the calculations amid the arithmetic details.

5.2.1 Nature of Interval Estimates

For both the reaction time and the SAT-V examples, we would like to know how precise an estimate $\overline{Y}$ is of the parameter μ. How large is the difference between $\overline{Y}$ and μ? A confidence interval provides a way of answering this question. Stated informally, a *confidence interval* is a range of values that "probably" includes the value of μ. As noted at the beginning of this chapter, confidence intervals have their informal counterpart in everyday language. If asked the driving distance between New York and Boston, someone might answer "between 200 and 220 miles." The person may not know the exact mileage, but they are able to give a range within which they feel confident the true distance lies. Results of opinion polls are often presented in terms of a confidence interval—a politician's approval rating might be quoted as "55% plus or minus 4%" or "the rating is accurate to within 4%." Both these statements describe a confidence interval of 51% to 59%.

In statistical data analysis, terms such as *probably* and *confident* need to be specified in terms of an exact probability. For example, we might select a probability of .95 as the desired level of confidence and then calculate an interval that allows us to be 95% confident that the interval contains μ. Just how the interval is calculated will be described shortly; but to give an immediate example of a confidence interval, we will assume the appropriate calculations have been made. For the braking reaction time data, for example, such an interval would be a statement such as

The probability is .95 that the interval 676 ± 38 milliseconds contains μ.

Or, equivalently,

The probability is .95 that the interval 638 to 714 milliseconds contains μ.

This statement tells us that for braking reaction time, 676 milliseconds is "probably" within 38 milliseconds of μ, where, in this example, "probably" is specified as .95. The interval 676 ± 38 or 638 to 714 is known as a confidence interval and constitutes an interval estimate of the mean. The value .95 is known as the *confidence level*, and the interval itself is therefore referred to as the 95% confidence interval.

> *A confidence interval provides an interval estimate by stating a range of values that, with a specified probability such as .95, includes the true value.*

The use of .95 as the level of confidence in this example reflects the most commonly used level, but other levels such as .90 or .99 are also used. The choice of confidence level depends on the judgment of the investigator as to how much uncertainty can be tolerated.

Interval estimates have an advantage over point estimates in that they provide information about how much error is associated with the point estimate. By itself, the point estimate of 676 milliseconds for the mean braking reaction time gives no information as to its proximity to μ; the point estimate could be close, or it could be way off

Furthermore,

> *The width of a confidence interval provides a basis for deciding whether the data provide an adequately precise estimate.*

The width of the confidence interval is simply the difference between its upper and lower bounds. In the reaction time example, the width is $714 - 638 = 76$ milliseconds. If the interval is expressed as 676 ± 38, then the width can be calculated simply as 2×38. Clearly, the smaller the width, the more precise the estimate. An experiment that provides a 95% interval of 680 to 700 milliseconds, a width of 20 milliseconds, locates the value of μ much more precisely than one that provides a 95% interval of 600 to 800 milliseconds, a width of 200 milliseconds.

The same kind of thinking is also relevant to informal, everyday confidence intervals. The interval estimate of 200 to 220 miles for the driving distance between New York and Boston has a width of 20 miles, which is probably precise enough for most purposes. On the other hand, an estimate of 100 to 300—an interval width of 200 miles—is much less precise and much less useful.

5.2.2 Calculating Confidence Intervals When σ_Y Is Known

σ_Y denotes population standard deviation.

Although it is not common to have a situation in which σ_Y is known, the following simple problem illustrates the basic steps for calculating a confidence interval. These basic steps can then be transferred to the more realistic cases in which σ_Y is unknown. The steps themselves are essentially the same as those used in Section 4.4.4. That section explained how to derive an interval of scores that marked off designated areas under the normal curve. Calculating a confidence interval is performing precisely that operation. In Section 4.4.4, the variable was Y; in this section, the variable is $\overline{Y}$.

IQ Scores

As noted previously, IQ scores have a mean $\mu = 100$ and a standard deviation $\sigma = 15$. Suppose an educator wishes to know the mean IQ score for students in her school district, wondering if it might be different from 100. To address this question, a random sample of 100 IQ scores from the district is obtained. The mean of these 100 scores is found to be 102. The population standard deviation of the IQ scores in her school district is assumed not to differ from 15.

Our goal is to obtain an interval such that we can claim (with a specified level of confidence) that the interval includes the true value μ. In this case, μ is the population mean IQ of students in the director's district. We will take .95 to be the desired confidence level. The goal, then, is to calculate the 95% confidence interval.

Figure 5.4 shows a normal curve that is the sampling distribution of the random variable $\overline{Y}$. In this example, $\overline{Y}$ is the variable representing the mean IQ score for all possible samples of size $n = 100$ from the school district. Our observed sample mean ($\overline{Y} = 102$) is just one observation from this sampling distribution. The mean of this sampling distribution, μ, is unknown.

In Figure 5.4, the center portion of the distribution contains 95% of the area, leaving 2.5% in each tail. The task is to calculate the distance on either side of the unknown mean (μ) needed to enclose this 95%. We will denote this distance by w. Thus the probability is .95 that a sample mean will fall within this interval of $\mu \pm w$. If we were to draw repeated samples of size $n = 100$ from the school district, 95% of the resulting sample means would fall within the range $\mu \pm w$.

Our immediate task is to calculate the value of w. To do this, we first obtain its value in z-score units, then convert this z-score into units of the original scale—IQ score units.

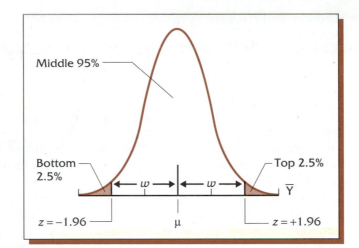

Figure 5.4
Sampling distribution of the mean, with unknown mean μ. The central area, $\mu \pm w$, contains 95% of the area, leaving 2.5% in each tail.

Consulting Table 5.1, a portion of the table of the normal curve, we find that the z-scores that mark off these areas are ± 1.96. That is, the value of w in z-score units is 1.96. Notice that the relevant table entry has an area .975 to the left and .025 to the right.

To convert this z-score of 1.96 into IQ score units, we multiply the z-score by the standard deviation of the distribution. Recall that this distribution is the distribution of the random variable $\overline{Y}$, so the relevant standard deviation is the standard error, $\sigma_{\overline{Y}}$. We have, then,

$$w = 1.96 \times \sigma_{\overline{Y}}$$

Table 5.1 Portion of the normal distribution table showing relevant entry for obtaining 95% confidence interval

z	Area to the left of z	Area to the right of z
. . .	. . .	. . .
1.91	.9719	.0281
1.92	.9726	.0274
1.93	.9732	.0268
1.94	.9738	.0262
1.95	.9744	.0256
1.96	.9750	.0250
1.97	.9756	.0244
1.98	.9761	.0239
1.99	.9767	.0233
. . .	. . .	. . .

The standard error is

$$\sigma_{\overline{Y}} = \frac{\sigma_Y}{\sqrt{n}} = \frac{15}{\sqrt{100}} = 1.5$$

It follows that

$$w = 1.96 \times 1.5 = 2.94$$

We therefore conclude that the probability is .95 that $\overline{Y}$ is within 2.94 of the population mean μ, in other words, that 95% of all sample means will fall within the interval $\mu \pm 2.94$.

The final step is to take the claim that $\overline{Y}$ is within 2.94 of μ and assume that it is equivalent to the claim that μ is within 2.94 of $\overline{Y}$. The statement that "on 95% of occasions, the interval $\mu \pm 2.94$ will contain $\overline{Y}$" is assumed to be the same as the statement that "on 95% of occasions, the interval $\overline{Y} \pm 2.94$ will contain μ." The interval $\overline{Y} \pm 2.94$ IQ units is therefore the required 95% confidence interval.

The reasonableness of treating these statements as equivalent may be clearer if we consider the example of estimating the distance between New York and Boston. One form of the statement would be, "I am 95% sure that my estimate of 210 miles is within 10 miles of the true distance." The equivalent version would be, "I am 95% sure that the true distance is within 10 miles of my estimate of 210 miles."

Three Steps in Calculating a Confidence Interval

The following steps should be followed in calculating a confidence interval.

Step 1 Establish the center of the interval. The required interval is centered on the point estimate $\overline{Y}$; that is, the interval will be $\overline{Y} \pm w$. (The remaining task is to find the value of w.)

Step 2 Obtain the z-score appropriate to the required level of confidence. For a 95% confidence interval, this value is 1.96; for a 99% confidence interval, the z-value is 2.58. These values are obtained from the table of the normal distribution.

Step 3 Convert the z-score into units of the original scale by multiplying the z-score by the standard error. In brief, $w = z \times \sigma_{\overline{Y}}$.

For our IQ example, $w = z \times \sigma_{\overline{Y}} = 1.96 \times 1.5 = 2.94$. The 95% confidence interval is therefore 102 ± 2.94, or 99.06 to 104.94. Rounding these figures to whole numbers, we have $w = 3$, and the investigator can claim that, with a probability of .95, the interval 99 to 105 contains the true (population) mean IQ. Note that the width of this 95% confidence interval is six IQ points.

On the basis of the preceding discussion, we can write a formula for calculating a confidence interval when σ_Y (and therefore $\sigma_{\overline{Y}}$) is known. The confidence interval (CI) is

$$CI = \overline{Y} \pm (z \times \sigma_{\overline{Y}})$$

where z is obtained from tables of the normal curve and the standard score corresponding to the designated confidence level.

CI is a convenient abbreviation that will be used in the remainder of this chapter. The confidence level can be indicated with a subscript. Thus CI$_{.95}$ indicates the 95%

The required confidence interval is $\overline{Y} \pm w$.

w denotes the half-width of the confidence interval.

CI$_{.95}$ is a convenient shorthand for the 95% confidence interval.

confidence interval; CI$_{.99}$ indicates the 99% confidence interval; and so forth. For the two most commonly used intervals,

$$CI_{.95} = \overline{Y} \pm (1.96 \times \sigma_{\overline{Y}})$$

$$CI_{.99} = \overline{Y} \pm (2.58 \times \sigma_{\overline{Y}})$$

5.2.3 Calculating Confidence Intervals When σ_Y Is Unknown

We are now in a position to consider the more common situation in which σ_Y is unknown. We return to the example of the braking reaction time data (Section 5.1). Because we do not know the value of the parameter σ_Y (the population standard deviation for reaction times), we cannot calculate the value of the standard error, $\sigma_{\overline{Y}}$, because $\sigma_{\overline{Y}} = \sigma_Y/\sqrt{n}$. How do we overcome this obstacle?

Estimating the Standard Error

Although we do not know the value of the standard deviation, σ_Y, we can use a point estimate in its place. We simply replace σ_Y with its sample-based estimate, s_Y. This estimate, you will remember, is

$$s_Y = \sqrt{\frac{SS_Y}{n-1}} = \sqrt{\frac{\Sigma(Y - \overline{Y})^2}{n-1}}$$

To estimate the standard error, replace σ_Y with its estimate, s_Y.

To obtain an estimate of the standard error, we replace σ_Y with this estimate of the standard deviation. We will denote the estimated standard error by $s_{\overline{Y}}$. Then the *estimated* standard error of the mean is

s_Y denotes standard deviation of the sample.

$$s_{\overline{Y}} = \frac{s_Y}{\sqrt{n}}$$

For our reaction time example, the standard deviation of the ten observations was

$$s_Y = \sqrt{\frac{25{,}932}{9}} = 53.68$$

$s_{\overline{Y}}$ denotes *estimated* standard error of the mean.

The estimate of the standard error is therefore

$$s_{\overline{Y}} = \frac{s_Y}{\sqrt{n}} = \frac{53.7}{\sqrt{10}} = 16.97$$

The *estimated* standard error of the mean is $s_{\overline{Y}} = s_Y/\sqrt{n}$

It is tempting to think that calculating the confidence interval is now a simple matter of using $s_{\overline{Y}}$ instead of $\sigma_{\overline{Y}}$ in the previously used formula for w, obtaining the relevant value of z from the normal curve tables, and proceeding as before. Unfortunately, the situation is not quite so simple.

In the formula $w = z \times \sigma_{\overline{Y}}$, the value of z was obtained from the table of the normal distribution. This use of the normal curve tables was justified because $\overline{Y}$ has a normal distribution; therefore, using the z-score was the appropriate method of locating the values that marked off the relevant areas of the distribution.

The problem that arises when $\sigma_{\overline{Y}}$ is unknown and replaced by its estimate, $s_{\overline{Y}}$, is that *the estimate $s_{\overline{Y}}$ is not a constant*. Remember, $\sigma_{\overline{Y}}$ is a parameter, $s_{\overline{Y}}$ is not. Instead, both s_Y and $s_{\overline{Y}}$ (remember, $s_{\overline{Y}}$ is based on s_Y) are *variables*. They are variables in the same sense that $\overline{Y}$ is a variable. That is, s_Y (and therefore $s_{\overline{Y}}$) varies from one sample to another, just as $\overline{Y}$ does. In brief, rather than being a constant, as are σ_Y and $\sigma_{\overline{Y}}$, the

Unlike $\sigma_{\overline{Y}}$, $s_{\overline{Y}}$ is not a constant; like all estimates, it is subject to variability across different samples.

estimates s_Y and $s_{\bar{Y}}$ *are random variables.* The upshot of all this is that, when the normally distributed random variable $z = (\bar{Y} - \mu)/\sigma_{\bar{Y}}$ is replaced with $(\bar{Y} - \mu)/s_{\bar{Y}}$, this resulting variable does *not* have a normal distribution. Rather, this new variable is a ratio formed by dividing one random variable ($\bar{Y}$) by a second random variable ($s_{\bar{Y}}$). The random variable formed by the ratio of these two random variables does *not* have a normal distribution.

Student's *t*-Distribution

What distribution describes the ratio $(\bar{Y} - \mu)/s_{\bar{Y}}$? The answer to this important question was first reported in 1908 and came from a source that may seem unlikely to present-day students—a brewery employee. The employee was William Gossett, one of a growing number of scientists hired by the Guinness Company, the famed Irish brewers of stout. Brewery policy prevented Gossett from publishing under his own name, so he published the paper under the pseudonym "Student." Student used the letter *t* to denote the probability distribution (density function) that describes the ratio $(\bar{Y} - \mu)/s_{\bar{Y}}$. The distribution is often referred to as *Student's t-distribution* and even more often as simply the *t-distribution*.

Why should a brewery require the services of a statistician, and what possible interest could a brewery have in the *t*-distribution? The brief answer is that a brewery, as with any manufacturing process that must be concerned with quality control, is interested in keeping variability within acceptable limits. In this regard, quality control has the same purpose as experimental design. The first step in controlling variability is to be able to estimate its effects. This is where the *t*-distribution can play an important role.

The *t*-distribution depends on a single parameter: the degrees of freedom.

What does the *t*-distribution look like? As Figure 5.5 shows, it looks very similar to the standardized normal distribution. The *t*-distribution is actually a family of distributions, as was the normal distribution. With the normal distribution, the various members of the family were distinguished by the values of two parameters, the mean and the standard deviation. For the *t*-distribution, members of the family are distinguished by a single parameter. This parameter is the degrees of freedom on which the estimate of σ_Y is based. For a single set of data such as our reaction time observations, or the SAT-V scores, the degrees of freedom are $df = n - 1$. (If you have forgotten

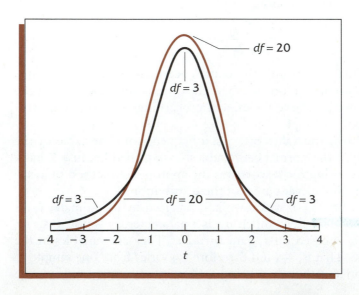

Figure 5.5
Two *t*-distributions with different degrees of freedom.

about degrees of freedom, you should review Section 2.2.2.) Notice that in the preceding calculation of s_Y for the ten reaction times, the degrees of freedom are $n - 1 = 9$.

Figure 5.5 shows two particular t-distributions, one for $df = 3$ and one for $df = 20$. Notice first that, like the normal distribution, the t-distribution is symmetrical and bell shaped. The effect of the parameter df can be seen clearly in the tails of the distribution. With $df = 3$, the tails approach the x-axis more slowly than with $df = 20$. Because both these curves, along with all probability distributions, have a total area of 1, this added area in the tails of the $df = 3$ distribution must be compensated for by less area in the center. This compensation accounts for the lower height of the $df = 3$ distribution over the central region. The general rule is that, as the degrees of freedom become smaller, the area under the t-distribution is more spread out.

As the degrees of freedom increase, the t-distribution becomes closer and closer to the normal distribution. To see why this is so, recall that the reason for any discrepancy between the t-distribution and the normal distribution is the fact that we have to use $s_{\bar{Y}}$ rather than $\sigma_{\bar{Y}}$. But as the number of observations (n) becomes large (and so too the degrees of freedom), $s_{\bar{Y}}$ becomes an increasingly precise and stable estimate of $\sigma_{\bar{Y}}$. In the limit—as n becomes infinitely large—$s_{\bar{Y}}$ and $\sigma_{\bar{Y}}$ become equal, and the t-distribution is then identical to the normal distribution. If you inspect the table of the t-distribution (Statistical Table 3), you will notice that with large degrees of freedom, the values change only slightly from one row to the next.

Using the t-Distribution to Calculate Confidence Intervals

The general form of the confidence interval for the mean is $\bar{Y} \pm w$. When $\sigma_{\bar{Y}}$ was known, the value of w was $z \times \sigma_{\bar{Y}}$, where the value of z was obtained from tables of the normal distribution and depended on the desired level of confidence. For the 95% confidence interval, this value of z was 1.96.

When $\sigma_{\bar{Y}}$ is unknown and is replaced by its estimate $s_{\bar{Y}}$, the confidence interval has the same basic form; but now the value of w is

$$w = t \times s_{\bar{Y}}$$

so the confidence interval is

$$CI = \bar{Y} \pm (t \times s_{\bar{Y}})$$

where t is a value obtained from tables of the t-distribution. Like the value for z, the precise value of t depends on the level of confidence desired. It also depends on *which* t-distribution is used; that is, it depends on the degrees of freedom. Figure 5.6 shows the 95% confidence interval for our reaction time data. For these data, $n = 10$; so the relevant distribution is the t-distribution with $df = 9$.

To obtain the value of t that marks off 95% in the middle and 2.5% in each tail, we must consult the table of the t-distribution. A section of this table is shown in Table 5.2. The full table is Statistical Table 3. Each row of the table gives values for a specific t-distribution defined by the degrees of freedom listed in the first column. The three remaining columns give values of t for three different areas. The column headed .10 gives the value of t that marks off 90% in the center of the distribution and 5% in each tail. The value of .10 (10%) at the head of the column is the combined area of the two tails (5% + 5% = 10%). This column would be used to calculate 90% confidence intervals. Similarly, the column headed .05 gives the value of t that marks off 95% in the center of the distribution and 2.5% in each tail. Again, the value of .05

When $\sigma_{\bar{Y}}$ must be estimated by $s_{\bar{Y}}$, the confidence interval is based on the t-distribution.

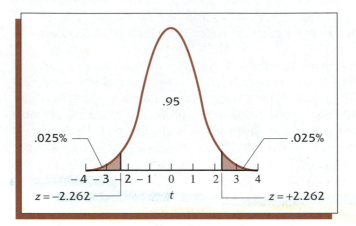

Figure 5.6
A *t*-distribution with *df* = 9, showing a central area of .95 and .05 in the combined tails. With 9 degrees of freedom, a *t*-value of 2.262 is needed to mark off this area.

at the head of the column is the combined area of the two tails (2.5% + 2.5% = 5%). This column would be used to calculate 95% confidence intervals. The column headed .01 gives *t* values that mark off 99% in the center of the distribution and .005 (0.5%) in each tail. This column would be used to calculate 99% confidence intervals. The tabled *t*-values that mark off these various areas are often referred to as *critical* values.

Figure 5.6 shows a *t*-distribution with *df* = 9. The critical values that mark off the central area of .95 and leave a combined area of .05 in the two tails can be read

Table 5.2 Portion of the table of critical values of the *t*-distribution

	Area in two tails		
df	.10	.05	.01
1	6.314	12.706	63.657
2	2.920	4.303	9.925
3	2.353	3.182	5.841
4	2.132	2.776	4.604
5	2.015	2.571	4.032
6	1.943	2.447	3.707
7	1.895	2.365	3.499
8	1.860	2.306	3.355
9	1.833	2.262	3.250
10	1.812	2.228	3.169
11	1.796	2.201	3.106
12	1.782	2.179	3.055
. . .	. . .	. . .	. . .

from the table by consulting the row corresponding to 9 *df* and locating the column headed .05. The value in this cell of the table is 2.262. As noted, the three columns give *t* values needed to calculate 90%, 95%, and 99% confidence intervals, respectively.

The table of the *t*-distribution is unlike that of the normal distribution in two ways. First, it is organized differently. In the tables of the normal distribution (see Statistical Table 1), you start with the value of *z* and read off the area from the body of the table. The *t*-distribution works in the opposite direction. You start with an area (.1, .05, or .01) and from the body of the table read off the value of *t* that marks off those areas. Second, the table of the *t*-distribution lists values of *t* for just these three areas, whereas the normal distribution lists areas for a very wide range of *z* values.

There are good reasons for these differences. On the practical side, if the organization used for the table of the normal distribution were used for the *t*-distribution, there would have to be a separate table for every degrees of freedom, an enormous volume of printing. But, economy aside, the values of the *t*-distribution that are commonly used in practice are those listed in the table. It would be rare to calculate a confidence interval other than 90%, 95%, or 99%. Moreover, other applications to be discussed in following chapters likewise use only these critical areas.

Inspection of the full table for the *t*-distribution (Statistical Table 3) reveals that, with larger degrees of freedom, the values of *t* change only slightly with changes in degrees of freedom. Beyond 40 degrees of freedom, the table therefore records values only in steps of 10 degrees of freedom. Often, however, the value of *t* needed is for an intermediate number of degrees of freedom. In such cases, it is preferable to use the closest available degrees of freedom *below* the value required. Thus, if a value for *t* with 57 degrees of freedom is needed, use *df* = 50. This strategy is a conservative one in that it assumes fewer rather than more degrees of freedom than you really have. This assumption amounts to assuming slightly fewer observations than are actually present, an assumption that is preferable to assuming more data than really exist.

> It is preferable to use the closest tabled degrees of freedom *below* the value required.

Braking Reaction Time

We can now complete our calculation of the confidence interval for the reaction time example with which we began. We know that the value of $\overline{Y}$ is 676 milliseconds. The estimated standard error was found to be

$$s_{\overline{Y}} = 16.97$$

The 95% confidence interval is $\overline{Y} \pm w$, where

$$w = t \times s_{\overline{Y}} = 2.262 \times 16.97$$

$$= 38 \text{ milliseconds (to the nearest whole number)}$$

The 95% confidence interval is therefore

$$CI_{.95} = 676 \pm 38, \text{ or } 638 \text{ to } 714$$

SAT-V Scores

The directors of a large school district would like to know how the scores of students in this district compare with the national average on the verbal form of the Scholastic Aptitude Test, the SAT-V. To address this question, the directors need to know the population mean of the students in that district. A random sample of $n = 100$ students is selected and their SAT-V scores obtained.

The value of $\overline{Y}$ for this sample was found to be 479. The estimated standard deviation was $s_Y = 96.2$. The estimated standard error is therefore

$$s_{\overline{Y}} = \frac{s_Y}{\sqrt{n}} = \frac{96.2}{\sqrt{100}} = 9.62$$

When the degrees of freedom are large, the value of *t* is close to the corresponding value of *z*.

The remaining value needed to complete the calculation of the confidence interval is the value of t. Note that in this case the degrees of freedom are large: $df = 99$. But Statistical Table 3 does not give the explicit value required. The tabulated values jump from 90 to 100. What should we do in cases like this, when the table does not give the exact value? One strategy would be to use the closest available value. In this case, it would be $df = 100$. However, as noted previously, a preferable strategy is to use the closest available degrees of freedom *below* the needed value. For our example, this value would be $df = 90$. The tabulated value of t for $df = 90$ and a 95% confidence interval is 1.987.

We can now complete the calculation. The 95% confidence interval is $\overline{Y} \pm w$, where

$$w = t \times s_{\overline{Y}} = 1.987 \times 9.62 = 19 \text{ (to the nearest whole number)}$$

The 95% confidence interval for the mean of the SAT-V scores is therefore

$$CI_{.95} = 479 \pm 19, \text{ or } 460 \text{ to } 498$$

General Form of a Confidence Interval

The confidence interval for a single mean, μ, has the general form

$$CI = \overline{Y} \pm w$$

When the standard error of the mean ($\sigma_{\overline{Y}}$) is known, then w is calculated by taking the value of z obtained from the tables of the normal curve and multiplying it by the standard error. That is,

$$CI = \overline{Y} \pm (z \times \sigma_{\overline{Y}})$$

When the standard error of the mean must be estimated (because σ_Y is unknown), the relevant sampling distribution is the t-distribution rather than the normal distribution. The value of w is then the appropriate value of the t statistic multiplied by the estimated standard error. That is,

$$CI = \overline{Y} \pm (t \times s_{\overline{Y}})$$

The value of t obtained from the tabled values of the t-distribution depends not only on the level of confidence required, but also on the degrees of freedom $(n - 1)$ used to estimate the value of σ.

Notice that in both cases the confidence interval has the general form of

■ a point estimate $(\overline{Y})$

■ $\pm$ the product of a critical value from the table of the appropriate sampling distribution (e.g., z or t)

■ $\times$ the appropriate standard deviation (e.g., $\sigma_{\overline{Y}}$, or $s_{\overline{Y}}$).

This general form can be thought of as a generic confidence interval in the sense that every confidence interval contains these same three components. When we consider further examples, such as the difference between two means, the confidence interval will have this same general form.

Comprehension Check 5.2

Important Concepts

1. Interval estimates have their counterpart in everyday language, as when someone states, "I am highly confident that my grade in this course will be between 70% and 80%."

2. A confidence interval is a range of values that claims to include μ with a specified probability, such as .95. Such an interval would be referred to as a 95% confidence interval. Other confidence levels commonly used are 90% and 99%.

3. The general form of the confidence interval of the mean is

$$CI = \overline{Y} \pm w$$

When σ_Y is known, $w = z \times \sigma_{\overline{Y}}$. The value for z comes from tables of the normal curve and depends on the level of confidence desired. For the 95% confidence interval, $z = 1.96$. The value of 1.96 is the z-score that leaves an area of .05 in the combined tails of the distribution. For a 99% confidence interval, the value of z is 2.58.

4. When σ_Y is unknown, the standard error must be estimated. Like all estimates, the estimated standard error is subject to sampling variability: $s_{\overline{Y}}$ is a variable in the same way that $\overline{Y}$ is a variable. The consequence of this fact is that, unlike the usual ratio for the z-score, which is $z = (\overline{Y} - \mu)/\sigma_{\overline{Y}}$, the ratio $(\overline{Y} - \mu)/s_{\overline{Y}}$ is *not* normally distributed. Instead of the normal distribution, it has a t-distribution.

5. The t-distribution has one parameter, the degrees of freedom. For large degrees of freedom, the t-distribution is well approximated by the normal distribution. If the t-table does not include the exact value of the needed degrees of freedom ($df = 87$, for example), then use the closest value *below* the one needed ($df = 80$ in this example).

6. When $\sigma_{\overline{Y}}$ must be estimated by $s_{\overline{Y}}$, the t-distribution must be used to calculate confidence intervals. In this case, the value of w in the general form of a confidence interval is $w = t \times s_{\overline{Y}}$. The value of t is obtained from tables of the t-distribution and therefore depends on the degrees of freedom.

7. The distinction between s_Y and $s_{\overline{Y}}$, and between the t-distribution and the normal distribution, gives rise to two commonly asked questions. These two questions are addressed in Box 5.1.

Worked Examples

For these examples, we return to Problem 2 of Comprehension Check 5.1. In that problem, 50 high school students from one school district and 20 high school students from another school district took the verbal component of the Scholastic Aptitude Test (SAT-V). Recall that scores on the SAT are scaled to have a mean of $\mu = 500$ and a standard deviation of $\sigma = 100$.

Box 5.1

Two Commonly Asked Questions

1. When do I use s_Y and when $s_{\overline{Y}}$?

First determine whether the variable you need a probability for is a score (Y) or the mean $\overline{Y}$. The answer then lies in the subscripts. The subscripts indicate that s_Y is the standard deviation of the distribution of Y, and $s_{\overline{Y}}$ is the standard deviation (the standard error) of the distribution of $\overline{Y}$. If you need to find the probability for values of Y, then use the standard deviation, s_Y. If you need to find the probability for values of $\overline{Y}$, then use the standard error, $s_{\overline{Y}}$.

2. When do I use z and when t?

The answer to this question depends on whether the population variance is known or whether the standard error is a sample-based estimate. If the value of σ^2 is known, then the population value of the standard error can be calculated and the normal distribution (z) is appropriate. If the variance is unknown and must be estimated from the data, then the t-distribution is the appropriate distribution.

Note that this distinction between t and z becomes an issue only for questions about the probability of values of $\overline{Y}$. The t-distribution is not used to answer questions about the probability of values of Y, the variable itself.

In Problem 2 of Comprehension Check 5.1, it was assumed that the samples from both school districts were random samples from a population with $\mu = 500$ and $\sigma = 100$. Suppose the investigators now reject this assumption. They claim that each sample was randomly chosen from the populations defined as their respective school districts, but they suspect that both the mean and the standard deviation of the SAT-V scores for these two school districts differ from each other and from the general population. In short, samples must be treated as having been drawn from different populations and the values of μ and σ are unknown for both these populations.

One school district had a larger sample than the other: $n = 50$ versus $n = 20$. For ease of identification, we will refer to the population from which the larger sample was drawn as the "large-sample population" and to the other population as the "small-sample population."

Example 1   SAT-V scores

Describe the implications of this new assumption for calculating the 95% confidence interval of the mean SAT-V scores for the respective populations from which these samples were drawn.

Answer Because the standard deviations are now unknown, they must be estimated from the data. The effect of using estimates ($s_{\overline{Y}}$) rather than the parameter value ($\sigma_{\overline{Y}}$) is that, when $\overline{Y}$ is converted to standard score form by forming the ratio $(\overline{Y} - \mu)/s_{\overline{Y}}$, the value of this ratio is no longer normally distributed but follows the *t*-distribution instead. For the larger sample, the ratio will follow a *t*-distribution with 49 degrees of freedom; for the smaller sample, it follows a *t*-distribution with 19 degrees of freedom.

Example 2 **SAT-V scores**

The following results were obtained for the SAT-V scores from the samples of students tested.

Population	n	$\overline{Y}$	s_Y
Large sample	50	527	93
Small sample	20	480	110

a. Calculate the estimated standard error of the mean for each population.

b. Calculate the 95% confidence interval for the mean SAT score of each population.

c. Calculate the 90% confidence interval for the mean SAT score of each population.

Answer

a. The estimated standard error for the *large-sample population* is

$$s_{\overline{Y}} = \frac{s_Y}{\sqrt{n}} = \frac{93}{\sqrt{50}} = 13.15$$

For the *small-sample population*, it is

$$s_{\overline{Y}} = \frac{s_Y}{\sqrt{n}} = \frac{110}{\sqrt{20}} = 24.60$$

b. For the *large-sample population*, the 95% confidence interval for the mean SAT score is $\overline{Y} \pm w$, where $\overline{Y} = 527$ and

$$w = t \times s_{\overline{Y}}$$

$$= 2.021 \times 13.15$$

$$= 27 \text{ SAT score units (to the nearest whole number)}$$

(*Note:* The values for $df = 49$ are not included in the table, so the conservative strategy of rounding down to $df = 40$ has been used. Thus $t = 2.021$ is the tabled value for $df = 40$ that marks off a combined area of .05 in the tails and .95 in the center.) The 95% confidence interval is therefore 527 ± 27 or 500 to 554.

For the *small-sample population*, the 95% confidence interval for the mean SAT score is $\overline{Y} \pm w$, where $\overline{Y} = 480$ and

$$w = t \times s_{\overline{Y}}$$

$$= 2.093 \times 24.60$$

$$= 51 \text{ SAT-V score units (to the nearest whole number)}$$

(*Note:* $t = 2.093$ is the tabled value for $df = 19$ that marks off a combined area of .05 in the tails and .95 in the center.) The 95% confidence interval is therefore 480 ± 51, or 429 to 531.

c. For the *large-sample population*, the 90% confidence interval for the mean SAT score is $\overline{Y} \pm w$, where $\overline{Y} = 527$ and

$$w = t \times s_{\overline{Y}} = 1.684 \times 13.15$$

$$= 22 \text{ SAT-V score units (to the nearest whole number)}$$

(*Note:* $t = 1.684$ is the tabled value for $df = 40$ that marks off a combined area of .10 in the tails and .90 in the center.) The 90% confidence interval is therefore 527 ± 22, or 505 to 549. For the *small-sample population*, the 90% confidence interval for the mean SAT score is $\overline{Y} \pm w$, where $\overline{Y} = 480$ and

$$w = t \times s_{\overline{Y}} = 1.729 \times 24.60$$

$$= 43 \text{ SAT-V score units (to the nearest whole number)}$$

(*Note:* $t = 1.729$ is the tabled value for $df = 19$ that marks off a combined area of .10 in the tails and .90 in the center.) The 90% confidence interval is therefore 480 ± 43, or 437 to 523.

Example 3   SAT-V scores

A further review of the situation leads to the claim that, although the two populations defined by the school districts are probably different with respect to their *mean* SAT-V scores, it is safe to assume that their *standard deviations* are the same and equal to that of the general population. Accepting this claim that $\sigma = 100$ for both populations, calculate the 95% confidence interval for the mean SAT-V score of each population.

Answer If the population standard deviation is known, then the standard errors no longer need to be estimated. For the *large-sample* population, the standard error will be

$$\sigma_{\overline{Y}} = \frac{\sigma_Y}{\sqrt{n}} = \frac{100}{\sqrt{50}} = 14.14$$

For the *small-sample* population, the standard error will be

$$\sigma_{\overline{Y}} = \frac{\sigma_Y}{\sqrt{n}} = \frac{100}{\sqrt{20}} = 22.36$$

For the *large-sample* population, the 95% confidence interval for the mean SAT-V score is $\overline{Y} \pm w$, where $\overline{Y} = 527$ and

$$w = z \times \sigma_{\overline{Y}} = 1.96 \times 14.14$$

$$= 28 \text{ SAT-V score units (to the nearest whole number)}$$

The 95% confidence interval is therefore 527 ± 28, or 499 to 555.

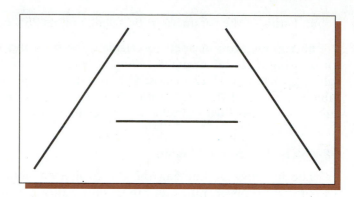

Figure 5.7
Ponzo illusion.

For the *small-sample* population, the 95% confidence interval for the mean SAT score is $\overline{Y} \pm w$, where $\overline{Y} = 480$ and

$$w = 1.96 \times 22.36$$

$$= 44 \text{ SAT-V score units (to the nearest whole number)}$$

The 95% confidence interval is therefore 480 ± 44, or 436 to 524.

Problems

Problem 1   Ponzo illusion

The Ponzo illusion presents two horizontal lines within two sloping lines (Figure 5.7). Although the horizontal lines are equal in length, most observers report that the upper line is longer. To measure the size of the illusion, the investigator asks observers to adjust one of the lines until the two lines *appear* equal. The effect of the illusion is that observers adjust the line lengths such that the bottom line is physically longer than the top line. With this adjustment, the lines *appear* to be of equal length. The magnitude of the illusion for each of these judgments is therefore measured as the difference, after the observer has made the adjustment, between the actual length of the bottom line and that of the top line.

Data Set 5.1 reports estimates by observers of the size of the Ponzo illusion. These observations can be thought of as a random sample of $n = 40$ measures from a population of such measures. A minus sign indicates that on that particular trial the bottom line was judged longer than the top line.

Data Set 5.1   Ponzo illusion estimates for Problem 1

−2	1	5	6	−7	17	6	13	18	14
−10	10	−1	14	17	12	−4	−4	5	13
−5	8	25	11	10	14	−11	14	13	−10
0	1	−1	−2	8	9	2	6	20	5

The mean and the sum of squares for these observations is respectively $\overline{Y} = 6.0$ and $SS_Y = 3078.0$.

a. Estimate the parameter μ by calculating its 95% confidence interval.

b. Suppose you decided to calculate the 90% and the 99% confidence intervals for μ, using these same data. (i) Would the lower bound of the 90% confidence interval be greater than 3.17 or less? (ii) Would the upper bound of the 99% confidence interval be greater than 8.83 or less? (iii) Confirm your answers to (i) and (ii) by calculating both the 90% and 99% confidence intervals.

Problem 2   Ponzo illusion

The investigator studying the Ponzo illusion obtains a second random sample, also of $n = 40$ observations. For these observations, $\overline{Y} = 7.20$ and $SS_Y = 3974.0$.

a. Calculate the 90% confidence interval on the basis of this new set of data.

b. Explain to someone who has never taken a course in statistics why this confidence interval is different from the 90% interval calculated in the previous problem.

5.3   Interpreting Confidence Intervals

5.3.1   What Does a Confidence Interval Mean?

The exact meaning of a confidence interval has been the subject of extensive debate among statisticians. The point at issue is this: Under a strict relative frequency interpretation of probability, it would be meaningless to make direct probability statements about μ. Statements such as $P(\mu > 12) = .95$ or $P(\mu < 8) = .05$ would be meaningless because μ is a constant, not a random variable. If probabilities are to be interpreted as long-run relative frequencies, then statements such as $P(\mu > 12) = .95$ could only mean that $\mu > 12$ on 95% of occasions. But because μ is a constant and cannot vary, it is either always greater than 12 or it is always less than 12. It must be one or the other—it cannot be greater than 12 on a certain proportion of occasions and less than 12 on the remainder.

Interval estimates are probability statements about the interval rather than directly about μ.

The usual way around this difficulty is to regard μ as fixed and the confidence interval itself as variable. According to this view, a 95% confidence interval amounts to the claim that, if repeated samples were drawn and a confidence interval calculated for each of these samples, then 95% of these confidence intervals would include the parameter μ. The interval 638 to 714 milliseconds therefore is a 95% confidence interval in the sense that the probability is .95 that this is one of the intervals that does include μ.

This point can be illustrated by using the analogy of estimating the distance between New York and Boston. Suppose a large number of people each make an interval estimate of this distance. The claim of 95% confidence would be that 95% of these individual estimates include the true distance. Therefore if one of the estimates is selected, there is a probability of .95 that it will be an estimate that includes the true value. The distance between New York and Boston remains fixed; it is the interval that varies from one occasion to another.

The idea that it is the confidence interval itself that is variable, not μ, is illustrated more formally in Figure 5.8, which shows what might happen if a number of samples of the same size were drawn and the 95% confidence interval calculated for each. The

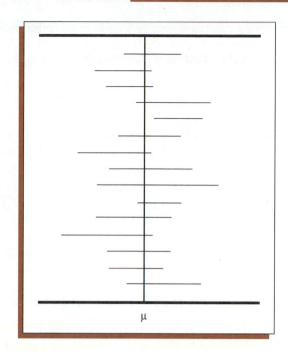

Figure 5.8
Set of 95% confidence intervals based on 15 different samples of the same size. Note that they differ in width and location relative to μ. Note also that one of the intervals does not cover μ.

vertical line represents the value of μ, the horizontal lines the confidence intervals. Notice that the length of each line that represents the width of the confidence interval varies from one sample to another, as does its location relative to μ. The interval is a 95% interval in the sense that with such repeated sampling, 95% of the intervals would contain μ within their length.

5.3.2 Width of the Confidence Interval

As noted previously, the total width of the confidence interval is $2w$, the distance between the interval's lower bound of $\overline{Y} - w$ and its upper bound of $\overline{Y} + w$. For our reaction time data, the width was $638 - 714$, or 76 milliseconds.

The width of a confidence interval will vary, depending on the level of confidence desired. With everything else held constant, the greater the desired level of confidence, the wider the interval will need to be. This relationship is intuitively reasonable. If everything else is held constant, the only way to increase the probability that the interval will include μ is to make it wider. In estimating the distance between Boston and New York, the person estimating may feel comfortable with the estimate 210 ± 10 miles. But if a $500 penalty is imposed for stating an interval that does not include the true distance, a wise strategy would be to widen the interval. An estimate of 210 ± 50 miles would give much greater assurance of avoiding the penalty.

In graphical terms, increasing the desired level of confidence corresponds to decreasing the area in the tails of the distribution. This decrease is accomplished by lengthening the interval so that the ends of the interval move further into the tails.

This last point can be confirmed by examining the tables themselves. Consider our braking reaction time example. The w value for the 95% confidence interval was

$$w = t \times s_{\overline{Y}} = 2.262 \times 16.97$$

$$= 38 \text{ milliseconds}$$

> The width of a confidence interval is $2w$.

To calculate the 99% confidence interval, the value of t for 95% (2.262) must be replaced with the tabulated value for the combined tail area of .01. Consulting Statistical Table 3 ($df = 9$), we find this value to be $t = 3.250$. The new value of w is

$$w = t \times s_{\bar{Y}} = 3.250 \times 16.97$$

$$= 55 \text{ milliseconds}$$

The 99% confidence interval therefore has a width of 110 msec.

If a lower confidence level is considered satisfactory, then the confidence interval will be narrower. To calculate the 90% confidence interval, for example, we need the tabulated value of t for a combined tail area of .10. Consulting Statistical Table 3 ($df = 9$), we find this value to be $t = 1.833$. The new value of w is therefore

$$w = t \times s_{\bar{Y}} = 1.833 \times 16.97$$

$$= 31 \text{ milliseconds}$$

5.3.3 Factors Influencing the Width of a Confidence Interval

As mentioned previously, the width of the confidence interval is a measure of the precision with which μ has been estimated. For a given level of confidence, the narrower the interval, the greater the precision. In general, greater precision is desirable, although there is usually a point at which increasing precision is of no practical benefit. Nevertheless, in planning an investigation, it is desirable to do whatever is possible to ensure adequate precision; and, to this end, it is helpful to examine the factors (other than the confidence level) that influence the width of the confidence interval and through which precision might be increased.

The width of a confidence interval is defined as

$$2w = 2 \times t \times s_{\bar{Y}}$$

This formula suggests that one way of increasing precision is through decreasing the size of $s_{\bar{Y}}$. Recall that

$$s_{\bar{Y}} = \frac{s_Y}{\sqrt{n}}$$

This expression shows that precision can be increased (the size of $s_{\bar{Y}}$ reduced) in two ways: by reducing the size of s_Y or by increasing n.

Reducing the Size of s_Y

We can reduce the size of s_Y by reducing the size of the residuals. (Recall that s_Y^2 is the mean of the squared residuals. In Chapter 8, we will discuss methods for achieving this end.) This strategy amounts to reducing the noisiness of the data through improved experimental control over extraneous influences. This strategy is obviously inappropriate when the response measure is intended to measure individual differences such as height or IQ; in this case, variability among the measures is the phenomenon of interest, not something to be reduced.

For a given confidence level, the width of the confidence interval is determined by the variability of the data and the sample size.

Increasing n

This strategy is simply a matter of making more observations, usually by using more participants. It is a straightforward exploitation of the law of large numbers and is by far the most commonly used method of improving precision. Later chapters will discuss methods of obtaining a desired degree of precision through using an appropriate value of n.

In sum, the relationship between the confidence level and the width of a confidence interval are related as follows:

- For a fixed level of confidence, the width of the confidence interval will depend on the data: the size of s_Y and the value of n, because these are the values that determine $s_{\bar{Y}}$.

- For given values of s_Y and n, the more confidence required, the wider must be the confidence interval. The 99% confidence interval will always be wider than the 95% confidence interval for the same data.

5.3.4 Using Confidence Intervals to Make Decisions

SAT-V Scores

The SAT-V example used in Section 5.2.3 asked how SAT-V data might be used to answer the question about a possible difference between students in this district and the national average of 500. The mean SAT-V score for the sample is 21 points lower than the national average. Does this observed difference of 21 points lead to the conclusion that the *population* mean for the district is below the national average?

We know that the 95% confidence interval for the population mean for the school district is

$$CI_{.95} = 479 \pm 19, \text{ or } 460 \text{ to } 498$$

To answer the directors' question, we must note that any decision will be cast in probabilistic terms. With this understanding, we can use the confidence interval to give an answer.

- First, we take the 95% confidence interval of 460 to 498 as the range of "plausible" values for μ.

- Second, we note that the value in question (500) lies outside this range of plausible values. In this sense, 500 can be considered an implausible value for the population mean of this school district.

- Third, we conclude that, because 500 is an implausible value for μ, the data from this sample provide evidence that the population mean of this school district is different from 500.

IQ Scores

A second example was introduced in Section 5.2.2. In this example, an educator asked whether the mean IQ score for students in her school district might be different from 100. To address this question, a random sample of $n = 100$ IQ scores was obtained. The mean of these 100 scores was found to be 102, and the 95% confidence interval was calculated and found to be 99 to 105. What should the educator conclude? Is the mean IQ score for students in her school district different from 100?

■ First, we will take the 95% confidence interval of 99 to 105 as the range of "plausible" values for μ, the population mean of this school district.

■ Second, we note that the value in question (100) lies within this range of plausible values. In this sense, the value of 100 can be considered plausible.

■ Third, we conclude that, because 100 remains a plausible value for μ, the data from this sample provide no convincing evidence that the population mean (μ) of this school district is different from 100.

Plausible and Implausible

The confidence interval specifies a range of plausible values for μ.

In these two examples, the terms *plausible* and *implausible* have a precise meaning linked to the .95 level chosen for the confidence interval. The criterion for implausibility would be more stringent if we used the 99% confidence interval. Alternatively, the criterion would be less stringent if we used the 90% confidence interval. Which criterion to use is a matter of judgment on the part of the investigator, although scientists conventionally employ either the 95% or 99% levels as the decision criterion.

This choice of confidence levels is related to the issue of parsimony discussed in Chapter 1. This idea, you will remember, is that science is conservative in the sense that it retains the simplest hypothesis compatible with the data. Only if the data render such simplicity implausible is a simpler hypothesis rejected in favor of one that is more complex.

When we use the 95% confidence interval as a criterion, the SAT-V data suggest such implausibility. Because 500 is an implausible value for the mean of this population, the hypothesis that the mean for this population is no different from the national average is no longer tenable. It would seem that there is something about the SAT-V scores for this district that needs explanation.

In our IQ example, the educator retains the simpler hypothesis that her school district is no different from normal, because the data fail to render this hypothesis implausible. The hypothesis of no difference is a simpler hypothesis, because, unlike the alternative hypothesis (that her school district *is* different from normal), it needs to invoke no special explanatory mechanism for this particular district. By demanding high levels such as 95% for the confidence interval, the educator is applying the stringent criterion for implausibility that is normal practice in scientific data analysis.

There is more to be said about the rationale and meaning of hypothesis testing and decision making, and the discussion will be continued in Chapter 6. Such hypothesis testing is more commonly found in experimental situations in which data are used to evaluate differences between two or more conditions—such as the difference between experimental and control conditions.

Comprehension Check 5.3

Important Concepts

1. Precisely how to interpret a confidence interval has been a controversial matter. The usual interpretation within the context of a frequency interpretation of probability is that the confidence level (such as 95%) should be thought of as the long-run proportion of intervals that, over repeated sampling, would include the population mean, μ.

2. The width of a confidence interval is $2w$, the difference between the upper and lower bound of the interval. The width of a confidence interval is a measure of the precision with which μ has been estimated. Narrower intervals reflect higher precision.

3. Several factors influence the width of a confidence interval. With everything else held constant, the greater the confidence demanded, the wider the interval must be. For a fixed level of confidence, the greater the variability of the data (measured by s_Y^2), the wider the interval. With everything else held constant, the larger the sample size, the narrower the interval.

4. Confidence intervals can be used to make decisions about plausible values of μ. A simple definition of plausibility is that any value lying within the confidence interval remains a plausible value. Values outside the interval can be declared implausible. Note that plausibility and implausibility are relative concepts depending on the degree of confidence of the interval.

Worked Examples

The following examples illustrate the relationship between n, w, and confidence level.

The IQ scores in a certain school district are known to have the same standard deviation as that in the general population ($\sigma = 15$), but school board members claim that the population mean for this high school district is higher than 100. To evaluate this claim, an investigator decides to measure the IQ of a random sample from the high school population and obtain a 95% confidence interval as an estimate of the school district's true mean.

How large should the sample be? The investigator knows that the larger the sample, the more precise will be the estimate as measured by the width of the confidence interval. However, testing is expensive, so the sample should be no larger than is necessary to achieve the desired level of precision.

Example 1   **Sample size and confidence interval width**

To help decide on the sample size, calculate the value of w that would be achieved by using samples of size $n = 20, 40, 60, 100$, and 200. Remember w is the half-width of the confidence interval.

Answer To calculate the values of w, we first need the standard error, $\sigma_{\bar{Y}}$, for each of the sample sizes. The standard error is $\sigma_{\bar{Y}} = \sigma_Y/\sqrt{n} = \sigma_Y/\sqrt{20}$, $\sigma_Y/\sqrt{40}$, $\sigma_Y/\sqrt{60}$, and so on. The values of w are then obtained by using the formula

$$w = z \times \sigma_{\bar{Y}}$$

These calculations yield the values shown in Table 5.3.

Example 2   **Graphing sample size and confidence interval width**

Plot a graph that has the value of n on the x-axis and the value of w on the y-axis. Represent each of the five calculated values of w with a point above the appropriate value of n.

Answer Figure 5.9 shows a plot of w as a function of n.

Table 5.3 Values of $\sigma_{\bar{Y}}$, and w for various sample sizes in Worked Example 1

n	$\sigma_{\bar{Y}}$	w
20	3.35	6.6
40	2.37	4.6
60	1.94	3.8
100	1.50	2.9
200	1.06	2.1

Example 3   Using the graph to obtain a sample size

The investigator decides that a w value of four IQ points is an adequate degree of precision. This value of w will yield a confidence interval of $\bar{Y} \pm 4$. Using your graph, read off the approximate sample size that will be needed to yield this value of w.

Answer Reading from the graph suggests a value of n approximately midway between 50 and 60. A value of $n = 55$ would seem to be a reasonable estimate. This result is illustrated in Figure 5.10.

Example 4   Checking the value for the sample size

Check the estimate from Example 3 by reworking the problem in the opposite direction: Calculate the value of w for $n = 55$.

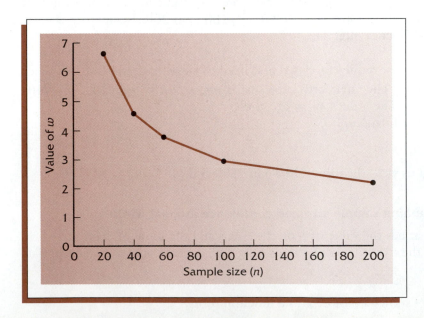

Figure 5.9
Plot of w as a function of sample size, n (worked Example 2).

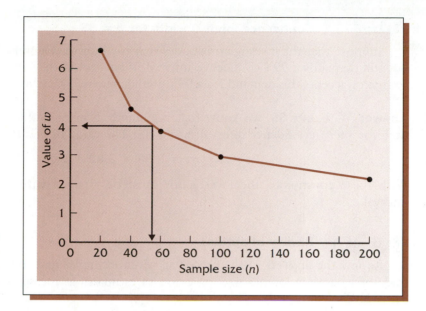

Figure 5.10
Estimating sample size for $w = 4$ (worked Example 3).

Answer For $n = 55$, the standard error will be

$$\sigma_{\bar{Y}} = \frac{\sigma_Y}{\sqrt{n}} = \frac{15}{\sqrt{55}} = 2.02$$

Then,

$$w = z \times \sigma_{\bar{Y}} = 1.96 \times 2.02$$
$$= 4.0$$

Example 5 Changing to a 99% confidence interval

Suppose the administrators decide that a 95% confidence interval is too risky and demand instead a 99% confidence interval. Given this new demand, what choices are open to the investigator?

Answer Either increase the sample size or increase the value of w that is acceptable.

Example 6 Sample size for a 99% confidence interval

A statistical consultant informs the investigator that, to keep $w = 4$ and have a 99% confidence interval, the sample size would have to be $n = 94$. Determine whether this advice is correct.

Answer With $n = 94$, we know that the standard error is

$$\sigma_{\bar{Y}} = \frac{\sigma_Y}{\sqrt{n}} = \frac{15}{\sqrt{94}} = 1.55$$

For the 99% confidence interval, $z = 2.58$; so

$$w = z \times \sigma_{\bar{Y}} = 2.58 \times 1.55 = 4.0$$

The consultant has given the correct advice.

Example 7   **Confidence interval width for *n* = 55**

Suppose that the investigator decides that the sample size must remain at $n = 55$ but still demands a 99% confidence interval. What would the value of w be if the investigator accepts this demand for a 99% confidence interval while keeping $n = 55$?

Answer With $n = 55$, we know that the standard error is 2.02 (Example 4) and that, for a 99% confidence interval, $z = 2.58$. The value of w is therefore

$$w = z \times \sigma_{\bar{Y}} = 2.58 \times 2.02 = 5.2$$

With these constraints, the investigator must be satisfied with a wider confidence interval.

Example 8   **Review of options**

Review the answers to the preceding seven examples and summarize the various trade-offs between sample size, precision of estimates as measured by w, and confidence levels.

Answer

■ If the confidence level is fixed, then increased precision (smaller w) can be achieved by increasing n.

■ If w (precision) is held constant, then an increase in confidence—say, from 95% to 99%—can be achieved by increasing n.

■ If the sample size is fixed, then the only option is a trade-off between w and the confidence level. A smaller value of w can be achieved only by reducing the confidence level. Conversely, a higher confidence level can be achieved only at the expense of increasing w.

Example 9   **Calculating a 95% confidence interval**

Having reviewed these various options, the investigator finally decides to use a sample of size 55 and calculate a 95% confidence interval. The data from this sample yield a mean of 103.2. Using the population value of 15 for σ_Y, calculate the 95% confidence interval for the mean of this population. Is there convincing evidence that the mean of this population is different from the general population mean of 100?

Answer The 95% confidence interval is

$$CI_{.95} = 103.2 \pm 4.0, \text{ or } 99.2 \text{ to } 107.2$$

Because this interval includes 100, the evidence that the population mean is different from 100 is unconvincing. The value of 100 remains plausible.

Problems

Problem 1   **Decision times**

This problem demonstrates the effect of the variance of the residuals on the width of the confidence interval. Table 5.4 shows data consisting of two hypothetical sam-

Table 5.4 Decision times in milliseconds for Problem 1

	A	B	A	B
	642	387	643	498
	643	401	644	610
	652	730	654	471
	633	547	632	560
	653	639	654	667
$\overline{Y} =$	645	601		
$s_Y =$	8.2	113.2		

ples of $n = 10$ decision times, along with the mean of each. These are computer-generated samples simulating a random selection from each of two populations, A and B. Both A and B have the same *population* mean but different variances. Suppose you were to calculate a 95% confidence interval for the mean of each population. By inspecting the data, judge which population would have the wider interval. Using the summary statistics provided at the end of the table, evaluate this judgment by calculating a 95% confidence interval for each population.

Problem 2   Ponzo illusion

Problem 2 of Comprehension Check 5.2 used a second set of Ponzo illusion data to calculate a 90% confidence interval. The interval was

$$CI_{.90} = 7.20 \pm 2.69, \text{ or } 4.51 \text{ to } 9.89$$

a. Suppose a reviewer of this study requests a more stringent 95% confidence interval for the same data. Without actually calculating this new interval, or even consulting the table of the t-distribution, which of the following intervals is the only plausible 95% confidence interval for these data?

3.97 to 10.43
5.11 to 9.29
3.27 to 9.73

b. Suppose another reviewer of this study requests an even more stringent 99% confidence interval. Using the answer to Problem 1, and once again without actually calculating this new interval, or even consulting the table of the t-distribution, choose which of the following intervals is the only plausible 99% confidence interval for these data.

4.37 to 10.03
2.88 to 11.52
1.18 to 9.82

c. For the second set of Ponzo illusion data, the 90% confidence interval is 7.2 ± 2.69, or 4.51 to 9.89. Which of the following statements best expresses the meaning of this confidence interval?

■ If many random samples of $n = 40$ observations were taken, the value of μ would fall within the interval 4.51 to 9.89 in 90% of these samples.

■ If many random samples of $n = 40$ observations were taken, the interval 4.51 to 9.89 would contain μ for 90% of these samples.

■ If many random samples of $n = 40$ observations were taken, and a 90% confidence interval calculated for each, 90% of these intervals would include μ.

d. For the second set of Ponzo illusion data, the 95% confidence interval is 3.97 to 10.43. If μ, the true value for the size of the illusion, is actually 0, then the illusion could be said not to exist. This null hypothesis of no effect (no illusion) is simpler than the alternative claim that the illusion exists. In the latter case, some special mechanism needs to be invoked to explain the illusory effect. Using the 95% confidence interval as a criterion of plausibility, do the data render the null hypothesis implausible? Does 0 remain a plausible value for the true size of the illusion? Suppose someone asked, "Does the Ponzo illusion really exist?" How would you answer?

If you had used the 99% confidence interval, would you have reached the same conclusion?

Chapter 5 Exercises

Exercise 1 Infant cognition

a. Use the results in the following table to calculate the estimated standard error for the mean for two experiments studying infant cognition. The data from these experiments were examined in Exercises 5 and 6 of Chapter 2.

b. Calculate the 95% confidence interval for the mean for each of these experiments.

c. Calculate the 99% confidence interval for the mean for each of these experiments

Experiment	n	$\overline{Y}$	SS_Y
Intermodal matching (Data Set 2.14)	40	69.27	16,434
Face recognition (Data Set 2.15)	48	62.00	17,324

Exercise 2 Role of smell in a neonate's recognition of its mother

A possible explanation of the result in the face recognition experiment is that the babies use smell rather than vision to identify their mother. Smell is thus a possible *confounding* variable. How might one control this possible confound? One technique would be to use a room deodorizer and see whether the same results are obtained. Another strategy is to ask whether, in fact, in this kind of experimental context, neonates respond to their mother's odor.

To answer this question, investigators repeat the experiment but remove visual cues by covering the apertures through which the face are visible with an open-weave fabric that nevertheless allows a free flow of air (and thus odor) between the women and the baby. If the babies used smell in the face recognition experiment as a basis for directing their gaze, then we should observe a mother preference under these new conditions. Fifty newborns participated in this experiment (Data Set 5.2). The 50 scores represent the percentage of total looking time spent by each infant focusing on his or her mother. Thus, the extent to which the score is above 50 is a measure of the degree of preference for mother's location over that of the stranger. This hypothetical experiment is modeled after the work reported by Bushnell, Sai, and Mullin (1989).

Data Set 5.2 Looking time scores for Exercise 2

70	61	78	79	61	68	56	56	73	81
52	23	15	61	36	37	17	30	59	25
67	42	35	45	64	42	69	67	16	48
78	53	51	48	77	46	47	49	87	27
28	51	47	43	34	98	83	17	53	49

a. Construct a stemplot for these data and check for features that might undermine data analysis.

b. Use the following results to calculate the estimated standard error for the mean: $n = 50$, $\overline{Y} = 51.98\%$, $SS_Y = 20{,}0141$.

c. Calculate the 95% confidence interval for the mean.

Exercise 3 Do infants discriminate?

Having calculated the 95% confidence intervals for the mean for the three experiments in Exercises 1 and 2, for each of these experiments state (and give reasons) whether the evidence indicates that infants are capable of the discrimination required by the experiment. Discrimination would be indicated by a population mean not equal to 50%.

Exercise 4 Confidence game

This exercise is actually a game aimed at increasing your understanding of the relationship between level of confidence and the width of a confidence interval. It is called the Confidence Game and is described in GameBox 5.1 on pages 252–253. It may be sufficient to play it just in your imagination, although with effort and a little ingenuity, it could be turned into a data analyst's version of a well-known board game.

Chapter 5 Review

Terms

confidence interval
confidence level
estimated standard error of the mean
mean of the sampling distribution of the mean
sampling distribution of the mean
standard error of the mean
t-distribution
unbiased estimate

GameBox 5.1

The Confidence Game

This game requires two or more players, one of whom is designated the dealer. The game consists of a series of turns. On each turn, the dealer selects a question and reads it to all the players. All questions require a number for an answer and come from one of six categories. Possible categories and some sample questions are listed later. [It is left to you to assemble a full set of questions, should you decide to develop a playable game. To help you understand the nature of confidence intervals, it may be sufficient simply to try a few examples against imaginary opponents.]

After the dealer has read the question, each player writes down an answer but does not show it to any of the other players. All answers must take the form, not of a single number, but of an interval of values within which the player believes the exact answer lies. For example, in answering the question "How many air miles is it from New York to Chicago?" you might answer "700 plus or minus 40 miles." All answers are to be given in this general form of a number plus or minus a value that gives the range within which you think the correct answer lies. If you think that you know the *exact* answer, you can make your range plus or minus 0.

The player who wins the turn is the player whose answer is both correct (the stated range includes the exact answer) and has the shortest range. For example, the correct answer to the question "How far is it from New York to Chicago?" is 714 miles. An answer "700 plus or minus 40 miles" and an answer "730 plus or minus 20 miles" are both correct because both answers quote a range that includes 714. However, the latter answer wins because it has a narrower range.

In answering each question, there are two goals:

■ Make sure that your range actually contains the correct value.

■ Make the range as narrow as is compatible with achieving the first goal.

Obviously the first goal can be achieved by making the range very large—for example, saying that the distance between New York and Chicago is 700 plus or minus 500 miles. Such a wide range reflects only

Formulas

population standard error of the mean: $\sigma_{\overline{Y}} = \dfrac{\sigma_Y}{\sqrt{n}}$

converting a sample mean to a z-score: $z = \dfrac{\overline{Y} - \mu}{\sigma_{\overline{Y}}}$

confidence interval: $CI = \text{point estimate} \pm w$

■ When the standard error is known, $CI = \overline{Y} \pm (z \times \sigma_{\overline{Y}})$, where the value of z is obtained from the table of normal distribution and depends on the desired level of confidence.

GameBox 5.1 (*continued*)

vague knowledge of the actual distance. Making your range very large may increase your confidence in achieving the first goal, but you will probably lose because another player will display more precise knowledge with a smaller correct range.

This game has instructional value because it illustrates two important features of confidence intervals.

1. The trade-off between confidence level and width. Confidence can be increased at the expense of increasing the width; width can be narrowed at the expense of decreased confidence level.

2. The only way to avoid this trade-off is through more knowledge or more data. With more knowledge or data, width can be narrowed without sacrificing confidence or confidence can be increased without widening the interval.

Here are a few sample questions of the kind that might be used in this game.

Geography	How far is it from New York to Chicago?
	How high is the highest mountain in North America?
History	In what year did George Washington die?
Sports	What is the highest number of runs scored by one side in a major league baseball game?
	What is the current world record for the 100-meter sprint?
Entertainment	How many movies has Sean Connery appeared in?
Science and medicine	How many bones are in the human body?
Arts and letters	How many plays did William Shakespeare write?

■ When the standard error is unknown and has been estimated, $CI = \overline{Y} \pm (t \times s_{\overline{Y}})$, where the value of t is obtained from the table of the t-distribution and depends on degrees of freedom and the desired level of confidence.

$$\text{width of confidence interval} = 2w$$

Quiz

Question 1

Complete each sentence with a term from the following list. Not all terms may be needed, and some may be used more than once.

central limit theorem	sampling distribution	z-score
random variable	t-ratio	normal distribution
t-distribution	n − 1	standard error
n	standard deviation	

The mean of a sample can be considered a _____ because its value can be thought of as a single random selection from a hypothetical population of sample means. The probability distribution of the sample mean is called the _____ of the mean. Under very general conditions, the form of this distribution is the _____, a result that reflects the impact of the _____. The standard deviation of this distribution is called the _____ and its value is the _____ of the original variable divided by the square root of _____.

How you obtain probabilities for values of $\bar{Y}$ depends on whether or not you know the population _____. If this value is known, then $\bar{Y} - \mu$ is divided by this value to form a _____ and probabilities can be obtained from tables of the _____. If the value is unknown and must be estimated, then $\bar{Y} - \mu$ is divided by this estimated value to form a _____ and probabilities can be obtained from tables of the _____.

Question 2

A set of problems, covering different variables, asks for the probability that a sample mean will exceed a certain value. In your own words, state under what conditions you would use the t-distribution as opposed to the normal distribution to solve each problem.

Question 3

In calculating a confidence interval, an investigator mistakenly uses the normal distribution when the t-distribution should have been used. Will this mistake result in a confidence interval that is wider or narrower than it should be?

Question 4

An experimenter calculates the mean, the variance, and the 95% confidence interval for the mean for data from a perception experiment with $n = 45$ participants. However, closer examination of the raw data shows that, whereas 42 of these subjects obtained scores ranging from 53% to 89% correct responses, 3 subjects scored only 2%, 4%, and 0% correct. The experimenter decides to remove the data for these subjects and to recalculate various statistics with the reduced sample of $n = 42$. Which one of the following statements is true?

The effect of eliminating these three scores will be to

a. Decrease the mean, the variance, and the width of the 95% confidence interval.

b. Decrease the mean and the variance, and increase the width of the 95% confidence interval.

c. Increase the mean and decrease both the variance and the width of the 95% confidence interval.

d. Increase the mean, decrease the variance, and increase the width of the 95% confidence interval.

Chapter 6 Preview

The purpose of Chapter 5 was to examine the difference between $\overline{Y}$ and μ. We cannot know for certain what that difference is, but knowing the sampling distribution of the estimate makes it possible to talk about the magnitude of the difference in probabilistic terms. Chapter 5 described the confidence interval as a way of making such a statement.

Chapter 6 builds on this rationale in a straightforward way. Its goal is to handle the more common situation in which our interest lies in the *difference between two means,* rather than in the value of a single mean. We want to say something useful about $\mu_1 - \mu_2$ rather than about μ, where the subscripts refer to the two conditions of an experiment, or two distinct populations.

In addition to calculating a confidence interval as an estimate of $\mu_1 - \mu_2$, most researchers also wish to make a specific decision as to whether or not the value of $\mu_1 - \mu_2$ is 0. Is there a difference between the two conditions? Any such decision will, of course, be cast in probabilistic terms, and just how this decision should be made has been a matter of considerable debate. Chapter 6 gives a brief overview of the main issues in this debate.

6 EXPERIMENTS WITH TWO INDEPENDENT GROUPS

The procedures described in Chapter 5 were relevant to response measures obtained under a single condition or from a single sample. For example, the reaction time measurements for a driver's braking were taken in order to estimate mean reaction time under one set of conditions. This chapter extends the coverage to situations in which response measures are compared under two conditions. Instead of estimating a single mean such as a driver's braking time, we now want to estimate the difference between two means—the difference in braking time, say, between drivers with a .05% blood alcohol level and drivers in a zero-alcohol control condition. Chapter 7 carries this development still further to situations in which there are three or more conditions. Both these chapters will cover only experiments with categorical predictor variables. Experiments with quantitative predictor variables are described in Chapter 9.

6.1 Independent-Groups Designs

Published descriptions of experiments in the behavioral sciences usually contain a section describing the "experimental design." So far, we have used the term *experimental design* in a very general way to refer to the conditions of an experiment, the various methods that are used to eliminate bias (Section 1.3), and methods (see Chapter 8) for ensuring adequate precision. The term *experimental design* can also be used in a somewhat narrower sense to refer to the basic structure of an experiment: the number and type of conditions, and how participants are assigned to those conditions.

The experiments discussed in this chapter all use two independent groups. Such designs are often referred to as *between-subjects designs*. The requirement that the groups be independent has two implications:

■ Each subject is in one and only one of the conditions.

■ The subjects are assigned independently of one another. The selection or assignment of a subject to one condition has no influence on the condition to which any other subject is assigned.

Independent-groups, or between-subjects, experiments can be contrasted with designs—called *repeated measures* designs, or *within-subjects* designs—in which the same subject participates in both conditions. Consider an experiment to investigate whether common, frequently used words are more easily remembered than are rare, infrequently used words. The experiment consisted of two conditions, common words and rare words. A total of 22 volunteers participated. Each participant studied a list of 40 words made up of 20 common words and 20 rare words. The response measure was the proportion (out of 20) of words of each kind remembered in a recall test. In this within-subjects experiment, every participant takes part in *both* conditions. Each participant will contribute two scores: one for common words and one for rare words.

Between-subjects designs can also be contrasted with *matched-pair designs*. For example, an experimental study of reaction to stress has two conditions, an experimental condition and a control condition. The investigator recruits 20 pairs of identical twins and uses a coin toss to assign one twin from each pair to the experimental condition, the other to the control condition. In this matched-pair experiment, each participant is in only one condition, but the assignment of participants to groups is not independent. The assignment of one twin determines the assignment of the other. This method of assignment directly contradicts the requirement of independence that states that the assignment of a subject to one condition has no influence on the condition to which any other subject is assigned.

Completely Randomized Design

The completely randomized design is a form of between-subjects design in which participants are assigned randomly to the conditions.

> *The completely randomized design is one in which each participant is assigned independently to one, and only one, of the conditions of the experiment by a simple process of randomization.*

Recall from Section 1.3 that random assignment ensures that each participant has an equal chance of being assigned to any one of the conditions.

Consider the description of an experiment that uses a completely randomized design, a description that might be found in the experimental design section of a published paper. The essential feature of a completely randomized design is emphasized by italics.

This experiment investigated the question of whether common, frequently used words are more easily remembered than are rare, infrequently used words. The experiment consisted of two conditions. In one condition, participants studied a list of 40 common words. In a second condition, participants studied a list of 40 rare words. A total of 44 volunteers participated. *Each participant was assigned randomly and independently to one of the two conditions* such that there were 22 participants in each. The response measure was the proportion of words remembered in a recall test.

Studies with Natural Predictor Variables

Section 1.3 pointed out that a natural predictor variable makes the random assignment of participants to conditions logically impossible. Experiments that do not use random assignment are sometimes referred to as *quasi-experiments*. Despite the absence of randomization, quasi-experiments qualify as independent-groups designs if the selection of a participant as a member of one group has no influence on who might be selected for the other group. For example, a study comparing the learning speed of 4- and 6-year-olds would qualify as an independent-groups design if the selection of the particular children for the 4-year-old sample had no influence on which children were chosen for the 6-year-old sample. It would not qualify as an independent-groups design if, for example, the groups were formed by using younger and older siblings.

> Experiments that do not use random assignment are called quasi-experiments.

Comprehension Check 6.1

Important Concepts

1. An independent-groups design is one in which each subject takes part in only one condition and subjects are assigned independently of one another.

2. A completely randomized experimental design is an independent-groups design in which participants are randomly assigned to the conditions of an experiment.

3. Natural predictor variables preclude random assignment of participants to conditions. However, such studies can qualify as independent-groups designs. The data are analyzed in the same way as data from a completely randomized design, but the causal interpretation of the results of the analysis must be more cautious.

Worked Examples

Example 1   Motor skill

Read the description of the following experiment and explain why it is *not* an example of a completely randomized design.

This experiment evaluated improvement with practice of a simple motor skill. Performance was measured at the commencement of training and again after 20 training trials.

Answer In this experiment, every participant takes part in *both* conditions. In a completely randomized design, each participant takes part in one and only one condition.

Example 2   Tranquilizer effects

Compare the following two versions of an experiment. Which version conforms to the principles of a completely randomized design? Explain the difference.

This experiment investigated the effect of a commonly used tranquilizer on mental functioning as measured by its effect on the speed of solving simple anagrams. The experiment consisted of two conditions, experimental and placebo control. A total of 30 volunteers participated. Participants were randomly assigned to one of the two conditions, 15 participants in each.

This experiment investigated the effect of a commonly used tranquilizer on mental functioning as measured by its effect on the speed of solving simple anagrams. The experiment consisted of two conditions, experimental and control. A total of 30 volunteers participated, 15 participants in each. Participants in the experimental group were 15 volunteers who in an interview stated that they had been taking the tranquilizer for at least the past month. The control group were 15 volunteers who in a similar interview stated that they had never taken the tranquilizer.

Answer The first version of the experiment conforms to the principles of a completely randomized design. In the second version of the experiment, assignment of participants to conditions is not random. Indeed, the predictor variable in this version of the experiment (tranquilizer users versus non-tranquilizer users) is best thought of as a natural rather than a manipulated variable. It is left as a further exercise to speculate on the possible sources of bias and confounding in this version.

Problems

Problem 1   Aggression

An experimental study of aggression has two conditions, an experimental condition and a control condition. The investigator considers two possible experimental designs.

Design A: A total of 40 participants will be used; 20 participants will be randomly assigned to each condition.

Design B: The investigator will recruit 20 pairs of same-sex siblings. One sibling from each pair will be assigned to the experimental condition, the other to the control condition.

Why is Design B not a completely randomized design?

Problem 2   Sex differences in aggression

The investigator from the previous problem predicts that there are sex differences in reaction to stress caused by sex-linked genetic influences on temperament. To evaluate this claim, the stress reaction of 30 female and 30 male randomly selected volunteers is measured.

If the investigator does obtain a difference between the two groups in reaction to stress, what can be concluded about the hypothesis of sex-linked genetic influences on temperament?

6.2 Analyzing Data from Independent-Groups Designs with Two Treatments

The analysis of data from independent-groups designs is always the same, regardless of whether randomization was possible. A difference arises, however, not in the analysis of the data, but in the interpretation of the results. Recall from Section 1.3 that without randomization, causal interpretations can be quite ambiguous.

The difference between quasi-experiments and completely randomized designs is not in the data analysis but in the causal interpretation of the difference between the means.

6.2.1 Review of Basic Concepts

Phobia Treatment

We now have the necessary background to complete the analysis of the data from the experiment designed to evaluate desensitization therapy in the treatment of a phobia. The data for this experiment were originally introduced in Section 3.3.1 as Data Set 3.1. The response measure is anxiety as measured by increase in heart rate. The control condition is designated Y_1 and the experimental condition Y_2. What do we already know about this experiment? What would we like to learn from the analysis of the data?

Design The experiment has a completely randomized design. Eighteen participants were randomly assigned to each of the two conditions, for a total of 36 participants in the experiment.

Estimates of $\mu_1 - \mu_2$ The primary question that data analysis should address is the difference in anxiety between the two conditions as measured by elevation in heart rate. By how much does the therapy affect heart rate? The elevation in heart rate for the control condition is symbolized by μ_1 and that for the experimental condition by μ_2. The data analysis will answer this question by estimating the value of $\mu_1 - \mu_2$. Consider first a *point* estimate of $\mu_1 - \mu_2$. We already know that the best point estimate for $\mu_1 - \mu_2$ is $\overline{Y}_1 - \overline{Y}_2$. For the data in Data Set 3.1, we have

$$\overline{Y}_1 - \overline{Y}_2 = 10.2 - 5.2 = 5.0$$

How close is this estimate of 5.0 to the value of $\mu_1 - \mu_2$? The point estimate itself gives no information on this question. An *interval estimate* provides such information in the form of a confidence interval. Chapter 5 introduced the concept of an interval estimate for a single parameter μ. We now extend this procedure to obtain a confidence interval for the difference between two parameters.

Which Model? A second, more specific, question is whether the therapy brings about any change at all. How strong is the evidence that $\mu_1 \neq \mu_2$? The answer to this question amounts to deciding between the two models described in Section 3.3. The first model, dubbed the "full" model, hypothesizes that $\mu_1 \neq \mu_2$. This model claims that, for the control condition, the observation Y_1 is a "noisy" measurement of μ_1 and, for the experimental condition, the observation Y_2 is a "noisy" measurement of μ_2. In symbols, we have, for the control condition,

$$Y_1 = \mu_1 + e$$

and, for the experimental condition,

$$Y_2 = \mu_2 + e$$

The alternative and simpler model hypothesizes that $\mu_1 = \mu_2$. Because it asserts that there is no difference, this hypothesis is termed the *null hypothesis;* the corresponding model can be termed the *null model.* If this null hypothesis is true, then μ_1 and μ_2 are equal and can be replaced by a single symbol μ.

$$Y_1 = Y_2 = \mu + e$$

Our task is to decide between these two models. Obtaining an interval estimate and deciding between the two rival models involves a simple extension of the rationale used in Chapter 5. It is, in fact, the identical logic now applied to differences between conditions rather than to the parameter of a single condition. In Chapter 5, we learned how to make probability statements about $\overline{Y}$. In this chapter, we will explain how to make probability statements about $\overline{Y}_1 - \overline{Y}_2$. In more technical terms, in Chapter 5, we learned how to treat $\overline{Y}$ as a random variable; in this chapter, we will explain how $\overline{Y}_1 - \overline{Y}_2$ can be treated as a random variable. The first application of these ideas is the calculation of the confidence interval for $\mu_1 - \mu_2$.

Residuals and Goodness of Fit In Section 3.3.1, we fitted both the full and the null models to the data, obtained the residuals, and calculated the variance of these residuals in each case. For the full model, the fitted model was

$$Y_1 = 10.2 + e \quad \text{(control condition)}$$

$$Y_2 = 5.2 + e \quad \text{(experimental condition)}$$

For the null model, the fitted model for both the control and experimental conditions was

$$Y_1 = Y_2 = 7.7 + e$$

Table 6.1 gives the residuals for both the null and full models.

Recall that in Chapter 3 we calculated the sum of squares of the residuals for each model. This calculation showed that the full model produced a 56% reduction ($R^2 = .56$) in the sum of squares for the residuals. This reduction may seem a substantial improvement in the goodness of fit, but how do we know whether it is sufficient to warrant rejecting the null hypothesis? If subjective judgments are to be avoided, we need a more formal method of deciding whether a given value of R^2 reflects a difference between the two models that is large enough to justify adopting the full model. Such a method will be developed in this chapter.

In calculating the variance of the residuals under the full model, we made the important assumption that the population variance of these residuals was the same for both conditions. This was the assumption of homogeneity of variance. On the basis of this assumption, we obtained a single estimate of this variance by averaging the sum of squares (more explicitly, the sum of the squared residuals) to obtain a single value of MS_e for the two conditions. The sum of the squared residuals was 59.6 for the

Table 6.1 Observations (Y_1 and Y_2) from the phobia treatment experiment for control and experimental conditions

Control condition			Experimental condition		
$Y_1{}^a$	$e_F{}^b$	$e_N{}^c$	$Y_2{}^a$	$e_F{}^d$	$e_N{}^e$
8.4	− 1.8	+ 0.7	5.2	+ 0.0	− 2.5
10.8	+ 0.6	+ 3.1	8.5	+ 3.3	+ 0.8
8.2	− 2.0	+ 0.5	1.9	− 3.3	− 5.8
9.6	− 0.6	+ 1.9	6.5	+ 1.3	− 1.2
5.5	− 4.7	− 2.2	8.8	+ 3.6	+ 1.1
12.6	+ 2.4	+ 4.9	5.5	+ 0.3	− 2.2
10.8	+ 0.6	+ 3.1	2.3	− 2.9	− 5.4
14.0	+ 3.8	+ 6.3	3.7	− 1.5	− 4.0
11.3	+ 1.1	+ 3.6	7.9	+ 2.7	+ 0.2
8.9	− 1.3	+ 1.2	1.9	− 3.3	− 5.8
9.8	− 0.4	+ 2.1	6.0	+ 0.8	− 1.7
10.1	− 0.1	+ 2.4	5.2	0.0	− 2.5
10.6	+ 0.4	+ 2.9	7.2	+ 2.0	− 0.5
11.3	+ 1.1	+ 3.6	0.0	− 5.2	− 7.7
9.7	− 0.5	+ 2.0	7.8	+ 2.6	+ 0.1
9.4	− 0.8	+ 1.7	2.4	− 2.8	− 5.3
10.5	+ 0.3	+ 2.8	4.7	− 0.5	− 3.0
12.1	+ 1.9	+ 4.4	8.1	+ 2.9	+ 0.4

a. Y_1 and Y_2 are measures of increase in heart rate (in beats per minute).
b. Residuals for full model: $e_F = Y_1 − 10.2$.
c. Residuals for null model: $e_N = Y_1 − 7.7$.
d. Residuals for full model: $e_F = Y_2 − 5.2$.
e. Residuals for null model: $e_N = Y_2 − 7.7$.

control group and 120.3 for the experimental group. Each of these values is based on $n − 1 = 17$ degrees of freedom. Recall that the value of MS_e is obtained by adding these two values and dividing by the summed degrees of freedom:

$$MS_e = \frac{59.6 + 120.3}{17 + 17} = 5.3$$

6.2.2 Obtaining a Confidence Interval for $\mu_1 − \mu_2$

In Section 5.2, we noted that a confidence interval has the general form

$$CI = \text{point estimate} \pm w$$

where w = a critical tabulated value $\times$ the appropriate standard deviation.

Review of Confidence Intervals for a Single Mean

Before proceeding with an account of how to apply this general form to the confidence interval for the difference between two means, we will review its application to a single mean, μ (see Section 5.2.3). The confidence interval has three basic components:

■ **Point estimate** For the confidence interval of a single mean, the point estimate is $\overline{Y}$.

■ **Critical tabled value** If σ is unknown and must be estimated, then the critical tabulated value is obtained by using the t-distribution and depends on the level of confidence required (.95, for example) and the degrees of freedom on which the estimate of σ is based $(n - 1)$.

■ **Appropriate standard deviation** The appropriate standard deviation is the estimated standard error, $s_{\overline{Y}}$, the estimated standard deviation of the sampling distribution of $\overline{Y}$.

Form of a Confidence Interval for $\mu_1 - \mu_2$

The confidence interval for $\mu_1 - \mu_2$ will have the same three components as the general form.

■ **Point estimate** The point estimate of $\mu_1 - \mu_2$ is $\overline{Y}_1 - \overline{Y}_2$.

■ **Critical tabled value** We will consider only cases in which the value of σ is unknown. In practice, this is almost always the case. As with a single mean, the need to estimate σ demands the use of the t-distribution; and, as before, when consulting the tables for the value of t, we will need to know two values: the level of confidence desired and the degrees of freedom.

For the single mean, the degrees of freedom were $n - 1$, the number of independent observations used to estimate the value of σ. Exactly the same principle applies in the case of the difference between two means. As described in Section 3.3.1, each condition contributes $n - 1$ degrees of freedom; so, for two conditions, the degrees of freedom will be $2(n - 1)$. If there is an unequal number of observations in each condition, then the degrees of freedom are $(n_1 - 1) + (n_2 - 1) = N - 2$.

For our phobia treatment experiment, $n = 18$; so each condition contributes 17 degrees of freedom for a total degrees of freedom of $2 \times 17 = 34$. If a 95% confidence interval is required, then, from the tables of the t-distribution, the critical value is found to be 2.032. The relevant excerpt of the full table is shown in Table 6.2.

The degrees of freedom are $2(n - 1)$.

■ **Appropriate standard deviation** For a single mean, the appropriate standard deviation was the estimated standard error, $s_{\overline{Y}}$, that is, the estimated standard deviation of the sampling distribution of $\overline{Y}$. For the difference between two means, the appropriate standard deviation is again an estimated standard error, this time the estimated standard deviation of the sampling distribution of $\overline{Y}_1 - \overline{Y}_2$. Notice that, in both cases, the appropriate standard deviation is the estimated standard error of the point estimate.

Estimated Standard Error of the Difference Between Two Means

What is the estimated standard error of the sampling distribution of $\overline{Y}_1 - \overline{Y}_2$? We will denote this standard error by $s_{\overline{Y}_1 - \overline{Y}_2}$. As before, the subscript indicates the random

Table 6.2 Portion of t-distribution

	Proportion in two tails		
df	.10	.05	.01
⋮	⋮	⋮	⋮
32	1.694	2.037	2.738
33	1.692	2.035	2.733
34	1.691	2.032	2.728
35	1.690	2.030	2.724
36	1.688	2.028	2.719
⋮	⋮	⋮	⋮

variable whose standard deviation is being estimated. The formula for the standard error for the difference between two means is

$$s_{\bar{Y}_1 - \bar{Y}_2} = \sqrt{\frac{2MS_e}{n}}$$

where n is the number of observations in each condition. If there is an unequal number of observations in each condition, then this formula becomes

$$s_{\bar{Y}_1 - \bar{Y}_2} = \sqrt{\frac{MS_e}{n_1} + \frac{MS_e}{n_2}}$$

An important feature of both these formulas is what they tell us about the factors that determine the size of the standard error. These factors are the same two that determined the standard error in the case of a single mean: the variability of the residuals and the sample size, n.

For the phobia treatment example, we know that $MS_e = 5.3$ and $n = 18$; so the standard error is

$$s_{\bar{Y}_1 - \bar{Y}_2} = \sqrt{\frac{2 \times 5.3}{18}} = 0.767$$

Confidence Intervals for the Phobia Treatment Experiment

The 95% confidence interval is

$$CI_{95} = (\bar{Y}_1 - \bar{Y}_2) \pm (t \times s_{\bar{Y}_1 - \bar{Y}_2})$$
$$= 5.00 \pm (2.032 \times 0.767) = 5.00 \pm 1.559 = 3.441 \text{ to } 6.559$$

Rounding the interval to one decimal place, the probability is .95 that the interval 3.4 to 6.6 contains the true value of $\mu_1 - \mu_2$. The effect of therapy on anxiety as measured by increased heart rate is "almost certainly" a reduction of 3.4 to 6.6 beats per minute in heart rate increase. Equivalently, we can say that the probability is only .05 that the interval 3.4 to 6.6 does not contain the true value of the difference.

Obtaining a 99% confidence interval requires only that we replace the .95 value from the t-distribution with the corresponding .99 value. Consulting Table 6.2, we see that 2.728 is the value we want. The 99% confidence interval then becomes

$$CI_{.99} = 5.00 \pm (2.728 \times 0.767) = 5.00 \pm 2.092 = 2.908 \text{ to } 7.092$$

Again rounding the numbers to one decimal place, we can claim that the probability is .99 that the interval 2.9 to 7.1 contains the true value of $\mu_1 - \mu_2$.

Notice that this confidence interval is wider than the 95% interval, a widening that reflects the cost of increased confidence.

Tranquilizer Effects

Now consider the experiment described in Example 2 at the end of Section 6.1. This experiment was designed to investigate the effect of a commonly used tranquilizer on mental functioning. Mental functioning is measured in terms of time (measured in seconds) taken to solve simple anagrams. The completely randomized version of this experiment consisted of two conditions, an experimental condition and a placebo control. A total of 30 volunteers participated. The experiment uses a completely randomized design: Participants were randomly assigned to the two conditions, $n = 15$ participants in each. Note that each participant was randomly assigned to one and *only* one of the two conditions. The data for this experiment are shown in Data Set 6.1.

Data Set 6.1   Data from tranquilizer effects experiment

$$\underline{Y_1 \text{ (control)}, \overline{Y}_1 = 9.06}$$

7.3	8.0	9.4	10.1	11.6	7.8	10.2	6.4
9.9	10.3	11.2	8.9	7.9	7.6	9.3	

$$\underline{Y_2 \text{ (experimental)}, \overline{Y}_2 = 10.41}$$

10.2	11.2	9.9	13.3	9.5	10.0	9.6	10.7
10.8	9.3	8.2	9.5	11.9	11.3	10.7	

Estimates of $\mu_1 - \mu_2$

The primary question concerns the difference in time taken to solve anagrams in the two conditions. This question is answered by estimating the value of $\mu_1 - \mu_2$. The point estimate of $\mu_1 - \mu_2$ is $\overline{Y}_1 - \overline{Y}_2$. For the data, we have

$$\overline{Y}_1 - \overline{Y}_2 = 9.06 - 10.41 = -1.35$$

Notice that this difference is negative, reflecting the fact that participants in the control condition took less time than those in the experimental condition. Notice also that the negative difference is a result of the quite arbitrary decision to call the control condition Y_1 and the experimental condition Y_2. It could just as reasonably be the other way around. For no more important a reason than that it simplifies the

If the difference between the sample means is negative, work with the absolute difference.

arithmetic, we will ignore the minus sign and work with the *absolute* difference of 1.35. An absolute difference is written $|\overline{Y}_1 - \overline{Y}_2|$ and denotes the difference between the two means regardless of sign. The important thing to keep in mind is that the value of 1.35 represents a difference in which the mean for the experimental group is larger than the mean for the control group.

Our general confidence interval is CI = point estimate $\pm$ w, where w = a critical tabled value $\times$ the appropriate standard deviation. In this case, the point estimate is 1.35. We will calculate a 95% confidence interval so that the appropriate value of t from the tables of the t-distribution is one with $2(n - 1) = 28$ degrees of freedom. Consulting the tables gives us a value for t of 2.048.

The "appropriate standard deviation" is $s_{\overline{Y}_1 - \overline{Y}_2}$, the estimated standard error of the difference between two means. To calculate the value of $s_{\overline{Y}_1 - \overline{Y}_2}$, we need to estimate the variance of the residuals, σ_e^2. As before, it is obtained by adding together the sum of the squared residuals for the two conditions and dividing by the combined degrees of freedom ($df = 28$). Routine computation gives $SS_1 = 32.2$ and $SS_2 = 21.2$. Thus the mean square of the residuals is

$$MS_e = (32.2 + 21.2)/28 = 1.907$$

We can now obtain the estimated standard error.

$$s_{\overline{Y}_1 - \overline{Y}_2} = \sqrt{\frac{2MS_e}{n}} = \sqrt{\frac{2 \times 1.907}{15}} = 0.504$$

The 95% confidence interval is therefore

$$CI_{.95} = |\overline{Y}_1 - \overline{Y}_2| \pm (t \times s_{\overline{Y}_1 - \overline{Y}_2}) = 1.35 \pm (2.048 \times 0.504)$$
$$= 1.35 \pm 1.032 = 0.318 \text{ to } 2.382$$

Thus, rounding the numbers to one decimal place, the probability is .95 that the interval 0.3 to 2.4 contains the true value of $|\mu_1 - \mu_2|$. According to this confidence interval, the possible effect of the tranquilizer ranges from a decrement in performance (increase in time taken to solve the anagram) of 0.3 second to a decrement of 2.4 seconds.

As before, obtaining a 99% confidence interval requires only that we replace the .95 value from the t-distribution with the corresponding .99 value. Thus 2.048 is replaced by 2.763. The 99% confidence interval is

$$CI_{.99} = 1.35 \pm (2.763 \times 0.504) = 1.35 \pm 1.393 = -0.043 \text{ to } 2.743$$

Rounding the numbers to two decimal places, the probability is .99 that the interval -0.04 to 2.74 contains the true value of $|\mu_1 - \mu_2|$. According to this confidence interval, the possible effect of the tranquilizer ranges from an improvement in performance (reduction in time taken) of 0.04 second to a decrement in performance (increase in time taken) of 2.74 seconds.

Ponzo Illusion

As part of a research program to understand the Ponzo illusion, an investigator asks whether the size of the illusion might depend on whether the observer is forced to make a judgment after only a brief period of viewing or after a long period of viewing. One possibility is that the illusion takes time to establish itself; another possibility is that the effect of the illusion dissipates with sustained inspection; a third possibility is that viewing time makes no difference at all.

To investigate this question, an experiment with two conditions was designed. In one condition, observers were required to give their judgment after just 5 seconds of viewing. In the second condition, observers were required to study the illusion for 1 minute before making their judgment.

Twenty-four observers were used in the experiment. They were assigned randomly to the conditions, 12 in each. Thus the design conforms with the criteria for a completely randomized design with two conditions. If the illusion does depend on the length of the observation period, then a full model will be required to account for the data. If, on the other hand, the data do not establish beyond a reasonable doubt that there is a difference between the two conditions, then there are no grounds for rejecting the more parsimonious null model.

Rather than set out the raw data, we have summarized the results from a computer analysis of the data:

Condition	n	$\overline{Y}$	SS_Y
Short	12	9.74	2218
Long	12	6.63	2874

First we calculate the mean square of the residuals:

$$MS_e = \frac{2218 + 2874}{11 + 11} = 231.45$$

Then the estimated standard error of the difference between the means is

$$s_{\overline{Y}_1 - \overline{Y}_2} = \sqrt{\frac{2MS_e}{n}} = \sqrt{\frac{2 \times 231.45}{12}} = 6.211$$

For the 95% confidence interval, the critical value of $t(22)$ is 2.074. We now have the necessary components to calculate the 95% confidence interval.

$$CI_{.95} = |\overline{Y}_1 - \overline{Y}_2| \pm w$$

(where $w = t \times s_{\overline{Y}_1 - \overline{Y}_2}$)

$$CI_{.95} = |9.74 - 6.63| \pm (2.074 \times 6.211) = 3.11 \pm 12.88 = -9.77 \text{ to } 15.99$$

Rounding to whole numbers, the probability is .95 that the interval -10 to 16 contains the true value of $|\mu_1 - \mu_2|$.

6.2.3 Using the Confidence Interval to Decide Between Models

Confidence intervals can be used to make judgments about whether or not the conditions of an experiment are having a genuine effect. A confidence interval can be thought of as a range of plausible values for the parameter it estimates. Values lying outside that interval can be considered implausible. This kind of reasoning is used in everyday thinking. If you strongly believe that the driving distance between New York and Boston is 210 ± 10 miles (between 200 and 220 miles), then you would regard an estimate of 250 miles, or any other estimate outside this interval, as implausible. The interval 200 to 220 expresses your conviction about what constitutes a range of plausible distances.

With statistical data analysis, the terms *plausible* and *implausible* are defined in terms of the level of confidence. For example, a 95% confidence interval of 3.4 to 6.6 for the difference between the therapy and control conditions in the phobia treatment experiment indicates that a true difference of less than 3.4 or more than 6.6 is implausible. It is implausible in the sense that, for this to be the case, the true value of the difference would have to lie outside the interval. However, the confidence interval specifies that the probability is only .05 that the interval 3.4 to 6.6 does not contain the true value.

Notice that, if the confidence interval is expressed as $|\overline{Y}_1 - \overline{Y}_2| \pm w$, then the interval will include 0 whenever the value of $|\overline{Y}_1 - \overline{Y}_2|$ is less than w. If $|\overline{Y}_1 - \overline{Y}_2|$ is greater than w, then the interval will not include 0. Consider the following examples.

- If $|\overline{Y}_1 - \overline{Y}_2| = 2$ and $w = 3$, then 2 ± 3 will include 0. In this case, the observed difference is less than w.

- If $|\overline{Y}_1 - \overline{Y}_2| = 4$ and $w = 3$, then the interval would be 4 ± 3, which does not include 0. In this case, the observed difference is greater than w.

> *In addition to being the half-width of the confidence interval, w represents the minimum value of $|\overline{Y}_1 - \overline{Y}_2|$ needed to declare 0 an implausible value.*

Thus there is a simple answer to the question "How large an observed difference do you need to discard as implausible the claim that the true difference is 0?" The answer is w.

A 99% confidence interval imposes a more demanding definition of implausibility. Such an interval requires that the probability that the interval does not contain the true value should be as low as .01. In the phobia treatment example, implausible is now defined as being less than 2.9 or more than 7.1. Plausibility is a relative concept that depends on just how much confidence is demanded.

With this background, we can take up the issue of deciding between our two competing models. One of these models, the full model, claims that $\mu_1 \neq \mu_2$ and that the model therefore needs separate parameters μ_1 and μ_2 for the control and experimental conditions, respectively. The competing model, the null model, claims that $\mu_1 = \mu_2$ and that the model therefore needs only one parameter, μ, that is common to both control and experimental conditions. Because it has one less parameter, the null model is the simpler, more parsimonious of the two. The choice between models amounts to the question of whether the null hypothesis claim is plausible. Remember, in these circumstances, science adheres to the principle of parsimony. In broad terms, this principle states that the scientist should choose the simpler model unless the data render that model clearly implausible.

Phobia Treatment

Do the data from the phobia treatment experiment render the null model clearly implausible? For the null model to be plausible, the claim that $\mu_1 = \mu_2$ (or equivalently, that $\mu_1 - \mu_2 = 0$) must be plausible. The 95% confidence interval, however, makes it clear that a true difference of 0 is not plausible. The specific value of 0 lies well outside the 3.4 to 6.6 range of plausible values. In brief, the data render the null model implausible. A model with a single parameter may be parsimonious, but such simplicity is not compatible with the data. We are therefore led to reject the null model in favor of the alternative, the full model.

Plausibility is a relative concept that depends on just how much confidence is demanded.

For the phobia treatment experiment, 0 is an implausible value for $\mu_1 - \mu_2$.

If we had adopted a more stringent criterion of implausibility by using a 99% confidence interval, we would have reached the same conclusion. Even this wider interval of 2.9 to 7.1 does not include 0 within its range of plausible values. In this case, $w = 2.092$; so, with the .99 criterion of implausibility, any difference greater than 2.092 would be declared implausible.

On the basis of the confidence interval, we can conclude that the data provide strong evidence in favor of the effectiveness of the therapy. These are not the results you would expect to obtain if the therapy were, in fact, ineffective and the true value of $\mu_1 - \mu_2$ was 0. It is not *impossible* that an ineffective therapy might have resulted in these data, but it is *highly improbable*. In the world of noisy data, certainty does not exist, and "highly improbable" is the best that one can hope for. The conclusion then is that, under the conditions of this experiment, desensitization therapy reduces the person's anxiety reaction to a frightening experience. In round figures, the therapy produces a reduction in average heart rate elevation of between $3\frac{1}{2}$ and $6\frac{1}{2}$ beats per minute. This reduction is from a control condition level estimated at 10.2 beats per minute.

This conclusion that the therapy is effective confirms what might have been suspected on the basis of the previously noted fact that the full model achieves a substantially better fit than does the null model—a 56% reduction in the residual sum of squares. However, whereas the value of R^2 quantifies the difference between the conditions, it does not provide a direct basis on which to decide formally whether the improvement in fit is sufficient to justify the full model.

Tranquilizer Effects

Our second example of the effect of a tranquilizer on mental functioning presents a less clear-cut picture. The 95% confidence interval is 0.318 to 2.382; and, using this interval, we would reject the null hypothesis because the value of 0 is outside the interval. On the other hand, the 99% confidence interval is -0.04 to 2.74, which *does* include 0; so, according to this more stringent criterion, the null hypothesis value of 0 remains plausible. We have then a situation in which a value of 0 is implausible according to the less stringent criterion, but not according to the more stringent criterion.

The situation in which one criterion leads to rejection and another more stringent criterion does not is by no means uncommon. It underlines the point that in statistical data analysis decisions are based on probabilities, not certainties. Remember that the scientist will reject the null hypothesis in favor of the less parsimonious full model only if the evidence places the matter "beyond a reasonable doubt." The difference between using a 95% and a 99% confidence interval involves a difference in judgment as to what constitutes reasonable doubt. This is an important matter that will be discussed further, but such a discussion is best left until we have described other procedures for deciding between models.

Ponzo Illusion

In our third example, the experiment investigating the Ponzo illusion, the 95% confidence interval is -9.77 to 15.99. This interval provides no grounds for rejecting the null hypothesis; the value of 0 is inside the interval, suggesting that 0 is an entirely plausible value for $|\mu_1 = \mu_2|$.

Comprehension Check 6.2

Important Concepts

1. The basic concepts from Chapter 5 can be applied to experiments with two conditions. We consider only experiments that have a completely randomized design or that are quasi-experiments comparing measures from independent random samples from two populations. We assume that the population variance is unknown but equal for the two conditions or groups.

2. A confidence interval for the difference between two population means has the same general form as that described in Chapter 5 for a single mean:

$$CI = \text{point estimate} \pm w$$

In this case, the point estimate is $\bar{Y}_1 - \bar{Y}_2$, and w is $t \times$ the estimated standard error of the difference between two means, $s_{\bar{Y}_1 - \bar{Y}_2}$.

3. The degrees of freedom for the t-statistics are $2(n - 1)$. Each of the two conditions contributes $n - 1$ degrees of freedom. If there is an unequal number in each condition, then the degrees of freedom are $(n_1 - 1) + (n_2 - 1)$ or $N - 2$.

4. The estimate of the standard error of the difference between two means is obtained by the formula $s_{\bar{Y}_1 - \bar{Y}_2} = \sqrt{2MS_e/n}$, where n is the number of participants in each condition.

5. The confidence interval can be used to decide whether the null hypothesis that $\mu_1 - \mu_2 = 0$ remains plausible in light of the data. The value of w is the minimum observed difference needed to render the null hypothesis implausible.

Worked Examples

Example 1 Investigation of induced happiness

This experiment is modeled after one reported by Laird (1974). The experiment asks whether an induced smile actually has the effect of making a person feel happier. In the experimental condition, participants were instructed to move facial muscles to mimic a smile while looking at a picture of children playing. In a second control condition, participants simply looked at the picture with a neutral facial expression. No mention was made of smiling to any of the participants; participants believed the purpose of the experiment was to evaluate the effect of facial muscles on perception. A total of 40 volunteers participated in the experiment. They were assigned randomly to the two conditions, 20 participants in each. The response measure was a "happiness score" obtained by administering a mood questionnaire.

Hypothetical data are shown in Data Set 6.2.

a. In calculating a confidence interval for the difference between the means of the two conditions, which sampling distribution would you use, the normal distribution or the t-distribution? Why?

b. Calculate the 95% and the 99% confidence intervals.

c. On the basis of the 95% confidence interval, do the results support the claim that an induced facial expression can change mood? Explain your reasoning.

Data Set 6.2 Happiness scores from the induced happiness experiment

Control condition: $n = 20$, $\overline{Y}_1 = 12.0$, $SS_Y = 686$

2	3	20	10	15	8	14	6	11	17
18	5	11	5	16	13	12	24	19	11

Experimental condition: $n = 20$, $\overline{Y}_2 = 16.0$, $SS_Y = 500$

15	10	14	19	16	26	23	12	20	13
17	3	13	17	23	14	20	15	13	17

Answer

a. The sampling distribution you would use is the t-distribution because the population variance is unknown and must be estimated.

The main calculation is that of the estimated standard error of the difference between means $s_{\overline{Y}_1 - \overline{Y}_2}$. To obtain this, we first calculate the mean square of the residuals:

$$MS_e = \frac{686 + 500}{19 + 19} = 31.21$$

Then the estimated standard error of the difference between the means is

$$s_{\overline{Y}_1 - \overline{Y}_2} = \sqrt{\frac{2MS_e}{n}} = \sqrt{\frac{2 \times 31.21}{20}} = 1.77$$

b. *Confidence intervals* For the 95% confidence interval, the critical value of $t(38)$ is 2.024. We now have the necessary components to calculate the 95% confidence interval.

$$CI_{.95} = |\overline{Y}_1 - \overline{Y}_2| \pm w \ (\text{where } w = t \times s_{\overline{Y}_1 - \overline{Y}_2})$$
$$= |12.0 - 16.0| \pm (2.024 \times 1.77) = 4.0 \pm 3.58 = 0.42 \text{ to } 7.58$$

For the 99% confidence interval, the critical value of $t(38)$ is 2.712. We now have the necessary components to calculate the 99% confidence interval.

$$CI_{.99} = |\overline{Y}_1 - \overline{Y}_2| \pm w \ (\text{where } w = t \times s_{\overline{Y}_1 - \overline{Y}_2})$$
$$= |12.0 - 16.0| \pm (2.712 \times 1.77) = 4.0 \pm 4.80 = -0.80 \text{ to } 8.80$$

c. Yes, the results do support the claim that an induced facial expression can change mood. The 95% confidence interval of 0.42 to 7.58 does not include 0, and in this sense, 0 is an implausible value for the population mean difference. According to this criterion, any difference larger than 3.58 is incompatible with the claim that the true difference is 0. Note, however, that the conclusion for the 99% confidence interval would be different from that for the 95% confidence interval; with this more stringent criterion, an obtained difference of 4.80 would be needed before the observed difference would be declared incompatible with a true difference of 0.

Problems

Problem 1   Induced anger (Data Set 6.3)

This experiment is also modeled after one reported by Laird (1974). The experiment asks whether an induced frown has the effect of making a person feel angrier. In this version of the experiment, participants in the experimental condition were instructed to move facial muscles to mimic a frown while looking at a picture of children playing. In the control condition, participants simply looked at the picture with a neutral facial expression. No mention was made of frowning to any of the participants; again, participants believed the purpose of the experiment was to evaluate the effect of facial muscles on perception. A total of 36 volunteers participated in the experiment. They were assigned randomly to the two conditions, 18 participants in each. The response measure was an "anger score" obtained by administering a mood questionnaire. The results of basic computations are shown in Data Set 6.3.

Data Set 6.3   Anger data for Problem 1

Control condition: $n = 18$, $\overline{Y}_1 = 6.89$ words, $SS_Y = 49.78$

5	7	5	5	7	5	9	7	7
8	3	8	9	8	8	8	9	6

Experimental condition: $n = 18$, $\overline{Y}_2 = 8.61$ words, $SS_Y = 70.28$

8	6	7	9	8	13	10	7	12
9	8	5	9	8	11	7	10	8

a. In calculating a confidence interval, what are the degrees of freedom for obtaining the value of the appropriate t-statistic from the t-distribution?

b. Calculate the 95% and the 99% confidence intervals.

c. On the basis of the 95% confidence interval, do the results support the claim that an induced facial expression such as frowning can change mood? Explain your reasoning.

Problem 2   Intentional versus incidental remembering (Data Set 6.4)

This experiment compares intentional with incidental remembering. In one condition, participants saw a list of 40 common words and were instructed to study them carefully for a subsequent memory test. Participants in a second condition saw the same list of words but were told nothing about a subsequent memory test. Instead, they were asked to rate each word for pleasantness on a seven-point scale. All participants saw each word for 5 seconds.

Following the presentation of the words, participants in both conditions were asked to recall as many words as they could in any order. A total of 52 volunteers participated in the experiment. They were assigned randomly to the two conditions, 26 participants in each. The results of basic computations for the two conditions are shown in Data Set 6.4.

Data Set 6.4 Memory data for Problem 2

Control condition: $n = 26$, $\overline{Y}_1 = 10.65$ words, $SS_Y = 241.9$

5	6	11	11	13	10	13	7	11	12	13	11	16
11	12	11	13	13	10	9	11	14	13	13	4	4

Experimental condition: $n = 26$, $\overline{Y}_2 = 10.15$ words, $SS_Y = 201.4$

14	8	11	7	10	6	9	12	13	5	9	5	12
10	9	16	13	8	7	9	12	11	13	13	10	12

a. In calculating a confidence interval, what are the degrees of freedom for obtaining the value of the appropriate t-statistic from the t-distribution?

b. Calculate the 95% and the 90% confidence intervals.

c. On the basis of the 95% confidence interval, do the results support the claim that intentional and incidental study differ in their effectiveness for subsequent remembering? Explain your reasoning.

6.3 Using the t-Distribution Directly to Decide Between Models

Using the confidence interval to decide between the full model and the null model is a procedure that has much to recommend it. The confidence interval provides not only a sound rationale for making the decision, but also an estimate of the true difference that is more informative than a simple point estimate. Nevertheless, many researchers consider it unnecessary to report confidence intervals, preferring to conduct a more direct test of the plausibility of the null model.

6.3.1 An Intuitive Example of Statistical Hypothesis Testing

Before giving a formal description of statistical hypothesis testing, consider an intuitive example. Suppose that a person claims to be able to identify reliably two well-known brands of cola. To evaluate this claim, a skeptical friend gives the cola drinker a series of tests, each test consisting of sips from two identical unmarked glasses, one containing Brand A cola, the other Brand B cola. Imagine the following results.

■ The cola drinker correctly identifies the brand of cola on the first two tests.

■ The cola drinker is correct on the first ten tests.

Both these situations confirm the cola drinker's original claim to be able to identify the two brands of cola, but only the second result is convincing; the first is not. Your reasoning may have been along the following lines:

Even a person who was unable to identify the colas might be correct on two tests just by guessing—it would not take a great deal of luck. But if the cola drinker were just guessing, it is very unlikely that the person would be correct ten times in a row.

This informal line of reasoning contains the basic rationale of statistical hypothesis testing that is commonly used to decide between models. Expressed more formally, the reasoning is

If the person is guessing, then being correct twice is not very unlikely; in fact, the probability is .25. In this sense, the data are not incompatible with the hypothesis of guessing; so there are no strong grounds for rejecting it. However, if the person really is just guessing, then being correct ten times in a row is extremely unlikely; in fact, the probability is less than .001. This result is quite incompatible with the hypothesis of guessing; thus the result provides strong grounds for rejecting the hypothesis.

The hypothesis that the person is just guessing corresponds to the null hypothesis and its associated model. The hypothesis that the person can identify the brands corresponds to the full model. We can now give a more formal expression to the argument for rejecting the null hypothesis on the basis of the sequence of ten tests.

If the null hypothesis (guessing) is true, then the data (ten correct answers) are highly unlikely ($p < .001$). The choice is therefore either to retain the null hypothesis and believe that a highly improbable event has occurred or to reject the null hypothesis in favor of one more compatible with the data (the full model).

In the following sections of this chapter, the null hypothesis is the hypothesis that two means are equal and that a model with a single parameter, μ, is therefore sufficient. To apply the rationale of the preceding paragraph, we will need to specify in a precise way whether believing the null hypothesis renders the data probable or improbable. If the data are not what would be expected (if they are improbable) for a situation in which the null hypothesis is true, then the null hypothesis should be rejected.

6.3.2 The *t*-Ratio for the Difference Between Two Means

The data from the phobia treatment experiment gave a 95% confidence interval of 3.4 to 6.6 heart beats per minute as the estimated difference between experimental and control conditions. The decision to adopt the full model and reject the null model was based on the fact that the value of 0 posited by the null hypothesis was outside this interval and therefore deemed implausible. The direct approach to making this decision is to ask whether the observed difference $\bar{Y}_1 - \bar{Y}_2$ is too large to have arisen from a situation in which the null hypothesis is true. Are the data compatible with the claim that $\mu_1 - \mu_2 = 0$? Is an observed difference of 5.0 heart beats per minute in our therapy experiment compatible with the claim that the therapy makes no difference? If the data are judged to be incompatible, then the simpler null model should be rejected in favor of the full model. Remember, data are real, whereas the null hypothesis is a conjecture; so, in the case of incompatibility, conjecture gives way to data. What we need is to give the informal idea of incompatibility a precise meaning.

The basis of statistical hypothesis testing is to ask how probable the observed difference is if the null hypothesis is true.

The *t*-ratio answers the question: Is $(\bar{Y}_1 - \bar{Y}_2)$ too large to have arisen from a situation in which the null hypothesis is true?

Intuitively some outcomes are clearly more compatible with the null hypothesis than others. If our cola taster had been correct on only six of the ten tests, then the outcome would have been judged more compatible with the null hypothesis (guessing). In this case, the null hypothesis of guessing predicts five out of ten as the single most likely outcome, and six correct is closer to this predicted value than is ten correct. The smaller the difference between the data and what the hypothesis predicts, the more compatible are the data with that hypothesis. If the hypothesis predicts that the *true* difference between the means is actually 0, the smaller the difference between the observed sample means, the more compatible are the data with that hypothesis. An obtained difference between $\overline{Y}_1$ and $\overline{Y}_2$ of 1.0 seems more compatible with the hypothesis that $\mu_1 - \mu_2 = 0$ than does a difference of 8.0. An obvious question remains, however. At what point does an obtained difference become so large as to be judged incompatible? Not surprisingly, the criterion is formulated in probabilistic terms.

Stated briefly, the data and the null hypothesis are deemed incompatible if the difference $\overline{Y}_1 - \overline{Y}_2$ is so large that it is unlikely to have arisen from a situation in which the true difference is 0. Is an observed difference of 5.0 heart beats per minute compatible with a true difference of 0? How probable is it that a difference as large as 5.0 could arise from a therapy that is ineffective? In short, how probable is it that noise alone could produce a difference as large as 5.0 heart beats per minute.

A judgment of compatibility requires that we establish a probability that a difference as large as $\overline{Y}_1 - \overline{Y}_2$ could have arisen under conditions in which $\mu_1 - \mu_2 = 0$. Incompatibility implies that this probability is small—that our observations are not likely to have arisen from a situation in which the null hypothesis is true. Establishing a probability for $\overline{Y}_1 - \overline{Y}_2$ involves a familiar routine: We treat $\overline{Y}_1 - \overline{Y}_2$ as a random variable and, having specified the appropriate probability distribution, obtain whatever probability is required.

For a single mean, the probabilities associated with values of $\overline{Y}$ were obtained by using the ratio

$$t = \frac{\overline{Y} - \mu}{s_{\overline{Y}}}$$

This ratio followed a t-distribution with $n - 1$ degrees of freedom. We now need the corresponding ratio for the difference between two means. This ratio is

$$t = \frac{(\overline{Y}_1 - \overline{Y}_2) - (\mu_1 - \mu_2)}{s_{\overline{Y}_1 - \overline{Y}_2}}.$$

This formula has the same form as for a single mean; the only change is that $\overline{Y}$ is replaced by $\overline{Y}_1 - \overline{Y}_2$, μ is replaced by $\mu_1 - \mu_2$, and $s_{\overline{Y}}$ is replaced by $s_{\overline{Y}_1 - \overline{Y}_2}$. This ratio also follows the t-distribution, but now the degrees of freedom are

$$df = 2(n - 1)$$

If there is an unequal number on each condition, then the degrees of freedom are $(n_1 - 1) + (n_2 - 1)$, or $N - 2$.

We are interested in finding probabilities for values of $\overline{Y}_1 - \overline{Y}_2$ under the assumption that $\mu_1 - \mu_2 = 0$. If $\mu_1 - \mu_2 = 0$, then the preceding ratio simplifies to

$$t = \frac{\overline{Y}_1 - \overline{Y}_2}{s_{\overline{Y}_1 - \overline{Y}_2}}$$

again with $df = 2(n - 1)$.

In purely descriptive terms, the ratio $t = (\overline{Y}_1 - \overline{Y}_2)/s_{\overline{Y}_1-\overline{Y}_2}$ is an index of how much the value of $\overline{Y}_1 - \overline{Y}_2$ differs from the zero value specified by the null hypothesis. It measures this discrepancy between data and hypothesis in units of the standard error. The great virtue of this particular measure is that (thanks to William Gossett) we know that its probability distribution is the *t*-distribution. We can therefore use this distribution to establish probabilities associated with different values of *t*, that is, different degrees of discrepancy between data and hypothesis. In particular, our interest is in using this distribution to decide whether our observed discrepancy, as measured by *t*, is plausible or improbable. If the discrepancy is plausible, then the null hypothesis will be retained; if improbable, then the null hypothesis will be rejected.

How the *t*-ratio and its associated probability should be used to decide between these competing hypotheses has been a matter of much debate, and even today the issue is far from settled. Current practice among behavioral scientists reflects the influence of two major traditions. One tradition is associated with Ronald Fisher (1890–1962), the other with two of Fisher's contemporaries: Jerzy Neyman (1899–1981) and Egon Pearson (1895–1980).

6.3.3 *p*-Values and Statistical Significance: The Fisher Tradition

Obtaining the *p*-Value for a Particular *t*-Ratio

Suppose that we have completed an experiment and that the data have been appropriately analyzed, giving a *t*-ratio of 1.5 with 20 degrees of freedom. To evaluate the null hypothesis for this experiment, we need to know the probability of observing a value of *t* as large as 1.5 (or larger). We will refer to this probability as the *p-value*. The *p*-value for this value of *t* is represented by the shaded area in the tails of the distribution shown in Figure 6.1. The shaded area is the probability that the value of *t* is below − 1.5 or above + 1.5. Stated more succinctly, it is the probability that the *absolute* value of *t* is greater than 1.5.

When calculating confidence intervals, we saw that the table of the *t*-distribution gives values of *t* for just three probabilities: .1, .05, and .01. Thus the table does not provide the information necessary to establish the exact probability for every given value of *t*, although many computer packages do provide exact probabilities. How-

> The *p*-value is the probability of observing a value of *t* as large as that actually obtained.

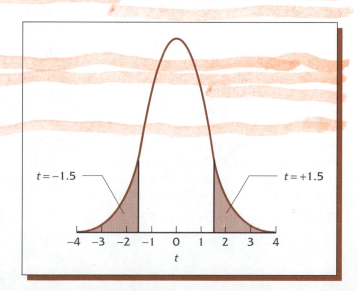

Figure 6.1
t-Distribution with 20 degrees of freedom, showing the *p*-value (shaded area) for a *t*-value of ± 1.5.

Table 6.3 Portion of *t*-distribution

df	Proportion in two tails		
	.10	.05	.01
⋮	⋮	⋮	⋮
18	1.734	2.101	2.878
19	1.729	2.093	2.861
20	1.725	2.086	2.845
21	1.721	2.080	2.831
22	1.717	2.074	2.819
⋮	⋮	⋮	⋮

The *t*-table enables the *p*-value of the *t*-ratio to be located relative to benchmark probabilities of .1, .05, and .01.

ever, the tabled values of .1, .05, and .01 are sufficient if all we need to establish is where the obtained value of *t* falls in relation to these benchmark probabilities. The tabled values are sufficient to establish whether the *p*-value is less than .1, between .1 and .05, between .05 and .01, or less than .01.

Recall that the *t*-table reports the area in the combined tails (the two extremes of the distribution). For example, the value of *t* corresponding to a probability of .10 marks a point such that values of *t* more extreme than this point (in either direction, positive or negative) are values that occur with a probability of less than .10. To obtain the *p*-value for $t = 1.5$ with 20 degrees of freedom, we consult the tables of the *t*-distribution, the relevant section of which is reproduced in Table 6.3. The value of *t* required for a *p*-value of .10 is 1.725. Our *t*-ratio of 1.5 is even smaller than this value, so although the table does not give us the exact probability, it indicates that the probability must be greater than .10. Thus the *p*-value for $t = 1.5$ with 20 degrees of freedom can be reported as $p > .10$. As we will soon see, this value provides no support for the full model. In other words, we cannot reject the null hypothesis.

How are *p*-values used to make a decision? Remember first that descriptively the *t*-ratio is a measure of $\overline{Y}_1 - \overline{Y}_2$ expressed in units of the standard error, $s_{\overline{Y}_1-\overline{Y}_2}$. Thus a small *p*-value indicates a difference between means that is improbable if the true difference is actually 0. Just as a fair coin is unlikely to yield nine heads in ten tosses, a true difference of 0 is unlikely to yield a large value of the *t*-ratio. Thus, if the *t*-ratio is sufficiently improbable, then the null hypothesis becomes implausible, just as the hypothesis of a fair coin becomes implausible if it yields nine heads in ten tosses. The obvious next question is the criterion for "sufficiently improbable." We will tackle this question in the context of a specific example, the phobia treatment experiment.

Phobia Treatment (Data Set 3.1)

The *t*-ratio for the phobia treatment experiment is

$$t = \frac{\overline{Y}_1 - \overline{Y}_2}{s_{\overline{Y}_1-\overline{Y}_2}} = \frac{5.0}{0.767} = 6.52$$

To decide on the plausibility of the null hypothesis, we need to know the probability of obtaining a *t*-value as large as 6.52. What is the *p*-value for $t = 6.52$? Consulting the *t*-tables with 34 degrees of freedom, we note that the most extreme value tabled is 2.728 for the .01 area (Table 6.2). Our *t*-value of 6.52 is larger than 2.728 and therefore even less probable. We conclude that, for $t = 6.52$, the *p*-value is less than .01 ($p < .01$) and that the null hypothesis is implausible. We therefore reject the null model in favor of the full model. The *t*-ratio of 6.52 tells us that a difference of 5.0 is very unlikely to have arisen from a situation in which the null hypothesis is true.

The *p*-value is illustrated in Figure 6.2, which shows how a value of 6.52 extends very far into the right-hand tail and is therefore less probable than the smallest probability included in the table.

Significance Level

How improbable does the obtained *t*-value need to be to justify rejecting the null hypothesis? The common convention is that the probability should be less than .05. Why this particular value? Why not .06 or .02? The reasons are largely historical. The value of .05 seems to have become conventional following Ronald Fisher's declaration that the .05 was an appropriate level of improbability. Fisher suggested .05 as a reasonable value to demand as a criterion for rejecting the null hypothesis, and this was the value for which tabled values of *t* were published. Had Fisher recommended that .06 should be the minimum probability instead of .05, and published *t*-values for *that* probability, then .06 rather than .05 would no doubt be the current convention. It should be noted that Fisher intended the value of .05 to serve merely as a guideline to help scientists interpret their data; elsewhere he refers to it as a "convenient" figure. Later forces turned the .05 level into something more rigid.

When the obtained *t*-value leads to a rejection of the null hypothesis, then the *t*-value is said to be *statistically significant*. The *p*-value on which the rejection is based is referred to as the *level of significance*. In our example of the phobia treatment experiment, the *t*-value of 6.52 yielded a *p*-value less than .01. We could therefore claim that this value was *statistically significant at the .01 level*. This expression is commonly abbreviated to "significant at the .01 level." Such expressions are shorthand for the claim that the observed mean-difference between the conditions is so large that the probability is less than .01 that it would occur if the null hypothesis were true.

The conventional minimum p-value needed to reject the null hypothesis is .05.

When the obtained t-value leads to a rejection of the null hypothesis, then the t-value is said to be statistically significant.

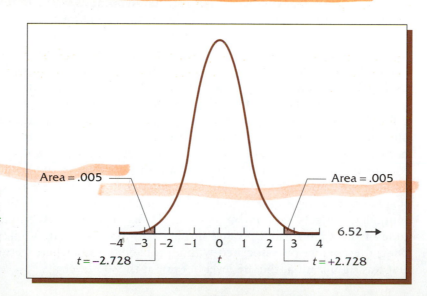

Figure 6.2
t-Distribution with 34 degrees of freedom, showing the *t*-value for the p-value of .01 (shaded area).

Area = .005   Area = .005

6.52 →

−4 −3 −2 −1 0 1 2 3 4

$t = -2.728$ *t* $t = +2.728$

Tranquilizer Effects

Consider the experiment investigating the effect of a tranquilizer on mental functioning described in Section 6.2.2 (Data Set 6.1). For this experiment, we have

$$t = \frac{\overline{Y}_1 - \overline{Y}_2}{s_{\overline{Y}_1 - \overline{Y}_2}} = \frac{1.35}{0.504} = 2.68$$

In this experiment, remember, there were 15 observations in each condition, so the relevant t-distribution is one with $2(n - 1) = 28$ degrees of freedom. Consulting the tables of the t-distribution (Statistical Table 3 in Appendix C) gives a value of $t = 2.048$ for a p-value of .05 and a value of $t = 2.763$ for the .01 level. Our obtained difference yielded a t-value of 2.68, greater (less probable) than the critical value for .05 but less than the value for .01. Thus the value of 2.68 has a p-value somewhere between .05 and .01. In this situation the convention is to report "$p < .05$."

Ponzo Illusion

Consider next the experiment investigating the effect of viewing time on the Ponzo illusion described in Section 6.2.2. For this experiment, we have

$$t = \frac{\overline{Y}_1 - \overline{Y}_2}{s_{\overline{Y}_1 - \overline{Y}_2}} = \frac{3.11}{6.211} = 0.501$$

In this experiment, remember, there were 12 observations in each condition, so the relevant t-distribution is one with $2(n - 1) = 22$ degrees of freedom. Consulting the tables of the t-distribution (Statistical Table 3) gives a critical value of $t = 2.074$. Our obtained difference yielded a t-value of 0.501, a value that is less than the critical value of 2.074 needed for a p-value of .05 and less than the 1.717 value needed for a p-value of .1. Thus the p-value of 0.501 is greater than .10 and therefore not significant at the .05 level, or even at the .10 level. The data provide no grounds on which to reject the null hypothesis.

Failure to reject the null hypothesis does not amount to a claim that the null hypothesis is true.

What does it mean *not* to reject the null hypothesis? Failure to reject the null hypothesis does not amount to a claim that the null hypothesis is true. For Fisher, not rejecting the null hypothesis meant simply that the data provided insufficient support for such a rejection. Whether or not the null hypothesis was *actually* false was a matter on which no definite statement could be made. Failure to reject the null hypothesis did not amount to an assertion that this hypothesis was true, just as failing to find an accused person guilty may not amount to an assertion of innocence, but may mean merely that the prosecution's case has not been established. Thus, in interpreting the results of the Ponzo illusion experiment, it would be inappropriate to assert that inspection time has no effect on the size of the illusion. Careful wording would describe the results as "providing no support for the claim that inspection time has an effect on the size of the illusion." In the absence of evidence to the contrary, parsimony demands that we retain the simpler null hypothesis.

The essence of the Fisher tradition was that judgments about the implausibility of the null hypotheses should be based on the p-value. In these terms, the results from the phobia treatment experiment are statistically more significant than those from the tranquilizer effects experiment. In the phobia treatment experiment, the obtained value of the t-ratio had a p-value smaller than .01. In the tranquilizer effects experiment, the t-value was associated with a probability somewhere between .05 and .01, so it was significant at the .05 level but not at the .01 level.

Many research papers report the results of their statistical data analyses in this Fisherian style. The typical method of reporting is to indicate the different levels at which various statistical tests are significant, that is, whether the probability is less than .05 or .01. Some publications report values of less than .001 or even .0001, although, as noted previously, there is little to be gained by reporting such small values to this level of exactness. In these terms, the results of the statistical analysis from our three examples might read

> In the experiment designed to study the effectiveness of desensitization therapy for treating phobias, there was a significant difference between the experimental and the control conditions; $t(34) = 6.52$, $p < .01$. There was also a significant difference between the experimental and the control conditions in the experiment designed to study the effect of a tranquilizer on mental functioning: $t(28) = 2.68$, $p < .05$. In the experiment designed to study the effect of viewing time on the Ponzo illusion, the effect of viewing time was not significant; $t(22) = 0.501$, $p > .10$.

The values in parentheses refer to the degrees of freedom for that *t*-value. Note that in a published report such results of the statistical analysis should be reported only after first reporting the means and standard deviations on which the analysis was based.

Comprehension Check 6.3

Important Concepts

1. A decision between the hypothesis underling the null model and the hypothesis underlying the full model can, if desired, be made without the intermediate step of calculating a confidence interval. This direct method uses a *t*-ratio that reflects the magnitude of the observed difference between the sample means.

2. In evaluating the null hypothesis of zero mean-difference, the *t*-ratio is the observed difference between the sample means divided by the estimated standard error of the difference between two means.

3. The logic underlying statistical hypothesis testing is to reject the null hypothesis of no difference if the observed difference is larger than might have plausibly arisen from a situation in which the null hypothesis is true.

4. The *t*-ratio provides the basis on which this plausibility of the observed difference can be given a precise meaning.

5. In using the *t*-ratio, two major traditions can be found in current practice. One is usually termed the Fisher tradition after its major advocate, Ronald Fisher. The second tradition is that of Neyman and Pearson. This section (6.3) describes the Fisher tradition; Section 6.4 describes the Neyman-Pearson tradition.

6. The Fisher tradition bases the decision about the null hypothesis on the probability associated with the obtained *t*-ratio. This value is termed the *p*-value. If the *p*-value is judged to be sufficiently small, then the null hypothesis is rejected; that is, the observed difference is declared to be too improbable to have arisen from a situation in which there is really no difference. The conventional minimum level of the *p*-value required to reject the null hypothesis is a probability of .05.

7. In reporting their results, researchers following the Fisher tradition typically report the value of the obtained t-ratio and its p-value. The p-value is usually reported relative to the tabled t-values of .1, .05, and .01.

Worked Examples

Example 1   **Induced happiness (Data Set 6.2)**

Confidence intervals were calculated for this experiment in Example 1 at the end of Section 6.2. The sample means for the control and the experimental conditions respectively were 12.0 and 16.0 seconds. The estimated standard error of the difference between means was found to be $s_{\overline{Y}_1 - \overline{Y}_2} = 1.77$.

a. What is the t-ratio you would calculate to evaluate the null hypothesis that there is no difference between the population means of the two conditions?

b. Using the tables of the t-distribution, establish the p-value for the value of the t-ratio calculated in (a).

c. Given this p-value, would you accept or reject the null hypothesis? Explain the reasoning behind the decision.

d. Write a sentence that expresses this conclusion as it might appear in a published article.

Answer

a.
$$t = \frac{\overline{Y}_1 - \overline{Y}_2}{s_{\overline{Y}_1 - \overline{Y}_2}} = \frac{4.0}{1.77} = 2.26$$

b. To obtain the p-value for a t-ratio of 2.26, we note first that the ratio is based on 38 degrees of freedom. Consulting Table 6.4, which shows a portion of the t-dis-

Table 6.4 Portion of the t-distribution

df	Proportion in two tails		
	.10	.05	.01
⋮	⋮	⋮	⋮
36	1.688	2.028	2.719
37	1.687	2.026	2.715
38	1.686	2.024	2.712
39	1.685	2.023	2.708
40	1.684	2.021	2.704
50	1.676	2.009	2.678
⋮	⋮	⋮	⋮

tribution, we find that a value of 2.26 is greater than the value of 2.024 required for a probability of .05, but less than the value of 2.712 required for a probability of .01. We therefore report the *p*-value as "$p < .05$."

c. The null hypothesis is rejected at the .05 level of significance. The reasoning behind this rejection is that the *t*-ratio indicates that a difference as large as 4.0 seconds is highly unlikely to be observed (the probability is less than .05) if the true difference is actually 0.

d. There was a significant difference between the experimental and the control conditions; $t(38) = 2.26$, $p < .05$.

Problems

Problem 1   Induced anger

Confidence intervals were calculated for the induced anger experiment in Problem 1 at the end of Section 6.2. There were $n = 18$ participants in each condition. The sample means for the control and experimental conditions respectively were 6.9 and 8.6, and the estimated standard error of the difference between means was found to be 0.626.

a. What is the *t*-ratio you would calculate to evaluate the null hypothesis that there is no difference between the population means of the experimental and control conditions?

b. Using the tables of the *t*-distribution, establish the *p*-value for the value of the *t*-ratio calculated in (a).

c. Given this *p*-value, would you accept or reject the null hypothesis? Explain the reasoning behind the decision.

d. Write a sentence that expresses this conclusion as it might appear in a published article.

Problem 2   Intentional versus incidental remembering

This experiment compared intentional with incidental remembering. It was used as Problem 2 at the end of Section 6.2. The sample means for the incidental and intentional conditions respectively were 10.65 and 10.15, and the estimated standard error of the difference between means was found to be 0.826. Using results from that analysis, answer the same four questions asked in Problem 1.

Problem 3   Two levels of incidental remembering

The results of the experiment in Problem 2 do not imply that all forms of incidental remembering are equally effective. In a new experiment, all participants again see a list of 40 common words for 5 seconds each. In one condition, the participants are asked to rate each of these words for pleasantness, as in Problem 2. In a second condition, participants are asked to report the number of syllables in each word. Following the presentation of the words, participants in both conditions were asked to recall as many words as they could in any order. A total of 44 volunteers participated in the experiment. They were assigned randomly to the two conditions, 22 participants in each. The results of basic computations are shown in the following table.

Condition	n	$\overline{Y}$	SS_Y
Pleasantness rating	22	12.2	171.9
Syllable count	22	6.9	234.6

a. Which model would you consider appropriate for these data: a null model for which $\mu_1 = \mu_2$ or a full model in which $\mu_1 \neq \mu_2$? Answer this question by calculating the appropriate t-ratio and establishing its p-value.

b. Write a sentence that expresses this conclusion as it might appear in a published article.

6.4 Decision Error Rates: The Neyman-Pearson Tradition

Although the basic method of calculating the t-value is not in dispute, Neyman and Pearson criticized Fisher's particular method of deciding whether to reject the null hypothesis, his interpretation of statistical significance, and especially the ambiguity that remains after a decision has been made to retain the null hypothesis. Although the following account of the Neyman-Pearson arguments is a somewhat simplified version, it captures the essence of their position, especially as that position has been adopted by behavioral scientists.

6.4.1 Two Types of Errors

Neyman and Pearson argued that the idea of statistical significance should be developed into a more formal analysis that made explicit the full nature of the decision-making process. According to this analysis, the researcher is confronted with a choice: to accept the null hypothesis (H_0) or to reject it in favor of a competing hypothesis (H_1). In making this decision, two kinds of errors are possible. In terms of the two-condition experiments discussed in this chapter, these hypotheses would be

$$H_0: \mu_1 = \mu_2$$

$$H_1: \mu_1 \neq \mu_2$$

■ The first kind of error occurs when the null hypothesis (H_0) is actually true and H_1 is false, but the decision is made to reject H_0 in favor of H_1. This form of error is referred to as a *Type-1 error*. This kind of error can be thought of as a false alarm, that is, claiming a difference when in fact none exists.

■ The second kind of error occurs when the H_0 is false and H_1 is true but the decision is to accept H_0 and reject H_1. This form of error is termed a *Type-2 error*.

This kind of error can be thought of as a miss, that is, failing to detect a difference when in fact there is one.

The possibilities are

Decision	H_0 true (no difference)	H_1 true (difference exists)
Reject H_0, accept H_1	Type-1 error (false alarm)	Correct decision
Accept H_0, reject H_1	Correct decision	Type-2 error (miss)

These possibilities represent a decision-making situation that is extremely common. For example, it represents the options facing a jury, as shown in the following chart. In this case, the Type-1 error corresponds to finding an innocent person guilty, and a Type-2 error to failing to find guilty a person who really was guilty. In terms of the signal and noise metaphor, a Type-1 error is the mistaken declaration of a signal when in reality there is only noise. In this sense, a Type-1 error is a false alarm.

Decision	Actually innocent	Actually guilty
Find guilty	Type-1 error	Correct conviction
Find innocent	Correct acquittal	Type-2 error

The Neyman-Pearson argument was that data analysis should specify the probability of making each of these types of errors and ensure that they are acceptably low.

6.4.2 Type-1 Error Rate: The Risk of a False Alarm

The Type-1 error rate is commonly designated α (Greek lowercase alpha). It corresponds to Fisher's significance level. Thus "a significance level of .05" in Fisher's terminology becomes "set $\alpha = .05$" in the Neyman-Pearson terminology. Unlike Fisher's significance level, however, the Type-1 error rate must be specified prior to the data analysis and fixed at that level. It would be inappropriate to use the p-value as a post hoc index of the degree of significance or to use phrases such as a "highly significant" or, even worse, "marginally significant."

Phobia Treatment

Suppose that in our phobia treatment experiment the Type-1 rate had been set at $\alpha = .05$. This statement would mean that we are willing to tolerate a probability of .05 of mistakenly rejecting a true null hypothesis, that is, of making the false alarm of claiming a difference when there is none. This decision rule is represented in Figure 6.3, which shows a t-distribution with 34 degrees of freedom. This t-distribution is divided into two regions, an *accept* region and a *reject* region. The accept region in Figure 6.3 is the central interval between -2.032 and $+2.032$. If the t-ratio falls within this interval, the decision is to accept the null hypothesis. The area of the distribution between these values is .95. The reject region is the area in the two tails corresponding to values of t more extreme than 2.032. The combined area in these two tails is .05. If the t-ratio falls into either of these tail areas, then the null hypothesis is rejected.

The Type-1 error rate should be specified prior to the data analysis.

α denotes Type-1 error rate.

The Type-1 error rate establishes acceptance and rejection regions of the t-distribution.

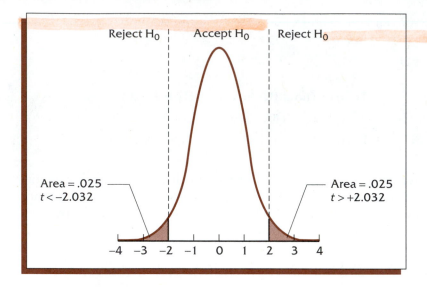

Figure 6.3

t-Distribution with *df* = 34, showing the accept and reject regions for a Type-1 error rate of $\alpha = .05$.

The decision rule is then

> *If $|t| < 2.032$, then retain H_0, reject H_1.*
>
> *If $|t| > 2.032$, then reject H_0, accept H_1.*

This decision rule can (and should) be established before the data have been analyzed. Then, once analyzed, the decision rule is applied strictly. In our phobia treatment example, we would calculate the value of the *t*-ratio in the same manner as before and would find it to be 6.52. Because 6.52 is greater than 2.032, this value is clearly outside the "accept" region and is located in the rejection region in the right-hand tail.

Note that if we had defined our rejection region by setting $\alpha = .01$, the value of 6.52 would still fall into this more stringently defined rejection region. However, strict adherence to the Neyman-Pearson procedure makes this an irrelevant observation. Unlike Fisher's approach, the Neyman-Pearson procedure makes it inappropriate to quantify the degree of significance. The decision rule was set with $\alpha = .05$, the *t*-value falls into the rejection region, the decision to reject the null hypothesis follows automatically, and that is the end of the matter. What might have been the case had another error rate been set is irrelevant.

Tranquilizer Effects

Consider the experiment investigating the effect of a tranquilizer on mental functioning. For this experiment, we obtained (in Section 6.3.3) a *t*-value of 2.68 based on 28 degrees of freedom. If we set a Type-1 error rate of .05, the rejection region would comprise the areas in the tails of the distribution to the right of $t = +2.048$ and to the left of $t = -2.048$. The value of 2.68 falls into the rejection region in the right-hand tail of this distribution, so the decision is to reject the null hypothesis.

Suppose the Type-1 error rate had been set at .01. In this case, the critical *t*-value obtained from Statistical Table 3 is 2.763. The rejection region comprises the areas in the tails of the distribution to the right of $t = +2.763$ and to the left of $t = -2.763$.

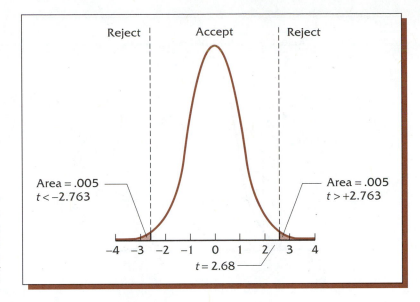

Figure 6.4
t-Distribution with
df = 28, showing
the accept and
reject regions for a
Type-1 error rate of
$\alpha = .01$.

This *t*-distribution is shown in Figure 6.4. In this case, the obtained *t*-value of 2.68 falls into the acceptance region, so the decision is *not* to reject the null hypothesis.

Remember that strict adherence to the Neyman-Pearson procedure means that the choice of error rate of .05 or .01 must be made prior to obtaining the results. In particular, the following chain of reasoning would be inappropriate:

■ Set the Type-1 error rate at $\alpha = .01$ prior to the experiment.

■ After the data have been analyzed, note that the value of *t* would have been significant had the error rate been set at .05.

■ Switch the error rate to .05 and reject the null hypothesis.

Ponzo Illusion

Consider the experiment designed to investigate the effect of viewing time on the Ponzo illusion. For this experiment, we obtained a *t*-value of 0.501, based on 22 degrees of freedom. If we set a Type-1 error rate of .05, the rejection region comprises the areas in the tails of the distribution to the right of $t = +2.074$ and to the left of $t = -2.074$. The value of .501 therefore falls into the nonrejection region of this distribution, so the decision is not to reject the null hypothesis (Figure 6.5).

Directional Tests

In setting the Type-1 error, the rejection region was located in the two tails of the distribution. The alternative to the null hypothesis was

$$H_1 : \mu_1 \neq \mu_2$$

This alternative to the null hypothesis indicates that it does not matter whether the difference between the means was positive or negative. A difference in either direction could be grounds for rejecting the null hypothesis. Thus, in setting an $\alpha = .05$, each tail contained an area of .025. A sufficiently large negative difference would fall into the left-hand rejection region, and a sufficiently large positive difference would fall into the right-hand rejection region.

Some data analysts argue for the possibility of locating the entire rejection region on one side of the distribution.

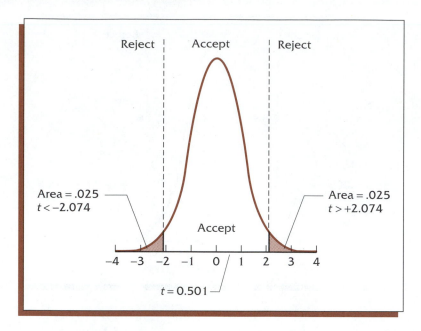

Figure 6.5
t-Distribution with $df = 22$, showing the accept and reject regions for a Type-1 error rate of $\alpha = .05$.

There are situations, however, when an investigator might claim that a difference in only one direction is relevant to rejecting the null hypothesis. For example, in the phobia treatment experiment, an investigator might claim that only a difference in the direction of improvement is a relevant contradiction of the null hypothesis. This contradiction of the null hypothesis can be expressed as $\mu_1 > \mu_2$, that is, that the level of anxiety in the control condition is higher than that in the experimental condition. The null hypothesis itself is that the control condition mean is equal to *or less than* the mean for the experimental condition. That is,

$$H_0 : \mu_1 \leq \mu_2$$

$$H_1 : \mu_1 > \mu_2$$

This one-tailed, or directional, location of the rejection region is illustrated in Figure 6.6. Note, however, that in accordance with the Neyman-Pearson method, this directional location of the rejection region must be decided prior to gathering the data.

The tabled values of the t-distribution are two-tailed values. The probability that heads each column is the combined tail area. However, it is a simple matter to use these tables to obtain values for a one-tailed Type-1 error rate of $\alpha = .05$. To obtain this value, use the column headed .10. Values in this column, being two-tailed, give the t-value for an area of .05 in each tail, exactly what is needed for the one-tailed Type-1 error rate of .05.

One-tailed tests should be used rarely, if ever.

Directional tests, or one-tailed tests, are not frequently used, nor should they be. Strong arguments can be made that they should *never* be used. Neither Fisher, Neyman, nor Pearson suggested the use of such a test, and all three would probably have disapproved of it. It is not possible to enter into the details of these arguments, but the major difficulty can be described. It is not appropriate to use a one-tail test merely because a difference in one direction is the only form of difference that is interesting, or because it is the direction of difference that is expected. In the phobia treatment experiment, for example, the researcher may argue that, if the therapy has *any* effect, it will almost certainly be in the direction of improvement. But what would happen if, contrary to expectations, the therapy had resulted in a substantial

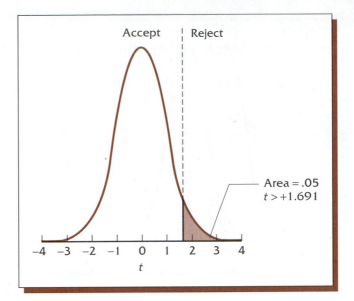

Figure 6.6
t-Distribution with *df* = 34, showing a one-tailed rejection region for a Type-1 error rate of $\alpha = .05$.

detrimental effect? Suppose the calculated value of *t* had been -2.2, a value that would lead to a rejection of the null hypothesis for a two-tailed test. In setting up the one-sided rejection region, the researcher is precluding the possibility of declaring this result to be statistically significant. Strict adherence to the Neyman-Pearson procedure would require that in such a case the researcher retain the null hypothesis. It is doubtful whether any researcher, confronted with such a result, would ignore the apparent negative effect of the therapy and treat the result as a nondifference. Nor would a good scientist ignore it. The possibility that a therapeutic procedure is doing more harm than good is not something to be ignored in interests of adhering to formal rules.

One way of avoiding this conflict between formal rules and sound scientific judgment is to set up two-tailed rejection regions no matter how unlikely a difference in one direction is judged to be.

6.4.3 The Type-2 Error Rate: The Risk of Missing a Real Difference

The Type-2 error rate is relevant when, in fact, the null hypothesis is false, that is, when there really is a difference and the full model is appropriate. Under these circumstances, an error is made if the null hypothesis is not rejected. Thus, whenever the decision is to retain the null hypothesis, there is the potential for a Type-2 error, a failure to detect a true difference; it is a signal that has been lost in noise. Perhaps inspection time really does make a difference to the size of the Ponzo illusion.

The concept of a Type-2 error rate was not part of the Fisher approach. As we have seen, for Fisher, failure to reject the null hypothesis meant simply that the data provided no support for such a rejection; whether or not the null hypothesis was actually false was a matter on which no definite statement could be made.

Neyman and Pearson attempted to go further and quantify the risk of making such an error. This Type-2 error rate is commonly denoted by β, the Greek lowercase letter beta. Figure 6.7 illustrates the Neyman-Pearson concept of a Type-2 error rate.

> The Type-2 error rate is the probability of failing to reject a false null hypothesis.

> β denotes the Type-2 error rate.

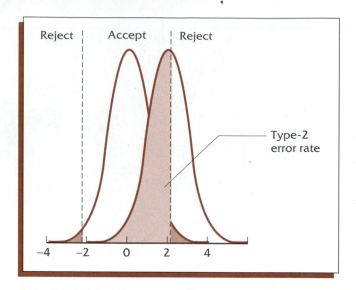

Figure 6.7

Distributions showing Type-1 error rates (darker areas) and Type-2 errors (lightly shaded areas).

The distribution to the left is a replica of the t-distribution of Figure 6.5, with the $\alpha = .05$ rejection region marked off as before and now indicated by the dark areas. The distribution to the right represents the probablity distribution of outcomes (the values of the t-ratio) for a case in which the null hypothesis is false.

The decision rule states that the null hypothesis should be accepted if the obtained value of the t-ratio falls within the interval -2.032 to $+2.032$. However, if the null hypothesis is actually false, then whenever the calculated t-ratio falls within the interval -2.032 to $+2.032$, the null hypothesis will be accepted and a Type-2 error will be made. What is the probability of this happening? The lightly shaded area represents this probability. Note that, because the right-hand distribution designates probabilities for the t-ratio when the null hypothesis is false, it will be the areas within *this* distribution that specifies the Type-2 error. To state the matter briefly, the left-hand distribution defines the acceptance region; but when the null hypothesis is false, it is the right-hand distribution that describes how the t-ratio will behave and thus how likely it is to fall in the acceptance region.

What factors determine the Type-2 error rate? What factors influence the size of the area corresponding to the lightly shaded portion of Figure 6.7? Three factors can be identified: the Type-1 error rate, the magnitude of $|\mu_1 - \mu_2|$, and the value of the standard error.

Type-1 Error Rate

This factor is the most obvious and the least interesting. If everything else is held constant, one error rate can be traded off against the other. If the Type-1 error rate is made more stringent—say, reduced from .05 to .01—then the cost is an increase in the Type-2 error rate. In Figure 6.7, for example, if the rejection region (the dark areas) is made smaller by moving the criterion further into the tails of the distribution, then the effect is to increase the lightly shaded area corresponding to the Type-2 error rate.

In everyday terms, the more evidence you demand before rejecting the null hypothesis, the greater the risk of mistakenly retaining a false null hypothesis. The more evidence a jury demands before finding an accused person guilty, the greater the risk of a guilty person getting off. In medical diagnosis, the stronger the evidence a physician demands before declaring a condition serious, the greater the risk that a genuinely serious condition will go untreated. A skeptic who demands strong evidence before sounding the alarm is more likely to miss a genuine emergency.

Conversely, a lower Type-2 error rate could be achieved at the cost of increasing the Type-1 error rate. A jury that demands less evidence will convict more criminals, but at the expense of convicting more people who are innocent. A physician who demands only minimal evidence before declaring a condition to be serious reduces the risk that a genuinely serious condition will go untreated, but at the expense of treating as serious conditions that are not serious at all. A suspicious person who demands only minimal evidence before sounding the alarm will miss few emergencies at the cost of creating many false alarms.

The trade-off between Type-1 and Type-2 errors is settled in different domains by considering the cost of each kind of error. As a general policy, science and jurisprudence consider Type-1 errors to be more serious than Type-2 errors. In jurisprudence, strong evidence is demanded before finding an accused person guilty. It is deemed preferable that some guilty people should go free than that the innocent should be found guilty. The moral cost of jailing (let alone executing) an innocent person is judged to outweigh the moral cost of letting some guilty people go free. In medicine, the opposite is often the case—even if there is only slight evidence that a condition is serious, treat it as if it were serious. It is usually preferable to administer a treatment unnecessarily (Type-1 error) than to fail to treat a genuinely sick person (Type-2 error).

In science, a Type-1 error results in the acceptance of a full model when the simpler null model would suffice. As discussed in Chapter 1, science typically abides by the principle of parsimony, and retaining the null model is more parsimonious. There are other costs associated with Type-1 errors. Type-1 errors are more likely to mislead fellow scientists into a serious waste of effort. Science seeks causes, and when a scientist claims to have found one (as revealed in differences between conditions of an experiment) fellow scientists are likely to follow this lead or modify their own research program to take this new discovery into account. If the claim is untrue (Type-1 error), then the cost in terms of wasted and misdirected effort can be enormous. On the other hand, Type-2 errors are usually considered less serious. If a genuine difference exists, then, although it might be missed on one occasion (a Type-2 error), it will be detected on a later occasion. The cost of a Type-2 error may be no more than a slight delay in making a discovery.

Magnitude of $|\mu_1 - \mu_2|$

If everything else is held constant, the greater the value of $|\mu_1 - \mu_2|$, the lower the Type-2 error rate. In commonsense terms, the larger the difference, the easier it is to detect and the less likely it is that the difference will remain undetected. If the decision to retain the null hypothesis in the Ponzo illusion experiment was a Type-2 error, perhaps it was because the difference was very small. In terms of the distributions in Figure 6.7, the magnitude of $|\mu_1 - \mu_2|$ is represented by the distance between the two distributions. As the right-hand distribution moves further away from the distribution under the null hypothesis, the overlap between the two distributions becomes less and the area corresponding to the Type-2 error rate becomes smaller.

One error rate can be traded off against the other.

The trade-off between Type-1 and Type-2 errors is settled in different domains by considering the cost of each kind of error.

The larger the difference between μ_1 and μ_2, the less likely it is that the difference will go undetected.

The actual magnitude of $|\mu_1 - \mu_2|$ is, of course, a feature of the phenomenon under investigation. How big an effect, if any, viewing time has on the Ponzo illusion is a feature of human perception; except by altering the conditions of the experiment it is not a value that can be adjusted by the experimenter in the interests of lowering the Type-2 error rate. It is important, however, to understand that specifying a value for the Type-2 error rate will be relative to a specified value for $|\mu_1 - \mu_2|$. Consider again the decision to retain the null hypothesis in the Ponzo illusion experiment. Did we commit a Type-2 error? Posed in these absolute terms, this question cannot be answered. However, questions of the following form *can* be answered:

Type-2 error rates are always relative to a hypothetical true difference.

■ If viewing time produces a true difference of 1 millimeter in the size of the illusion (that is, $|\mu_1 - \mu_2| = 1$ millimeter), what is the probability that the experiment will lead to a decision to retain the null hypothesis?

■ If viewing time produces a true difference of 5 millimeters in the size of the illusion (that is, $|\mu_1 - \mu_2| = 5$ millimeters), what is the probability that the experiment will lead to a decision to retain the null hypothesis?

The answers for the two cases would be different. The first statement asks for β relative to a hypothetical difference of 1 millimeter. The second statement asks for β relative to a much larger difference of 5 millimeters. The probability in the first case would therefore be higher than in the second. Failure to detect a small difference is more likely than failure to detect a larger one.

This example reveals a fundamental asymmetry between Type-1 and Type-2 errors. An experimenter following the Neyman-Pearson rationale can (indeed, must) fix α at a specific level such as .05 or .01. However, for β, the level is always relative to some hypothetical value of the true difference between the conditions. This hypothetical value is usually specified in terms of the value of this difference expressed in units of the standard deviation: $|\mu_1 - \mu_2|/\sigma$. You may recognize this ratio from Chapter 3. It is the measure of effect size referred to in that chapter as Cohen's **d**.

Cohen's d measures effect size in units of the standard deviation.

The fact that the Type-2 error rate is expressed relative to some value of Cohen's **d** is illustrated by statements such as, "For $\mathbf{d} \geq 1.0$, the probability of a Type-2 error is .10." Such a statement means that, if **d** is as large as 1.0, then the probability (β) is .10 that the null hypothesis will be mistakenly retained. Equivalently, the statement claims that the probability is .90 that the null hypothesis will be correctly rejected. The value .90 is simply $1 - \beta$. The probability ($1 - \beta$) that the null hypothesis will be correctly rejected is known as the *power* of a statistical test. The power of a statistical test is simply its capacity to detect a real difference. It is rather like the power of a telescope. A telescope with low power will detect only the brightest stars; weak stars will remain unseen. A test with low power (high β-rate) will detect only large differences; small difference will remain undetected.

The probability $1 - \beta$ is known as the power of a statistical test.

How can an experimenter ensure that an experiment is designed to yield data that will support a statistical test of adequate power? The answer to this question brings us to the third factor that influences the Type-2 error rate: the value of the standard error.

Value of the Standard Error

For a given Type-1 error rate and a specified value of effect size, the Type-2 error decreases as the standard error decreases.

Expressed informally, this relationship states that the less noisy the data, the easier it is to detect genuine differences. High levels of noise make the detection of signals more difficult, especially weak signals. Distant stars are more difficult to see in a hazy atmosphere, and the whispered message is more difficult to hear at a noisy party than in a quiet living room.

Apart from settling for a higher Type-1 error rate or detecting only larger effect sizes, reducing the size of the standard error is the one way in which an experimenter can reduce β and increase power. Methods for reducing the size of the standard error were introduced as part of the discussion of factors influencing the width of the confidence interval. The concept of power $(1 - \beta)$ is really the Neyman-Pearson counterpart to the concept of precision as measured, for example, by confidence interval width. Any factors that reduce the size of the standard error will increase both precision and power.

In designing an experiment, investigators working within the Neyman-Pearson tradition might state their goal as

> For $\alpha = .05$, the experiment is designed to achieve a power of .9 to detect an effect size of $d \geq 1.0$."

Investigators using confidence intervals might state their goal as

> The experiment should have sufficient precision to estimate the true difference to within 0.5 standard deviation units with 95% confidence.

In both cases, the overall goal is to ensure that the standard error is small enough to provide an adequate answer to the investigators' question. The first statement reflects the decision-making goal of the Neyman-Pearson tradition. The investigators want to be highly confident (90%) that, if the size of the effect is as large as 1.0, then the null hypothesis will be appropriately rejected. The second statement reflects a primary concern with estimating the size of the difference rather than with decision making. In this case, the investigators want the 95% confidence interval to be no wider than $\overline{Y} \pm w$, where w is 0.5σ.

As we saw in the earlier discussion, the two major methods of reducing the size of the standard error are

- increasing the number of observations (n)

- reducing the size of the residuals

Chapter 8 describes how these two methods can be used to achieve adequate power and precision.

Power and the width of a confidence interval are closely related concepts.

Comprehension Check 6.4

Important Concepts

1. The distinguishing feature of the Neyman-Pearson tradition was to place statistical hypothesis testing in a rigorous decision-making framework in which a decision rule was established prior to the data analysis.

2. They formalized the concept of decision error rates and distinguished between Type-1 and Type-2 errors.

3. A Type-1 error occurs when the null hypothesis is mistakenly rejected. In this case, a difference has been claimed when none exists. The probability of making a Type-1 error, the Type-1 error rate, is denoted by α. It is usually set at $\alpha = .05$.

4. A Type-2 error occurs when a decision is made to retain the null hypothesis even though it is actually false—there really is a difference. The probability of making a Type-2 error, the Type-2 error rate, is denoted by β. The Type-2 error is always relative to a specified size of the true difference between the two population means.

5. Three factors influence β: the chosen level of α, the size of the difference between the two population means, and the standard error of the difference between the means.

6. The power of a statistical test is the complement of the Type-2 error; it is $1 - \beta$, the probability of detecting a true difference.

Worked Examples

Example 1 Induced happiness

Confidence intervals were calculated for this experiment in Example 1 at the end of Section 6.2, and the null hypothesis was evaluated through a direct use of the t-distribution in Example 1 at the end of Section 6.3. The sample means for control and experimental conditions respectively were 12.0 and 16.0. The estimated standard error of the difference between means was found to be $s_{\bar{Y}_1 - \bar{Y}_2} = 1.77$. There were $n = 20$ participants in each condition.

a. What is the null hypothesis for this experiment?

b. What is the alternative to the null hypothesis for this experiment?

c. Sketch a t-distribution and, using the appropriate t-values, mark off the acceptance and rejection regions for a Type-1 error rate of .05. Locate the position on the sketch of the obtained t-value. Ensure that the region into which it falls (acceptance versus rejection) coincides with the judgment made in Example 1 at the end of Section 6.3.

Answer

a. The null hypothesis for this experiment is $H_0: \mu_1 - \mu_2 = 0$.

b. The alternative to the null hypothesis is $H_1: \mu_1 - \mu_2 \neq 0$.

c. Figure 6.8 marks off the acceptance region (95%) between $t = \pm 2.024$, the value of t for $df = 38$ and a combined area of .05 in the tails. The rejection regions are the tail areas more extreme than 2.024. The obtained value of 2.26 falls into the rejection region in the right-hand tail.

Example 2 Intentional versus incidental remembering (Data Set 6.4)

Confidence intervals were calculated for this experiment in Problem 2 at the end of Section 6.2, and the null hypothesis was evaluated through a direct use of the t-distribution in Problem 2 at the end of Section 6.3. The sample mean was 10.65 for

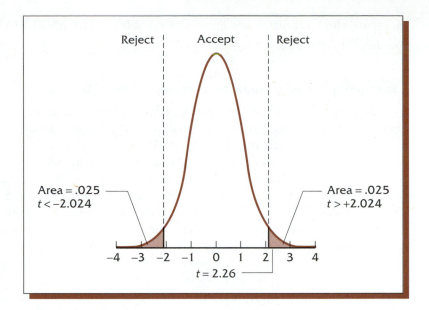

Figure 6.8
t-Distribution with $df = 38$, showing rejection region for $\alpha = .05$.

the incidental conditions and 10.15 for the intentional condition. The estimated standard error of the difference between means was found to be $s_{\bar{Y}_1 - \bar{Y}_2} = 0.826$. There were $n = 26$ participants in each condition.

Sketch a t-distribution and, using the appropriate t-values, mark off the acceptance and rejection regions for a Type-1 error rate of .05. Locate the position on the sketch of the obtained t-value. Ensure that the region into which it falls (acceptance versus rejection) coincides with the judgment made in Problem 2 at the end of Sections 6.2 and 6.3.

Answer Figure 6.9 marks off the acceptance region (95%) between $t = \pm 2.009$, the value of t for $df = 50$ and a combined area of .05 in the tails. The rejection re-

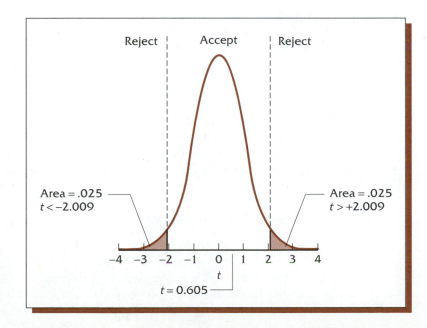

Figure 6.9
t-Distribution with $df = 50$, showing rejection region for $\alpha = .05$.

gions are the tail areas more extreme than 2.009. The obtained value of $t = 0.605$ falls into the acceptance region.

Example 3   Social interaction among toddlers (Data Set 2.6)

This experiment from child psychology was first used in Problem 2 at the end of Section 2.1. It is based on results from an experimental study of social interaction among toddlers by Jacklin and Maccoby (1978).

The experiment asks whether infants as young as 33 months are sensitive to whether their same-age playmate is the same or the opposite sex. To answer this question, pairs of 33-month-old infants were placed in a playroom and given a single desirable toy to play with. Does the amount of social interaction between the two depend on whether they are of the same sex or of different sexes? This question might be answered by observing paired infants and recording how often they interact with each other. Some pairs were same-sex pairs; some were different-sex pairs.

Notice that the predictor variable is natural and that the term *participant* does not refer to an individual infant but to a pair. For the purposes of this experiment, each pair constitutes a single observational unit in the sense that each pair yields a single measurement. Thus the value of n is 30, the number of pairs in each condition.

Analyses from previous exercises have yielded the following results, where the subscript 1 refers to the same-sex pairs and the subscript 2 to the different-sex pairs: $\overline{Y}_1 = 31.0$, $\overline{Y}_2 = 22.0$, $SS_1 = 446$, $SS_2 = 484$.

a. What is the estimated standard error of the difference between the means?

b. Using $\alpha = .05$ evaluate the null hypothesis of no difference between the means.

c. Which model do you judge to be appropriate for these data: the full model or the null model? Give reasons.

d. A commentator reviewing this experiment makes the claim, "Although this experiment convincingly establishes the phenomenon that same-sex pairs interact more with each other than do different-sex pairs, it tells us little about the cause of this difference." Explain the justification for this comment.

Answer

a. To calculate the value of $s_{\overline{Y}_1 - \overline{Y}_2}$, we need to estimate the variance of the observations, which we assume to be the same for both conditions. This estimate is denoted by MS_e and is obtained by adding together the sum of the squared residuals for the two conditions and dividing by the combined degrees of freedom ($df = 58$).

$$MS_e = (446 + 484)/58 = 16.03$$

We can now obtain the estimated standard error:

$$s_{\overline{Y}_1 - \overline{Y}_2} = \sqrt{\frac{2MS_e}{n}} = \sqrt{\frac{2 \times 16.03}{30}} = 1.03$$

b.
$$t = \frac{\overline{Y}_1 - \overline{Y}_2}{s_{\overline{Y}_1 - \overline{Y}_2}} = \frac{9.0}{1.03} = 8.74$$

The degrees of freedom are $2(n-1) = 58$. Consulting Statistical Table 3 gives us a value for t of 2.009 (using $df = 50$ as the closest tabled value *below* 58). Because the obtained value of t is greater than this critical value, the null hypothesis must be rejected.

c. The full model is required to provide an adequate fit for these data. The null hypothesis is untenable because the t-ratio falls into the rejection region. If there really were no difference between the conditions, a difference as large as 9.0 would be improbable.

d. The result leaves open many possible causal explanations, a situation typical of quasi-experiments. Is it some inborn disposition? A result of early experience? Or some other factor? Despite its causal ambiguity, the finding is of obvious importance. It tells us that infants as young as 33 months can distinguish the sex of fellow infants and respond differently on the basis of that knowledge. Thus an important phenomenon has been established, and further research aimed at establishing the cause is justified.

Problems

Problem 1   Potential errors

Review the conclusions you drew about the null hypothesis for Problems 1, 2, and 3 of Comprehension Check 6.3. In which of these experiments is it possible that you might have made a Type-1 error? In which experiments might you have made a Type-2 error?

Problem 2   Comparing intentional and incidental remembering

The results from the experiments used in Problems 2 and 3 of Comprehension Check 6.3 suggest both an obvious inference and an interesting speculation. One form of incidental remembering (rating pleasantness) seems to be as effective a study method as intentional study. However, another form of incidental remembering (counting syllables) is less effective than rating pleasantness. The obvious prediction is that counting syllables is a less effective study method than intentional study. Problem 2 describes an experiment to test this inference. Problem 3 explores the "interesting speculation."

The experiment to evaluate the prediction that counting syllables is a less effective study method than intentional study used a completely randomized design with 23 participants in each of two conditions. Participants in the intentional study condition were instructed "to study the words because you will be required to recall them." Participants in the incidental condition were told nothing of the memory test and simply responded to each word by indicating the number of syllables. Other details of the experiment are the same as in Problems 2 and 3 of Comprehension Check 6.3.

a. If μ_1 is the mean for the intentional study condition and μ_2 is the mean for the incidental (syllable counting) condition, what is the null hypothesis for this experiment?

b. What is the alternative to the null hypothesis for this experiment?

c. Using a Type-1 error rate of $\alpha = .05$, draw a sketch of a t-distribution that sets out the acceptance and rejection regions for the null hypothesis.

d. Analysis of the data gave the following results: $\overline{Y}_1 = 11.7$, $\overline{Y}_2 = 7.2$, $s_{\overline{Y}_1 - \overline{Y}_2} = 1.55$. Use these values to obtain the value of the t-ratio and then establish whether this value falls in the acceptance or rejection region of your sketch.

Problem 3   A better form of incidental remembering

The interesting speculation is that if different forms of incidental remembering are differentially effective, there might be a form of incidental remembering that is more effective than rating pleasantness and therefore more effective than intentional study. If so, then we have found an incidental task that produces better remembering than that produced when participants make a conscious effort to remember. Participants will have remembered better without even trying (to remember)!

This experiment used a completely randomized design with $n = 31$ participants in each of two conditions. Participants in both conditions were shown a list of 40 single-word personality descriptors—adjectives such as "attractive," "aggressive," and so on. One condition was the intentional study condition in which participants were instructed "to study the words because you will be required to recall them." Participants in the incidental condition were told nothing of the memory test but were asked to rate each word on a five-point scale as to how well the adjective described their own personality. Other details of the experiment are the same as in Problems 2 and 3 of Comprehension Check 6.3.

a. Using a Type-1 error rate of $\alpha = .05$, draw a sketch of a t-distribution that sets out the acceptance and rejection regions for the null hypothesis for this experiment.

b. Analysis of the data gave the following results: $\overline{Y}_1 = 13.7$, $\overline{Y}_2 = 17.8$, $s_{\overline{Y}_1 - \overline{Y}_2} = 1.71$. Use these results to calculate the value of the t-ratio, and then establish whether this value falls in the acceptance or rejection region of your sketch.

c. Express in words the conclusion you draw from these results.

6.5   Overview and Evaluation

Although the different approaches have much in common and will usually lead to the same conclusion, important differences remain.

Although this chapter has presented three alternative approaches to answering questions about $\mu_1 - \mu_2$, all three performed the same basic analysis. They all made use of the same estimate of the standard error of the difference between the sample means, and they all used the same t-distribution with $2(n - 1)$ degrees of freedom. Both the Fisher and the Neyman-Pearson approaches permit the calculation of confidence intervals; and although they interpreted these intervals somewhat differently, this difference is not one that need concern us here.

Moreover, despite their differences, the decision to reject or not reject the null hypothesis will usually be the same regardless of which approach is adopted. The decisions will usually be the same, but not always. In our tranquilizer effects experiment, we saw that if an α-rate of .01 had been set, the experimenter using the Neyman-Pearson procedure would not have rejected the null hypothesis, whereas Fisher's approach allows the flexibility of waiting until the t-value has been computed before deciding. One way of avoiding this potential difference is always to set the Type-1 error rate at $\alpha = .05$. In practice, this is exactly what most investigators do.

Given this apparent resolution of any conflict between the procedures, it may appear that there is nothing of importance left to discuss. The differences between the various approaches seem too minor and hair-splitting to have any relevance to the practical matter of scientific progress or to warrant further discussion in an introductory textbook. Some aspects of the discussion are indeed best left to professional theoreticians, but there are other aspects of the decision-making process that have an impact on how experiments are designed, how data are interpreted, and whether or not the results of an experiment will be acceptable for publication.

Rather than engage in an abstract discussion of the strengths and weaknesses of the various approaches, we will describe a situation that arises quite often in everyday research.

6.5.1 "Marginally Significant" Difference

Jill has just completed an experiment for her honors thesis. The experiment was designed to evaluate the effectiveness of training students to use visual imagery in learning geometry. The experiment used a completely randomized design with two conditions, an experimental condition in which participants received training in visual imagery and a control group in which participants were taught by conventional methods. There were 20 students in each condition. The response measure was the score (expressed as a percentage) obtained on a final geometry exam.

Jill has been trained in the Neyman-Pearson tradition, so before starting the experiment, she formulated her hypotheses

$$H_0: \mu_1 - \mu_2 = 0$$

$$H_1: \mu_1 - \mu_2 \neq 0$$

and set a Type-1 error rate of $\alpha = .05$ as the basis for deciding between the two hypotheses. Consulting the tables of the t-distribution, she found that with $2(n - 1) = 38$ degrees of freedom, a t-value of 2.024 was needed to reject the null hypothesis.

On analyzing the data, the mean for the control group is 66% and the mean for the experimental group is 71%, an improvement of 5% that seems to confirm Jill's belief in the effectiveness of the new method.

The mean square of the residuals for the data is found to be $MS_e = 65.0$, a value leading to an estimated standard error for the difference between means of

$$s_{\bar{Y}_1 - \bar{Y}_2} = \sqrt{\frac{2MS_e}{n}} = \sqrt{\frac{2 \times 65}{20}} = 2.55$$

Jill then calculates a t-ratio:

$$t = \frac{(\bar{Y}_1 - \bar{Y}_2) - (\mu_1 - \mu_2)}{s_{\bar{Y}_1 - \bar{Y}_2}} = \frac{5.0 - 0}{2.55} = 1.96$$

Jill's initial excitement over the result suddenly turns to despair when she obtains this result; the obtained t-value of 1.96 is just slightly below the value of 2.024 needed to reject the null hypothesis. Her frustration increases when she calculates that if the difference between the two conditions had been 5.2% rather than 5.0%, the obtained t-value would have been 2.039 and the null hypothesis could have been rejected.

Adhering to Neyman-Pearson principles, Jill's only alternative is to retain the null hypothesis. Fisher's approach would have given her greater flexibility. A t-value of 1.96 has an associated probability of .06, just short of the traditional .05 level of significance. As a Fisherian, Jill might have described this result as "marginally significant," an expression that can still be found in the literature. She might even have argued, perhaps using evidence from previous studies, that a probability of .06, although larger than the traditional .05, is small enough to reject the null hypothesis. Although Fisher might have approved of this kind of reasoning, few journal editors today (or thesis supervisors) would accept it.

A common criticism of the flexibility of the Fisher approach takes the form of the slippery slope argument. If .06 is improbable enough, why not .07, and if .07, why not .08, or .09, or . . . ? The line has to be drawn somewhere; but if the criterion can be adjusted, depending on how the data turn out and what the experimenter hopes to prove, objectivity has been lost, and the idea of a fixed and objective Type-1 error rate becomes meaningless.

There is considerable merit to this argument against undisciplined flexibility. On the other hand, strict decision making can lead to some troubling situations. Suppose someone repeats Jill's experiment, finds an improvement of 4.7%, but obtains a slightly smaller estimated standard error. (Remember $s_{\overline{Y}_1 - \overline{Y}_2}$ is subject to sampling variability and would vary from one repetition of the experiment to another, just as $\overline{Y}_1 - \overline{Y}_2$ does.) The net result is that the 4.7% difference now leads to a rejection of the null hypothesis. This second experimenter writes up the experiment, and it is accepted for publication on the grounds that it demonstrates a reliable method of improving the learning of geometry. Meanwhile, Jill wonders what she should do next. The troubling aspect to this situation (a not uncommon one) is that, from any reasonable point of view, these two versions of the experiment have produced virtually identical results. Yet applying the Neyman-Pearson decision rule creates a situation in which two experiments with almost identical results lead to different decisions.

Before resolving Jill's dilemma, we will consider a second example. Bill is a fellow honors student in the same laboratory, also working on his thesis. He, too, is interested in improving geometry instruction, but he has adopted an approach different from Jill's. Bill has devised a tutorial system, and he tests the system with an experiment similar to Jill's. The only difference between the two experiments is that students in Bill's experimental condition receive the tutorial system instead of the imagery training. Bill uses a different group of students, with 40 students in each condition. The experiment has a completely randomized design. As in Jill's experiment, the response measure is the score (expressed as a percentage) obtained on a final geometry exam.

Bill has also been trained in the Neyman-Pearson tradition; so before starting the experiment, he, too, set a Type-1 error rate of $\alpha = .05$ as the basis for deciding between the null and the full models. Consulting the tables of the t-distribution, he found that with $2(n - 1) = 78$ degrees of freedom, a t-value of 1.991 was needed to reject the null hypothesis.

On analyzing the data, the mean for the control group is 68% and the mean for the experimental group is 70%, an improvement of 2%. The value of MS_e for the data is found to be 18.5, leading to an estimated standard error for the difference between means of 0.962. The resulting t-ratio is therefore

$$t = \frac{2.0 - 0}{0.962} = 2.079$$

This value of t is greater than the 1.991 value needed to reject the null hypothesis. Bill therefore concludes that the tutorial system improves the learning of geometry.

6.5.2 Comparison and Evaluation

There are important lessons to be learned from a careful comparison of the results of Jill's and Bill's experiments. An uncritical account of the results might summarize them by concluding that imagery training does not improve geometry learning but the tutorial system does. If both experiments were to be published, it is highly likely that this summary is what would be found in subsequent reviews of the literature, textbook accounts, and theories developed to explain the learning of geometry. Although such a summary would seem to have the support of rigorous statistical hypothesis testing, it presents what is probably a seriously distorted picture of what is really happening in geometry learning.

> *The difficulty with a summary that merely records significant versus not significant results is that it fails to make any reference to the size of the difference between the two conditions.*

Suppose we calculate a 95% confidence interval for both experiments. The interval will be

$$CI_{.95} = (\overline{Y}_1 - \overline{Y}_2) \pm (t \times s_{\overline{Y}_1 - \overline{Y}_2})$$

For Jill's experiment, this expression gives

$$CI_{.95} = 5.0 \pm (2.024 \times 2.55) = 5.0 \pm 5.16 = -0.16 \text{ to } 10.16$$

Notice that this interval includes 0 (barely), corresponding to the "very nearly significant" status of the t-statistic. For Bill's experiment, the confidence interval is

$$CI_{.95} = 2.0 \pm (1.991 \times 0.962) = 2.0 \pm 1.92 = 0.08 \text{ to } 3.92$$

Notice that this interval does not include 0, a result that corresponds to the rejection of the null hypothesis using the t-statistic.

The most obvious feature of these two 95% confidence intervals is that Jill's is much wider than Bill's. In round figures, Jill's data suggest that the effect of the imagery training could plausibly be anywhere between 0 and 10%. For Bill's data, the corresponding range is 0 to 4%. Bill's experiment leads to a much more precise estimate, a consequence of a larger number of participants ($n = 40$ versus $n = 20$) and an experimental procedure that led to less noisy data as reflected in the value of MS_e (65.0 versus 18.5). Another way of making the same point is to say that Bill's experiment has greater power to detect a difference of a given size.

An interpretation of Jill's data that is more constructive than dismissing it as a nonsignificant result is to conclude that the experiment lacks sufficient precision to make *any* decision about the null hypothesis. Notice that the same criterion that supports the conclusion that 0 is a plausible value for the effect of imagery also supports the conclusion that a 10% improvement is plausible. Both values fall within the 95% confidence interval. The best interpretation of Jill's data therefore is simply that the data are too noisy to support a conclusion either way. Her best course of action is therefore to redesign the experiment, or recruit more participants, to reduce the standard error and obtain a narrower confidence interval and greater power.

An educator might judge that any method for improving geometry teaching must show an improvement of at least 5% to justify the extra time and expense of initiating it. Looking at the results from these two experiments, the educator concludes that Bill's tutorial method is not worth pursuing, but Jill's method cannot be ruled out. It

The two experiments differ in their power to detect a difference of a given size.

is at least plausible that imagery training yields improvement greater than 5%. In brief, the educator concludes that Bill's tutorial system leads to a reliable improvement, but one that is too small to be practically useful. Jill's results are unreliable but suggest that they *could* lead to levels of improvement that would justify implementation. Had the educator been unwilling to specify a minimum level of worthwhile improvement and paid attention only to the decisions to reject or not reject the null hypothesis, quite the opposite conclusion might have been reached.

It is also important to note that the *p*-value is not a good index of the *size* of an effect. Published papers sometimes quote *p*-values of .001 or even .0001. However, the number of zeros should not be interpreted as an index of the size of an effect, or even of its scientific importance. This sort of thinking is sometimes encouraged in reports that describe differences as "highly" significant. However, the size of the difference is only one of the determinants of the value of *t* and thus of the *p*-value. The other determinant is the size of the standard error. The *p*-value is an index of the *reliability* of the difference, not its magnitude, and certainly not its scientific importance.

> The *p*-value is not a good index of the size of an experimental effect.

This analysis of various interpretations of Jill's experiment is a critique of scientific practice more than it is of the Neyman-Pearson or the Fisher approach as such. It is unfortunate that the Neyman-Pearson principles have led to a practice that classifies results as either significant or not, and then equates this all-or-none classification with a simple all-or-none conviction about whether there is, or is not, a real difference. Neither Fisher, Neyman, nor Pearson would have approved of such a practice, albeit for different reasons.

Advantages of Confidence Intervals

Many of the difficulties associated with statistical decision making can be avoided by the use of confidence intervals. The advantages of confidence intervals are

1. A confidence interval provides information about the likely *magnitude* of a difference. This information tends to be lost in a methodology that focuses on decision making. It is important to note that the significance level is not a good index of an effect's magnitude.

2. If a judgment does need to be made about the null hypothesis, a confidence interval provides sufficient information to do so. Such a judgment might be needed in the context of deciding whether the data demand a full model.

3. The width of a confidence interval provides information about the precision of the estimate. In Jill's experiment, the width of the confidence interval indicated an estimate that was so imprecise as to make it obvious that the appropriate next step was, not to give up, but to reduce the standard error.

4. A confidence interval provides a better basis for making comparisons across different experiments than does a simple box score of significant versus nonsignificant differences. In integrating findings across similar experiments, it is important to take into account different levels of precision. Suppose, for example, that Jill repeats her experiment with a design that increases precision and that it yields a 95% confidence interval of 4.1 to 5.8. It would be poor scientific thinking to integrate the findings of her two experiments by saying that one experiment found a nonsignificant difference, one found a significant difference, so the score is 1 to 1. This interpretation suggests that the two experiments support incompatible conclusions, whereas the confidence interval makes it clear that the results are highly compatible.

6.5.3 Describing the Magnitude of an Effect

An important conclusion from this critical overview is that statistical significance, whether in the Fisher or the Neyman-Pearson tradition, does not tell us everything we need to know about the results of even the simplest of experiments. Although it is often desirable to decide whether or not the data demand a full model, there is other important information that this all-or-none decision fails to convey. Such information aims to go beyond simply deciding whether or not an experimental manipulation has had an effect. Its goal is to quantify the *magnitude* or *strength* of an experimental effect. We will conclude this section with a summary of previously mentioned methods of achieving this goal.

The most important information that statistical hypothesis testing fails to convey is an estimate of the *magnitude* of the difference between the means. To report only the decision with respect to the null hypothesis is rather like being told that you passed a course, but not whether your grade was 50% or 95%. A significant difference does not imply a large difference, even if the *p*-value is "highly significant." Even the smallest difference will be detected if the experiment has sufficient precision. Conversely, an experiment with low precision may fail to detect a very large difference.

We have seen that the magnitude of the difference between the means can be estimated in either point or interval form. The *point estimate* may take either of two forms:

1. The simple difference between the means: $\mu_1 - \mu_2$ is estimated by $\overline{Y}_1 - \overline{Y}_2$.

2. Cohen's "effect size" **d**, defined as $\mathbf{d} = (\mu_1 - \mu_2)/\sigma$. Its estimate is

$$\hat{\mathbf{d}} = \frac{\overline{Y}_1 - \overline{Y}_2}{\sqrt{MS_e}}$$

This index was described in Section 3.3.4. Recall that its major advantage over the simple difference is that, by expressing the difference in units of the estimated standard deviation, it becomes possible to compare differences across different experiments. However, as point estimates, neither conveys information about the precision of the estimate. Such information is provided by an interval estimate.

The *interval estimate* of $\mu_1 - \mu_2$ has the following form:

$$CI = (\overline{Y}_1 - \overline{Y}_2) \pm (t \times s_{\overline{Y}_1 - \overline{Y}_2})$$

where $s_{\overline{Y}_1 - \overline{Y}_2}$ is the estimated standard error of the difference between means. The value of t is determined by the degrees of freedom and the desired level of confidence.

A second form of information not conveyed by statistical hypothesis testing is the degree to which the full model reduces the residuals and thereby provides an improved fit. Rejection of the null hypothesis implies that the data demand a full model, but the degree of improvement in fit can range from small to substantial.

The simplest index of improvement in fit is the proportional reduction in the sum of squared residuals that the full model achieves relative to the null model. This index was described in Section 3.3.3, and in this chapter its value was calculated for both the phobia treatment experiment and the tranquilizer effects experiment. Expressed as a proportion, this ratio was

$$R^2 = \frac{SS_{model}}{SS_{total}}$$

The most important information that statistical hypothesis testing fails to convey is an estimate of the *magnitude* of the difference between the means.

Recall that in this formula, SS_{model} is $SS_{total} - SS_e$, where SS_{total} is the sum of the squared residuals under the null model.

Comprehension Check 6.5

Important Concepts

1. Although all the various approaches to statistical decision making will usually lead to the same conclusion, each approach has its own strengths and weaknesses.

2. The problem of "marginal significance" highlights the difference between the Fisher and the Neyman-Pearson approaches. Differences that are "almost significant" pose no special problem if the researcher is content with quoting a confidence interval or the *p*-value, as in the Fisher tradition. From these perspectives, there is really no need to make a decision at all. The Neyman-Pearson tradition, on the other hand, would reject the concept of "marginal significance" as lacking objectivity; it allows too much flexibility.

3. An unfortunate practice is to ignore the problem of Type-2 errors and to regard retention of the null hypothesis as equivalent to an assertion that no difference exists. Neither tradition would endorse this view.

4. Summarizing the results of experiments simply in terms of significance/nonsignificance is unsatisfactory for several reasons, all of which stem from the same source: Such a box-score summary fails to take into account the *magnitude* of the effect of the predictor variable. The major problems posed by such box-score summaries are

- With poor precision (low power), a true difference may not be detected, even though it is quite large.

- With very high precision, a trivially small difference may be statistically significant.

- Box-score summaries of significant/nonsignificant results can lead to serious distortions when used to integrate findings over a number of different experiments.

5. The three major indices of the *magnitude* of the effect of the predictor variable are

- the standardized point estimate of the difference (estimated Cohen's **d**)

- the confidence interval estimate of the difference

- the reduction in the variance of the residuals achieved by the full model, expressed as a proportion of the variance of the residuals for the null model.

Worked Examples

Example 1   **Summary table**

Table 6.5 provides a convenient summary of the results of basic computations for three of our familiar experiments.

Table 6.5 Summary of results for Worked Example 1a

Experiment	n	$\overline{Y}_1$	$\overline{Y}_2$	SS_{total}	SS_e	MS_e	$s_{\overline{Y}_1-\overline{Y}_2}$
Phobia	18	10.2	5.2	404.9	179.9	_____	_____
Tranquilizer	15	9.06	10.41	67.0	53.4	_____	_____
Ponzo	12	9.74	6.63	5092	5034	_____	_____

a. Complete the entries for the last two columns.

b. Use these results to complete Table 6.6. Many of these values have already been calculated. However, you should use this example as a means of assuring yourself that you understand how the various values were obtained. The column headed t asks for the obtained value of the t-ratio. The column headed $t_{.95}$ asks for the tabulated value of the t-ratio for $\alpha = .05$.

Answer We obtain the value of MS_e by dividing SS_e by the degrees of freedom. Recall that SS_e is $SS_1 + SS_2$.

For the phobia treatment experiment, $MS_e = 179.9/34 = 5.29$.
For the tranquilizer effects experiment, $MS_e = 53.4/28 = 1.91$.
For the Ponzo illusion experiment, $MS_e = 5034/22 = 228.82$.

We obtain the value of $s_{\overline{Y}_1-\overline{Y}_2}$ by using the formula

$$s_{\overline{Y}_1-\overline{Y}_2} = \sqrt{\frac{2MS_e}{n}}$$

For the phobia treatment experiment, $s_{\overline{Y}_1-\overline{Y}_2} = \sqrt{\dfrac{2 \times 5.29}{18}} = 0.77$.

For the tranquilizer effects experiment, $s_{\overline{Y}_1-\overline{Y}_2} = \sqrt{\dfrac{2 \times 1.91}{15}} = 0.50$.

For the Ponzo illusion experiment, $s_{\overline{Y}_1-\overline{Y}_2} = \sqrt{\dfrac{2 \times 228.82}{12}} = 6.18$.

Table 6.6 Results for Worked Example 1b

Experiment	df	$t_{.95}$	t	p-value	$\hat{d}$	$CI_{.95}$ for $|\mu_1 - \mu_2|$	R^2
Phobia	_____	_____	_____	_____	_____	_____	_____
Tranquilizer	_____	_____	_____	_____	_____	_____	_____
Ponzo	_____	_____	_____	_____	_____	_____	_____

Table 6.7 Summary of results for Worked Example 1

Experiment	df	$t_{.95}$	t	p-value	$\hat{d}$	$CI_{.95}$ for $|\mu_1 - \mu_2|$	R^2
Phobia	34	2.032	6.52	$<.01$	2.17	3.44 to 6.56	.56
Tranquilizer	28	2.048	2.68	$<.05$	0.98	0.32 to 2.38	.20
Ponzo	22	2.074	.501	$>.10$	0.21	-9.70 to 15.92	.01

b. The procedure for finding the listed values for the columns headed df, $t_{.95}$, t, p-value, and $CI_{.95}$ will be found earlier in the chapter. If you have any difficulty in obtaining the current values, consult the relevant section.

We obtain the estimates of **d** by using the formula

$$\hat{d} = \frac{\overline{Y}_1 - \overline{Y}_2}{\sqrt{MS_e}}$$

For the phobia treatment, $\hat{d} = \dfrac{5.0}{2.30} = 2.17$.

For the tranquilizer effects experiment, $\hat{d} = \dfrac{1.35}{1.38} = 0.98$.

For the Ponzo illusion experiment, $\hat{d} = \dfrac{3.11}{15.13} = 0.21$.

We obtain the value of R^2 by using the formula

$$R^2 = \frac{SS_{model}}{SS_{total}} = \frac{SS_{total} - SS_e}{SS_{total}}$$

For the phobia treatment experiment, $R^2 = \dfrac{404.9 - 179.9}{404.9} = .556$.

For the tranquilizer effects experiment, $R^2 = \dfrac{67.0 - 53.4}{67.0} = .203$.

For the Ponzo illusion experiment, $R^2 = \dfrac{5092 - 5034}{5092} = .011$.

The results of these calculations are compiled in Table 6.7.

Problems

Problem 1 **Summary of worked examples and problems**

Table 6.8 provides a convenient summary of the results of other experiments used as worked examples and problems throughout this chapter.

a. Complete the entries for the last two columns in Table 6.8.

b. Using the results from Table 6.8, complete Table 6.9. As in Table 6.6, the column headed $t_{.95}$ asks for the tabled value of the t-ratio for $\alpha = .05$.

Table 6.8 Summary of results for Problem 1

Experiment	Reference	n	$\overline{Y}_1$	$\overline{Y}_2$	SS_{total}	SS_e	MS_e	$s_{\overline{Y}_1 - \overline{Y}_2}$
Induced happiness	Section 6.2 Example 1	20	12.0	16.0	1346.0	1186.0	_____	_____
Induced anger	Section 6.2 Problem 1	18	6.9	8.6	146.7	120.1	_____	_____
Intentional vs. incidental remembering	Section 6.2 Problem 2	26	10.65	10.15	446.5	443.3	_____	_____
Two levels of incidental remembering	Section 6.3 Problem 3	22	12.2	6.9	715.5	406.5	_____	_____
Social interaction	Section 6.4 Example 3	30	31.0	22.0	2145.0	930.0	_____	_____

Table 6.9 Second summary of results for Problem 1

Experiment	df	$t_{.95}$	t	p-value	$\hat{d}$	$CI_{.95}$ for $|\mu_1 - \mu_2|$	R^2
Induced happiness	_____	_____	_____	_____	_____	_____	_____
Induced anger	_____	_____	_____	_____	_____	_____	_____
Intentional vs. incidental remembering	_____	_____	_____	_____	_____	_____	_____
Two levels of incidental remembering	_____	_____	_____	_____	_____	_____	_____
Social interaction	_____	_____	_____	_____	_____	_____	_____

Chapter 6 Exercises

The following exercises involve the analysis of data from a number of experiments. Many of these data sets were reviewed as exercises in Chapter 2 for the kinds of anomalies that might preclude the routine methods of analysis that have been described in this chapter. Remember that such a review should always precede the analysis of any data set.

For each experiment, you should perform the following tasks.

1. State the null hypothesis H_0, its alternate hypothesis H_1, and the model corresponding to each.

2. If a Type-1 error rate is set at .05, find the critical value of the t-statistic on which you would base a decision to reject or retain the null hypothesis.

3. Calculate the following values, using the computational results provided with each exercise.

a. an estimate of Cohen's **d**

b. R^2, the percentage reduction in the sum of squared residuals achieved by the full model relative to the null model

c. the 95% confidence interval

d. the t-ratio and its associated p-value

4. What conclusion would you draw about the effect of the experimental manipulation?

Exercise 1   Opinion change (Data Set 2.12)

Recall that in this experiment (Chapter 2, Exercise 2), there are two conditions, each with $n = 24$ participants. Participants were randomly assigned to the two conditions. All participants do the initial task. One condition is a control condition. Participants in this condition subsequently complete the rating scale but do not engage in any activity of persuasion. Participants in the experimental condition attempt to persuade others but do not complete the rating scale until afterward.

Condition	n	Mean	SS_Y	SS_{total}
1. Control	24	5.0	82.0	152.0
2. Experimental	24	6.0	58.0	

Note that in this and the following exercises, SS_{total} is the sum of squared residuals under the null model. Recall that SS_{model} is $SS_{total} - SS_e$

Exercise 2   Undermining intrinsic motivation (Data Set 2.13)

In this experiment (Chapter 2, Exercise 3), there are two conditions, each of $n = 18$ participants. (Recall that two outliers were removed in the Chapter 2 exercise.)

Participants were randomly assigned to the two conditions. In one condition, the participants expect a reward. Participants in the other condition do not expect a reward.

Condition (X)	n	Mean	SS_Y	SS_{total}
1. Reward	18	5.18	118.64	
2. No reward	18	10.27	41.36	392.57

Exercise 3 Effect of threat on desirability (Data Set 3.2)

In this experiment (Chapter 3, Exercise 3), 7-year-old children play with a set of toys and are then asked to rank them by choosing their favorite toy, their next favorite, and so on. The experimenter then designates the child's second preference as a *forbidden* toy, telling the child that he or she is not to play with this particular toy when left alone with the toys. There are two conditions. Half the children receive a threat of mild disapproval should they play with the forbidden toy; the other half receive a threat of very severe disapproval. Each child then has a period in which he or she is left alone with the toys. During this period, none of the children actually plays with the forbidden toy, but this conformity is not itself the result of major interest; rather we are interested in whether this conformity has produced any change in the perceived desirability of the forbidden toy. After this "temptation period," the children are asked to rate the desirability of each of the toys, including the forbidden toy. This toy, you will remember, was their original second preference. They perform this rating task by awarding each toy a number of stars ranging from 0 stars (most undesirable) to 10 stars (highly desirable). Forty children are used, 20 in each condition. They are assigned randomly to the two conditions.

Condition	n	Mean	SS_Y	SS_{total}
1. Mild threat	20	6.3	48.2	
2. Severe threat	20	7.8	63.2	133.9

Exercise 4 Infant perception of partly occluded stationary objects (Data Set 2.16)

This experiment (Chapter 2, Exercise 7) uses the habituation technique to answer a question about object perception in 4-month-old infants. A total of 46 infants were tested. Half of the infants (Group 1) were shown the single nonoccluded rod. The other 23 infants (Group 2) were shown the two short, separated, aligned rods, again without any occluding. Infants were assigned randomly to the two groups. If infants perceived the initial habituating stimulus as a single rod, then infants in this group should show a novelty preference. The response measure is the length of time spent looking at the test stimulus. Remember that the longer the looking time, the greater the novelty preference. The following results are from the reduced data set (outliers removed).

Condition	n	Mean	SS_Y	SS_{total}
1. Nonoccluded rod	23	23.39	2577	
2. Separated sections	23	20.96	1877	4522

Exercise 5 Infant perception of partly occluded moving objects (Data Set 6.5)

This experiment uses the habituation technique to answer the same question asked in the infant perception experiment in Exercise 4, except now, instead of being stationary, the rod is seen moving back and forth horizontally, left to right, right to left. Will infants perceive this pattern of movement as that of a single rod or as two rods moving in unison?

The experiment used a total of 44 infants, ranging in age from 14 to 18 weeks. Half the infants (22) were shown the single nonoccluded rod. The other 22 infants were shown the two short, separated, aligned rods, again without any occluding rectangle. Infants were randomly assigned to the conditions (Data Set 6.5). If infants perceived the initial habituating stimulus as a single unbroken rod, then infants in this group should show a novelty preference to this stimulus, despite the fact that what they literally were shown in the habituation phase of the experiment were two short aligned rods, moving in unison, but separated by the rectangle.

The response measure is the length of time spent looking at the test stimulus. Remember that the longer the looking time, the greater the novelty preference.

Data Set 6.5 Perception data for Exercise 5

Group 1: Shown nonoccluded rod

| 40 | 35 | 52 | 23 | 25 | 37 | 57 | 63 | 0 | 49 | 87 |
| 8 | 57 | 20 | 36 | 69 | 44 | 23 | 10 | 8 | 54 | 59 |

Group 2: Shown separated aligned sections

| 15 | 10 | 9 | 15 | 26 | 25 | 45 | 34 | 41 | 3 | 34 |
| 16 | 52 | 0 | 24 | 17 | 7 | 0 | 54 | 29 | 5 | 10 |

Condition	n	Mean	SS_Y	SS_{total}
1. Nonoccluded rod	22	38.91	10,730	19,730
2. Separated sections	22	21.41	5631	

Exercise 6 Memory and mental imagery (Data Set 6.6)

This experiment compared the effect on remembering of two different study conditions. In one condition (normal instructions), participants were given 50 pairs of words (depicting an object or event) and instructed simply to "try to remember" each pair so that if given one of the words they could recall the other. In the other condition (imagery instructions), participants studied the same 50 pairs but were instructed to form a mental image of the objects or events depicted, and to form as vivid an image as possible of them interacting in some way. If the words were *house* and *grass,* they might imagine a house with grass growing on the roof. One day later, participants were tested; they were given one word from each of the pairs and asked to recall the other element of the pair.

There were 60 participants in the experiment. They were assigned randomly to the two conditions: 30 participants in each. The response measure was the number of responses correctly recalled out of 50 (Data Set 6.6).

Data Set 6.6   Memory data for Exercise 6

Condition 1: Normal instructions

16	37	23	27	23	30	30	28	22	34
36	21	22	26	13	21	37	19	18	21
24	15	26	17	34	27	29	26	10	23

Condition 2: Imagery instructions

36	24	26	41	36	26	34	28	34	33
37	41	38	26	29	35	37	34	26	32
31	29	26	43	36	25	36	47	35	31

Condition	n	Q_1	Md	Q_3	Mean	SS_Y	SS_{total}
1. Normal instructions	30	20.5	23.5	29.0	24.5	1427.5	
2. Imagery instructions	30	27.5	34.0	36.0	33.1	983.9	3512

Before proceeding with tasks 1 through 4 outlined at the beginning of the exercises, sketch the following graphs.

a. Plot back-to-back stemplots for these data. Given the values for the first and third quartiles, use the $1.5 \times IQR$ rule to check that the data do not contain outliers.

b. Given the values for the median and the first and third quartiles, draw side-by-side boxplots for these data.

Exercise 7   Method of loci (Data Set 6.7)

One of the oldest mnemonic techniques is known as the method of loci. It was recommended for use in memorizing the ordered set of topics in a speech. The mnemonic would also be a useful technique for students who want to be able to remember an ordered set of points for an essay exam. Suppose you must remember a shopping list consisting of 12 items. The first step in using the method of loci is to think of a set of locations that are naturally ordered. A simple example would be a route you commonly follow to get from one place to another (home to school, for instance). Along this route are various familiar locations such as a stoplight where you cross the street or a busstop where you catch the bus; you will need 12 such locations. The next step is to associate each location with one item on the shopping list. Then, when you need to recall the items simply travel (mentally, of course) along your route, retrieving each item in turn as you reach its location.

An experiment with two conditions was conducted to evaluate the mnemonic. In one condition (normal instructions), participants were given 24 words and instructed simply to "try to remember" each so that they could later recall the words. In the other condition (mnemonic instructions), participants studied the same 24 words but were instructed in the method of loci. One day later, participants were tested by being asked to recall the list of 24 items.

There were 36 participants in the experiment. They were assigned randomly to the two conditions, 18 participants in each. The response measure was number of responses correctly recalled out of 24 (Data Set 6.7).

Data Set 6.7   Memory data for Exercise 7

Condition 1: Normal instructions

9	5	7	11	9	15	13	7	12
7	9	5	7	10	13	8	12	7

Condition 2: Mnemonic instructions

11	14	14	16	12	16	9	14	15
17	14	20	14	15	14	16	13	10

Condition	n	Mean	SS_Y	SS_{total}
1. Normal instructions	18	9.22	143.1	472.0
2. Mnemonic instructions	18	14.11	113.8	

Chapter 6 Review

Terms

accept-reject region
bias
completely randomized design
experimental design
homogeneity of variance
independent-groups design
matching

one-tailed test
power
precision
p-value
quasi-experiment
significance level
standard error of the difference between independent means
Type-1 error
Type-2 error

Formulas

Estimated standard error of the difference between independent means:

$$s_{\overline{Y}_1 - \overline{Y}_2} = \sqrt{\frac{2MS_e}{n}}$$

Confidence interval for the difference between independent means:

$$\text{CI} = \text{point estimate} \pm w$$

$$= |\overline{Y}_1 - \overline{Y}_2| \pm (t \times s_{\overline{Y}_1 - \overline{Y}_2})$$

$$t = \frac{\overline{Y}_1 - \overline{Y}_2}{s_{\overline{Y}_1 - \overline{Y}_2}} \text{ (assuming the null hypothesis is } H_0\colon \mu_1 - \mu_2 = 0)$$

Quiz

Question 1

In the following paragraphs, there are pairs of terms set within braces {·}. In each case, choose which of the two terms you consider appropriate.

An investigator wants to estimate the vocabulary size of 6-year-old boys and girls and evaluate the difference between the two. A random sample of 50 girls and 50 boys has been chosen for this purpose. However, the investigator decides to test only a randomly chosen subset (15 girls and 15 boys) from the original sample. This smaller sample will result in a {*biased, less precise*} estimate of vocabulary size for each sex. If, instead of choosing the subset at random, the investigator had asked for volunteers and tested the first 15 of each sex to volunteer, then the estimate is likely to be {*biased, less precise*} as well.

Because this study has a {*natural, manipulated*} predictor variable, it is an example of a {*completely randomized, independent-groups*} design. To evaluate sex differences, the investigator decides to calculate a 95% confidence interval for the difference between the means of boys and girls. As the first step, the value of SS_e is calculated and divided by {28, 29} degrees of freedom to obtain the value of MS_e. The formula $(\bar{Y}_{boys} - \bar{Y}_{girls})/\sqrt{MS_e}$ is then used to estimate {*Cohen's* **d**, *the t-ratio*}. Next, the formula {$\sqrt{2MS_e}/\sqrt{15}$, $\sqrt{2MS_e}/\sqrt{30}$} is used to obtain the {*estimated standard error of the difference, mean square of the residuals*}. The table of the {*t, normal*} distribution is then consulted, using {14, 28} degrees of freedom; w, the half-width of the confidence interval, is then obtained by multiplying this critical tabulated value by {*estimated standard error of the difference, mean square of the residuals*}.

If the 95% confidence interval does not contain the value 0, the null hypothesis of zero difference can be {*rejected, retained*} at the {*.05, .95*} level of significance. This decision rule is equivalent to setting a {*Type-1, Type 2*} error rate of .05. If the null hypothesis is rejected, then the decision might constitute a {*Type-1, Type-2*} error. If, on the other hand, the null hypothesis is retained, then this decision might constitute a {*Type-1, Type-2*} error.

Question 2

Decide whether each of the following statements is true or false.

a. Increasing the precision of an experiment by increasing the sample size would increase the likelihood of committing a Type-1 error.

b. Holding everything else constant, decreasing the Type-1 error rate increases the likelihood of committing a Type-2 error.

c. If the null hypothesis is false, you can never commit a Type-2 error, no matter how small the sample.

d. In testing hypotheses about differences between two means, an experimenter mistakenly uses 36 instead of 20 degrees of freedom when looking up the tables of the *t*-distribution to find the critical value. Assuming all other calculations are correct, the effect of this error will be to increase the probability of a Type-1 error.

e. An experimenter sets $\alpha = .05$ as the significance level, obtains a *t*-statistic less than the critical value, and therefore does not reject the null hypothesis. The significance level of .05 means that the probability of this decision being erroneous is .05.

f. If the null hypothesis is true, you can never commit a Type-2 error, no matter how small the sample.

g. Increasing the sample size reduces the likelihood of committing a Type-1 error.

Chapter 7 Preview

Chapter 7 takes the ideas of Chapter 6 and develops them one step further—to experiments in which there are more than two conditions. But this extension introduces a complication, namely, that the impact of an experimental manipulation can no longer be expressed as a single difference between a pair of means. Even with just three conditions, there are three pairs and therefore three differences; with four conditions there are six differences. The problem to be addressed therefore is to find a single measure of the overall influence of the conditions of the experiment. As we will see, the rationale for such a measure has already been introduced.

7 LARGER EXPERIMENTS WITH INDEPENDENT GROUPS: ANALYSIS OF VARIANCE

In this chapter, we will take the basic concepts developed in Chapter 6 and extend their application to experiments with more than two conditions and independent-groups designs. Recall from Chapter 6 that there are two forms of this design: completely randomized designs in which the participants have been randomly assigned to the conditions and designs using a natural predictor variable such as age or sex to form independent groups.

Although the generalization to larger experiments introduces some new concepts, the resulting differences in the analysis of data should not be allowed to obscure the fundamental similarities. The fundamental design is the same, and the central concerns remain that of obtaining confidence intervals as estimates of differences between conditions and of deciding between null and full models. As in the previous examples using the t-distribution, these goals are achieved by using the variance of the residuals as the estimate of the noise in the data against which the possible presence of signals is evaluated.

7.1 Models for Experiments with More Than Two Conditions

Using an extended version of the phobia treatment experiment as an example, we begin by setting out the null and full models, fitting them to data, and calculating the sum of squared residuals. These steps are a straightforward extension of the methods used for two-condition experiments analyzed in Chapter 6, and they were described briefly in Chapter 3. Much of the material in Sections 7.1.1 and 7.1.2 may therefore seem familiar. However, the importance of the concepts covered in these sections justifies their review.

7.1.1 Full and Null Models

Data Set 7.1 gives data from an extension of the phobia treatment experiment. The extended version has three conditions; the additional condition is another form of therapy known as counterconditioning, in which classical conditioning is used to train the person to react to the feared stimulus with a response that is incompatible with the fear response. Thus a child's fear of a dog might be overcome by pairing the presence of a dog with a pleasurable stimulus such as an attractive toy. The response measure is rated anxiety level. There were 45 participants randomly assigned to conditions, 15 in each.

Data Set 7.1   Data for the three-condition phobia treatment experiment.

Y_1 (general counseling), $\overline{Y}_1 = 10.0$

| 10 | 8 | 10 | 12 | 10 | 14 | 13 | 9 | 12 | 8 | 10 | 4 | 8 | 10 | 12 |

Y_2 (systematic desensitization), $\overline{Y}_2 = 6.0$

| 4 | 6 | 4 | 10 | 4 | 6 | 4 | 8 | 8 | 4 | 2 | 4 | 10 | 8 | 8 |

Y_3 (counterconditioning), $\overline{Y}_3 = 5.0$

| 3 | 9 | 7 | 5 | 3 | 3 | 7 | 1 | 1 | 3 | 5 | 7 | 7 | 9 | 5 |

With these three conditions, there are three differences between pairs to be estimated:

- $\mu_1 - \mu_2$, the difference between general counseling and desensitization
- $\mu_1 - \mu_3$, the difference between general counseling and counterconditioning
- $\mu_2 - \mu_3$, the difference between desensitization and counterconditioning

The difference between a pair of means is called a comparison.

It is common to refer to such differences between pairs of means as *comparisons*. Notice that just the first of these three comparisons corresponds to our previous two-condition example.

In Section 3.3, we noted that the *full model* for this three-condition experiment can be set out as

$$Y_1 = \mu_1 + e \qquad Y_2 = \mu_2 + e \qquad Y_3 = \mu_3 + e$$

The *null hypothesis* for this experiment is that *all three* of the comparisons (differences between pairs) are 0. That is,

$$H_0: \mu_1 = \mu_2 = \mu_3 = \mu$$

where μ is the overall mean. The null model can therefore be written as

$$Y_1 = Y_2 = Y_3 = \mu + e$$

This method of writing the models by explicitly listing the conditions becomes quite cumbersome when the number of conditions becomes at all large. Rather than list the conditions as we have in this example, it is simpler to use subscripts:

$$Y_i = \mu_i + e$$

Model writing can be simplified by using the subscript *i*.

For our three-condition phobia treatment experiment, the subscript i can be 1, 2, or 3: $i = 1$ indicates the counseling condition; $i = 2$, the desensitization condition; and $i = 3$, the counterconditioning condition.

Fitting the Full Model

The model is fitted in exactly the same way it was fitted for the two-condition case. The fitted full model is

$$Y_i = \overline{Y}_i + e$$

and the fitted null model is

$$Y_i = \overline{Y} + e$$

where $\overline{Y}$ is the mean of all the observations; it is the estimate of the grand mean, μ.

For the phobia treatment experiment, the fitted full model is therefore

$$Y_1 = 10.0 + e \qquad Y_2 = 6.0 + e \qquad Y_3 = 5.0 + e$$

The fitted full model is set out explicitly in Table 7.1.

Table 7.1 Fitted full model $Y_i = \overline{Y}_i + e$ for the phobia treatment experiment

$Y_1 = \overline{Y}_1 + e$	$Y_2 = \overline{Y}_2 + e$	$Y_3 = \overline{Y}_3 + e$
$10 = 10 + 0$	$4 = 6 - 2$	$3 = 5 - 2$
$8 = 10 - 2$	$6 = 6 + 0$	$9 = 5 + 4$
$10 = 10 + 0$	$4 = 6 - 2$	$7 = 5 + 2$
$12 = 10 + 2$	$10 = 6 + 4$	$5 = 5 + 0$
$10 = 10 + 0$	$4 = 6 - 2$	$3 = 5 - 2$
$14 = 10 + 4$	$6 = 6 + 0$	$3 = 5 - 2$
$13 = 10 + 3$	$4 = 6 - 2$	$7 = 5 + 2$
$9 = 10 - 1$	$8 = 6 + 2$	$1 = 5 - 4$
$12 = 10 + 2$	$8 = 6 + 2$	$1 = 5 - 4$
$8 = 10 - 2$	$4 = 6 - 2$	$3 = 5 - 2$
$10 = 10 + 0$	$2 = 6 - 4$	$5 = 5 + 0$
$4 = 10 - 6$	$4 = 6 - 2$	$7 = 5 + 2$
$8 = 10 - 2$	$10 = 6 + 4$	$7 = 5 + 2$
$10 = 10 + 0$	$8 = 6 + 2$	$9 = 5 + 4$
$12 = 10 + 2$	$8 = 6 + 2$	$5 = 5 + 0$

As with the two-condition case, we will assume that the population variance of these residuals is the same for each condition. This assumption is an extended version of the assumption of homogeneity of variance to more than two conditions. The calculation of the mean square of the residuals described briefly in Chapter 3, follows exactly the same procedure used in the two-condition case. We add the sums of squares for each condition and divide by the total degrees of freedom. Each condition contributes $n - 1$ degrees of freedom; so, for the three-condition example, the degrees of freedom are $3 \times 14 = 42$. The sum of the squared residuals for each condition is

$$SS_1 = (0)^2 + (-2)^2 + \ldots = 86$$

$$SS_2 = (-2)^2 + (0)^2 + \ldots = 88$$

$$SS_3 = (-2)^2 + (+4)^2 + \ldots = 96$$

The sum of squares of all residuals for this full model is

$$SS_e = SS_1 + SS_2 + SS_3 = 86 + 88 + 96 = 270$$

The mean square of the residuals is then

$$MS_e = \frac{SS_e}{3(n-1)} = \frac{270}{42} = 6.43$$

Fitting the Null Model

For the null model, $Y_i = \overline{Y} + e$. The value of $\overline{Y}$ is 7.0. Note that $\overline{Y}$ is also the average of the means of the three conditions. The fitted version of the null model is therefore

$$Y_1 = Y_2 = Y_3 = 7.0 + e$$

It is set out in detail in Table 7.2. For the null model, the sum of the squared residuals is the sum of all 45 squared residuals about the overall mean. This is the total sum of squares.

$$SS_{total} = 3^2 + 1^2 + \ldots + (-2)^2 = 480$$

Thus the full model reduces the sum of the squared residuals by $SS_{model} = SS_{total} - SS_e = 480 - 270 = 210$. This is a proportional reduction of

$$R^2 = \frac{210}{480} = .44$$

General Formulas

In Section 3.3, we gave the formulas for calculating SS_{total}, SS_e, and MS_e for two- and three-condition experiments using an independent-groups design. The generalization to independent-groups designs with more than three conditions is a straightforward extension of these formulas.

Suppose that an experiment has k conditions, each with n observations. The experiment therefore contains a total of $n \times k$ observations. Then the sum of squares for the residuals for the full model would be

$$SS_e = SS_1 + SS_2 + SS_3 + \ldots + SS_k$$

and

Table 7.2 Fitted null model $Y_i = \bar{Y} + e$ for the phobia treatment experiment ($\bar{Y} = 7$)

$Y_1 = \bar{Y} + e$	$Y_2 = \bar{Y} + e$	$Y_3 = \bar{Y} + e$
$10 = 7 + 3$	$4 = 7 - 3$	$3 = 7 - 4$
$8 = 7 + 1$	$6 = 7 - 1$	$9 = 7 + 2$
$10 = 7 + 3$	$4 = 7 - 3$	$7 = 7 + 0$
$12 = 7 + 5$	$10 = 7 + 3$	$5 = 7 - 2$
$10 = 7 + 3$	$4 = 7 - 3$	$3 = 7 - 4$
$14 = 7 + 7$	$6 = 7 - 1$	$3 = 7 - 4$
$13 = 7 + 6$	$4 = 7 - 3$	$7 = 7 + 0$
$9 = 7 + 2$	$8 = 7 + 1$	$1 = 7 - 6$
$12 = 7 + 5$	$8 = 7 + 1$	$1 = 7 - 6$
$8 = 7 + 1$	$4 = 7 - 3$	$3 = 7 - 4$
$10 = 7 + 3$	$2 = 7 - 5$	$5 = 7 - 2$
$4 = 7 - 3$	$4 = 7 - 3$	$7 = 7 + 0$
$8 = 7 + 1$	$10 = 7 + 3$	$7 = 7 + 0$
$10 = 7 + 3$	$8 = 7 + 1$	$9 = 7 + 2$
$12 = 7 + 5$	$8 = 7 + 1$	$5 = 7 - 2$

$$MS_e = \frac{SS_e}{k(n - 1)}$$

k denotes number of conditions in an experiment.

The denominator $k(n - 1)$ is the degrees of freedom for k conditions, each with n observations. Each of the k conditions contributes $n - 1$ degrees of freedom. Recall from Section 3.3.2 that if there is an unequal number of observations in each condition, then the degrees of freedom can be obtained by using the more general formula $N - k$, where N is the total number of observations across all conditions.

The sum of squares for the residuals for the null model would be the sum of all $n \times k$ squared residuals, each residual being the difference between that observation and the overall, or grand, mean of the $n \times k$ observations. Remember, that with equal numbers of observations in all conditions, the grand mean of all $n \times k$ observations is arithmetically equivalent to the average of the individual means for all conditions. The condition means in the phobia treatment experiment (see Data Set 7.1) were 10, 6, and 5. The average of these three means is $(10 + 6 + 5)/3 = 7$. This "mean of the means" is also the mean of all 45 observations.

Comparing Models

As in the analysis of two-condition experiments, we will usually want to know whether the data demand anything more complicated than the null model, and Section 7.2 will describe how this question is answered. However, we will first describe a method for calculating confidence intervals for the differences between the means of each pair of conditions.

7.1.2 Calculating Confidence Intervals

A confidence interval is calculated for each difference between pairs of means.

For the three-condition phobia treatment experiment, we need a confidence interval for each of the comparisons

$$\mu_1 - \mu_2$$

$$\mu_1 - \mu_3$$

$$\mu_2 - \mu_3$$

In Section 5.2.3 and Section 6.2.2, we described the general form of the confidence interval as

$$CI = \text{point estimate} \pm w$$

where w = a critical tabled value × the appropriate standard deviation. The point estimates will be

$$\overline{Y}_1 - \overline{Y}_2 = 4$$

$$\overline{Y}_1 - \overline{Y}_3 = 5$$

$$\overline{Y}_2 - \overline{Y}_3 = 1$$

The "appropriate standard deviation" is the estimated standard error of the difference between two means, and its formula is the same as described in Chapter 6. Moreover, because of the assumption of homogeneity of variance, this estimated standard error is the same for any comparison within an experiment. That is,

$$s_{\overline{Y}_1 - \overline{Y}_2} = s_{\overline{Y}_1 - \overline{Y}_3} = s_{\overline{Y}_2 - \overline{Y}_3} = \sqrt{\frac{2MS_e}{n}}$$

Note that the 2 in the numerator of this formula reflects the fact that the formula gives the standard error of the difference between two means. However, the value of MS_e in this formula is based on the data from *all* the conditions, not just the two conditions whose mean difference is being estimated.

The remaining component of the confidence interval is the "critical tabled value." Obtaining this critical value raises the first conceptual difference between two-condition experiments and those with three or more conditions.

There are two different meanings for the confidence level of an interval estimate.

Suppose we decide to calculate 95% confidence intervals for our three differences. What does a probability of .95 mean in this case? There are two distinct possibilities. One possibility is that the probability refers to each confidence interval separately. The second possibility is that the probability refers to the entire set of confidence intervals (three, in our example). The difference between these two possibilities may not be immediately apparent and is best explained with an everyday example.

Six-and-You-Lose

Imagine a game that might be called Six-and-You-Lose. In this game, ordinary six-sided dice are rolled. You can choose to roll as many dice as you wish. Let this number be N. If *none* of the N dice lands six, then you win N hundred dollars; if *any one* of them lands six, you lose, and the penalty of losing is that you must pay $200.

How many dice should you choose to roll? Rolling more dice promises greater winnings, so why not roll a great many dice? The catch, of course, is that the more dice you roll, the greater the risk of losing and paying the $200 penalty. Remember, one six is all it takes to lose.

Notice first that, for each die considered individually, the probability is 1/6 of landing six. So if you choose to roll just one die ($N = 1$), then the probability of winning is 5/6 and the probability of losing is 1/6. If you choose to roll two dice, then the probability for each die landing six remains 1/6, but the probability of winning the game is no longer 5/6. This is so because the probability that *at least one* of the two dice will land six is greater than 1/6. You may win $200, but the risk of losing is greater than it was with $N = 1$. (In fact, it is approximately .3.) Intuitively, some increase in the probability of losing seems plausible, because with two dice there are two opportunities of obtaining a six rather than one. If you choose $N = 10$, then you stand to win $1000; but with 10 dice, the probability of *at least one* of them landing six is quite high—about .84, in fact.

The important distinction that this game illustrates is the distinction between the probability of each die taken individually, and the probabilities of outcomes for the entire set of N dice considered collectively. The probability of an individual die landing six is 1/6, but the probability that at least one die out of a set of N dice will land six is larger than 1/6; just how much larger depends on the size of N.

The same distinction arises with confidence intervals whenever the number of conditions is greater than two and there is thus more than one possible comparison. Should the confidence levels refer to each interval taken individually, or to the entire set of intervals considered collectively?

The 95% confidence level may apply to the intervals considered either separately or collectively.

Individual Confidence Intervals

If the confidence levels refer to each interval *taken individually*, then a confidence level of .95 means that the probability is .95 that the interval contains the true difference ("you win") and .05 that it does not ("you lose"). This probability is analogous to the probability for each die considered individually. However, if each confidence interval has a probability of .95, then the probability that at least one of these intervals does not contain the true difference is greater than .05, just as the probability is greater than 1/6 that at least one die from a set of N dice will land six. When there is more than one interval, or more than one die, there are more chances for the unlikely event to occur, that is, there is a greater probability of there being an interval that does not contain the true difference, or of a die landing six.

Simultaneous Confidence Intervals

Suppose, however, that we want the confidence levels to refer to *the entire set of intervals*, that is, to all the intervals from an experiment considered collectively. In other words, we would like to say that a confidence level of .95 means that the probability is .95 that *all* confidence intervals contain their respective true values. Equivalently, this would mean that the probability is no greater than .05 that any one of the intervals does not contain the true difference. Such intervals are usually referred to as *simultaneous confidence intervals* because the confidence level refers to the entire set of intervals considered simultaneously. Simultaneous confidence intervals are preferable to individual confidence intervals because they provide a clearly specified level of confidence for the entire set of intervals. In the game Six-and-You-Lose, the assurance needed is expressed in the probability that *no dice* will land six, not the probability associated with each die considered separately. In both cases, the probabilities needed refer to the entire set of intervals or the entire set of dice, not to the individual elements.

This distinction between simultaneous and individual confidence intervals has an important implication for the "critical tabled value" in our general formula for confidence intervals. To obtain simultaneous confidence intervals with a confidence level of .95, we need a critical tabled value different from the t-value used in the two-condition case. The previously used t-value would be appropriate only if we wished to calculate intervals for which the confidence level referred to the differences considered individually. In the two-condition case, this is quite appropriate because there is only one difference.

Value of w for Simultaneous Confidence Intervals

A number of proposals have been made for the appropriate critical tabled value. Although each is based on a slightly different rationale, they all address the same problem. We will describe one method developed by the statistician John Tukey. The method is based on a distribution called the *Studentized range distribution* and is denoted by the letter q. The actual value needed in calculating w is not q itself, but $q/\sqrt{2}$. Thus the value of w is given by the formula

w = a critical tabled value × the appropriate standard deviation

$$= \frac{q}{\sqrt{2}} \times \sqrt{\frac{2MS_e}{n}}$$

This expression simplifies to

$$w = q \times \sqrt{\frac{MS_e}{n}}$$

q denotes Studentized range statistic.

Studentized Range Statistic

The distribution of the Studentized range statistic, q, has two parameters:

■ the number of conditions in the experiment, which we will denote by the letter k

■ The degrees of freedom which, as noted earlier, are $k(n-1)$

The Studentized range statistic is basically the sampling distribution of the difference between the largest and the smallest sample means. Tables of the Studentized range statistic are set out to reflect the two parameters needed to define its values. It is usual to provide values for only 95% and 99% confidence intervals. An excerpt from this table is given in Table 7.3. To obtain the required value, locate the row with the appropriate degrees of freedom and then scan across this row until reaching the column with the appropriate value of k. At the intersection of this row and column are two values, one in ordinary lightfaced type, the other in boldface type. Lightface values are q for a 95% confidence interval; boldface values are q for a 99% confidence interval.

Table 7.3 Portion of the table of the distribution of the Studentized range statistic, q

	Number of conditions, k						
df	2	3	4	5	6	7	8
15	3.02	3.68	4.08	4.37	4.60	4.78	4.94
	4.18	**4.84**	**5.26**	**5.56**	**5.80**	**6.00**	**6.17**
16	3.00	3.65	4.05	4.33	4.56	4.74	4.90
	4.14	**4.79**	**5.20**	**5.50**	**5.73**	**5.92**	**6.09**
17	2.99	3.63	4.02	4.30	4.52	4.71	4.86
	4.11	**4.75**	**5.15**	**5.44**	**5.66**	**5.85**	**6.01**
18	2.97	3.61	4.00	4.28	4.50	4.67	4.83
	4.08	**4.71**	**5.10**	**5.39**	**5.61**	**5.79**	**5.95**
19	2.96	3.59	3.98	4.25	4.47	4.65	4.80
	4.06	**4.68**	**5.06**	**5.34**	**5.56**	**5.74**	**5.89**
20	2.95	3.58	3.96	4.23	4.45	4.62	4.77
	4.03	**4.65**	**5.02**	**5.30**	**5.52**	**5.69**	**5.84**
25	2.91	3.52	3.89	4.15	4.36	4.53	4.67
	3.95	**4.53**	**4.89**	**5.15**	**5.35**	**5.52**	**5.66**
30	2.89	3.49	3.85	4.10	4.30	4.47	4.60
	3.90	**4.46**	**4.80**	**5.05**	**5.25**	**5.41**	**5.54**
40	2.86	3.44	3.79	4.04	4.23	4.39	4.52
	3.83	**4.37**	**4.70**	**4.94**	**5.12**	**5.27**	**5.40**
60	2.83	3.40	3.74	3.98	4.16	4.31	4.44
	3.77	**4.29**	**4.60**	**4.82**	**5.00**	**5.14**	**5.26**

The intersection of the shaded row and column gives the values of q for a three-condition experiment with 40 degrees of freedom for MS_e. Lightface values of q are for a 95% confidence interval; boldface values are for a 99% confidence interval.

Phobia Treatment

For our phobia treatment experiment, the degrees of freedom are $3 \times 14 = 42$ and $k = 3$. The value of q is obtained by using the row for $df = 40$ (the closest available value below the exact value); and in the column for $k = 3$, we have values of 3.44 for the 95% confidence interval and 4.37 for the 99% confidence interval.

We now have all the necessary ingredients to complete the calculation of the confidence intervals. Note that the value of w will be the same for all three intervals. For the 95% confidence interval,

$$w = q \times \sqrt{\frac{MS_e}{n}} = 3.44 \times \sqrt{\frac{6.43}{15}} = 2.25$$

For $\mu_1 - \mu_2$, $CI_{.95} = 4 \pm 2.25 = 1.75$ to 6.25.
For $\mu_1 - \mu_3$, $CI_{.95} = 5 \pm 2.25 = 2.75$ to 7.25.
For $\mu_2 - \mu_3$, $CI_{.95} = 1 \pm 2.25 = -1.25$ to 3.25.

Just as in the two-condition case, these confidence intervals can be used to make decisions about plausible true values of differences between conditions. In particular, we can decide whether 0 remains a plausible value for such differences. For our phobia treatment experiment, we could conclude that 0 remains a plausible value for the difference between conditions 2 and 3, but not between 1 and 2 or between 1 and 3. In short, the two therapies differ from general counseling, but there is no evidence to support the conclusion that the two therapies differ from each other.

7.1.3 Testing Null Hypotheses Directly

In Section 6.3, the t-distribution was used to test directly the null hypothesis of no difference between the means of two conditions. When there are more than two conditions, a statistic such as t can again be used to conduct such direct tests. However, under these circumstances, the concept of a Type-1 error rate has an ambiguous interpretation similar to that of the confidence level of the interval estimate. The error rate could refer to each decision separately or to the complete set of decisions.

Suppose there are three conditions and thus three differences between pairs of means about which decisions will be made. Suppose further, that in all three cases the true difference is actually 0: The null hypothesis is true in all cases. If the Type-1 error rate is set at $\alpha = .05$ and if this error rate refers to each decision considered separately, then $\alpha = .05$ implies that, *for each difference,* the probability is .05 that the observed difference will fall into the rejection region, resulting in a Type-1 error. (Remember, we are assuming that all the differences are 0.) However, when the three decisions are considered *collectively,* there are three opportunities for a Type-1 error to occur, so the probability of at least one of the three happening is greater than .05. Think of the decision process as analogous to rolling three dice, each with a probability of 1/6 of landing six. For each of the three dice, the probability is 1/6, but the probability of at least one of the three dice landing six is greater than 1/6.

Stated succinctly, the point of the preceding analysis is this: If the Type-1 error rate is set at $\alpha = .05$ for the decision about each comparison considered separately, then the probability of at least one false rejection among the entire set of decisions will be greater than .05. Just as simultaneous confidence intervals were preferred, cautious experimenters usually demand that the Type-1 error rate be set with respect to the entire set of decisions, not with respect to each decision considered separately. An error rate that is set with respect to the entire set of decisions in an experiment is termed the *error rate per experiment*. An error rate that is set with respect to each individual decision is termed the *error rate per comparison*. It follows from the preceding discussion that, as soon as there are two or more decisions to be made, the error per experiment will be larger than the error rate per comparison. Thus if we want to achieve an error rate per experiment of, say, .05, then the error rate per comparison would have to be lower than .05.

To achieve an error rate per experiment of, say, .05, the error rate per comparison would have to be lower than .05.

Returning to our dice example, suppose landing six is analogous to a Type-1 error and four dice are rolled. The *error rate per comparison* would be 1/6; it is simply the probability that any specified die will land six. The *error rate per experiment* is the probability that at least one of the four dice will land six, and this probability is larger than 1/6. As claimed in the previous paragraph, the error rate per experiment is larger than the error rate per comparison; four dice considered collectively provide more opportunities for a six.

Consider a second analogy. A physician tells a seriously ill person that he will need a surgical procedure consisting of four separate operations. For each of these operations, the chance of survival is .95, the risk of dying is .05. The .05 probabilities correspond to the error rate per comparison. Think of it as the death rate per operation. The chance of surviving the whole procedure of four operations is less than .95. Equivalently, the probability of dying during the entire procedure from one of these operations is greater than .05 because there are four opportunities, each with a probability of .05. Think of it as the death rate per procedure. This probability corresponds to the error rate per experiment. The more opportunities an error has to occur, the higher the overall probability of it happening.

The usual strategy in evaluating experimental data is to set the Type-1 error rate with respect to error per experiment rather than error per comparison. We set the error rate per experiment at the desired level—say, $\alpha = .05$. The error rate per comparison would then be less than .05. Just how much lower than .05 depends on how many comparisons are to be tested. The more tests, the greater the risk of at least one mistaken rejection of the null hypothesis, so the greater is the necessary reduction.

Bonferroni Method

A direct application of this line of reasoning leads to one method of setting the error rate per experiment known as the *Bonferroni method*. We will not describe the method in detail, but it is helpful to understand its rationale as an example of the general problem of controlling error rates per experiment. The Bonferroni method lowers the error rate per comparison so that the error rate per experiment is at or below the desired level of, say, .05. For example, if the plan is to test just two comparisons, then the Bonferroni method sets the significance level for each decision (the error rate per comparison) at a probability of .05 divided by 2, that is, at .025. Then the probability that *either* comparison will lead to a Type-1 error (error rate per experiment) will be no more than .05. If the plan is to test three comparisons, then you would set the significance level for each decision at a level equal to .05 divided by 3, that is, at .017. The probability that any one of comparisons will lead to a Type-1 error will then be no more than .05.

> *In general, for k decisions, the error rate per comparison is set at α/k.*

Suppose we apply the Bonferroni logic to our surgery example. If the surgeon's goal is that the overall procedure should have a death risk rate of .05, then each separate operation will have to be made safer than .05 so that the death rate per procedure is no greater than .05. There are four operations, so, for the death rate per procedure of .05 or less, the death rate per operation would have to be reduced to $.05/4 = .0125$.

The preferred strategy is to set the Type-1 error rate with respect to error per experiment rather than to the error per comparison.

Planned Comparison

The Bonferroni method is appropriate only if the investigator does not intend to test all the possible comparisons and is willing to specify in advance of the analysis exactly which comparisons are to be evaluated. This procedure involving the advance specification of a limited number of comparisons is an example of a general strategy known as *planned comparisons*. Methods of planned comparisons require (1) that the investigator test just a subset of all the possible differences and (2) that this subset be specified before the data are collected. Methods such as the Bonferroni procedure are therefore appropriate under circumstances in which the investigator can designate precisely which differences are of scientific interest.

Planned comparisons involve the advance specification of a limited number of comparisons.

Post Hoc Comparisons

Methods of planned comparisons are inappropriate in exploratory studies in which the investigator wishes to allow the possibility that a difference between any two conditions could exist. Methods that allow for the testing of all differences are known as *post hoc* ("after the event") procedures. Post hoc procedures allow the investigator to explore the data and evaluate whatever differences appear interesting. Advance specification is not required, as it is with methods of planned comparison.

Post hoc comparisons allow the testing of all possible comparisons.

Tukey's HSD

One method of conducting post hoc evaluations of the null hypothesis is to calculate the minimum difference needed to reject the null hypothesis and then compare this value to the obtained differences. One such method uses the q-statistic to calculate w, as described in Section 7.1.2. Remember from Chapter 6 that w is the minimum difference needed to reject the null hypothesis. When used for the purpose of making post hoc comparisons and calculated using the q-statistic, the value of w has been dubbed (by the statistician John Tukey) the *honestly significant difference*, or HSD. That is,

HSD denotes honestly significant difference.

$$\text{HSD} = w = q \times \sqrt{\frac{\text{MS}_e}{n}}$$

For the phobia treatment example in Section 7.1.2, w was found to be 2.25. Thus any difference between two conditions greater than 2.25 would be declared "significantly different from 0." A difference larger than 2.25 is deemed incompatible with the null hypothesis that the true difference is 0. Using this criterion, we would declare that differences between conditions 1 and 2 and between 1 and 3 are significantly different from 0, but not for conditions 2 and 3. These three decisions are made with an error rate per experiment of .05.

Tukey's HSD specifies the minimum difference needed to be significant.

The HSD method is equivalent to basing decisions on the simultaneous confidence intervals calculated according to the method described in Section 7.1.2. The null hypothesis would be rejected if the confidence interval did not include 0.

7.1.4 Simultaneous Confidence Intervals and Decision Error Rates

Beginning with the concepts of parsimony, we pointed out in early chapters that science demands strong evidence in order to reject the null hypothesis and replace it with a less simple hypothesis. The general concern to avoid Type-1 errors reflects this demand. Science considers it costly to make a false alarm by declaring that a difference exists when there is none.

The preference for simultaneous confidence intervals, or for error rates per experiment, reflects this emphasis on controlling Type-1 error rates. If error rates per comparison were used, then in a large experiment in which many decisions are being made, the probability would be quite high that at least one false rejection of the null hypothesis would occur. In this sense, the use of error rates per experiment provides the investigator with protection against an inflated Type-1 error rate. An experiment that quotes an error rate per comparison of .05 could have an error rate per experiment as high as .5!

The Bonferroni method and Tukey's HSD are but two examples of the many methods available to test comparisons. These two methods have been chosen as commonly used examples of planned and post hoc methods, respectively. With one exception, a detailed description of other methods is beyond the scope of this introductory text. The one exception is a method known as Fisher's LSD, which will be described briefly in Section 7.2. Its description is delayed because, unlike either of the aforementioned methods, this procedure depends on a prior overall analysis of the data. Such an overall analysis is the topic of that section.

Per-experiment error rates provide the investigator with protection against what would otherwise be an inflated Type-1 error rate.

LSD denotes least significant difference.

Dangers of Hunting Expeditions

The different methods of testing comparisons have a common goal to protect the investigator against an inflated Type-1 error rate. An appreciation of the problem can be gained by considering another example of coin tossing. Suppose our concern is to establish whether or not a coin is fair by tossing it a certain number of times and observing the number of heads. What outcomes would lead to a rejection of the null hypothesis of a fair coin?

The binomial distribution tells us that outcomes as extreme as no heads or six heads in six tosses will occur with a probability of .03. Suppose that you therefore decide that either six or zero heads in six tosses provides grounds for rejecting the null hypothesis. Consider next the following two experiments and their results.

Experiment 1: The coin is tossed six times and lands heads every time. By prior agreement, this outcome is too improbable to be compatible with the hypothesis of a fair coin.

Experiment 2: The coin is tossed 100 times. The investigator examines the entire sequence of 100 outcomes and notices that the six tosses from toss number 63 to toss number 68 all landed heads. Using the same criterion, does this sequence of six successive heads provide grounds for rejecting the null hypothesis?

It should be clear from the discussion of per-decision and per-experiment error rates that Experiment 2 does not provide good grounds for rejecting the null hypothesis. Whereas the probability of such an extreme outcome is indeed .03 for any single sequence of six tosses, the probability of obtaining six successive heads *anywhere* within a sequence of 100 tosses is much higher than .03. Experimenter 2 engaged in what amounts to "data snooping": a hunting expedition through the data, looking for the previously designated improbable outcome. With enough tosses, this improbable outcome becomes a near certainty. With one million tosses, it is virtually certain that *somewhere* within the sequence there will be six successive heads or six successive tails. Within the context of the entire experiment of a million tosses, either of these outcomes is not at all improbable. The relevant probability for Experiment 2 is not the probability of six heads or tails in six tosses, but rather the probability of six successive heads or tails occurring anywhere within a sequence of 100 tosses. The difference between the two outcomes is essentially that between per-decision and per-experiment error rates. With 100 tosses, there are more opportunities of obtaining a sequence of six heads than in just six tosses.

A similar danger exists in experiments with many conditions and thus many comparisons between pairs. If a simple error rate per comparison is set and the hunting expedition begun, then, with enough comparisons, it is highly likely that at least one will turn out to be significant. Thus an investigator wishing to embark on a post hoc examination of the data needs the extra protection provided by procedures such as that of Tukey's HSD. Although the rationales for various post hoc methods differ, all methods share a common goal of avoiding an inflated Type-1 error rate. The protection they offer is the result of their demand for stronger evidence in order to reject the null hypothesis.

Notice that the situation is rather different if the investigator designates a specific outcome in advance. Suppose, *prior to conducting the experiment,* the coin-tossing investigator in Experiment 2 hypothesizes that in the sequence of 100 tosses, the thirty-third through thirty-eighth tosses will be either all heads or all tails. Now the correct probability of this extreme outcome is .03. The distinction is between the probability of obtaining six heads or tails on a predesignated sequence of six tosses versus obtaining a sequence of six heads or tails *anywhere* in the experiment. It is this distinction that underlies the difference in rationale between planned comparisons and post hoc comparisons.

The protection against an inflated Type-1 error rate offered by post hoc methods comes at a cost: an increase in the Type-2 error rate. This fact is another example of the general principle that the more stringent the criterion for rejecting the null hypothesis, the greater the risk of failing to detect a genuine difference. Thus the advantage of a planned comparisons procedure is that it offers greater power to detect a true difference, at least for the limited number of predesignated comparisons.

7.1.5 Graphs with Error Bars

With three or more conditions, it is sometimes helpful to display the results of an experiment in the form of a bar chart, the height of each bar indicating the mean for that condition. In these cases it is informative to indicate the precision with which the condition means have been estimated by adding vertical lines across the top of each bar, as shown in Figure 7.1.

These vertical lines are commonly referred to as *error bars*. The distance of the error bar above and below the top of the graph bar is an indication of precision. A common convention (and the one used in Figure 7.1) is to indicate precision in terms of the standard error of the mean; in this case, the error bar extends a distance of $s_{\bar{Y}}$ above and below the top of the graph bar. Recall that $s_{\bar{Y}} = \sqrt{MS_e/n}$; so, for the data in Data Set 7.1, we have

$$s_{\bar{Y}} = \sqrt{\frac{6.43}{15}} = 0.65$$

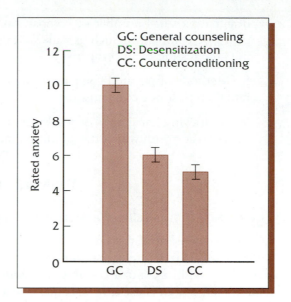

Figure 7.1

Graph of the results (mean rated anxiety) for the three-condition phobia treatment experiment showing error bars. The error bar extends a distance of one standard error of the mean above and below the top of the bar.

Comprehension Check 7.1

Important Concepts

1. When independent-groups designs have more than two conditions, the full model is a straightforward extension of the two-condition case. It is convenient to use subscripts rather than to list all the conditions. Thus the model can be written as $Y_i = \mu_i + e$.

2. The sum of squared residuals for the full model is also a straightforward extension of the two-condition case. It is formed by adding together the sum of squared residuals for each of the k conditions.

3. The value of MS_e is obtained in the usual way by dividing the sum of squared residuals by the degrees of freedom. There are $n - 1$ degrees of freedom for each of the k conditions, that is, $k(n - 1)$ degrees of freedom in total.

4. In calculating confidence intervals for the difference between the means of pairs of conditions, it is important to distinguish between confidence levels (such as .95) applied to differences considered individually and the complete set of differences within an experiment. It is preferable to obtain simultaneous intervals for which the confidence level applies to the entire set of intervals collectively.

5. One method of calculating such simultaneous intervals, called Tukey's HSD method, uses the q-statistic obtained from the Studentized range distribution. The Studentized range distribution has two parameters: the number of conditions, k, and the degrees of freedom, $k(n - 1)$.

6. Hypotheses about comparisons (differences between pairs of means) can be tested directly. In doing so, a distinction is drawn between error rates per comparison and error rates per experiment.

7. A distinction is also drawn between planned and post hoc methods of testing comparisons. A method of planned comparison such as the Bonferroni method designate a small number of comparisons prior to the experiment. A method of post hoc comparison such as Tukey's HSD (honestly significant difference) permits the testing of all comparisons.

8. Methods of planned comparison have the advantage of a smaller Type-2 error rate than post hoc comparisons.

9. In drawing bar graphs of results, it is informative to add error bars to indicate the precision with which the condition means have been estimated.

Worked Examples

Example 1 Tranquilizer effects (Data Set 7.2)

In an extension of the tranquilizer effects example used previously, the investigator evaluates two different tranquilizers, designated T1 and T2. They are to be evaluated along with a control condition, yielding three conditions in all. A completely randomized design is used, with 16 participants randomly assigned to each condition. As before, the response variable is time taken to complete the task. Longer times mean poorer performance. The resulting data are given in Data Set 7.2.

Analysis of these data yields the results shown for each condition. A further calculation gives the sum of squares of the residuals for the null model as $SS_{total} = 154.76$.

a. Use the distribution of the Studentized range (Statistical Table 4 in Appendix C) to obtain simultaneous 95% confidence intervals for each of the three comparisons between the pairs of means of the conditions.

b. What is the value of Tukey's HSD?

c. Using a Type-1 error rate of $\alpha = .05$, identify which conditions differ from each other.

d. What is the value of R^2 for this experiment?

Data Set 7.2 Tranquilizer effects data for Example 1

Y_1 (control), $\overline{Y}_1 = 8.95$, $SS_Y = 27.22$

8.8	7.6	8.4	9.8	8.8	11.3	10.6	8.1
10.0	8.2	9.1	5.8	8.3	9.2	10.7	8.5

Y_2 (T1), $\overline{Y}_2 = 10.25$, $SS_Y = 36.34$

12.7	10.2	10.5	10.3	11.0	11.0	10.1	9.3
10.2	11.8	11.3	10.9	6.9	7.1	11.6	9.1

Y_3 (T2), $\overline{Y}_3 = 11.77$, $SS_Y = 27.51$

12.1	10.3	10.0	10.7	10.9	11.6	11.7	12.4
11.3	10.6	10.5	14.6	14.3	12.4	13.1	11.8

Answer

a. To calculate the 95% confidence interval, we need to calculate

$$w = q \times \sqrt{\frac{MS_e}{n}}$$

The value of q is obtained from the table of the Studentized range (Statistical Table 4). The parameter values are $k = 3$ and the degrees of freedom are $df = 3 \times 15 = 45$. Using $df = 40$ as the closest tabled value below 45, we find a value of $q = 3.44$ for the .95 confidence level (in lightface type in the table).

The value of MS_e is $(27.22 + 36.34 + 27.51)/45 = 91.07/45 = 2.024$. Thus

$$w = q \times \sqrt{\frac{MS_e}{n}} = 3.44 \times \sqrt{\frac{2.024}{16}} = 1.22$$

For point estimates, we have

$$|\overline{Y}_1 - \overline{Y}_2| = 1.30$$
$$|\overline{Y}_1 - \overline{Y}_3| = 2.82$$
$$|\overline{Y}_2 - \overline{Y}_3| = 1.52$$

Thus the required 95% confidence intervals are

For $|\mu_1 - \mu_2|$, $CI_{.95} = 1.30 \pm 1.22 = 0.08$ to 2.52.
For $|\mu_1 - \mu_3|$, $CI_{.95} = 2.82 \pm 1.22 = 1.60$ to 4.04.
For $|\mu_2 - \mu_3|$, $CI_{.95} = 1.52 \pm 1.22 = 0.30$ to 2.74.

b. Tukey's HSD is simply w. Thus the minimum difference required to reject the null hypothesis is 1.22.

c. Because all three differences exceed 1.22, all are incompatible with a true difference of 0. Thus with an error rate per experiment of .05, all three null hypotheses are rejected. Notice that these decisions are also derivable from the fact that none of the 95% confidence intervals includes 0.

d. The reduction in the sum of squares by the full model is $SS_{model} = 154.76 - 91.07 = 63.69$. Expressed as a proportion of SS_{total}, this reduction gives

$$R^2 = \frac{63.69}{154.76} = .41$$

Example 2   Induced emotion (Data Set 7.3)

In an extension of the induced emotion experiment (Chapter 6), four emotional states were investigated: anger, sadness, happiness, and disgust. Participants were required to follow instructions about moving their facial muscles in ways that mimicked each of these four emotions. While forming these facial expressions, heart rate change was measured in beats per minute. A completely randomized design is used, with $n = 14$ participants randomly assigned to each condition (emotion). The resulting data are given in Data Set 7.3 along with the results of the basic computations.

Using Tukey's HSD as a criterion and with a Type-1 error rate of .05, decide which pairs of emotions differ from each other as measured by mean heart rate change.

Data Set 7.3   Induced emotion data for worked Example 2

Y_1 (anger), $\overline{Y}_1 = 8.09$, $SS_Y = 44.84$

11.5	4.2	7.4	6.3	9.4	8.0	7.6
9.6	8.8	9.1	5.9	7.1	9.7	8.6

Y_2 (sadness), $\overline{Y}_2 = 5.83$, $SS_Y = 65.75$

10.0	2.0	5.0	5.7	4.7	5.1	6.8
4.8	10.2	4.2	5.0	4.0	6.6	7.5

Y_3 (happiness), $\overline{Y}_3 = 1.55$, $SS_Y = 45.87$

1.3	2.3	-1.1	1.0	5.5	0.6	0.1
1.0	1.8	-0.6	2.5	0.0	4.7	2.6

Y_4 (disgust), $\overline{Y}_4 = 0.12$, $SS_Y = 42.42$

1.9	-3.3	-1.0	-0.7	-1.2	-1.5	0.8
1.1	-0.5	0.3	4.3	0.1	1.5	-0.1

Answer   To calculate the HSD, we need to calculate

$$\text{HSD} = w = q \times \sqrt{\frac{\text{MS}_e}{n}}$$

The value of q is obtained from the table of the Studentized range (Statistical Table 4 in Appendix C). The parameter values are $k = 4$ and degrees of freedom $= 4 \times 13 = 52$. Using $df = 40$ as the closest tabled value below 52, we find a value of $q = 3.79$ for the .95 confidence level (in lightface type in Statistical Table 4).

The value of MS_e is $(44.84 + 65.75 + 45.87 + 42.42)/52 = 198.88/52 = 3.82$. Thus

$$\text{HSD} = q \times \sqrt{\frac{\text{MS}_e}{n}} = 3.79 \times \sqrt{\frac{3.82}{14}} = 1.98$$

We conclude that any absolute comparison between pairs larger than 1.98 will lead to a rejection of the null hypothesis for those two conditions. Inspection of the four means indicates that the means for the anger and sadness conditions differ from the two other conditions, and from each other, by at least 1.98.

These decisions are made with an error rate per experiment of $\alpha = .05$. Happiness and disgust do not differ significantly from each other.

Problems

Problem 1   Intentional remembering (Data Set 7.4)

Problems presented at the end of Sections 6.2, 6.3, and 6.4 examined the effect on remembering of various orienting tasks performed by participants during the study phase of the experiment. Problem 1 describes an experiment designed to explore these findings further.

The experiment is an extension of Problem 3 at the end of Section 6.4. That experiment showed that a suitable incidental task could be more effective than intentional instructions that simply ask participants to "try to remember." A remaining question is whether participants who are given the rating task *and* told that their memory will be subsequently tested do better than participants who do not expect a test of their memory. The incidental task instructions may be better than intentional instructions, but perhaps the two combined constitute an even better method.

To evaluate this hypothesis, an experiment is conducted with three conditions. One is the simple intentional instruction condition without an orienting task. Participants are instructed to study the words so that they can later recall as many of the words as possible. The second condition asks participants to perform an orienting task consisting of the following *self-reference rating* instruction: "Rate each adjective according to how well you think it describes you personally." No mention is made of a later recall test. Participants in the third condition are given both the self-reference orienting task and are warned of the subsequent memory test.

There are 25 randomly assigned participants in each condition, for a total of 75 participants in the experiment. The results consist of the proportion of adjectives recalled by each participant and are given in Data Set 7.4.

a. Obtain simultaneous 95% confidence intervals for each of the three comparisons.

b. What is the value of Tukey's HSD?

c. Using a Type-1 error rate of $\alpha = .05$, use Tukey's HSD to identify which conditions differ from each other.

Data Set 7.4   Intentional remembering data for Problem 1

Y_1 (intentional study), $\overline{Y}_1 = .383$, $SS_Y = 1.080$

.32	.42	.20	.40	.38	.40	.22	.10	.38
.72	.26	.30	.64	.70	.36	.62	.54	
.60	.26	.08	.76	.22	.06	.08	.56	

Y_2 (incidental rating), $\overline{Y}_2 = .577$, $SS_Y = 1.158$

.26	.74	.70	.48	.46	.72	.66	.56	.72
.78	.74	.84	.24	.68	.14	.78	.16	
.30	.70	.80	.36	.58	.72	.82	.48	

Y_3 (intentional study and incidental rating), $\overline{Y}_3 = .597$, $SS_Y = 1.288$

.93	.35	.75	.55	.67	.49	.67	.39	.39
.43	.59	.97	.45	.55	.33	.25	.49	
.79	.47	.19	.89	.65	.93	.81	.95	

Problem 2   Age and vocabulary

As part of a study of the effect of aging on various cognitive tasks, the verbal abilities of three age groups were compared by using a test of vocabulary that asks for the meaning of 50 different words. The groups were

A   High school seniors (average age 17 years)
B   Members of a social organization (average age 40 years)
C   Members of a retirement community (average age 70 years)

There were 30 participants at each age level, and the results of a basic analysis of the data gave the following values. The response measure was the number of correctly defined words out of the total of 50. The computations are based on DS07_05.dat in the *ASCII Files*. (Raw data are not listed for every problem and exercise. However, as stated in the Preface, all designated data sets are available as an ASCII file. Thus the data set for this problem, not typeset as Data Set 7.5, is available in the ASCII file DS07_05.dat.)

Group	$\overline{Y}$	SS_Y
A	28.9	1224
B	33.9	1220
C	33.2	1224

a. Obtain 95% confidence intervals for each of the three comparisons between pairs of means of the groups.

b. What is the value of Tukey's HSD?

c. Using a Type-1 error rate per experiment of $\alpha = .05$, identify which conditions differ from each other.

7.2 Evaluating the Null Model: Analysis of Variance

Analysis of variance is used to conduct an overall test of the null hypothesis.

If an investigator wants merely to evaluate the comparisons between pairs of means of the conditions in an experiment, then the methods described in Section 7.1 are all that are needed. It is common practice, however, to conduct an overall evaluation of the plausibility of the null model relative to the full model. In the analysis of experiments with categorical predictor variables, the procedure commonly used to perform this overall evaluation is *analysis of variance*. The reason for this term will become apparent as we proceed.

7.2.1 Estimating the Overall Effect of the Predictor Variable

In experiments with just two conditions, the influence of the predictor variable on the response variable can be measured in terms of the difference between the means of the two conditions. Both Cohen's **d** and the *t*-statistic are based on this difference. For Cohen's **d**, the estimate of d is the observed mean difference expressed in units of the estimated standard deviation; for the *t*-distribution, the observed difference is expressed in units of the estimated standard error.

When an experiment has three or more conditions, no single comparison between pairs of means will provide the required overall measure. We have, however, already introduced one measure that provides the necessary overall estimate. This measure is SS_{model}, the difference between the sums of squared residuals of the null and the full models. This difference formed the numerator in the calculation of R^2. The greater the reduction in the residuals brought about by the full model relative to the null model, the stronger is the effect of the predictor variable. It is now time to examine in greater detail this difference in the sums of squared residuals. To do so, we will use the data from the three-condition phobia treatment experiment (see Data Set 7.1).

The terminology commonly used in analysis of variance is slightly different from that already introduced. For the full model, the sum of the squared residuals is the sum of squared deviations of the observations about the mean of each condition. In the phobia treatment experiment, SS_1 is the sum of squared deviations of the observations about the mean of the first condition, SS_2 is the sum of squared deviations of the observations about the mean of the second condition, and so forth. For this reason, SS_e, the sum of the squared residuals for the full model, is referred to as the *sum of squares within conditions*, or simply the *within-condition sum of squares*. We can write this as SS_{within}, noting that this is nothing more than a more specific descriptive label for SS_e. In the phobia treatment experiment (Data Set 7.1), the within-condition sum of squares was $SS_{within} = 270.0$.

For the null model, the sum of the squared residuals is the variance of the observations about the mean of the entire set of observations. In the phobia treatment experiment, this mean was 7.0, the mean of all 45 observations. We have referred to this "sum of squared residuals for the null model" simply as the *total sum of squares* (SS_{total}), and we will continue to do so. In the phobia treatment experiment, the total sum of squares was $SS_{total} = 480.0$.

The difference between the total sum of squares and the within-condition sum of squares represents the reduction in the total sum of squares due to the full model. We have referred to this as SS_{model}. In the phobia treatment experiment, the full model reduces the total sum of squares by $480 - 270$, or 210. The full model achieves this reduction by incorporating parameters μ_i, thereby allowing for a different mean for each condition. This reduction in the sum of squares achieved by the model is therefore referred to as the *between-condition sum of squares*. It can be denoted by $SS_{between}$. In this alternative terminology, the previously used relationship $SS_{model} = SS_{total} - SS_e$ becomes

$$SS_{between} = SS_{total} - SS_{within}$$

Rearranging the terms in this equation, we obtain an equivalent relationship:

$$SS_{total} = SS_{between} + SS_{within}$$

In the phobia treatment experiment, this relationship is $480 = 210 + 270$.

The sum of the squared residuals for the full model is termed SS_{within}.

SS_{within} (SS_e) denotes sum of squares within conditions.

SS_{total} denotes sum of squared residuals under null model.

$SS_{between}$ (SS_{model}) denotes sum of squares between conditions.

Although $SS_{between}$ can be defined simply as the difference between SS_{total} and SS_{within}, its numerical value has a very simple relationship to the differences among the observed means of the conditions. It should not be surprising that there is some relationship, because, as noted, $SS_{between}$ is an alternative label for SS_{model}, reflecting the extent to which the full model accounts for variability. What may be surprising is just how direct this relationship is.

7.2.2 Between-Conditions Sum of Squares

It is helpful at this point to introduce a minor change in the notation we have been using for the full model. The full model has been written $Y_i = \mu_i + e$. The null model has been written $Y_i = \mu + e$, where μ is the overall, or grand, mean. The change in notation is a simple one. We will express each μ_i in the full model as a deviation from the overall mean μ. This change is rather like expressing the daily temperature as "5 degrees above the average of 70" rather than "75 degrees" or a person's IQ as "an IQ of 20 above the average of 100" rather than "an IQ of 120." Both forms express the same information.

In terms of sample estimates for the phobia treatment experiment, the overall mean was 7.0. The mean of 10.0 for condition 1 is now expressed as 7.0 + 3.0 (3.0 above the estimated grand mean of 7.0); the mean for condition 2 becomes 7.0 − 1.0 (1.0 less than the estimated grand mean); and so forth.

For the full model, the notation commonly used to express this new form is

$$\mu_i = \mu + \alpha_i$$

where α_i is the difference between the mean of the condition and the grand mean. Thus α_i is the difference between μ_1 and μ. Its estimated value for condition 1 in the phobia treatment experiment is +3.0. The model statement for the full model then becomes

$$Y_i = \mu + \alpha_i + e$$

The null model asserts that all the α_i are 0. Note that the symbol α used in this context has nothing to do with the α used to denote the Type-1 error rate. It is unfortunate that tradition leads to the same symbol, but in any particular situation, the symbol's referent will be clear. Moreover, when used as a symbol for a factor, α will usually have a subscript.

The meaning of this change in notation will be clearer if we work through the corresponding procedures for fitting the model in this new form. We will use the letter $\mathbf{a}$ to refer to the estimate of α. Thus, for the fitted model, μ is replaced by $\bar{Y}$ and α is replaced by $\mathbf{a}$. This substitution gives

$$Y_i = \bar{Y} + \mathbf{a}_i + e$$

The various values of the $\mathbf{a}_i$ are simply the deviations of the condition means from the estimated overall mean:

$$\mathbf{a}_i = \bar{Y}_i - \bar{Y}$$

Thus

$$\mathbf{a}_1 = 10.0 - 7.0 = 3.0$$

$$\mathbf{a}_2 = 6.0 - 7.0 = -1.0$$

$$\mathbf{a}_3 = 5.0 - 7.0 = -2.0$$

Each μ_i in the full model is expressed as a deviation from the overall mean μ.

$\alpha_i = \mu_i - \mu$

$\mathbf{a}_i$ denotes the estimate if α_i.

$\bar{Y}_i$ denotes condition mean.

Expressed in this new notation, the fitted model for the phobia treatment experiment is

$$Y_1 = 7.0 + 3.0 + e$$

$$Y_2 = 7.0 - 1.0 + e$$

$$Y_3 = 7.0 - 2.0 + e$$

The fitted model for each of the 45 observations is given in Table 7.4.

Expressing the mean for each condition as a deviation from the grand mean implies that $a_1 + a_2 + a_3 = 0$. Notice that what we have done is equivalent to expressing three scores as deviations from their mean. In this case, the "scores" are the condition means. Thus the fact that $a_1 + a_2 + a_3 = 0$ is an example of the zero-sum principle introduced in Chapter 2. In our example, $3 - 1 - 2 = 0$.

The values of a_i will always sum to 0.

Expressing the observed condition means as deviations from their own mean (the grand mean) enables us to state the relationship between the sum of squares between conditions, $SS_{between}$, and the difference between the observed condition means. The relationship is

$$SS_{between} = n \times \Sigma a_i^2$$

For the phobia treatment experiment,

$$n \times \Sigma a_i^2 = 15 \times [3^2 + (-1)^2 + (-2)^2] = 210$$

which is the previously calculated value for $SS_{between}$.

Table 7.4 Fitted full model $Y_i = \bar{Y} + a_i + e$ for the phobia treatment experiment

$Y_1 = \bar{Y} + a_1 + e$	$Y_2 = \bar{Y} + a_2 + e$	$Y_3 = \bar{Y} + a_3 + e$
$10 = 7 + 3 + 0$	$4 = 7 - 1 - 2$	$3 = 7 - 2 - 2$
$8 = 7 + 3 - 2$	$6 = 7 - 1 + 0$	$9 = 7 - 2 + 4$
$10 = 7 + 3 + 0$	$4 = 7 - 1 - 2$	$7 = 7 - 2 + 2$
$12 = 7 + 3 + 2$	$10 = 7 - 1 + 4$	$5 = 7 - 2 + 0$
$10 = 7 + 3 + 0$	$4 = 7 - 1 - 2$	$3 = 7 - 2 - 2$
$14 = 7 + 3 + 4$	$6 = 7 - 1 + 0$	$3 = 7 - 2 - 2$
$13 = 7 + 3 + 3$	$4 = 7 - 1 - 2$	$7 = 7 - 2 + 2$
$9 = 7 + 3 - 1$	$8 = 7 - 1 + 2$	$1 = 7 - 2 - 4$
$12 = 7 + 3 + 2$	$8 = 7 - 1 + 2$	$1 = 7 - 2 - 4$
$8 = 7 + 3 - 2$	$4 = 7 - 1 - 2$	$3 = 7 - 2 - 2$
$10 = 7 + 3 + 0$	$2 = 7 - 1 - 4$	$5 = 7 - 2 + 0$
$4 = 7 + 3 - 6$	$4 = 7 - 1 - 2$	$7 = 7 - 2 + 2$
$8 = 7 + 3 - 2$	$10 = 7 - 1 + 4$	$7 = 7 - 2 + 2$
$10 = 7 + 3 + 0$	$8 = 7 - 1 + 2$	$9 = 7 - 2 + 4$
$12 = 7 + 3 + 2$	$8 = 7 - 1 + 2$	$5 = 7 - 2 + 0$

This relationship becomes intuitively reasonable upon reflection. Each value of **a** is the deviation of a score (the condition mean) from the mean of those scores (the mean of the condition means—the grand mean). Although there are just three deviations, each occurs n times in each condition. Thus the formula $n \times \Sigma a_i^2$ can be expressed in words as the sum of the squared deviations (over all the scores) of the condition means. Just as the sum of squares for a set of ordinary scores (Y) quantifies the differences among those scores, the sum of squares for a set of condition means quantifies the variability of those means.

Another way of thinking about $SS_{between}$ is that it is the predictable part of the data—the signal; SS_{within}, then, is the noise. Thus the analysis partitions the data into sums of squares corresponding to a model, or signal, component and a residual, or noise, component.

7.2.3 Mean Squares and the Analysis of Variance Summary Table

Sections 7.2.1 and 7.2.2 explain how the total sum of squares can be broken down into two elements: the sum of squares between conditions and the sum of squares within conditions, or model plus residual sums of squares. The next step is to convert these elements to mean squares. Converting sums of squares to mean squares is, as we have seen, a matter of dividing the sum of squares by the appropriate degrees of freedom. For the sum of squares within conditions, we have already noted that the degrees of freedom are $k(n-1)$ and that the mean square, which we denoted MS_e, was therefore

$$MS_{within} = MS_e = \frac{SS_{within}}{k(n-1)}$$

For the sum of squares between conditions, $SS_{between}$, the degrees of freedom are $k-1$. The principle in deriving this value is the same as in previous examples. There are k different scores (condition means, in this case) and, because the mean of these scores (the grand mean) is fixed, the degrees of freedom are one less than the number of different scores. Thus the mean square between conditions is

$$MS_{between} = \frac{SS_{between}}{k-1}$$

As is true for all mean squares, the mean square between conditions is a variance. $MS_{between}$ is the variance of the condition means.

These results can be set out in a convenient summary table, as shown in Table 7.5. The results for the therapy evaluation experiment are shown in Table 7.6.

Notice that the mean square for the total sum of squares has not been calculated. No use will be made of this mean square. Notice, however, that the degrees of freedom for the total sum of squares equals the total number of observations minus 1. Remember that the total sum of squares is the sum of squared residuals for the null model and that this sum of squares is the sum of the 45 squared deviations of each score from the single grand mean. Thus there are $45 - 1 = 44$ degrees of freedom.

It is important to note that, just as the between-condition and within-condition sums of squares add up to the total sum of squares, the degrees of freedom for each of these components add up to the degrees of freedom for the total sum of squares. In the phobia treatment example, these values are $2 + 42 = 44$. Thus analysis of variance can be thought of as a breakdown, not only of the total sum of squares into two components, but also of their corresponding degrees of freedom.

Analysis of variance partitions the data into sums of squares corresponding to a model (signal) component and a residual (noise) component.

Sums of squares are converted to mean squares by dividing by the degrees of freedom.

$MS_{between}$ is the variance of the condition means.

Sums of squares and degrees of freedom are additive; mean squares are not.

Table 7.5 General analysis of variance summary table for a completely randomized design with k conditions and n participants in each

Source	SS	df	MS
Model: Between conditions	$SS_{between}$	$k - 1$	$\dfrac{SS_{between}}{k - 1}$
Residual: Within condition	SS_{within}	$k(n - 1)$	$\dfrac{SS_{within}}{k(n - 1)}$
Total	SS_{total}	$nk - 1$	—

Table 7.6 Analysis of variance summary table for phobia treatment experiment with $k = 3$ conditions and $n = 15$ participants in each

Source	SS	df	MS
Model: Between conditions	210	2	105.00
Residual: Within condition	270	42	6.43
Total	480	44	—

Notice, however, that, unlike the sum of squares, the mean squares are not additive. The mean square within conditions and the mean square between conditions cannot be added together to form a total mean square.

7.2.4 Evaluating the Null Hypothesis: The *F*-Distribution

The mean square between conditions is a measure of the variance of the condition means. What factors influence its size? The most obvious factor is the true, or population, difference among the condition means. Although an experiment yields only estimates of the values of μ_i, the greater the difference among these true values, the greater will be the typical differences among their estimates. The second factor is noise. Even if the null hypothesis is true and there is no difference among the condition means (the μ_i are all equal), the observed condition means (the $\overline{Y}_i$) would still vary. Thus, of the two factors contributing to the mean square between conditions, one is potential, the other is inevitable. The potential contributing factor is the variability of the μ_i. If the null hypothesis is false and the full model appropriate, then this potential becomes real. If the null hypothesis is true, then there is no contribution from this source. But regardless of whether the null hypothesis is true or false, the mean square between conditions will always be influenced by noise.

The mean square between conditions has two contributing factors: the true difference among the condition means and noise.

In summary, the mean square between conditions is a mixture of signal (if there is one) and noise. On the other hand, MS_e is a measure of noise alone. This difference between the two mean squares gives us the basic rationale for evaluating the null hypothesis. We form a ratio

$$\frac{MS_{between}}{MS_{within}}$$

This ratio has components

$$\frac{signal + noise}{noise}$$

Now, if the null hypothesis is true (no signal), then this ratio should be 1.0, because the only contributor to $MS_{between}$ is noise—the variability measured by the residual mean square, MS_e, or equivalently, MS_{within}. Another way of making the same point is to say that, if the null hypothesis is true, then $MS_{between}$ and MS_{within} should not differ systematically, and their ratio should therefore approximate 1.0. Thus the rationale for testing the null hypothesis is to evaluate the ratio of these two mean squares and establish whether or not it is compatible with a true value of 1.0.

If the null hypothesis is false, and genuine differences between the condition means are contributing to the value of $MS_{between}$, then the ratio should be significantly greater than 1.0.

The basic method for making this evaluation is the same as for testing pairs of means by using the t-distribution. Recall that the t-ratio formed a descriptive index of the discrepancy between the observations and the prediction of the null hypothesis that $\mu_1 - \mu_2 = 0$. This ratio was then treated as a random variable, and relevant probabilities were obtained from the table of the t-distribution. In the present case, the statistic that measures the discrepancy between the data and the prediction under the null hypothesis is the ratio of the two mean squares. In purely descriptive terms, the larger this ratio, the greater the apparent contribution of differences among the conditions. We need to know whether the ratio is large enough to be incompatible with the claim that its true value is 1.0. To answer this question, we need to treat the ratio $MS_{between}/MS_{within}$ as a random variable. Given the appropriate probability distribution, we can then answer questions about whether the observed discrepancy is plausible in a situation in which the null hypothesis is true.

When the null hypothesis is true, the probability distribution of the ratio $MS_{between}/MS_{within}$ is known as the F-distribution. The use of the letter F acknowledges the contribution of Ronald Fisher, who not only derived the distribution but was the main driving force behind the development of analysis of variance. We then have a random variable, the F-ratio, defined as

$$F = \frac{MS_{between}}{MS_{within}}$$

For the phobia treatment experiment,

$$F = \frac{MS_{between}}{MS_{within}} = \frac{105.00}{6.43} = 16.33$$

The F-distribution has two parameters. Both are degrees of freedom. The first parameter is the degrees of freedom for the mean square between conditions, the numerator of the F-ratio. The second parameter is the degrees of freedom for the mean

When the null hypothesis is true, both $MS_{between}$ and MS_{within} have the same expected value.

When the null hypothesis is true, the probability distribution of the ratio $MS_{between}/MS_{within}$ is the F-distribution.

square within conditions, the denominator of the *F*-ratio. For the therapy evaluation experiment, the *F*-ratio has 2 degrees of freedom in the numerator and 42 degrees of freedom in the denominator. It is common to indicate the degrees of freedom by writing $F_{(2,42)}$. The first number in parentheses refers to the degrees of freedom of the numerator, the second to the degrees of freedom of the denominator.

F-distributions for various degrees of freedom are shown in Figure 7.2. Notice that the *F*-ratio cannot be negative. This constraint follows from the fact that it is a ratio of variances, and a variance can never be negative because it is based on a sum of *squares*. In general, the *F*-distribution is a positively skewed distribution. It becomes increasingly symmetrical as the numerator degrees of freedom increase. As they become increasingly large, the *F*-distribution approaches the normal distribution.

The table of the *F*-distribution (Statistical Table 5) is organized like the table of the *q*-statistic. A portion of the full table is shown in Table 7.7. The table is read by

> The *F*-distribution has two parameters: the degrees of freedom of the numerator and of the denominator.

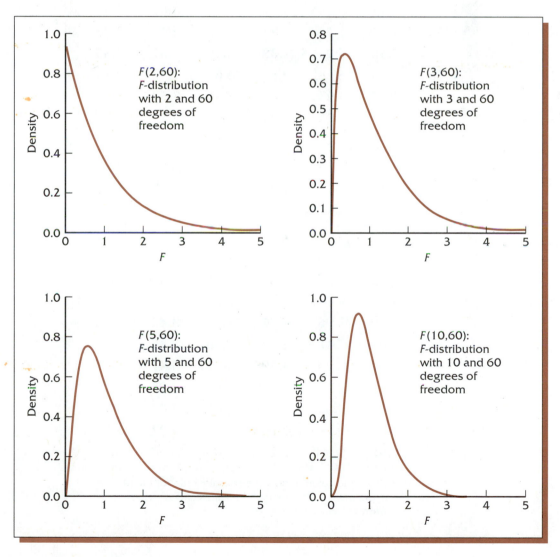

Figure 7.2
F-distributions with different degrees of freedom. The smaller of the two degrees of freedom is for the numerator mean square, the larger for the denominator mean square. The means of all distributions are 1.0.

Table 7.7 Portion of the table of the F-distribution

	Numerator degrees of freedom (df_1)					
df_2	1	2	3	4	5	6
30	4.17	3.32	2.92	2.69	2.53	2.42
	7.56	**5.39**	**4.51**	**4.02**	**3.70**	**3.47**
32	4.15	3.29	2.90	2.67	2.51	2.40
	7.50	**5.34**	**4.46**	**3.97**	**3.65**	**3.43**
34	4.13	3.28	2.88	2.65	2.49	2.38
	7.44	**5.29**	**4.42**	**3.93**	**3.61**	**3.39**
36	4.11	3.26	2.87	2.63	2.48	2.36
	7.40	**5.25**	**4.38**	**3.89**	**3.57**	**3.35**
38	4.10	3.24	2.85	2.62	2.46	2.35
	7.35	**5.21**	**4.34**	**3.86**	**3.54**	**3.32**
40	4.08	3.23	2.84	2.61	2.45	2.34
	7.31	**5.18**	**4.31**	**3.83**	**3.51**	**3.29**
42	4.07	3.22	2.83	2.59	2.44	2.32
	7.28	**5.15**	**4.29**	**3.80**	**3.49**	**3.27**
44	4.06	3.21	2.82	2.58	2.43	2.31
	7.25	**5.12**	**4.26**	**3.78**	**3.47**	**3.24**
46	4.05	3.20	2.81	2.57	2.42	2.30
	7.22	**5.10**	**4.24**	**3.76**	**3.44**	**3.22**
48	4.04	3.19	2.80	2.57	2.41	2.29
	7.19	**5.08**	**4.22**	**3.74**	**3.43**	**3.20**
50	4.03	3.18	2.79	2.56	2.40	2.29
	7.17	**5.06**	**4.20**	**3.72**	**3.41**	**3.19**
55	4.02	3.16	2.77	2.54	2.38	2.27
	7.12	**5.01**	**4.16**	**3.68**	**3.37**	**3.15**
60	4.00	3.15	2.76	2.53	2.37	2.25
	7.08	**4.98**	**4.13**	**3.65**	**3.34**	**3.12**

The shaded row and column mark the critical F-ratio for the phobia treatment experiment. Lightface type indicates critical values for $\alpha = .05$, **boldface** values for $\alpha = .01$.

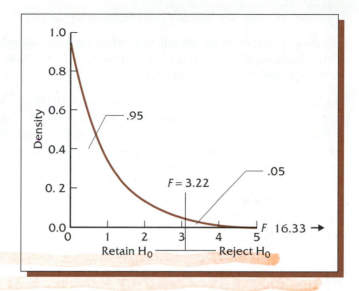

Figure 7.3
F-distribution with 2 and 42 degrees of freedom. This distribution is the appropriate sampling distribution for the phobia treatment experiment. The value $F = 3.22$ marks off the critical region for $\alpha = .05$. The obtained *F*-ratio of 16.33 is far into the rejection region in the right-hand tail of the distribution.

locating the row corresponding to the denominator degrees of freedom, moving across that row until the column corresponding to the numerator degrees of freedom is reached. The intersection of this row and column contains two values. The value in lightface type indicates the critical value for $\alpha = .05$; the one in boldface type indicates the critical value for $\alpha = .01$.

For the phobia treatment experiment, the obtained *F*-ratio was 16.33. Consulting the tables, we find that, with 2 and 42 degrees of freedom, the critical value is 3.22 for $\alpha = .05$ and 5.15 for $\alpha = .01$. The critical value for $\alpha = .05$ is shown in Figure 7.3.

For either the .05 or the .01 criterion, the obtained value of 16.33 exceeds the critical value and is therefore significant. An *F*-ratio as large as 16.33 is highly improbable if the null hypothesis is true. The data are incompatible with the null model. This conclusion corresponds to the decisions made using the confidence intervals or Tukey's HSD, which showed that the data were incompatible with the hypothesis of no differences among the condition means.

7.2.5 Fisher's LSD (Protected *t*)

Imagine an experiment with four conditions. With four condition means, there are six possible comparisons between pairs of means. One way of testing each of these differences would be to conduct a separate *t*-test for each of the six. The obvious criticism of this practice is that if each of these tests is conducted with $\alpha = .05$, the probability of a Type-1 error for the entire set of six decisions is greater than .05.

One method that offers some protection against an inflated error rate is known as Fisher's least significant difference, briefly mentioned in Section 7.1.4. In a nutshell, the rationale behind this method is to perform the *t*-tests, *but only if the analysis of variance has first established a significant F-ratio*. As noted earlier, one way of proceeding would be to calculate a separate *t*-ratio for each difference. A more efficient method is to establish the minimum difference (the LSD, or least significant difference) between any two means that would be needed to cause the *t*-ratio to be significant. This procedure is analogous to that used for Tukey's HSD.

LSD denotes least significant difference.

The rationale for Fisher's LSD has two steps:

Step 1 Perform an overall analysis of variance. Conduct tests of comparisons *only* if this analysis of variance leads to a rejection of the null hypothesis. That is, proceed to Step 2 only if the F-ratio is significant.

Step 2 If the F-ratio is significant, then establish the w value by using an error rate per comparison as a criterion, rather than the error rate per experiment of Tukey's method. The value of w is obtained by using the table of the t-distribution. In fact, the LSD procedure amounts to conducting individual t-tests on pairs of means, the error rate or significance level referring to each comparison.

Consider the phobia treatment experiment once more. Because the F-ratio was significant, the results satisfy Fisher's criterion for proceeding to conduct tests of comparisons.

$$w = \text{a critical tabled value} \times \text{the appropriate standard deviation}$$

Now the critical tabled value will be obtained from the t-distribution rather than from the distribution of the q-statistic. For 42 degrees of freedom, the critical value of t for $\alpha = .05$ is 2.021 (see Statistical Table 3). The appropriate standard deviation is the standard error of the difference between two means, which is calculated in the usual way:

$$\text{standard error} = \sqrt{\frac{2MS_e}{n}} = \sqrt{\frac{2MS_{within}}{n}} = \sqrt{\frac{2 \times 6.43}{15}} = 0.926$$

Thus we have

$$w = 2.021 \times 0.926 = 1.87$$

Thus the minimum difference needed for significance is LSD = 1.87. Using this criterion, we would declare that differences between conditions 1 and 2 and between 1 and 3 are significantly different from 0 but not for conditions 2 and 3. This conclusion coincides with that made by using Tukey's HSD criterion (Section 7.1.2). Notice, however, that the LSD value is less than the HSD criterion of 2.25. In general, the LSD criterion is less conservative (demands a smaller difference) than the HSD criterion, so the two methods can sometimes lead to different decisions.

Fisher's LSD procedure uses a critical t-value corresponding to an error rate per comparison. The defense of this procedure is that the tests are conducted only if the overall F-ratio is significant. Situations can exist in which the F-ratio is not significant, but one or more of the obtained differences exceeds the LSD criterion. However, if the LSD procedure is applied properly, these differences would not be declared significant; in fact, they would never be tested, because the initial criterion of a significant F-ratio has not been met. This two-stage testing procedure thereby offers some protection against the inflated Type-1 error rate that would exist if multiple t-tests were applied without first demanding a significant F-ratio. For this reason, the t-value used in Fisher's LSD procedure is sometimes described as a "protected t."

7.2.6 Analysis of Variance, the *F*-Distribution, and the *t*-Test

It may have occurred to you that there is a close relationship between the use of the t-distribution for two-condition experiments (Chapter 6) and the use of the F-distribution for experiments with more than two conditions. One way of describing this relationship is to ask what happens if the analysis of variance procedures described in this chapter are applied to a two-condition experiment such as the phobia treatment experiment of Section 6.2.1 (Data Set 3.1).

Most of the necessary calculations for the analysis of variance of this two-condition experiment have been completed in the course of its analysis using the t-distribution. The sum of the squared residuals was 179.9 with $df = 34$, giving a value for MS_e of 5.3. The two means were $\overline{Y}_1 = 10.2$ and $\overline{Y}_2 = 5.2$. The grand mean is therefore $(10.2 + 5.2)/2 = 7.7$, so

$$a_1 = +2.5 \quad \text{and} \quad a_2 = -2.5$$

$$SS_{between} = 18 \times [2.5^2 + (-2.5)^2] = 225$$

The analysis of variance summary is shown in Table 7.8, and the F-value is

$$F = \frac{225}{5.3} = 42.5$$

If we take the square root of this F-ratio, we have $\sqrt{42.5} = 6.52$. This was the value of the t-ratio calculated in Chapter 6. It is a general rule that, for an independent-groups design with two conditions, the value of the t-ratio is the square root of the F-ratio from an analysis of variance performed on the same data. In other words, for an F-ratio with 1 degree of freedom in the numerator and degrees of freedom in the denominator the same for both tests, $F = t^2$. If you have any doubt about this relationship, it is easily checked by consulting the F- and t-tables (Statistical Tables 5 and 3). For a given α level and the same degrees of freedom, you will find the entries in the F-table for numerator $df = 1$ are exactly the square of the corresponding value in the t-table.

Another aspect of this relationship is the equation that relates MS_e to the standard error of the difference between two means. As noted in Section 7.2.5, this relationship is

$$s_{\overline{Y}_1 - \overline{Y}_2} = \sqrt{\frac{2MS_e}{n}}$$

For our example, $s_{\overline{Y}_1 - \overline{Y}_2} = \sqrt{2 \times 5.3/18} = 0.767$. This is the value of the standard error of the difference between two means for these results that we obtained in Chapter 6.

> With 1 degree of freedom in the numerator, $F = t^2$.

Table 7.8 Analysis of variance summary table for the original phobia treatment experiment

Source	SS	df	MS
Model: Between conditions	225.0	1	225.0
Residual: Within condition	179.9	34	5.3
Total	404.9	35	—

Comprehension Check 7.2

Important Concepts

1. The procedure described in this section is known as analysis of variance. It introduces new terminology for some familiar concepts.

■ The difference in the sum of squared residuals between the null and the full model provides a measure of the overall differences (variability) among the condition means. It is termed the between-condition sum of squares, and written $SS_{between}$.

■ The sum of squared residuals for the full model is termed the within-condition sum of squares and is written SS_{within}.

■ The sum of squared residuals for the null model is termed the total sum of squares and is written S_{total}.

2. The important equation is $SS_{total} = SS_{between} + SS_{within}$.

3. The sum of squares between conditions and the sum of squares within conditions can be converted to mean squares by dividing the sum of squares by their respective degrees of freedom. For the mean square within conditions (MS_{within}), the degrees of freedom are $k(n - 1)$; for the mean square between conditions ($MS_{between}$), the degrees of freedom are $k - 1$. Note that MS_{within} is the same as MS_e.

4. The full model was rewritten by expressing each condition mean as a deviation from the grand mean. This rewriting led us to express the model as

$$Y_i = \mu + \alpha_i + e$$

where α_i is the difference between μ_i and the grand mean, μ. The estimate of α_i is $\mathbf{a}_i$ and is equal to $\overline{Y}_i - \overline{Y}$.

5. The values of $\mathbf{a}_i$ are related to $SS_{between}$ in a very simple way:

$$SS_{between} = n \times \Sigma \mathbf{a}_i^2$$

6. The null hypothesis can be evaluated by using the ratio

$$F = \frac{MS_{between}}{MS_{within}}$$

This ratio has a probability distribution known as the F-distribution, which has two parameters: the degrees of freedom for the numerator mean square and the degrees of freedom for the denominator mean square.

7. If the F-ratio leads to a rejection of the null hypothesis, then Fisher's LSD (least significant difference) procedure can be used to evaluate differences between pairs of means. This procedure is less conservative than is Tukey's HSD method.

8. When analysis of variance procedures are applied to an independent-groups design with just two conditions, the resulting F-ratio equals the square of the corresponding t-ratio.

Worked Examples

Example 1   **Tranquilizer effects (see Data Set 7.2)**

This example uses the expanded tranquilizer effects experiment analyzed in Example 1 at the end of Section 7.1. For this experiment, $n = 16$. The basic results from Section 7.1 were

Condition	$\overline{Y}$	SS_Y
Y_1 (control)	8.95	27.22
Y_2 (T1)	10.25	36.34
Y_3 (T2)	11.77	27.51

The sum of squares for the null model is $SS_{total} = 154.8$.

a. Write out the full and null models for this experiment and use the preceding results to estimate the parameters μ and α_i for the full model.

b. Conduct an analysis of variance on the data from this experiment and decide whether using Fisher's LSD procedure is justified.

c. If using Fisher's LSD procedure is justified, use it to evaluate the differences between the means of the three conditions.

d. What is the value of R^2 for this experiment?

Answer

a. The full model is $Y_i = \mu + \alpha_i + e$. The null model is $Y = \mu + e$. The fitted full model is $Y = \overline{Y} + a_i + e$. The estimate of μ is $\overline{Y} = (8.95 + 10.25 + 11.77)/3 = 10.32$. This estimate gives the following values for the a_i:

$$a_1 = 8.95 - 10.32 = -1.37$$

$$a_2 = 10.25 - 10.32 = -0.07$$

$$a_3 = 11.77 - 10.32 = +1.45$$

Note that, apart from rounding error, the a_i sum to 0.

b. The analysis of variance requires that we obtain $SS_{between}$ and SS_{within}. We have already calculated SS_{within} as

$$SS_{within} = 27.22 + 36.34 + 27.51 = 91.1$$

The total sum of squares, SS_{total}, is the sum of squares of the residuals for the null model. Its value was 154.8. The sum of squares between conditions corresponds to the difference between SS_{total} and SS_{within}. Thus

$$SS_{between} = 154.8 - 91.1 = 63.7$$

This value could also have been obtained by using the values of the a_i. Using this method,

$$SS_{between} = n \times \Sigma a_i^2 = 16 \times 3.98 = 63.7$$

Table 7.9 Analysis of variance summary table for phobia treatment experiment (Worked Example 1)

Source	SS	df	MS
Model: Between conditions	63.7	2	31.850
Residual: Within condition	91.1	45	2.024
Total	154.8	47	—

Note: the value 3.98 is $(-1.37)^2 + (-0.07)^2 + (1.45)^2$. We can now set up an analysis of variance summary table (Table 7.9). The sum of squares between conditions is based on $k - 1 = 2$ degrees of freedom. The sum of squares within conditions is based on $k(n - 1) = 3 \times 15 = 45$ degrees of freedom. The total degrees of freedom is therefore $2 + 45 = 47$, 1 less than the total number of observations.

The *F*-ratio is

$$F = \frac{31.850}{2.024} = 15.7$$

Consulting the *F*-tables (Statistical Table 5), we find that, for a Type-1 error rate of .05, the critical *F*-value for 2 and 45 degrees of freedom is 3.20. Thus our *F*-ratio of 15.7 reflects differences among the means that is larger than could be plausibly expected if the null hypothesis were true.

c. Given this conclusion, Fisher's LSD procedure allows us to proceed with establishing the value for this version of the least significant difference. We need t for 45 degrees of freedom. We will use the closest tabled value below the exact number of degrees of freedom required. With $\alpha = .05$, the critical value of t with 40 degrees of freedom is 2.021. The appropriate standard deviation is the standard error of the difference between two means, which is calculated in the usual way:

$$\text{standard error} = \sqrt{\frac{2MS_e}{n}} = \sqrt{\frac{2 \times 2.024}{16}} = 0.503$$

Thus we have

$$w = 2.021 \times 0.503 = 1.0$$

So the minimum difference needed for significance is LSD = 1.0. Using this criterion, we would declare that all three differences between conditions are significantly different from 0.

d. The value of R^2 for this experiment is $R^2 = SS_{model}/SS_{total} = SS_{between}/SS_{total}$. Thus $R^2 = 63.7/154.8 = .41$.

Example 2   Induced emotion (see Data Set 7.3)

For the induced emotion experiment used in Example 2 of Section 7.1, $n = 14$ and the basic computations led to the values given in the following table.

Condition	$\bar{Y}_i$	SS_Y
Y_1 (anger)	8.09	44.84
Y_2 (sadness)	5.83	65.75
Y_3 (happiness)	1.55	45.87
Y_4 (disgust)	0.12	42.42

The total sum of squares (the sum of the squared residuals for the null model) is $SS_{total} = 773.5$.

a. Obtain estimates for μ and α_i in the full model for this experiment:

$$Y = \mu + \alpha_i + e$$

b. Complete the analysis of variance summary table.

c. Calculate the appropriate F-ratio and use it to evaluate the plausibility of the null hypothesis against a criterion of $\alpha = .05$.

d. If the F-ratio is significant, calculate Fisher's LSD and decide which comparisons are significant.

e. What is the value of R^2 for this experiment?

Answer

a. The estimate of the overall mean is $\bar{Y} = (8.09 + 5.83 + 1.55 + 0.12)/4 = 3.90$. This mean value gives the following estimates:

$$a_1 = 8.09 - 3.90 = +4.19$$

$$a_2 = 5.83 - 3.90 = +1.93$$

$$a_3 = 1.55 - 3.90 = -2.35$$

$$a_4 = 0.12 - 3.90 = -3.78$$

b. The analysis of variance requires that we obtain $SS_{between}$ and SS_{within}. SS_{within} is $(44.84 + 65.75 + 45.87 + 42.42) = 198.9$. The total sum of squares, SS_{total} is the sum of squares of the residuals for the null model. Its value was 773.5. The sum of squares between conditions corresponds to the difference between SS_{total} and SS_{within}. Thus $SS_{between} = 773.5 - 198.9 = 574.6$. This value could also have been obtained by using the values of the a_i.

$$SS_{between} = n \times \Sigma a_i^2 = 14 \times 41.04 = 574.6$$

We can now construct an analysis of variance summary table (Table 7.10). The sum of squares between conditions is based on $k - 1 = 3$ degrees of freedom. The sum of squares within conditions is based on $k(n - 1) = 4 \times 13 = 52$ degrees of freedom. The total degrees of freedom is $3 + 52 = 55$, which is 1 less than 56, the total number of observations in the experiment.

c. The F-ratio is

$$F = \frac{191.53}{3.82} = 50.14$$

Table 7.10 Analysis of variance summary table for induced emotion experiment (Worked Example 2)

Source	SS	df	MS
Model: Between conditions	574.6	3	191.53
Residual: Within condition	198.9	52	3.82
Total	773.5	55	—

Consulting the F-tables (Statistical Table 5), we find that for a Type-1 error rate of .05, the critical F-value for 3 and 50 degrees of freedom is 2.79 ($df = 50$ is the closest tabulated value below $df = 52$). Thus our F-ratio of 50.14 reflects differences among the condition means that are larger than could be plausibly expected if the null hypothesis were true.

d. Given this conclusion, Fisher's LSD procedure allows us to proceed with establishing the value for the least significant difference. With $\alpha = .05$, the critical value of t for 50 degrees of freedom is 2.009. The appropriate standard deviation is the standard error of the difference between two means, which is calculated in the usual way:

$$\text{standard error} = \sqrt{\frac{2\text{MS}_e}{n}} = \sqrt{\frac{2 \times 3.82}{14}} = 0.74$$

Thus we have $w = 2.009 \times 0.74 = 1.49$, so minimum difference needed for significance is LSD = 1.49. Inspection of the four means indicates that the means for the anger and sadness conditions differ from the two other conditions and from each other by at least 1.49 (see Table 7.5). Happiness and disgust do not differ significantly from each other.

e. The value of R^2 for this experiment is $R^2 = \text{SS}_{\text{between}}/\text{SS}_{\text{total}}$. Thus $R^2 = 574.6/773.5 = .74$.

Problems

Problem 1   **Intentional remembering (see Data Set 7.4)**

The data reported as part of Problem 1 at the end of Section 7.1 gave the following results ($n = 25$):

Condition	$\overline{Y}$	SS_Y
Y_1 (intentional study)	.383	1.080
Y_2 (incidental rating task)	.577	1.158
Y_3 (intentional study and rating task)	.597	1.288

Calculation of the sum of squares residuals under the null model gives $\text{SS}_{\text{total}} = 4.225$.

a. Obtain estimates for μ and α_i in the full model for this experiment:

$$Y = \mu + \alpha_i + e$$

b. Complete the analysis of variance summary table.

c. Calculate the appropriate F-ratio and use it to evaluate the plausibility of the null hypothesis against a criterion of $\alpha = .05$.

d. If the F-ratio is significant, calculate Fisher's LSD and decide which comparisons are significant.

e. What is the value of R^2 for this experiment?

Problem 2   **Aging and memory (DS07_06.dat in the *ASCII Files*)**

In a further study of the effects of aging on cognitive performance, memory performance was investigated for the same three groups as those specified in Problem 2 of Section 7.1. There were $n = 21$ participants at each age level, and the results of a basic analysis of the data gave the following results. The response measure was the number of items recalled in a free recall memory task.

Condition	$\overline{Y}$	SS_Y
A (average age 17 years)	13.7	158.0
B (average age 40 years)	12.6	161.0
C (average age 70 years)	8.2	193.0

The total sum of squares (the sum of the squared residuals for the null model) is $SS_{total} = 872.0$.

a. The full model for this experiment is

$$Y = \mu + \alpha_i + e$$

Obtain estimates for μ and α_i in this model.

b. Complete the analysis of variance summary table.

c. Calculate the appropriate F-ratio and use it to evaluate the plausibility of the null hypothesis against a criterion of $\alpha = .05$.

d. If the F-ratio is significant, calculate Fisher's LSD and decide which comparisons are significant.

7.3 Analysis of Variance of Factorial Designs

The extensions to the two-condition experiments considered thus far have involved simply adding more conditions. In principle, the number of such conditions can be increased indefinitely. In practice, larger experiments usually involve conditions that have some organization rather than consisting of a simple unstructured list. We therefore turn our attention to designs in which the conditions can be organized in a way that reflects their underlying structure.

7.3.1 Experiment with Four Conditions Arranged in a 2×2 Factorial Design

Consider a study of driver safety that investigates the effects of alcohol consumption and sleep deprivation on the time it takes to apply a car's brakes after the sudden appearance of an unexpected object. Suppose that two preliminary experiments have been completed. The first of these small experiments studied the effect of alcohol consumption and established that the consumption of 1 ounce of alcohol increased the mean reaction time by 200 milliseconds relative to a control condition of no alcohol consumption. The second experiment studied sleep deprivation and established that 24 hours without sleep increased the mean reaction time by 120 milliseconds relative to a control (no sleep deprivation) condition in which drivers had been awake 6 hours after a normal night's sleep.

The investigator now asks about the *combined* effect of these two factors. For example, what would be the reaction time of a driver who has consumed 1 ounce of alcohol *and* gone 24 hours without sleep? For convenience, we will refer to the alcohol factor as factor A and to sleep deprivation as factor B. In our example, each of these factors has two values, or two *levels*. The levels of the A factor are no alcohol (denoted A_1) and 1 ounce of alcohol (denoted A_2); the two levels of the B factor are no sleep deprivation (denoted B_1) and 24 hours of sleep deprivation (denoted B_2).

To answer the question about the combined effects of A and B, the investigator designs an experiment with the following four conditions.

The four conditions can be arranged as two factors, each with two levels.

A factor is a set of conceptually related conditions. Each condition within this set is called a level of the factor.

■ No alcohol consumed and no sleep deprivation (A_1B_1).

■ One ounce of alcohol consumed and no sleep deprivation (A_2B_1).

■ No alcohol consumed and 24 hours of sleep deprivation (A_1B_2).

■ One ounce of alcohol consumed and 24 hours of sleep deprivation (A_2B_2).

These four conditions can be arranged in a two-dimensional, or "two-way," table as shown in Table 7.11. One dimension of the table is the alcohol consumption factor,

Table 7.11 Effects of alcohol and sleep deprivation on a driver's braking reaction time

		B (sleep deprivation)	
		B_1 (none)	B_2 (24 hours)
A (alcohol consumption)	A_1 (none)	A_1B_1 (μ_{11})	A_1B_2 (μ_{12})
	A_2 (1 ounce)	A_2B_1 (μ_{21})	A_2B_2 (μ_{22})

The four conditions of the experiment have been arranged in a 2×2 factorial layout. The population mean in each cell is denoted by μ_{11}, μ_{12}, etc.

the other is the sleep deprivation factor. This arrangement of the factors is referred to as a *factorial design,* or a factorial layout; and because there are two levels of each factor, it would be described as a 2×2 ("two-by-two") factorial design. More generally, an experiment with *a* levels of the A factor and *b* levels of the B factor would be described as an $a \times b$ factorial design.

Such an arrangement is called a 2×2 factorial design.

The term *two-way* to describe the arrangement of the conditions in Table 7.11 distinguishes the factorial layout from *one-way* designs. (One-way designs are designs such as those considered in Sections 7.1 and 7.2 in which the conditions are treated as a single unstructured set.) The first column of this 2×2 arrangement, containing A_1B_1 and A_2B_1, corresponds to the previously described preliminary experiment that studied the effect of alcohol consumption. The first row of this 2×2 arrangement, containing A_1B_1 and A_1B_2, corresponds to the other preliminary experiment that studied the effect of sleep deprivation. The novel feature of the factorial design is the inclusion of the A_2B_2 condition. Participants in this condition are subject to the joint influence of alcohol consumption and sleep deprivation.

How might performance in this A_2B_2 condition be predicted from the individual effects of the two contributing factors? There are two broad possibilities: The first possibility is that the two effects combine *additively.* The second is that they *interact.* An analogy might help clarify the distinction between these alternatives. Consider the following question. If two level teaspoons (10 milliliters) of sugar are added to a cup (200 milliliters) of coffee, by how much (if at all) does the volume increase? The additivity assumption predicts that the volume increases by an amount equal to the volume of sugar. The new volume would be 210 milliliters. However, if the sugar and coffee combined in a way that resulted in a volume other than 210 milliliters—say, 205 milliliters—then the relation between coffee and sugar would be described as *nonadditive.* This nonadditive outcome reflects an interaction between the two factors.

The two factors may combine additively or interactively.

As we consider each of these two possibilities, we will use population values for the cell means, not because we could ever know such values in practice, but because it is helpful to see additivity and nonadditivity in their "pure" form before analyzing real data along with their inevitable residuals.

Additivity

The first and simpler possibility is that the effects of alcohol consumption and sleep deprivation simply add to each other, in which case the factors can be described as additive. The effect of alcohol consumption is to add 200 milliseconds; the effect of sleep deprivation is to add 120 milliseconds. Additivity implies that the combined effect of alcohol consumption and sleep deprivation should be to increase a driver's reaction time by $200 + 120 = 320$ milliseconds relative to a control condition in which the driver has had no alcohol and is not sleep deprived. If the reaction time for this control group were $\mu_{11} = 650$ milliseconds, then the mean reaction times for each of the four conditions would be those shown in Table 7.12. If we plot these four cell means with the response measure (reaction time) on the *y*-axis, we have Figure 7.4.

Some data analysts might object to the fact that data points in Figure 7.4 have been connected with a straight line, claiming that the data should be graphed on a bar chart because the predictor variable is categorical. This objection is valid if the lines are interpreted as indicating values of Y (response measures) corresponding to values of the predictor variables intermediate between the values 0 and 24 hours of

Additivity implies that the lines joining the points depicting a factor will be parallel.

Table 7.12 Cell means under conditions of additivity

		Sleep deprivation		
		None	24 hours	Row mean
Alcohol consumption	None	$\mu_{11} = 650$	$\mu_{12} = 650 + 120 = 770$	710
	1 ounce	$\mu_{21} = 650 + 200 = 850$	$\mu_{22} = 650 + 120 + 200 = 970$	910
	Column mean	750	870	810

Response measure is braking reaction time in milliseconds.

sleep deprivation. The lines do not indicate such values because the predictor variable is being treated as categorical. The function of the lines is merely pictorial; they serve to stress the factorial layout by guiding the eye to connect those points that depict the same factor.

Notice that the lines that join the points for no sleep deprivation and 24 hours without sleep are parallel. This feature is a direct consequence of additivity. Additivity means that the difference between the two levels of one factor is the same at each level of the other factor. The difference in reaction time between no alcohol consumption and 1 ounce is 200 milliseconds for both levels of sleep deprivation. Similarly, additivity implies that the difference in reaction time between no sleep deprivation and 24 hours of sleep deprivation is 120 milliseconds for both 0 and 1 ounce of consumed alcohol.

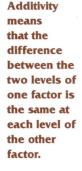

Additivity means that the difference between the two levels of one factor is the same at each level of the other factor.

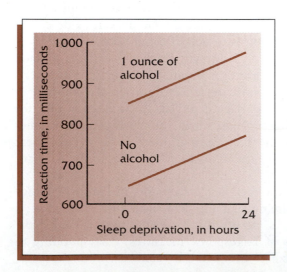

Figure 7.4
Plot of cell means from Table 7.12 for the four conditions under the assumption of additivity of effects.

Table 7.12 contains values labeled "row mean" and "column mean." These values are the means for each level of one factor averaged over the levels of the other. For example, the row mean of 710 milliseconds is the mean reaction time for the no alcohol condition averaged over the two levels of sleep deprivation; the mean of the second column (870 milliseconds) is the mean reaction time of the 24-hour sleep deprivation condition averaged over both levels of the alcohol factor, and so forth.

The relationship of additivity can be expressed in terms of a model that is a straightforward extension of the model used in Section 7.2. For the required model, we use as building blocks the models for the two preliminary experiments described at the beginning of this section.

For the preliminary experiment conducted to evaluate the effect of alcohol, a model would be

$$\mu_i = \mu + \alpha_i \quad (i = 1,2)$$

For the preliminary experiment conducted to evaluate the effect of sleep deprivation, a model would be

$$\mu_j = \mu + \beta_j \quad (j = 1,2)$$

To distinguish the two factors, we have used β and j to denote the two levels of the sleep deprivation factor instead of α and i, which now refer only to the two levels of the alcohol factor.

If the two factors combine additively, then each cell has the following value:

$$\mu_{ij} = \mu + \alpha_i + \beta_j \quad (i = 1,2; j = 1,2)$$

For example, the model for the condition in which participants have no alcohol and no sleep deprivation would be

$$\mu_{11} = \mu + \alpha_1 + \beta_1$$

Similarly,

$$\mu_{21} = \mu + \alpha_2 + \beta_1$$

$$\mu_{12} = \mu + \alpha_1 + \beta_2$$

$$\mu_{22} = \mu + \alpha_2 + \beta_2$$

As with previously considered models, the values for α and β are expressed as deviations from the grand mean. Thus the parameter values are

■ The grand mean is

$$\mu = (\mu_{11} + \mu_{12} + \mu_{21} + \mu_{22})/4 = (650 + 770 + 850 + 970)/4 = 810$$

■ The mean for the first level of the alcohol factor (no alcohol) is 710 milliseconds, so

$$\alpha_1 = 710 - 810 = -100 \text{ milliseconds}$$

$$\alpha_2 = 910 - 810 = +100 \text{ milliseconds}$$

■ For the sleep deprivation factor.

$$\beta_1 = 750 - 810 = -60$$

$$\beta_2 = 870 - 810 = +60$$

Table 7.13 Cell means for the four conditions from Table 7.14, expressed in terms of their additive model components

		Sleep deprivation	
		None	**24 hours**
Alcohol consumption	**None**	$\mu_{11} = 650 = 810$ $- 100 - 60$	$\mu_{12} = 770 = 810$ $- 100 + 60$
	1 ounce	$\mu_{21} = 850 = 810$ $+ 100 - 60$	$\mu_{22} = 970 = 810$ $+ 100 + 60$

Each cell mean can be expressed as the sum of the relevant parameter values.

With these results, we can express each cell mean as the sum of the relevant parameter values.

$$\mu_{11} = 650 = \mu + \alpha_1 + \beta_1 = 810 - 100 - 60$$

$$\mu_{21} = 850 = \mu + \alpha_2 + \beta_1 = 810 + 100 - 60$$

$$\mu_{12} = 770 = \mu + \alpha_1 + \beta_2 = 810 - 100 + 60$$

$$\mu_{22} = 970 = \mu + \alpha_2 + \beta_2 = 810 + 100 + 60$$

Table 7.13 shows these values in their appropriate cells of the 2×2 table.

Interactions

An interaction can take different forms.

The second possibility is that the effects are not additive but interactive. For our example, such an interaction might take either of two forms. In one plausible form of the interaction, one factor could exaggerate the effect of the other; so the combined effect is larger than the sum of the parts. For example, the braking reaction time for the combined alcohol and sleep-deprived condition might be 500 milliseconds greater than that of the control condition, a value greater than the 320 milliseconds predicted by additivity. Such a result would be obtained if sleep deprivation exaggerates the influence of the alcohol; in other words, if the driver is sleep deprived, then the effect of alcohol consumption is greater than 200 milliseconds. This is the sense in which alcohol consumption and sleep deprivation interact in a way that makes their combined effect greater than the sum of their separate effects. Table 7.14 gives an example of this form of an interaction.

Nonadditivity implies that the difference between the two levels of one factor is not the same at each level of the other factor.

If we plot the four cell means from Table 7.14 with the response measure (reaction time) on the y-axis, we have Figure 7.5. Notice that, in Figure 7.5, the lines are no longer parallel. This feature is a direct consequence of nonadditivity. Nonadditivity implies that the difference between the two levels of one factor is not the same at each level of the other factor. The difference in reaction times between no alcohol and 1 ounce is 200 milliseconds for no sleep deprivation, but 500 milliseconds with 24 hours of sleep deprivation. Similarly, nonadditivity implies that the difference in reaction times between no sleep deprivation and 24 hours of sleep deprivation is dif-

Table 7.14 Cell, row, and column means under conditions of nonadditivity

		Sleep deprivation		
		None	24 hours	Row mean
Alcohol consumption	None	$\mu_{11} = 650$	$\mu_{12} = 770$	710
	1 ounce	$\mu_{21} = 850$	$\mu_{22} = 1150$	1000
	Column mean	750	960	855

ferent for no alcohol consumption from what it is for 1 ounce of consumed alcohol. The former difference is 120 milliseconds; the latter is 300 milliseconds.

In a second possible form of the interaction, the combined effect is *less* than that predicted by simple additivity. Suppose, for example, that the reaction time for the combined condition is 250 milliseconds greater than in the control condition. This combined effect is less than the 320 milliseconds predicted by additivity. In this case, the effect of one factor is to reduce the influence of the other. Or we could say that this form of the interaction reflects a degree of redundancy or overlap between the two influences. Such an interaction might arise with two forms of therapy—say, drug treatment and psychotherapy. Each treatment may be effective, but, if a patient undergoes both forms, the combined benefits may be little better than either alone.

The cell means in Table 7.15 provide an example of this form of an interaction. If we plot these four values with the response measure (reaction time) on the *y*-axis, we have Figure 7.6.

Figure 7.5

Plot of cell means from Table 7.14 for the four conditions showing nonadditivity of effects.

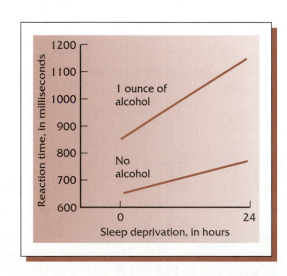

Table 7.15 Cell means under conditions of nonadditivity

		Sleep deprivation	
		None	24 hours
Alcohol consumption	None	$\mu_{11} = 650$	$\mu_{12} = 770$
	1 ounce	$\mu_{21} = 850$	$\mu_{22} = 900$

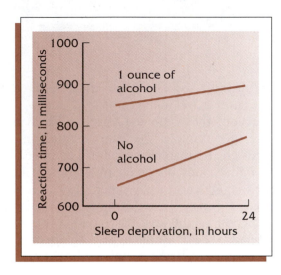

Figure 7.6
Plot of cell means from Table 7.15 for the four conditions, showing a different form of nonadditivity from that shown in Figure 7.5.

Adding the Interaction Term to the Model

Attempting to fit the additive model to nonadditve parameters results in wrong predictions.

If we attempted to fit the additive model to the population cell means in either Table 7.14 or Table 7.15, we would find that the fit is imperfect. Suppose, for example, that we attempt to fit an additive model to the data in Table 7.14.

■ The grand mean is

$$\mu = (\mu_{11} + \mu_{12} + \mu_{21} + \mu_{22})/4 = (650 + 770 + 850 + 1150)/4 = 855$$

■ The mean for the first level of the alcohol factor (no alcohol) is 710 milliseconds, so

$$\alpha_1 = 710 - 855 = -145 \text{ milliseconds}$$

$$\alpha_2 = 1000 - 855 = +145 \text{ milliseconds}$$

■ For the sleep deprivation factor,

$$\beta_1 = 750 - 855 = -105$$

$$\beta_2 = 960 - 855 = +105$$

With these results, we can attempt to express each cell mean as the sum of the relevant parameter values. For example, the prediction of the additive model for μ_{11} is $\mu + \alpha_1 + \beta_1 = 855 - 145 - 105 = 605$. The actual value of μ_{11}, however, is

650. Thus the model's prediction for this cell is too low by 45 milliseconds. Similarly, the model makes inaccurate predictions for the other three cells. For example, the prediction of the additive model for μ_{21} is

$$\mu_{21} = \mu + \alpha_2 + \beta_1 = 855 + 145 - 105 = 895$$

whereas the actual value is 850. Thus the prediction of the additive model for this cell is too high by 45 milliseconds. Similar calculations give the additive model's predicted value for μ_{12} as $855 - 145 + 105 = 815$, a value 45 milliseconds greater than the actual value of 770 milliseconds. Finally, the predicted value for μ_{22} is $855 + 145 + 105 = 1105$, which is 45 milliseconds below the actual value of 1150.

The failure of the additive model dictates that an extra term be included in the model, an interaction term that adjusts or compensates for nonadditivity. This interaction term is denoted by $\alpha\beta_{ij}$, where values of the subscripts i and j pick out particular cells. The interaction term for the A_1B_1 cell, for example, would be $\alpha\beta_{11}$; for the A_1B_2 cell, it would be $\alpha\beta_{12}$; and so forth. Thus the model for the population mean for the A_1B_1 cell is

$$\mu_{11} = \mu + \alpha_1 + \beta_1 + \alpha\beta_{11}$$

More generally, the model with an interaction term is

$$\mu_{ij} = \mu + \alpha_i + \beta_j + \alpha\beta_{ij}$$

The $\alpha\beta_{ij}$ term indicates the degree of nonadditivity or, in equivalent terms, the magnitude of the interaction. The terms α_i and β_j are commonly referred to as *main effects*. Thus α_i denotes the main effect of alcohol consumption (the effect of alcohol consumption averaged over the two levels of sleep deprivation) and β_j denotes the main effect of sleep deprivation (the effect of sleep deprivation averaged over the two levels of alcohol consumption). Thus the new model partitions the between-condition sum of squares into main effects and an interaction effect. An additive model is one containing only main effects.

The idea that an interaction is the discrepancy between the true cell mean and the prediction of additivity can be expressed explicitly by simply rearranging the terms of the model:

$$\alpha\beta_{ij} = \mu_{ij} - (\mu + \alpha_i + \beta_j)$$

The terms within the parentheses make up the additive prediction. This is the relationship used previously to calculate the inaccuracy of the additive model for the

More generally, the model with an interaction term is $\mu_{ij} = \mu + \alpha_i + \beta_j + \alpha\beta_{ij}$

There is a distinction between main effects and interaction effects.

Table 7.16 Degree of nonadditivity (interaction) for each of the four conditions for the parameter values in Table 7.16

		Sleep deprivation	
		None	24 hours
Alcohol consumption	None	$\alpha\beta_{11} = +45$	$\alpha\beta_{12} = -45$
	1 ounce	$\alpha\beta_{21} = -45$	$\alpha\beta_{22} = +45$

alcohol consumption and sleep deprivation example. This inaccuracy of the additive model is precisely what is meant by the interaction term. Those results can be presented in a 2×2 table, as shown in Table 7.16 (page 361).

7.3.2 Analyzing Data from a 2×2 Factorial Design

So far the discussion of factorial designs has been in terms of parameters. We will consider again the alcohol consumption and sleep deprivation example, this time with data of the type that might be obtained from an actual experiment.

Suppose that the alcohol consumption and sleep deprivation experiment was conducted with $n = 10$ participants randomly assigned to each of the four conditions, a total of 40 participants. Although the response times from such an experiment would normally be recorded in milliseconds, for purposes of this example they are shown in seconds, rounded to the nearest tenth of a second. The data are presented in this cruder form simply to avoid large numbers (see Table 7.17). The bottom two rows of Table 7.17 give the mean and sum of squares for that condition.

Analyzing the Braking Reaction Time Data as a One-Way Design with Four Conditions

One method of analyzing the data from this experiment would be to use the methods described in Sections 7.1 and 7.2. The experiment can be treated as a completely randomized one-way design with four conditions. As we will see, this one-way form of analysis is not the usual one, but it is perfectly legitimate and quite instructive.

Table 7.17 Means and sum of squares for the braking reaction time experiment, with four conditions

	A_1B_1	A_1B_2	A_2B_1	A_2B_2
	0.9	0.8	0.9	1.4
	0.4	0.5	0.9	1.2
	0.6	0.8	0.9	1.1
	0.7	0.9	0.7	1.3
	0.6	1.1	0.7	1.3
	0.8	0.8	0.9	1.2
	0.8	0.8	0.7	1.1
	0.5	0.7	1.0	0.9
	1.0	0.7	0.6	1.2
	0.5	0.6	0.8	1.1
Mean	0.68	0.77	0.81	1.18
SS_Y	0.336	0.241	0.149	0.176

The model for such a one-way analysis would be

$$Y_i = \mu + \alpha_i + e \quad (i = 1, 2, 3, 4)$$

If we perform this analysis, we obtain

$$SS_{within} = 0.336 + 0.241 + 0.149 + 0.176 = 0.902$$

The degrees of freedom are $k(n - 1) = 4 \times 9 = 36$, so

$$MS_{within} = 0.902/36 = 0.025$$

An investigator could use this value to calculate simultaneous confidence intervals for differences between pairs of condition means. The investigator could also evaluate all the comparisons between pairs of conditions by using Tukey's HSD; or, if a smaller number of these comparisons has been specified in advance, a method of planned comparisons such as the Bonferroni method could be employed.

Alternatively, the investigator could calculate a sum of squares for between conditions and use analysis of variance to evaluate the null hypothesis. Computing the sum of squares for between conditions gives a value of $SS_{between} = 1.454$. The analysis of variance summary table would then contain the values given in Table 7.18. The F-ratio from this table is $0.485/0.025 = 19.4$. This F-ratio has $df = 3$ in the numerator and $df = 36$ in the denominator. Consulting Statistical Table 5 of the F-distribution indicates that, with these degrees of freedom, the critical value of the F-ratio for $\alpha = .05$ is 2.87. Thus the null hypothesis must be rejected.

Although either of these two forms of the analysis is entirely permissible—and, in some cases, may even be preferable—they both fail to capture the 2×2 factorial arrangement of the conditions. Both these analyses treat the experiment simply as one with four conditions, ignoring the idea that there are two factors, each with two levels. For this reason, these analyses also fail to offer an explicit account of the concept of interaction—the distinction between additivity and nonadditivity.

Table 7.17 shows the same data (from DS07_07.dat in the *ASCII Files*) shown in Table 7.19, but in a 2×2 factorial arrangement. The following analysis captures the factorial structure of the conditions. It obtains sums of squares corresponding to the main effects and interaction terms in the model. This principle of correspondence between sums of squares and the terms in the model is one that we have seen in all our previous examples of analysis of variance.

The full model, complete with interaction term, is

$$Y_{ij} = \mu_{ij} + e = \mu + \alpha_i + \beta_j + \alpha\beta_{ij} + e$$

Table 7.18 One-way analysis of variance summary table for the braking reaction time experiment

Source	SS	df	MS
Model: Between conditions	1.454	3	0.485
Residual: Within condition	0.902	36	0.025
Total	2.356	39	—

Table 7.19 Data for the four conditions (from Table 7.17) arranged in a 2×2 factorial layout

		Sleep deprivation (B)	
		B_1 (none)	**B_2 (24 hours)**
Alcohol consumption (A)	**A_1 (none)**	0.9 0.4 0.6 0.7 0.6 0.8 0.8 0.5 1.0 0.5 $\overline{Y}_{11} = 0.68$	0.8 0.5 0.8 0.9 1.1 0.8 0.8 0.7 0.7 0.6 $\overline{Y}_{12} = 0.77$
	A_2 (1 ounce)	0.9 0.9 0.9 0.7 0.7 0.9 0.7 1.0 0.6 0.8 $\overline{Y}_{21} = 0.81$	1.4 1.2 1.1 1.3 1.3 1.2 1.1 0.9 1.2 1.1 $\overline{Y}_{22} = 1.18$

Equivalently,

$$Y_{ij} - \mu = \alpha_i + \beta_j + \alpha\beta_{ij} + e$$

The difference between this model and the one used for the previous analysis (Table 7.18) is that the single factor α used to denote all four conditions is partitioned into two separate factors (two main effects) and their interaction. Recall that the symbol α is used to denote the A factor (the main effect of alcohol consumption) and β is used to denote the B factor (the main effect of sleep deprivation).

The sum of squares between conditions is correspondingly partitioned into the two factors and their interaction.

$$SS_{between} = SS_A + SS_B + SS_{AB}$$

The total sum of squares then becomes

$$SS_{total} = SS_{between} + SS_{within} = SS_A + SS_B + SS_{AB} + SS_{within}$$

This partitioning of the total sum of squares is represented in Figure 7.7.

The between-conditions sum of squares can be partitioned into its main effects and interaction.

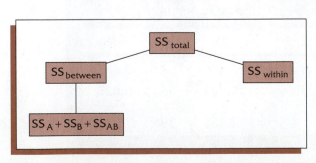

Figure 7.7
Partitioning of the total sum of squares into between-condition and residual sums of squares and the further partitioning of the between-condition sum of squares into main effects and their interaction.

The 2×2 factorial arrangement of the conditions and the corresponding partitioning of the sum of squares has no effect on the *within*-condition sum of squares. This fact becomes obvious when you consider the meaning of the within-condition sum of squares. It is the variability of scores within a condition about the mean of that condition, averaged over the conditions. This variability within each condition is the same, regardless of whether or not the conditions are arranged factorially.

The within-condition sum of squares is unchanged.

The first step in obtaining the partitioned between-condition sum of squares is to fit the expanded full model. We do this by estimating the various components. Although these calculations would normally be done on a computer, they will be performed explicitly on this simple data set so that the underlying logic of the computations becomes apparent.

In performing the calculations, it is helpful to set out the obtained cell means in a simple table. As Table 7.20 indicates in the bottom right-hand cell, the estimate of μ, the grand or overall mean, is 0.860.

The estimate of α_1 and α_2 (alcohol consumption main effect) are denoted by a_1 and a_2. For the no alcohol level of this factor, the estimate of α_1 is

$$a_1 = 0.725 - 0.860 = -0.135$$

For the 1-ounce alcohol level of this factor, the estimate of α_2 is

$$a_2 = 0.995 - 0.860 = +0.135$$

Notice that $a_1 + a_2 = 0$, a simple example of the zero-sum principle.

The estimate of β_1 and β_2 (sleep deprivation main effect) are denoted by b_1 and b_2. For no sleep deprivation, the estimate of β_1 is

$$b_1 = 0.745 - 0.860 = -0.115$$

For 24-hours sleep deprivation, the estimate of β_2 is

$$b_2 = 0.975 - 0.860 = +0.115$$

Notice that $b_1 + b_2 = 0$.

The estimates of interaction terms are denoted by ab_{11}, ab_{21}, etc. As the subscripts indicate, there is one such term for each of the four cells. The value of each of

Table 7.20 Cell means for the four conditions

		Sleep deprivation		
		None	24 hours	Row mean
Alcohol consumption	None	$\overline{Y}_{11} = 0.68$	$\overline{Y}_{12} = 0.77$	0.725
	1 ounce	$\overline{Y}_{21} = 0.81$	$\overline{Y}_{22} = 1.18$	0.995
	Column mean	0.745	0.975	0.860

Table 7.21 Estimates of the nonadditivity (interaction) components of the full model for the alcohol consumption and sleep deprivation experiment

		Sleep deprivation		
		None	24 hours	Row sum
Alcohol consumption	None	$ab_{11} = +0.070$	$ab_{12} = -0.070$	0
	1 ounce	$ab_{21} = -0.070$	$ab_{22} = +0.070$	0
	Column sum	0	0	0

these interaction terms represents the departure from additivity for that cell—the difference between the observed cell mean and the value for that cell predicted by the additive model. Their values can therefore be obtained by subtraction, just as they were in the previous example using parameter values. Thus the estimate of $\alpha\beta_{11}$ is

$$ab_{11} = \overline{Y}_{11} - (\overline{Y} + a_1 + b_1) = 0.680 - (0.860 - 0.135 - 0.115) = +0.070$$

The remaining estimates are obtained in a similar fashion.

$$ab_{21} = \overline{Y}_{21} - (\overline{Y} + a_2 + b_1) = 0.810 - (0.860 + 0.135 - 0.115) = -0.070$$
$$ab_{12} = \overline{Y}_{12} - (\overline{Y} + a_1 + b_2) = 0.770 - (0.860 - 0.135 + 0.115) = -0.070$$
$$ab_{22} = \overline{Y}_{22} - (\overline{Y} + a_2 + b_2) = 1.180 - (0.860 + 0.135 + 0.115) = +0.070$$

Note that the row and column sums of Table 7.21 must be 0. This property holds for all tables of interaction estimates.

Obtaining the Sum of Squares for the 2×2 Factorial Design

The values of SS_A, SS_B, and SS_{AB} can be obtained in the usual way.

■ For the alcohol factor,

$$SS_A = 20[a_1^2 + a_2^2] = 20[(-0.135)^2 + 0.135^2)] = 0.729$$

The multiplier 20 is the number of observations for each level of A, ignoring the B factor.

■ For the sleep deprivation factor,

$$SS_B = 20[b_1^2 + b_2^2] = 20[(-0.115)^2 + 0.115^2)] = 0.529$$

The multiplier 20 is the number of observations for each level of B, ignoring the A factor.

■ For the interaction between the two factors,

$$SS_{AB} = 10[ab_{11}^2 + ab_{21}^2 + ab_{12}^2 + ab_{22}^2]$$
$$= 10[(0.07^2) + (-0.07)^2 + (-0.07)^2 + (0.07)^2] = 0.196$$

The multiplier 10 is the number of observations for each of the four cells of the 2×2 table.

Adding together these sums of squares for A, B, and AB gives a total for the sum of squares for between conditions:

$$SS_{between} = SS_A + SS_B + SS_{AB}$$
$$= 0.729 + 0.529 + 0.196 = 1.454$$

Notice that this value of 1.454 is a familiar one. It is exactly the value obtained for the between-condition sum of squares in the previous one-way analysis reported in Table 7.18. That analysis considered the experiment as having one factor with four levels, yielding a between-condition sum of squares of 1.454. This new analysis partitions this between-condition sum of squares of 1.454 into component elements of $0.729 + 0.529 + 0.196$, corresponding respectively to the main effects of A, B and their interaction, $A \times B$.

This relationship between $SS_{between}$ and its contributing components offers an alternative method of calculating the interaction of sum of squares. If the values of $SS_{between}$, SS_A, and SS_B are known, then the interaction sum of squares can be obtained by subtraction:

$$SS_{AB} = SS_{between} - (SS_A + SS_B)$$

Degrees of Freedom

For one-way designs, the degrees of freedom for between conditions were the number of conditions minus 1, denoted $k - 1$. This same principle applies to the degrees of freedom for the main effects in factorial designs. The degrees of freedom for the A factor will be the number of levels of the A factor minus 1; the degrees of freedom for the B factor will be the number of levels of the B factor minus 1. In our 2×2 example, application of this principle results in $df = 1$ for both the alcohol consumption and sleep deprivation factors. For designs with factors that have more than two levels, the same general relationship holds. If the A factor has a levels, then there are $a - 1$ degrees of freedom for SS_A; if the B factor has b levels, then there are $b - 1$ degrees of freedom for SS_B.

You might expect that the degrees of freedom for the interaction term would be 3 because there are four values of ab_{ij}, but this expectation is wrong. The correct number of degrees of freedom is 1. One method of obtaining this number is by subtraction. Degrees of freedom can be added up, as can sums of squares.

Degrees of freedom are additive.

$$df_{between} = df_A + df_B + df_{AB}$$

Thus

$$df_{AB} = df_{between} - (df_A + df_B)$$

In the 2×2 case, the between-condition sum of squares, $SS_{between}$, has 3 degrees of freedom. In breaking down this value into sums of squares for the two main effects and their interaction, the two main effects account for a total of 2 degrees of freedom, 1 degree of freedom for the A main effect and 1 degree of freedom for the B main effect. This leaves 1 degree of freedom for the remaining interaction sum of squares.

A second way of deriving the degrees of freedom for the interaction is to notice the constraints on the four values, as illustrated in Table 7.21. For the main effects, the constraint is that the elements must sum to 0: $a_1 + a_2 = 0$, $b_1 + b_2 = 0$. With

Table 7.22 Analysis of variance summary table for the factorial version of the braking reaction time experiment

Source	SS	df	MS
Model: Between conditions	1.454	3	—
A (alcohol consumption)	0.729	1	0.729
B (sleep deprivation)	0.529	1	0.529
A × B	0.196	1	0.196
Residual: Within condition	0.902	36	0.025
Total	2.356	39	—

the interaction terms, there are similar constraints. Both rows *and* columns must sum to 0. It follows that once one of the values in the 2×2 table has been calculated, the remaining three values are determined. In a 2×2 factorial design, there is therefore just 1 degree of freedom for SS_{AB}.

For designs with factors that have more than two levels, the degrees of freedom for the interaction between A (with a levels) and B (with b levels) are $(a - 1)(b - 1)$.

Just as the sum of squares for the residuals (SS_{within}) is unaffected by the arrangement of the conditions, so too are the degrees of freedom. The degrees of freedom remain $n - 1$ times the number of conditions. When the conditions are arranged factorially, the number of conditions is $a \times b$. For the 2×2 design, there are four conditions; so the degrees of freedom of the residuals are $4(n - 1)$. The general formula for residual degrees of freedom is

$$df_e = a \times b(n - 1)$$

These various results can be set out in an analysis of variance summary table such as that shown in Table 7.22. The mean squares in the column headed "MS" are obtained in the usual way, by dividing the sum of squares by the corresponding degrees of freedom.

Evaluating *F*-Ratios for Main Effects and Interaction

Section 7.2 described the rationale for the use of the *F*-ratio and the *F*-distribution. This same rationale can be used to evaluate each of the condition mean squares in Table 7.22. An *F*-ratio is obtained for each of the three terms A, B, and A×B by dividing the mean square for the condition by the MS_{within}. For example, the *F*-ratio for the A factor is

There are separate *F*-ratios for each main effect and the interaction.

$$F_A = \frac{MS_A}{MS_{within}} = \frac{0.729}{0.025} = 29.16$$

The *F*-ratio for the B factor is

$$F_B = \frac{MS_B}{MS_{within}} = \frac{0.529}{0.025} = 21.16$$

The *F*-ratio for the AB interaction factor is

$$F_{AB} = \frac{MS_{AB}}{MS_{within}} = \frac{0.196}{0.025} = 7.84$$

The rationale for testing the null hypothesis in the case of the one-way design was described in Section 7.2.4. This same rationale can be applied to each of the three *F*-ratios in the two-way factorial design.

The null hypothesis for the A factor is that all the $\alpha_i = 0$. If this null hypothesis is true, then MS_A and MS_{within} are both determined only by noise, so their ratio should not differ significantly from 1.0. The *F*-distribution provides the basis for making this evaluation. For F_A, the degrees of freedom are 1 and 36. The critical *F*-value against which this obtained *F*-ratio should be compared is obtained from the table of the *F*-distribution (Statistical Table 5). Using $\alpha = .05$, the critical *F* value for $df = 1$ and 36 is 4.11. The F_A of 29.16 exceeds this critical value, so the null hypothesis for the A factor is rejected.

The null hypothesis for the B factor is that all the $\beta_j = 0$. If this null hypothesis is true, then the ratio of MS_B and MS_{within} should not differ significantly from 1.0. Again, the *F*-distribution provides the basis for making this evaluation. For F_B, the degrees of freedom are 1 and 36. The critical *F* value for $df = 1$ and 36 is 4.11. The obtained F_B of 21.16 exceeds this critical value, so the null hypothesis for the B factor is also rejected.

The null hypothesis for the AB interaction is that all the $\alpha\beta_{ij} = 0$. If this null hypothesis is true, then the ratio of MS_{AB} and MS_{within} should not differ significantly from 1.0. For F_{AB}, the degrees of freedom are 1 and 36, the same as for F_A and F_B. The critical *F* value is therefore again 4.11. The obtained F_{AB} of 7.84 exceeds this critical value, so the null hypothesis for the B factor is also rejected.

The rejection of all three null hypotheses indicates that, to account for the data, the model must retain parameters for all three components: the main effects, α_i and β_j, and the interaction term, $\alpha\beta_{ij}$.

R^2 is the proportion of the total sum of squares accounted for by the model. For the analysis reported in Table 7.24, we have

$$R^2 = \frac{SS_{model}}{SS_{total}} = \frac{1.454}{2.356} = .62$$

7.3.3 A Closer Look at Main Effects and Interactions

The data for the braking reaction time experiment required a full model containing parameters for both main effects and for the interaction. Results from other experiments might demand fewer parameters. At the other extreme from the full model is the null model:

$$\text{null model:} \quad Y_{ij} = \mu + e$$

An analysis of variance result that failed to reject any of the null hypotheses would make this model appropriate. In this case, there would be no evidence that either factor or any combination of the two factors influences the response measure.

It is possible that the results might demand any combination of α_i, β_j, and $\alpha\beta_{ij}$ to be retained. For example, if the only significant *F*-ratio were F_A, then the appropriate model would be

model requiring only a pararameter
for the A factor: $\qquad$ $Y_{ij} = \mu + \alpha_i + e$

If both main effects F_A and F_B were significant, but the interaction F_{AB} were not, then the appropriate model would be the additive model:

additive model: $\quad Y_{ij} = \mu + \alpha_i + \beta_j + e$

Only one of the main effects—F_B, say—and the interaction F_{AB} might be significant. In this case, the appropriate model would be

model requiring a pararameter
for the B factor and its interaction: $\quad Y_{ij} = \mu + \beta_j + \alpha\beta_{ij} + e$

It is possible for the interaction F_{AB} to be significant without either of the main effects being significant. In this case, the appropriate model would be

model requiring only a pararameter
for the interaction factor: $\qquad$ $Y_{ij} = \mu + \alpha\beta_{ij} + e$

Imaginary Drug and Therapy Experiment

To make the various model possibilities more concrete, we will take a hypothetical experiment and consider examples of various combinations of present and absent parameters. This imaginary experiment was designed to evaluate the effectiveness of two factors in the treatment of depression. Factor A is a drug treatment factor with two levels: A_1, drug; A_2, placebo control. Factor B is a psychotherapy factor and also has two levels: B_1, therapy; B_2, no therapy control. The conditions can thus be arranged in a two-way (2×2) factorial form. The experiment is to be conducted using a completely randomized design.

■ Participants in the drug/therapy condition (Y_{11}) receive both the drug and accompanying psychotherapy.

■ Participants in the placebo/therapy condition (Y_{21}) do not receive the drug but *do* receive psychotherapy.

■ Participants in the drug/no therapy condition (Y_{12}) receive the drug but no psychotherapy.

■ Participants in the placebo/no therapy condition (Y_{22}) receive neither the drug nor the accompanying psychotherapy.

The response variable is a measure of well-being; the larger the score, the more beneficial the treatment. The full model is

$$Y_{ij} = \mu + \alpha_i + \beta_j + \alpha\beta_{ij} + e$$

The full model's specification for each condition of this experiment is set out in Table 7.23.

Consider the following situations in which only some of the parameters remain in the model. These situations illustrate the range of possible results that might be obtained from such an experiment.

Situation 1. Main effect for B, no A effect, and no interaction The model is

$$Y_{ij} = \mu + \beta_j + e$$

Table 7.23 Components of the full model for the 2×2 factorial design of the imaginary drug/therapy experiment

		B (therapy factor)	
		B_1 (therapy)	**B_2 (no therapy)**
A (drug) factor	**A_1 (drug)**	$\begin{aligned} Y_{11} &= \mu_{11} + e \\ &= \mu + \alpha_1 + \beta_1 \\ &\quad + \alpha\beta_{11} + e \end{aligned}$	$\begin{aligned} Y_{12} &= \mu_{12} + e \\ &= \mu + \alpha_1 + \beta_2 \\ &\quad + \alpha\beta_{12} + e \end{aligned}$
	A_2 (placebo)	$\begin{aligned} Y_{21} &= \mu_{21} + e \\ &= \mu + \alpha_2 + \beta_1 \\ &\quad + \alpha\beta_{21} + e \end{aligned}$	$\begin{aligned} Y_{22} &= \mu_{22} + e \\ &= \mu + \alpha_2 + \beta_2 \\ &\quad + \alpha\beta_{22} + e \end{aligned}$

Suppose that the population cell means were those shown in Table 7.24. In this case,

$$\mu = (7 + 7 + 3 + 3)/4 = 5$$

$$\beta_1 = 7 - 5 = +2$$

$$\beta_2 = 3 - 5 = -2$$

The values of α_1, α_2, and all $\alpha\beta_{ij}$ are 0.

Figure 7.8 gives a graph of these cell means. These parameter values would describe a situation in which therapy was beneficial but the drug had no effect at all. The absence of an interaction indicates that the effect of therapy and the drug are additive. The effect of the therapy is the same for both levels of the A factor, that is, the effect is the same for both drug and placebo—a difference of 4 Y-units in both cases. Equivalently, the absence of an interaction reflects the fact that the drug has the same effect (none) for both levels of the B factor.

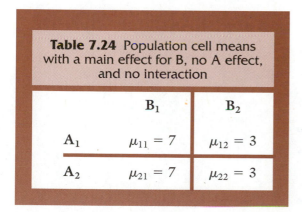

Table 7.24 Population cell means with a main effect for B, no A effect, and no interaction

	B_1	**B_2**
A_1	$\mu_{11} = 7$	$\mu_{12} = 3$
A_2	$\mu_{21} = 7$	$\mu_{22} = 3$

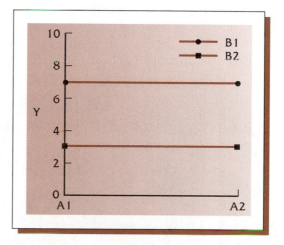

Figure 7.8
Graph of the data in Table 7.24, showing a main effect for B but no A effect and no interaction.

Table 7.25 Population cell means with main effects but no interaction

	B_1	B_2
A_1	$\mu_{11} = 8$	$\mu_{12} = 5$
A_2	$\mu_{21} = 4$	$\mu_{22} = 1$

Situation 2. Main effect for A and B, but no interaction The model is

$$Y_{ij} = \mu + \alpha_i + \beta_j + e$$

There is no interaction, so the $\alpha\beta_{ij}$ are all 0. Suppose that the population cell means were those shown in Table 7.25. In this case,

$$\mu = 4.5$$
$$\alpha_1 = 6.5 - 4.5 = +2$$
$$\alpha_2 = 2.5 - 4.5 = -2$$
$$\beta_1 = 6 - 4.5 = +1.5$$
$$\beta_2 = 3 - 4.5 = -1.5$$

The data given in Table 7.25 and graphed in Figure 7.9 show additive main effects.

Figure 7.9 gives a graph of these parameter values, which describe a situation in which drug treatment and therapy are both beneficial. The absence of an interaction indicates that both these effects are the same for both levels of the other factor. For example, therapy produces the same degree of improvement for both drug and placebo participants (3 Y-units in both cases). Equivalently, the absence of an interaction reflects the fact that the drug has the same effect for both levels of the B factor.

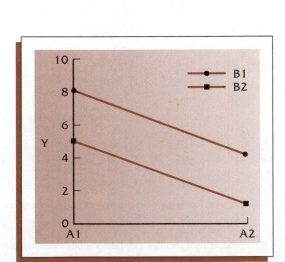

Figure 7.9
Graph of the data in Table 7.25, showing a main effect for A and B, but no interaction.

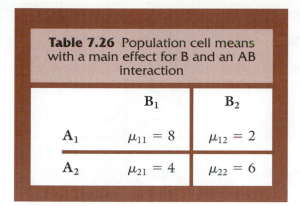

Table 7.26 Population cell means with a main effect for B and an AB interaction

	B_1	B_2
A_1	$\mu_{11} = 8$	$\mu_{12} = 2$
A_2	$\mu_{21} = 4$	$\mu_{22} = 6$

Table 7.27 AB ($\alpha\beta_{ij}$) interaction terms for the cell means in Table 7.28

	B_1	B_2
A_1	$\alpha\beta_{11} = +2$	$\alpha\beta_{12} = -2$
A_2	$\alpha\beta_{21} = -2$	$\alpha\beta_{22} = +2$

There is an improvement of 4 Y-units for participants in both the therapy and no therapy conditions.

It was previously stated that, when no interaction is present, the main effects are described as *additive*. In this example, the meaning of this term is clear.

The drug produces an improvement of 4 Y-units and therapy produces an improvement of 3 Y-units. Participants who receive both the drug and therapy improve by an amount of 3 + 4 = 7 Y-units relative to participants who receive neither. The effects of drug and therapy combine additively.

Situation 3. Main effect for B and an AB interaction The model is

$$Y_{ij} = \mu + \beta_j + \alpha\beta_{ij} + e$$

In this example, there is no A effect. Suppose the cell means were those shown in Table 7.26. The interaction components of the model ($\alpha\beta_{ij}$) are given in Table 7.27.

Figure 7.10 gives a graph of the cell means and the interaction parameter values. Because there is an interaction parameter, no simple interpretation of the main effects is possible. There is no drug main effect, for example, because, *averaged across the*

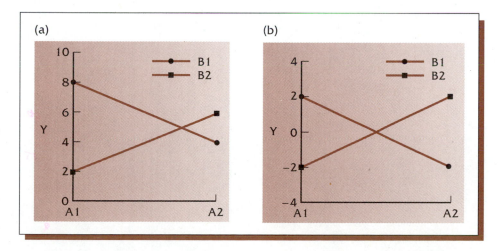

Figure 7.10
(a) Plot of cell means from Table 7.26, showing a main effect for B and an AB interaction, but no A effect. (b) Graph of the AB interaction (Table 7.27).

Table 7.28 Parameter values (population condition means) with no main effects but an AB interaction

	B_1	B_2
A_1	$\mu_{11} = 4$	$\mu_{12} = 6$
A_2	$\mu_{21} = 6$	$\mu_{22} = 4$

Table 7.29 AB ($\alpha\beta_{ij}$) interaction terms for the cell means in Table 7.30

	B_1	B_2
A_1	$\alpha\beta_{11} = -1$	$\alpha\beta_{12} = +1$
A_2	$\alpha\beta_{21} = +1$	$\alpha\beta_{22} = -1$

It is often very misleading to interpret main effects when there is an interaction.

levels of B, the drug and placebo conditions yield the same mean of 5. Yet the drug does make a difference, *depending on whether it is accompanied by therapy*. When accompanied by therapy, the drug enhances the beneficial effects of therapy. Without therapy, the drug has a negative effect. This positive effect with therapy combined with the negative effect without therapy results in the average (main) effect of 0. However, it is obviously seriously misleading to describe this absence of a main effect with a claim that "the drug has no effect in the treatment of depression."

The interaction can also be described from the perspective of the B factor. It is quite misleading to describe the main effect of therapy as "therapy produces beneficial effects," because this statement is not true for both the drug and placebo levels of the A factor. The effects of therapy differ, depending on whether or not therapy is accompanied by drug treatment.

Situation 4. No main effects but an AB interaction The model is

$$Y_{ij} = \mu + \alpha\beta_{ij} + e$$

There is no A effect and no B effect, so the α_i and the β_j are all 0. Suppose that the parameter values were those shown in Table 7.28. The interaction terms are shown in Table 7.29, and Figure 7.11 gives a graph of the cell means and the interaction pa-

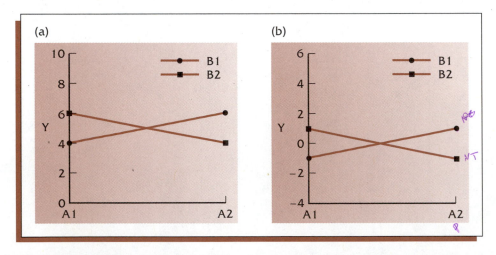

Figure 7.11
(a) Plot of cell means in Table 7.28, showing an AB interaction, but no A or B main effects. (b) Graph of the interaction (Table 7.29).

rameter values. As in the previous example, because there is an interaction parameter, there is no simple interpretation of the main effects. There is no drug or therapy main effect because, averaged across the levels of B, the drug and placebo conditions yield the same mean of 5; and averaged across the levels of A, the therapy and no therapy conditions yield the same mean, also of 5. Yet both the drug and therapy *do* make a difference, depending on how they are combined. When therapy and the drug are administered in combination, they interact in a way that is detrimental relative to either therapy or drug administered alone. In fact, drug and therapy combined yield the same outcome as administering neither; one appears to cancel the effect of the other.

The form of the interaction shown in Figures 7.10 and 7.11 is sometimes described as a "strong" or "crossover" interaction. In this case, the interaction reflects, not just a difference in the magnitude of the effect of one factor at the levels of the other, but a reversal of order. In Figure 7.11, for A_1 (drug), no therapy (B_2) is better than therapy (B_1); but for A_2 (placebo), this order is reversed, that is, B_1 is better than B_2. Again, it is obviously seriously misleading to describe this absence of a main effect with a claim that "neither therapy nor the drug is beneficial in the treatment of depression."

Patterns of Nonadditivity

A significant interaction effect in analysis of variance indicates that the interaction term $\alpha\beta$ should be kept in the model. However, the story does not end at this point. The interaction can reflect a number of quite different patterns of nonadditivity, just as a significant overall main effect can correspond to different patterns of differences and nondifferences between the means of pairs of conditions. The interaction implies simply that *somewhere* among the pattern of cell means, additivity has been violated.

Even a simple 2×2 interaction can take several forms and needs further clarification. Consider the three possibilities shown in Figure 7.12. The graphs depict population cell means, and all three reveal the presence of an interaction. Graph (a) shows a case in which B_1 is greater than B_2 for both A_1 and A_2. The interaction is a consequence of the difference being greater for A_1 than for A_2. Graph (b) shows a case in which B_1 is greater than B_2 for A_1 but not different for A_2. Graph (c) depicts a crossover interaction in which there is a difference between B_1 and B_2 for both A_1 and A_2, but in the opposite direction.

> The interaction can reflect a number of quite different patterns of nonadditivity.

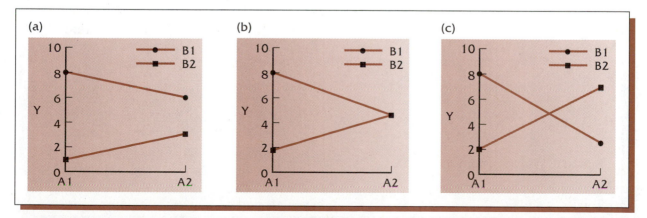

Figure 7.12
Three examples of an interaction in a 2×2 factorial design.

These examples make the obvious point that to report merely that "the interaction was significant" is to leave open a very wide range of possibilities and that such a statement needs to be followed up with a more explicit analysis of the exact form that the interaction takes. In the case of the 2×2 interaction, this analysis involves evaluation of the difference between the two levels of a factor at each level of the other factor: Is there a difference between B_1 and B_2 at A_1? Is there a difference between B_1 and B_2 at A_2? Tukey's procedure or some other post hoc procedure could be used to answer such questions.

7.3.4 General Two-Way Factorial Design

Thus far, all the examples of factorial designs have had just two levels of each factor, although we have stated that, in general, such designs may have any number of levels. We used a to indicate the number of levels of factor A and b, the number of levels of factor B. The general analysis of variance summary table is shown in Table 7.30.

Consider now an experiment with three levels of the A factor and two levels of the B factor—a 3×2 factorial design. We have already considered a number of examples of experiments designed to investigate the effectiveness of therapy for the treatment of anxiety or fear. The last example was an experiment that included two kinds of therapy as well as a counseling-only control condition. Consider now a further extension of this investigation. The therapy and counseling programs have been conducted over a number of sessions and the investigator asks whether more sessions might bring further improvements. The goal then is to compare two treatment lengths: the original and an extended version. For convenience, we will refer to these two lengths respectively as "short" (S) and "long" (L).

Table 7.30 Analysis of variance summary table for a general two-way factorial design

Source	SS	df	MS	F-ratio
Model: Between conditions	SS_{model}	$ab - 1$	—	—
A	SS_A	$a - 1$	$\dfrac{SS_A}{a - 1}$	$\dfrac{MS_A}{MS_{within}}$
B	SS_B	$b - 1$	$\dfrac{SS_B}{b - 1}$	$\dfrac{MS_B}{MS_{within}}$
A×B	SS_{AB}	$(a - 1)(b - 1)$	$\dfrac{SS_{AB}}{(a - 1)(b - 1)}$	$\dfrac{MS_{AB}}{MS_{within}}$
Residual: Within condition	SS_{within}	$ab(n - 1)$	$\dfrac{SS_{within}}{ab(n - 1)}$	—
Total	SS_{total}	$abn - 1$	—	—

As a practitioner, the investigator wants to answer questions such as

■ The previous experiment provided no evidence that the two therapies differed. However, will a difference emerge with more sessions? Perhaps one therapy, but not the other, will yield further improvement.

■ The previous experiment provided evidence that the two therapies were more beneficial than counseling alone. Will the counseling-only condition prove more beneficial with more sessions?

The experiment is a completely randomized design with six conditions. Three of the six conditions are the same as those of the earlier experiment: counseling, systematic desensitization therapy, and counterconditioning administered for the short duration. The other three conditions use the same three forms of treatment, but administer them for the longer duration. The investigator uses a total of 60 participants. They are assigned randomly to the six conditions, $n = 10$ participants in each. The response measure is rated anxiety level. The data are in DS07_08.dat in the *ASCII Files*.

Hypothetical cell means from such an experiment are given in Table 7.31. Another way of displaying this structure of the conditions is through a graph, so a plot of these six condition means is given in Figure 7.13.

Application of the formulas given in Section 7.3.2 gives $SS_A = 480.0$; $SS_B = 60.0$; $SS_{AB} = 40.0$; $SS_{within} = 244.0$. With these values, we can complete the analysis of variance summary table. The *F*-ratios in the last column of Table 7.32 were obtained in the same way as before, by dividing the mean square for the factor by the MS_{within}. For example, the *F*-ratio for the A factor is

$$F_A = \frac{MS_A}{MS_{within}} = \frac{240}{4.52} = 53.1$$

There are separate *F*-ratios for each main effect and the interaction.

Table 7.31 Cell means based on the data for the expanded therapy evaluation experiment arranged in a 3×2 factorial layout ($n = 10$ participants in each cell)

		B (duration of therapy)		
		B_1 (short)	B_2 (long)	Row Mean $\overline{Y}_A$
A (form of therapy)	A_1 (counseling)	$\overline{Y}_{11} = 11$	$\overline{Y}_{12} = 11$	11
	A_2 (systematic desensitization)	$\overline{Y}_{21} = 7$	$\overline{Y}_{22} = 3$	5
	A_3 (counter-conditioning)	$\overline{Y}_{31} = 6$	$\overline{Y}_{32} = 4$	5
	Column mean $\overline{Y}_B$	8	6	$\overline{Y} = 7$

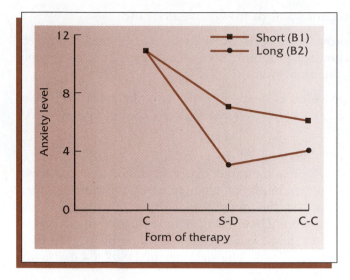

Figure 7.13
Plot of means for the six conditions from Table 7.31: C, counseling (A_1); S-D, systematic desensitization (A_2); C-C, counterconditioning (A_3).

The null hypothesis for the A factor is that all three of the $\alpha_i = 0$. If this null hypothesis is true, then MS_A and MS_{within} reflect only noise, so their ratio should not differ significantly from 1.0. The F-distribution provides the basis for making this evaluation. For F_A, the degrees of freedom are 2 and 54. The critical F-value against which this obtained F-ratio should be compared is obtained from the table of the F-distribution (Statistical Table 5). Using $\alpha = .05$, the critical F-value for $df = 2$ and 54 is 3.18. The F_A exceeds this critical value, so the null hypothesis for the A factor is rejected.

The null hypothesis for the B factor is that both $\beta_j = 0$. If this null hypothesis is true, then the ratio of MS_B and MS_{within} should not differ significantly from 1.0. Again, the F-distribution provides the basis for making this evaluation. For F_B, the degrees of freedom are 1 and 54. The critical F-value for $df = 1$ and 54 is 4.03. The obtained F_B of 13.3 exceeds this critical value, so the null hypothesis for the B factor is also rejected.

Table 7.32 Analysis of variance summary table for the 3×2 factorial phobia treatment experiment

Source	SS	df	MS	F-ratio
Model: Between conditions	580	5	—	—
A (form of therapy)	480	2	240	53.1
B (duration)	60	1	60	13.3
A×B	40	2	20	4.4
Residuals: Within condition	244	54	4.52	—
Total	824	59	—	—

The null hypothesis for the AB interaction is that all the $\alpha\beta_{ij} = 0$. If this null hypothesis is true, then the ratio of MS_{AB} and MS_{within} should not differ significantly from 1.0. For F_{AB}, the degrees of freedom are 1 and 54, the same as for F_B. The critical F-value is therefore again 4.03. The obtained F_{AB} of 4.4 exceeds this critical value, so the null hypothesis for the B factor is also rejected.

The interpretation of interactions in factorial experiments larger than 2×2 can become quite complex. Often the investigator will be more interested in differences between individual cell means than in the overall interaction. These more detailed analyses are beyond the scope of this introductory text. However, even at the introductory level, the important point to be remembered is that the accurate communication of results demands that interactions need to be "unpacked" and interpreted with greater specificity than is provided by a simple statement that the analysis of variance shows that an interaction exists.

If an investigator's interest is only in differences between individual cell means, then, once the value of MS_{within} has been calculated, the overall analysis of variance can be bypassed in favor of directly calculating confidence intervals for the relevant cell mean differences. Section 7.1 demonstrated this strategy with respect to one-way designs. Although this direct attack has much to recommend it, by far the most common practice among investigators is to perform the overall analysis of variance.

The rejection of all three null hypotheses indicates that, to account for the data, the model must retain parameters for all three components: the main effects, α_i and β_j, and the interaction term, $\alpha\beta_{ij}$.

As with other designs, we can calculate R^2:

$$R^2 = \frac{SS_{model}}{SS_{total}} = \frac{580}{824} = .70$$

R^2 is the proportion of the total sum of squares accounted for by the model.

Comprehension Check 7.3

Important Concepts

1. Larger experiments are often designed with a factorial layout consisting of two (or more) factors, with each factor having two or more levels. In a two-factor experiment, the factors can be labeled A and B, and subscripts i and j are used to indicate the levels of A and B, respectively (see Box 7.1). If the A factor has a levels and the B factor has b levels, then the experiment is described as an $a \times b$ factorial design. The examples considered in this section were 2×2 and 3×2 designs.

2. Models of factorial designs distinguish between main effects and their interaction. In a two-factor experiment, main effects are differences among the means of levels of one factor averaged over the levels of the other factor. An interaction reflects the nonadditivity of the main effects, that is, the influence of one factor is different at different levels of the other factor.

3. Estimates of the main effect for each level of a factor are obtained by subtracting the grand mean from the mean for that level. An estimate of interaction effect for a condition is obtained by subtracting the grand mean and the sum of main effects from the condition mean.

Box 7.1

Summary of Notation for Two-Way Factorial Designs

- A and B are labels for the two factors.

- a is the number of levels for Factor A.

- b is the number of levels for Factor B.

- i is the subscript used to indicate the level of the A factor; $i = 1, 2, \ldots, a$.

- j is the subscript used to indicate the level of the B factor; $j = 1, 2, \ldots, b$.

  Thus,

- Y_{ij} are the observations for the cell corresponding to the ith level of factor A and the jth level of factor B.

- $\overline{Y}_{ij}$ is the mean of the observations for the cell corresponding to the ith level of factor A and the jth level of factor B.

  The full model for the two-way factorial design is

  $$Y_{ij} = \mu + \alpha_i + \beta_j + \alpha\beta_{ij} + e$$

  where

- μ is the grand mean; its estimate is $\overline{Y}$.

- α_i is the effect of the ith level of factor A; its estimate is $\mathbf{a}_i$.

- β_j is the effect of the jth level of factor B; its estimate is $\mathbf{b}_j$.

4. The analysis of variance summary table records the partitioning of the $SS_{between}$ term into its three contributing components (SS_A, SS_B, and SS_{AB}) and the corresponding partitioning of the degrees of freedom.

5. Mean squares are obtained by dividing the sums of squares by their degrees of freedom. Values for these degrees of freedom are $df_A = a - 1$; $df_B = b - 1$; $df_{AB} = (a - 1)(b - 1)$. Note that these degrees of freedom sum to $df_{between} = ab - 1$.

6. F-ratios for each of MS_A, MS_B, and MS_{AB} are obtained by dividing the mean square by MS_{within}. The three null hypotheses are tested by comparing these obtained F-ratios with the critical F-values for a given significance level obtained from the table of the F-distribution. Note that each of the three mean squares will have its own F-ratio.

7. Decisions about the three null hypotheses determine which parameters of the full model—all of them, none, or any combination of them—should be retained.

Box 7.1 *(continued)*

- $\alpha\beta_{ij}$ is the interaction effect of the ijth condition; its estimate is $\mathbf{ab}_{ij}$.
- e is the residual associated with each observation.

- SS_A is the sum of squares for the A factor.
- SS_B is the sum of squares for the B factor.
- SS_{AB} is the sum of squares for the interaction between A and B.
- $SS_{model} = SS_{between} = SS_A + SS_B + SS_{AB}$.
- $SS_{within} = SS_e$, the sum of squares within conditions.
- $SS_{total} = SS_{model} + SS_{within}$.

- df_A is the degrees of freedom for the A factor; $df_A = (a - 1)$.
- df_B is the degrees of freedom for the B factor; $df_B = (b - 1)$.
- df_{AB} is the degrees of freedom for the AB interaction; $df_{AB} = (a - 1)(b - 1)$.

- MS_A is the mean square for the A factor; $MS_A = SS_A / df_A$.
- MS_B is the mean square for the B factor; $MS_B = SS_B / df_B$.
- MS_{AB} is the mean square for the AB interaction; $MS_{AB} = SS_{AB} / df_{AB}$.

- F_A is the F-ratio for the A factor; $F_A = MS_A / MS_{within}$.
- F_B is the F-ratio for the B factor; $F_B = MS_B / MS_{within}$.
- F_{AB} is the F-ratio for the interaction between A and B; $F_{AB} = MS_{AB} / MS_{within}$.

Worked Examples

Example 1   Tranquilizer Effects (DS07_09.dat in the *ASCII Files*)

This example is a further investigation of the tranquilizer T1 used in the Example 1 at the end of Sections 7.1 and 7.2. An investigator hypothesizes that T1 might show sex differences in its effect on cognitive functioning. To test this hypothesis, the investigator uses a 2×2 design. The two levels of factor A are A_1, placebo control; A_2, tranquilizer. The two levels of factor B are B_1, female; B_2, male. There are 40 women and 40 men participating in the experiment, with 20 of each sex assigned randomly to the tranquilizer and placebo conditions. The response variable is time taken to complete the task.

The means and sums of squares are given in Table 7.33. The sum of squared residuals for the null model is $SS_{total} = 1312.64$. The combined $SS_{between} = 339.22$, and it breaks down into

$$SS_A = 315.22$$

$$SS_B = 16.56$$

$$SS_{AB} = 7.44$$

Table 7.33 Cell means and sums of squares for the four conditions for the tranquilizer effects experiment (Worked Example 1)

		B (sex)	
		B_1 (female)	B_2 (male)
A (treatment)	A_1 (placebo)	$\overline{Y}_{11} = 8.37$ $SS_{11} = 185.1$	$\overline{Y}_{12} = 8.67$ $SS_{12} = 283.9$
	A_2 (T1)	$\overline{Y}_{21} = 11.73$ $SS_{21} = 270.5$	$\overline{Y}_{22} = 13.25$ $SS_{22} = 233.9$

a. Draw a graph of the results in terms of the mean for each condition.

b. Estimate the value of all parameters of the full model.

c. Complete the analysis of variance summary table.

d. What is the value of R^2 for this experiment?

Answer

a. See Figure 7.14.

b. The full model is $Y_{ij} = \mu + \alpha_i + \beta_j + \alpha\beta_{ij} + e$. Estimates of the components of this model are

$$\mu: \quad \overline{Y} = (8.37 + 11.73 + 8.67 + 13.25)/4 = 10.505$$
$$\alpha_i: \quad a_1 = (8.37 + 8.67)/2 - 10.505 = -1.985$$
$$a_2 = (11.73 + 13.25)/2 - 10.505 = +1.985$$
$$\beta_j: \quad b_1 = (8.37 + 11.73)/2 - 10.505 = -0.455$$
$$b_2 = (8.67 + 13.25)/2 - 10.505 = +0.455$$

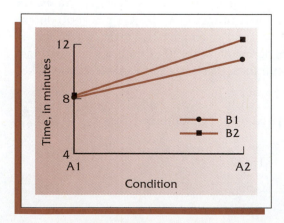

Figure 7.14
Plot of the results of tranquilizer effects experiment. A1 = Placebo; A2 = T1; B1 = Female; B2 = Male.

Table 7.34 Two-way analysis of variance summary table for the tranquilizer effects experiment

Source	SS	df	MS	F
Model: Between conditions	339.22	3	—	—
A (tranq./plac.)	315.22	1	315.22	24.6
B (sex)	16.56	1	16.56	1.29
A×B	7.44	1	7.44	0.58
Residual: Within condition	973.42	76	12.81	—
Total	1312.64	79	—	—

$\alpha\beta_{ij}$: $\quad ab_{11} = 8.37 - (10.505 - 1.985 - 0.455) = +0.305$

$\quad ab_{21} = 11.73 - (10.505 + 1.985 - 0.455) = -0.305$

$\quad ab_{12} = 8.67 - (10.505 - 1.985 + 0.455) = -0.305$

$\quad ab_{22} = 13.25 - (10.505 + 1.985 + 0.455) = +0.305$

Note that these estimates can be used to calculate SS_A, SS_B, and SS_{AB}.

$$SS_A = 40[(-1.985)^2 + 1.985^2] = 315.22$$

$$SS_B = 40[(-0.455)^2 + 0.455^2] = 16.56$$

$$SS_{AB} = 20[0.305^2 + (-0.305)^2 + (-0.305)^2 + 0.305^2] = 7.44$$

c. To complete the sums of squares column of the analysis of variance summary table (Table 7.34), we need SS_{within} in addition to the results provided.

$$SS_{within} = 185.1 + 270.5 + 283.9 + 233.9 = 973.4$$

d. The value of R^2 is $SS_{model}/SS_{total} = 339.22/1312.64 = .26$.

Example 2   State-dependent retrieval (Data Set 7.10)

This experiment examines state-dependent retrieval where the "state" is mild alcohol intoxication. According to the state-dependent hypothesis, words studied in a state of intoxication should be better recalled in that state than in a sober state, and words studied in the sober state should be better recalled in the sober state. A total of 80 participants are used, 20 being assigned to each of the four conditions. Half of these participants (40) study a list of words while sober, the other half after having consumed a fixed quantity of alcohol sufficient to produce mild intoxication. After a 48-hour retention interval, all participants are required to recall the words. Half of the participants who studied the words while sober attempt this recall test while mildly intoxicated, the other half while sober. Similarly, half of the participants who studied the words while intoxicated attempt recall while sober, the other half while mildly intoxicated. Data Set 7.10 gives the proportion of words recalled by each subject in each of the four conditions. For a discussion of results such as those presented here, see Eich (1980).

Data Set 7.10   Data for the four conditions in the state-dependent retrieval experiment (Worked Example 2)

Acquisition in sober state (A_1)

B_1 (recall in sober state), $\overline{Y}_{11} = .442$, $SS_{11} = .3365$

.13	.43	.43	.35	.38	.48	.50	.30	.40	.73
.43	.60	.53	.50	.28	.30	.50	.58	.55	.43

B_2 (recall in intoxicated state), $\overline{Y}_{12} = .291$, $SS_{12} = .4102$

.21	.26	.01	.43	.31	.46	.21	.23	.38	.33
.43	.11	.21	.43	.21	.18	.53	.53	.28	.08

Acquisition in intoxicated state (A_2)

B_1 (recall in sober state), $\overline{Y}_{21} = .201$, $SS_{21} = .5057$

.20	.15	.35	.40	.12	.02	.37	.22	.07	.00
.00	.22	.00	.07	.55	.05	.35	.25	.20	.42

B_2 (recall in intoxicated state), $\overline{Y}_{22} = .299$, $SS_{22} = .5553$

.46	.53	.06	.31	.03	.48	.16	.16	.58	.18
.46	.26	.18	.38	.08	.36	.21	.38	.18	.53

The sum of squared residuals for the null model is $SS_{total} = 2.4029$. The combined $SS_{between} = 0.5952$, and it breaks down into

$$SS_A = 0.2726$$

$$SS_B = 0.0138$$

$$SS_{AB} = 0.3088$$

a. Draw a graph of the results in terms of the mean for each condition.

b. Complete the analysis of variance summary table. Using $\alpha = .05$, decide which terms should remain in the model.

c. Suppose you had no table for the F-distribution. Use the table of the t-distribution to derive the critical F-value for $\alpha = .05$, checking that it corresponds to the value used in answering (b).

d. What is the value of R^2 for this experiment?

e. Provide a verbal description of the results.

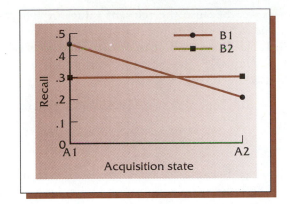

Figure 7.15
Plot of the results of the state dependent retrieval experiment. A1, sober at acquisition; A2, intoxicated at acquisition; B1, sober at recall; B2, intoxicated at recall.

Answer

a. See Figure 7.15.

b. In a 2×2 design, the degrees of freedom for the main effects and interaction are 1, as in the previous example. The SS$_{within}$ is .3365 + .4102 + .5057 + .5553 = 1.8077. The degrees of freedom for SS$_{within}$ are $ab(n − 1) = 4 \times 19 = 76$. [Each of the 2×2 = 4 conditions contributes $(n − 1) = 19$ degrees of freedom.] With this result, we can complete the analysis of variance summary table (Table 7.35). The critical value of the F-ratio can be obtained from the tables of the F-distribution. Because all three components have the same degrees of freedom in the numerator ($df = 1$) and identical denominators (MS$_{within}$), the critical value of the F-ratio will be the same for all three. From Statistical Table 5 this value is found to be 3.97, using $df = 75$, the closest lower tabled value.

The obtained F-values for the A factor and the AB interaction exceed this critical value; the F-value for the B factor does not. Thus the data require a parameter for the A effect and for the AB interaction. The model would therefore be

$$Y_{ij} = \mu + \alpha_i + \alpha\beta_{ij} + e$$

Table 7.35 Two-way analysis of variance summary table for the state-dependent retrieval experiment (Worked Example 2)

Source	SS	df	MS	F
Model: Between conditions	.5952	3	—	—
A	.2726	1	.2726	11.46
B	.0138	1	.0138	0.58
A×B	.3088	1	.3088	12.98
Residual: Within condition	1.8077	76	.0238	—
Total	2.4029	79	—	—

c. Because the relevant values of F have 1 degree of freedom in the numerator, the value of F will be equivalent to t^2 with degrees of freedom 76. From Statistical Table 3, we find that, for $df = 76$, the value of t is between 1.990 ($df = 80$) and 1.994 ($df = 70$). Squaring each of these gives t-values of 3.96 and 3.98. The F-value used in (b) was 3.97.

d. The value of R^2 for this experiment is

$$R_2 = \frac{SS_{between}}{SS_{total}} = \frac{.5952}{2.4029} = .248$$

e. Because of the interaction, care needs to be taken in describing the results. The interaction supports the hypothesis of state-dependent remembering. This is the claim that recall is better if it occurs in the same state as that in which the material was studied. However, in addition to this interactive effect, there is a main effect of A, which indicates that sobriety is better than intoxication. Thus the best single condition is one that combines state identity with being sober: It is best to be sober both when studying and when remembering.

Example 3   Drug treatment experiment

An experiment is designed to evaluate the effects of four different drug treatments (including a placebo control) on three different clinical populations. The experiment uses a 4×3 factorial design. Independent samples, each of 36 volunteers from each of the three clinical populations, are chosen. Each of these samples is randomly divided among the four drug conditions, 9 volunteers in each.

a. Complete the analysis of variance summary table (Table 7.36), ignoring the shaded portions and using a Type-1 error rate of .05 for the values of $F_{critical}$.

b. What model is appropriate for these data?

c. What is the value of R^2?

Table 7.36 Two-way analysis of variance summary table for the drug treatment experiment (Worked Example 3)

Source	SS	df	MS	F	$F_{critical}$
Model: Between conditions					
A (drugs)	29.6				
B (clinical group)	6.1				
A×B	18.2				
Residual: Within condition	196.4				
Total					

Answer

$$SS_{model} = SS_A + SS_B + SS_{AB} = 29.6 + 6.1 + 18.2 = 53.9$$

$$SS_{total} = SS_{model} + SS_{within} = 53.9 + 196.4 = 250.3$$

$$df_A = 4 - 1 = 3$$

$$df_B = 3 - 1 = 2$$

$$df_{AB} = 3 \times 2 = 6$$

$$df_{model} = 3 + 2 + 6 = 11$$

$$df_{within} = 4 \times 3 \times 8 = 96$$

$$df_{total} = df_{model} + df_{within} = 11 + 96 = 107$$

$$MS_A = 29.6/3 = 9.87$$

$$MS_B = 6.1/2 = 3.05$$

$$MS_{AB} = 18.2/6 = 3.03$$

$$MS_{within} = 196.4/96 = 2.05$$

$$F_A = MS_A/MS_{within} = 9.87/2.05 = 4.81$$

$$F_B = MS_B/MS_{within} = 3.05/2.05 = 1.49$$

$$F_{AB} = MS_{AB}/MS_{within} = 3.03/2.05 = 1.48$$

For evaluating F-ratios, we use the table of the F-distribution for $\alpha = 05$. The degrees of freedom for the denominator are 96, so we use 90 as the closest tabled value *below* that needed:

$$\text{For } F_A, F(3,96) = 2.71$$

$$\text{For } F_B, F(2,96) = 3.10$$

$$\text{For } F_A, F(6,96) = 2.20$$

b. The only obtained F-ratio to exceed its critical value is F_A, so the main effect for drugs is the only significant effect. The appropriate model would therefore be $Y_{ij} = \mu + \alpha_i + e$.

c. $R^2 = SS_{model}/SS_{total} = 53.9/250.3 = .22$

Problems

Problem 1   Aging and memory (DS07_11.dat in the *ASCII Files*)

In a further study of the effects of aging on cognitive performance, memory performance was investigated for the same three groups specified in Problem 2 at the end of Section 7.2. Recall that these groups were

■ A_1: High school seniors (average age 17 years)

■ A_2: Members of a social organization (average age 40 years)

■ A_3: Members of a retirement community (average age 70 years)

Table 7.37 Cell means for the aging and memory experiment

		B (rate)	
		B_1	B_2
	A_1	14.1	16.1
A (age)	A_2	13.5	15.2
	A_3	7.9	10.4

It is hypothesized that the lower performance for the elderly might have been a consequence of this group being unduly penalized by the fast presentation rate at which words were presented. To evaluate this hypothesis, an experiment is designed in which participants at each age level are randomly divided into two groups, one group receives the words at the original fast rate (designated B_1), the other half at a slow rate (B_2). There were 34 participants at each age level, giving $n = 17$ at each rate. The response measure was the number of items recalled in a free recall memory task. The cell means for the six conditions are shown in Table 7.37.

a. Draw a graph of these results.

b. Some entries of the analysis of variance summary table appear in Table 7.38. Fill in the missing entries. The column headed $F_{critical}$ refers to the tabulated value of the F-statistics against which you would test the null hypothesis for that effect with $\alpha = .05$. No values should be entered into the shaded portions.

Table 7.38 Two-way analysis of variance summary table for the aging and memory experiment

Source	SS	df	MS	F	$F_{critical}$
Model: Between conditions					
A	708.9				
B	104.0				
A×B	2.5				
Residual: Within condition	843.4				
Total					

c. What is the value of R^2 for this experiment?

d. Given the results from the F tests, what terms should be dropped from the full model?

e. What conclusion do you draw about the hypothesis that the lower performance for the elderly was a consequence of this group being unduly penalized by the fast presentation rate with which words were presented?

Chapter 7 Exercises

Exercise 1 Extension of the opinion change experiment
(DS07_12.dat in the *ASCII Files*)

This experiment extends the opinion change experiment by adding a control condition. The original experiment (Data Set 2.12) was described in detail in Exercise 2 at the end of Chapter 2 and analyzed as Exercise 1 at the end of Chapter 6. In that version of the experiment, participants in the two conditions received, respectively, a $1 and a $100 reward for attempting to persuade someone that a boring task was actually interesting. Participants in the added control condition do not engage in any act of persuasion. After performing the initial task, they complete the same rating scale as participants in the $1 and $100 payment conditions.

What predictions might you make about the ratings of participants in the control condition compared with those in the two other conditions? Will their ratings be closer to the $1 condition or the $100 condition? Before making your prediction, review the attribution-based analysis of this experiment given in Exercise 2 at the end of Chapter 2.

There were $n = 15$ participants in each condition of this experiment. They were assigned randomly to the three conditions. The basic results from the data analysis are

Condition (Y)	Mean	SS_Y
Control	4.40	69.60
$1 payment	6.47	55.73
$100 payment	4.60	35.60

The value of SS_{total} was found to be 199.91.

a. Using Tukey's HSD procedure, evaluate the differences among the three conditions.

b. Write out the full model for this experiment.

c. Use analysis of variance to evaluate the justification for the full model over the null model. Compare this model with your initial predictions.

d. Calculate the value of R^2 for these data.

Exercise 2 Extension of the undermining intrinsic motivation experiment
(DS07_13.dat in the *ASCII Files*)

This experiment extends the experiment analyzed as Exercise 2 at the end of Chapter 6 with one additional condition. Children in this third condition are given the "Good Player Award" *after* completing the initial 6-minute drawing session.

Thus, unlike the other rewarded condition, these children engage in the initial drawing session unaware that they will be subsequently rewarded. The experiment therefore addresses the question of whether expectation of a reward is critical to the effect observed in the original experiment. The response measure was the time, in minutes, each child spent drawing during the 1-hour test period. There were 48 participants in this experiment. They were assigned randomly to the three conditions, $n = 16$ participants in each. The basic results from the data analysis are

Condition (Y)	Mean	SS_Y
Reward expected	5.64	105.96
No reward	9.67	57.81
Surprise reward	10.13	201.19

The value of SS_{total} was found to 560.48.

a. Write out the full model for this experiment.

b. Use analysis of variance to evaluate the justification for the full model over the null model.

c. If appropriate, use Fisher's LSD to investigate the comparisons between pairs of means among the three conditions.

d. Calculate the value of R^2 for these data.

Exercise 3 Further extension of the undermining intrinsic motivation experiment (DS07_14.dat in the *ASCII Files*)

This experiment further extends the experiment analyzed in Exercise 2 by asking whether the results of that experiment are the same for boys and girls. The experiment was repeated, but the participants in each of the three conditions (factor A) are divided into two groups, boys and girls (factor B). There were 72 participants in this experiment, 36 girls and 36 boys. Within each of these groups, children were assigned randomly to the three conditions, $n = 12$ in each. The cell means (time, in minutes, spent drawing) for the six conditions are shown in the following table.

		Sex (B)	
		Girls	Boys
	Reward expected	4.83	5.92
Condition (A)	No reward	8.92	10.25
	Surprise reward	10.25	9.00

a. Draw a graph of these results.

b. Analysis of the data gives the following results: $SS_A = 286.19$, $SS_B = 2.72$, $SS_{AB} = 24.36$ and $SS_{total} = 651.28$. Write out the complete summary table of the factorial analysis of variance and, with $\alpha = .05$, evaluate the main effects and interaction. What terms should be retained in a model for these data?

c. What is the value of R^2 for this experiment?

Chapter 7 Review

Terms

additivity
analysis of variance
between-condition sum of squares (special case of SS_{model})
Bonferroni method
comparison
error bar
error rate per comparison
error rate per experiment
factor
factorial arrangement of conditions
Fisher's LSD (least significant difference)
HSD (Tukey's honestly significant difference)
interaction
levels of a factor
main effect
planned comparisons
post hoc comparisons
simultaneous confidence intervals
Studentized range distribution
total sum of squares
within-condition sum of squares (special case of SS_e)

Formulas

$$MS_{within} = MS_e = \frac{SS_e}{k(n-1)}$$ For an experiment with k conditions and n participants in each.

$$HSD = q \times \sqrt{\frac{MS_e}{n}}$$ This is also the value of w for simultaneous confidence intervals.

$$SS_{between} = n \times \Sigma a_i^2 \qquad \text{where} \quad a_i = \overline{Y}_i - \overline{Y}$$

$$MS_{between} = \frac{SS_{between}}{(k-1)}$$

$$F = \frac{MS_{between}}{MS_{within}}$$

$$F = t^2$$

$$SS_{model} = SS_{between} = SS_A + SS_B + SS_{AB}$$

$$SS_{total} = SS_{between} + SS_{within} = SS_A + SS_B + SS_{AB} + SS_{within}$$

$$df_{between} = df_A + df_B + df_{AB}$$

Quiz

At various points in the following paragraphs are pairs of italicized terms set within braces {·}. In each case, choose the term you consider appropriate.

95% simultaneous confidence intervals calculated using the Studentized range statistic will be {*wider, narrower*} than individual 95% confidence intervals calculated using the *t*-distribution. This difference in width reflects the fact that if the probability is .95 that each interval contains the true difference, the probability is {*less, more*} than .95 that all intervals considered collectively will simultaneously contain the true differences.

In an analysis of variance of an experiment with four independent groups, the {*null, full*} model is based on the assumption that all four groups have equal population means. For the null model, the mean square of the residuals is called {MS_{total}, MS_{within}}, whereas, for the full model, the mean square of the residuals is called {MS_{total}, MS_{within}}. The difference between MS_{total} and MS_{within} is {MS_e, MS_{model}}. MS_{model} is also known as {MS_{within}, $MS_{between}$}.

If the experiment has 12 participants in each of the four conditions, then MS_{within} is based on {*3, 44*} degrees of freedom, whereas MS_{model} is based on {*3, 44*} degrees of freedom. The *F*-ratio would be found by dividing {MS_{within}, $MS_{between}$} by {MS_{within}, $MS_{between}$}. The tabled value of the *F*-statistic that would be used to test the null hypothesis ($\alpha = .05$) is {*2.82, 2.58*}.

A factorial design consists of at least two {*factors, levels*} each with two or more {*factors, levels*}. An analysis of variance partitions the {*within-, between-*} conditions sum of squares into main effects and interactions. If there is no interaction, then the main effects are said to be {*additive, nonadditive*}. If there is an interaction, then the effect of one factor {*is, is not*} the same at the different levels of the other factor. Graphically, an interaction implies that the lines connecting the means are {*parallel, nonparallel*}.

Chapter 8 Preview

Chapter 7 concludes the discussion of completely randomized designs. In Chapter 8 we turn our attention to the matter of precision and power. Earlier chapters introduced the relevant concepts but said very little about how, in planning an experimental study, an investigator can ensure that estimates will be sufficiently precise and decision made with adequate protection against a Type-2 error.

8 INCREASING THE PRECISION OF AN EXPERIMENT

At the end of Section 6.5, we discussed the problem faced by Jill, the senior undergraduate, whose thesis data showed "marginally significant" results. Jill's experiment was designed to evaluate the effectiveness of teaching students to use visual imagery in learning geometry. The group using visual imagery showed a 5% improvement, but with a Type-1 error rate set at $\alpha = .05$, the obtained t-value of 1.96 was just slightly below the value of 2.024 needed to reject the null hypothesis.

This example of experimental results for which an effect is almost, but not quite, significant is not at all uncommon. Faced with this situation, investigators are sometimes tempted to resort to questionable practices (such as retrospectively switching to a one-tailed test or eliminating "bad" data) in an effort to achieve statistical significance. There is a saying that, if tortured long enough, data will confess to almost anything.

In this chapter, we address the problem posed by Jill's experiment. The basic cause of the difficulty with this experiment was low precision. We will discuss how she might have anticipated and thereby avoided her frustrating situation. The family of concepts relevant to this matter have all been introduced: power, precision, confidence interval widths, Type-2 error rates. This chapter is a "how to" account of ways in which experiments can be designed to improve precision, obtain a narrower confidence interval, and reduce the Type-2 error rate.

From the viewpoint of scientific method, the case of the marginally significant difference is relatively straightforward. Jill's situation, for example, is one in which the evidence for an effect has not reached the level demanded by the scientific community. The imagery training *may* improve performance, but the effect has not been established beyond a reasonable doubt. Jill, on the other hand, may be convinced that, in failing to reject the null hypothesis, she has made a Type-2 error.

Consider Jill's results again. The experimental condition produced an improvement of 5 percentage points. In thinking about this result, there is a temptation to regard the quantity 5 as fixed and to believe that the problem is one of increasing precision so that the observed improvement of 5 "becomes significant." This is a bad way of thinking about the matter. The value of 5 is a point *estimate*, just *one* value of a random variable. The basic claim of the statistical analysis is that values other than 5 remain plausible, in other words, that repeating the experiment would almost certainly yield a value other than 5. In the case of Jill's experiment, the 95% confidence interval tells us that even 0 is not an implausible value; it tells us that a repetition of the experiment might produce no improvement at all. The confidence interval also tells us that the value of 5 might underestimate the true amount of improvement, that an improvement by as much as 10% is not implausible. The purpose in increasing precision is not to "make the improvement of 5 significant" but to narrow the range of plausible values, that is, to narrow the 95% confidence interval. If, in fact, the null hypothesis is true, then increasing precision will only make this truth more apparent.

If Jill is convinced imagery really *does* make a difference, and wishes to convince the scientific community of the fact, then she has little choice but to repeat the experiment, on this occasion planning the experiment so that the results provide a more precise estimate of the true difference. In so doing, of course, it may turn out that Jill was mistaken in her conviction and that the improvement that she observed in the original experiment was a chance fluctuation of 5 from a true value of or near 0.

In Chapter 6, we noted that precision and Type-2 error rates can be manipulated via the value of the standard error. In turn, the value of the standard error can be influenced either through the value of n or through the value of MS_e (also referred to as MS_{within}). The first possibility is a relatively straightforward matter that asks the question, "How large should n be to ensure adequate precision?" Section 8.1 addresses this question for independent-groups designs. Reducing the value of MS_e takes us into new realms of experimental design that are discussed in the remainder of the chapter.

8.1 Choosing an Appropriate Value of n in Two-Condition Experiments

The specification of an appropriate value of n will always be an approxmation.

The examples at the end of Section 5.3 illustrated how the width of a confidence interval could be systematically changed by choosing different values of n. But the specification of an appropriate value of n will always be an approximation. There is never enough information to be certain that the chosen value of n will achieve precisely the desired power level. However, the methods to be described, even if they yield only an approximation, are to be preferred over a purely intuitive judgment about the appropriate sample size.

8.1.1 Choosing n to Achieve a Desired Value of w

In estimating the needed sample size, the normal distribution will be used as an approximation to the t-distribution.

We know that the half-width of the confidence interval is w, which is the product of a critical tabled value and the appropriate standard deviation. In a two-condition experiment such as Jill's the critical tabled value was the t-statistic and the appropriate standard deviation was the estimated standard error of the difference between the means. The method presented here for choosing n takes the simplifying step of equating the estimate of the standard error of the difference between the means with the population value and thus approximating the t-distribution by the normal distribution.

The value of w for a 95% confidence interval is therefore

$$w = z \times s_{\overline{Y}_1 - \overline{Y}_2} = z \times \sqrt{\frac{2MS_e}{n}}$$

Squaring both sides of this equation and rearranging the terms, we have

$$n = 2\text{MS}_e \left(\frac{z}{w}\right)^2$$

Note two implications of this equation. First, the larger the value of MS_e, the larger will be the value of *n*. In brief, the larger the residuals, the larger the sample size needed to attain a specified value of *w*. Second, the smaller the value of *w*, the larger the value of *n*. In other words, larger sample sizes are needed to achieve narrower confidence intervals.

If the confidence level is set at .95, then the critical tabled value is $z = 1.96$. From Jill's original experiment, we have $\text{MS}_e = 65.0$. Suppose that Jill decides that the experiment should result in a 95% confidence interval with $w = 4.0$. (In Jill's original experiment, *w* was calculated as 5.2.) To achieve $w = 4.0$, we substitute the values of *z*, MS_e, and *w* into the equation for *n*:

$$n = 2 \times 65 \times \left(\frac{1.96}{4}\right)^2 = 31.2$$

Thus $n = 32$ is the approximate number of participants that Jill should use to achieve a value of $w = 4.0$. If Jill repeats the experiment with $n = 32$, then she can expect an estimate of mean improvement that is within 4 units of the true value. Notice that when the calculation of *n* yields a decimal fraction, as it usually does, we round up to the next whole number. This is a conservative strategy erring on the side of using too many rather than too few participants.

8.1.2 Choosing *n* to Achieve Desired Power

Suppose that Jill conducts the experiment with $n = 32$. A reasonable question to ask of this new experiment is this: If the true difference is 4.0, what is the probability of failing to detect it, that is, of failing to reject the null hypothesis? In other words, what is the Type-2 error rate? The answer to this question may come as something of a surprise: The Type-2 error rate is $\beta = .5$. The power of this test is $1 - \beta$, so the power is also .5.

This value of β may seem very high. A value of $\beta = .5$ means that with 32 participants in each group, there is only a 50-50 chance of detecting a difference, even if the true difference is as large as 4. Thinking about the meaning of a 95% confidence interval, however, reveals the plausibility of this result. Imagine repeating the experiment many times and calculating a 95% confidence interval for each. The results from this kind of simulation were graphed in Figure 5.8. If the true difference is 4, then the long-run average of these 95% confidence intervals for the difference will be centered on a value of 4 and extend 4 (the value of *w*) on either side. That is, the lower end of this average interval will just touch the value of 0. Any fluctuation toward the low end will result in a confidence interval that includes 0. A confidence interval that includes 0 would lead to a decision to retain the null hypothesis—and a Type-2 error. Assuming that fluctuations toward the low and high ends are equally likely, 50% of the fluctuations will be toward the low end. It follows that half of the 95% confidence intervals will include the value of 0. On these occasions, the null hypothesis will be retained. That is, with $\alpha = .05$ and $w = 4$, the Type-2 error is $\beta = .5$.

Suppose Jill wishes to set $\beta = .2$. This error rate would give a power level of $1 - \beta = .8$. How many participants are needed in each condition? Investigators answer such questions by consulting published tables. To use these tables, two items of information are needed:

If *w* is the half-width of the confidence interval, then the power of the test to detect a difference as large as *w* is .5.

■ A measure of the magnitude of the minimum difference that the investigator wishes to detect at the specified β level. One measure commonly used to make this specification is Cohen's d. Recall that $d = (\mu_1 - \mu_2)/\sigma_e$. It is also useful at this point to review the conventions for describing effect sizes (Chapter 3). According to Cohen, a d-value of 0.8 or more is a *large* effect; a d-value of 0.5 is considered a medium effect; a d-value of 0.2 is considered small.

■ To calculate d, we need to know the value of σ_e, the standard deviation of the residuals. Remember that σ_e is assumed to be the same for each condition. The value of σ_e is typically unknown. Substituting an estimate, $\sqrt{MS_e}$, leads to an approximate value for the desired sample size.

Where does this estimate of σ_e come from? The answer is not obvious, because the general goal is to decide on the value of the sample size *before* conducting the experiment. But how can an estimate of $\sqrt{MS_e}$ be obtained unless data have been collected? The only way of obtaining an estimate of σ_e is to use the results from a pilot study or the results from previous experiments that used the same response measure under similar conditions. The resulting estimation of σ_e may not be as good as the investigator would like, but even if it is little more than an educated guess, it will almost certainly be better than obtaining no estimate at all and deciding on a value of n on some intuitive basis that ignores the whole issue of precision and power.

In Jill's case, we have an estimate of σ_e from her original experiment. That value was $\sqrt{MS_e} = 8.06$. So, for a difference of 4 in Jill's experiment, we have

Estimates of σ_e must be obtained by using the results from a pilot study or the results from previous experiments.

$$d = \frac{4}{8.06} = 0.50$$

Table 8.1 gives the value of n needed for a given power level and effect size. The values of d in Table 8.1 range from 0.15 to 1.0. Although d can be greater than 1.0, large values are rarely needed for the purpose of estimating sample size. Values in this table are based on the normal distribution as an approximation to the t-distribution. Use of the normal distribution rather than the formally correct t-distribution is justified on the grounds that the approximation will be satisfactory in most cases. Remember that, because of the uncertainty surrounding the value of σ_e, the estimates of n are always educated guesses rather than precise estimates; so, in this context, the inaccuracies introduced by using the normal distribution rather than the t-distribution are negligible. An investigator who is concerned over the potential inaccuracy of the procedure might use a value of n somewhat greater than the value obtained from the table, treating the tabled value as a minimum n needed to achieve the desired level of power. As in other matters, deciding on sample size often demands experienced judgment in addition to the mechanical application of formulas.

Table 8.1 can be used in reverse to obtain the power level for an experiment after it has been conducted.

Consulting Table 8.1, we look for the column headed .8, the desired power level. We then look for the row headed .5, the designated value of d. The intersection of this column and row gives the required value of n. For $d = 0.5$, and n of 63 is needed to achieve a power of $1 - \beta = .8$.

It is interesting to ask about the Type-2 error rate in Jill's original experiment. Given that this experiment used $n = 20$, what was the value of β relative to a true difference of $\mu_1 - \mu_2 = 4$? What was the power of this experiment to detect a true difference of 4 ($d = 0.5$)? We can use Table 8.1 in the reverse direction to obtain an approximate answer to this question. Consulting the row for $d = 0.5$, we look for a value near $n = 20$. What we find is that $n = 17$ corresponds to a power of $1 - \beta = .3$ and that $n = 24$ corresponds to $1 - \beta = .4$. Jill's $n = 20$ is intermediate

Table 8.1 Sample sizes (n) needed to achieve a specified power ($1 - \beta$) for different effect sizes (**d**) in a completely randomized design with two conditions

Effect size, d	Power ($1 - \beta$)									
	.1	.2	.3	.4	.5	.6	.7	.8	.9	.95
0.15	41	112	184	259	342	436	549	698	934	1156
0.20	24	63	104	146	193	245	309	393	526	650
0.25	15	41	66	94	123	157	198	252	337	416
0.30	11	28	46	65	86	109	138	175	234	289
0.35	8	21	34	48	63	80	101	129	172	213
0.40	6	16	26	37	49	62	78	99	132	163
0.45	5	13	21	29	38	49	61	78	104	129
0.50	4	11	17	24	31	40	50	63	85	104
0.55	4	9	14	20	26	33	41	52	70	86
0.60	3	7	12	17	22	28	35	44	59	73
0.65	3	6	10	14	19	24	30	38	50	62
0.70	2	6	9	12	16	20	26	33	43	54
0.75	2	5	8	11	14	18	22	28	38	47
0.80	2	4	7	10	13	16	20	25	33	41
0.85	2	4	6	9	11	14	18	22	30	36
0.90	2	4	6	8	10	13	16	20	26	33
0.95	2	3	5	7	9	11	14	18	24	29
1.00	1	3	5	6	8	10	13	16	22	26

The intersection of the shaded row and column indicates that a sample size of $n = 63$ is needed to achieve a power ($1 - \beta$) of .8 to detect **d** = 0.5, a medium effect size.

between 17 and 24, so the power of the original experiment to detect a difference of 4 was somewhere between .3 and .4. This result leads to the rather disturbing conclusion that even if there exists a true difference of 4 between the conditions, Jill's original experiment had so little power that the probability of the experiment detecting this difference (rejecting the null hypothesis) was less than .4.

8.1.3 Comments on Power and Precision

It is tempting to dismiss the insufficient power in Jill's experiment as the kind of mistake made only by an inexperienced investigator. Unfortunately, Jill's mistake is not at all uncommon, even among experienced researchers. Published experiments often lack sufficient power to detect even quite large differences.

Many published experiments lack sufficient power to detect even quite large differences.

In 1962, Jacob Cohen (to whom we owe the **d** measure of effect size) analyzed the statistical power of studies published in the 1960 volume of the *Journal of Abnormal and Social Psychology* (Cohen, 1962). The first point he noted was that these studies paid virtually no attention to the power, or Type-2 error rates, of their statistical tests. Cohen calculated the power of these studies, just as we did for Jill's original experiment. He found that, for a small effect size ($d = 0.2$), not a single study had a better than 50-50 chance of rejecting the null hypothesis and that the typical Type-2 error rate was greater than .8, a power level below .2. Only when large effects were present ($d = 0.8$ or more) did the investigator have a reasonable chance of detecting it.

Despite this and subsequent articles making the same point, matters seem to have improved little since Cohen's original paper. Sedlmeier and Gigerenzer (1989) examined the power of studies published in the *Journal of Abnormal Psychology* and found power levels no higher than those found by Cohen 27 years earlier.

Perhaps part of the explanation for this persistence of inadequate power is that many investigators appear to have a mistaken belief in the accuracy of their intuitions about what constitutes an adequate sample size. Tversky and Kahneman (1971) asked experienced researchers to give intuitive estimates of the sample sizes needed to achieve a specified power level in experiments designed to obtain a general replication of a previously observed difference. These intuitive estimates of sample size were far smaller than would have been needed to achieve the designated level of power. Even experienced researchers underestimated the impact of random variation.

A further reason why experimenters badly underestimate the danger of Type-2 errors and conduct seriously underpowered experiments is a reluctance to specify quantitatively how large a difference they wish to detect. Yet, as we have seen, specification of power or of a Type-2 error rate can be made only relative to some specified effect size. In response to this demand for a minimum effect size, the temptation may be to respond, "I wish to detect *any* difference, no matter how small." To gauge how unrealistic this demand is, you need only consult the values in Table 8.1. Consider an effect size of $d = 0.15$, a small but not a trivial difference to an investigator who wishes to detect "any difference." To achieve a power level of .8 to detect this difference, an experiment with $n = 698$ is needed. If you demand the capability of detecting even smaller effects, the value of n needed to achieve reasonable power levels soon becomes impossibly large.

> Intuitive estimates of sample sizes often underestimate the value of n needed to achieve the desired level of power.

> Detecting *any* difference, no matter how small, is an unrealistic goal.

Comprehension Check 8.1

Important Concepts

1. The precision of an experiment can be increased either by increasing the size of n or by lowering the value of MS_e. (Section 8.1 considered the first of these two options.)

2. It is possible to estimate a value of n that will yield an approximation to some desired value of w, where w is the half-width of the confidence interval. This sample size will give an approximate power level of .5 to detect a true difference of w.

3. Using published tables, we can estimate a value of n needed to yield an approximation to some desired level of power $(1 - \beta)$ relative to a designated effect size, **d**.

4. Many published studies lack sufficient power to detect even moderately large effects.

Worked Examples

Example 1 **Induced happiness**

The study of induced happiness used in Chapter 6 (Data Set 6.2) obtained an estimate for the residual mean square of $MS_e = 31.21$. In designing a replication of this experiment, the investigator wishes to obtain a 95% confidence interval with a w (half-width) of 3.0.

a. Use the estimate $MS_e = 31.21$ to estimate the number of participants (n) that should be used in each condition.

b. Using this value of n, what is the power of the t-test to detect a difference of 3.0?

c. If the investigator wants to detect a difference of 3.0 with a power level of .7, how many participants (n) should be used in each condition?

Answer

a. We will use the normal distribution approximation to the t-distribution.

$$n = 2MS_e \left(\frac{z}{w}\right)^2 = 2 \times 31.21 \left(\frac{1.96}{3}\right)^2 = 26.6$$

Thus $n = 27$ participants should be used in each condition.

b. The power is .5. The value of n needed to obtain a specified value of w will always be the n corresponding to a power of .5 to detect a difference equal to w. The relationship can be confirmed for this example by consulting Table 8.1. A difference of 3.0 corresponds to a value of **d** of $3/\sqrt{MS_e} = 3/5.59 = 0.54$. For the column headed $1 - \beta = .5$ and the row headed .55 (the closest tabled value), we read off a value for n of 26.

c. Consulting Table 8.1, for a value of $\mathbf{d} = 0.54$ and $1 - \beta = .7$, (using $\mathbf{d} = 0.55$, the closest tabled value), we read off a value for n of 41.

Example 2 **Induced anger**

In designing a replication of the induced anger experiment (Problem 1, Section 6.2), the investigator seeks advice on how large n needs to be to achieve satisfactory power. The original experiment provides an estimate of $\sqrt{MS_e} = 1.88$, on which an estimate for n can be based. The investigator would like to detect any difference greater than 1.5 and do so with a power of .8. However, the investigator is willing to settle for a power of .7 if the n required for .8 exceeds the available resources.

a. To provide the investigator with the information needed to decide on a value for n, find the value of n that would be needed for both the .8 and the .7 power levels.

b. The investigator decides on a value for n corresponding to the power level of .8. With this number of participants, what is the estimated power of the experiment to detect a difference of 1.0?

Answer

a. The specified difference of 1.5 corresponds to an effect size of

$$d = \frac{1.5}{1.88} = 0.80$$

Table 8.1 indicates that for an effect size of $d = 0.8$ and a power level of .8, $n = 25$ participants are needed. For a power level of .7, $n = 20$ are needed to detect an effect size of $d = 0.8$.

b. A difference of 1.0 gives an effect size of $d = 1.0/1.88 = 0.53$. Using Table 8.1 to obtain the power to detect this value of d requires some search and estimation because the table gives values for $d = 0.5$ and 0.55 but not $d = 0.53$. Starting with $d = 0.5$, we note that a value of $n = 24$ gives a power of .4. Then with $d = 0.55$, a value of $n = 26$ gives a power of .5. The power with $n = 25$ and $d = 0.53$ is thus intermediate between .4 and .5. In summary, the power to detect a difference of 1.0 is just under 50%.

Problems

Problem 1   Ponzo illusion

Critically examine the power of the statistical test used in the Ponzo illusion experiment described and analyzed in Chapter 6. That experiment asked whether the size of the illusion was influenced by the viewing time (short versus long). The basic results of the experiment were

Condition	n	$\overline{Y}$	SS_Y
Short	12	9.74	2218
Long	12	6.63	2874

These results led to a value of 15.2 for $\sqrt{MS_e}$. The null hypothesis was retained. Using this value of $\sqrt{MS_e}$, answer the following questions.

a. What value of n would have been needed to detect a true difference of 10.0 with a probability of $1 - \beta = .7$?

b. With $n = 12$, how large would the true difference need to be for it to be detected with a power of $1 - \beta = .6$?

Problem 2   Intentional versus incidental remembering

Problem 2, Section 6.2 described an experimental study of intentional versus incidental remembering. The estimated residual mean square was $MS_e = 8.865$. In designing a replication of this experiment, the investigator wishes to obtain a 95% confidence interval with a w value (half-width) of 1.5.

a. Use the estimate of $MS_e = 8.865$ to estimate the number of participants (n) that should be used in each condition.

b. Using this value of n, what is the power of the t-test to detect a difference of 1.5?

c. If the investigator wants to detect a difference of 1.5 with a power level of .8, how many participants (n) should be used in each condition?

Problem 3	Incidental remembering

Problem 3, Section 6.3 described an experimental study comparing two different forms of incidental remembering. The estimated residual mean square was $MS_e = 9.677$. The investigator is planning a similar experiment to compare two other incidental tasks. The value of MS_e from this prior study is thought to provide a reasonable estimate of the residual mean square in this new experiment.

a. In designing this experiment, the investigator wishes to be able to detect a difference of $|\mu_1 - \mu_2| = 2.5$ with a probability (power) of $1 - \beta = .8$. How many participants should be used in each condition?

b. If the experiment is conducted with this number of participants, what is the approximate power of the experiment to detect a difference of 2.0?

8.2 Reducing Residuals by Using Matched Pairs

In Jill's experiment, individual students *within* each condition differ in their level of performance. The residuals are the direct reflection of this within-condition variability. Although all students in the experimental condition receive the same imagery training, each student yields a different score. Certain factors are not being held constant, so strict replication fails: The same experimental condition does not yield the same measurement. The magnitude of this uncontrolled variability is measured by MS_e. In this section, we discuss a method for reducing the size of MS_e.

Major contributors to the variability measured by MS_e are individual differences among the participants on the attribute measured by the response variable. In Jill's experiment, participants differ in geometry ability. In a completely randomized design, the random assignment of participants to the conditions ensures that these differences in ability are randomly distributed across the two conditions. This method of assignment eliminates bias, but the variability produced by the differences remains among observations within each condition as well as among observations from different conditions. Using matched pairs is a method of isolating this source of variability and removing it from MS_e.

In the completely randomized design, residuals are the direct consequence of within-condition variability.

Major contributors to MS_e are stable individual differences among the participants.

Two observations form a matched pair if the source of those observations (two participants, for example) have been equated on some other variable.

8.2.1 ## Why and How to Form Matched Pairs

We begin by considering observations from two participants in the experimental condition of Jill's original experiment. One of these two participants scored 75%, the other 64%, a difference of 11%. These two observations are from the same condition, so *any* difference between them is interpreted as unwanted noise, that is, a failure of strict replication. More concretely, it is a difference that contributes to the size of MS_e and thus to the lowering of precision. The goal is to use the matching strategy described at the beginning of Chapter 6 to reduce the contribution of such differences to MS_e. The strategy is to identify a known source of the differences and make a comparison between the two conditions, holding this source constant.

Matching by Using a Measured Attribute

As noted earlier, a major source of the 11% difference between our two sample participants is likely to be each student's prior ability in geometry. It may not be the only source, but it is likely to be a major one. Both students may benefit from the imagery training, but if they benefit equally (they both improve by 4), then the difference between them will remain the same.

Consider two other students. One was a participant in the experimental condition who scored 80%, the other was a participant in the control condition who scored 66%. This difference between them of 14% also could be the result of the first student being better at geometry than the second. But the difference could also be the result of the beneficial effects of the imagery training; remember that one member of the pair receives training, the other does not. In this case, the two sources—one noise and the other a potential signal—are obviously confounded, and the stronger the noise (individual differences in geometry ability), the more difficult it will be to detect the signal.

When applied to Jill's experiment, matched pairs is a strategy that would control individual differences in geometry ability by setting up pairs of students who are matched on geometry ability as measured by a suitable test in geometry. One member of the pair would be randomly assigned to the experimental condition, the other to the control condition. Suppose the scores for these two participants are 71 and 68, a difference of 3. Whatever the cause of this difference, it cannot be differences in geometry ability because the two participants have equal ability, at least as measured by the test on which the matching was based. For the comparison between these two students, geometry ability has been held constant.

In the case of Jill's experiment, geometry ability is an obvious choice for a variable on which to match. However, it is important to understand the general principle underlying this choice. What property of a matching variable makes it effective in gaining precision? We know that the matching variable should measure an attribute that influences the experiment's response variable. The goal is to match (hold constant) a variable that would produce unwanted differences. This factor can then no longer contribute to any difference between the two members of the matched pair. With matching, one source of the variability among the difference scores has been controlled. The effect of this matching is therefore to reduce the variability of the difference scores among the *n* pairs.

To see how this design strategy works, consider the unrealistic but instructive case of an ideal match for five imaginary pairs of response measures (Table 8.2). Notice first that there is considerable variability among observations within each of the two

> The goal of the matched-pair design is to match (hold constant) a variable that otherwise would produce unwanted differences.

Table 8.2 Example of ideal matching				
Matched pair	Experimental condition	Control condition	Pair mean	Pair difference
1	72	68	70	4
2	76	72	74	4
3	64	60	62	4
4	56	52	54	4
5	69	65	67	4

Although there is variability among the observations within each condition, the difference between the members of a matched pair is constant. The response measure is a score on a math test.

conditions. Next, note that there is also variability in the overall performance level of the five pairs. This variability is apparent if you examine the means for each pair in the shaded column of Table 8.2. For example, the first and especially the second pairs perform well on this task; the fourth pair performs relatively poorly. However, the *difference* between each pair is a constant. For any given pair, the experimental participant's score is simply the control participant's score plus 4. Thus, although the measures *within each condition* are highly variable, the effect of the experimental manipulation *within each pair* is perfectly uniform. The experimental manipulation adds 4 to a participant's score. In this ideal example, the experimental manipulation is the only source of difference between the two members of each pair.

Compare the situation in Table 8.2 with one in which the same participants are not matched on a relevant variable but are paired at random. The resulting data are shown in Table 8.3. The scores in Table 8.3 are exactly the same as those in

Table 8.3 Data from Table 8.2, randomly rearranged				
Random pair	Experimental condition	Control condition	Pair mean	Pair difference
1	56	60	58	− 4
2	64	65	64.5	− 1
3	76	68	72	8
4	72	52	62	20
5	69	72	70.5	− 3

In this arrangement, the pairs are no longer matched. The same data values now give highly variable pair differences.

Table 8.2, so the mean difference between the conditions is still 4, but now there is great variability in the differences. The effect of the experimental manipulation that was perfectly clear in Table 8.2 is totally obscured by variability (noise) in Table 8.3.

A matching variable is effective to the extent that it makes the pair-difference scores less variable than they would be if participants were paired at random. It will achieve this goal to the extent that it measures those factors that produce the variability among participants *within* each condition. If different levels of geometry ability produce variability within a condition, then matching on geometry ability will be effective in gaining precision. Once measurements on the matching variable have been taken, the results can be used to form matched pairs, thereby equating the members of the pair on what are otherwise noise-producing influences.

Other Bases for Forming Matched Pairs

There are other ways to form matched pairs besides using values on a continuous measure such as geometry ability. Matched pairs can often be formed on the basis of a relevant categorical variable. For example, using same-sex sibling pairs will ensure a degree of matching on both environmental and genetically influenced measures. This matching will be imperfect but, depending on the response measure, such partial matching of pairs may be effective in reducing MS_e relative to the independent-groups design. If genetic influences are a strong source of within-condition variability, then the use of identical twin pairs would be an especially effective basis for matching; although setting up such an experiment would be a time-consuming process unless the investigator has ready access to a twin sample.

Whether matching is based on a continuous or a categorical measure, the principle is the same: Form pairs so as to "hold constant" some attribute that would otherwise contribute to the difference between the two members of the pair.

New Version of Jill's Experiment, Using Matched Pairs

For the complete version of Jill's new experiment, a number of matched pairs would be established. One member of each pair is randomly assigned to the experimental condition, the other to the control condition. Each of these n pairs would provide a single measure of the difference between the experimental and control conditions, uncontaminated by differences in geometry ability. Thus, for this matched-pair design, the basic data are n difference scores, one score for each pair. The mean of these difference scores will be denoted by $\overline{D}$ and their standard deviation by s_D.

For this experimental design, the estimate of Cohen's effect size is

$$\hat{d} = \frac{\overline{D}}{s_D}$$

To make comparisons with Jill's first experiment, we will suppose that this new experiment also uses a total of 40 participants, consisting of 20 matched pairs. This sample size was established by using Table 8.4, which is the matched-pair counterpart of Table 8.1. Table 8.4 indicates that, for this matched-pair design, an experiment with 20 pairs will give a power of approximately .6 (a Type-2 error rate of .4) to detect a difference of $d = 0.5$. This level of power is probably less than ideal, but, as we will see, it is a considerable improvement over the first experiment.

Table 8.4 Sample sizes needed to achieve a specified power $(1 - \beta)$ for different effect sizes (**d**) in a matched-pair design

Effect size, d	Power $(1 - \beta)$									
	.1	.2	.3	.4	.5	.6	.7	.8	.9	.95
0.15	21	56	92	130	171	218	275	349	467	578
0.20	12	32	52	73	97	123	155	197	263	325
0.25	8	21	33	47	62	79	99	126	169	208
0.30	6	14	23	33	43	55	69	88	117	145
0.35	4	11	17	24	32	40	51	65	86	107
0.40	3	8	13	19	25	31	39	50	66	82
0.45	3	7	11	15	19	25	31	39	52	65
0.50	2	6	9	12	16	20	25	32	43	52
0.55	2	5	7	10	13	17	21	26	35	43
0.60	2	4	6	9	11	14	18	22	30	37
0.65	2	3	5	7	10	12	15	19	25	31
0.70	1	3	5	6	8	10	13	17	22	27
0.75	1	3	4	6	7	9	11	14	19	24
0.80	1	2	4	5	7	8	10	13	17	21
0.85	1	2	3	5	6	7	9	11	15	18
0.90	1	2	3	4	5	7	8	10	13	17
0.95	1	2	3	4	5	6	7	9	12	15
1.00	1	2	3	3	4	5	7	8	11	13

The intersection of the shaded row and column indicates that a sample size of $n = 20$ is needed to achieve a power $(1 - \beta)$ of .6 to detect an effect size of **d** = 0.5.

Data Set 8.1 gives the actual data from Jill's second experiment. The final column, headed D, gives the difference between the two test scores for each pair.

8.2.2 Analyzing the Matched-Pair Design as a Set of *n* Difference Scores

A straightforward way of analyzing these results is to consider the column of difference scores (D) in Data Set 8.1 as a set of $n = 20$ scores and calculate a confidence interval for μ_D, their mean. This confidence interval is calculated by using the methods described in Chapter 5. We estimate the variance of the scores, use this value to calculate the estimated standard error, and then use the t-distribution to obtain the

A confidence interval can be calculated for μ_D.

Data Set 8.1 Test scores from the matched-pair version of Jill's experiment

Pair	Experimental ($\bar{Y}_1 = 71$)	Control ($\bar{Y}_2 = 67$)	D ($\bar{D} = 4$)	Pair	Experimental (cont.)	Control (cont.)	D (cont.)
1	62	56	6	11	71	69	2
2	76	60	16	12	68	68	0
3	75	73	2	13	73	69	4
4	52	58	−6	14	75	69	6
5	69	67	2	15	66	72	−6
6	71	63	8	16	59	57	2
7	76	62	14	17	72	66	6
8	69	77	−8	18	80	66	14
9	89	91	−2	19	78	60	18
10	66	70	−4	20	73	67	6

μ_D denotes population mean of difference scores.

desired confidence interval. Note that with 20 difference scores, there are 19 degrees of freedom.

Computer output gives us the sum of squared deviations of the difference scores as

$$\text{SS}_D = (6 - 4)^2 + (16 - 4)^2 + (2 - 4)^2 + \ldots + (6 - 4)^2 = 1048$$

so

$$s_D = \sqrt{\frac{1048}{19}} = 7.427$$

The estimated standard error is

$$s_{\bar{D}} = \frac{s_D}{\sqrt{n}} = \frac{7.427}{\sqrt{20}} = 1.661$$

For a 95% confidence interval, the t-distribution for $df = 19$ gives a value of $t = 2.093$. The 95% confidence interval is therefore

$$\text{CI}_{.95} = \bar{D} \pm (2.093 \times 1.661) = 4 \pm 3.48 = 0.52 \text{ to } 7.48$$

There are several features of this 95% confidence interval worth noting. First, the standard error, $s_{\bar{D}}$, is smaller than the standard error, $s_{\bar{Y}_1 - \bar{Y}_2}$, obtained in Jill's first experiment. Second, this reduction in the standard error results in a narrower 95% confidence interval. Third, the interval does not include the value of 0, so the null hypothesis can be rejected; 0 is an implausible value for μ_D. Finally, notice that the null hypothesis is rejected even though chance differences in the samples result in a point estimate of $\bar{D}$ (4.0) that is actually smaller than the difference obtained in the original experiment (5.0).

The null hypothesis can be tested directly, using the t-distribution.

An alternative but equivalent procedure for evaluating the null hypothesis would be to test it directly by using the t-distribution. As a firm adherent to the Neyman-Pearson tradition, Jill states the null and alternative hypotheses. The null hypothesis is

$$H_0: \mu_D = 0$$

and the alternative hypothesis is

$$H_1: \mu_D \neq 0$$

Before beginning the new experiment, the Type-1 error rate is set at $\alpha = .05$.

The data yield a t-ratio of

$$t = \frac{\overline{D} - 0}{s_{\overline{D}}} = \frac{4}{1.661} = 2.41$$

As noted when calculating the 95% confidence interval, the t-distribution for $df = 19$ gives $t = 2.093$ as the critical value. Our t-ratio of 2.41 exceeds this critical value, so it falls into the rejection region. The null hypothesis is therefore rejected.

8.2.3 A Closer Look at the Matched-Pairs Design

The analysis of the matched-pair design as a set of n difference scores is simple and intuitive. Each pair-difference provides an estimate of the difference between the two conditions that is uncontaminated by the factor on which the pair is matched. The t-test then establishes whether these observed differences are compatible with a true mean difference of 0. However, the very simplicity of this analysis helps conceal the details of why this design improves precision. Moreover, the strategy of taking difference scores will run into obvious difficulties when the number of conditions is more than two. Deeper insight into the rationale for the matched-pair design can be gained by constructing a model that explicitly sets out the components of each observation.

As a first step in constructing this model, we will consider again the data for the first pair of participants in Jill's second experiment. The data are

Pair	Experimental	Control	D
1	62	56	6

The rationale for the matched-pair design can be understood in terms of a model that explicitly sets out the ingredients of each observation.

What factors contribute to the score of 62 for the participant in the experimental condition? The potential factors are

■ being in the experimental condition (receiving the imagery training) rather than in the control condition

■ prior level of ability in geometry

■ other uncontrolled factors

Parameters of a Model for the Matched-Pairs Design

If we express the three preceding factors in a simple additive model, then, for this observation, we have

$$Y = \mu + \alpha_1 + \pi_1 + e$$

The various elements are

■ μ As before, μ is the parameter representing the overall (grand) mean.

■ α_1 The parameter α_1 indicates the effect of condition 1. In this case, the subscript 1 denotes the experimental condition. A positive value of α_1 would indicate that the experimental condition increases the value of Y relative to the overall mean.

π_j denotes average performance level of one pair relative to all other pairs.

■ π_1 The parameter π_1 measures the average performance level of the first pair of participants relative to other pairs. Because it is a characteristic of the pair, this parameter is the same for each member of this pair. A positive value of π_1 would indicate that the average performance of this pair in the experiment is above the overall mean. A major source of this superiority is assumed to be attributable to the pair's above-average ability in geometry—the variable on which the two participants are matched. A negative value of π_1 would suggest that this pair is below average in geometry ability and that their geometry ability therefore decreases the value of Y for this pair relative to the overall mean.

■ e As before, e is the residual.

Estimates of the Parameters

Parameters are estimated as in previous models. The parameters α_i and π_j and their estimates a_i and p_j are expressed as deviation from the grand mean.

The parameters are estimated in much the same way we estimated them for the independent-groups design. First, the estimate of μ is $\overline{Y}$, the mean of all scores. For the data in Data Set 8.1, $\overline{Y} = 69$.

The subscript of a_i designates the condition.

p_j denotes estimate of π_j.

The subscript of π_j designates the pair.

The residual is obtained by subtraction.

The estimate of α_1 is a_1 and, as before, this estimate is expressed as a deviation from the grand mean. The mean of the 20 observations in the experimental condition is 71, so $a_1 = 71 - 69 = +2$. The mean of the 20 observations in the control condition is 67, so $a_2 = 67 - 69 = -2$. Notice that $a_1 + a_2 = 0$.

The estimate of π_1 is denoted by p_1. As with other parameters, this estimate is also expressed as a deviation from the grand mean. The mean performance of the first pair is $(62 + 56)/2 = 59$. This value of 59 is below the overall mean of 69, so, averaged over the two conditions, these two participants are below average in performance on the response measure. Thus $p_1 = 59 - 69 = -10$. Note that this value is the same for the control group member of the pair; there is just one π parameter for each pair. The subscript designates the pair, not the condition.

As before, the residuals are obtained by subtraction. The residual is the difference between the observation and the prediction based on the parameter estimates. For the experimental group member of the first pair,

$$e = Y - (\overline{Y} + a_1 + p_1) = 62 - (69 + 2 - 10) = +1$$

For the control group member of the first pair,

$$e = Y - (\overline{Y} + a_2 + p_1) = 56 - (69 - 2 - 10) = -1$$

Putting these values together, we have the following model estimates for the two members of the first pair:

For the member who was assigned to the experimental condition,

$$Y = \overline{Y} + a_1 + p_1 + e$$
$$62 = 69 + 2 - 10 + 1$$

Table 8.5 Estimates of parameters in the model for the data from Data Set 8.1

Pair (j)	Experimental Group					Control Group				
	Y_1	$\overline{Y}$	a_1	p_j	e	Y_2	$\overline{Y}$	a_2	p_j	e
1	62 = 69 + 2			−10	+1	56 = 69 − 2			−10	−1
2	76 = 69 + 2			−1	+6	60 = 69 − 2			−1	−6
3	75 = 69 + 2			+5	−1	73 = 69 − 2			+5	+1
4	52 = 69 + 2			−14	−5	58 = 69 − 2			−14	+5
5	69 = 69 + 2			−1	−1	67 = 69 − 2			−1	+1
6	71 = 69 + 2			−2	+2	63 = 69 − 2			−2	−2
7	76 = 69 + 2			0	+5	62 = 69 − 2			0	−5
8	69 = 69 + 2			+4	−6	77 = 69 − 2			+4	+6
9	89 = 69 + 2			+21	−3	91 = 69 − 2			+21	+3
10	66 = 69 + 2			−1	−4	70 = 69 − 2			−1	+4
11	71 = 69 + 2			+1	−1	69 = 69 − 2			+1	+1
12	68 = 69 + 2			−1	−2	68 = 69 − 2			−1	+2
13	73 = 69 + 2			+2	0	69 = 69 − 2			+2	0
14	75 = 69 + 2			+3	+1	69 = 69 − 2			+3	−1
15	66 = 69 + 2			0	−5	72 = 69 − 2			0	+5
16	59 = 69 + 2			−11	−1	57 = 69 − 2			−11	+1
17	72 = 69 + 2			0	+1	66 = 69 − 2			0	−1
18	80 = 69 + 2			+4	+5	66 = 69 − 2			+4	−5
19	78 = 69 + 2			0	+7	60 = 69 − 2			0	−7
20	73 = 69 + 2			+1	+1	67 = 69 − 2			+1	−1

For the control group member of this first pair,

$$Y = \overline{Y} + a_2 + p_1 + e$$
$$56 = 69 - 2 - 10 - 1$$

Notice that the two residuals are the same except for a change in sign. In fact, for every pair, one residual is the negative of the other. Across rows and down columns (for each pair and each condition), the residuals must sum to 0. Estimating the parameters for all 40 participants gives the values shown in Table 8.5.

The general full model for this design is

$$Y_{ij} = \mu + \alpha_i + \pi_j + e$$

The subscript i indicates the condition ($i = 1$ or 2), and the subscript j indicates the pair (in our example, $j = 1, 2, \ldots, 20$). We can rearrange the terms of this equation and write

$$Y_{ij} - \pi_j = \mu + \alpha_i + e$$

Viewed in this form, π_j can be thought of as an adjustment to Y_{ij}. The adjustment produces a revised score that equates ("levels the playing field") for preexisting differences on the matching variable.

The null model corresponding to the claim that $\alpha_1 = \alpha_2 = 0$ becomes

$$Y_{ij} = \mu + \pi_j + e$$

Normally, we will want to distinguish between this reduced model and the full model, which includes α.

Calculating the Standard Error of the Mean Difference Score

If we calculate the various sums of squares for the values in Table 8.5, we obtain some interesting results. First, if we sum the squares of the residuals of the full model, we have

for the experimental condition: $SS_e = 1^2 + 6^2 + (-1)^2 + \ldots$
for the control condition: $SS_e = (-1)^2 + (-6)^2 + 1^2 + \ldots$

Notice that these two sums will be the same, because the numbers are the same except for a change in sign. For any pair, one residual is the negative of the other. Because squaring removes the distinction between $+$ and $-$, the two sums must be equal. Thus, for the conditions combined,

$$SS_e = 2(1^2 + 6^2 + 1^2 + \ldots + 1^2) = 2(262) = 524$$

The sum within the parentheses contains 20 terms and thus 19 degrees of freedom. The mean square of the residuals is therefore

$$MS_e = \frac{524}{19} = 27.6$$

This result leads directly to the standard error of the difference between the two condition means:

$$s_{\overline{D}} = \sqrt{\frac{2MS_e}{n}} = \sqrt{\frac{2 \times 27.6}{20}} = 1.66$$

The standard error is a measure of a model's failure to account for the data.

Notice that the value of 1.66 is the same value as the denominator of the t-test we calculated in Section 8.22. That value of the standard error was based on the standard deviation difference scores. Once again, we have an example of a very important general principle. The standard error is a direct reflection of the magnitude of the residuals; it is a measure of the model's failure to account for the data.

The analysis based on the model also enables us to gain insight into just how much precision was gained by the matched-pair design over that of an independent-groups design. Suppose we were to drop the π_j component from the model. It is this component that distinguishes the matched-pair design from the independent-groups design. To obtain the residuals for the fitted version of this reduced model, we would simply combine the **p** and e components for each score in Table 8.5. If we form the sum of squares of these revised residuals, we obtain a value of 2400. Using the procedures of Chapter 6, we find that this sum of squares leads to a value of

$MS_e = 2400/38 = 63.2$, considerably larger than the value of 27.6 obtained when the π_j component is added to the model.

8.2.4 Analysis of Variance of Matched Pairs

In Chapter 7, we saw that for an independent-groups design, analysis of variance could be applied to designs with just two conditions, although it is typically used only for designs with three or more conditions. In this sense, the t-test could be regarded as a special case of analysis of variance in which matters are simplified by virtue of there being just a single difference between pairs. A similar relationship holds between two-condition matched-pair designs and designs that use matching but have more than two conditions—designs with three conditions that use matched triples, for example. The latter designs will be considered in Section 8.3. However, to lay the foundation for that discussion, it is useful to see how the principles of analysis of variance can be applied in the simpler two-condition matched-pair case.

The breakdown of the scores in Table 8.5 suggests how analysis of variance might be applied to the matched-pair design. We have seen that the analysis of variance summary table contains sums of squares and mean squares corresponding to the various terms in the full model. In the factorial design, for example, α, β, $\alpha\beta$, and e lead to MS_A, MS_B, MS_{AB}, and MS_e, respectively. The same general principle applies to the matched-pair design. The full model $Y_i = \mu + \alpha_i + \pi_j + e$ will lead to sums of squares and mean squares corresponding to α, π, and e.

The sum of squares corresponding to α is the sum of squares between conditions. It is calculated exactly as before:

$$SS_{between} = n \times \Sigma a_i^2$$

For the data in Table 8.5,

$$n \times \Sigma a_i^2 = 20 \times [2^2 + (-2)^2] = 160$$

The sum of squares corresponding to π is the sum of squares of the means of the pairs. It is calculated in the usual way:

$$SS_{pairs} = 2 \times \Sigma p_j^2$$

The subscript j ranges from 1 to n. For the data in Table 8.5, this sum of squares is the sum of the squared p_j values consisting of two identical columns of 20 numbers each—hence, the initial multiplier value of 2.

$$SS_{pairs} = 2 \times \Sigma p_j^2 = 2 \times [(-10)^2 + (-1^2) + 5^2 + \ldots + 1^2] = 1876$$

The sum of squares corresponding to the e component of the model is the sum of squares of the residuals. SS_e was calculated in Section 8.2.3 and found to be $SS_e = 524$.

The value of SS_{total} can be obtained by simply adding up the three sums of squares we have just calculated:

$$SS_{total} = SS_{between} + SS_{pairs} + SS_e = 160 + 1876 + 524 = 2560$$

Alternatively, and as in previous cases, SS_{total} can be obtained by fitting the model $Y_i = \mu + e$ and calculating the sum of squares of the resulting residuals. Computer analysis gives the result of this operation as 2560.

We can now complete the analysis of variance summary table as shown in Table 8.6. Notice that, if the sum of squares for the pairs (1876) is added to the residual

Table 8.6 Analysis of variance summary table for the data in Data Set 8.1

Source	SS	df	MS
Model	2036	20	—
Between conditions	160	1	160
Pairs	1876	19	98.7
Residual	524	19	27.6
Total	2560	39	—

sum of squares (524), we obtain a value of 2400. This value is the same as that obtained in Section 8.2.3 when the π_j parameter was dropped from the model and the residual sum of squares recalculated for this reduced model. The straightforward way of looking at this correspondence is to see that the sum of squares for the pairs (1876) is the variability that matching has removed from the residual sum of squares of the independent-groups design. It represents the gain in precision—the noise reduction—that matching has achieved over randomization. If the pairings were to be ignored and the data analyzed as an independent-groups design, then SS_e would be 2400 and the value of MS_e would be $2400/38 = 63.2$. As noted previously, this mean square is considerably greater than the value of 27.6 obtained when the design exploits matching.

Another way of evaluating the effectiveness of the matching strategy is to calculate the value of R^2. For the matched-pair analysis,

$$R^2 = \frac{SS_{model}}{SS_{total}} = \frac{2036}{2560} = .80$$

If the π_j parameter were dropped from the model, then only α remains, so SS_{model} is equivalent to $SS_{between}$. Then,

$$R^2 = \frac{SS_{model}}{SS_{total}} = \frac{160}{2560} = .06$$

These various ways of looking at the effect of matching all make it clear that the matching strategy has brought about a substantial reduction in the residuals. Designing the experiment with matched pairs so that π_j can be added to the model provides a much better fit than does the model corresponding to the independent-groups design.

As was the case in the independent-groups design, if $\mu_D = 0$, then $MS_{between}$ and MS_e are both estimates of σ_e^2 and their ratio should not vary systematically from a value of 1.0. The probability distribution that describes the ratio of these two estimates will be the F-distribution. The degrees of freedom will be 1 in the numerator and $n - 1 = 19$ in the denominator.

For our example, the F-ratio is

$$F = \frac{MS_{between}}{MS_e} = \frac{160}{27.6} = 5.80$$

Recall that the F-ratio with 1 degree of freedom in the numerator is the square of the corresponding t-ratio. Thus $\sqrt{5.80} = 2.41$ is the t-ratio calculated in Section 8.22. Note also that, as we have seen before, the standard error of the difference is easily derived from MS_e.

$F = t^2$

$$s_{\overline{D}} = \sqrt{\frac{2MS_e}{n}} = \sqrt{\frac{2 \times 27.6}{20}} = 1.66$$

This value of 1.66 is the same as that obtained in Section 8.2.3. For a Type-1 error rate of $\alpha = .05$, the critical tabled value of the F-ratio for 1 and 19 degrees of freedom is 4.38. Because the calculated F-ratio of 5.80 is greater than this critical value, we conclude that the hypothesis that $\mu_D = 0$ is implausible and therefore that $\mu_D \neq 0$.

8.2.5 A Special Case of Matched Pairs: Within-Subjects (Repeated Measures) Designs

Suppose that Jill had decided on a very different design for her new experiment. Suppose that, instead of forming matched pairs, she measures performance *before* giving the imagery instruction and then reassesses performance of the same participants *after* the instruction. In this "before-after" design, each participant would contribute two measures—a "before measure" and an "after measure." These two measures could be used to obtain a difference score and the data analyzed in the same way as the data for the matched-pair design were.

This "before-after" design is an example of a whole class of experimental designs called within-subjects or repeated measures designs. In the two-condition version of this design, each participant is measured under both conditions of the experiment. In our example, the "before" measure provides the data corresponding to the control condition; the "after" measure serves as the experimental condition. Within-subjects designs can be generalized to more than two conditions, and these larger experiments will be considered in Section 8.3.

A within-subjects design can be thought of as an extreme form of matching, and data from such experiments are usually analyzed in exactly the same way as are data from experiments using matched pairs of different individuals. In a *within-subjects design*, the matched pair is replaced by the same person measured under two different conditions. Rather than two distinct individuals who have been matched on just one variable (such as geometry ability), there is now complete identity—matching on *every* variable. In fact, "every" is something of an exaggeration. Even when using the same person, matching is not perfect because there is an important sense in which an individual is not quite the same from one occasion to the next. This one source of imperfection turns out to be important and will be discussed shortly.

As an example of a within-subjects design, consider the experimental investigation of induced happiness described in Worked Example 1 at the end of Section 6.2. This experiment, modeled after one reported by Laird (1974), asked whether an induced smile actually has the effect of making a person feel happier. In the experimental condition, participants were instructed to move facial muscles to mimic a smile while looking at a picture of children playing. Participants in the control condition simply looked at the same picture but maintained a neutral facial expression. No mention was made of smiling to any of the participants; participants believed the purpose of the experiment was to evaluate the effect of facial muscles on perception.

In a within-subjects design, the matched pair is replaced by the same person measured under two different conditions.

Repeated measures can be thought of as an extreme form of matching.

In a within-subjects version of this experiment, all participants would be measured under both smile-mimic and neutral-expression conditions. These measurements must take place on different occasions, and we will assume that the order in which a participant receives these conditions is random. If order of the condition makes a difference, this randomization ensures that its effects will not bias estimates.

A total of 22 volunteers participated in the experiment. The power values in Table 8.4 indicate that $n = 22$ will give a power $(1 - \beta)$ of .8 to detect an effect size of $d = 0.6$. As in the original version of the experiment, the response measure was a "happiness score" obtained by administering a mood questionnaire. Hypothetical data for this version of the experiment are shown in Data Set 8.2. These data can be analyzed either by using the t-distribution or by analysis of variance.

Data Set 8.2 Happiness scores for the within-subjects version of the induced happiness experiment

Participant	Happy ($\overline{Y}_1 = 16$)	Neutral ($\overline{Y}_2 = 13$)	D ($Y_1 = 3$)	Participant	Happy (cont.)	Neutral (cont.)	D (cont.)
1	16	12	4	12	20	9	11
2	15	17	−2	13	15	9	6
3	23	18	5	14	17	17	0
4	20	15	5	15	6	9	−3
5	23	15	8	16	15	7	8
6	21	16	5	17	15	15	0
7	23	18	5	18	7	4	3
8	23	27	−4	19	15	19	−4
9	18	11	7	20	7	3	4
10	8	8	0	21	13	13	0
11	18	11	7	22	14	14	0

Using the t-distribution, we begin by calculating the standard deviation of the difference scores and then use this value to calculate the standard error of the mean difference score. Computer output gives us the sum of squared deviations as

$$SS_D = (4 - 3)^2 + (-2 - 3)^2 + (5 - 3)^2 + \ldots + (0 - 3)^2 = 377$$

so

$$s_D = \sqrt{\frac{377}{21}} = 4.237$$

The standard error is

$$s_{\overline{D}} = \frac{s_D}{\sqrt{n}} = \frac{4.237}{\sqrt{22}} = 0.903$$

95% Confidence Interval

For a 95% confidence interval, the t-distribution for $df = 21$ gives a value of $t = 2.080$. The 95% confidence interval is therefore

$$CI_{.95} = \overline{D} \pm (2.080 \times 0.903) = 3.0 \pm 1.9 = 1.1 \text{ to } 4.9$$

Because this interval does not include 0, we can reject the null hypothesis at the .05 significance level.

t-Statistic

An alternative but equivalent procedure for evaluating the null hypothesis would be to test it directly, using the t-distribution. The null hypothesis is $H_0 : \mu_D = 0$. The alternative hypothesis is $H_1 : \mu_D \neq 0$. We will set $\alpha = .05$. The data yield a t-ratio of

$$t = \frac{\overline{D}}{s_{\overline{D}}} = \frac{3.0}{0.903} = 3.3$$

As noted when calculating the 95% confidence interval, the t-distribution for $df = 21$ gives a value of $t = 2.080$ as the critical value. Our t-ratio of 3.3 exceeds this critical value, so it falls into the rejection region. The null hypothesis is therefore rejected.

Analysis of Variance

If we apply analysis of variance, then the computations would follow those for the matched-pair design. The only difference is that the label "participants" replaces the label "pairs." Computation gives the analysis of variance summary table shown in Table 8.7.

The F-ratio for evaluating the difference between the conditions is

$$F = \frac{\text{MS}_{\text{between}}}{\text{MS}_e} = \frac{96.02}{8.98} = 10.70$$

This value of F, apart from rounding error, is the square of the t-ratio calculated previously. Note also that, as noted earlier, the standard error of the difference is easily derived from MS_e:

$$s_{\overline{D}} = \sqrt{\frac{2\text{MS}_e}{n}} = \sqrt{\frac{2 \times 8.98}{22}} = 0.903$$

Table 8.7 Analysis of variance summary table for the data in Data Set 8.2

Source	SS	df	MS
Model	1148.50	22	—
Between conditions	96.02	1	96.02
Participants	1052.48	21	50.12
Residual	188.48	21	8.98
Total	1336.98	43	—

Carryover Effect

Within-subjects designs can be thought of as a very powerful form of matching. Moreover, the analysis of the data is the same as for matched pairs of different individuals. These similarities should not be allowed to mask one important difference between matched pairs and within-subjects. In measuring the same participant in both conditions, there is the possibility that the participants' experience in whatever condition they receive first might influence their performance on the second. An obvious example would be some form of practice effect in which the experience gained in the first condition changes performance in the second condition and makes it different from what it would have been otherwise. This kind of cross talk, or *carryover effect,* between conditions can seriously bias the measurement of the second condition. It is a problem that cannot arise in the case of matched pairs of different individuals.

The possibility of such carryover effects could be a matter of concern in the experiment we have just described. Participants who have already been in one condition are now familiar with various aspects of the experimental procedure. They may be more relaxed on the second occasion, they may be more bored, or they may be resentful at having to appear at a second session. On the basis of their experience in the first session, participants may develop some new strategy for performing the task or for using the rating scale.

Sometimes carryover problems can be overcome by randomly determining (separately for each participant) the order in which conditions are presented. In the induced happiness experiment, the flip of a coin might determine whether the participant received the happy or neutral condition first. Alternatively, a matching strategy could be used by presenting each condition first to exactly half the participants and second to the other half. In this case, the order of the conditions would be described as "balanced."

As with other aspects of experimental control, managing carryover effects depends heavily on the researcher's experience in the area under investigation. However, if carryover effects are known to pose a serious problem, then within-subjects designs should not be used.

Carryover effect occurs in a within-subjects design when the experience of the first condition influences performance on the second.

Disadvantages of Matching

The danger of carryover effects in within-subjects designs may suggest that matching is the better strategy. Matching, however, has its own drawbacks. In many applications, establishing an effective matching variable can be a difficult and time-consuming task. Moreover, even after the matching variable has been devised, the practical difficulties in establishing matched pairs can also be time consuming. It is often the case that when carryover effects pose a genuine threat to sound experimentation, the least expensive way of increasing precision is to resort to the strategy of Section 8.1—simply increase n.

Comprehension Check 8.2

Important Concepts

1. A strategy for reducing MS_e and thereby increasing precision is to form matched pairs.

2. Matching will be effective in reducing MS_e to the extent that pairs are matched on a factor that is responsible for variability among participants *within* a condition.

3. In choosing the sample size needed to achieve a desired power level, a table of power values appropriate for matched-pair designs must be used.

4. A simple form of analysis for matched pairs is to take difference scores, calculate the standard error of their mean, and use the t-distribution to calculate a confidence interval or to evaluate the statistical significance of $\overline{D}$ directly.

5. The full model for the matched-pair design is $Y = \mu + \alpha_i + \pi_j + e$. This model forms the basis of an analysis of variance in which SS_{within} of the independent-groups design is partitioned into two components: a reduced SS_{within} and SS_{pairs}. This removal of the SS_{pairs} is responsible for the increased precision.

6. An experimental design that can be thought of as a special case of matching is known as within-subjects. Although the analysis of within-subjects designs is usually performed in exactly the same way as matched pairs, care must be taken with within-subjects to ensure that results are not contaminated by unwanted carry-over effects.

Worked Examples

Example 1   **Tranquilizer effects (Data Set 8.3)**

In Chapter 6, we analyzed data from an experiment designed to investigate the effect of a tranquilizer on mental functioning, which was measured in terms of time (in seconds) taken to solve simple anagrams. Data were analyzed from an experiment that had an independent-groups design. Consider now a matched-pair version of this experiment.

Pairs of participants are matched on the basis of a prior test of anagram-solving ability. Pairs of participants are formed such that the two members of each pair have

Data Set 8.3   Data for the first matched-pair version of the tranquilizer effects experiment (Worked Example 1)

Pair	Experimental ($\overline{Y}_1 = 10.86$)	Control ($\overline{Y}_2 = 9.59$)	D ($\overline{D} = 1.27$)	Pair	Experimental (cont.)	Control (cont.)	D (cont.)
1	10.7	10.4	0.3	9	10.7	10.6	0.1
2	10.4	9.1	1.3	10	10.6	8.7	1.9
3	10.4	9.9	0.5	11	10.6	10.3	0.3
4	11.2	11.4	−0.2	12	7.1	5.5	1.6
5	11.3	10.8	0.5	13	10.8	9.3	1.5
6	13.0	11.9	1.1	14	9.7	8.4	1.3
7	12.3	9.4	2.9	15	13.7	11.4	2.3
8	10.4	6.7	3.7				

the same anagram-solving ability, as measured by this prior test. One member of each pair is assigned randomly to the experimental (tranquilizer) condition, the other member of the pair to the control (placebo) condition. The experiment uses $n = 15$ matched pairs. This is the same number of participants used in the independent-groups version of this experiment. The data are shown in Data Set 8.3, which also gives the means for each column. Computation gives the estimated standard deviation of the difference scores (D) as $s_D = 1.096$.

a. If the model $Y = \mu + \alpha_i + \pi_j + e$ is fitted to these data, find the estimated values of (i) μ; (ii) α_1; (iii) π_4; (iv) all four components of the model for the experimental condition member of pair 7.

b. Given the values for the two sample means and the standard deviation of the difference scores, calculate a 95% confidence interval for μ_D, the difference between the means of the two conditions. On the basis of this 95% confidence interval, would you reject the hypothesis that $\mu_D = 0$?

c. What is the value of the t-ratio you would calculate to evaluate the hypothesis that $\mu_D = 0$? Using $\alpha = .05$, check that this value leads to a decision consistent with that made in (b).

d. If the data were to be analyzed using analysis of variance, what value of the F-ratio would you get when $MS_{between}$ is divided by MS_e?

e. The data in Data Set 8.3 are analyzed by using analysis of variance. Partial results from this analysis are given in Table 8.8, an analysis of variance summary table. (i) Complete the missing entries. (ii) Calculate the F-ratio for testing $MS_{between}$ and check that it equals the value you obtained in (d). (iii) Use the table of the F-distribution to establish the critical value of the F-ratio for $\alpha = .05$. Check that it equals the square of the critical t-value used in (b) to calculate the 95% confidence interval. (iv) Use the value of MS_e to derive the estimate of the standard error of the difference between the means and check that it equals the value you obtained in (b).

f. What is the value of R^2 for this experiment? Examine the gain in precision achieved through matching by calculating a value for R^2 with the matching factor (π) removed from the model.

Table 8.8 Incomplete analysis of variance summary table for the data in Data Set 8.3 (Worked Example 1)

Source	SS	df	MS
Model	_____	_____	—
Between conditions	12.160	_____	_____
Pairs	66.209	_____	_____
Residual	8.405	_____	_____
Total	_____	_____	—

g. In the original version of this experiment, which used an independent-groups design, the value of w, the half-width of the confidence interval, was 1.03; the value of MS_e was 1.91, and R^2 was .203. By comparing these values with the corresponding values in the matched-pairs design, convince yourself that in this case the matching strategy has achieved increased precision.

Answer

a. (i) The estimate of μ is the grand mean (the mean of all 30 observations), which is $(10.86 + 9.59)/2 = 10.22$. (ii) The estimate of α_1 is $a_1 = 10.86 - 10.22 = 0.64$. (iii) The estimate of π_4 is the difference between the mean for that pair and the grand mean: $p_4 = (11.2 + 11.4)/2 - 10.22 = 1.08$. (iv) The estimate of μ is 10.22; the estimate of α_1 is $a_1 = 0.64$; the estimate of π_7 is the difference between the mean for that pair and the grand mean: $p_7 = (12.3 + 9.4)/2 - 10.22 = 0.63$. The estimate of the residual, e, is obtained by subtraction, so $e = 12.3 - (10.22 + 0.64 + 0.63) = 0.81$. Thus the breakdown of this participant's score is $12.3 = 10.22 + 0.64 + 0.63 + 0.81$.

b. The first step in calculating the 95% confidence interval for the difference between the means of the two conditions is to obtain the standard error of the mean difference: $s_{\overline{D}} = s_D/\sqrt{n} = 1.096/\sqrt{15} = 0.283$. For a 95% confidence interval, the t-distribution for $df = 14$ gives a value of $t = 2.145$. The 95% confidence interval is therefore $CI_{.95} = \overline{D} \pm (2.145 \times 0.283) = 1.27 \pm 0.61 = 0.66$ to 1.88. Because this interval does not include 0, we can reject the null hypothesis at the .05 significance level.

c. The value of the t-ratio needed to evaluate the hypothesis that $\mu_D = 0$ is $t = \overline{D}/s_{\overline{D}} = 1.27/0.283 = 4.5$. As we noted when calculating the 95% confidence interval, the t-distribution for $df = 14$ gives a critical value of $t = 2.145$. Our t-ratio of 4.5 exceeds this critical value, so it falls into the rejection region. The null hypothesis is therefore rejected, a decision consistent with that made on the basis of the 95% confidence interval.

d. If the data were to be analyzed by using analysis of variance, the value of the F-ratio obtained when $MS_{between}$ was divided by MS_e would be t^2. That is, we should obtain an F-ratio of $4.5^2 = 20.3$.

e. (i) Table 8.9 gives the missing entries. The mean squares were obtained by dividing the sum of squares by the degrees of freedom on which it is based. (ii) The F-ratio for testing $MS_{between}$ is $F = MS_{between}/MS_e = 12.16/0.600 = 20.3$. This value equals the value obtained in (d). (iii) The critical F-ratio is obtained from the tables of the F-distribution for $df = 1$ and 14. This value is 4.60. Note that $\sqrt{4.60} = 2.145$, the critical value of the t-ratio used to calculate the 95% confidence interval. (iv) The value of MS_e can be used to derive the estimate of the standard error of the difference between the means: $s_{\overline{D}} = \sqrt{2MS_e/n} = 0.283$. This is the value we obtained in (b).

f. The value of R^2 for this experiment is $R^2 = SS_{model}/SS_{total} = 78.369/86.774 = .90$. If the π_j parameter were dropped from the model, then only α would remain, so SS_{model} would be equivalent to $SS_{between}$. Then $R^2 = SS_{model}/SS_{total} = 12.160/86.774 = .14$.

g. For the matched pair design, w and MS_e are smaller, and R^2 is larger.

Table 8.9 Analysis of variance summary table for the data in Data Set 8.3 (Worked Example 1)

Source	SS	df	MS
Model	78.369	15	—
Between conditions	12.160	1	12.16
Pairs	66.209	14	4.73
Residual	8.405	14	0.60
Total	86.774	29	—

Example 2 **Incidental remembering**

Problem 3 at the end of Section 6.3 used an independent-groups design to compare two levels of incidental remembering. A new version of this experiment uses a within-subjects design. Participants again see a list of 40 common words for 5 seconds each. Each word is preceded by an instruction. Half of the words are preceded by an instruction to rate each of the words for pleasantness. The other half are preceded by an instruction to report the number of syllables the word contains. The order of the words and their preceding instruction is random.

Following the presentation of the words, participants were asked to recall as many words as they could in any order. A total of 17 volunteers participated in the experiment. The resulting data are shown in Data Set 8.4.

a. What are the estimates for α_1 and α_2 based on these data? Use these values to obtain the value of $SS_{between}$ for the analysis of variance of these data.

Data Set 8.4 Recall scores for the within-subjects version of the incidental remembering experiment (Worked Example 2)

Pair	Rate pleasantness ($\overline{Y}_1 = 8.59$)	Count syllables ($\overline{Y}_2 = 5.88$)	Pair	Rate pleasantness (cont.)	Count syllables (cont.)
1	9	6	10	4	4
2	5	3	11	7	7
3	8	4	12	1	0
4	10	4	13	7	4
5	8	5	14	11	5
6	14	10	15	13	12
7	12	11	16	8	5
8	8	3	17	10	9
9	11	8			

Table 8.10 Incomplete analysis of variance summary table for the data in Data Set 8.4 (Worked Example 2)

Source	SS	df	MS
Model	_____	_____	—
Between conditions	62.2	_____	_____
Participants	309.1	_____	_____
Residual	28.8	_____	_____
Total	_____	_____	—

b. These data were analyzed by using analysis of variance. Table 8.10 gives part of the results of this analysis. Complete the missing parts.

c. What is the value of the F-ratio for testing the hypothesis that $\mu_D = 0$? Using $\alpha = .05$, what is the critical tabled value of the F-ratio against which this obtained value should be compared? Should the hypothesis that $\mu_D = 0$ be rejected?

d. Use the value of MS_e to calculate the standard error of the difference between the means. Use this result to calculate a 95% confidence interval for μ_D.

Answer

a. The grand mean for these data is $(8.59 + 5.88)/2 = 7.235$. The estimate for α_1 is therefore $a_1 = 8.59 - 7.235 = 1.355$, and the estimate for α_2 is $a_2 = -1.355$. The value of $SS_{between}$ for the analysis of variance of these data is therefore

$$SS_{between} = n \times \Sigma a_i^2 = 17 \times [1.355^2 + (-1.355^2)] = 62.4$$

(Rounding error makes this value 62.4 rather than 62.2.)

b. The missing entries for the analysis of variance summary table are shown in Table 8.11. Each mean square was obtained by dividing the sum of squares by the degrees of freedom on which it is based.

c. The value of the F-ratio for testing the hypothesis that $\mu_D = 0$ is $F = MS_{between}/MS_e = 62.2/1.8 = 34.6$. For $\alpha = .05$ and $df = 1$ and 16, the critical tabled value of the F-ratio against which this obtained value should be compared is 4.49. The hypothesis that $\mu_D = 0$ should therefore be rejected.

d. The value of the standard error of the difference between the means is $s_{\overline{D}} = \sqrt{2MS_e/n} = (2 \times 1.8)/17 = 0.46$. For a 95% confidence interval, we use the t-distribution with $df = 16$. The table of the t-distribution gives a value of $t = 2.120$. (Note that $2.12 = \sqrt{4.49}$, the square root of the critical F-ratio used in the analysis of variance.) The difference between the condition means is $\overline{D} = 8.59 - 5.88 = 2.71$. The 95% confidence interval is therefore $CI_{.95} = \overline{D} \pm (2.120 \times 0.46) = 2.71 \pm 0.98 = 1.73$ to 3.69. Because this interval does not include 0, we can reject the null hypothesis at the .05 significance level.

Table 8.11 Analysis of variance summary table for the data in Data Set 8.4 (Worked Example 2)

Source	SS	df	MS
Model	371.3	17	—
Between conditions	62.2	1	62.2
Participants	309.1	16	19.3
Residual	28.8	16	1.8
Total	400.1	33	—

Problems

Problem 1   Tranquilizer effects (Data Set 8.5)

In Worked Example 1, pairs of participants were matched on the basis of a prior test of anagram-solving ability; pairs were formed so that two members of each pair had the same anagram-solving ability as measured by this prior test. Consider a new version of this experiment. Rather than give a prior test of anagram-solving ability, the investigator decides to make use of existing information. The investigator has the GPA of each participant and uses this measure to form matched pairs. Pairs are formed so that the two members of each pair have approximately the same GPA.

The data for the new version are shown in Data Set 8.5. The standard deviation of the difference scores is $s_D = 1.433$.

a. If the model $Y = \mu + \alpha_i + \pi_j + e$ is fitted to these data, what are the estimated values of (i) μ; (ii) α_2; (iii) π_1; (iv) all four components of the model for the control condition member of pair 9.

Data Set 8.5   Anagram solution times for a second matched-pair version of the tranquilizer effects experiment in which pairs are matched on the basis of GPA scores (Problem 1)

Pair	Experimental ($\overline{Y}_1 = 11.21$)	Control ($\overline{Y}_2 = 9.71$)	D ($\overline{D} = 1.51$)	Pair (cont.)	Experimental (cont.)	Control (cont.)	D (cont.)
1	9.6	9.4	0.2	9	11.3	9.5	1.8
2	13.7	12.5	1.2	10	13.1	12.0	1.1
3	10.6	9.1	1.5	11	12.3	9.5	2.8
4	10.7	7.9	2.8	12	10.6	11.1	− 0.5
5	10.4	9.1	1.3	13	11.8	11.7	0.1
6	11.7	9.5	2.2	14	11.3	7.4	3.9
7	11.6	7.8	3.8	15	8.6	9.5	− 0.9
8	10.9	9.6	1.3				

Table 8.12 Incomplete analysis of variance summary table for the data in Data Set 8.5 (Problem 1)

Source	SS	df	MS
Model	_____	_____	—
Between conditions	17.025	_____	_____
Pairs	40.712	_____	_____
Residual	14.375	_____	_____
Total	_____	_____	—

b. Given the values for the two sample means and the standard deviation of the difference scores, calculate a 99% confidence interval for μ_D, the difference between the means of the two conditions. On the basis of this 99% confidence interval, would you reject the hypothesis that $\mu_D = 0$?

c. What is the value of the t-ratio you would calculate to evaluate the hypothesis that $\mu_D = 0$? Using $\alpha = .01$, check that this value leads to a decision consistent with that made in (b).

d. If the data were to be analyzed by using analysis of variance, what value of the F-ratio would you get when $MS_{between}$ is divided by MS_e?

e. The data for this experiment are analyzed by using analysis of variance. Partial results from this analysis are given in Table 8.12. (i) Complete the missing entries. (ii) Calculate the F-ratio for testing $MS_{between}$ and check that it equals the value you obtained in (d). (iii) Use the table of the F-distribution to establish the critical value of the F-ratio for $\alpha = .01$. Check that it equals (within rounding error) the square of the critical t-ratio used in (b) to calculate the 99% confidence interval. (iv) Use the value of MS_e to derive the estimate of the standard error of the difference between the means and check that it equals the value you obtained in (b).

f. What is the value of R^2 for this experiment? Examine the gain in precision achieved through blocking by calculating a value for R^2 with the matching factor (π) removed from the model.

g. Using whatever measures you consider relevant, decide which of the two matched-pair versions of this experiment (Example 1 or this one) achieves the greater gain in precision relative to the original independent-groups design.

Problem 2   **Evaluation of typing speed (Data Set 8.6)**

In an experiment designed to evaluate a computer program aimed at increasing typing speed, the typing speed of novice typists is measured before using the program and then again after 10 hours of practice with the program. Typing speed is measured in words per minute, suitably corrected for errors. Data Set 8.6 gives the data from the experiment, which used 14 participants. The column headed "Improvement" is the difference score for each participant (After − Before). Given the standard devia-

Data Set 8.6 Data for the typing evaluation experiment (Problem 2)

P	Before ($\overline{Y}_1 = 22.36$)	After ($\overline{Y}_2 = 30.43$)	Improvement ($\overline{D} = 8.07$)
1	18	24	6
2	20	30	10
3	21	30	9
4	35	41	6
5	15	16	1
6	23	30	7
7	24	30	6
8	27	31	4
9	25	28	3
10	18	30	12
11	25	36	11
12	22	40	18
13	23	32	9
14	17	28	11

The response measure is typing speed, in words per minute.

tion of the improvement (difference) scores (4.323), calculate a 95% confidence interval for the population mean improvement score, μ_D. Discuss the justification for an advertising claim that 10 hours of practice with the program produces an average improvement of ten words per minute.

8.3 Matching and Within-Subjects Designs with More Than Two Conditions

A block is a set of matched elements equal in number to the number of conditions.

The randomized block design with *k* conditions has *n* blocks of *k* matched participants.

The matching principle can be extended to more than two conditions. When matching involves more than a pair, the set of matched elements is called a *block*. An experiment with three conditions, for example, would require blocks of matched triples rather than matched pairs. A prior measure could be used to match participants in blocks of three. Alternatively, a block might represent some categorical grouping such as members of the same household; in an animal study, the category might be littermates. For each of these blocks, the three participants would be assigned randomly to the three conditions, one participant in each. The general name for such a design is a *randomized block design*. If an experiment has *k* conditions, then *n* blocks, each of size *k*, would be formed and the *k* members of each block assigned randomly to the *k* conditions.

In the behavioral sciences, the most common form of this design is the special case of repeated measures or within-subjects design in which each participant takes part in all conditions. We will therefore use a within-subjects design as an example.

Within-Subjects Design with Three Conditions

Social psychologists have documented ways in which our behavior is influenced by what we believe about ourselves and by our impression of what others believe we are capable of. If someone convinces you that you are good at science, your performance in science will improve.

Consider an experiment in which second grade students were told repeatedly that they were good at math. Does this attribution manipulation lead to improved math scores? To answer this question, $n = 17$ second graders were given different but equivalent math tests on three occasions. The first occasion was a pretest given before beginning the attribution manipulation. The second test was given immediately after the attribution manipulation; and the third was given a few weeks later. The conditions of this experiment are the three occasions: pretest, immediate posttest, and delayed posttest. Each of the 17 students contributes three observations, one for each condition. Hypothetical data from this experiment are given in Data Set 8.7. This example is based on part of an experiment reported by Miller, Brickman, and Bolen (1975).

Data Set 8.7   Data from the experiment evaluating the effect of attribution manipulation on math performance of second graders

Student	Pretest ($\overline{Y}_1 = 15.3$)	Immediate posttest ($\overline{Y}_2 = 18.2$)	Delayed posttest ($\overline{D} = 18.9$)	Student	Pretest (cont.)	Immediate posttest (cont.)	Delayed posttest (cont.)
1	18	21	20	10	10	19	19
2	15	16	15	11	23	17	22
3	14	16	20	12	15	24	23
4	11	16	16	13	16	13	14
5	15	15	19	14	10	18	21
6	26	21	27	15	12	22	18
7	9	18	19	16	20	20	19
8	14	21	14	17	17	18	18
9	15	15	18				

The response measure is test score.

The full model for this experiment is the same as that for a two-condition experiment, the only difference being that the subscript i now has three possible values corresponding to the three conditions:

$$Y_i = \mu + \alpha_i + \pi_j + e$$

The null hypothesis is that $\alpha_1 = \alpha_2 = \alpha_3 = 0$, so the model corresponding to this hypothesis is

$$Y_i = \mu + \pi_j + e$$

The usual method of analyzing these results is to evaluate the full model by using analysis of variance. However, as was the case for the independent-groups design, it is

The full model for this experiment is the same as that for the two-condition case.

also possible to calculate a confidence interval for each of the three differences between pairs of means by using a procedure such as Tukey's (see Section 8.3.2).

The analysis of variance summary has the same form as that for the two-condition case.

The analysis of variance summary table is shown as Table 8.13. It has the same form as that for the two-condition case. Although such calculations would usually be done by using computer software, it is important to have some understanding of how the numbers were obtained. The between-condition and the between-participant sums of squares are calculated in the usual way. For the between-condition sum of squares,

$$SS_{between} = n \times \Sigma a_i^2$$

The values of a_i are obtained exactly as they were in Section 8.2.4. The grand mean for the data in Data Set 8.7 is 17.4, so, for example, a_1 is $15.3 - 17.4 = -2.1$. There are three conditions, so the degrees of freedom for $SS_{between}$ is 2. In an experiment with k conditions, $SS_{between}$ would have $k - 1$ degrees of freedom.

The sum of squares corresponding to π is the sum of squares among the mean scores (averaged over the three occasions) of the 17 participants. It is calculated in the same way as in Section 8.2.4.

$$SS_{participants} = k \times \Sigma p_j^2$$

The sums of squares are obtained in the same way they are calculated for the two-condition case.

For this experiment, $k = 3$. The values of the p_j are also obtained exactly as before. For example, the mean for the first participant in Data Set 8.7 is $(18 + 21 + 20)/3 = 19.7$, so

$$p_1 = 19.7 - 17.4 = +2.3$$

There are 17 participants, so the degrees of freedom for $SS_{participants}$ is 16. In an experiment with n participants, $SS_{participants}$ would have $n - 1$ degrees of freedom.

The residuals would be obtained by subtraction in the usual way. The degrees of freedom for these residuals is $df = 32$. There are two ways of deriving this value. The first is by subtraction. The total degrees of freedom for the entire experiment is the total number of observations less one: $(3 \times 17) - 1 = 50$. The between-condition and between-participant sum of squares have a combined degrees of freedom of $2 + 16 = 18$, thus leaving $50 - 18 = 32$ degrees of freedom for the residual.

Table 8.13 Analysis of variance summary table for the data reported in Data Set 8.7

Source	SS	df	MS
Model	485.9	18	—
Between conditions	127.2	2	63.6
Participants	358.7	16	22.4
Residual	288.8	32	9.025
Total	774.7	50	—

The second way of obtaining the residual degrees of freedom is to use the general formula

$$df_{residual} = (k - 1)(n - 1)$$

That is, the degrees of freedom for the residual sums of squares is the product of the degrees of freedom for between conditions and the degrees of freedom for between participants. In this example, $(k - 1)(n - 1) = 2 \times 16 = 32$.

This general formula provides some insight into the nature of the residuals in within-subjects and randomized block designs. One way of thinking about the model statement and its corresponding analysis of variance summary table is to regard this design as a $k \times n$ two-way factorial design without an interaction term. One factor is the conditions, with $k - 1$ degrees of freedom; the other factor is the block or participant factor with $n - 1$ degrees of freedom. These two factors are assumed to be additive in the sense defined in the discussion of factorial designs:

The model for the randomized block design assumes that there is no interaction between blocks and conditions or, in the case of repeated measures, between participants and conditions.

Consider what it would mean to have an interaction between participants and conditions. Interactions you will recall are present when the effects of one factor are different at the different levels of the other factor. For a within-subjects design, an interaction between participants and conditions would mean that the effect of the conditions is different for different participants. In an attribution experiment affecting math ability, for example, it would mean that the effect of the attribution was different for different participants—that some participants benefited more than others, or that some benefited and others did not. Any such interaction would simply be incorporated into the residual sum of squares and thus into MS_e. In short, an interaction between participants and conditions (or between blocks and conditions in a randomized block design) is confounded with the residual variance—a signal is confounded with noise—and therefore inflates its measure, MS_e.

To understand this confounding of signal and noise, note one important difference between the present design and the completely randomized factorial design. In the completely randomized factorial design, MS_e is the average variability *within* each cell. However, unlike the completely randomized factorial design, when the within-subjects design is considered as a conditions × participants factorial design, *there is only one observation within each cell*. It is therefore impossible to estimate any variability within a cell; estimating variability demands at least two observations. The only estimate of noise is variability among the residuals, with one residual in each of the $n \times k$ cells. If a systematic interaction is also contributing to the variability among these residuals, then there is no way of separating out their relative contributions.

Table 8.14 gives the general form of the analysis of variance summary table for a randomized block or within-subjects design. As with the matched-pair design, or the two-condition within-subjects design, the F-distribution can be used to evaluate the mean square between conditions. To review the logic underlying the use of the F-ratio, recall that two components can contribute to the size of $MS_{between}$—one potential, the other inevitable.

The existence of a real participant × condition interaction will inflate the size of MS_e.

Table 8.14 General form of the analysis of variance summary table for a randomized block or within-subjects design with k conditions and n blocks or participants

Source	SS	df	MS
Model			
Between conditions	$SS_{between}$	$k - 1$	$\dfrac{SS_{between}}{(k - 1)}$
Blocks participants	SS_{blocks}	$n - 1$	$\dfrac{SS_{blocks}}{n - 1}$
Residual	SS_e	$(k - 1)(n - 1)$	$\dfrac{SS_e}{(k - 1)(n - 1)}$
Total	SS_{total}	$nk - 1$	—

The potential contributor is any differences among the population condition means. The null hypothesis is that these population condition means are all equal:

$$H_0 : \mu_1 = \mu_2 = \mu_3 = \ldots$$

Any difference among these means, even if it is between just a single pair, falsifies the null hypothesis and serves as a basis for increasing the value of $MS_{between}$. The inevitable contribution is from noise. Remember that even if the null hypothesis were true and that the *population* values of the condition means were all equal, the *sample* condition means would differ somewhat among themselves.

By comparing the value of $MS_{between}$ with the value of MS_e, the *F*-ratio enables us to decide whether the value of $MS_{between}$ is significantly larger than MS_e. If the null hypothesis is true, then the *F*-ratio should not differ significantly from a value of 1.0. As before, the probability distribution that describes the ratio of these two mean squares will be the *F*-distribution. The degrees of freedom are $k - 1$ in the numerator (2, in our example) and $(k - 1)(n - 1) = 32$ in the denominator.

For the present example, the *F*-ratio is

$$F = \frac{MS_{between}}{MS_e} = \frac{63.6}{9.025} = 7.05$$

For a Type-1 error rate of $\alpha = .05$, the critical tabulated value of the *F*-ratio for 2 and 32 degrees of freedom is 3.29. The obtained *F*-ratio of 7.05 is greater than this critical value, so we conclude that the hypothesis that the *F*-ratio has an expected value of 1.0 is implausible; the evidence indicates that the claim that $\alpha_i = 0$ for every i is untenable.

8.3.2 Simultaneous Confidence Intervals

When there are three or more conditions in a randomized block or within-subjects design, the distinction between confidence levels considered singly and simultaneously arises just as it did in Section 7.1.2 for the independent-groups design. With individual confidence intervals, the confidence level refers to each interval considered separately. If each of these levels is set at 95%, the probability that *all* the intervals will include their true values will be less than .95. With simultaneous confidence intervals, the confidence level refers to the entire set of intervals, that is, the probability that they all contain the true difference. For the three-condition attribution experiment, we would usually want the confidence level to apply to all intervals simultaneously.

Simultaneous confidence intervals in a randomized block or within-subjects design can be obtained in exactly the same way as we calculated them for the independent-groups design. We will apply the Tukey method that uses the Studentized range distribution (see Section 7.1.2). The confidence interval for each difference will be the point estimate of the difference $\pm w$, for example, $|\overline{Y}_1 - \overline{Y}_2| \pm w$ where, as before,

$$w = q \times \sqrt{\frac{MS_e}{n}}$$

The value of q is obtained from the table of the Studentized range distribution. Recall that use of the tables requires values for two parameters: k, the number of conditions, and df, the degrees of freedom on which MS_e is based. For this design, $df = (k - 1)(n - 1)$. For the attribution and math performance experiment, $k = 3$ and $df = 32$. Consulting the table of the Studentized range distribution (Statistical Table 4 in Appendix C) gives a value of $q = 3.49$ (using $df = 30$ as the closest tabled value). We therefore have

$$w = q \times \sqrt{\frac{MS_e}{n}} = 3.49 \times \sqrt{\frac{9.025}{17}} = 2.5$$

The condition means in Data Set 8.7 give the following point estimates of the mean differences:

$$|\overline{Y}_1 - \overline{Y}_2| = 2.9$$
$$|\overline{Y}_1 - \overline{Y}_3| = 3.6$$
$$|\overline{Y}_2 - \overline{Y}_3| = 0.7$$

The three 95% confidence intervals are thus

for $|\mu_1 - \mu_2|$, $CI_{.95} = 2.9 \pm 2.5 = 0.4$ to 5.4
for $|\mu_1 - \mu_3|$, $CI_{.95} = 3.6 \pm 2.5 = 1.1$ to 6.1
for $|\mu_2 - \mu_3|$, $CI_{.95} = 0.7 \pm 2.5 = -1.8$ to 3.2

These 95% confidence intervals provide a way of evaluating the null hypothesis for each of the differences between pairs of means, with a Type-1 error rate per experiment of $\alpha = .05$. The first two intervals do not include 0, so, in these two cases, the null hypothesis of zero difference would be rejected. The interval estimate for $|\mu_2 - \mu_3|$ *does* include 0, so the difference between these conditions is not significant.

Recall from Section 7.1.3 that w is also the minimum difference needed to reject the null hypothesis. This minimum difference was termed the HSD, the honestly significant difference. In our example, HSD = 2.5, so any difference between pairs of means greater than 2.54 would, according to this criterion, be declared significant. Both $|\overline{Y}_1 - \overline{Y}_2|$ and $|\overline{Y}_1 - \overline{Y}_3|$ exceed 2.5, so, as the confidence intervals have already indicated, these two differences are incompatible with a true difference of 0. We

The null hypothesis can be tested directly against *w*, Tukey's honestly significant difference, HSD.

therefore conclude that the attribution manipulation improves performance and that this improvement remains constant over the following few weeks.

Therapy Follow-Up Study

In a follow-up study of people who received desensitization therapy to reduce phobia, an investigator measures anxiety levels of 20 participants at three time intervals after the end of therapy: 1 week, 3 months, and 1 year. As before, the response measure is rated anxiety level. The data are shown in Data Set 8.8. We will use analysis of variance to evaluate these data and then calculate 95% confidence intervals for the three differences. The results from the analysis of variance are given in the summary table shown in Table 8.15. Check that you understand the values for the various degrees of freedom and how the MS values are obtained from the SS values.

Data Set 8.8 Data for the therapy follow-up study

P	1 week ($\bar{Y}_1 = 6.0$)	3 months ($\bar{Y}_2 = 6.3$)	1 year ($\bar{D} = 5.9$)	P	1 week (cont.)	3 months (cont.)	1 year (cont.)
1	5	7	4	11	8	6	7
2	4	4	2	12	3	1	0
3	6	6	7	13	6	6	5
4	6	6	7	14	7	7	5
5	6	6	6	15	10	8	9
6	9	10	9	16	5	5	5
7	8	9	9	17	6	7	7
8	5	5	4	18	4	7	8
9	6	9	7	19	4	5	5
10	6	5	6	20	6	7	6

The response measure is rated anxiety level.

The null hypothesis of no difference among the conditions ($H_0: \alpha_i = 0$) can be evaluated by using the F-ratio based on the between-conditions mean square:

$$F = \frac{MS_{between}}{MS_e} = \frac{0.865}{0.972} = 0.89$$

Because the null hypothesis was retained, precision and the probability of the Type-2 error is a matter of concern.

We could consult the table of the F-distribution to obtain the critical value of the F-ratio for 2 and 38 degrees of freedom, but because the obtained value of the F-ratio is less than 1.0, it is unnecessary. Obviously, an F-ratio that is less than 1.0 cannot be significantly *greater* than 1. Therefore, the null hypothesis is not rejected.

Although the data provide no evidence that rated anxiety levels have changed over the 12-month period, a cautious investigator might be concerned that this failure to reject the null hypothesis reflects the low precision of the estimated differences. Although a detailed account of power calculations for this design is beyond the scope of this book, some insight into precision can be gained by looking at the width of the confidence intervals of the differences between the mean ratings. To this end, we will calculate the value of *w* for simultaneous 95% confidence intervals, using the Stu-

Table 8.15 Analysis of variance summary table for the data in Data Set 8.8

Source	SS	df	MS
Model	196.8	21	—
Between conditions	1.73	2	0.865
Participants	195.07	19	10.27
Residual	36.9	38	0.972
Total	233.7	59	—

dentized range statistic. The relevant value of q is for $k = 3$ and $df = 38$, and the table gives an approximate value of 3.44. Thus

$$w = q \times \sqrt{\frac{MS_e}{n}} = 3.44 \times \sqrt{\frac{0.972}{20}} = 0.76$$

Although a satisfactory value of w is always a matter for an experienced researcher to decide, the value of $w = 0.76$ suggests a high degree of precision. Even if the investigator demands a 99% confidence interval, the value of w for this interval is only $4.37 \times \sqrt{0.972/20} = 0.96$. Thus the investigator can feel highly confident that the obtained differences in mean rating are accurate to within 1 rating-scale point of the true difference.

The high precision is also reflected in the value of R^2, which indicates that the nonresidual components of the model account for a high proportion of the variability as measured by the sums of squares. For this experiment, $R^2 = SS_{model}/SS_{total} = 196.8/233.7 = .84$.

Comprehension Check 8.3

Important Concepts

1. The matched-pair design can be extended to experiments with more than two conditions.

2. If the experiment uses blocks of matched participants, then the design is described as a randomized block design. An experiment with k conditions would consist of n blocks, each made up of k matched participants.

3. If the experiment obtains an observation from each participant under all of the k conditions, then the experiment is described as a within-subjects or repeated measures design.

4. As in the two-condition case, both randomized block and within-subjects (repeated measures) designs are analyzed in the same way.

5. Both the model and the analysis of variance summary table have exactly the same form as in the two-condition case.

6. When there are three or more conditions, the problem of multiple confidence intervals arises, as it did in independent-groups designs. The solution to this problem is the same as for independent-groups designs. The Studentized range statistic can be used to obtain simultaneous confidence intervals and to obtain Tukey's honestly significant difference.

Worked Examples

Example 1   Improving geometry teaching (Data Set 8.9)

Consider an experiment designed to directly compare Jill's imagery training with Bill's tutorial system as a means of improving geometry instruction. The experiment is designed with three conditions: a control condition and two experimental conditions representing the imagery and tutorial procedures.

With three conditions, it is necessary to form blocks of size three, that is, matched triples rather than matched pairs. In this example, such blocks are formed by using a preliminary test of geometry ability. The number of such blocks used is $n = 18$, so there are $3 \times 18 = 54$ participants in total. The data from this experiment are shown in Data Set 8.9.

Data Set 8.9   Test scores for the three-condition experiment evaluating two different techniques to improve geometry teaching (Worked Example 1)

Block	Control ($\overline{Y}_1 = 64.9$)	Imagery ($\overline{Y}_2 = 71.5$)	Tutorial ($\overline{Y}_3 = 70.2$)	Block	Control (cont.)	Imagery (cont.)	Tutorial (cont.)
1	49	66	62	10	61	73	64
2	75	77	81	11	66	65	65
3	62	78	63	12	60	69	74
4	78	80	87	13	90	86	76
5	70	54	57	14	67	71	69
6	58	68	70	15	75	67	85
7	56	71	71	16	67	79	71
8	56	61	66	17	47	66	65
9	67	78	63	18	65	78	74

a. Is this experiment appropriately described as a within-subjects design or a randomized block design?

b. Write out the full model for this experiment and calculate the estimates for all components except the residuals. Calculate the residual for just the first score in the control condition.

c. Given the following three values, set up the analysis of variance summary table for this experiment and complete all entries.

$$SS_{between} = 432 \qquad SS_{blocks} = 2724 \qquad SS_e = 1344$$

d. What is the F-ratio for evaluating the null hypothesis that $\alpha_i = 0$ for all three values of i? What is the critical tabled F-ratio for evaluating the null hypothesis with $\alpha = .05$? Does this comparison lead to the rejection of the null hypothesis?

e. Using the Studentized range statistic, calculate simultaneous 95% confidence intervals for the three comparisons of pairs of means in this experiment. What is the value of Tukey's HSD for these data?

Answer

a. This experiment provides an example of a standard randomized block design. Each individual participant takes part in only one condition.

b. The full model is $Y_i = \mu + \alpha_i + \pi_j + e$. It can be fitted to these data in exactly the same way as we fitted it for the two-condition case. The top row of Data Set 8.9 gives the means of each condition. Rounding to one decimal place, the grand mean is $\overline{Y} = (64.9 + 71.5 + 70.2)/3 = 68.9$.

Calculating the $\mathbf{a}_i$:

$$\mathbf{a}_1 = 64.9 - 68.9 = -4.0 \quad \mathbf{a}_2 = 71.5 - 68.9 = +2.6 \quad \mathbf{a}_3 = 70.2 - 68.9 = +1.3$$

Notice that, apart from rounding error, these three values sum to 0.

Calculating the $\mathbf{p}_j$: Consider the first block. The mean of this block is $(49 + 66 + 62)/3 = 59.0$. The value of $\mathbf{p}_1$ is therefore $59.0 - 68.9 = -9.9$. The mean of the second block is 77.67, so $\mathbf{p}_2 = 77.7 - 68.9 = +8.8$. The remaining values of the $\mathbf{p}_j$ are calculated similarly:

Block	1	2	3	4	5	6	7	8	9
$\mathbf{p}_j$	-9.9	8.8	-1.2	12.8	-8.5	-3.5	-2.9	-7.9	0.5

Block	10	11	12	13	14	15	16	17	18
$\mathbf{p}_j$	-2.9	-3.5	-1.2	15.1	0.1	6.8	3.5	-9.5	3.5

Remember that positive values of $\mathbf{p}$ reflect a block with a higher than average score, whereas negative values of $\mathbf{p}$ reflect a block with a lower than average score. Notice that apart from rounding error, these 18 values sum to 0.

Calculating the residuals: The residuals are calculated for each of the 54 scores by using the normal subtraction method. For the first score in the control condition, $e = 49 - (68.9 - 4.0 - 9.9) = -6.0$.

c. The analysis of variance summary table is shown in Table 8.16.

d. The F-ratio for evaluating the null hypothesis that $\alpha_i = 0$ for all three values of i is $F = \text{MS}_{\text{between}}/\text{MS}_e = 216/39.5 = 5.47$. The critical tabulated F-ratio for evaluating the null hypothesis with $\alpha = .05$ is F with 2 and 34 degrees of freedom. The table of the F-distribution (Statistical Table 5) gives $F(2,34) = 3.28$. The obtained value of 5.47 is greater than this tabled value, so the null hypothesis is rejected.

e. The Studentized range statistic, q, will be used to calculate simultaneous 95% confidence intervals. For our example, $k = 3$ and $df = 34$. Consulting the table of

Table 8.16 Analysis of variance summary table for the data shown in Data Set 8.9 (Worked Example 1)

Source	SS	df	MS
Model	3156	19	—
Between conditions	432	2	216
Blocks	2724	17	160
Residual	1344	34	39.5
Total	4500	53	—

the Studentized range distribution (Statistical Table 4) gives a value of $q = 3.49$ (using $df = 30$ as the closest lower tabled value).

$$w = q \times \sqrt{\frac{MS_e}{n}} = 3.49 \times \sqrt{\frac{39.5}{18}} = 5.2$$

From the condition means in Data Set 8.9, we have the following point estimates of the mean differences:

$$|\overline{Y}_1 - \overline{Y}_2| = 6.6 \qquad |\overline{Y}_1 - \overline{Y}_3| = 5.3 \qquad |\overline{Y}_2 - \overline{Y}_3| = 1.3$$

The three 95% confidence intervals are thus

for $|\mu_1 - \mu_2|$, $CI_{.95} = 6.6 \pm 5.2 = 1.4$ to 11.8
for $|\mu_1 - \mu_3|$, $CI_{.95} = 5.3 \pm 5.2 = 0.1$ to 10.5
for $|\mu_2 - \mu_3|$, $CI_{.95} = 1.3 \pm 5.2 = -3.9$ to 6.5

The first two intervals do not include 0, so, in these two cases, the null hypothesis of zero difference would be rejected. The interval estimate for $|\mu_2 - \mu_3|$ *does* include 0, so the difference between these conditions is not significant.

The honestly significant difference, HSD, is simply w, so for these data, HSD = 5.2. Any difference between pairs of means greater than 5.2 would, according to this criterion, be declared significant. Both $|\overline{Y}_1 - \overline{Y}_2|$ and $|\overline{Y}_1 - \overline{Y}_3|$ exceed 5.2, so, as the confidence intervals have already indicated, these two differences are incompatible with a true difference of 0. The results therefore support the conclusion that both methods improve performance, but they themselves do not differ.

Example 2 **Extending the therapy follow-up study (Data Set 8.10)**

Consider an extension of the therapy follow-up study described in Section 8.3.2 (Data Set 8.8). In a follow-up of the same participants, a fourth evaluation was taken 2 years after the end of therapy. The data for all four evaluations are given in Data Set 8.10. Note that the values in the first three conditions are identical to those in Data Set 8.8.

a. Is this experiment appropriately described as a within-subjects design or a randomized block design?

Data Set 8.10 Data for the 2-year follow-up of the therapy evaluation experiment (Worked Example 2)

P	1 week ($\bar{Y}_1 = 6.00$)	3 months ($\bar{Y}_2 = 6.30$)	1 year ($\bar{Y}_3 = 5.90$)	2 years ($\bar{Y}_4 = 6.35$)	P	1 week (cont.)	3 months (cont.)	1 year (cont.)	2 years (cont.)
1	5	7	4	5	11	8	6	7	6
2	4	4	2	4	12	3	1	0	3
3	6	6	7	61	13	6	6	5	6
4	6	6	7	8	14	7	7	5	7
5	6	6	6	7	15	10	8	9	8
6	9	10	9	11	16	5	5	5	5
7	8	9	9	9	17	6	7	7	8
8	5	5	4	5	18	4	7	8	5
9	6	9	7	9	19	4	5	5	3
10	6	5	6	6	20	6	7	6	6

The response measure is rated anxiety level.

b. Given the following three values, set up the analysis of variance summary table for this experiment and complete all entries.

$$SS_{between} = 2.94 \qquad SS_{blocks} = 260.24 \qquad SS_e = 52.31$$

c. What is the F-ratio for evaluating the null hypothesis that $\alpha_i = 0$ for all four values of i. What is the critical tabled F-ratio for evaluating the null hypothesis with $\alpha = .05$? Does this comparison lead to the rejection of the null hypothesis?

d. Calculate the value of Tukey's HSD for these data with $\alpha = .05$.

Answer

a. This experiment has a within-subjects design.

b. The analysis of variance summary table is shown in Table 8.17. Note that there are now 3 degrees of freedom for between conditions and that there is a corresponding increase in the degrees of freedom for MS_e.

c. The F-ratio for evaluating the null hypothesis that $\alpha_i = 0$ for all four values of i is $F = MS_{between}/MS_e = 0.979/0.918 = 1.067$. The critical tabled F-ratio for evaluating the null hypothesis with $\alpha = .05$ is F with 3 and 57 degrees of freedom. The table of the F-distribution gives $F(3,57) = 2.77$. The obtained value of 1.067 is less than this tabled value, so the null hypothesis is not rejected.

d. The Studentized range statistic, q, will be used to calculate Tukey's HSD. For our example, $k = 4$ and $df = 57$. Consulting the table of the Studentized range distribution gives a value of $q = 3.79$ (using $df = 40$ as the closest lower tabled value).

$$HSD = q \times \sqrt{\frac{MS_e}{n}} = 3.79 \times \sqrt{\frac{0.918}{20}} = 0.81$$

Table 8.17 Analysis of variance summary table for the data in Data Set 8.10 (Worked Example 2)

Source	SS	df	MS
Model	263.18	22	—
Between conditions	2.94	3	0.979
Participants	260.24	19	13.697
Residual	52.31	57	0.918
Total	315.49	79	—

Problems

Problem 1   Levels of processing (Data Set 8.11)

In an experiment demonstrating the principle of "levels of processing" in memory, Craik and Tulving (1975) presented participants with 60 different to-be-remembered words. Each word (shown here in bold type) was presented just once, preceded by a question. The question could be one of three types:

Appearance: Is the word typed in capital letters?   **HOUSE**
Sound: Does the work rhyme with "teak"?   **CREEK**
Meaning: Is the word something hot?   **FLAME**

The correct answer to each of these questions is "yes." For other questions, the correct answer was "no." After this encoding phase, participants were given a recognition-memory test. For this test phase, the words studied in the encoding phase were mixed with a number of previously unseen words to serve as distractors, and participants were required to identify the words that had been previously presented. The response variable was the number of words correctly identified as

Data Set 8.11 Data for the within-subjects experiment to examine levels of processing in memory (Problem 1)

P	Appearance ($\overline{Y}_1 = 3.88$)	Sound ($\overline{Y}_2 = 6.28$)	Meaning ($\overline{Y}_3 = 7.84$)	P	Appearance (cont.)	Sound (cont.)	Meaning (cont.)
1	4	6	8	8	2	5	9
2	3	4	6	9	7	8	9
3	2	7	8	10	5	5	9
4	3	6	7	11	3	7	8
5	7	9	9	12	6	8	9
6	1	3	5	13	5	8	10
7	3	6	8	14	6	7	9

Data Set 8.11 (*continued*)

P	Appearance (cont.)	Sound (cont.)	Meaning (cont.)	P	Appearance (cont.)	Sound (cont.)	Meaning (cont.)
15	2	5	7	21	0	1	6
16	4	7	6	22	3	6	5
17	7	7	10	23	6	8	9
18	6	7	10	24	1	5	5
19	2	5	7	25	5	7	8
20	4	8	9				

The response measure is the number of words correctly identified.

having been previously presented for each of the three encoding conditions. The data in Data Set 8.11 are for words to which, in the encoding phase, the correct answer was "yes." There were ten such words for each question type and $n = 25$ participants.

a. Analysis of the data gives a value of 42.37 for the sum of squares of the residuals (SS_e). Calculate the value of Tukey's HSD with $\alpha = .05$ and use it to test the null hypothesis for each of the three differences between pairs of means. Then calculate a 95% confidence interval for each of the three differences between pairs of means.

b. The values of $SS_{between} = 198.96$ and $SS_{participants} = 204.67$. Write out the complete analysis of variance summary table for these data.

c. What is the *F*-ratio you would use to evaluate the null hypothesis that all $\alpha_i = 0$? Using a Type-1 error rate of .05, what is the critical tabled value of the *F*-ratio against which you would compare this obtained *F*-ratio?

Problem 2 Stimulus generalization (Data Set 8.12)

This experiment investigates stimulus generalization in pigeons. Pigeons were originally trained to peck at a yellow light. They were then tested with lights of four different colors as well as the original yellow. Each of the $n = 12$ pigeons is thus tested under all five color conditions. The response measure is pecks per minute.

a. Draw a simple bar graph of the five condition means, setting out the conditions on the *x*-axis in the order given in Data Set 8.12.

b. Analysis of the data gives a value of 1866 for the sum of squares of the residuals (SS_e). Calculate the value of Tukey's HSD with $\alpha = .05$, and then use it to evaluate the differences between pairs of means.

c. Use what you know about the color spectrum to interpret the results in terms of stimulus generalization.

d. The values of $SS_{between} = 3586$ and $SS_{pigeons} = 3181$. Write out the complete analysis of variance summary table for these data.

Data Set 8.12   Data for experiment investigating stimulus generation (Problem 2)

Pigeon	Red ($\overline{Y}_1 = 19.9$)	Orange ($\overline{Y}_2 = 28.0$)	Yellow ($\overline{Y}_3 = 37.4$)	Green ($\overline{Y}_4 = 22.6$)	Blue ($\overline{Y}_5 = 14.7$)
1	14	16	41	23	1
2	15	22	36	16	14
3	9	34	18	8	3
4	31	33	47	26	30
5	24	25	50	22	25
6	12	18	29	13	12
7	17	31	41	13	10
8	39	33	43	42	21
9	29	31	27	22	15
10	12	20	37	25	18
11	7	30	34	22	0
12	30	43	46	39	28

The response measure is pecks per minute.

Chapter 8 Exercises

Exercise 1   Recognition of photographs of faces (Data Set 8.13)

Can 3-month-old infants distinguish a photograph of their mother's face from that of a stranger? The response variable is a measure of viewing preference, the assumption being that, if recognized, an infant will view its mother's face longer. In this experiment, the infant sees only one face at a time (actually, a photograph of a face), and the length of time the infant spends looking at the face is recorded. On some tri-

Data Set 8.13   Data for photograph recognition experiment (Exercise 1)

Infant	Time looking at mother ($\overline{Y}_1 = 75.06$)	Time looking at stranger ($\overline{Y}_2 = 46.94$)	Infant	Time looking at mother (cont.)	Time looking at stranger (cont.)
1	103	30	10	99	69
2	84	19	11	104	43
3	57	59	12	93	67
4	44	0	13	92	89
5	47	43	14	58	45
6	75	51	15	42	11
7	65	70	16	90	49
8	47	9	17	88	65
9	88	79			

The response measure is looking time, in seconds.

als, the infant is shown a photograph of mother; on other trials, the photograph of a stranger.

The data in Data Set 8.13 give looking times (in seconds) at mother versus stranger for 17 infants ranging in age from 85 to 100 days. The hypothetical results are based on the work of Barrera and Maurer (1981b).

a. Which of the following terms best describes the design of this experiment: (i) independent-groups design; (ii) within-subjects; (iii) matched pairs?

b. The standard deviation of the difference scores for the 17 infants is $s_D = 23.51$. Calculate the 95% confidence interval for the difference between the means of these conditions, μ_D.

c. Would you conclude that there is a difference between the length of time the infants spend looking at mother compared with that spent looking at a stranger?

Exercise 2   Perception of facial expressions (Data Set 8.14)

This experiment studied the infant's perception of facial expressions. Can 3-month-old infants distinguish between a smiling face and a frowning face? To answer this question, 26 infants ranging in age from 88 to 101 days were shown pictures of a female face (a stranger) that had either a frowning, angry expression or a smiling, happy expression. The technique for measuring discrimination is different from the viewing-preference method used previously. The new method is known as *habituation,* and it makes use of the fact that, with repeated exposure to a stimulus, infants will look at it less and less. They display habituation to the stimulus. If the infant is now given a choice between viewing the old (habituated) stimulus and a novel stimu-

Data Set 8.14   Data for experiment investigating perception of facial expression (Exercise 2)

Infant	Habituated stimulus	Novel stimulus	Infant	Habituated stimulus	Novel stimulus
1	60	26	14	24	30
2	55	72	15	38	81
3	20	54	16	39	51
4	67	69	17	51	131
5	55	55	18	59	128
6	32	41	19	56	80
7	44	66	20	60	102
8	31	52	21	49	97
9	60	89	22	46	64
10	49	78	23	51	77
11	65	99	24	74	43
12	47	55	25	80	91
13	81	55	26	47	33

The response measure is viewing time, in seconds.

lus, he or she will show a strong viewing preference for (will look longer at) the novel stimulus. Of course, this *novelty preference* can be obtained only if the infant can discriminate between the old and the novel stimulus. Thus novelty preference following habituation is evidence of discriminability. In this experiment, half the infants are habituated to the smiling face and half to the frowning face. Following habituation, all infants are shown each of the faces, habituated and novel, and their viewing time for each is recorded. The data are shown in Data Set 8.14. For present purposes, we will ignore whether the habituation was to the frowning or smiling expression. The hypothetical data are based on Barrera and Maurer (1981a).

a. The mean viewing times for habituated and novel stimuli are 51.5 and 70.0 seconds, respectively. The standard deviation of the difference scores for the 26 infants is $s_D = 27.186$. Calculate a *t*-ratio and use it to evaluate the null hypothesis that $\mu_D = 0$ with $\alpha = .05$.

b. Calculate the 95% confidence interval for μ_D, the difference between the means of these conditions.

c. Would you conclude that 3-month-old infants can distinguish between a smiling face and a frowning face?

Exercise 3 Infant perception of partly occluded stationary objects (Data Set 8.15)
This experiment studied the perception of partly occluded stationary objects. It is the same as the one described in Exercise 4 at the end of Chapter 6 except for a change in design. Participants were 22 infants ranging in age from 14 to 18 weeks. As in the previous version, they were habituated to the stationary occluded rod through repeated exposure. However, instead of the infants being divided into two groups, all infants (on different trials) are shown the two short, separated, aligned rods (on one trial) and, on a different trial, the single nonoccluded rod. If infants perceived the ini-

Data Set 8.15 Data for infant perception experiment (Exercise 3)

Infant	Time 1[a] ($\overline{Y}_1 = 24.91$)	Time 2[b] ($\overline{Y}_2 = 21.91$)	Infant	Time 1[a] (cont.)	Time 2[b] (cont.)
1	33	49	12	23	2
2	19	0	13	18	17
3	29	21	14	35	0
4	20	23	15	3	24
5	13	8	16	0	0
6	34	39	17	55	35
7	32	36	18	10	7
8	19	47	19	0	21
9	22	31	20	40	30
10	36	26	21	41	15
11	32	21	22	34	30

a. Time 1, viewing time (in seconds) for separated aligned rods.
b. Time 2, viewing time (in seconds) for single rod.

Table 8.18 Incomplete analysis of variance summary table for data in Data Set 8.15 (Exercise 3)

Source	SS	df	MS
Model	―――	―――	—
Between conditions	99.0	―――	―――
Pairs	6094.6	―――	―――
Residual	2697.0	―――	―――
Total	―――	―――	—

tial habituating stimulus as a single rod, then they should show no novelty preference when shown the single nonoccluded rod because they are seeing something that is essentially the same as what they *perceived* during the habituation trials. However, if infants did perceive the initial habituating stimulus as a single rod, they should show a novelty preference when shown the two short, separated, aligned rods. Again, remember that the longer the looking time, the greater the novelty preference. The data are given in Data Set 8.15.

   a. The data were analyzed by using analysis of variance (see summary in Table 8.18). Complete the missing entries.

   b. Evaluate the null hypothesis that there is no difference in viewing time between the two conditions.

   c. The investigator is concerned about the power of this statistical test. The standard deviation of the difference scores is 16.0. Use this value to estimate the power $(1 - \beta)$ of the experiment to detect a difference of 10 seconds.

Exercise 4   Infant perception of partly occluded moving objects (Data Set 8.16)
   This experiment studied the perception of partly occluded *moving* objects. It is a modified version of the experiment described in Exercise 5 at the end of Chapter 6. This new version uses a within-subjects design. Participants were 22 infants ranging in age from 14 to 18 weeks. They were habituated to the moving partially occluded rod through repeated exposure. However, instead of the infants being divided into two groups as in the Chapter 6 version of the experiment, all infants (on different trials) are shown the two short, separated, aligned rods (on one trial) and, on a different trial, the single nonoccluded rod. If infants perceived the initial habituating stimulus as a single rod, then they should show no novelty preference when shown the single nonoccluded rod because they are seeing something that is essentially the same as what they *perceived* during the habituation trials. Consequently, if infants did perceive the initial habituating stimulus as a single rod, they should show a novelty preference when shown the two short, separated, aligned rods.

   a. The data for this experiment are given in Data Set 8.16. The standard deviation of the difference scores for the 22 infants is $s_D = 13.70$. Calculate a *t*-ratio and use it to evaluate the null hypothesis that $\mu_D = 0$ with $\alpha = .05$.

Data Set 8.16 Data for experiment investigating infant perception of partly occluded moving objects (Exercise 4)

Infant	Aligned rods ($\bar{Y}_1 = 41.5$)	Single rod ($\bar{Y}_2 = 23.7$)	Infant	Aligned rods (cont.)	Single rod (cont.)
1	40	22	12	36	21
2	67	54	13	45	27
3	22	1	14	25	18
4	48	36	15	37	6
5	27	0	16	16	4
6	50	40	17	72	41
7	65	23	18	19	21
8	0	0	19	66	48
9	41	58	20	75	42
10	38	15	21	26	10
11	63	34	22	36	0

The response measure is viewing time, in seconds.

b. Calculate a 95% confidence interval for the difference, μ_D.

Exercise 5   Scrambled faces (Data Set 8.17)
Within an hour of birth, infants were shown (on different occasions) three different faces: a schematic face, a scrambled face, or a blank, unfilled outline of a face. Each of these stimuli was moved across the infant's field of view. The response measure was the extent to which the infant rotated head and eyes to follow the stimulus.

Data Set 8.17   Data for scrambled faces experiment (Exercise 5)

Infant	Face ($\bar{Y}_1 = 49.95$)	Scrambled ($\bar{Y}_2 = 41.53$)	Black ($\bar{Y}_3 = 18.11$)	Infant	Face (cont.)	Scrambled (cont.)	Black (cont.)
1	67	56	41	11	29	18	16
2	45	50	21	12	55	37	7
3	53	45	20	13	50	50	16
4	71	34	38	14	74	42	35
5	41	20	−7	15	50	46	16
6	46	48	30	16	61	39	7
7	54	57	27	17	48	77	34
8	32	13	2	18	41	40	22
9	46	37	−1	19	61	41	17
10	25	39	3				

The response measure is degrees of rotation of the infant's head and eyes.

The measurement is in degrees of rotation. A total of 19 infants were used. The resulting data are given in Data Set 8.17.

a. Given the following three values, set up the analysis of variance summary table for this experiment and complete all entries.

$$SS_{between} = 10345 \qquad SS_{blocks} = 7137 \qquad SS_e = 3393$$

b. What is the F-ratio for evaluating the null hypothesis that $\alpha_i = 0$ for all three values of i? What is the critical tabled F-ratio for evaluating the null hypothesis with $\alpha = .05$? Does this comparison lead to the rejection of the null hypothesis?

c. Calculate the value of Tukey's HSD for these data with $\alpha = .05$.

Chapter 8 Review

Terms

additivity
block
carryover effect
matched-pair design
power $(1 - \beta)$
precision
randomized block design
within-subjects (repeated measures) design

Formulas

The general form of the analysis of variance summary table for a matched pair, randomized block, or within-subjects design with k conditions and n blocks or participants is shown in Table 8.19.

Table 8.19 General form of an analysis of variance summary table

Source	SS	df	MS
Model			
Between conditions	$SS_{between}$	$k - 1$	$\dfrac{SS_{between}}{(k - 1)}$
Pairs blocks participants	SS_{blocks}	$n - 1$	$\dfrac{SS_{blocks}}{n - 1}$
Residual	SS_e	$(k - 1)(n - 1)$	$\dfrac{SS_e}{(k - 1)(n - 1)}$
Total	SS_{total}	$nk - 1$	—

approximate sample size needed to obtain a confidence interval width of $2w$

$$n = 2MS_e \left(\frac{z}{w} \right)^2$$

estimated effect size for matched pairs (difference scores) $\hat{d} = \dfrac{\overline{D}}{s_D}$

standard error of the mean difference score $s_{\overline{D}} = \dfrac{s_D}{\sqrt{n}} = \sqrt{\dfrac{2MS_e}{n}}$

t-ratio for testing the null hypothesis that $\mu_D = 0$ $t = \dfrac{\overline{D}}{s_{\overline{D}}}$

full model for matched pair, randomized block, and within-subjects designs
$$Y_i = \mu + \alpha_i + \pi_j + e$$

Quiz

Question 1

Complete each sentence with a term from the following list. The same term may be used more than once.

β	$1 - \beta$	a decrease	an increase
blocks	blocks/subjects	carryover effects	conditions
half-width	larger	matched	MS_e
power	randomized block	randomly	residual
response measure	sample size	smaller	within
within-condition			

Increasing the precision of an estimate is reflected in a _____ value of w, the _____ of the confidence interval, and in an increase in _____, denoted by _____.

There are two general strategies for achieving a desired degree of precision in an experiment. One strategy is to obtain a prior approximation of the _____ needed to achieve the desired degree of precision. Increasing the sample size will result in a _____ value of w and _____ in the power to detect a difference of a given size.

A second strategy for increasing precision is to reduce _____ variance as measured by _____. This reduction can be accomplished by forming _____ of subjects who have been _____ on an extraneous variable known to influence (contribute variability to) the _____. The contribution of the extraneous variable is thereby eliminated as an influence on differences between the participants _____ a block.

An experimental design that uses blocks of matched subjects is known as a _____ design. In this design, the number of participants within each block is equal to the number of _____ and the participants of each block are assigned _____ among the conditions.

A special case of the matching strategy is the within-subjects design in which each participant is measured under all the conditions. This design is usually very effective in reducing the size of _____, but it introduces the danger of unwanted _____.

In the analysis of variance for a randomized block/within-subjects design, the within-condition sum of squares is broken down into two components. One component is the sum of squares reflecting the differences among means of the _____, averaged over _____. The second component is the _____ sum of squares—the within-condition variability not accounted for by differences among the means of blocks/subjects.

Chapter 9 Preview

Chapters 6 through 8 have been concerned with data for which the predictor variable is categorical and the response variable quantitative. The next two chapters consider two other cases. Chapter 9 considers data for which both predictor and response variables are quantitative. Chapter 10 considers data for which both predictor and response variables are categorical.

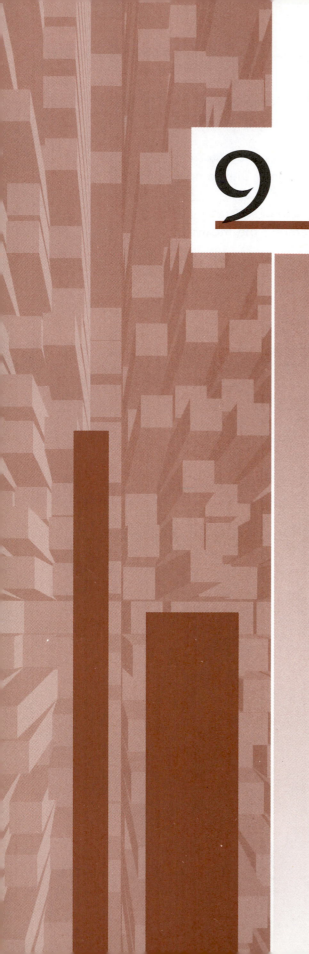

9 QUANTITATIVE PREDICTOR VARIABLES: LINEAR REGRESSION AND CORRELATION

I n all the examples considered in Chapters 6, 7, and 8, the predictor variable was treated as categorical. We turn now to a consideration of designs in which the predictor variable can be modeled as a continuous quantitative variable. The general approach to the development of models for quantitative predictor variables was set out briefly in Sections 1.1.3 and 3.3.5. Although this chapter does not assume that you have remembered the details, it may be helpful to review these sections before proceeding.

9.1   Fundamentals of Regression and Correlation

Data for which both the predictor and response variables are quantitative are common in the behavioral sciences. A standard example is a dose–response function: a function that describes the relationship between the quantity of a drug administered and a behavioral measure such as anxiety level, degree of depression, or blood pressure. How does anxiety level change with increasing dosage levels? Another example would be the relationship between IQ and grade point average. Do students with high IQ scores obtain high grade point averages?

There are two closely related goals in analyzing such data. One goal is to construct an equation for *predicting* values of the response variable. For a dose–response function, the equation might predict anxiety level for a specified dose level. The second goal is to describe the *strength* of the predictive relationship between two variables. An investigator may be less interested in making direct use of the rule for predicting GPA on the basis of IQ than in simply knowing how strongly the two variables are related. Different studies may emphasize one of these goals rather than the other. We will illustrate the two goals with three examples.

The general term to describe the analysis that fulfills these goals is *regression analysis.* When the focus of the analysis is largely, or even entirely, on the second goal of knowing how strongly the two variables are related, the analysis is sometimes termed a *correlation* analysis.

The primary goal of regression analysis is to formulate a prediction rule of correlation analysis to establish the strength of the relationship between two variables.

9.1.1 Three Examples

Example 1. Regression with a Manipulated Predictor Variable

The following experiment was designed to study the relationship between sleep deprivation and ability to concentrate on a difficult task. The investigator records the number of errors made by participants after 8, 16, 24, 32, or 40 hours without sleep. Ten participants are assigned to each of the five degrees of sleep deprivation for a total of 50 participants in all.

In this problem, the number of hours of sleep deprivation is clearly the predictor variable and number of errors the response variable. Moreover, the values of the predictor variable were set by the experimenter as 8, 16, 24, 32, and 40. So too was the number of cases (ten) for each of these values. Thus hours of sleep deprivation is a manipulated variable. The feature of this example that distinguishes it from the two examples that follow is that the values of the predictor variable were determined by the experimenter.

Example 2. Regression with a Natural Predictor Variable

In developing aptitude and performance tests for use with children, a common requirement is to establish age norms. Such norms require information about how performance changes with age. Suppose an investigator has developed a test of verbal comprehension consisting of 50 carefully chosen items. The test is intended for children in grades 1 through 6. The investigator wishes to establish a rule that predicts performance level as a function of age. To this end, the investigator selects a sample of 100 grade school children. Each child takes the verbal comprehension test. The test score and the age of each child in the sample is recorded.

This example is different from the first regression problem in that both variables are natural and their values are not directly controlled by the investigator. Nevertheless, this example is basically the same as the first in that the two variables—age and test score—play distinct roles. Age is the predictor variable, test score the response variable. The goal of the investigation is to derive a rule that expresses performance on the test as a function of age.

This example does not control the number of cases at different age levels. The number of participants aged 80 months, for example, is not fixed in advance as was the number of participants at each level of sleep deprivation. In that example, the investigator ensured that there was an equal number of observations at each level of sleep deprivation. In Example 2, the investigator exerts no such control over the distribution of age, and there almost certainly would not be an equal number of cases at each age level. Of course, the investigator could have designed the study along the lines of the sleep deprivation example and selected equal-sized samples at predetermined fixed age levels: exactly ten children at 60 months of age, ten at 70 months of age, and so on. From a practical point of view, this sampling method would be more difficult to implement and might not be worth the added effort.

Example 3. Correlation Problem

Suppose an investigator wishes to establish the relationship between IQ and GPA. How strongly related are the two measures? To answer this question, an investigator might collect data consisting of IQ and GPA scores for a sample of senior students. This example is different from the first regression problem but similar to the second in that both variables are natural and their values are outside the direct control of the investigator.

The difference between this third example and the first two is that, for this example, there is no longer a sharp distinction between the predictor and response variables. Examples such as this, in which either variable might serve as predictor or response variable, are likely to be the subject of a correlation analysis. In the first two examples, levels of sleep deprivation and of age were clearly the predictor variables and the performance measures were clearly the response variables. It would make no sense to reverse these roles. However, in this third example, either variable can play either role. IQ could be used as a basis for predicting GPA, or vice versa. The difference between this and the earlier examples may be taken further. In terms of the interests of the investigator, the distinction between predictor and response may be irrelevant. Rather than predict one variable from the other, the investigator may merely wish to know how strongly the two variables are correlated, or indeed whether they are correlated at all.

Despite the differences, the data analysis for these three examples is highly similar. We will proceed with a step by step analysis of the data for each example, performing the steps for each example in turn, developing the common principles, and pointing out differences when appropriate.

9.1.2 Scatterplots of the Data and Conditional Distributions

Example 1. Sleep Deprivation and Ability to Concentrate

Hypothetical data for the sleep deprivation example are given in Data Set 9.1. The row heading H represents hours of sleep deprivation and E represents the number of errors. Because there are just five distinct levels of the predictor variable, the data can be conveniently reorganized into columns representing each level of sleep deprivation (Table 9.1).

Data Set 9.1 Sleep deprivation data for Example 1

H	8	40	24	8	16	8	16	24	32	40
E	10	32	42	27	36	18	16	26	28	41
H	24	40	8	40	8	24	32	24	32	40
E	31	44	18	33	24	32	37	29	29	49
H	16	24	8	40	16	40	32	8	16	24
E	13	31	10	42	19	43	26	24	20	32
H	32	40	40	16	24	16	16	40	32	8
E	27	39	38	29	32	25	10	50	37	21
H	24	32	32	16	24	16	32	32	8	8
E	29	27	46	27	33	32	36	39	17	26

These data can be plotted as a *scatterplot*, which is a graph that places the values of the predictor variable on the *x*-axis and values of the response variable on the *y*-axis. Each data point is represented by a point in this two-dimensional space. For example, a participant in the 8-hour condition with an error score of 10 would be

Table 9.1 Data from Data Set 9.1, grouped in columns defined by the value of the predictor variable

Hours of sleep deprivation				
8	**16**	**24**	**32**	**40**
24	13	29	39	49
10	27	32	26	43
18	19	26	27	41
10	29	32	36	44
21	25	33	29	39
26	36	29	37	50
17	20	42	27	32
27	32	31	37	42
24	16	31	28	33
18	10	32	46	38

represented by a point defined by X = 8, Y = 10. Figure 9.1 is a scatterplot for the data in Data Set 9.1 and Table 9.1.

Figure 9.1 shows a distribution of error scores for each of the five different levels of sleep deprivation included in the experiment. Such individual distributions are often referred to as *conditional distributions*. Conditional distributions are distributions of the response variable, conditional on a specified value of the predictor variable.

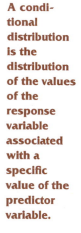

A conditional distribution is the distribution of the values of the response variable associated with a specific value of the predictor variable.

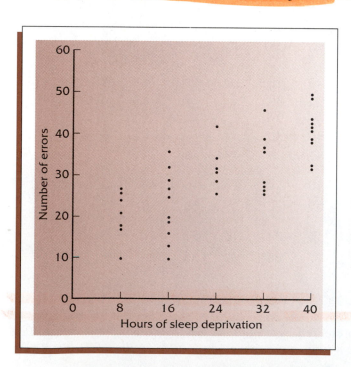

Figure 9.1
Scatterplot of the data from an experiment studying the effect of sleep deprivation on number of errors made while performing a difficult task. (Some points represent two data points of identical value; hence the plot does not show ten distinct points for each condition.)

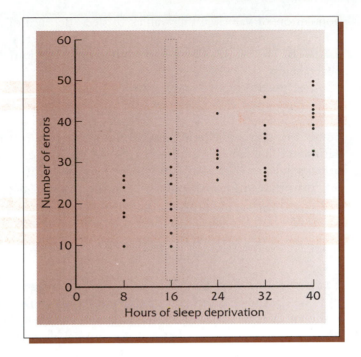

Figure 9.2
Copy of Figure 9.1. The dotted box marks off the conditional distribution of errors for 16 hours of sleep deprivation.

Figure 9.2 reproduces Figure 9.1 with the conditional distribution of errors for participants in the 16-hour condition marked off as an example. The overall distribution of Y (the distribution of all 50 observations regardless of which value of X they come from) is known as the *marginal distribution*.

Assumptions of Regression Analyses. The various procedures about to be covered assume that

■ Each of these conditional distributions is a sample from a normally distributed random variable.

■ These normal distributions have the same variance. This is the already familiar assumption of homogeneity of variance.

For the analyses discussed in this chapter, the additional assumption will be made that

■ The population means of the conditional distributions lie along a straight line, called a *regression line*.

The assumption that the means of the conditional distributions lie along a straight line is referred to as the *assumption of linear regression*. We will discuss linear regression at length in Section 9.1.3. More advanced analyses allow for regression that is not linear. The problem of deciding whether or not the linearity assumption is justified will also be discussed later in this chapter.

Figures 9.1 and 9.2 show the conditional distributions at the five levels of sleep deprivation used in the experiment. These are sample distributions with just ten observations each. However, it is important to imagine the theoretical or population distribution from which these samples were drawn. It has already been mentioned that these population distributions are assumed to have normal distributions with equal variances. What you must also imagine is that the particular values of the predictor variable used—8, 16, 24, 32, and 40 hours—are themselves sample values from a

The marginal distribution is the complete distribution of the response variable.

The assumption of linear regression is that the means of the conditional distributions lie on a straight line.

population of values. Other values of sleep deprivation might have been selected—10, 15.3, or 26.8 hours, for example. The lengths of sleep deprivation actually used—8, 16, 24, 32, 40—are obviously not a random sample, but they are a sample nevertheless.

The upshot of this point is that you must imagine a conditional distribution of performance scores for every possible value of the predictor variable within the range of 8 to 40 hours. Because the predictor variable is continuous, there will be an infinite number of such conditional distributions, of which just five were sampled for the experiment. The five distributions can be thought of as slices cut out of a three-dimensional solid made up of infinitely many normal distributions packed, side by side, with one distribution for each point within the range of possible sleep deprivation values. In the analysis that follows, it is assumed that *all* these conditional distributions of the response variable—not only the five distributions actually sampled—are normal and have equal variances, and that their means lie along a straight line.

The sample conditional distributions are drawn from an underlying continuum of conditional distributions.

Example 2. Test Scores as a Function of Age

The data for the second example are shown in Data Set 9.2, and their scatterplot is shown in Figure 9.3. The only difference between this scatterplot and that for the sleep deprivation data is that the conditional distributions no longer fall into neat columns. No effort was made to constrain the ages to a small number of specific values, so values of the predictor variable are scattered across the range of sampled age values rather than falling neatly into columns. The sample marginal distribution of test scores is the single distribution of all 100 test scores, ignoring age.

Data Set 9.2 Data for Example 2, consisting of (X,Y) pairs of observations for 100 participants (X, age in months; Y, test score)

X	100	74	90	121	101	137	132	83	125	86
Y	26	24	27	37	28	33	31	38	46	30
X	107	81	87	109	133	92	124	96	75	108
Y	37	26	28	31	48	26	28	27	19	32
X	78	80	107	84	109	79	83	112	83	118
Y	21	24	34	31	40	23	31	26	30	38
X	130	127	125	125	132	90	123	77	92	97
Y	44	36	33	32	39	29	45	19	19	22
X	115	80	114	65	96	103	118	97	135	92
Y	34	22	36	23	43	23	36	28	45	32
X	100	93	111	112	89	75	91	126	119	110
Y	33	37	38	40	25	26	37	41	33	38
X	60	121	123	72	96	65	87	62	75	105
Y	14	32	43	22	34	27	31	25	23	39

Data Set 9.2 *(continued)*

X	111	61	72	124	100	81	76	133	112	70
Y	35	21	20	35	31	23	25	26	29	23

X	66	74	109	97	115	111	82	102	126	109
Y	20	29	35	35	36	33	28	26	36	34

X	70	125	103	111	74	74	102	68	65	72
Y	22	34	26	26	26	23	34	17	17	32

Once again, it is important to imagine the theoretical or population distributions from which these samples were drawn. They are assumed to have the same general form as in the first example. The marginal distribution and all conditional distributions of test scores are assumed to be normally distributed random variables with equal (homogeneous) variances. Graphically, the population distribution will be a three-dimensional solid made up of infinitely many normal distributions of equal variance packed side by side. The assumption of linear regression is that the *y*-axis values representing the means or peaks of these distributions lie along a straight line.

The only difference between Example 2 and the previous example is the method of sampling from the theoretical distribution. For Example 2, values of the predictor variable (age) were not constrained to a limited number of fixed values; so, rather than sampling from a small number of predetermined slices from the solid, each observation is free to come from any slice within the solid. However, whatever age-defined slice an observation has been drawn from, all slices (conditional distributions) are assumed to be normal distributions with equal variance.

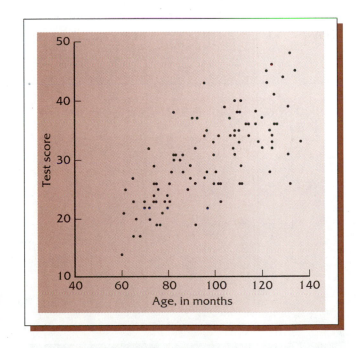

Figure 9.3
Scatterplot for the data from Table 9.3 for Example 2 (test performance as a function of age).

Example 3. Relationship Between IQ and GPA

Consider a data set consisting of the IQ and GPA scores of 50 students (Data Set 9.3). These data can be represented in the form of a scatterplot, as shown in Figure 9.4. Because there is no longer a sharp distinction between the response and predictor variables, either IQ or GPA might appear on the *x*-axis. The fact that in Figure 9.4 IQ is plotted on the *x*-axis and GPA on the *y*-axis is an arbitrary decision.

Data Set 9.3 Data for Example 3, consisting of (IQ, GPA) pairs of observations for 50 participants (P)

P	1	2	3	4	5	6	7	8	9	10
IQ	121	107	110	136	119	86	110	135	111	110
GPA	3.3	3.6	1.9	2.0	2.8	1.0	3.8	3.9	3.9	3.1

P	11	12	13	14	15	16	17	18	19	20
IQ	132	134	102	123	110	95	103	112	105	117
GPA	3.3	2.4	1.0	1.5	3.6	0.9	3.1	1.8	1.3	2.5

P	21	22	23	24	25	26	27	28	29	30
IQ	92	104	115	83	111	123	110	101	102	110
GPA	0.1	2.3	3.8	0.6	3.9	2.0	2.1	2.7	1.0	2.7

P	31	32	33	34	35	36	37	38	39	40
IQ	113	114	116	103	95	92	109	106	121	110
GPA	2.9	3.3	2.0	0.9	2.7	1.5	0.6	1.5	2.8	1.3

P	41	42	43	44	45	46	47	48	49	50
IQ	121	105	127	116	103	108	111	92	108	110
GPA	4.0	2.1	3.9	1.3	2.2	1.5	2.5	0.3	1.7	2.3

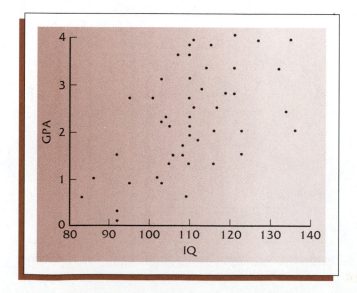

Figure 9.4

Scatterplot of the data from a study of the relationship between IQ and GPA.

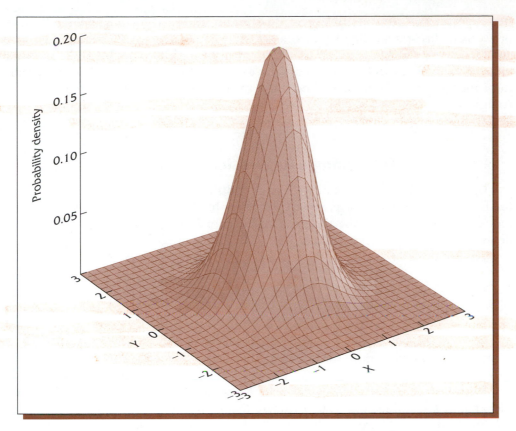

Figure 9.5

Representation of a bivariate normal probability distribution. Both variables have been converted to standard scores. The contour lines are sections parallel to either the *x*- or *y*-axis. They represent conditional distributions that are normal with equal (homogeneous) variances. The vertical axis represents probability density.

Another aspect of the difference between this example and the previous two examples is that both IQ and GPA will be considered to be random variables. In the previous examples, there would have been no purpose and very little meaning in treating the predictor variable as a random variable. The studies were not designed to make probability statements about values of the predictor variable, but only about values of the response measure. Thus, assumptions about normal distributions and equal variances were relevant only to the response variable. When both predictor and response variables are considered to be random variables, such assumptions are applied to both variables. When this happens, the resulting probability distribution is known as the *bivariate normal distribution.*

Figure 9.5 offers a graphical depiction of the bivariate version of the normal distribution. We will assume that the data in the scatterplot (Figure 9.4) have been drawn from such a distribution. The important feature of the bivariate normal distribution is that all the conditional distributions, as well as both marginal distributions, are normal distributions, not just the conditional distributions for one of the variables. Figure 9.5 is rather like an oddly shaped loaf of thinly sliced bread. If the loaf is sliced parallel to the GPA (*y*-axis), then each slice is a conditional distribution of GPA for a particular value of IQ. All these slices have the shape of the normal distribution;

In correlation problems, both variables are treated as random variables.

In a bivariate normal distribution, the two marginal distributions and all conditional distributions are normal distributions.

they all have the same variance; and their means all lie on a straight line. As noted previously, this straight line is called a regression line. If the loaf is sliced parallel to the IQ (x-axis), then each slice is a conditional distribution of IQ for a particular value of GPA. These IQ distribution slices also have the shape of the normal distribution; they all have the same variance; and their means all lie on a straight line. This straight line is a second regression line. Note that the variance of the IQ conditional distributions may be different from the variance of the GPA distributions.

9.1.3 Fitting a Regression Line to Data

In Sections 1.1.3 and 3.3.5, we introduced the concept of a linear (straight line) prediction rule and gave a graphical example. In this section, we will express this model algebraically, describe the meaning of its parameters, and then use the sleep deprivation example to explain how the model can be fitted to data.

The equation of the regression line has the general form $Y = \alpha + \beta X$.

The equation of a straight-line regression rule has the general form

$$Y = \alpha + \beta X$$

In this equation, commonly referred to as the regression line, X is the value of the variable represented on the x-axis and Y is the corresponding value of the variable represented on the y axis. The variable X will normally be the predictor variable (hours of sleep deprivation, for example) and Y the response variable (number of errors, for example).

The constants β and α are parameters. These two parameters are needed to define the straight line uniquely. It is unfortunate that convention has adopted the repeated use of α and β for different situations, but the context will usually leave no room for ambiguity. The use of α in the straight-line regression model is unrelated to its use in the model for the completely randomized design, and, of course, the use of α and β in the regression model has nothing to do with the use of these symbols to denote Type-1 and Type-2 errors.

The intercept parameter, α, represents the overall height of the line.

The slope of the line, β, is called the regression coefficient.

In the linear regression model, the parameter α specifies the overall height of the line in terms of the point at which the line crosses the y axis, a point known as the *intercept*. The other parameter (β) corresponds to the *slope* of the line. It is called the *regression coefficient*, or *regression weight*. To see the effect of varying these parameters, examine the four lines drawn in Figure 9.6. These lines are parallel—they have the same slope of $\beta = 0.4$—but differ in their intercept.

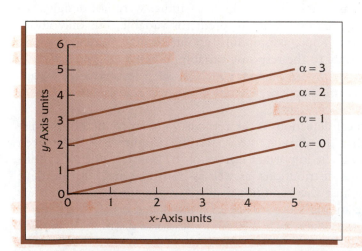

Figure 9.6
Four straight lines with the same slope parameter, $\beta = 0.4$, and four different values of the intercept parameter, α.

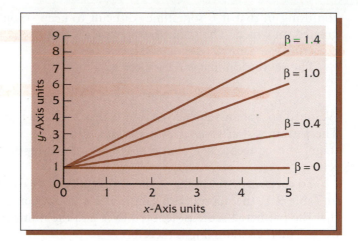

Figure 9.7
Four straight lines with a
constant intercept parameter,
$\alpha = 1$, and four different values
of the slope parameter, β.

What happens if the intercept parameter α is held constant but the value of the regression coefficient, β, is varied? The answer is given in Figure 9.7. In this case, the four lines vary in slope but have the same intercept value of 1. The regression coefficient reflects the rate at which values on the y-axis are changing for a unit increase in the value of the x-axis variable. Thus a slope of $\beta = 1.4$ indicates an increase of 1.4 y-axis units for an increase of 1 x-axis unit.

Figures 9.6 and 9.7 show how the parameters of a model can be thought of as the knobs or dials of the model and estimating their values as a form of fine tuning—"tweaking" the fit of the model to provide the most accurate predictions possible. In fitting the straight-line model, for example, the estimated values of β and α can be tweaked to adjust the slope and the overall height of the line until the "best" line is obtained.

The fitted version of the linear model is

$$\hat{Y} = a + bX$$

The Roman letter b replaces the Greek β and a replaces α. This usage corresponds to the switch from Greek to Roman letters used previously to distinguish parameters such as the mean and the variance from their sample-based estimates.

Fitting a Regression Line to the Sleep Deprivation Data

We will use the sleep deprivation study (Example 1) to illustrate the basic regression analysis in some detail. The principles learned from this example can then be applied to the other two examples. The goal of all the analyses is to estimate the parameters of a model that predicts the response variable as a linear function of a given value of the predictor variable. For Example 1, the model would predict the error score as a function of hours of sleep deprivation.

When the regression model is applied to the sleep deprivation data, X is the value of the predictor variable (hours of sleep deprivation). The value of a in this equation is the estimated value of intercept of the line, that is, the point at which it crosses the y-axis. The value of b is the estimated regression coefficient, that is, the slope of the line. As noted previously, the line itself is called the regression line. The value of b is known as the (estimated) regression coefficient, or the regression weight.

It is common to describe the regression line as "the regression of Y on X." Our analysis will regress errors (Y) on sleep deprivation (X). The expression can be

The regression line is usually described as "the regression of Y on X." The response variable is regressed on the predictor variable.

confusing in that it is sometimes difficult to keep straight which variable is being regressed on which. The point to remember is that the response variable is regressed on the predictor variable, not the other way round.

The regression line will have the general form

for this example

predicted error score = a + (b × hours of sleep deprivation)

We need to obtain values for a and b that produce the "best fitting" regression line. The formulas that generate such values of a and b will be described shortly. At this stage, the conceptual underpinnings are more important than the formulas themselves.

To review the meaning of "best fitting," accept for the moment that, for the data in Table 9.1, the appropriate values of a and b are a = 13.53 and b = 0.671. Recall that the predicted score is denoted by $\hat{Y}$ and the number of hours of sleep deprivation by X. The regression line is therefore

$$\hat{Y} = 13.53 + 0.671X$$

If X = 24 hours, for example, then the predicted number of errors is

$$\hat{Y} = 13.53 + (0.671 \times 24) = 29.6$$

Predicted values are sometimes called fitted values.

The predicted values for the other levels of sleep deprivation are shown in the right-hand column of Table 9.2. Predicted values such as these are sometimes referred to as *fitted values.*

Expressed in words, these values of a and b (rounded to 13.5 and 0.67, respectively) give a rule that states: Starting with an error rate of 13.5 for 0 hours of sleep deprivation, the number of errors increases by 0.67 errors for every hour of sleep deprivation. For example, the increase in errors for an 8-hour increase in sleep deprivation is 8 × 0.671 = 5.4 errors. Apart from rounding error, this is the difference between adjacent values in the $\hat{Y}$ row of Table 9.2, each of which represents an increase of 8 hours over the preceding value. The total increase in errors over the full range 8 to 40 hours is 32 × 0.671 = 21.5. Note that 21.5 is the difference between the last and first values of $\hat{Y}$ in Table 9.2. Figure 9.8 shows the regression line superimposed on the scatterplot from Figure 9.1.

Table 9.2 Linear regression predictions for the number of errors for the values of X included in the experiment

Hours of sleep deprivation (X)	Predictions ($\hat{Y}$)
8	18.9
16	24.3
24	29.6
32	35.0
40	40.4

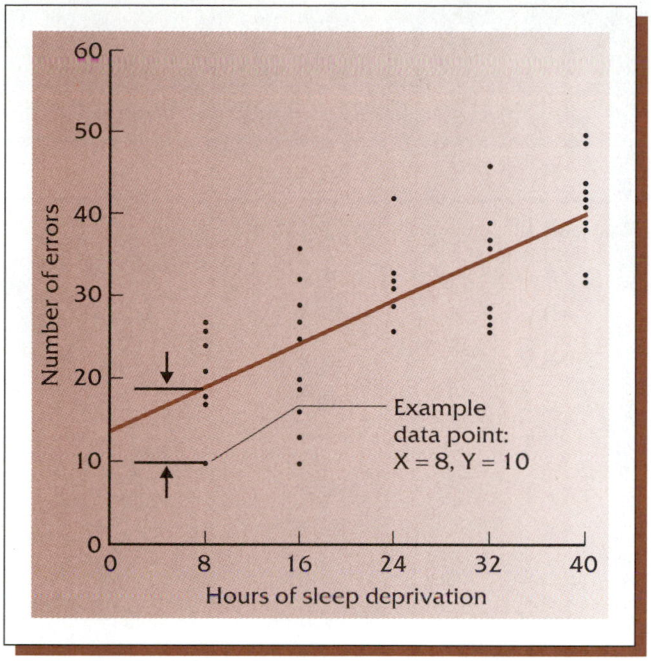

Figure 9.8
Scatterplot of the data in Data Set 9.1, with the least squares regression line. The intercept of the line is a = 13.53, and the slope is b = 0.671. An observation of ten errors for a participant in the 8-hour condition is labeled. The residual for this observation is the vertical distance of this point from the regression line — the distance between the two arrows.

Calculating Residuals

Once we know the values of a and b, residuals can be calculated. As always, the residual is the difference between the observed value and the value predicted by the model:

$$e = \text{observation} - \text{fit}$$

For the linear prediction rule, the residual for a particular observation is

$$e = Y - \hat{Y} = Y - (a + bX)$$

For the sleep deprivation data in Data Set 9.1,

$$e = Y - (a + bX) = Y - (13.53 + 0.671X)$$

For example, for the 8-hour condition,

$$e = Y - [13.53 + (0.671 \times 8)] = Y - 18.9$$

so, for the first observation (Y = 10) in this condition,

$$e = 10 - 18.9 = -8.9$$

Figure 9.8 can be used to indicate the graphical depiction of this residual. The label points to the first data point listed in Data Set 9.1. This is an observation of 10 errors (Y = 10) for the 8-hour condition. Graphically, the residual for this observation is the vertical distance between the observation (10) and the regression line. The height of the regression line for X = 8 is 18.9. The negative value of the residual reflects the fact that the data point is below the regression line. Note that the mean of *all* residuals is 0; there is no constraint that the mean residual be 0 for each conditional distribution. The residuals for each of the observations in Table 9.1 are shown in Table 9.3.

The residual is the vertical distance between the observation and the regression line.

Table 9.3 Residuals for each data point for the sleep deprivation experiment

8	16	24	32	40
−8.9	−11.3	−.6	4.0	8.6
5.1	2.7	2.4	−9.0	2.6
−0.9	−5.3	−3.6	−8.0	0.6
−8.9	4.7	2.4	1.0	3.6
2.1	0.7	3.4	−6.0	−1.4
7.1	11.7	−.6	2.0	9.6
−1.9	−4.3	12.4	−8.0	−8.4
8.1	7.7	1.4	2.0	1.6
5.1	−8.3	1.4	−7.0	−7.4
−0.9	−14.3	2.4	11.0	−2.4

The mean of the 50 residuals is 0.

Meaning of N

N denotes the total number of observations.

Before proceeding, we need to clarify a point of notation. We will use the symbol N to refer to the total number of observations, the total number of (X,Y) pairs. In the sleep deprivation example, $N = 50$. It is important to avoid confusion with n, the symbol we have used in previous chapters to denote the number of observations at each level of the predictor variable. In regression problems, N is the value that enters into formulas. Although, for this example, we could write $N = nk$ (where n is the number of observations for each of the k levels of X), no explicit use is made of the number of observations at each level of X. Moreover, in Examples 2 and 3, the concept of the number of observations at each level of X would have no useful meaning because in these cases the values of X are free to vary.

Sum of Squares and Mean Square of the Residuals

The degrees of freedom for the mean square of the residuals is $df = N - 2$.

The sum of squares of the residuals in Table 9.3 can be calculated in the usual way. SS_e is obtained by squaring each of the 50 values and finding their sum. To obtain the value of the corresponding mean square, MS_e, we divide by the appropriate degrees of freedom, which are $N - 2$, or 48 for the sleep deprivation example. The rationale for this value of $N - 2 = 48$ is as follows. There are $N = 50$ observations in all. One degree of freedom is lost estimating the intercept parameter, α, just as in the completely randomized design, 1 degree of freedom was lost in estimating the overall mean. Remember that a, the estimate of α, establishes the overall height of the regression line. A second degree of freedom is lost estimating the slope parameter, β. This leaves 48 degrees of freedom for the residuals. In general, the degrees of freedom for the mean square of the residuals will be $N - 2$, where N is the total number of observations.

Least Squares Criterion

The values of a and b that produce the best fitting straight line are those that produce the minimum sum of squared residuals. This is the "least squares" criterion of goodness of fit defined in Chapter 3. The method for obtaining the values of a and b is analogous to the method used in Chapter 3 to demonstrate that the sample mean was a least squares estimate of μ. The method is to write out an algebraic expression for the sum of squared residuals, then use the differential calculus to obtain the values of a and b that minimize the value of this expression. In the sleep deprivation study, the sum of squares of the residuals in Table 9.3 is 1969.8. If we were to use any values for a and b other than a = 13.53 and b = 0.671, and then use these alternative values to recalculate the residuals, the resulting sum of squares would always be greater than 1969.8.

Although the computations are usually onerous and would be performed by computer, the formulas for a and b will be given. The sum of squares for the marginal distributions are defined in the usual way. For the marginal distribution of the Y variable,

$$SS_Y = \Sigma(Y - \overline{Y})^2$$

where $\overline{Y}$ is the mean of the marginal distribution of the response variable. Because X, the predictor variable, is also a quantitative variable, we can form the sum of squares for the marginal distribution of X:

$$SS_X = \Sigma(X - \overline{X})^2$$

where $\overline{X}$ is the mean of the marginal distribution of the predictor variable.

Sum of Products

The formula for b involves just one new concept, that of the sum of products. The sum of products, denoted SP_{XY}, is also based on deviations from the mean and is analogous to the sum of squares. Remember that "sum of squares" is shorthand for the sum of the squared deviations of scores about their mean. The *sum of products* is defined as

$$SP_{XY} = \Sigma(X - \overline{X})(Y - \overline{Y})$$

There is one such product term, $(X - \overline{X})(Y - \overline{Y})$, for each observation in Table 9.1. For example, the first observation in the table is for X = 8 and Y = 10. This participant made 10 errors after 8 hours without sleep. We can express these X and Y scores as deviations from $\overline{X}$ and $\overline{Y}$, respectively. The mean of the 50 X values is $\overline{X} = 24.0$, and the mean of the 50 Y values is 29.6. Thus the product term for this participant is

$$(8.0 - 24.0) \times (10.0 - 29.6) = 313.6$$

The value of SP_{XY} is obtained by calculating such a product term for each observation and summing over the resulting 50 products. For the sleep deprivation data, the sum of products is 4294.4.

The formula for the least squares estimate of β in the regression equation is

$$b = \frac{SP_{XY}}{SS_X}$$

This value fixes the slope of the line.

The least squares solution for estimating the intercept, α, is the value of a that makes the line pass through the point $(\overline{X}, \overline{Y})$. In brief, the least squares regression line

---

Margin notes:

Values of a and b are chosen to satisfy the least squares criterion.

SP_{XY} denotes sum of products.

The sum of products is the sum of products of pairs of scores expressed as deviations from their respective means.

The formula for b, the least squares estimate of β, is

$$b = \frac{SP_{XY}}{SS_X}$$

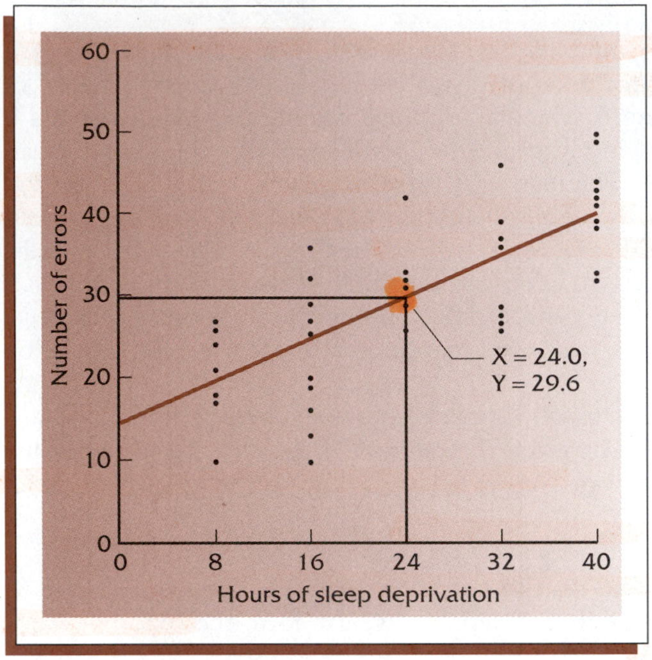

Figure 9.9
Scatterplot of the data in Data Set 9.1, with the least squares regression line. Note that the line passes through the point ($X = 24.0$, $Y = 29.6$), the means of X and Y, respectively.

The formula for a, the least squares estimate of α, is $a = \overline{Y} - b\overline{X}$.

always passes through the point defined by the means of the predictor and response variables. Figure 9.9 illustrates this requirement. This criterion makes some intuitive sense if you think of the point $(\overline{X}, \overline{Y})$ as the center of the scatterplot. The regression line is anchored so as to pass through this center point. The value of α is then the point at which this line crosses the *y*-axis. Given that the lines passes through $(\overline{X}, \overline{Y})$, the estimate of α is

$$a = \overline{Y} - b\overline{X}$$

Calculation of the Values of b and a for Example 1

For the sleep deprivation data, $SS_X = 6400$, so

$$b = \frac{SP_{XY}}{SS_X} = \frac{4294.4}{6400} = 0.671$$

and

$$a = \overline{Y} - b\overline{X} = 29.64 - (0.671 \times 24) = 13.53$$

There is much more to be said about this regression line. How accurate is the estimate of the regression coefficient? How is the regression equation used to make predictions? How strong is the relationship between the predictor and response variables? Is there a relationship at all? We will consider all these questions, but before doing so, we will review the basic procedures that have just been described by applying them to the remaining two examples.

9.1.4 Regression Lines for Examples 2 and 3

As further examples of the procedures described in Section 9.1.3, we will derive regression equations for Examples 2 and 3.

Example 2. Test Scores as a Function of Age

For Example 2, the regression line will have the general form

$$\text{predicted test score} = a + (b \times \text{age})$$

Again using Y to denote the response variable and X the predictor variable, we will use the following computational results obtained from computer output based on the formulas given in Section 9.1.3.

mean of the marginal distribution of test scores: $\overline{Y} = 30.35$ items correct
mean of the marginal distribution of ages: $\overline{X} = 98.14$ months
sum of squares of the test scores: $SS_Y = 5208.8$
sum of squares of the age values: $SS_X = 43{,}658.0$
sum of products: $SP_{XY} = 10{,}926.0$

The least squares estimates for b and a are therefore

$$b = \frac{SP_{XY}}{SS_X} = \frac{10{,}926}{43{,}658} = 0.25$$

and

$$a = \overline{Y} - b\overline{X} = 30.35 - (0.25 \times 98.14) = 5.81$$

Thus the regression of test score on age gives the least squares regression rule:

$$\text{predicted test score} = 5.81 + (0.25 \times \text{age})$$

or

$$\hat{Y} = 5.81 + (0.25 \times X)$$

The predicted test score of a child aged 100 months is

$$\hat{Y} = 5.81 + (0.25 \times 100) = 30.81$$

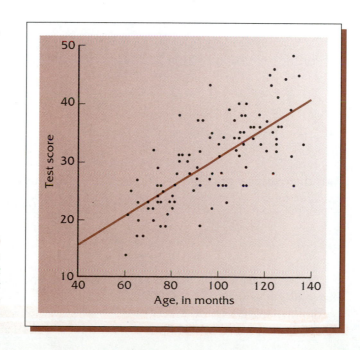

Figure 9.10
Scatterplot of the data from Example 2, with the least squares regression line for test score regressed on age. Note that the x-axis begins at 40 and the y-axis at 10.

The scatterplot with this fitted regression line is shown in Figure 9.10. There is a feature of this plot that sometimes causes confusion. You may have noticed that the points at which the regression lines intersect the x- and y-axes do not correspond to the values of the estimated intercept parameter a. This is because the x- and y-axes do not themselves intersect at $Y = 0$ and $X = 0$. To obtain the correct graphical representation of the values of a, you would move the y-axis to the left so that it was located at $X = 0$ rather than $X = 40$ and lower the x-axis from its present value of $Y = 10$ to a value $Y = 0$.

The residuals associated with this fit are, as in the previous example, the vertical distances between the data point and the regression line. The sum of the squared residuals for this analysis is $SS_e = 2474.3$. This value will be used in a later analysis of these data.

Example 3. Relationship Between IQ and GPA

For Example 3, it is possible to derive two regression lines by reversing the roles of predictor and response variables. Consider first IQ as the predictor variable and GPA the response variable. The regression line when GPA is thus regressed on IQ will have the general form:

$$\text{predicted GPA} = a + (b \times IQ)$$

Reversing the roles, when IQ is regressed on GPA,

$$\text{predicted IQ} = a + (b \times GPA)$$

It is important to note that the values of a and b will be different for these equations.

With switch-hitting roles of predictor and response variables, the designation of one variable as X and the other Y is arbitrary. We will use X to designate IQ and Y to designate GPA. For this designation, we get the following computational results:

mean of the marginal distribution of IQ scores: $\overline{X} = 110.18$
mean of the marginal distribution of GPA scores: $\overline{Y} = 2.26$
$SS_X = 6811.38$
$SS_Y = 56.96$
$SP_{XY} = 332.82$

For the regression of Y on X,

$$b = \frac{SP_{XY}}{SS_X} = \frac{332.82}{6811.38} = 0.0494$$

and

$$a = \overline{Y} - b\overline{X} = 2.26 - (0.0494 \times 110.18) = -3.12$$

Thus the regression of GPA on IQ gives the least squares regression rule:

$$\text{predicted GPA} = -3.12 + (0.0494 \times IQ)$$

or

$$\hat{Y} = -3.12 + (0.0494 \times X)$$

The residuals for this model can be calculated and their sum of squares obtained. The resulting value is $SS_e = 40.69$.

For the regression of X (IQ) on Y (GPA), we reverse the roles of SS_Y and SS_X. This places SS_Y rather than SS_X in the denominator for calculating b. The general rule

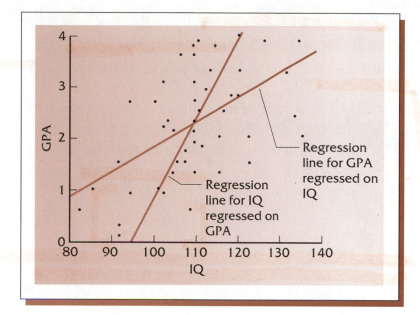

Figure 9.11
Scatterplot of the data from Example 3, with the least squares regression lines for GPA regressed on IQ and for IQ regressed on GPA.

is that the sum of squares in the denominator is the sum of squares for whatever variable is serving as the *predictor* variable. This is a case where it is even more important than usual not to memorize a formula without thinking about what role the symbols are playing. When Y (GPA score) is serving as the predictor variable,

$$b = \frac{SP_{XY}}{SS_Y} = \frac{332.82}{56.96} = 5.84$$

and

$$a = \overline{X} - b\overline{Y} = 110.18 - (5.84 \times 2.26) = 96.98$$

Thus the regression of GPA on IQ gives the least squares regression rule:

$$\text{predicted IQ} = 96.98 + (5.84 \times \text{GPA})$$

or

$$\hat{X} = 96.98 + (5.84 \times Y)$$

The residuals for this model can be calculated and the sum of squares obtained. The resulting value is $SS_e = 4866.5$.

Note that in continuing to use X to designate IQ and Y to designate GPA, we have reversed the convention of using X for the predictor variable and Y for the response variable. Recall that the denominator in the formula for b is always the sum of squares for the variable serving as the *predictor* variable. The scatterplot with both fitted regression lines is shown in Figure 9.11.

9.1.5 Interval Estimates of the Regression Coefficient

The formula given in the preceding section provides a *point* estimate of the population regression coefficient, β. It is sometimes useful to obtain a confidence interval for this parameter. Such an interval can be obtained by using the basic procedure that should now be familiar.

The confidence interval for β will have the usual general form:

$$\text{CI} = \text{point estimate} \pm w$$

In this case, the point estimate of β is b, so $\text{CI} = b \pm w$. The value of w will be $t \times s_b$, where

■ t is the critical value of the t-ratio obtained from the table of the t-distribution. The degrees of freedom for this t-ratio are $N - 2$.

■ s_b is the standard error of the estimated slope, b.

The standard error of the estimated regression coefficient, b, is

$$s_b = \sqrt{\frac{\text{MS}_e}{\text{SS}_X}}$$

Deriving the formula for the standard error of b is beyond the scope of this text. We will simply state it:

$$s_b = \sqrt{\frac{\text{MS}_e}{\text{SS}_X}}$$

In this formula, MS_e is the mean square of the residuals obtained, as usual, by dividing the sum of squares, SS_e, by its degrees of freedom, $N - 2$.

For the sleep deprivation data, we have $\text{SS}_e = 1969.8$ and $\text{SS}_X = 6400$. Thus,

$$\text{MS}_e = \frac{\text{SS}_e}{N - 2} = \frac{1969.8}{48} = 41.04$$

Therefore,

$$s_b = \sqrt{\frac{\text{MS}_e}{\text{SS}_X}} = \sqrt{\frac{41.04}{6400}} = 0.080$$

Suppose we wish to obtain the 95% confidence interval for β. For $df = 40$ (the closest tabled value below $df = 48$), the value of the t-ratio for a 95% confidence interval is $t = 2.021$. The value of w for such an interval would be

$$w = t \times s_b = 2.021 \times 0.080 = 0.16$$

The 95% confidence interval for β is therefore

$$\text{CI}_{.95} = 0.671 \pm 0.16$$

Rounding to two decimal places, we have

$$\text{CI}_{.95} = 0.51 \text{ to } 0.83$$

If desired, this confidence interval can be used in the normal way to evaluate the null hypothesis that the true value of β is 0 by noting whether the interval includes 0. In this example, the interval does not include 0, and, at the .05 significance level, we can conclude that the slope is nonzero; there is a significant linear change in error rate as a function of number of hours of sleep deprivation.

Example 2.   Test Scores as a Function of Age

For these data, $\text{SS}_e = 2474.3$ and $\text{SS}_X = 43{,}658.0$:

$$\text{MS}_e = \frac{2474.3}{98} = 25.25$$

Thus

$$s_b = \sqrt{\frac{\text{MS}_e}{\text{SS}_X}} = \sqrt{\frac{25.25}{43{,}658.0}} = 0.024$$

To obtain the 95% confidence interval for β, we obtain the value of the t-ratio with $df = 98$. For a 95% confidence interval using $df = 90$ as the closest lower value, $t = 1.987$. The value of w for such an interval would be

$$w = t \times s_b = 1.987 \times 0.024 = 0.05$$

The 95% confidence interval for β is therefore $CI_{.95} = 0.25 \pm 0.05$. Thus $CI_{.95} = 0.20$ to 0.30.

Example 3. Relation Between GPA and IQ Scores

In this example, there are two regression coefficients, and each will have its own confidence interval. When GPA is the response variable,

$$MS_e = \frac{40.69}{48} = 0.848$$

and so when GPA is regressed on IQ, the standard error of b is

$$s_b = \sqrt{\frac{MS_e}{SS_X}} = \sqrt{\frac{0.848}{6811.38}} = 0.011$$

To obtain the 95% confidence interval for β, we obtain the value of the t-ratio with $df = 48$. For a 95% confidence interval, using $df = 40$ as the closest lower value, $t = 2.021$. The value of w for such an interval would be

$$w = t \times s_b = 2.021 \times 0.011 = 0.022$$

The 95% confidence interval for β is therefore $CI_{.95} = 0.049 \pm 0.022$. This gives $CI_{.95} = 0.027$ to 0.071.
When IQ is the response variable,

$$MS_e = \frac{4866.5}{48} = 101.4$$

and so when IQ is regressed on GPA, the standard error of b is

$$s_b = \sqrt{\frac{MS_e}{SS_Y}} = \sqrt{\frac{101.4}{56.96}} = 1.334$$

The t-ratio is the same with $df = 48$. The value of w for such an interval would be

$$w = t \times s_b = 2.021 \times 1.334 = 2.70$$

The 95% confidence interval for β is therefore $CI_{.95} = 5.84 \pm 2.70$. This gives $CI_{.95} = 3.14$ to 8.54.
    The preceding examples are instructive for three reasons. First, they illustrate that the rationale for calculating confidence intervals that was used for means also applies to regression coefficients. In both cases, the interval is centered on the point estimate, and the semi-width (w) is the relevant tabulated statistic multiplied by the standard error. Second, once again the confidence intervals provide a basis for evaluating the null hypothesis. If the interval does not include 0, then the hypothesis that $\beta = 0$ can be rejected. Third, the width of the interval provides information that an investigator can use to evaluate the precision with which β has been estimated.

Comprehension Check 9.1

Important Concepts

1. When both predictor and response variables are quantitative, the goals of the data analysis can be (a) to construct a regression equation for predicting values of the response variable and (b) to describe the strength of the relationship between the two variables.

2. This section considers three examples that differ slightly in their design and purpose, but share common procedures of analysis.

3. A scatterplot is a graph that locates each data point in a space defined by the values of the predictor and response variables.

4. A conditional distribution is the distribution of the response variable associated with a specified value of the predictor variable. The marginal distribution is the distribution of all the values of one variable regardless of values of the other variable.

5. The procedures described in this chapter assume that (a) the conditional distributions of the response variable are samples from normally distributed random variables, (b) these distributions have equal variances (homogeneity of variance assumption), and (c) the means of these conditional distributions fall along a straight line. This last assumption is the assumption of linear regression.

6. For applications in which both variables can be considered random variables and treated as either predictor or response variable, the sample scatterplot is assumed to have been drawn from a bivariate normal probability distribution. In such a distribution, all the conditional distributions of both variables are normal distributions.

7. The fitted version of the least squares linear regression rule is $\hat{Y} = a + bX$. The value a is the intercept of the line and b is the slope. The values of a and b are chosen to minimize the sum of squared residuals. The value of b is known as the estimated *regression coefficient,* or *regression weight.* The sum of squares of the residuals for the fitted model has $N - 2$ degrees of freedom.

8. The sum of products is defined as $SP_{XY} = \Sigma(X - \overline{X})(Y - \overline{Y})$. This value enters into the formula for the least squares estimate of the regression weight, b.

9. For the bivariate normal model, two regression lines can be obtained. One is for the regression of Y on X, the other for the regression of X on Y.

10. The standard error of the estimated regression weight can be calculated and used to obtain a confidence interval for β. This confidence interval can be used in the normal way to evaluate the null hypothesis that the true value of β is 0.

Worked Examples

Example 1 **Alcohol and simple motor coordination (Data Set 9.4)**

In a study of the relationship between blood alcohol level and a simple motor coordination task, an investigator measures performance under five levels of alcohol consumption: 0, 0.5, 1, 2, and 3 ounces of consumed alcohol. The motor coordination task requires the participants to maintain contact with a moving target for as long as possible. Fifteen participants are assigned to each of the five alcohol-level conditions for a total of 75 participants in all. The response variable is time measured in seconds.

a. Set out the axes you would use for a scatterplot of these data. Plot the scatter for the conditional distribution for X = 0.5 ounces.

b. The mean for the marginal distribution of all 75 X values (alcohol consumed) is $\overline{X} = 1.30$; for the marginal distribution of the 75 Y values (time on target), the mean is $\overline{Y} = 59.92$. To obtain the least squares regression line, we need the sum of products. For the first observation in each of five levels of alcohol consumption, calculate the product terms that would enter into the entire sum of products.

c. Regression analysis gives the following values: $SP_{XY} = -990.2$, $SS_X = 87.0$. Use these results to calculate the least squares estimates of b and a.

Data Set 9.4 Alcohol consumption data for alcohol and motor coordination experiment (Worked Example 1)

0 ounces (conditional mean 73.7)

77	64	72	88	75	57	88	78
71	70	63	61	91	84	67	

0.5 ounces (conditional mean 68.4)

69	68	61	74	54	70	67	58
56	83	75	71	71	76	73	

1 ounce (conditional mean 66.3)

63	69	66	85	43	63	62	55
63	71	82	70	73	53	77	

2 ounces (conditional mean 50.5)

77	48	55	43	47	63	47	48
34	68	42	44	70	21	50	

3 ounces (conditional mean 40.7)

23	32	40	39	51	44	27	32
40	44	26	61	38	60	53	

The response variable is time, in seconds.

d. Use these values of b and a to draw the regression line. Use the axes you set out previously for the scatterplot. Calculate the residuals for the first five observations in each category of Data Set 9.4 (page 471).

e. Express in words the meaning of the regression coefficient b. That is, describe how performance changes with increased alcohol consumption.

f. What is the predicted time-on-target score for a person who has consumed 1.5 ounces of alcohol?

g. Given the result $SS_e = 9217.45$, calculate a 95% confidence interval for the regression coefficient, β. The regression line suggests a decline in performance with increased alcohol consumption. Is this decline statistically significant?

Answer

a. The complete scatterplot is shown in Figure 9.12. The scatter for the conditional distribution for X = 0.5 ounces has been enclosed in the dotted rectangle.

b. For any observation (X,Y), the product term is $(X - \overline{X})(Y - \overline{Y})$. The product terms for the data points in the first observation in each category of the data set are as follows

■ For X = 0, $(X - \overline{X})(Y - \overline{Y}) = (0 - 1.30)(77 - 59.92) = -22.20$.

■ For X = 0.5, $(X - \overline{X})(Y - \overline{Y}) = (0.5 - 1.30)(69 - 59.92) = -7.26$.

■ For X = 1, $(X - \overline{X})(Y - \overline{Y}) = (1 - 1.30)(63 - 59.92) = -0.92$.

■ For X = 2, $(X - \overline{X})(Y - \overline{Y}) = (2 - 1.30)(77 - 59.92) = 11.96$.

■ For X = 3, $(X - \overline{X})(Y - \overline{Y}) = (3 - 1.30)(23 - 59.92) = -62.76$.

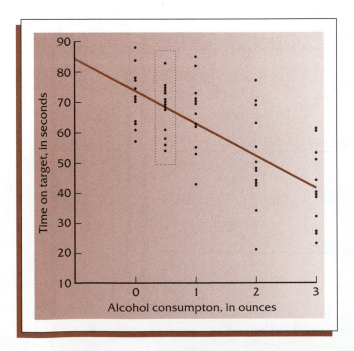

Figure 9.12
Scatterplot of the data in Data Set 9.4. The dotted rectangle encloses the scatter for the conditional distribution for X = 0.5 ounces.

Table 9.4 Residuals for the first observation in each category of Data Set 9.4 (Worked Example 1)

Alcohol consumption (ounces)	Observed values (Y)	Predicted values ($\hat{Y}$)	Residuals (observed − predicted)
0	77.00	74.72	2.28
0.5	69.00	69.03	− 0.03
1.0	63.00	63.34	− 0.34
2.0	77.00	51.96	25.04
3.0	23.00	40.58	− 17.58

c.
$$b = \frac{SP_{XY}}{SS_X} = \frac{-990.2}{87.0} = -11.381$$

and

$$a = \overline{Y} - b\overline{X} = 59.92 - (-11.381 \times 1.30) = 74.72$$

d. The regression line is shown on the scatterplot in Figure 9.12. Note that the negative value of b results in a line with negative slope: performance (Y) decreases with increasing values of X.

To calculate the residuals, we need the predicted values that the model generates for each level of alcohol consumption. The regression equation is

$$\hat{Y} = 74.72 - 11.38X$$

Substituting 0, 0.5, 1, 2, 3 for X in this equation gives the predicted values in the third column of Table 9.4. The residuals are the differences between the observed and predicted values.

e. Over the range 0 to 3 ounces, performance declines at the rate of 11.38 seconds per ounce of alcohol consumed.

f. The predicted time-on-target score for a person who has consumed 1.5 ounces of alcohol is $\hat{Y} = 74.72 - (11.38 \times 1.5) = 57.65$.

g. The value of $MS_e = 9217.45/73.0 = 126.27$. The standard error of b is

$$s_b = \sqrt{\frac{MS_e}{SS_X}} = \sqrt{\frac{126.27}{87.0}} = 1.20$$

To obtain the 95% confidence interval for b, note that, for $df = 73$, the value of the t-ratio for a 95% confidence interval is $t = 1.994$ (using $df = 70$). The value of w for the interval would therefore be

$$w = t \times s_b = 1.994 \times 1.20 = 2.40$$

The 95% confidence interval for b is $CI_{.95} = -11.38 \pm 2.40$. Rounding to two decimal places, we have $CI_{.95} = -13.78$ to -8.98. In this example, the interval does not include 0; and at the .05 significance level, we can therefore conclude that the slope is nonzero; there is a significant linear change in performance as a function of amount of alcohol consumed.

Example 2. Age and vocabulary size

How rapidly does a child's vocabulary increase between the ages of 3 and 6 years? To answer this question, vocabulary size was estimated for 35 children at each of the four age levels 3, 4, 5, and 6 years. The investigator claims that a regression analysis of the data from this study shows that at age 3 years the predicted average vocabulary is 800 words and that vocabulary size increases linearly at the rate of 550 words per year.

    a. What was the regression coefficient on which the investigator based this claim?

    b. Draw a graph of the regression line over the range 3 to 6 years.

    c. What is the estimated vocabulary size for 6-year-olds?

    d. A 5-year-old from the study has a vocabulary of 2000 words. What is the residual associated with this observation?

Answer

    a. The estimated regression coefficient is b = 550.

    b. A graph of the regression line is shown in Figure 9.13.

    c. A linear increase adds 550 words per year. Thus, if the vocabulary size is 800 at age 3, for age 6, 3 years later, it will be 800 + (550 × 3) = 2450.

    d. For age 5, the model predicts a vocabulary size of 800 + (550 × 2) = 1900. Thus an observed vocabulary size of 2000 at this age level has an associated residual of 2000 − 1900 = 100 words.

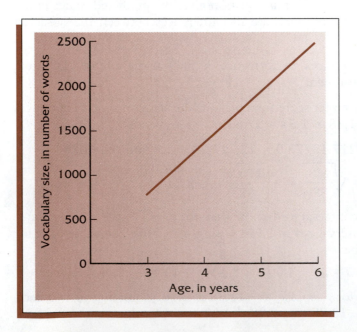

Figure 9.13
Regression line for Example 2.

Example 3. Verbal comprehension and numerical ability (Data Set 9.5)

Is there any relationship between verbal comprehension, as measured by a test of verbal comprehension, and numerical ability, as measured by simple arithmetic problems? To answer this question, an investigator administered tests to a sample of 80 junior high school students. The verbal comprehension test has a maximum score of 75 and the numerical ability test has a maximum score of 50. We will denote the verbal comprehension score by X and the numerical ability score by Y. The data (Data Set 9.5) yield the following computational results:

mean verbal comprehension score: $\overline{X} = 53.9$
mean numerical ability score: $\overline{Y} = 30.5$
$SS_X = 6542.8$
$SS_Y = 2465.9$
$SP_{XY} = 2071.0$

a. Obtain the regression line for numerical ability regressed on verbal comprehension.

Data Set 9.5 Data for verbal comprehension and numerical ability experiment (Worked Example 3)

V	68	38	53	56	51	54	61	52	69	50
N	39	26	37	33	38	31	25	36	43	29
V	53	48	60	65	72	63	54	54	55	34
N	26	29	28	40	37	29	34	30	28	22
V	63	58	53	55	36	58	44	57	41	47
N	24	31	26	24	30	31	23	35	32	36
V	71	47	44	57	52	58	66	44	58	51
N	28	31	33	35	32	30	37	19	37	27
V	57	58	62	63	51	55	58	66	42	59
N	33	37	32	28	29	30	30	34	35	25
V	54	40	67	46	65	34	49	69	57	61
N	19	28	38	23	44	25	33	41	28	40
V	50	41	54	43	46	57	70	38	56	42
N	28	20	28	28	33	29	40	20	26	30
V	58	42	45	65	58	46	56	49	56	55
N	29	25	31	33	24	27	32	23	31	33

The measure for verbal comprehension is a score out of a maximum of 75. The measure for numerical ability is a score out of a maximum of 50.

b. Obtain the regression line for verbal comprehension regressed on numerical ability.

c. Plot these two regression lines, setting verbal comprehension on the *x*-axis and numerical ability on the *y*-axis.

d. What is the point at which these two lines intersect?

Answer

a. For numerical ability (Y) regressed on verbal comprehension (X),

$$b = \frac{SP_{XY}}{SS_X} = \frac{2071.0}{6542.8} = 0.317$$

and

$$a = \overline{Y} - b\overline{X} = 30.5 - (0.317 \times 53.9) = 13.4$$

The regression line for numerical ability regressed on verbal comprehension is $\hat{Y} = 13.4 + (0.317 \times X)$.

b. To obtain the regression line of verbal comprehension (X) regressed on numerical ability (Y), we have

$$b = \frac{SP_{XY}}{SS_Y} = \frac{2071.0}{2465.9} = 0.840$$

and

$$a = \overline{X} - b\overline{Y} = 53.9 - (0.840 \times 30.5) = 28.3$$

Thus the regression line for verbal comprehension regressed on numerical ability is $\hat{X} = 28.3 + (0.840 \times Y)$.

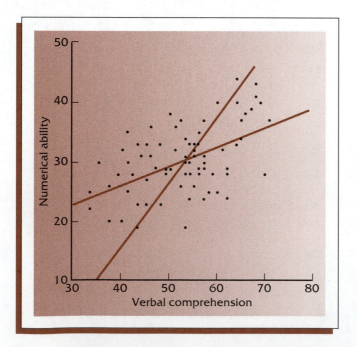

Figure 9.14
Scatterplot and regression lines for the data in Example 3.

c. The plot in Figure 9.14 gives both regression lines. Although the scatterplot was not requested, it is added as a further illustration of the relation between data points and least squares fitted regression lines.

d. The two regression lines intersect at $Y = \bar{Y}$ (30.5) and $X = \bar{X}$ (53.9). Remember that the least squares criterion requires that the regression lines pass through this point. Because both lines must pass through this point, it is the point they have in common—their point of intersection.

Problems

Problem 1   **Memory and marijuana (Data Set 9.6)**

In an investigation of the effects of marijuana on retention of learned material, 48 participants learned lists of words after having eaten cookies containing different quantities of THC (the active ingredient in marijuana). They were then tested a week later to see how much of the learned material had been retained. In this hypothetical version of the experiment, there were 12 participants at each of four dosage levels of THC: 4, 8, 12, and 16 milligrams of THC. The response measure is percentage of words recalled (Data Set 9.6).

Data Set 9.6   Data for memory experiment in Problem 1

4 mg THC (conditional mean 35.1)

33	34	36	36	34	31	43	34	34	31	40	35

8 mg THC (conditional mean 26.7)

23	28	27	30	23	35	26	26	27	25	24	27

12 mg THC (conditional mean 18.9)

13	25	15	23	18	25	21	19	18	12	19	19

16 mg THC (conditional mean 7.8)

11	6	10	9	7	9	14	10	8	3	1	6

The response measure is percentage of words recalled.

a. Set out the axes you would use to construct a scatterplot of the data in Data Set 9.6. Plot the scatter for the conditional distribution $X = 12$ milligrams.

b. The mean of the X values (milligrams of THC consumed) is $\bar{X} = 10.0$; for all 48 Y values (percentage of words retained), the mean is $\bar{Y} = 22.15$. Calculate the product terms that would enter into SP_{XY} for the first observation in the 4-mg and 8-mg conditions.

c. Regression analysis gives the following values: $SP_{XY} = -2150.0$, $SS_X = 960.0$. Use these results to calculate the least squares estimates of b and a.

d. Use these values of b and a to draw the regression line. Use the axes you set out previously for the scatterplot. Calculate the residuals for the first observation in the 4mg and 8mg conditions of Data Set 9.6.

e. Express in words the meaning of the estimated regression coefficient b. That is, describe how performance changes with increased THC consumption.

f. Given the result $SS_e = 614.87$, calculate a 95% confidence interval for the regression coefficient, β. The regression line suggests a decline in performance with increased THC consumption. Is this decline statistically significant from 0?

Problem 2   Total time hypothesis (Data Set 9.7)

An investigator claims that if participants are given a list of foreign language words to learn, the number of words they can learn will be a linear function of the total length of time they are given to study the list. To evaluate this "total time hypothesis," different groups of participants were given either 10, 15, 20, 25, or 30 minutes to study the word list. Memory for the words was then tested. There were 12 participants in each of the five study time conditions. The response measure is the number of words recalled (Data Set 9.7). The overall mean is $\bar{Y} = 23.78$ words recalled. Fitting a least squares regression line gives the following results: $SS_X = 3000.00$, b = 1.303.

Data Set 9.7   Data for the investigation of the total time hypothesis (Problem 2)

10 min study time (conditional mean 10.8)

| 14 | 15 | 21 | 7 | 4 | 14 | 15 | 9 | 14 | 3 | 3 | 11 |

15 min study time (conditional mean 16.0)

| 7 | 19 | 3 | 14 | 18 | 21 | 15 | 15 | 21 | 18 | 23 | 18 |

20 min study time (conditional mean 25.6)

| 33 | 30 | 23 | 27 | 15 | 26 | 15 | 24 | 25 | 25 | 31 | 33 |

25 min study time (conditional mean 30.2)

| 30 | 32 | 28 | 21 | 36 | 28 | 21 | 32 | 37 | 34 | 25 | 38 |

30 min study time (conditional mean 36.3)

| 47 | 32 | 28 | 27 | 42 | 37 | 36 | 36 | 41 | 36 | 36 | 38 |

a. Calculate the value of $\overline{X}$; then derive the full linear regression equation and use it to predict the number of words that would be recalled after 12 and after 27 minutes of study.

b. Provide a verbal description of the total time hypothesis.

Problem 3   Happiness and income (DS09_08.dat in the *ASCII Files*)

Is higher income associated with greater happiness? To answer this question, a sample of $N = 100$ participants was chosen, covering a wide range of annual incomes. Each participant was given a questionnaire that resulted in a measurement on a 20-point scale of their happiness with life. Income is measured in $1000 units. That is, an income score of 25 represents an annual income of $25,000. Regressing the happiness rating (Y) on income (X) gave the following results: $SS_Y = 1354.7$, $SS_X = 43,021.2$, $SP_{XY} = 477.7$, $SS_e = 1349.4$.

Calculate a 95% confidence interval for the regression coefficient and decide whether the data provide any evidence that income and happiness are related.

Problem 4   Maternal attention and infant attractiveness (Data Set 9.9)

Three independent judges rated a sample of 50 3-week-old infants for physical attractiveness. Their ratings were combined to give a total attractiveness score out of 30 for each of the 50 infants. Observers also measured the length of time each mother spent looking at her infant during a 30-minute observation period. Thus each infant has two scores, one for attractiveness and one for time looked at by the mother. The data are shown in Data Set 9.9.

Is there a relation between the two measures?

Data Set 9.9   Data for maternal attention and infant attractiveness experiment (Problem 4)

Rating (X)	20	15	19	16	11	16	18	30	15	11
Time (Y)	9	9	7	5	7	8	7	12	13	4
Rating (X)	20	14	16	21	9	12	17	16	4	19
Time (Y)	6	4	2	11	3	11	5	7	0	6
Rating (X)	17	12	15	21	16	9	21	17	15	14
Time (Y)	9	3	5	4	10	1	6	11	1	5
Rating (X)	11	10	22	19	13	17	13	18	22	18
Time (Y)	0	2	9	7	8	8	2	5	9	8
Rating (X)	26	14	21	21	22	19	17	19	16	21
Time (Y)	7	11	7	13	12	7	6	5	7	4

The response measure for infant attractiveness (X) is the judges' combined rating (out of a maximum rating of 30). The response measure of maternal attention (Y) is time (minutes).

Basic computations gave the following results.

mean attractiveness rating score: $\overline{X} = 16.70$
mean looking time: $\overline{Y} = 6.56$
$SS_X = 1042.52$
$SS_Y = 550.32$
$SP_{XY} = 399.40$

a. Obtain the regression line for looking time regressed on attractiveness rating.

b. Obtain the regression line for attractiveness rating regressed on looking time.

c. Plot these regression lines, setting looking time on the y-axis and attractiveness rating on the x-axis.

d. When looking time is regressed on attractiveness rating, the sum of squares of the residuals is $SS_e = 397.30$. Calculate a 95% confidence interval for the regression coefficient of looking time regressed on attractiveness rating.

e. When attractiveness rating is regressed on looking time, the sum of squares of the residuals is $SS_e = 752.63$. Calculate a 95% confidence interval for the regression coefficient of attractiveness rating regressed on looking time.

f. Do the data support the claim that a mother's looking time is influenced by her infant's rated attractiveness?

9.2 Evaluating the Fit of the Linear Regression Model

We have seen how to obtain the best fitting (in the least squares sense) regression lines. But, to repeat a question asked previously, how good is "best"? How good is the fit between data and model? This section extends the coverage regression analysis to address this question, using the same three examples. We will see that regression analysis is a simple variant of analysis of variance and that such an analysis can be used to evaluate goodness of fit, along with the usual measure (R^2) of the strength of the relationship between predictor and response variables. The analysis can also be used to examine the adequacy of a linear prediction rule as opposed to a curvilinear rule.

9.2.1 Regression Analysis of the Sleep Deprivation Example

The sleep deprivation experiment is particularly simple because there is just a small number of fixed values of the predictor variable and an equal number of observations at each of these levels. This simplicity allows for a straightforward application of the principles of analysis of variance of the kind used in Chapters 7 and 8.

The only difference between the example to be presented in this chapter and previous applications of analysis of variance is a change in the model. The model for completely randomized designs with a categorical predictor variable was $Y_i = \mu + \alpha_i + e$. In that model, each condition had its own distinct parameter value, α_i. For such a model, the categorical prediction rule was simply that the best (least squares) prediction is the sample mean of that condition: $\hat{Y}_i = \overline{Y} + \mathbf{a}_i = \overline{Y}_i$. In this chapter, we introduce a different model, with a correspondingly different prediction rule.

Linear Regression Model

The model for linear regression uses the linear prediction rule to replace the categorical prediction rule $(\mu + \alpha_i)$ in the earlier model. Thus, conceptually, the new model is

$$Y = \text{line} + \text{residual}$$

The formal expression for "line" is $(\alpha + \beta X)$. Thus the model is

$$Y = \alpha + \beta X + e$$

where, you will recall, α is the parameter representing the intercept (the point that the regression line crosses the y-axis) and β is the regression coefficient (the slope of the regression line). Notice that with a continuous quantitative predictor variable the subscript i, used previously to identify the values of a categorical predictor variable, is no longer needed.

The intercept parameter, α, in the regression model is really analogous to the parameter μ in the completely randomized, and in the randomized block, designs. Both α and μ are parameters that indicate the overall level of performance. The slope parameter, β, reflects the rate at which values of Y are changing as X changes.

We have seen that the fitted version of the model is

$$Y = \text{fit} + \text{residual} = a + bX + e$$

As noted in Section 9.1.3, application of the least squares criterion of fit for the sleep deprivation data gives a value of $a = 13.53$ and $b = 0.67$. The residuals resulting from this least squares fit were set out in Table 9.3 and had a total sum of squares of 1969.8.

Sum of Squares for Linear Regression

It is possible to derive a sum of squares that measures the variability accounted for by the regression line. This sum of squares is the counterpart of the between-condition sum of squares that was used in the one-way analysis of variance. In that analysis, the estimated condition means were expressed as deviations from the grand mean: $a_i = \overline{Y}_i - \overline{Y}$. These values of a_i were squared and added, one squared value for each data point (n for each condition).

In the regression analysis, the condition mean, $\overline{Y}_i$, is replaced by the estimate based on the regression line, $\hat{Y} = a + bX$. The values of $\hat{Y}$ are the fitted values that were used to obtain the residuals in Table 9.6. Each of these fitted values differs from the overall mean, $\overline{Y}$. This difference (the counterpart of the a_i) can be denoted by $\hat{Y} - \overline{Y}$. As in the full analysis of variance, there is one such difference for each of the 50 observations. The sum of the squares of these 50 differences is the sum of squares that measures the variability accounted for by the regression line.

$$SS_{\text{regression}} = \Sigma(\hat{Y} - \overline{Y})^2$$

For the sleep deprivation example, the value of this sum of squares is 2883.7. The corresponding regression analysis summary table takes the form shown in Table 9.5. Notice that there is just 1 degree of freedom for the linear regression model. This single degree of freedom corresponds to the slope of the regression line. Given the intercept value (or, alternatively, given $\overline{Y}$) that fixes the overall level of the response variable, the only measure of the difference between conditions (values of X) is the

Table 9.5 Regression analysis summary table for Example 1			
Source	SS	df	MS
Model: Linear regression	2883.7	1	2883.7
Residual	1969.8	48	41.0
Total	4854.5	49	—

slope of the regression line. The value of b is all that is needed to obtain an estimate of the difference between the means of any two conditional distributions. For example, in the sleep deprivation experiment, the value of b was 0.67. The estimated difference in mean error scores between two conditions X_1 and X_2 is simply $b \times (X_1 - X_2)$. If X_1 is 32 hours and X_2 is 8 hours, then the estimated difference in mean error scores between two conditions is $0.67 \times 24 = 16.1$ errors. In brief, the model expresses the differences among all the conditions by just a single number: the estimated regression coefficient, b.

The values for residual sum of squares and residual mean square are, of course, the same as those given in Section 9.1. The total sum of squares is simply the sum of squares for the entire (marginal) distribution of Y values. Thus, if SS_{total} is divided by its degrees of freedom, $N - 1$, we obtain the variance of the marginal distribution:

The total sum of squares is the sum of squares for the marginal distribution of Y values.

$$s_Y^2 = \frac{4854.5}{49} = 99.05$$

This result means that the breakdown of sum of squares in the regression table (Table 9.5) is a partitioning of the sum of squares of the response measures (Y) into two components: a component that measures the variability accounted for by the regression line and a residual component reflecting variability *not* accounted for by the line.

Standard Error of Estimate

The square root of MS_e is known as the standard error of estimate.

There is a special term for the square root of the mean square of the residuals. It is known as the *standard error of estimate:*

$$\text{standard error of estimate} = \sqrt{MS_e}$$

Although it is not widely used in the practical business of making predictions (for reasons to be explained shortly), the standard error of estimate does provide an overall measure of the variability of the data points about the regression line in units of the response variable. For the sleep deprivation example, the standard error of estimate is $\sqrt{41} = 6.4$ errors.

Evaluating the Null Hypothesis

Recall from Section 9.1 that the null hypothesis of zero slope is $H_0: \beta = 0$. This null hypothesis corresponds to a horizontal regression line representing a situation in which the response variable Y is the same regardless of the value of X, that is, that the value of Y does not vary as a function of the value of X.

This null hypothesis can be evaluated by forming the *F*-ratio:

$$F = \frac{MS_{regression}}{MS_e}$$

For our example,

$$F = \frac{2884}{41} = 70.3$$

where $MS_{regression}$ is shorthand for the mean square for linear regression. This ratio could be compared with the tabled value for $F(1,48)$; although, even without consulting the tables, it is obvious that an *F*-ratio as large as 70 will exceed the critical value at either the .05 or .01 levels. This result is consistent with the conclusion drawn from the confidence interval in Section 9.1.5. The null hypothesis that $\beta = 0$ is rejected. As in previous chapters, the two procedures are formally equivalent.

$MS_{regression}$ denotes mean square for linear regression.

In regression problems such as the sleep deprivation example, testing the null hypothesis is often not the primary purpose of the analysis. It may already be well established that the null hypothesis is false—that the predictor variable has *some* effect on the response variable—and the purpose of the experiment is to establish the parameters of the linear prediction rule, or merely to estimate the strength of the relationship between the two variables.

The strength of the relationship between the two variables can be described in terms of R^2, the proportion of the total sum of squares accounted for by the model. For the sleep deprivation data,

R^2 is the proportion of the total sum of squares accounted for by the regression line.

$$R^2 = \frac{SS_{regression}}{SS_{total}} = \frac{2884}{4854} = .594$$

9.2.2 Regression Analysis for Examples 2 and 3

We can now apply the methods of regression analysis to the other two examples.

Example 2. Test Scores as a Function of Age

The regression analysis for Example 2 follows exactly the same procedure as that used for Example 1. The regression analysis summary is given in Table 9.6. The standard error of estimate $= \sqrt{MS_e} = \sqrt{25.25} = 5.02$ items correct.

Table 9.6 Regression analysis summary table for Example 2

Source	SS	*df*	MS
Model: Linear regression	2734.4	1	2734.4
Residual	2474.3	98	25.25
Total	5208.7	99	—

Evaluation of the null hypothesis is probably not a matter of great interest in this example in that it is scarcely news that verbal skill increases with age. Rather, interest is in measuring the rapidity of increase, and this information is given by the regression coefficient, b. However, the null hypothesis that $\beta = 0$ could be evaluated by forming the F-ratio:

$$F = \frac{MS_{\text{regression}}}{MS_e} = \frac{2734.4}{25.25} = 108.3$$

This F-ratio has 1 and 98 degrees of freedom and is obviously significant at either the .05 or .01 levels. This result is consistent with the conclusion drawn on the basis of the confidence interval calculated in Section 9.1.5.

The proportion of the total sum of squares accounted for by the model is

$$R^2 = \frac{SS_{\text{regression}}}{SS_{\text{total}}} = \frac{2734.4}{5208.7} = .525$$

Example 3. Relationship Between IQ and GPA

This example differs from the first two in that, as noted in Section 9.1, two regression lines can be obtained by reversing the roles of predictor and response variables. We will complete each of these regression analyses in turn. It will be important to note the similarities and differences between the two analyses.

When GPA is considered the response variable and regressed on IQ, the regression analysis gives the summary table shown in Table 9.7. Notice that, within rounding error, $SS_{\text{total}} = SS_Y$ as reported in Example 3 of Section 9.1. The null hypothesis that $\beta = 0$ can be evaluated in terms of the F-ratio:

$$F = \frac{MS_{\text{regression}}}{MS_e} = \frac{16.26}{0.848} = 19.2$$

This F-ratio has 1 and 48 degrees of freedom and is significant at either the .05 or the .01 level.

The proportion of the total sum of squares accounted for by the model is

$$R^2 = \frac{SS_{\text{regression}}}{SS_{\text{total}}} = \frac{16.26}{56.95} = .286$$

Table 9.7 Regression analysis summary table for Example 3, GPA regressed on IQ

Source	SS	df	MS
Model: Linear regression	16.26	1	16.26
Residual	40.69	48	0.848
Total	56.95	49	—

Table 9.8 Regression analysis summary table for Example 3, IQ regressed on GPA

Source	SS	df	MS
Model: Linear regression	1944.9	1	1944.9
Residual	4866.5	48	101.4
Total	6811.4	49	—

When IQ is considered the response variable and regressed on GPA, the regression analysis gives the summary table shown in Table 9.8. The null hypothesis can be evaluated in terms of the F-ratio:

$$F = \frac{MS_{regression}}{MS_e} = \frac{1944.9}{101.4} = 19.2$$

The proportion of the total sum of squares accounted for by the model is

$$R^2 = \frac{SS_{regression}}{SS_{total}} = \frac{1944.9}{6811.4} = .286$$

Measures of Strength of Relationship in Example 3

Notice that the values for the F-ratio and R^2 are identical for both analyses. This result is not coincidence but a mathematical necessity. Although it may at first seem little more than an odd curiosity, a moment's reflection shows that the equivalence makes intuitive sense. Both the F-ratio and R^2 are measures of the strength of the relationship between the two variables. The F-ratio compares $MS_{regression}$ to MS_e, whereas R^2 compares $SS_{regression}$ to SS_{total}. It makes intuitive sense that these measures of strength of relationship should be symmetrical. It would be difficult to understand how IQ could be related to GPA, but GPA not related to IQ. A measure such as R^2 can be thought of as the variance common to, or shared by, the two variables, that is, the variance that supports the prediction of one variable on the basis of the other. The fact that there are differences in the values of a and b between the regression equations is a consequence of the predictor and response variables having different means and standard deviations.

The R^2 statistic has special meaning when applied to data for which the bivariate normal distribution is relevant—data such as those in Example 3. The square root of R^2 is known as the correlation coefficient, or, more fully, the *Pearson product-moment correlation coefficient*. The Pearson in this case is not the Egon Pearson of Neyman-Pearson fame, but his father, Karl Pearson, who first formulated the correlation coefficient in 1896. The correlation coefficient is denoted by the symbol r. For Example 3, the correlation coefficient between GPA and IQ is r = $\sqrt{.286}$ = .535.

Although convention dictates that we use the lowercase r, it is important to remember that r is simply $\sqrt{R^2}$. Note that because R^2 is a proportion of the total sum of squares, it can never be more than 1.0. Thus 1.0 is also the maximum value of the

The square root of R^2 is known as the correlation coefficient, or the Pearson product-moment correlation coefficient, r.

r = $\sqrt{R^2}$, so it ranges in size from −1.0 to +1.0.

r and b always have the same sign.

correlation coefficient, r. Note also that $\sqrt{R^2}$ can be $+r$ or $-r$. Whether the value of r is positive or negative can be inferred from the regression coefficient. The sign for r and b will be the same: A negative regression coefficient implies a negative correlation coefficient. Putting these facts together tells us that the correlation coefficient can range in value from -1.0 to $+1.0$. These extreme values correspond to values of $R^2 = 1$, meaning that, in these cases, the linear relationship accounts for *all* the variance; the residuals would be all 0.

ρ denotes correlation coefficient for the population.

The correlation coefficient, r, is a sample statistic calculated from sample data. The corresponding population parameter is denoted by ρ, the Greek letter rho.

9.2.3 Evaluating the Linearity Assumption

Although we have described the rationale for obtaining estimates of the parameters of the linear prediction rule, there remains the question of whether a straight line is the appropriate rule. Perhaps some other function, such as a curvilinear relationship, would provide better predictions. How can this question be answered? The claim that we wish to evaluate is that the linear prediction rule captures the entire signal—that there are no other systematic components to the data—and that the residuals therefore consist purely of noise or random variation about the regression line.

There are several ways of tackling this question. We will consider first some graphical methods that provide a visual inspection of the data and can reveal the inappropriateness of the linear rule. When the linear rule proves inappropriate, alternative models must be formulated. Although the fitting and evaluation of nonlinear models is beyond the scope of this text, even at an introductory level it is important to be aware of the dangers of analyzing data in terms of linear regression without checking on the appropriateness of the linear model.

Residual Plots

Residual plots can be used to evaluate the randomness of the residuals.

Careful investigators often construct graphical plots of the residuals, and many computer packages provide the option of calculating and plotting residuals. A residual plot for the data in Table 9.1 is shown in Figure 9.15. The residual for each observation is represented by its distance from the horizontal line at a y-axis (residual) value of 0, which is the overall mean of the residuals. Each residual is plotted above the appropriate value of $\hat{Y}$, the predicted (fitted) error score. Although in this graph the residuals are plotted against fitted values, residuals can also be plotted against observed values of the predictor variable.

If the residuals represent nothing but random variation about the regression line, then the residual plot should show no systematic trends across the x-axis. No such trend is apparent in Figure 9.15; the points seem scattered unsystematically about 0. Later in this section, we will examine a case in which the residual plot makes it readily apparent that the linear prediction rule is inadequate.

When the predictor variable is manipulated—as in the sleep deprivation example—and just a small number of values are included in the experiment, there is a second way of graphically evaluating the adequacy of the linear model. The method is to plot the sample means of the conditional distributions against the values of the predictor variable. Such a plot is shown in Figure 9.16. This plot also supports the appropriateness of the linear prediction rule. The five conditional means do not seem to depart from the regression line in any systematic way.

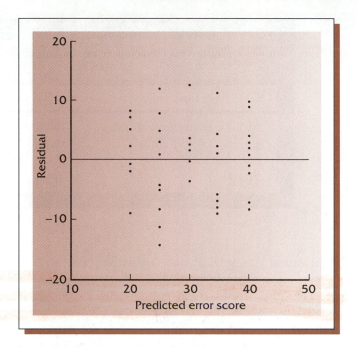

Figure 9.15
Residual plot for the sleep deprivation data of Example 1.

When values of the predictor variable are free to vary—as in Examples 2 and 3—it is not possible to make such a straightforward plot of conditional means against values of the predictor variable. In this situation, one strategy is to approximate the type of plot in Figure 9.16 by grouping values of the predictor variable into class intervals. It is then possible to calculate the mean of the response measures within the class interval and plot these means against the midpoints of the class intervals.

Although visual inspection of residual plots or of conditional means may seem to lack objectivity, it can be a powerful method of detecting systematic departures from linearity. However, for a manipulated predictor variable such as that in the sleep

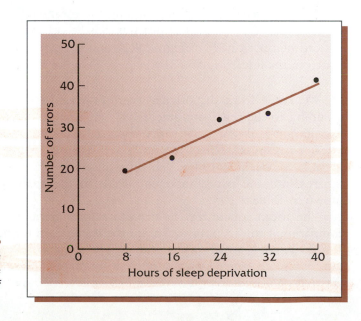

Figure 9.16
Plot of the means of the sample conditional distributions for the sleep deprivation data of Example 1.

Table 9.9 Analysis of variance summary table for Example 1

Source	SS	df	MS
Model: Between conditions	2992.3	4	748.1
Residual	1861.2	45	41.4
Total	4854.5	49	—

deprivation example, a more objective method is also available. This method is to compare the regression analysis with an analysis of variance that sets aside the assumption of a linear prediction rule and treats the predictor variable as categorical. The analysis is then based on the full model for the independent groups design. Essentially, the method determines whether the departures of the means from the regression line in Figure 9.16 result from only random variation. To do this, we consider the five levels of sleep deprivation as five values of a categorical variable and perform an analysis of variance as described in Chapter 7. The resulting analysis of variance summary table is shown in Table 9.9.

This analysis gives a sum of squares for between conditions of 2992.3. This value is based on 4 degrees of freedom, and it captures *all* the variability among the five means. This variability can be broken down into two components:

1. the variability accounted for by the straight line, and estimated in the original regression analysis completed at the beginning of Section 9.2.1 (Recall that this component reflects the variability among the values of $\hat{Y}$, that is, the predicted value for each condition based on the regression line.)

2. the remaining variability among the means reflecting the extent to which the means of the conditional distributions lie off the regression line (This variability can be seen clearly in Figure 9.16 and is the average squared distance of a point from the line.)

We know from the original regression analysis that the sum of squares corresponding to the regression line is 2883.7. Thus the sum of squares for the between-condition variability that is *not* captured by the regression line is the between-condition sum of squares less the linear regression sum of squares (see Table 9.5): $2992.3 - 2883.7 = 108.6$. This partitioning of the between-condition sum of squares into the two components leads to the analysis of variance summary table shown in Table 9.10.

The mean square for the departure from linear regression can be evaluated by comparing it to the mean square for the residuals in terms of an *F*-ratio. The *F*-ratio is $F = 36.2/41.4$, which is less than 1. The variability of the means about the regression line is no larger than the residual variation. Thus, there is no evidence that the departure from linearity is anything but noise.

Table 9.10 Analysis of variance summary table showing partitioning of the between condition sum of squares

Source	SS	df	MS
Model	2992.3	4	—
Linear regression	2883.7	1	2883.7
Departure from linear regression	108.6	3	36.2
Residual	1861.2	45	41.4
Total	4854.5	49	—

Yet another way of confirming the adequacy of the linear regression model is to compare the value of R^2 for the two models. For the regression model, we found R^2 to be .59. The completely randomized design analysis yields a value of

$$R^2 = \frac{2992.3}{4854.5} = .62$$

Thus moving from the linear regression model to the full categorical model yields negligible increase in the proportion of variability accounted for by the model.

Advantages of Linear Regression Model

These various analyses support the adequacy of the linear regression model; the residuals for this model appear to be entirely noise. However, by this same criterion, the full categorical model is also adequate. The two models appear to fit the data equally well. It is therefore reasonable to ask why the linear regression model is considered superior to the full categorical model.

Note first that there is nothing "illegal" about the fact that the full model treats each condition in the experiment—each level of sleep deprivation—as one value of a categorical variable. Although the predictor variable is obviously quantitative, the quantities used in the experiment can be treated merely as values that define the category. Thus the reason for preferring the linear regression model over the full model is *not* that it is wrong to treat each level of sleep deprivation as a category.

The reason for preferring the linear regression model over the full categorical model is contained in a cluster of closely related concepts. If pressed to defend this preference, an investigator might give the following explanations:

■ The linear regression rule is a stronger rule in the sense that, unlike the categorical model, it predicts performance for *all* values of X between 8 and 40 hours of sleep deprivation, not just the particular values used in the experiment. The categorical model can make predictions only for those values of the predictor variable actually included in the experiment. Note, however, that even with the quantitative model, it would be unwise to extend predictions beyond the range of X-values (8 and 40 hours in this example) included in the experiment.

■ The linear regression rule is more parsimonious; all predictions are based on just two parameter estimates. The categorical full model, on the other hand, requires the estimation of five parameters, one for each condition.

■ The linear regression rule is more elegant and lawlike. It permits statements such as "the error rate increases by 0.67 errors for every hour of sleep deprivation." The categorical full model can do no better than to list the separate predictions for the five conditions included in the experiment.

Example 4.   Drug Dosage Level

Consider the effect of drug dosage level in the treatment of depression. The experiment was first described in Section 3.3.5 of Chapter 3. It included five conditions: 0, 2, 4, 6, and 8 units of the drug, and the response measure was level of depression. A total of 40 participants were used in the study, 8 in each of the five drug dosage conditions (DS09_10.dat in the *ASCII Files*).

A scatterplot of the resulting data is given in Figure 9.17, along with the best fitting (least squares) linear regression line. The estimated regression coefficient (the slope of the regression line) is b = -0.691. This negative value indicates that the slope is downward, that is, that depression decreases with increased dosage. The estimate for the intercept is 7.91. A regression summary analysis gives the results shown in Table 9.11. From this table, we can calculate an *F*-ratio to evaluate the hypothesis of zero slope:

$$F = \frac{MS_{regression}}{MS_e} = \frac{152.63}{4.67} = 32.65$$

This value is substantially greater than the tabled value for $F(1,38)$ for either $\alpha = .05$ or .01, so it is safe to conclude that the true slope of the regression line is not 0. However, there remains the question of whether the linear prediction rule is the most appropriate. Is there another rule that would make better predictions, that would

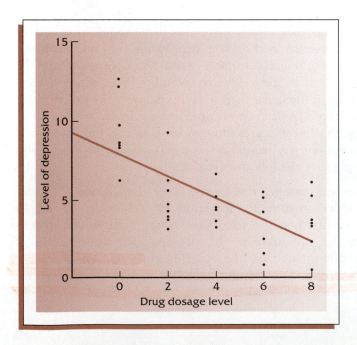

Figure 9.17
Scatterplot and least squares regression line for the study of drug dosage level and depression.

Table 9.11 Regression analysis summary table for drug dosage level example

Source	SS	df	MS
Model: Linear regression	152.63	1	152.63
Residual	177.63	38	4.67
Total	330.26	39	—

produce residuals with a significantly smaller mean square than the 4.67 obtained with the linear regression rule? There is, and we will now apply the various methods for addressing this question.

Appropriateness of the Linear Model. Figure 9.18 gives a residual plot of the linear regression analysis. In this plot, the residuals have been plotted against values of the predictor variable rather than against estimates. Notice that there appears to be a systematic trend such that at the extremes (0 and 8) the residuals are mostly above the line, whereas in the center they are mostly below the line. This trend is also evident in a plot of the means for each of the five levels (Figure 9.19).

If the data are analyzed assuming a categorical model, then the value of $SS_{between}$ is 197.89. This sum of squares has 4 degrees of freedom. Using this value along with the values from the regression analysis, we can calculate the sum of squares for departure from linearity as $SS_{between} - SS_{regression}$. This approach gives the summary table shown in Table 9.12.

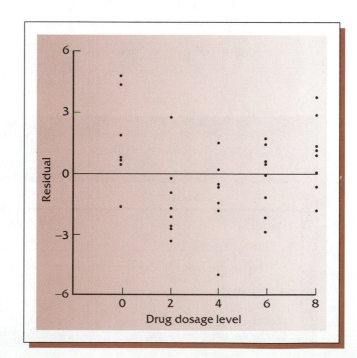

Figure 9.18
Residual plot for the study of drug dosage level and depression.

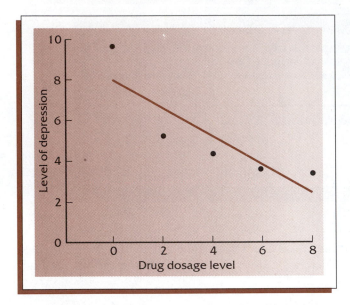

Figure 9.19
Plot of the sample means of the conditional distributions for the study of drug dosage level and depression.

We can evaluate the mean square for departure from linear regression by forming an F-ratio, which compares the mean square for departure from linear regression with the mean square of the residuals:

$$F = \frac{15.09}{3.78} = 3.99$$

Consulting the table of the F-distribution for $F(3,35)$, we find a critical value of 2.88 for the .05 significance level. This result confirms what is apparent in the graphical depiction of the residuals. There is significant departure from linearity.

Comparison of R^2 for the Two Models. Finally, we can compare the value of R^2 for the linear regression model with that of the full model. For the regression model,

$$R^2 = \frac{SS_{regression}}{SS_{total}} = \frac{152.63}{330.26} = .46$$

Table 9.12 Analysis of variance summary table for drug dosage level example

Source	SS	*df*	MS
Model	197.89	4	—
Linear regression	152.63	1	152.63
Departure from linear regression	45.26	3	15.09
Residual	132.37	35	3.78
Total	330.26	39	—

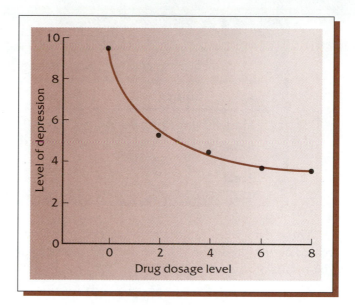

Figure 9.20
Smooth curve fitted to the sample means of the conditional distributions for the study of drug dosage level and depression.

For the full model,

$$R^2 = \frac{SS_{between}}{SS_{total}} = \frac{197.89}{330.26} = .60$$

Thus the linear regression model accounts for considerably less variability than the full model.

Nonlinear or Curvilinear Models. There are other alternatives besides the linear and the categorical full model. The graph shown in Figure 9.19 suggests a smooth curve, and Figure 9.20 shows such a curve. Fitting such *nonlinear* or *curvilinear* models is beyond the scope of this introductory text, but the basic principles underlying nonlinear regression are not. They are the same as for linear regression. The only difference is that the expression $\alpha + \beta X$ is replaced with some nonlinear expression, such as one involving the logarithm of X. The goal remains the same: Find least squares estimates of the parameters, calculate the sum of squares of the resulting residuals, and evaluate this sum of squares to ensure that it contains only noise.

When values of the predictor variable are free to vary, as they do in the studies of test scores as a function of age and the relation between GPA and IQ, the evaluation of linearity is not so straightforward. In this text, coverage of such situations will be limited to graphical methods of plotting residuals from the linear model.

Anxiety and Test Performance

This example provides a rather dramatic illustration of the value of graphical methods in examining data for nonlinearity. The application of linear regression would lead to gross misinterpretation of the data. The regression analysis summary table itself gives no hint of this danger, but a simple residual plot immediately reveals the inadequacy of the linear model.

In a study of the relationship between anxiety level and performance on a difficult math test, rated anxiety (measured on a 20-point scale) and scores on the test (score out of a maximum of 75) were obtained for 120 students who took the test (DS09_11.dat in the *ASCII Files*).

Table 9.13 Regression analysis summary table for the anxiety and test performance example

Source	SS	df	MS
Model: Linear regression	138.0	1	138.0
Residual	10,429.4	118	88.4
Total	10,567.4	—	—

These data were subject to a regression analysis in which anxiety level (X) was treated as the predictor variable and test performance (Y) as the response measure. The results of this analysis were

for anxiety level: $\overline{X} = 10.37$, $SS_X = 911.87$
for test performance: $\overline{Y} = 49.18$

The estimated regression weight was $b = -0.39$, and the intercept estimate was $a = 53.2$. The regression summary table is shown in Table 9.13.

The 95% confidence interval for b can be calculated as follows. The standard error of b is

$$s_b = \sqrt{\frac{MS_e}{SS_X}} = \sqrt{\frac{88.4}{911.87}} = 0.31$$

Note that, for $df = 100$ (an adequate approximation for $df = 118$), the value of the t-ratio for a 95% confidence interval is $t = 1.984$. The value of w for the interval would therefore be

$$w = t \times s_b = 1.984 \times 0.31 = 0.62$$

The 95% confidence interval for b is therefore $CI_{.95} = -0.39 \pm 0.62$. Rounding to two decimal places, we have $CI_{.95} = -1.01$ to 0.23. This interval includes 0, so there are no grounds for rejecting the null hypothesis that the true value of the regression coefficient is 0. The null hypothesis that $\beta = 0$ remains plausible.

The same conclusion is reached if we calculate an F-ratio from the regression analysis summary table:

$$F(1,118) = \frac{MS_{regression}}{MS_e} = \frac{138.0}{88.4} = 1.56$$

This F-ratio is well below the value needed for significance. For a Type-1 error rate of $\alpha = .05$, the nearest tabulated value below $df = (1,118)$ is for 1 and 100 degrees of freedom. The tabulated F-value is 3.94. Again, there is no convincing evidence that there is a significant linear relationship between anxiety level and test performance.

The value of R^2 is

$$R^2 = \frac{SS_{regression}}{SS_{total}} = \frac{138.0}{10,567} = .013$$

This very small value for R^2 is further evidence of the absence of a linear relationship between anxiety and performance.

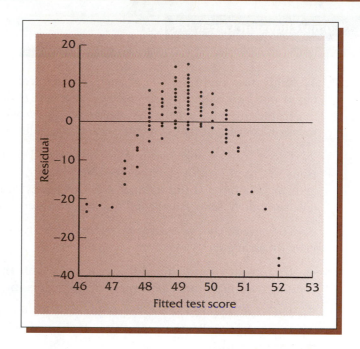

Figure 9.21
Residual plot for the study of
the effect of anxiety level on
test performance.

Remembering that the product-moment correlation is $r = \sqrt{R^2}$, we calculate that the correlation between anxiety and performance is $\sqrt{.013} = -.11$. Note that r is negative because the regression coefficient is negative.

A casual investigator might conclude from this analysis that anxiety has no effect on test performance. A regression line with a slope not significantly different from 0 indicates that performance is not a linear function of anxiety. Not only is the conclusion that anxiety has no effect on test performance unwarranted, but a simple graphical analysis shows that this conclusion is almost certainly false. Consider the residual plot shown in Figure 9.21 for the linear regression analysis. The residuals are plotted as a function of their fitted values.

It is immediately apparent that the residuals are not randomly distributed about the regression line. Residuals near the mean test score are positive, but they decrease systematically as they move away from the mean. These data show a strong curvilinear relationship, and an appropriate analysis would reveal a very strong relationship between anxiety level and performance. The data illustrate a relationship long known in psychology as the Yerkes-Dodson law. This law describes a relationship that is probably confirmed by your own experience. It states that, for a task of a given difficulty level, there is an optimal level of anxiety or arousal—too much anxiety, or too little, lowers performance relative to performance at the optimal level of anxiety. In brief, performance is a curvilinear function of anxiety, not a linear one. A linear relationship would mean that either the more anxiety, the better (a positive regression weight), or the more anxiety, the worse the performance (a negative regression weight). Neither of these claims is true.

Although the analysis of nonlinear regression is beyond the scope of this book, this example underlines the point that a correlation or regression coefficient based on linear regression may not give an accurate picture of the true relation between variables. This inaccuracy can be thought of as another example of misleading averaging. The linear regression model with zero slope claims that the best prediction of performance is the average performance over all the data; it fails to reflect the fact that this prediction averages over means that are genuinely different for different levels of anxiety.

A zero linear regression weight or correlation coefficient does not imply there is no relation between the two variables.

Comprehension Check 9.2

Important Concepts

1. Regression problems can be analyzed by partitioning the total sum of squares based on the model $Y = \alpha + \beta X + e$, where α is the parameter representing the intercept (the point where the regression line crosses the y-axis) and β is the regression coefficient (the slope of the regression line).

2. The regression analysis summary table based on the model in concept 1 partitions the total sum of squares into a linear regression sum of squares with 1 degree of freedom and the residual sum of squares with $N - 2$ degrees of freedom. The symbol N denotes the total number of observations.

3. The square root of the mean square of the residuals is known as the standard error of estimate.

4. The residual mean square from the regression analysis can be used to form an F-ratio to evaluate the hypothesis that the regression coefficient, β, is 0.

5. The sum of squares for regression can be compared with the total sum of squares to obtain R^2, the proportion of the variability accounted for by the linear regression model.

6. When the data are assumed to have an underlying bivariate normal distribution, $\sqrt{R^2}$ is denoted by r and is termed the Pearson product-moment correlation coefficient.

7. There are several ways in which to examine the validity of the linearity assumption. Graphically, residuals can be plotted against predicted values of the response variable, or against the conditional means of the predictor variable, and examined for systematic trends. More formal methods are available, but the only case considered in detail was the case in which the predictor variable is manipulated and the regression analysis can be compared with an analysis of variance based on the full model that treats the predictor variable as categorical.

8. When linearity is inappropriate, the linear regression model can give a false picture of the strength of the relationship between the variables.

Worked Examples

Example 1　Alcohol and simple motor coordination

This example continues the analysis of the data used in Example 1, Section 9.1. The total number of participants was $N = 75$.

a. Given the following results, set out a regression analysis summary table for these data.

$$SP_{XY} = -990.2 \qquad SS_X = 87.0 \qquad SS_Y = 20{,}487.5 \qquad SS_e = 9217.5$$

b. Calculate the standard error of estimate for these data.

c. Use the F-distribution to test the hypothesis that the true value of the regression coefficient is 0.

d. Calculate R^2 for the linear regression model fitted to these data.

e. If the five values of the predictor variable are treated as categorical and an analysis of variance is conducted, the resulting sum of squares for between conditions is $SS_{between} = 11,458.6$, with 4 degrees of freedom. Use this result to evaluate the appropriateness of the linear model relative to a nonlinear model.

Answer

a. The total sum of squares is $SS_Y = 20,487.5$. Thus the regression sum of squares is $SS_Y - SS_e = 20,487.5 - 9217.5 = 11,270.0$. These values are given in Table 9.14.

b. The standard error of estimate for these data is $\sqrt{126.3} = 11.2$.

c. The F-distribution to test the hypothesis that $\beta = 0$ is $F(1,73) = 11,270.0/126.3 = 89.2$.

d. $R^2 = \dfrac{SS_{regression}}{SS_{total}} = \dfrac{11,270.0}{20,487.5} = .55$

e. The sum of squares for departure from linear regression is the sum of squares between conditions, less the sum of squares for regression. This difference is $11,458.6 - 11,270.0 = 188.6$, with 3 degrees of freedom. The analysis of variance summary table is shown in Table 9.15. The F-ratio for departure from linear regression is less than 1, so it provides no evidence against the linearity assumption.

Table 9.14 Regression analysis for Worked Example 1

Source	SS	df	MS
Model: Linear regression	11,270.0	1	11,270.0
Residual	9217.5	73	126.3
Total	20,487.5	74	—

Table 9.15 Analysis of variance summary table for Worked Example 1

Source	SS	df	MS
Model	11,458.6	4	—
Linear regression	11,270.0	1	10,890.7
Departure from linear regression	188.6	3	62.9
Residual	9028.9	70	129.0
Total	20,487.5	74	—

Example 2 Verbal comprehension and numerical ability

This example continues the analysis of Example 3, Section 9.1. The verbal comprehension score was denoted by X and the numerical ability score by Y. There were $N = 80$ participants. The results of the basic analysis were $SS_X = 6542.8$, $SS_Y = 2465.9$, and $SP_{XY} = 2071.0$. Regressing numerical ability (Y) on verbal comprehension (X) gave a value for the sum of squares of residuals of $SS_e = 1810.1$.

a. Given the aforementioned results, set out the regression analysis summary table for this analysis.

b. Calculate the standard error of estimate for estimating numerical ability on the basis of verbal comprehension.

c. Use the F-distribution to test the hypothesis that the true value of the regression coefficient is 0.

d. Calculate R^2 for the linear regression model fitted to these data. What is the product-moment correlation coefficient between the two variables? What assumption underlies the use of the product-moment correlation coefficient?

e. Regressing verbal comprehension (X) on numerical ability (Y) gives a value for the sum of squares of residuals of $SS_e = 4802.8$. Set out the regression analysis summary table for this analysis.

f. Use the values from the table constructed for (e) to calculate the standard error of estimate for estimating verbal comprehension on the basis of numerical ability.

g. Use the values from the table constructed for (e) to calculate the F-ratio you would use to test the hypothesis that the true value of the regression coefficient is 0.

h. Use the values from the table constructed for (e) to calculate the value of R^2 for the linear regression model fitted to these data.

i. The values for the F-ratio and R^2 are the same as for the preceding analysis of the regression of numerical ability regressed on verbal comprehension, but the standard error of estimate is different. Why?

Answer

a. The value of $SS_{regression}$ is $SS_{total} - SS_e = 2465.9 - 1810.1 = 655.8$. The complete summary table appears in Table 9.16.

b. The standard error of estimate for these data is $\sqrt{23.2} = 4.82$.

c. The F-ratio to test the hypothesis that $\beta = 0$ is $F(1,78) = 655.8/23.2 = 28.3$. This value is greater than the tabled value of $F(1,78)$ for either the .05 or the .01 level. The null hypothesis that $\beta = 0$ must therefore be rejected.

d. $R^2 = \dfrac{SS_{regression}}{SS_{total}} = \dfrac{655.8}{2465.9} = .266$

The product-moment correlation coefficient between the two variables is $\sqrt{.266} = .516$. This correlation is positive because the regression coefficient was posi-

Table 9.16 Regression analysis summary table for Example 2 with numerical ability regressed on verbal ability

Source	SS	df	MS
Model: Linear regression	655.8	1	655.8
Residual	1810.1	78	23.2
Total	2465.9	79	—

tive. The assumption underlying the use of the product-moment correlation coefficient is that the data are a sample from a bivariate normal distribution.

e. The regression analysis summary table appears in Table 9.17.

f. The standard error of estimate for estimating verbal comprehension on the basis of numerical ability is $\sqrt{61.57} = 7.85$.

g. The F-ratio to test the hypothesis that the true value of the regression coefficient is 0 is $F = 1740.0/61.57 = 28.3$.

h. The value of R^2 is $1740.0/6542.8 = .266$.

i. The values for the F-ratio and R^2 are both measures of the strength of the relationship between two variables and are therefore the same for both the regression of verbal comprehension on numerical ability and vice versa. The standard error of estimates are different because they are standard deviations of the residuals about their respective regression lines and therefore scaled according to their own units of measurement. The standard deviation of verbal comprehension is larger than the standard deviation of numerical ability, so the standard error for the regression of verbal comprehension on numerical ability (which is in units of the verbal comprehension test) is correspondingly larger than the standard error for the regression of numerical ability on verbal comprehension.

Table 9.17 Regression analysis summary table for Worked Example 2 with verbal ability regressed on numerical ability

Source	SS	df	MS
Model: Linear regression	1740.0	1	1740.0
Residual	4802.8	78	61.57
Total	6542.8	79	—

Problems

Problem 1   Memory and marijuana

This problem continues the analysis of data from the investigation of the effects of marijuana on retention of learned material begun as Problem 1, Section 9.1. There were $N = 48$ participants in the experiment. The predictor variable (X) was dosage level and the response variable (Y) was recall score.

a. Use the following results to set out a regression analysis summary table for these data. $SS_X = 960.00$, $SS_Y = 5429.98$, $SS_e = 614.87$

b. Calculate the standard error of estimate for these data.

c. Use the F-distribution to test the hypothesis that the true value of the regression coefficient is 0.

d. Calculate R^2 for the linear regression model fitted to these data.

e. If the four values of the predictor variable are treated as categorical and an analysis of variance conducted, the resulting sum of squares for between conditions is $SS_{between} = 4846.23$. Use this result to evaluate the appropriateness of the linear regression model relative to a nonlinear model.

Problem 2   Total time hypothesis

This problem continues the analysis of data from Problem 2, Section 9.1. This investigation of the total time hypothesis examined the relation between the length of study time and the recall of foreign language vocabulary. There were $N = 60$ participants in the experiment. The predictor variable (X) was study time and the response variable (Y) was recall score. The overall mean recall score was $\bar{Y} = 23.78$ words recalled.

The following results were obtained: $SS_X = 3000.00$, $SS_Y = 6998.18$, $SS_e = 1902.15$. If the five values of the predictor variable are treated as categorical and an analysis of variance conducted, the resulting sum of squares for between conditions is $SS_{between} = 5157.27$.

a. Use this result to evaluate the appropriateness of the linear regression model relative to a nonlinear model.

b. Do the data support the total time hypothesis?

Problem 3   Happiness and income

This problem continues the analysis of data from the investigation of the relationship between happiness and income described in Problem 3, Section 9.1. There were $N = 100$ participants. Regressing the happiness rating (Y) on income (X) gave the following results: $SS_Y = 1354.7$, $SS_X = 43,021.2$, $SS_e = 1349.4$.

a. Set out a regression analysis summary table for these results.

b. Use this analysis to test the null hypothesis of zero regression coefficient. Check that your conclusion is consistent with that made on the basis of the confidence interval calculated in Section 9.1.

c. Calculate R^2 for the linear regression model fitted to these data.

| Problem 4 | Maternal attention and infant attractiveness |

This problem continues the analysis of data from the investigation of the relationship between maternal attention and infant attractiveness described in Problem 4, Section 9.1 (see Data Set 9.9). $SS_X = 1042.52$, $SS_Y = 550.32$.

a. When looking time is regressed on attractiveness rating, the sum of squares of the residuals is $SS_e = 397.3$. Set out a regression analysis summary table for these results.

b. Use this analysis to test the null hypothesis of zero regression coefficient. Check that your conclusion is consistent with that made on the basis of the confidence interval calculated in Section 9.1.

c. Calculate R^2 for the linear regression model fitted to these data. What is the correlation coefficient between the two variables?

d. When attractiveness rating is regressed on looking time, the sum of squares of the residuals is $SS_e = 752.63$. Set out a regression analysis summary table for this analysis.

e. Calculate R^2 for the linear regression model fitted to these data and check that it is the same value as that calculated for looking time regressed on attractiveness rating.

9.3 Correlation Coefficient

The product-moment correlation coefficient has had a dominant influence within the behavioral sciences for almost a century, and its influence remains unabated. Next to the mean and standard deviation, the product-moment correlation coefficient is probably the most commonly used statistic in the behavioral sciences. It is therefore appropriate that we examine this statistic in greater detail.

At a general level, the reason for the widespread use of the correlation coefficient is understandable. The behavioral sciences are interested in relationships, especially relationships among natural variables such as abilities, personality characteristics, aptitude test performance, job performance, and countless other attributes. The product-moment correlation coefficient measures the strength of such relationships. Other measures of the relationship between variables exist, and many are also called correlation coefficients. However, when the term *correlation coefficient* is used in this chapter, it will refer to the product-moment correlation coefficient.

9.3.1 A Closer Look at the Product-Moment Correlation Coefficient

Because of its widespread use, the correlation coefficient is often the focal point in textbook chapters on correlation and regression. We take a slightly different perspective: we make regression the focus and present the correlation coefficient as a subtopic within this broader context. The justification for this approach is the need to stress two important facts about the product-moment correlation coefficient.

The first fact is that the correlation coefficient is a *model-dependent* measure of the strength of the relationship between two variables. It is not a stand-alone statistic that can be used regardless of assumptions about the underlying structure of the data.

Despite its widespread use as a descriptive statistic, the product-moment correlation coefficient should be interpreted within the context of linear regression.

It provides an appropriate measure of the strength of a relationship only within the context of linear regression. As described previously, its interpretation assumes an underlying bivariate normal distribution, a distribution that implies *linear regression* and conditional distributions that are *normal* and have *equal variances*.

The second fact is that the correlation coefficient is a special case based on the more general statistic R^2, the measure of the proportion of the total variability that a model accounts for. In this regard, the use of the correlation coefficient is rather like the use of the *t*-ratio in testing the difference between two means. Both the correlation coefficient and the *t*-ratio are perfectly appropriate in the analysis of data with two variables or conditions; but presented in isolation, these statistics fail to offer any insight into how to analyze data with more than two variables or more than two conditions. By understanding the *t*-ratio as a special case of the *F*-ratio, and understanding the correlation coefficient as a special case of R^2, a foundation is established for the extension to more general situations. Designs using more than one predictor variable are called multiple regression and are described briefly in Chapter 11.

Analysis of variance, regression analysis, and the *t*-test are all closely related.

This emphasis on generality also serves to emphasize the interrelatedness of the various methods. The regression analysis described in this chapter is really a minor variant of the analysis of variance discussed in Chapters 7 and 8, and the *t*-test in turn is a special case of analysis of variance. All these applications have the same general form. Each proposes a model claiming that observations are the sum of various components, and R^2 provides a measure of how good a job the model does in accounting for the total variance in the data.

Formulas for the Product-Moment Correlation Coefficient

Although the correlation coefficient can be calculated as $\sqrt{R^2}$, there are other, equivalent, formulas. Several of these are listed below. They are given for two reasons:

■ One or the other formula may be the most convenient, depending on what data analysis has already been completed.

■ The formulas demonstrate the various relations between the product-moment correlation coefficient and other aspects of the data such as the regression coefficient.

Perhaps the most common formula is one using the sum of products, SP_{XY}. This formula is

$$r = \frac{SP_{XY}}{\sqrt{SS_X SS_Y}}$$

This formula can be applied to the data from the IQ and GPA example. We know from the original analysis that $SS_X = 6811.38$, $SS_Y = 56.96$, and $SP_{XY} = 332.82$. So

$$r = \frac{SP_{XY}}{\sqrt{SS_X SS_Y}} = \frac{332.82}{\sqrt{6811.38 \times 56.96}} = .534$$

Notice that this value when squared is $.534^2 = .285$. Within rounding error, these values are the same as those reported in Section 9.2.2.

If we divide both the numerator and denominator of this formula by $N - 1$ (thus leaving the ratio unchanged), we obtain the following results. The numerator becomes $SP_{XY}/N - 1$. This averaged sum of products is a statistic known as the *covariance*, written cov(X,Y). The denominator becomes

$$\frac{\sqrt{SS_X SS_Y}}{N-1} = \sqrt{\frac{SS_X}{N-1}} \times \sqrt{\frac{SS_Y}{N-1}} = s_X s_Y,$$

the product of the standard deviations. Thus another way of expressing the formula for the correlation coefficient is

$$r = \frac{cov(X,Y)}{s_X s_Y}$$

For the data from the IQ and GPA example, cov(X,Y) = 332.82/49 = 6.79. Thus r = cov(X,Y)/$s_X s_Y$ = 6.79/(11.79 × 1.08) = .533. Within rounding error this value is the same as that calculated previously. Another useful formula relates the correlation coefficient to the regression coefficient, b. The formula is

$$r = b \times \sqrt{\frac{SS_X}{SS_Y}}$$

Again, for the data from the IQ and GPA example,

$$r = 0.0488 \times \sqrt{\frac{6811.38}{56.96}} = .534$$

An equivalent version of this formula is obtained by dividing both SS_X and SS_Y by their degrees of freedom, which are $N - 1$ in both cases. This operation replaces SS_X and SS_Y with the variances of X and Y, so when the square root is taken, we have the standard deviations of each of the marginal distributions. The formula for r is then

$$r = b \times \frac{s_X}{s_Y}$$

This formula provides an important insight into the correlation coefficient. The correlation coefficient is the regression coefficient rescaled by the ratio of the standard deviations of the two marginal distributions. If these two distributions had the same standard deviation, then $s_X/s_Y = 1$, so r and b would have the same value. A special case of this equality of standard deviations exists if both X and Y are converted, each separately, to standard scores before calculating the correlation coefficient. In this case, the regression coefficient is called the *standardized regression coefficient*.

The relationship r = b × (s_X/s_Y) also holds for the corresponding population parameters. That is,

$$\rho = \beta \times \frac{\sigma_X}{\sigma_Y}$$

It follows from this equation that, if the regression coefficient β is 0, then the correlation coefficient ρ is also 0. Thus the procedure previously described to evaluate the null hypothesis that $\beta = 0$ is also a test of the null hypothesis that $\rho = 0$.

Scatterplots and the Size of the Correlation Coefficient

The size of the correlation coefficient is reflected in the general shape of the scatterplot. As noted in Section 9.2.2, the correlation coefficient ranges in value from −1.0 to +1.0.

The covariance between two variables is the average sum of products.

The covariance between X and Y is denoted by cov(X,Y).

A regression coefficient based on standard scores is called a standardized regression coefficient.

Testing the null hypothesis, $H_0: \beta = 0$, is equivalent to testing $H_0: \rho = 0$.

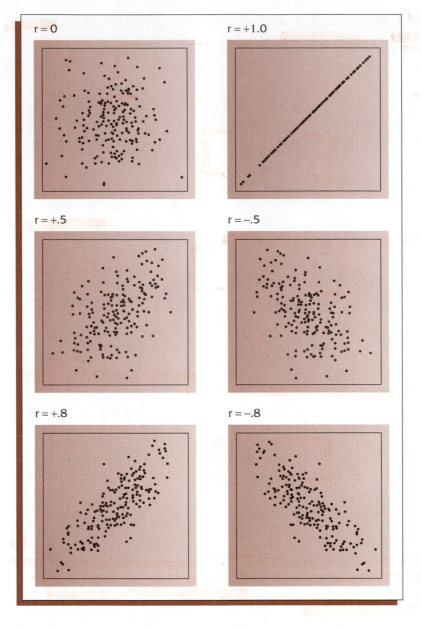

The higher the correlation, the more concentrated the scatter about the regression line.

Figure 9.22
Scatterplots for different values of the correlation coefficient.

With a negative correlation, high scores on one variable tend to be associated with low scores on the other.

Figure 9.22 shows scatterplots for different values of the correlation coefficient. Notice that, with zero correlation, the scatterplot has an overall circular shape. As the correlation increases, the pattern of scatter becomes more elliptical in form; the higher the correlation, the more concentrated the scatter about the regression line. When the correlation is perfect, the ellipse is concentrated along a line that is also the regression line. As noted previously, a correlation of 1.0 implies that all observations lie exactly on the regression line.

The same trends in the shape of the scatter exist for negative correlations, but now the elliptical shape is in the opposite orientation, extending from the top left to the bottom right corner. This orientation reflects the fact that, with a negative correlation (and thus a negative regression weight), high scores on one variable tend to be associated with low scores on the other.

9.3.2 Factors Influencing the Size of the Product-Moment Correlation Coefficient

Range Effects

In correlational studies, the sampling procedure, or the measuring instrument itself, sometimes leads to a restriction in the range of either or both of the variables. The following examples illustrate the point.

■ The height of professional basketball players is more restricted than height in the general population.

■ The IQ scores of college seniors is more restricted than IQ scores of the general population.

■ The vocabulary test scores of fifth graders is more restricted than the vocabulary test scores of all grade school children.

■ Tests that are extremely easy or difficult will restrict the range of scores relative to a test of intermediate difficulty. This example is really a case of ceiling and floor effects discussed in Chapter 2 in relation to the skewed frequency distributions. If a test is so easy that everyone scores above 75%, the range of scores will obviously be less than a test of moderate difficulty in which the scores range from 30% to 95%.

■ A similar restriction of range can arise with rating scales. Imagine a rating scale that allows just three values: 1 (agree), 2 (indifferent), or 3 (disagree). Suppose that, on the issue to be rated, almost everyone agrees but to varying degrees. The result will be restricted variability (most participants will score 1) relative to the variability accompanying a rating scale allowing more levels of agreement.

In terms of statistical measurement, restriction of range would be reflected in a smaller variance and standard deviation of one or both marginal distributions.

Restriction of range has a strong impact on the size of the correlation coefficient. Restriction of range reduces the size of the correlation coefficient. There are two ways of making this rule seem intuitively plausible. The first way is to consider an extreme example. Consider using height to predict basketball performance, as measured by points scored. Who is likely to score more, a person 62 inches tall or a person 82 inches tall? Nothing is certain, but a 6′10″ person seems a better bet than a 5′2″ person. Compare this situation with the question, "Who is likely to score more, a person 81 inches tall or a person 82 inches tall?" Here the prediction is much less certain. Predicting from the narrow range of 1 inch is extremely difficult compared with predicting from a range of 20 inches.

The second demonstration of the effect of restriction of range is graphical. Consider the scatterplot of a correlation of .8 shown in Figure 9.23. Suppose that the range of values on the x-axis is restricted to the values within the vertical lines. If the scatter within the vertical bars is treated as the entire scatterplot, the shape of the resulting scatter is no longer the elongated ellipse of original plot, but considerably more circular—indicative of a smaller correlation.

If reducing the variance of scores by restricting the range reduces the size of the correlation coefficient, then inflating the variance should increase it. It does. How might this happen? As with restriction of range, it can happen either through inappropriate sampling of participants, or because of the measurement instrument.

Restriction of range reduces the size of the correlation coefficient.

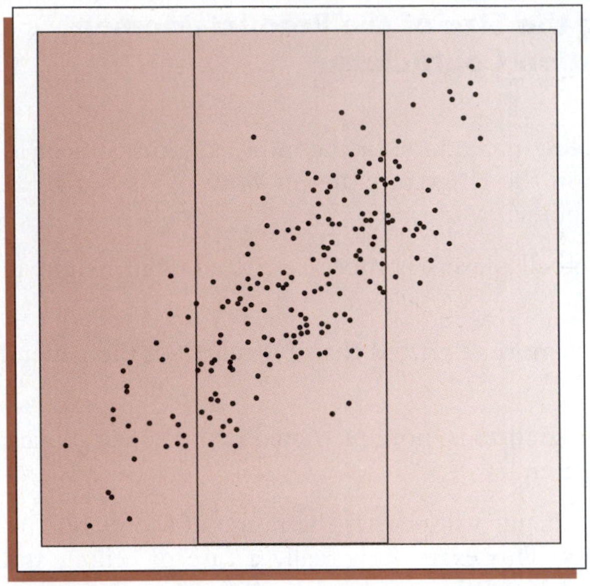

Figure 9.23
Scatterplot for two variables with a correlation coefficient of .8. The vertical lines denote the range restriction.

In the case of sampling, an inflated variance would occur if the only participants selected were those scoring at the extremes of the range. For example, a sample of children attending special education classes might consist of both gifted children with very high IQ scores and children needing special education because of their low IQ, but no children from the middle range of IQ scores. A concrete example of this type of selection effect forms part of Exercise 5 at the end of this chapter.

The measuring instrument can also achieve the same effect. For example, a test might consist of a mixture of very easy and very difficult items, but few items of intermediate difficulty. The effect of such item selection is to produce a distribution of scores that tends toward bimodality, that is, a cluster of low scores representing students who can pass only some of the easy items but none of the difficult ones, and a second cluster who pass all the easy ones and some of the difficult ones as well. Indeed, the factors that result in an inflated variance (and thus an inflated correlation coefficient) are precisely those factors described in Section 2.1.3 as producing bimodal frequency distributions.

Outliers

Outliers can influence the value of a regression coefficient and the correlation coefficient. The effect can be to increase or decrease their values, depending on the location of the outlier. The simplest way to think about this effect is in terms of the scatterplot. If the outlier is located so as to make the overall shape of the scatterplot more elongated, then the effect of the outlier will be to increase the value of the correlation coefficient. If, on the other hand, the effect is to make the overall shape more circular, then the effect of the outlier will be to decrease the value of the correlation coefficient. Exercise 4 at the end of this chapter contains an example of the latter case.

Nonlinearity of Regression

If an investigation reports a low correlation between two variables, then a critical reader might ask if this result is attributable to a violation of the assumption of linear regression. If the true structure of the data is nonlinear regression, then the correlation coefficient will underestimate the true relationship between the two variables.

This fact follows directly from the analysis that was described in Section 9.2.3 and discussed the evaluation of the linearity assumption. If the regression is really nonlinear, then a nonlinear (curvilinear) model will do a better job of predicting than the inappropriate linear model that underlies the correlation coefficient.

Measurement Reliability

The reliability of a measurement instrument is the stability of the measurement over different occasions. Thus an ability test is reliable to the extent that a person's score on the test does not fluctuate from one administration of the test to another. Although there are several methods of measuring reliability, the reliability of a test can be thought of as the correlation of the test with itself, and the quantification of reliability is usually expressed in the form of a correlation coefficient. In psychological measurement, a well-constructed ability test might have a reliability of .8 or more; scales measuring personality attributes are typically somewhat lower.

The important point for present purposes is that the reliability of the measurements places an upper bound on how high the correlation can be between that variable and any other variable. A general rule is that a variable cannot correlate more highly with another variable than it can with itself. Thus, a critical reader, when confronted with a low correlation coefficient between two variables, might ask about the reliability of each of the measures. A small correlation might reflect the low reliability of one or both of the measurements rather than the absence of a relationship.

Correlations in Everyday Thinking

We are surrounded by correlations. Tall parents have tall children; people who eat more, weigh more; families with higher incomes live in larger houses. Such correlations, although imperfect, govern many everyday predictions and expectations. How accurate are these subjective judgments? One aspect of this question, discussed in Box 9.1, is regression to the mean.

Comprehension Check 9.3

Important Concepts

1. Although the product-moment correlation coefficient is widely used as a descriptive statistic, it is important to interpret it within the wider context of linear regression. The correlation coefficient is a special case of $\sqrt{R^2}$ that is applicable when the data have an underlying bivariate normal distribution.

2. Linear regression itself is a special case of model fitting and model evaluation. It is closely related to the analysis of variance and t-tests described in earlier chapters.

3. Various formulas for the correlation coefficient demonstrate its relation to the sum of products and the estimated regression coefficient. In particular, r is equal to the regression coefficient multiplied by the ratio of the standard deviations of the marginal distributions.

4. The size of a correlation coefficient is reflected in the shape of the scatterplot. As the size of the correlation coefficient increases, the overall shape of the scatterplot becomes less circular and more elliptical.

5. Various factors can influence the size of the correlation coefficient. The factors covered in this chapter were selection factors that restrict or inflate variance, outliers, curvilinear regression, and measurement reliability.

Box 9.1

Regression to the Mean

Suppose that, for a particular population, the correlation between the height of fathers and their adult sons is .8. The height of one father from this population is 73 inches. What is the best prediction of the son's height?

An intuitively attractive answer to this question is 73 inches, with the less than perfect correlation being reflected in variation about this point estimate; the lower the correlation, the greater the variation and the more error-prone the prediction. This latter intuition is true, but the intuition underlying the point estimate is false. This false intuition is sufficiently compelling that even Pearson himself was surprised when he came to realize, in the course of his development of regression theory, that this intuition was mistaken.

To see why this intuition is false, we need only look at the regression equation using the standardized regression coefficient. Recall that if both predictor and response variables are standardized (each has a mean of 0 and a standard deviation of 1), then $r = b$. Because the means are 0, the regression equation is simply $\hat{Y} = rX$. Thus, if 73 inches is one standard deviation above the mean ($X = 1$), then $\hat{Y} = .8 \times 1 = .8$. In other words, the predicted height of a son whose father's height is one standard deviation above the mean is .8 of a standard deviation above the mean. That is, the prediction is that the son will be shorter than his father.

Imagine a second father whose height is one standard deviation *below* the mean. In this case, $\hat{Y} = rX = .8 \times (-1) = -.8$. Now the prediction is that the son will be *taller* than his father—only .8 standard deviations below the mean compared to 1.

In both these cases, the prediction is that the son's height will be closer to the mean than the father's—.8 of a standard deviation rather than 1. The general principle underlying these examples is this: *When the correlation is less than perfect, extreme values of the predictor variable will tend to be paired with less extreme values of the response variable*. This relationship is known as *regression to the mean*. Notice that the lower the correlation, the greater the regression to the mean.

Regression to the mean is more than a statistical curiosity. It is part of everyday experience, although it often passes unnoticed or is misinterpreted. Patients selected on one occasion because they are the most severely depressed among a group will be less severely depressed when evaluated on a later occasion. Brilliant parents have less brilliant children, just as brilliant children tend to have less brilliant parents. The students who top their freshman year tend not to be the top students in the sophomore year. Students who do extremely well on the first term test tend to do not quite so well on the second.

Kahneman and Tversky (1973) describe how instructors in a flight school followed the advice of psychologists and positively reinforced each successful completion of a flight maneuver. Contrary to their expectations, and those of the psychologists, high praise for these exceptional maneuvers resulted in poorer performance on the next try. Regression provides a simple explanation of this result. The instructors selected extreme performance, the correlation between one performance and the next is imperfect—exactly the ingredients for regression to the mean to occur.

Worked Examples

Example 1 Verbal comprehension and numerical ability

This example continues the analysis of Worked Example 3, Section 9.1, and Example 2, Section 9.2. The verbal comprehension score was denoted by X and the numerical ability score by Y.

a. Use the following values to calculate the product-moment correlation coefficient between verbal comprehension and numerical ability. $SS_X = 6543.0$, $SS_Y = 2466.0$, $SP_{XY} = 2071.0$

b. Use the value of the product-moment correlation coefficient you have just calculated to obtain the following regression coefficients: (i) the estimated regression coefficient when numerical ability is regressed on verbal comprehension; (ii) the estimated regression coefficient when verbal comprehension is regressed on numerical ability. (iii) Check your answers against the values previously obtained in Section 9.1.

c. A critic claims that numerical ability and verbal comprehension are correlated only over the low- and mid-range of verbal comprehension, not at higher levels. To demonstrate this claim, an investigator selects participants from the top 25% (the fourth quartile) of verbal comprehension and measures their numerical ability. The correlation between verbal comprehension and numerical ability for these participants is found to be near 0, apparently confirming the original claim. Comment on this conclusion.

d. On the basis of the value of the product-moment correlation coefficient, decide which of the scatterplots in Figure 9.24 is the actual scatterplot for these data.

Answer

a. $r = \dfrac{SP_{XY}}{\sqrt{SS_X SS_Y}} = \dfrac{2071}{\sqrt{6543 \times 2466}} = .516$

b. When numerical ability is regressed on verbal comprehension,

$$r = b \times \sqrt{\frac{SS_X}{SS_Y}}$$

Substituting values for r, SS_X, and SS_Y, we have $.516 = b \times 1.63$, so $b = .516/1.63 = 0.32$. When verbal comprehension is regressed on numerical ability,

$$r = b \times \sqrt{\frac{SS_Y}{SS_X}}$$

Substituting values for r, SS_X, and SS_Y, we have $.516 = b \times 0.613$, so $b = .516/0.613 = 0.84$.

c. The conclusion is highly suspect. The near-zero correlation could merely reflect the impact of the restricted range that would reduce the original correlation.

d. See Figure 9.24. The actual scatterplot is scatterplot a. This scatterplot is the only one that shows a moderate positive correlation. Scatterplot b has near zero correlation, scatterplot c has moderate negative correlation, and scatterplot d has a very high positive correlation.

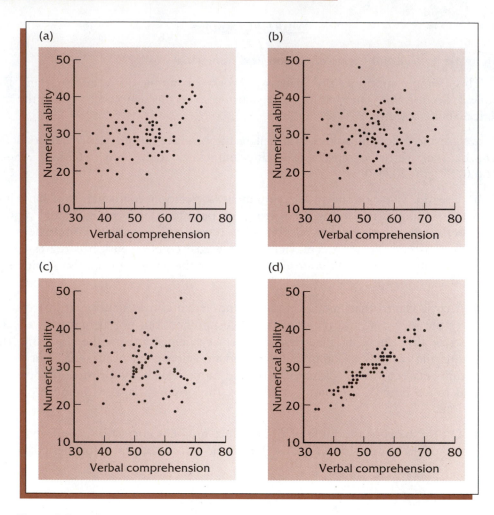

Figure 9.24
Possible scatterplots for Example 1.

Problems

Problem 1   Maternal attention and infant attractiveness

This problem continues the analysis of Problem 4, Sections 9.1 and 9.2. In this study, each of 50 infants had two scores, one for rated attractiveness (X) and one for time looked at by the mother (Y). The mean attractiveness rating score was $\overline{X} = 16.70$ and the mean looking time was $\overline{Y} = 6.56$ minutes.

a. Use the following (previously presented) values to calculate the product-moment correlation coefficient between infant attractiveness and maternal attention: $SS_X = 1042.52$, $SS_Y = 550.32$, $SP_{XY} = 399.40$. Check that, when squared, this correlation coefficient equals the value of R^2 obtained in Problem 4, Section 9.2.

b. Use the value of the product-moment correlation coefficient you have just calculated to obtain: (i) the estimated regression coefficient when looking time is regressed on attractiveness rating; (ii) the estimated regression coefficient when attractiveness rating is regressed on looking time ability. (iii) Check that these are the values previously obtained in Problem 4, Section 9.1.

Chapter 9 Exercises

Exercise 1. Practicing recall (Data Set 9.12)

One method of improving retention of learned material is to practice recalling it. How effective is this recall practice? To answer this question, $N = 80$ participants studied material for 30 minutes. This total study time was broken down into two different activities: silent study and recall practice. Different participants engaged in different proportions of these two activities—either 0%, 20%, 40%, 60%, or 80% of the 30 minutes was spent on recall practice. There were 16 participants in each of these five levels.

After the 30 minutes, recall for the material was tested and recorded as a percentage of the total possible recall. The data listed in Data Set 9.12 give the percentage of items recalled in the final test (Y) for each level of percentage of time spent in recall practice (X). Analysis gives the following basic results:

$$\overline{Y} = 54.51 \qquad \overline{X} = 40.00 \qquad SS_X = 64{,}000.0$$

$$SS_Y = 26{,}702.0 \qquad SS_e = 8533.08 \qquad SP_{XY} = 34{,}100.0$$

Complete the regression analysis of these results by completing the following steps.

Data Set 9.12 Percentage of items recalled for different amounts of recall practice in Exercise 1

0% time spent in recall practice (X; mean = 32.44)

34	22	37	25	48	38	41	37
15	34	48	32	35	22	16	35

20% time spent in recall practice (X; mean = 44.56)

50	36	51	42	35	38	43	44
30	57	45	53	58	54	27	50

40% time spent in recall practice (X; mean = 56.19)

47	64	67	62	43	43	53	63
41	57	76	60	60	64	35	64

60% time spent in recall practice (X; mean = 62.75)

72	46	57	59	56	55	67	68
60	64	84	63	70	62	56	65

80% time spent in recall practice (X; mean = 76.63)

89	87	63	73	77	80	56	63
91	74	98	81	88	55	68	83

a. Establish the least squares regression line for final recall regressed on percentage of time spent practicing recall.

b. Set out the regression analysis summary table.

c. Obtain a 95% confidence interval for the regression coefficient.

d. Calculate the value of R^2 and the standard error of estimate.

e. Plot the means of each of the five conditional distributions against their X values and then draw the regression line on the same axes. Does the graph provide any evidence of nonlinearity in the regression?

f. The data were reanalyzed, treating them as a completely randomized design with five levels of a categorical predictor variable. The value of $SS_{between}$ was found to be 18,334.9. Evaluate the departure from linearity by comparing its mean square with MS_e in the form of an F-ratio. Is the linear regression model appropriate?

Exercise 2. IQ correlations for twins

The following table gives basic computational results for the data sets reporting IQ scores for three different types of pairs of twins. The data set for T2 was also used in Chapter 2, Exercise 8.

T1: Fraternal twins reared together (DS09_13.dat in the *ASCII Files*)
T2: Identical twins reared apart (DS09_14.dat)
T3: Identical twins reared together(DS09_15.dat)

For each of these data sets, obtain the product-moment correlation coefficient between twins.

Data set	N	SS_A	SS_B	SP_{AB}
T1	200	34,483	41,673	21,898
T2	100	22,077	24,532	15,968
T3	150	32,811	35,349	28,923

Exercise 3. Subscales of the WAIS for a random sample (DS09_16.dat in the *ASCII Files*)

This exercise involves the analysis of the scores for a random sample of 110 participants on the two subscales of the Wechsler Adult Intelligence Test (WAIS). The results of basic computations are $N = 110$; $\overline{Y}$ (performance) $= 50.64$; $\overline{X}$ (verbal) $= 60.85$; $SS_Y = 12,261$; $SS_X = 21,680$; $SP_{XY} = 11,910$. When WAIS verbal is regressed on WAIS performance, the sum of squares for the residuals is $SS_e = 10,111$. When WAIS performance is regressed on WAIS verbal scores, the sum of squares for the residuals is $SS_e = 5718$.

a. Obtain the regression line for WAIS performance scores regressed on WAIS verbal scores.

b. Obtain the regression line for WAIS verbal scores regressed on WAIS performance scores.

c. Plot these two regression lines, setting performance scores on the y-axis and verbal scores on the x-axis.

d. What is the point at which these two lines intersect?

e. Given the preceding results, set out the regression analysis summary table for the regression of WAIS verbal scores on WAIS performance scores.

f. Calculate the standard error of estimate for estimating WAIS verbal scores on the basis of WAIS performance scores.

g. Use the *F*-distribution to test the hypothesis that the true value of the regression coefficient is 0.

h. Given the preceding results, set out the regression analysis summary table for the regression of WAIS performance scores on WAIS verbal scores.

i. Calculate the standard error of estimate for estimating WAIS verbal scores on the basis of WAIS performance scores.

j. Calculate R^2 for the linear regression model fitted to these data. What is the product-moment correlation coefficient between the two variables? What assumption underlies the use of the product-moment correlation coefficient?

Exercise 4.   Subscales of the WAIS for a restricted sample (DS09_17.dat in the *ASCII Files*)

This data set consists of total scores for the performance and verbal subtests of the WAIS for 104 participants aged 17 to 18 referred for testing because of extremely poor academic performance.

The scatterplot for the original data set (Data Set 2.18) is shown in Figure 9.25. In Exercise 9 of Chapter 2, the two marginal distributions for these data were examined, revealing outliers in the distribution of the performance scores. These outliers are also apparent in the scatterplot and have been circled and labeled. Outliers such as these exert a strong influence on the correlation coefficient, just as they did on the mean and variance. These four outliers have been removed, and all calculations have been performed on the reduced data set. Thus the value of *N* in the table of results is

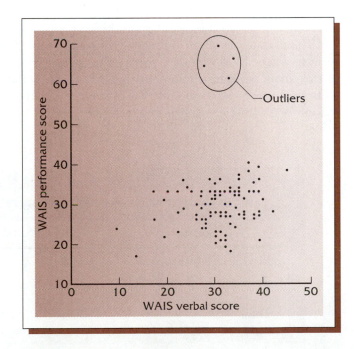

Figure 9.25
Scatterplot for the WAIS data of
Exercise 4 showing outliers.

100, not the original value of 104. The other statistics are $\overline{Y}$ (performance) = 29.40; $\overline{X}$ (verbal) = 30.72; SS_Y = 2434.0, SS_X = 3812.2, SP_{XY} = 784.2. When WAIS performance is regressed on WAIS verbal scores, the sum of squares for the residuals is SS_e = 2272.7. When WAIS verbal is regressed on WAIS performance, the sum of squares for the residuals is SS_e = 3559.5.

a. Obtain the regression line for WAIS verbal scores regressed on WAIS performance scores.

b. Obtain the regression line for WAIS performance scores regressed on WAIS verbal scores.

c. Plot these two regression lines, setting performance scores on the y-axis and verbal scores on the x-axis.

d. Given the preceding results, set out the regression analysis summary table for the regression of WAIS verbal scores on WAIS performance scores.

e. Calculate the standard error of estimate for estimating WAIS verbal scores on the basis of WAIS performance scores.

f. Use the F-distribution to test the hypothesis that the true value of the regression coefficient is 0.

g. Given the preceding results, set out the regression analysis summary table for the regression of WAIS performance scores on WAIS verbal scores.

h. Calculate the standard error of estimate for estimating WAIS verbal scores on the basis of WAIS performance scores.

i. Calculate R^2 for the linear regression model fitted to these data. What is the product-moment correlation coefficient between the two variables?

j. Examine the original scatterplot, including the outliers. If these outliers had been retained, what effect do you think their inclusion would have had on the correlation coefficient?

Exercise 5. WAIS subscales for combined sample (DS09_18.dat in the *ASCII Files*)
The data set used in Exercise 4 consisted of scores for the performance and verbal subtests of the WAIS for 100 participants aged 17 to 18 referred for testing because of extremely poor academic performance. The new data set for this exercise includes additional scores on these same WAIS subtests for 100 participants attending a special school for the intellectually gifted.

Table 9.18 Regression analysis summary table for Exercise 5

Source	SS	df	MS
Model: Linear regression	144,510	1	144,510
Residual	11,977	198	60.49
Total	156,486	199	—

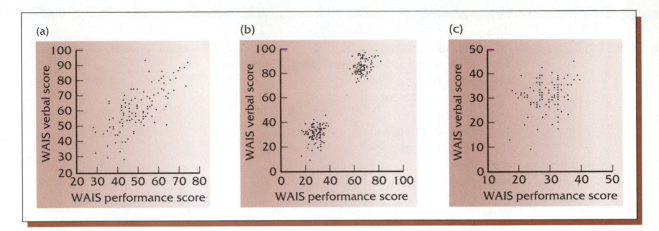

Figure 9.26
Scatterplots for Exercise 5.

Someone, not having had the benefit of a course such as the one you are taking, decides it would be a good idea to combine these data sets into a single set with $N = 200$ on the grounds that this larger sample size will give greater precision to the estimates. When WAIS verbal is regressed on WAIS performance for this combined data set (Data Set 9.5) the regression analysis summary table shown in Table 9.18 is obtained.

a. Calculate R^2 for the linear regression model fitted to these data. What is the product-moment correlation coefficient between the two variables? Why is the value of R^2 and the correlation coefficient between the WAIS performance and verbal subscales so much higher for the combined data set than for the data set in Exercise 3?

b. Exercises 3, 4, and 5 have obtained three quite different values for the correlation coefficient between WAIS verbal scores and WAIS performance scores. If someone asks what is the "real" correlation between the WAIS subscales, how would you answer?

In answering this question, it may be helpful to examine the three scatterplots in Figure 9.26. One scatterplot is for the data from Exercises 3, one for Exercise 4, and one for the combined data set analyzed in Exercise 5. The scatterplots are not in order, but, as part of the exercise, you should be able to identify which scatterplot is which.

Chapter 9 Review

Terms

bivariate normal distribution
conditional distribution
correlation analysis
correlation coefficient
covariance
homogeneity of variance

intercept
linear regression
marginal distribution
Pearson product-moment correlation coefficient
regression analysis
regression coefficient
regression line
regression to the mean
regression weight
residual plot
restriction of range
scatterplot
slope
$SS_{regression}$
standard error of estimate
standard error of a regression coefficient
standardized regression coefficient
sum of products

Formulas

Degrees of freedom for linear regression: $df = N - 2$

Sum of products: $SP_{XY} = \Sigma(X - \overline{X})(Y - \overline{Y})$

Estimate of β, the regression coefficient or slope parameter: $b = \dfrac{SP_{XY}}{SS_X}$

Estimate of α, the intercept parameter: $a = \overline{Y} - b\overline{X}$

$$s_b = \sqrt{\dfrac{MS_e}{SS_X}}$$

The regression analysis summary table has the general form shown in Table 9.19.

$$F = \dfrac{MS_{regression}}{MS_e}$$

Table 9.19 General form of a regression analysis summary table

Source	SS	df	MS
Model: Linear regression	$SS_{regression}$	1	$MS_{regression}$
Residual	SS_e	$N - 2$	MS_e
Total	$SS_{total} = SS_Y$	$N - 1$	

$$R^2 = \frac{SS_{regression}}{SS_{total}}$$

$$\text{standard error of estimate} = \sqrt{MS_e}$$

$$r = \frac{SP_{XY}}{\sqrt{SS_X SS_Y}}$$

$$r = \frac{cov(X,Y)}{s_X s_Y}$$

$$r = b \times \sqrt{\frac{SS_X}{SS_Y}}$$

$$r = b \times \frac{s_X}{s_Y}$$

Quiz

Complete each sentence with a term from the following list. The same term may be used more than once.

conditional distribution(s)	product-moment correlation coefficient
homogeneity of variance	regression coefficient
intercept	residuals
linear regression	response variable
marginal distribution	scatterplot
means	$SS_{regression}$
MS_e	SS_{total}
$MS_{regression}$	standard error of estimate
$N - 1$	sum of squared residuals
$N - 2$	total
overestimate	underestimate
predictor variable	variances

The graph of a sample bivariate frequency distribution is called a _____. In such a graph, the distribution of one variable for a fixed value of the other is called a _____, whereas the total distribution of the variable regardless of values of the other is called a _____. The assumption of _____ is that the _____ have _____ that lie on a straight line. Regression analysis also assumes that the conditional distributions have equal _____, another example of the assumption of _____.

The linear regression model has two parameters. One is an _____ parameter, α, that indicates the overall height of the line. The other is a slope parameter, β, called the _____. The regression analysis obtains estimates of α and β that minimize the _____ about the regression line. The analysis is said to regress the _____ on the _____. Regression analysis then partitions the _____ sum of squares into the sum of squares accounted for by the regression line, _____, and the sum of squares of the _____. The square root of the mean square of the residuals is called the _____. An F-ratio to test the significance of regression is obtained by dividing _____ by _____. This F-ratio has _____ degrees of freedom in the denominator.

The value of R^2 is _____ divided by _____. The square root of this value is known as the _____. This statistic is widely used to describe the strength of the relationship between two variables. In interpreting its value, researchers should be mindful of the factors that can influence its size. For example, if the regression is actually nonlinear, then the correlation coefficient will _____ the true strength of the relationship between the two variables. Restricting the range of scores will also _____ the value that would have been obtained with an unrestricted sample.

Chapter 10 Preview

Chapter 9 concludes the account of data analysis with a quantitative response variable. The class of data that remains to be discussed is the case in which the response variable is categorical. In such cases, the response measure consists of frequencies—a tally of the number of outcomes that fall into a defined set of categories.

10

CATEGORICAL RESPONSE VARIABLES AND DISTRIBUTION-FREE METHODS

The first two sections of this chapter introduce methods of analysis suitable for data in which all variables are categorical. The data take the form of frequency tallies, that is, the number of times certain events occur or the number of people who fall into certain categories. For this reason, the data to be discussed in this chapter are often referred to as *frequency data,* or *count data.* One important difference between the statistical tests described in this chapter and those of earlier chapters is that, with count data, assumptions about normal distributions and homogeneity of variance are no longer relevant. The final section of this chapter describes a number of other methods that are also free of these assumptions.

Consider a simple example of count data. In this example, college women ($N = 50$) were shown two photographs of themselves. One was an ordinary photograph of the participant, taken by the investigator before the experiment began. The other was the mirror image of this photograph.

Because the human face is never perfectly symmetrical, these two photographs are readily distinguishable, although highly similar. Each participant was asked to decide which of the two photographs of themselves they preferred. Seventeen of the 50 participants preferred the original, 33 the mirror image. In this example, the categorical nature of the response variable yields observations consisting of frequencies, that is, the numbers of cases or choices in each category.

As a second example of count data, consider the results of a survey conducted in an electoral district in which 200 randomly sampled voters were asked which of two presidential candidates, A or B, they favored. The investigator is interested in whether there is a difference between men and women in candidate preference.

The results of the survey can be arranged in a 2×2 table, as shown in Table 10.1. Each of the 200 survey respondents can be classified and assigned to one of the four cells in the table. For example, of the 97 men surveyed, 65 preferred candidate A, 32 preferred candidate B. Of the 103 women surveyed, 45 preferred candidate A, 58 preferred candidate B.

Categorical response variables yield frequency data, or count data.

Table 10.1 Frequency data for electoral survey

		Preferred Candidate	
		A	B
Gender	Male	65	32
	Female	45	58

Contingency refers to the relationship between two bases of classification such as gender and voting preference.

Do the results of this survey support the claim of a relationship, or *contingency*, between gender of voter and candidate preference? It appears as if men prefer candidate A, whereas women prefer candidate B. How strong is this contingency? Is it strong enough to reject the simpler claim that there is no gender difference in preference, in other words, that gender and voting preference are independent?

This chapter considers both of these kinds of problems. Section 10.1 considers problems of the first kind, in which there is a single basis of classification. Section 10.2 considers problems of the second kind, in which there are two factors and for which the major question of interest is whether the factors are independent or whether a contingency exists between them.

10.1 Count Data with a Single Basis of Classification: Goodness of Fit

In this section, we will consider examples, such as the photo-preference study, in which there is a single basis of classification—form of photograph, for example. This situation is analogous to the single-factor designs for quantitative response variables that we considered in Chapter 7. In this simple photo-preference example, there are just two categories, but we will also consider examples with more than two. Studies in which there are two bases of classification (such as those to be considered in Section 10.2) are analogous to the factorial designs for quantitative response variables also discussed in Chapter 7.

10.1.1 Models and Hypotheses for Count Data

The question to be answered in the photo-preference study is whether one form of the photograph is preferred over the other. Do the data provide any evidence to support this claim? The null hypothesis is that the choice between the two photographs is effectively random, equivalent to the mental toss of a fair coin. According to this hypothesis, the probability of choosing the original photograph is the same as choosing the mirror image. We can express the null hypothesis as

$$H_0: P(\text{original}) = P(\text{mirror image}) = .5$$

In this statement P(original) denotes the probability of choosing the original photograph and P(mirror image) denotes the probability of choosing the mirror image. If this null hypothesis is true, then with $N = 50$, the expected frequency of choices is 25 for each of the two photographs. The observed number of choices of the original photograph was 17 rather than this expected value of 25, and the question to be answered is whether this difference between the expected and observed frequency is larger than might be expected by chance.

The null hypothesis generates expected frequencies.

Using the Normal Distribution to Approximate the Binomial Distribution

One method of evaluating this difference and thereby testing the null hypothesis is to use the normal distribution as an approximation of the binomial distribution. We noted in Chapter 4 that the original purpose of de Moivre in deriving the equation of the normal distribution was to approximate binomial probabilities. The method of obtaining these approximations makes use of standard scores first discussed in Chapter 2 and used extensively in Chapter 4.

Recall that, in Section 2.3.2, the general form of standard score was given as

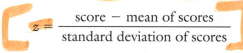

$$z = \frac{\text{score} - \text{mean of scores}}{\text{standard deviation of scores}}$$

The z-score we will use to obtain approximations of the binomial distribution will take this general form.

Before proceeding to analyzing the photo-preference data, consider the following question as an example of using the normal distribution to approximate a binomial probability. Assuming equal numbers of men and women in the population, suppose a sample of 100 people contains 55 women. What is the probability of obtaining 55 or more women in a random sample of 100? Note first that the probability distribution relevant to answering such a question is the binomial. However, with $N = 100$, the calculations would be overwhelming and so, along with de Moivre, we turn to the normal distribution to provide an approximation. That is, we now consider the random variable "number of women" to be continuous (approximately) and to be normally distributed (approximately). If we use the symbol f_o to denote the value of the random variable (observed frequency of women), then we are asked to find $P(f_o \geq 55)$.

To convert this value of f_o into a standard score, we need to know the mean of the random variable and its standard deviation. We make use of the following results. The mathematical deviation of these results will not be given:

When N is large, the normal distribution provides a satisfactory approximation to the binomial distribution.

f_o denotes observed frequency.

f_e denotes expected frequency.

N denotes sample size.

p denotes probability of the event.

- A binomial distribution for an event has parameters N and p, where N is the sample size and p is the probability of the event. The mean of the distribution is Np. We will use the symbol f_e to denote this expected value of the frequency. Thus, for a binomial distribution, $f_e = Np$.

- The standard deviation is $\sqrt{Np(1-p)}$.

The mean of the binomial distribution is $f_e = Np$.

In these formulas, p is the probability of the outcome that contributes to the tally of f_o. If the outcome of interest is "number of heads," then p refers to the probability of obtaining a head. If the outcome of interest is "number of people choosing the original photograph," then p refers to the probability of a person choosing the original photograph, and so forth.

The standard deviation of the binomial distribution is $\sqrt{Np(1-p)}$

Converting a Binomial Variable to a z-Score

The procedure for obtaining normal approximations is to convert the relevant value of f_o to z-scores. That is,

$$z = \frac{f_o - f_e}{\sqrt{Np(1-p)}} = \frac{f_o - Np}{\sqrt{Np(1-p)}}$$

For our example, $N = 100$ and $p = .5$, so $f_e = Np = 50.0$ and the standard deviation is $\sqrt{Np(1-p)} = \sqrt{100 \times .5 \times .5} = 5.0$. Thus the relevant z-score is

$$z = \frac{55 - 50}{5} = 1.0$$

and $P(f_o \geq 55)$ is thus equivalent to $P(z \geq 1.0)$. Consulting the table of the normal distribution (Statistical Table 1 in Appendix C) for $z = 1.0$ gives the answer .1587.

The approximation works best when N is large and p is close to .5. A common criterion for an adequate approximation is that both f_e and $N(1-p)$ should be greater than 10. This value of 10 is not a magic cutoff figure, merely a rule of thumb.

Photograph-Preference Experiment

We return now to the analysis of the data from the photo-preference experiment. Suppose f_o denotes the observed frequency of choosing the original version of the photograph. If the null hypothesis is true, then f_o has a binomial distribution with a mean (expected frequency) of $f_e = Np$. In our example, $f_o = 17$ and $f_e = Np = 50 \times .5 = 25$. The normal approximation of the binomial distribution gives the following z-score:

$$z = \frac{f_o - f_e}{\sqrt{Np(1-p)}}$$

This gives

$$z = \frac{17 - 25}{\sqrt{50 \times .5 \times .5}} = -2.26$$

The table of the normal distribution (Statistical Table 1) indicates that the critical value of z for the .05 level of significance is $z = \pm 1.96$, so the observed frequency of 17 is more discrepant from the expected frequency of 25 than would be expected by chance.

Although this method of analysis is perfectly appropriate for this example, it is a method that does not generalize beyond the simple case of two categories. In this respect, it warrants comments similar to those made about the t-test in Chapters 7 and 8. These methods offer a simple procedure for the two-condition case but fail to provide an adequate basis on which a more general procedure can be developed. What is needed is a rationale that will provide the basis for a more general method that is not limited to the simple case of two variables.

10.1.2 Using the Chi-Square Distribution to Test Hypotheses

The procedure about to be described follows a rationale that should be familiar by now. The method has the following steps:

Table 10.2 Intermediate results for the photo-preference study

Condition	f_o	f_e	$e\,(=f_o - f_e)$
Original photo	17	25	-8
Mirror image	33	25	$+8$

Standard Steps of Statistical Data Analysis

Step 1 State a model and the associated null hypothesis.

Step 2 Derive expected (predicted) values on the basis of the model.

Step 3 Calculate residuals as the discrepancy between the observations and the model's predictions.

Step 4 Evaluate the residuals.

For the photo-preference example, the model is

$$f_o = f_e + e$$

For the null model, $f_e = Np$. The values of f_o, the values of f_e under the null hypothesis, and the resulting residuals, e, for our photo-preference example are given in Table 10.2.

Pearson's Chi-Square, χ^2

Notice that the residuals sum to 0. The random variable we will use to evaluate the residuals takes the following form:

$$\Sigma \frac{(f_o - f_e)^2}{f_e} = \Sigma \frac{e^2}{f_e}$$

Provided certain assumptions (to be noted shortly) are satisfied, this random variable has a probability distribution known as the chi-square distribution and is denoted by χ^2 (χ is the Greek letter chi, pronounced "kye"). This distribution was first derived around the year 1900 by Karl Pearson (to whom we also owe the product-moment correlation coefficient). For the applications to be described in this chapter, chi-square is often referred to as *Pearson's chi-square*.

For our example, we have

$$\chi^2 = \Sigma \frac{e^2}{f_e} = \frac{(-8)^2}{25} + \frac{8^2}{25} = 5.12$$

To evaluate the null hypothesis, we need to know the probability of obtaining a χ^2 value of 5.12 or more if the true probability is .5. Such probabilities are obtained from tables of the chi-square distribution.

The χ^2 distribution has one parameter, the degrees of freedom.

The chi-square distribution is a probability distribution with one parameter consisting of its degrees of freedom. As with other statistics, such as t or F, it is customary to denote the degrees of freedom in parentheses. Thus $\chi^2(1)$ denotes χ^2 with 1 degree of freedom. To use the chi-square distribution for a particular problem, the degrees of freedom need to be established.

For the photograph-preference experiment, there is just 1 degree of freedom, so the relevant distribution is $\chi^2(1)$. Notice that once one of the expected frequencies is known, the second expected frequency is fixed because the two must sum to 50. Equivalently, once one of the residuals has been calculated, the second residual is fixed because the two must sum to 0.

The table of the chi-square distribution (Statistical Table 6) is set out in the same way as that of the t-distribution. Critical values of χ^2 are set out for various degrees of freedom for the critical regions of .1, .05, and .01. A section of the table is shown as Table 10.3. Figure 10.1 shows the .05 critical region for a chi-square distribution with $df = 1$. In this distribution, the value of χ^2 that marks off the critical region of .05 is 3.84.

The obtained value of χ^2 for the data from the photograph-preference experiment was 5.12. This value is greater than the critical value of 3.84, so the null hypothesis can be rejected at the .05 significance level. A χ^2 value as large as 5.12 reflects residuals larger than would be expected if the null hypothesis were true. It appears that participants showed a systematic preference for the mirror image photograph.

$\chi^2(1)$ is the distribution of z^2.

The χ^2 distribution is closely related to the normal distribution. Consider a normally distributed standardized variable, z. Suppose we sample z-scores from this distribution and square each of them. Imagine now sampling repeatedly in this way and plotting the resulting frequency distribution of these z^2 values. The population distribution corresponding to this distribution is a chi-square distribution with $df = 1$.

Table 10.3 Portion of the chi-square table showing critical values of chi-square for 1 through 6 degrees of freedom

	Proportion in critical region		
df	.10	.05	.01
1	2.71	3.84	6.63
2	4.61	5.99	9.21
3	6.25	7.81	11.34
4	7.78	9.49	13.28
5	9.24	11.07	15.09
6	10.64	12.59	16.81

The full table is Statistical Table 6 in Appendix C.

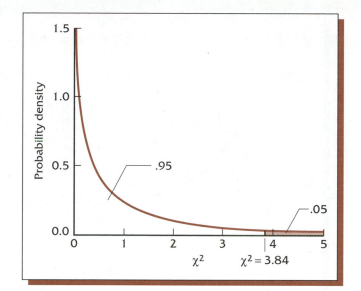

Figure 10.1
Chi-square distribution with 1 degree of freedom. The value $\chi^2 = 3.84$ marks off an area .05 to the right and .95 to the left.

Understood as the distribution of z^2, the unusual shape of the χ^2 distribution with $df = 1$ shown in Figure 10.1 makes sense. Note first that all negative z-scores (half the z-distribution) become positive when squared, so the value of χ^2 cannot be negative. Note second that, in the normal z-distribution, the scores are most heavily concentrated (the probability is most dense) around 0, the mean. When squared, this concentration is even greater, but always on the positive side. Thus a z-score of -0.06 becomes $+0.0036$. This effect of squaring produces the concentration of probability near the positive side of 0.

Notice that the value of χ^2 for our example is exactly the square of the z-value we obtained earlier when the normal distribution approximation was used ($2.26^2 = 5.12$). Notice also that with $df = 1$, the critical value of χ^2 for the .05 level is the square of the corresponding critical value of the normal distribution ($1.96^2 = 3.84$). These equalities are a direct consequence of the fact that $\chi^2(1) = z^2$.

The chi-square distribution with more than 1 degree of freedom is the distribution that results from adding two or more squared, normally distributed z-scores. Suppose we select two independent z-scores, z_1 and z_2, then square each and add together the two values to form a new variable, $z_1^2 + z_2^2$. Repeating this operation of selecting two z-scores, squaring each, and adding the squares would result in a frequency distribution, the population probability distribution for which would be a chi-square distribution with $df = 2$. In general, a chi-square distribution with k degrees of freedom is the distribution of k independent, squared, normally distributed z-scores.

Because χ^2 with $df = k$ is the sum of k independent random variables, it follows from the central limit theorem that as k becomes large, the chi-square distribution is increasingly well approximated by the normal distribution. This trend is apparent in Figure 10.2.

> With k degrees of freedom, χ^2 is the distribution of the sum of k independent values of z^2.

Assumptions

There are two assumptions that underlie the use of the chi-square distribution as the appropriate probability distribution of the statistic $\Sigma[(f_o - f_e)^2 / f_e]$.

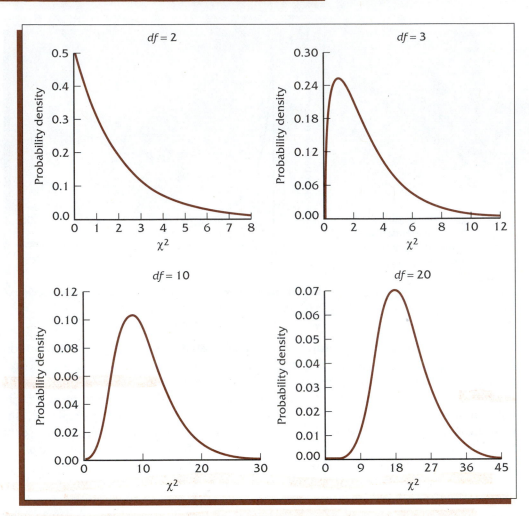

Figure 10.2
Chi-square distributions for 2, 3, 10, and 20 degrees of freedom.

The N observations must be independent.

■ The N observations must be mutually independent in the sense that each observation (each choice in our example) is uninfluenced by any other observation. This assumption would be violated if the same individual contributed more than one frequency count to the data, or if one individual's choice was influenced by another person's choice. In our example, the 50 frequencies come from 50 different individuals; and provided they were not allowed to interact in any way that would influence choice, the independence assumptions would be satisfied.

The expected frequencies must not be too small.

■ The expected frequencies must not be too small. This assumption is related to the previously described assumption under which the normal distribution provides an adequate approximation to the binomial distribution. In that case, the suggested rule of thumb was that both Np and $N(p - 1)$ should be at least 10. Although this rule may be appropriate for that very simple case, it is probably too stringent as a general rule covering the larger examples to be considered in the following sections.

The most widely accepted rule is that all expected frequencies should be at least 5. A generally held view is that the effect of lower expected frequencies is largely to reduce the power of the χ^2 test rather than to inflate the Type-1 error rate. Consequently, with low expected frequencies, it is even more difficult than usual to interpret a decision not to reject the null hypothesis.

10.1.3 Extending the Method to Three or More Categories

The method described in Section 10.1.2 is readily extended to more than two categories. Consider the following example. When constructing a multiple-choice test, it is usually desirable to make the incorrect alternatives (distractors) equally attractive. A four-alternative choice test has three wrong alternatives that we will label a, b, and c. Suppose $N = 84$ students answer one of the questions from the test incorrectly. The frequency of choice, f_o, among the three wrong answers was 22, 29, and 33 for distractors a, b, and c, respectively.

The null hypothesis is that the three distractors each have an equal probability (1/3) of being chosen:

$$H_0\text{: } P(a) = P(b) = P(c) = 1/3$$

The expected frequencies are therefore $f_e = N \times (1/3) = 84/3 = 28$. These values are set out in Table 10.4. The residuals, obtained by subtracting f_e from f_o, are shown in the bottom row.

Calculating χ^2 for a Three-Category Example

The χ^2 statistic can be calculated in the same way as the two-category example was, except that now there are three terms to be summed:

$$\chi^2 = \Sigma \frac{e^2}{f_e} = \frac{(-6)^2}{28} + \frac{1^2}{28} + \frac{5^2}{28} = 2.21$$

There are 2 degrees of freedom for this chi-square. Note that in Table 10.4, once two of the residuals have been calculated, the third is fixed by the constraint that the residuals must sum to 0. In general, for a single basis of classification with k categories, the degrees of freedom are $k - 1$. Consulting the χ^2 table (Statistical Table 6) for $df = 2$ indicates a critical value of $\chi^2 = 5.99$.

$df = k - 1$

Table 10.4 Observed and expected frequencies under the null hypothesis and residuals for the multiple-choice test-item example

Distractors	f_o	f_e	e
a	22	28	− 6
b	29	28	+ 1
c	33	28	+ 5
Total	84	84	0

Table 10.5 Outcome frequencies from 240 rolls of a die and the expected frequencies under the null hypothesis of a rectangular probability distribution

Outcome	f_o	f_e	e
1	45	40	5
2	36	40	−4
3	40	40	0
4	33	40	−7
5	36	40	−4
6	50	40	10
Total	240	240	0

Goodness of Fit

The two examples we have considered both consisted of a single basis of classification, and the chi-square distribution was used to compare observed with expected frequencies. Such applications are sometimes referred to as "goodness of fit." In the two examples, the null hypothesis was that each category was equally likely. This hypothesis is equivalent to postulating a rectangular distribution as the probability distribution underlying the observations.

Consider one further example in which the chi-square distribution is used to evaluate the null hypothesis of a rectangular distribution. Suppose an ordinary six-sided die is rolled 240 times to evaluate its fairness. The outcome for each roll is tallied, giving the data recorded in Table 10.5. The values of f_e are each 240/6.

Evaluating the residuals by calculating the χ^2 statistic, we have

$$\chi^2 = \Sigma \frac{e^2}{f_e} = \frac{5^2}{40} + \frac{(-4)^2}{40} + \frac{0^2}{40} + \frac{(-7)^2}{40} + \frac{(-4)^2}{40} + \frac{10^2}{40} = 5.15$$

This χ^2 has $k - 1 = 5$ degrees of freedom. Consulting the table of the χ^2 distribution (Statistical Table 6), we find a critical value of 11.07 is needed for significance at the .05 level. The obtained value is less than 11.07, so there is no evidence on which to reject the hypothesis of a fair die. The residuals appear to be well within the magnitude that could be expected to occur with a fair die.

Evaluating Goodness of Fit for a Binomial Distribution: A Quincunx

The use of the chi-square distribution to test goodness of fit is not limited to evaluating rectangular distributions. The following example tests goodness of fit for a binomial distribution. Suppose that a designer at a science museum has constructed a small quincunx to demonstrate the laws of probability to visitors. (Refer to Chapter 4 if you have forgotten the details of the quincunx.) This particular quincunx has five rows of pins and therefore six possible outcomes. The design specifications call for

Table 10.6 Outcome frequencies, probabilities, and the expected frequencies under the null hypothesis of a binomial probability distribution

Outcome	f_o	p	f_e	e
0	6	.031	4	+2
1	17	.156	20	−3
2	39	.313	40	−1
3	48	.313	40	+8
4	16	.156	20	−4
5	2	.031	4	−2
Total	128	1.00	128	0

128 balls. They also require that when a ball hits a pin, it has an equal chance of deflecting left or right.

The designer knows that, if the equal probability specification has been satisfied, then the 128 balls represent a sample from a binomial distribution with $p = .5$. To calculate the expected frequencies, we need to know the probability associated with each of the six possible outcomes. These probabilities are obtained from tables of the binomial distribution for $N = 5$ and $p = .5$ (Statistical Table 2). These values are recorded in Table 10.6 in the row labeled p.

To evaluate the hypothesis that the balls falling in the quincunx are governed by the binomial distribution, the 128 balls are passed through the quincunx and the number falling into each of the bins is tallied. For convenience, we will label the bins 0, 1, 2, 3, 4, and 5. The number of balls ending in each of the bins (f_o) is recorded in Table 10.6. The expected number of balls in each bin is simply the probability multiplied by 128. This multiplication gives the values of f_e shown in Table 10.6.

$$\chi^2 = \Sigma \frac{e^2}{f_e} = \frac{2^2}{4} + \frac{(-3)^2}{20} + \frac{(-1)^2}{40} + \frac{8^2}{40} + \frac{(-4)^2}{20} + \frac{(-2)^2}{4} = 4.875$$

This χ^2 has $k - 1 = 5$ degrees of freedom. Consulting the table of the χ^2 distribution (Statistical Table 6), we find a critical value of 11.07 is needed for significance at the .05 level. The obtained value is less than 11.07, so there is no evidence to reject the hypothesis that the quincunx is governed by the binomial distribution. The residuals appear to be well within the magnitude that would be expected for a quincunx built to the design specifications.

Comprehension Check 10.1

Important Concepts

1. With categorical variables, the data take the form of frequency counts. Such data is often termed count data.

2. Models for count data can be evaluated by comparing observed frequencies (f_o) with the expected frequencies (f_e) predicted by a model.

3. The models considered in this section involve a single basis of classification. Evaluating models of this type is often referred to as evaluating goodness of fit. When the data are binary (just two categories), the data can be analyzed by using the normal distribution approximation to the binomial distribution.

4. Residuals are, as usual, the differences between the observations and the predictions of the model. With count data, this principle takes the form of residuals that are the differences between observed and expected frequencies.

5. The residuals can be evaluated by using Pearson's χ^2 statistic. The chi-square distribution has one parameter, degrees of freedom.

6. The χ^2 distribution is appropriate if the observed frequencies are independent and the expected frequencies are not too small.

7. The χ^2 procedure can be applied to goodness of fit situations with any number of categories. The degrees of freedom for χ^2 are $k - 1$, where k is the number of categories.

Worked Examples

Example 1   Subjective randomness

Students in a large lecture class are asked to think of a single digit, 0 through 9, "at random," write it down, and hand it to the instructor without showing it to anyone. The instructor tallies the frequency with which each digit was chosen by the 270 members of the class. The results follow.

Chosen digit	0	1	2	3	4	5	6	7	8	9	Total
f_o	13	16	19	51	26	28	37	43	22	15	270

Evaluate the claim that, when asked to think of a number at random, people show a bias favoring the selection of some digits over others.

Answer If the participants in this study showed no bias in their selection of a digit, then each of the 10 digits would have an equal chance of being chosen. In other words, the sample data would come from a rectangular probability distribution, with the probability of the selection of each digit being .1. To evaluate this null hypothesis, we can generate expected frequencies and use the chi-square distribution to evaluate the differences between the observed and expected frequencies. If the probability of each digit being selected is .1, then the expected frequency of each digit is 27.

The residuals are shown in Table 10.7, and

$$\chi^2 = \Sigma \frac{e^2}{f_e} = \frac{(-14)^2}{27} + \frac{(-11)^2}{27} + \frac{(-8)^2}{27} + \frac{24^2}{27}$$

$$+ \frac{(-1)^2}{27} + \cdots + \frac{(-12)^2}{27} = 55.0$$

Table 10.7 Results for Worked Example 1

Chosen digit	f_o	f_e	e
0	13	27	-14
1	16	27	-11
2	19	27	-8
3	51	27	24
4	26	27	-1
5	28	27	1
6	37	27	10
7	43	27	16
8	22	27	-5
9	15	27	-12
Total	270	270	0

This χ^2 has $k - 1 = 9$ degrees of freedom. Consulting the χ^2 tables (Statistical Table 6) for $df = 9$, we find that the critical value for the .05 level is $\chi^2(9) = 16.92$. Thus the null hypothesis must be rejected. The data support the claim that, when asked to think of a random number, people do *not* behave as a genuine random number generator would.

Example 2 Distribution of sexes

Does the number of male and female children in families follow the binomial distribution? The question was investigated by using families with four children. The number of girls in each of 400 four-child families was recorded. The outcome frequencies follow.

Number of girls	0	1	2	3	4	Total
f_o	19	88	160	111	22	400

Answer The binomial probabilities are shown in the row labeled p in Table 10.8. The expected frequencies are obtained by multiplying the probabilities by $N = 400$. Thus $f_e = 25$ for zero girls is obtained by multiplying $1/16$ by 400. The residuals, $f_o - f_e$, are shown in the final column.

$$\chi^2 = \Sigma \frac{e^2}{f_e} = \frac{(-6)^2}{25} + \frac{(-12)^2}{100} + \frac{10^2}{150} + \frac{11^2}{100} + \frac{(-3)^2}{25} = 5.117$$

This χ^2 has $k - 1 = 4$ degrees of freedom. The χ^2 table (Statistical Table 6) gives a critical value of $\chi^2(4) = 9.49$ at the .05 level. The obtained value falls

Number of girls	f_o	p	f_e	e
Table 10.8 Results for Example 2				
0	19	1/16	25	-6
1	88	4/16	100	-12
2	160	6/16	150	10
3	111	4/16	100	11
4	22	1/16	25	-3
Total	400	16/16	400	0

below this critical value, so there are no grounds for rejecting the null hypothesis. The observed frequencies are compatible with having come from a binomial distribution.

Problems

Problem 1   Guessing in a multiple-choice test

A (desperate) student hopes to improve his chances of guessing correct answers in a multiple-choice test. The instructor in the course always uses six alternatives for each multiple-choice item, the alternatives being labeled a through f. Having looked over the past exams, the student suspects that the instructor favors locating the correct answer in the middle positions and tends to avoid making alternatives a or f the correct answer. If this observation is true, then, the student reasons, his correct guessing rate can be enhanced by choosing the favored middle positions. The data on which the student based his suspicion follow.

Location of correct alternative	a	b	c	d	e	f	Total
f_o	29	43	45	47	42	34	240

Is the student's suspicion justified, or is he a victim of the kind of wishful thinking that interprets noise as the desired signal?

Problem 2   Distribution of bird nests

In a study of animal behavior, nest location of a bird species is surveyed over a 10×10 kilometer area. To evaluate a claim that the nests are not uniformly distributed across this area, the total area is divided into four quadrants and the number of nest sites tallied for each. Of the 420 nests observed, the breakdown by quadrant was 120, 101, 93, and 106 nest sites.

Do these data support the claim that the nests are not uniformly distributed among the quadrants?

Problem 3   Length discrimination

In a study of length discrimination, participants are shown three lines side by side and asked to choose the longest. On one trial (a "catch" trial), all the lines are equal in length. The purpose of this trial is to discover whether there is a response bias. When no discrimination is possible, are participants biased in their choice with respect to the position of the alternatives—left, center, or right? The relevant data are positions of the line chosen on this catch trial for a sample of 66 participants. The results follow.

Line position	Left	Center	Right	Total
f_o	17	34	15	66

Do the data support the hypothesis of a response bias?

Problem 4   Litter size

An investigator claims that, for a species of rodent, the number of surviving offspring 2 weeks after birth follows a binomial distribution. The model is based on the assumption that, starting with a litter size of n offspring immediately after delivery, there is a fixed probability, p, that each of the offspring will survive for 2 weeks and a probability of $1 - p$ that they will die within that period. If this assumption is true, then the number of survivors after that time is formally equivalent to tossing a coin which has probability p of landing heads (= survival) and a probability of $1 - p$ of landing tails (= death). The number of heads represents the number of surviving offspring. To test this binomial model, the investigator records litter sizes at delivery (n) and again after 2 weeks (f_o). The data are for 100 litters that had an initial size of $n = 5$. The data show a survival probability of $p = 2/3$.

Litter size after 2 weeks	0	1	2	3	4	5	Total
f_o	4	5	13	19	50	9	100

Using this value of p, evaluate the investigator's binomial model. Are the data compatible with having come from a binomial distribution with $p = 2/3$?

10.2   Contingency Analysis: Count Data with Two Bases of Classification

In this section, we consider cases in which there are two categorical bases of classification. In these circumstances, the question of interest is whether there is any relationship, or contingency, between the two bases of classification. Is there a contingency between smoking and lung cancer, between gender and handedness, or between favoring capital punishment and membership in a conservative political party? Notice that with categorical data such as these, the questions are about relative

With categorical data, hypotheses about contingency are formulated in terms of relative frequencies.

frequencies of occurrence of events rather than about differences in the means as it might be with quantitative variables. Is the frequency of lung cancer higher among those who smoke than among those who do not? Is the proportion of left-handedness higher for men than for women? Is the percentage of conservatives who favor capital punishment higher than the percentage of liberals? The purpose of this section is to describe methods of evaluating data that address such questions.

10.2.1 Independence in a 2×2 Contingency Table

Consider a simple example. Is there a relationship between gender and handedness, or are the two independent? At the cost of oversimplifying matters slightly, we will assume that people can be classified as either left- or right-handed. This 2×2 set of possibilities can be set out in a table such as Table 10.9. Any individual can be classified and assigned to one of the four cells in the table. Such a table is commonly referred to as a contingency table because this arrangement of the data is the basis for examining the relationship or contingency between the two factors.

We would say that gender and handedness are independent outcomes if knowing whether a person was male or female did not improve our ability to predict whether or not the person was left- or right-handed. This would be the case if the incidence of left-handedness were the same for men and women. Under the assumption of independence, we would expect the proportion of left-handed men to be the same as the proportion of left-handed women.

If gender and handedness were *not* independent, then the incidence of left-handedness among men would be different from that among women. Suppose the incidence of left-handedness is higher among males than among females. Then knowing that a person is male makes it more likely that the person is left-handed, whereas knowing that a person is female makes it less likely that the person is left-handed. We could then say that there was a contingency or relationship between gender and handedness.

Two events are independent if the probability of their joint occurrence is the product of the probabilities of their separate occurrences.

The following statement is a formal definition of *independence:* Two events are independent if the probability of their joint occurrence is the product of the probabilities of their separate occurrences. We will refer to this rule as the *multiplication rule* for independent events.

Suppose a person is selected at random from the population. In this particular population, the proportion of left-handed people is .20 and the proportion of men is .5. Then, if gender and handedness are independent,

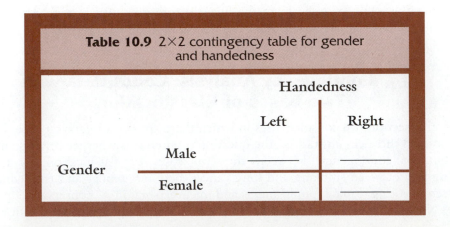

Table 10.9 2×2 contingency table for gender and handedness

		Handedness	
		Left	Right
Gender	Male	_____	_____
	Female	_____	_____

- The probability of being both male and left-handed is $.20 \times .5 = .1$.

- The probability of being both female and left-handed is $.20 \times .5 = .1$.

- The probability of being both male and right-handed is $.80 \times .5 = .4$.

- The probability of being both female and right-handed is $.80 \times .5 = .4$.

These probabilities can be entered into the four cells of Table 10.9 as shown in Table 10.10.

> **Stated more generally, the multiplication rule for independence is as follows: If E_1 and E_2 are two events, then E_1 and E_2 are independent if**
>
> $$P(E_1 \text{ and } E_2) = P(E_1) \times P(E_2)$$

As a second example, suppose E_1 denotes being in favor of capital punishment and E_2 denotes being in favor of making abortion illegal. Suppose that in a large town an opinion poll shows that 60% of people favor capital punishment and 30% favor making abortion illegal. If these two opinions are independent, then the probability of a sampled person being both in favor of capital punishment and in favor of making abortion illegal would be $.6 \times .3 = .18$. In other words, if opinions on these two issues are unrelated, then 18% of people would be in favor of both capital punishment and making abortion illegal. Similarly,

E_1 and E_2 are independent if $P(E_1$ and $E_2) = P(E_1) \times P(E_2)$.

- The probability of opposing capital punishment and being in favor of making abortion illegal is $.4 \times .3 = .12$.

- The probability of favoring capital punishment and being opposed to making abortion illegal is $.6 \times .7 = .42$.

- The probability of opposing both capital punishment and making abortion illegal is $.4 \times .7 = .28$.

Notice that the four probabilities sum to 1.0. This result follows from the fact that the four possible combinations of opinions on the two issues exhaust the possibilities. Everyone is assumed to fall into one of the four cells of the contingency table.

Table 10.10 Cell probabilities under the null hypothesis of independence in the 2×2 contingency table for gender and handedness

		Handedness	
		Left	Right
Gender	Male	.1	.4
	Female	.1	.4

If independence holds, then knowing a person's opinion on capital punishment is of no help in predicting their opinion on abortion. If, however, these two issues are *not* independent, then probabilities could not be derived by the multiplication rule. For example, independence would be violated if people who favor capital punishment are more likely to believe that abortion should be illegal than those who oppose capital punishment. Similarly, if smoking and lung cancer are independent, then the risk of lung cancer would be as high among nonsmokers as among smokers. The nonindependence of smoking and lung cancer—the contingency between the two—is reflected in the higher proportion of lung cancer victims among smokers than among nonsmokers.

10.2.2 Using the χ^2 Distribution to Evaluate Independence and the Strength of Contingency

To test the null hypothesis of independence, the multiplication rule is used to generate the expected frequencies for each of the four cells of the contingency table.

The procedure for evaluating independence follows the same logic as that used in the goodness of fit examples. The only difference is that now the multiplication rule of independence will be used to generate the expected frequencies for each of the four cells of the contingency table. However, having generated these frequencies, the procedure will be to calculate residuals, square them, and apply the standard formula for the chi-square statistic.

Expanded Photo-Preference Study

The following example is an extension of the photo-preference study described in Section 10.1. That study showed a preference for the mirror image photograph over the original. One explanation of this preference is that of familiarity. There is considerable evidence to support the general claim that, when making esthetic judgments, people express a preference for the familiar over the unfamiliar. In terms of your own face, the mirror image would be overwhelmingly more familiar to you than the face that is seen by your friends and appears in photographs. You rarely see your own face other than in the mirror, whereas your friends almost always see the real thing. If this explanation is correct, then close friends of the participants ought to prefer the *original* photograph.

To examine this matter, an experiment is designed in which 25 college women were shown two photographs of themselves, as in the original study. These same photographs were also shown to a close friend of each participant. As before, one of these photographs was the original photograph taken by the investigator before the experiment began. The other was the mirror image of this original. All participants ($N = 50$) judged which of the two photographs they preferred. There are now two bases of classification, each with two categories:

■ type of photograph: original versus mirror image

■ judge: self versus friend

A marginal frequency is the sum of a row or column of cell frequencies.

The data from such a study can be arranged in a 2×2 table, as shown in Table 10.11. Each entry in this table is the number of cases that fall into that cell. Thus, when the judge is the photographed person's friend, 21 of these friends prefer the original photograph and 4 prefer the mirror image photograph. When the judge is the photographed person herself, 9 prefer the original photograph and 16 the mirror image photograph. The row and column headed "Total" are *marginal frequencies*. They tell us, for example, that 30 out of 50 participants preferred the original photo-

Table 10.11 Data for the expanded photo-preference experiment

Judge	Original	Mirror image	Total
Friend	21	4	25
Self	9	16	25
Total	30	20	$N = 50$

"Total" is the marginal frequency.

graph over the mirror image. The row totals tell us that there were 25 participants of each type—friend and self.

The question we wish to answer is whether there is a contingency between the two bases of classification or whether the two bases of classification are independent. Is the probability of preferring the original over the mirror image photograph independent of whether the judge is the person in the photograph or a close friend? The hypothesis of independence serves as the null hypothesis.

To formulate this independence hypothesis, we use the multiplication rule of independence. Under the null hypothesis of independence, the proportion of friends choosing the original photograph is the marginal proportion of friends × the marginal proportion of choices of the original photograph.

In analyzing the data in the contingency table, we will proceed by the following steps.

Step 1 Use the marginal totals to form marginal proportions. These values are shown in Table 10.12.

Step 2 Use the marginal proportions to calculate the expected proportion in each cell under the null hypothesis of independence (Table 10.13).

> The hypothesis of independence serves as the null hypothesis.
>
> A marginal proportion is the sum of the frequencies in a row or column divided by N.

Table 10.12 Marginal proportions (boldface type) for the expanded photo-preference experiment

Judge	Original	Mirror image	Marginal proportion
Friend	21	4	25/50 = .5
Self	9	16	25/50 = .5
Marginal proportion	30/50 = .6	20/50 = .4	50/50 = 1.0

Table 10.13 Expected cell proportions under the null hypothesis			
Judge	Original	Mirror image	Marginal proportion
Friend	$.5 \times .6 = .3$	$.5 \times .4 = .2$	.5
Self	$.5 \times .6 = .3$	$.5 \times .4 = .2$	.5
Marginal proportion	.6	.4	1.0

Step 3 Convert proportions to frequencies by multiplying each cell proportion by the number of cases, 50. This operation gives the required table of expected frequencies, f_e (Table 10.14).

Step 4 Calculate the residuals by subtracting the expected frequencies from the corresponding observed frequencies. This operation gives the residuals shown in Table 10.15. Notice that both rows and columns sum to 0.

Step 5 Calculate the value of Pearson's chi-square statistic:

$$\chi^2 = \Sigma \frac{e^2}{f_e} = \frac{6^2}{15} + \frac{(-6)^2}{10} + \frac{(-6)^2}{15} + \frac{6^2}{10} = 12.0$$

Table 10.14 Expected frequencies under the null hypothesis			
Judge	Original	Mirror image	Total
Friend	$.3 \times 50 = 15$	$.2 \times 50 = 10$	25
Self	$.3 \times 50 = 15$	$.2 \times 50 = 10$	25
Marginal proportion	30	20	50

Table 10.15 Residuals			
Judge	Original	Mirror image	Total
Friend	$21 - 15 = +6$	$4 - 10 = -6$	0
Self	$9 - 15 = -6$	$16 - 10 = +6$	0
Total	0	0	0

Table 10.16 Expected frequencies calculated by using a single formula

Judge	Original	Mirror image	Total
Friend	$\dfrac{25 \times 30}{50} = 15$	$\dfrac{25 \times 20}{50} = 10$	25
Self	$\dfrac{25 \times 30}{50} = 15$	$\dfrac{25 \times 20}{50} = 10$	25
Total	30	20	50

The above calculations have been set out step-by-step to make clear the rationale underlying the calculation of the expected frequencies. However, the various steps are usually collapsed into a single formula. To obtain the expected frequency for a given cell, multiply the marginal frequencies (totals) for the row and the column of that cell and divide by N.

$$f_e = \frac{\textit{product of two marginal frequencies}}{N}$$

Thus, in this example, the expected frequency for the cell corresponding to the first row and first column is $(25 \times 30)/50 = 15$. The 25 in the numerator is the row total for "friend" and the 30 is the column total for "original." The complete table calculated in this way is shown in Table 10.16.

Step 6 Measure the strength of contingency by obtaining the phi coefficient. At a purely descriptive level, the size of the chi-square statistic is a measure of the extent to which the data depart from perfect independence. The larger the value of χ^2, the stronger the contingency. The value of χ^2 can therefore serve as the basis for a measure of contingency.

A commonly used measure for 2×2 contingency tables is the *phi* (ϕ) *coefficient:*

$$\phi = \sqrt{\frac{\chi^2}{N}}$$

The ϕ coefficient can be thought of as a categorical or count-data counterpart to the product-moment correlation coefficient. Both coefficients provide a measure of the strength of the relationship between two variables. The ϕ coefficient ranges from a value of 0 (complete independence) to 1.0 (complete dependence). The ϕ coefficient can also be thought of as a measure of effect size, the contingency counterpart to Cohen's **d**. Cohen (1988) suggests that $\phi = .1$ be interpreted as a small effect size, $\phi = .3$ a medium effect size, and $\phi = .5$ a large effect size.

For the photo-preference data,

$$\phi = \sqrt{\frac{\chi^2}{N}} = \sqrt{\frac{12}{50}} = .49$$

According to Cohen's convention this is a medium to strong contingency.

The various steps in calculating the expected frequencies can be collapsed into a single formula.

Step 7 Evaluate the null hypothesis of independence. In this example, the marginal proportions were used to calculate the expected frequencies. In such cases, the 2×2 table results in a χ^2 variable with just 1 degree of freedom. Notice that, in the table of expected frequencies, once one value of f_e has been calculated, the remaining three are fixed because the sum of each row and column must equal the observed marginal frequencies. Equivalently, notice that when one of the residuals has been calculated, the remaining three are fixed because each row and column of the residuals must sum to 0.

The critical tabled value of χ^2 with $df = 1$ for the .05 level is 3.84. The obtained value of $\chi^2 = 12.0$ is larger than this critical value, so the null hypothesis of independence must be rejected. The residuals are larger than might plausibly be expected by chance. Recall that the residuals are the differences between observed frequencies and those expected under the hypothesis of independence.

This rejection of the null hypothesis amounts to the claim that there is a contingency between photo preference and whether the person making the choice is the person in the photograph or the person's friend. This result is exactly what the familiarity hypothesis would predict. When the photograph is of oneself, the mirror image is a more familiar representation of one's face and therefore is preferred. When the same two photographs are viewed by a friend, the mirror image is the less familiar representation and therefore is judged less preferable than the original photograph.

10.2.3 R×C Contingency Tables

The procedure for analyzing a 2×2 contingency table readily generalizes to cases in which the number of rows and/or the number of columns is more than two. If R denotes the number of rows and C the number of columns, then the table is described as an *R×C contingency table*.

Consider first an example in which R = 2 and C = 3. This experiment studied whether the willingness of a bystander to offer assistance to a person in distress was influenced by the number of other bystanders. A confederate of the investigator, in a booth adjacent to the participant, pretends to have an asthma attack. In one condition of the experiment, the participant is alone in an adjacent booth. In a second condition, the participant is with one other person who, unknown to the participant, is also a confederate of the investigator. Participants in a third condition are with four other people—also confederates. The categorical response measure is whether or not the participant leaves the booth to assist the person having the apparent asthma attack. The confederates in conditions 2 and 3 have been instructed not to offer such assistance. There were 20 participants in each of the three conditions. Hypothetical data from such an experiment are shown in Table 10.17.

The null hypothesis is that the two bases of classification are independent, that is, that the probability of the participant leaving the booth to assist the person having the apparent asthma attack is independent of the number of other people in the group. As in the 2×2 case, the formal statement of this null hypothesis of independence employs the multiplication rule of independence.

The marginal proportions for these data are shown in Table 10.18, along with the expected cell proportions under the independence hypothesis. These expected cell

Table 10.17 Data for the bystander assistance experiment

		Number of bystanders[a]			
		1	2	5	Total
Action	Help	14	7	4	25
	No help	6	13	16	35
	Total	20	20	20	60

[a] The number of bystanders includes the participant.

Table 10.18 Expected cell proportions under the null hypothesis of independence

		Number of bystanders			
		1	2	5	Total
Action	Help	.139	.139	.139	.417 = 25/60
	No help	.194	.194	.194	.583 = 35/60
	Total	.333 = 20/60	.333 = 20/60	.333 = 20/60	1.0

proportions are obtained by multiplying the marginal proportions for the row and column that define that cell. For example, the expected cell proportion for the cell corresponding to the "Help" row and the single bystander is $(25/60) \times (20/60) = .139$. The expected cell proportion for the cell corresponding to the "No help" row and the single bystander is $(35/60) \times (20/60) = .194$.

The expected cell frequencies are obtained by multiplying the expected proportions by 60. Table 10.19 gives the values calculated in this step. These expected frequencies can be calculated with the same formula as that described in the 2×2 case. The expected frequency is the product of the marginal frequencies (totals) divided by N. Thus, for the first cell, the expected frequency is

$$f_e = \frac{25 \times 20}{60} = 8.33$$

Table 10.19 Expected cell frequencies under the null hypothesis of independence

		Number of bystanders			
		1	2	5	Total
Action	Help	8.33	8.33	8.33	25
	No help	11.67	11.67	11.67	35
	Total	20	20	20	60

Table 10.20 Residuals

		Number of bystanders			
		1	2	5	Total
Action	Help	$14 - 8.33$ $= 5.67$	$7 - 8.33$ $= -1.33$	$4 - 8.33$ $= -4.33$	0
	No help	$6 - 11.67$ $= -5.67$	$13 - 11.67$ $= 1.33$	$16 - 11.67$ $= 4.33$	0
	Total	0	0	0	0

The residuals are obtained as the difference between observed and expected frequencies. They appear in Table 10.20. The value of Pearson's χ^2 statistic is obtained by squaring each residual, dividing this squared residual by the expected frequency for that cell, and finding the total across the six cells:

$$\chi^2 = \Sigma \, \frac{e^2}{f_e}$$

$$= \frac{5.67^2}{8.33} + \frac{(-5.67)^2}{11.67} + \frac{(-1.33)^2}{8.33} + \frac{1.33^2}{11.67} + \frac{(-4.33)^2}{8.33} + \frac{4.33^2}{11.67} = 10.8$$

The Phi Coefficient for R×C Contingency Tables

A more general form of the phi coefficient is needed for tables that are larger than 2×2. This more general coefficient was proposed by the statistician Harald Cramér and is therefore commonly referred to as *Cramér's phi* and symbolized ϕ_c. Its value is

$$\phi_c = \sqrt{\frac{\chi^2}{N(k-1)}}$$

ϕ_c denotes Cramér's phi.

In this formula, N is the sample size and k is the smaller of R and C. In the bystander experiment, $k = 2$; so, for the bystander experiment,

$$\phi_c = \sqrt{\frac{\chi^2}{N(k-1)}} = \sqrt{\frac{10.8}{60 \times 1}} = .42$$

In the formula for Cramér's phi, k is the smaller of R and C.

According to Cohen's convention, this is a medium effect size. Notice that, in this special case in which $k = 2$, the formula for ϕ_c becomes the same as the formula for the ϕ in the 2×2 case.

Evaluating the Null Hypothesis of Independence

To make this evaluation, we need to know the degrees of freedom for χ^2 in larger contingency tables. The general answer is that, in an R×C table, the degrees of freedom are $(R-1) \times (C-1)$. In the case of the 3×2 table of our example, the degrees of freedom are therefore 2. Notice that, in the table of residuals or of expected frequencies, it takes only two entries to fix the remaining values because of the constraints on the row and column totals to sum to 0 in the case of the residuals or to the observed marginal frequencies in the case of the expected frequencies.

In an R×C table, the degrees of freedom for testing independence are $(R-1) \times (C-1)$.

The null hypothesis for the bystander example can be evaluated by comparing this obtained value of χ^2 with the tabled value of χ^2 with $df = 2$. For the .05 significance level, the critical value of $\chi^2(2)$ is 5.99. This value is less than the obtained value of 10.8, so the null hypothesis of independence should be rejected. It is appropriate to conclude that the number of other bystanders influences the probability that any one bystander will offer assistance.

Comprehension Check 10.2

Important Concepts

1. This section describes the analysis of data for which outcomes are classified with respect to their values on two attributes.

2. Such data can be arranged in a contingency table in which the categories of one attribute are represented in the rows and the categories of the second attribute are represented by the columns.

3. The null hypothesis to be tested is that of independence between the row and column classifications.

4. Independence is formally defined by the multiplication rule: The expected proportion in each cell is the product of that cell's marginal proportions.

5. The multiplication rule is used to generate expected frequencies in each cell.

6. Expected frequencies are used to calculate residuals that can then be evaluated by using Pearson's χ^2 statistic.

7. For a 2×2 table, the phi coefficient (ϕ) provides a measure of the strength of the contingency. For larger tables, a modified phi coefficient (ϕ_c, Cramér's phi) is used.

8. The degrees of freedom for testing the null hypothesis of independence are $(R - 1) \times (C - 1)$, where R is the number of rows and C is the number of columns.

Worked Examples

Example 1   Locus of control

Many personality theorists distinguish internal and external locus of control. People with an internal locus of control believe that their own actions will make a difference. People with an external locus of control believe that what happens is determined by outside forces. One prediction based on this distinction concerns the choices people will make when confronted with situations for which the outcome is either predominantly skill determined or predominantly luck determined. Kahle (1980) carried out such a study, using male participants. Table 10.21 presents hypothetical data similar to those obtained in that study. Participants were classified as having personalities with either internal or external locus of control. They were then given a choice between a task that involved largely skill and a task that involved largely luck.

Calculate Pearson's chi-square and the phi (ϕ) coefficient for these data. What evidence is there for a genuine contingency between choice and personality type in this situation?

Answer The expected frequencies under the null hypothesis of independence can be obtained by multiplying the marginal frequencies (totals) and dividing by 105. The results are given in Table 10.22.

Table 10.21 Data for Worked Example 1

		Task chosen		
		Skill	Chance	Total
Control locus	External	20	30	50
	Internal	34	21	55
	Total	54	51	105

Table 10.22 Expected frequencies for Example 1

		Task		
		Skill	Chance	Total
Control locus	External	$\dfrac{50 \times 54}{105}$ $= 25.7$	$\dfrac{50 \times 51}{105}$ $= 24.3$	50
	Internal	$\dfrac{55 \times 54}{105}$ $= 28.3$	$\dfrac{51 \times 55}{105}$ $= 26.7$	55
	Total	54	51	105

Table 10.23 gives the residuals. From these, we calculate

$$\chi^2 = \Sigma \frac{e^2}{f_e} = \frac{(-5.7)^2}{25.7} + \frac{5.7^2}{24.3} + \frac{5.7^2}{28.3} + \frac{(-5.7)^2}{26.7} = 5.0$$

$$\phi = \sqrt{\frac{\chi^2}{N}} = \sqrt{\frac{5}{105}} = .22$$

The χ^2 statistic has $df = 1$. The critical value of χ^2 for 1 degree of freedom at the .05 level of significance is 3.84. Thus the null hypothesis of independence can be rejected. This significant χ^2 indicates that although the phi coefficient is small, it is significantly different from 0.

Table 10.23 Residuals for Example 1

		Task		
		Skill	Chance	Total
Control locus	External	$20 - 25.7$ $= -5.7$	$30 - 24.3$ $= 5.7$	0
	Internal	$34 - 28.3$ $= 5.7$	$21 - 26.7$ $= -5.7$	0
	Total	0	0	0

Example 2   Sex, relationship, and violence

In a study of violent crimes, 400 violent crimes in a large city were reviewed and classified according to two attributes:

■ relation of the victim to the criminal: whether the victim of the crime was a stranger, a friend, or a relative

■ gender of the victim: whether the victim was male or female

The resulting hypothetical data are given in Table 10.24. Calculate Pearson's χ^2 and Cramér's phi (ϕ_c) for these data. Evaluate the null hypothesis that there is no contingency between the gender of the victim and the relation of the victim to the person who committed the crime.

Answer The expected frequencies under the null hypothesis of independence can be obtained from the product of the marginal frequencies (totals) divided by 400. The results are given in Table 10.25. The value in the first cell, for example, is obtained as $(240 \times 140)/400 = 84$. The residuals are obtained as the difference between the observed and expected frequencies. They are shown in Table 10.26.

Table 10.24 Data for Example 2

		Relation to victim			
		Stranger	Friend	Relative	Total
Gender of victim	Male	104	95	41	240
	Female	36	65	59	160
	Total	140	160	100	400

Table 10.25 Expected frequencies for Example 2

		Relation to victim			
		Stranger	Friend	Relative	Total
Gender of victim	Male	84	96	60	240
	Female	56	64	40	160
	Total	140	160	100	400

Table 10.26 Residuals for Example 2

		Relation to victim			
		Stranger	Friend	Relative	Total
Gender of victim	Male	$104 - 84$ $= 20$	$95 - 96$ $= -1$	$41 - 60$ $= -19$	0
	Female	$36 - 56$ $= -20$	$65 - 64$ $= 1$	$59 - 40$ $= 19$	0
	Total	0	0	0	0

The value of Pearson's χ^2 can then be obtained by using the standard formula:

$$\chi^2 = \Sigma \frac{e^2}{f_e} = \frac{20^2}{84} + \frac{(-1)^2}{96} + \frac{(-19)^2}{60} + \frac{(-20)^2}{56} + \frac{1^2}{64} + \frac{19^2}{40} = 27.0$$

This χ^2 has 2 degrees of freedom, so the critical value for $\alpha = .05$ is 5.99. The obtained value of χ^2 was 27.0, so the null hypothesis of independence is rejected.

Cramér's phi (ϕ_c) for these data is

$$\phi_c = \sqrt{\frac{\chi^2}{N(k-1)}} = \sqrt{\frac{27}{400 \times 1}} = .26$$

Thus there is a small but significant contingency between the relation to the victim and the gender of the victim with respect to the frequency of violent crimes.

Problems

Problem 1   Voter preference

At the beginning of the chapter, the data in Table 10.27 were used as an example of a contingency table and the following questions were asked.

Table 10.27 Data for Problem 1

		Preferred candidate	
		A	B
Gender	Male	65	32
	Female	45	58

Do the results of this survey support the claim of a relationship or contingency between gender of voter and candidate preference? It appears as if men prefer candidate A, whereas women prefer candidate B. How strong is this contingency? Is it strong enough to reject the simpler claim that there is no gender difference in preference, that is, that gender and voting preference are independent?

Answer these questions.

Problem 2   Incubation in problem solving

The data to be analyzed in this problem come from an experiment in which participants were asked to solve the following problem.

> Given match sticks that form five squares, as in the figure below, move just three sticks to form four squares.

The concept of "incubation" in problem solving asserts that if you cannot find a solution to a difficult problem, it is often helpful to take a period of rest in which work on the problem is set aside. In a study of this concept, two groups of participants worked on the match stick problem. One group worked for 15 minutes. Participants in a second group worked for 5 minutes and were then given a 30-minute rest period during which they watched a movie. They were then given a further 10 minutes to work on the problem. Thus all participants had 15 minutes to work actively on the problem. There were 30 participants in each group. The number of people solving and not solving the problem is shown in Table 10.28. Is there any evidence that the incubation group performed better than the control group?

Table 10.28 Data for Problem 2

		Group	
		Control	Incubation
Solved?	Yes	16	18
	No	14	12

Table 10.29 Data for Problem 3

		Group	
		Memory	Help
Solved?	Yes	39	29
	No	11	21

Problem 3 **Memorization and conceptualization in problem solving**

Katona (1940) used the match stick problem described in Problem 2 to compare the effectiveness of either memorization or conceptualization in problem solving. The experiment and data for Problem 3 are modeled loosely on Katona's original experiments. The experiment for Problem 3 contains two groups. Participants in group 1—the *memory group*—are shown the steps in solving the match stick problem. They are instructed to remember the steps involved in the solution, and the steps are repeated seven times. Participants in group 2—the *help group*—are given hints on solving the problem that encourage participants to discover general principles involved in such problems. Two days after this initial session, the participants were given the same problem to solve.

There were 50 participants in each condition. The data from this second session are shown in Table 10.29. Calculate the phi coefficient for this contingency table. Do these results provide evidence for a difference between the two groups in the proportion of participants solving the problem after a 2-day period?

Problem 4 **Problem solving after a 2-day period**

The experiment used in Problem 3 is repeated with one change. In this new version of the experiment, the task given after the 2-day period is a different match stick problem, although one that embodies the same general principles. There were 44 participants in each condition. The data from the second session are shown in Table 10.30.

Table 10.30 Data for Problem 4

		Group	
		Memory	Help
Solved?	Yes	10	26
	No	34	18

Table 10.31 Data for Problem 5

		Group		
		Memory	Help	Control
Solved?	Yes	18	17	4
	No	16	17	30

a. Calculate the phi coefficient for this contingency table. Do these results provide evidence for a difference between the two groups in the proportion of participants solving the problem after a 2-day period? b. Comparing the results from the experiments in Problems 3 and 4, what conclusions would you draw about training in problem solving?

Problem 5   **An extension of the Problem 4 experiment**

The experiment described in this problem is an extended version of the experiment used in Problem 4. This version of the experiment adds a control group. Participants in this group receive no help at all during the initial session. The other difference is that the interval between the two sessions is extended from 2 days to 3 weeks. At the second session, all participants attempt to solve exactly the same problem they worked on during the first session. There were 34 participants in each condition. The data from the second session are shown in Table 10.31.

Calculate Cramér's phi (ϕ_c) for this contingency table. Do these results provide evidence for a difference between the three groups in the proportion of participants solving the problem after a 3-week period?

Problem 6   **Another extension of the Problem 4 experiment**

This experiment is a repeat of the experiment used in Problem 5, except that, as in Problem 4, the task given after the 3-week period was a different match stick problem, not the one used in the initial session. There were 30 participants in each condition. The data from the second session are shown in Table 10.32.

Calculate Cramér's phi (ϕ_c) for this contingency table. Do these results provide evidence for a difference between the three groups in the proportion of participants solving the problem after a 3-week period?

Problem 7   **Further analysis of Problem 6 data**

The data in Table 10.32 strongly suggest that the significant χ^2 reflects the difference between the help condition and the other two. The memory condition does not appear to differ from the control condition. These observations can be tested by applying a χ^2 analysis to relevant subsections of the full table. For example, suppose we wish to compare the help condition with the control condition. The relevant portion of Table 10.32 is the 2×2 table shown in Table 10.33.

Table 10.32 Data for Problem 6

		Group		
		Memory	Help	Control
Solved?	Yes	3	16	4
	No	27	14	26

Table 10.33 2×2 table for Problem 7

		Group	
		Help	Control
Solution?	Yes	16	4
	No	14	26

a. Analyze this table as you would any 2×2 contingency table. Calculate a phi coefficient and evaluate whether the proportion of successful solutions is different for the help condition compared with that of the control condition.

b. Suppose we wish to compare the help condition with the memory condition. Set out the relevant portion of the full table that would be relevant to this evaluation, then calculate a phi coefficient and evaluate whether this portion of the table is compatible with the null hypothesis of independence.

10.3 Distribution-Free or Nonparametric Methods of Analysis

The methods described in the first two sections of this chapter required no assumptions about the form of the underlying distribution or about its parameters. With a categorical response variable that simply tallies frequencies, such considerations are either meaningless or irrelevant. By contrast, previous methods using the normal, t, or F distributions have, in one way or another, involved the assumptions of normal distributions and homogeneity of variance, and the tests have been based on estimates of means and variances.

Each of these assumption-based methods of testing hypotheses has a counterpart that does not rely on such assumptions. These methods are commonly referred to as *distribution-free* or *nonparametric* tests. Although some statisticians make a distinction between these two terms, they are often used interchangeably. The term *distribution-free* captures the important feature that the test does not depend on assumptions about the form of the underlying distribution. *Nonparametric* is a term that reflects the fact that such tests do not involve the estimation of the parameters (such as the mean and variance) of such distributions. Methods described in earlier chapters can therefore be referred to as *parametric tests,* because they do involve the estimation of parameters.

All the methods to be described in this section are based on the strategy of replacing scores with their ranks. The various procedures are therefore often described as *rank-order methods.* Consider as an example the following set of observations and their ranks.

Rank-order methods replace the original observations with their ranks.

Score	12	43	22	9	32	29	45	14	28	18
Rank	2	9	5	1	8	7	10	3	6	4

The effect of replacing scores with their ranks is to ignore the distances between adjacent scores. In this example, scores of 28 and 29 and scores of 32 and 43 are, when replaced by their ranks, equally separated by one rank. It is this property of ranks that makes them independent of the form of the distribution of the original scores. Scores may be severely skewed, bimodal, or have outliers, but, provided nothing is done to alter their ordering, a set of N scores will always yield the same set of ranks.

The virtues of nonparametric tests have been much debated. Those who favor using nonparametric tests argue that they have most of the virtues of traditional parametric tests, without the possible distortions that might arise if assumptions are violated. However, this advantage comes at a price. One disadvantage is that nonparametric methods tend to focus exclusively on null hypothesis testing. The goal of model fitting, obtaining confidence intervals, and so forth is set aside in favor of tests of significance.

In the final analysis, the choice between parametric and nonparametric tests will probably be made on the basis of the data. If the data do not seriously contradict the underlying assumptions, then parametric methods would normally be used. If, however, the data indicate a serious violation of the assumptions, then an investigator may judge it wiser to employ nonparametric methods.

The following methods will be described in just sufficient detail to convey their underlying rationale. For more coverage, formulas, and the arithmetic details of how to conduct these tests, you should consult a text such as Howell (1992). The methods have been organized in terms of their relationship to the corresponding parametric method.

Wilcoxon Rank-Sum Test

This test is the nonparametric counterpart of the *t*-test for two independent groups. Its rationale is quite straightforward and provides a good example of the general principles underlying nonparametric methods. An equivalent form of the Wilcoxon rank-sum test is called the Mann-Whitney U-test.

The goal of the analysis is to compare the scores from two independent groups, denoted group 1 and group 2, with n_1 observations in group 1 and n_2 observations in group 2. Suppose first that the null hypothesis is *false* and that the scores for group

2 are typically larger than those for group 1. If we now rank order the entire set of scores from lowest to highest, then group 1 scores will tend to receive low ranks and group 2 scores high ranks. To capture this fact, we could sum the ranks for group 1 scores and also for group 2 scores. We would expect the sum for group 1 to be smaller than the sum for group 2.

If we suppose the null hypothesis to be *true*, then there should be no systematic differences between the rankings of the two groups. In this case, the sum of the ranks for group 1 and group 2 scores should differ only by a chance amount.

The Wilcoxon rank-sum test uses as its test statistic the sum of the ranks for whichever group has the smaller n. If the two groups are equal ($n_1 = n_2$), then use the smaller of the two sums. The value of this smaller sum is then used as a test statistic (analogous to the t-ratio) and compared with the smallest value that would be expected by chance if the null hypothesis were true. These critical values are found in published tables.

Kruskal-Wallis One-Way Analysis of Variance

Just as the analysis of variance with which we are familiar can be thought of as a generalization of the t-test to more than two groups, the Kruskal-Wallis one-way analysis of variance is a generalization of the Wilcoxon rank-sum test. The method involves forming a single ranking of all observations regardless of group, then calculating the sum of ranks for each group. If the null hypothesis is true, then these sums should differ only by chance. We then calculate a test statistic (analogous to the F-ratio) that measures the extent to which these summed ranks differ from each other, and the probability associated with this statistic is established. If this probability is small, then the null hypothesis is rejected.

Wilcoxon's Matched-Pairs Signed-Ranks Test

This method is the nonparametric version of the t-test for matched pairs described in Chapter 8. Consider as an example an experiment that measures anxiety before and after therapy. The response measure is the change in anxiety from pretherapy to posttherapy. If the therapy is effective, then most of these differences should be positive and any differences that are negative should be relatively small. On the other hand, if the null hypothesis is true (the therapy is ineffective), then there should be about as many positive as negative differences, and they should be of approximately the same absolute size.

To test the null hypothesis, the differences are first ranked, ignoring the direction (sign) of the difference. Then the sign of each difference is restored to the rank of that difference, and the positive and negative ranks are summed separately. The test statistic, for which tables exist, is whichever of these two sums is smaller. Note that if the null hypothesis is false, then the sum of the negative ranks should be low because they should be both small in magnitude and in number.

Friedman's Rank Test for Matched Blocks

This method is the nonparametric counterpart of the randomized block or within-subjects design. It is the extension of Wilcoxon's matched-pair signed-ranks test to more than two conditions. Imagine an experiment that evaluates therapy by measuring anxiety before and immediately after therapy, and then again in a follow-up study six months after the end of therapy. Thus each participant has three scores. The null hypothesis is that there is no difference in anxiety levels among the three conditions.

The rationale underlying the Friedman rank test for matched blocks begins with ranking the scores *within* each block or, as in our example, within each subject. Suppose the null hypothesis is false and anxiety levels are high before therapy, low immediately after, and at an intermediate level after six months. If this effect is very strong, then most of the pretherapy scores will receive a ranking of 3, indicating they are the highest of the three scores for that participant. Scores for the immediate posttherapy will tend to be the lowest and thus receive a rank of 1. Scores in the six-month follow-up condition will tend to be intermediate and receive a rank of 2. If the ranks for each condition are now summed over the participants, then the sum of ranks should be high for the pretherapy condition, low for the posttherapy condition, and intermediate for the six-month follow-up. If, on the other hand, the null hypothesis is true, then these sums should be approximately equal because the ranks will be randomly ordered across the three measurement occasions. The test statistic for Friedman's rank test reflects the differences among these three sums of ranks.

Spearman's Rank-Order Correlation Coefficient

The product-moment correlation coefficient also has its rank-order counterpart called Spearman's rank-order correlation coefficient. In this case, the correspondence between the two statistics is very close. Spearman's rank-order coefficient simply replaces the scores in each measure with their ranks, and the formula for Pearson's product-moment correlation coefficient is applied to these ranks instead of the scores. Tables exist for testing whether a rank-order coefficient is significantly different from 0.

Concluding Comments

Notice that, as previously stated, all the methods described in this section replace the original scores with ranks. It is this step that makes them insensitive to the distributional assumptions of parametric methods. When the data clearly violate those assumptions, these rank-order methods have much to recommend them. However, two points should be kept in mind when deciding on their use.

■ Strictly speaking, the null hypothesis being tested by these methods is not about differences between the means of the conditions but about differences in rank ordering. It is logically possible for two conditions to have equal means but quite different sums of ranks. Thus, if a test such as the Wilcoxon rank-sum test yields a significant result, care must be taken in interpreting this as evidence of a difference between the *means* of the two conditions.

■ When data seriously violate the assumptions of parametric methods, it is sometimes wise to ask why such a violation has occurred rather than immediately deciding on a nonparametric method. Recall from Chapter 2 that badly skewed or bimodal distributions may be a consequence of inappropriate sampling or of problems with the measuring instrument. Nonparametric methods should not be used as a Band-Aid to cover up more serious problems in the data.

Chapter 10 Exercises

Exercise 1   The foot-in-the-door phenomenon

In this study (introduced in Exercise 1 of Chapter 2), each of 80 households was asked to mount a large antipollution sign. An interviewer visited a randomly selected half of these households just once and asked them to mount the large sign. The other 40 households were visited twice. On the first visit, the interviewer made a relatively innocuous request: to sign a petition promoting a clean environment. Then, a week later, the same interviewer returned with the more substantial request to mount the sign. Will households in this two-visit group be more willing to mount the sign than those in the one-visit group?

Tabulate the data for this experiment, which appear in Data Set 2.11 (Exercise 1, Chapter 2) and check that the frequencies in Table 10.34 are correct. Calculate the phi coefficient as a measure of the strength of the contingency between the experimental manipulation and the response of agree versus refuse.

Exercise 2   Familiarization and the foot-in-the-door phenomenon

One difficulty with the experiment in the Exercise 1 is that any differences in compliance between the two groups may have been due, not to any agreement to the initial request, but to the fact that, for the two-visit group, the interviewer was an already familiar figure at the time of the major request. To evaluate this possibility, this experiment adds a third condition. This condition consists of an additional group, termed the *familiarization* group. This group receives two visits, but the first visit contains no request; it serves merely to familiarize the household with the interviewer. A total of 108 households are used. They are randomly assigned to three groups of 36 each. Table 10.35 gives the tabulated results for this study, arranged in a 3×2 contingency table. The new data are recorded in DS10_01.dat in the *ASCII Files*.

Calculate Cramér's phi (ϕ_c) for this contingency table. Do these results provide evidence for a difference between the three conditions in the proportion of participants agreeing or refusing to mount the sign?

Table 10.34 Tabled data for Exercise 1

		Response	
		Refused	Agreed
Household	One-visit group	31	9
	Two-visit group	19	21

Table 10.35 Data for Exercise 2

		Response		
		Refused	Agreed	Total
Household	One-visit group	28	8	36
	Two-visit group with initial request	16	20	36
	Two-visit group for familiarization only	26	10	36
	Total	70	38	108

Table 10.36 Data for Exercise 3

		Response		
		Refused	Agreed	Total
Household	One-visit group	28	8	36
	Two-visit group with initial request	18	18	36
	Two-visit group with different interviewers	19	17	36
	Total	65	43	108

Exercise 3   Is familiarization necessary for the foot-in-the-door phenomenon?

The study in Exercise 2 addressed the question of whether familiarity was a *sufficient* condition to produce a "foot-in-the-door" effect. This next study asks whether it is a *necessary* condition. Can the effect be observed if the second visit is made by a different person, and, moreover, one who is "blind" as to whether or not the household has received a previous visit and request? As in Exercise 2, a total of 108 households are used, randomly assigned to three conditions (groups) of 36 each. Group 1 receives just one visit; group 2 receives two visits, at the first of which the small request is made; group 3 is the same as group 2, except that the second visit is made by a different interviewer who is unaware of whether or not the household has received a previous visit. Table 10.36 shows the data for this study, arranged in a 3×2 contingency table.

Calculate Cramér's phi (ϕ_c) for this contingency table. Do these results provide evidence for a difference between the three conditions in the proportion of participants agreeing or refusing to mount the sign?

Exercise 4   Is similarity of content important?

The final experiment in this series asked whether the content of the two requests needs to be similar in subject matter (e.g., both about the environment). Groups 1 and 2 are the same conditions as in Exercise 3, but for group 3, the initial minor request concerns a totally unrelated topic. Households were randomly assigned to the conditions. Table 10.37 shows the data for this study, arranged in a 3×2 contingency table.

Calculate Cramér's phi (ϕ_c) for this contingency table. Do these results provide evidence for a difference between the three conditions in the proportion of participants agreeing or refusing to mount the sign?

Table 10.37 Data for Exercise 4

		Response		
		Refused	Agreed	Total
Household	One-visit group	26	6	32
	Two-visit group with similar request	9	23	32
	Two-visit group with dissimilar request	17	15	32
	Total	52	44	96

Exercise 5   Imitation of gestures

Exercise 4 of Chapter 2 presented data from a study of imitation of gestures by 3-month-old infants. Each infant was shown four gestures and the responses to each gesture were classified into one of seven categories. These data are frequencies; however, the application of the procedures you have just used in the above exercises is highly questionable. Why?

Chapter 10 Review

Terms

chi-square (χ^2)
contingency
count data
Cramér's phi coefficient
distribution-free test
expected frequency (f_e)
frequency data
goodness of fit
independent events or outcomes
marginal frequency
marginal proportion
multiplication rule
nonparametric test
observed frequency (f_o)
order statistic
Pearson's chi-square
phi coefficient
rank-order method
residual (as $f_o - f_e$)

Formulas

$$f_e = Np$$

$$\chi^2 = \Sigma \frac{(f_o - f_e)^2}{f_e} = \Sigma \frac{e^2}{f_e}$$

$$P(E_1 \text{and} E_2) = P(E_1) \times P(E_2) \quad \text{Defintion of independent events}$$

$$f_e = \frac{\text{product of two marginal totals}}{N} \quad \text{Expected frequencies in a contingency table}$$

$$\phi = \sqrt{\frac{\chi^2}{N}} \quad \text{Phi coefficient}$$

$$\phi_c = \sqrt{\frac{\chi^2}{N(k-1)}} \quad \text{Cramér's phi (appropriate for larger contingency tables)}$$

Quiz

Complete each sentence with a term from the following list. The same term may be used more than once.

chi-square
degrees of freedom
independent
parametric tests
residuals

contingency
expected frequencies
nonparametric tests
phi coefficient

count
goodness of fit
observed frequencies
ranks

Observations for categorical variables are often described as _____ data. Such data are used to evaluate models by using the model to generate _____. The _____ are the differences between the _____ and those generated by the model. The test statistic calculated on the basis of these residuals is called _____. Its distribution has one parameter based on the _____.

Chapter 10 described two kinds of models. One kind, called _____, generates predictions for categories organized along a single dimension. The second kind of model is used to evaluate the _____ between two categorical factors. In this latter case, the _____ measures the strength of the relationship, and the null hypothesis is that the two factors are _____.

Another group of statistical procedures that do not require assumptions about underlying distributions are called _____. The strategy underlying these tests is to replace scores with their _____. These methods may be appropriate when the assumptions of _____ such as the *t*-test have been seriously violated.

11 REVIEW

We have now completed our account of the basic methodology of statistical data analysis. The purpose of this concluding chapter is twofold. The first section of the chapter reviews the various methods, partly as a summary, but, more especially, to emphasize their unity and close interconnectedness. The methods that have been covered are not a catalogue of unrelated techniques but variations built on a common underlying rationale.

The second section of the chapter offers a brief description of various extensions to these methods. The methods we have covered are not only useful in their own right, they are also the building blocks for more advanced methods.

11.1 Overview of Statistical Data Analysis

The various methods of statistical data analysis we have covered are all variations on a single theme. In every case, the overall goal of statistical data analysis has been to account for (explain) the variability in the response measure. The general method for achieving this goal has been to formulate, fit, and then evaluate models. Each model predicts the response measure as a function of the value of a predictor or explanatory variable. Models not only account for the sample data from which they were derived, they also provide estimates of what is true in the population. Science, remember, is concerned with the general rather than the particular.

All the methods we considered have involved the following components:

■ formulating a model

■ fitting a model to the data by estimating the value of its parameters

■ calculating residuals along with a summary measure of their magnitude, thereby providing an index of how well the model fits

■ evaluating the size of the residuals by asking (a) how much variability does the model account for and (b) whether the residuals are small enough to have plausibly arisen by chance—whether they can be regarded merely as noise

■ providing an account of differences among specific conditions

We will review each of these components in turn and then review the assumptions underlying the various methods we have covered.

11.1.1 Formulating Models

A model explains or predicts an observation by specifying the factors that contribute to its value. In stating models, it is customary to use X to refer to the predictor (explanatory) variable and Y to refer to the response variable.

Models for Independent-Groups Designs

Consider, for example, single-factor between-groups experiments with a categorical predictor variable. These designs were discussed in Chapters 6 and 7. The model for such experiments stated that an observation is the sum of a constant (the overall mean, μ) and a component (α_i) representing the influence of the particular condition under which the observation was made:

$$\hat{Y}_i = \mu + \alpha_i$$

If the experiment is expanded to include two factors, A and B, factorially arranged, then the model becomes

$$\hat{Y}_{ij} = \mu + \alpha_i + \beta_j + \alpha\beta_{ij}$$

In this model, α_i and β_j represent the effects of factors A and B, respectively. The term $\alpha\beta_{ij}$ represents nonadditivity: the extent to which $\hat{Y}$ cannot be predicted as the sum of α_i and β_j. $\alpha\beta_{ij}$ is called the interaction term. The need for an interaction term indicates that the influence of one factor is different for different levels of the other factor. If the effect of a drug depends on the age of the participant, then there is an interaction between drug effect and age. If no interaction is present, the factors are said to be additive.

In the world of real data, no such model will fit the data perfectly and make error-free predictions. The term *residual* was used to refer to the discrepancy between a model's prediction and an actual observation. Thus, when modeling actual data, we need to add a residual term, denoted by e, to acknowledge this discrepancy. The full models then become

> **Residuals must be added to the model to reflect the difference between an observation and the model's prediction.**

$$Y_i = \hat{Y}_i + e = \mu + \alpha_i + e$$

and

$$Y_{ij} = \hat{Y}_{ij} + e = \mu + \alpha_i + \beta_j + \alpha\beta_{ij} + e$$

for the two-way factorial design.

Model for Block or Within-Subjects Designs

For experiments using matched pairs, matched blocks, or a within-subjects design (Chapter 8), there are two predictor variables: the condition and the block or subject.

The model's prediction rule stated that each observation was the sum of a constant (the overall mean, μ), a component (α_i) representing the influence of the particular condition under which the observation was made, and a component (π_j) representing the influence associated with a particular block or individual (j). Adding the residual term gives the model

$$Y_{ij} = \mu + \alpha_i + \pi_j + e$$

Model for Linear Regression

When the predictor variable is quantitative (Chapter 9), then the straight-line prediction rule (linear regression) states that each observation is the sum of a constant (the intercept of the line) and a component that is the value of the predictor variable (X) multiplied by a constant, the regression coefficient β:

$$Y = \alpha + \beta X + e$$

Null Models

All these models have versions—special cases—called null models. Null models cover the case in which the predictor variable exerts no effect on (or is unrelated to) the response variable. One of the major goals of statistical data analysis is to evaluate whether the null model is compatible with the data. Because the null model is the simplest model, the principle of parsimony states that this model should be retained unless there is strong evidence against it.

In the case of one-way, independent-groups designs, the null model states that the α_i are all 0, so the null model is simply $Y_i = \mu + e$. For factorial designs, the null model is also $Y_{ij} = \mu + e$. Remember that the only difference between one-way and factorial designs is the arrangement of the conditions; so if the conditions have no effect, then the two (null) models are identical. If the null hypothesis is true, then the predictor variable accounts for none of the variance in the response measure.

For block and within-subjects designs, the null model also corresponds to a state of affairs in which all the α_i are 0. The null-condition model therefore becomes $Y_{ij} = \mu + \pi_j + e$. Notice that π_j remains in the model even though the conditions have no effect. In this case, blocks or individuals will usually account for some of the variability in the response measure, but this fact would already be known to the investigator and would therefore be of little interest.

For linear regression, the null hypothesis is that $\beta = 0$, so the null model is $Y = \alpha + e$. In this case, the parameter α is the overall mean of the response variable. Apart from using the symbol α rather than μ, this null model is the same as the null model for the independent-groups design. In both cases, the predicted value is a constant (μ or α), so the prediction is the same regardless of the value of the predictor variable.

Linear Models

You may have noticed that all the models we have considered have the same general form. Their prediction rules all consisted of components that were simply added together. Such models are referred to as *linear models*. Models are described as linear if the prediction rule is the *sum* of the contributing components. A nonlinear model might be one that involved the product of two or more contributing components.

Models for Frequency Data

The models described in Chapter 10 were for categorical data and do not fall into the general class of linear models as defined in the previous paragraph. However, even for categorical data, the basic rationale for statistical data analysis is the same: A model is formulated and residuals are evaluated. In this case, residuals were the differences between the observed frequencies f_0 and the frequencies predicted by the model. The latter are called the expected frequencies, f_e. We considered two kinds of models. One was referred to as goodness of fit, the other as contingency analysis.

With goodness of fit, the model is usually a probability distribution. The probability distribution specifies the expected proportion for each outcome category. This proportion is converted to an expected frequency by multiplying the proportion by N, the total number of observations. For example, if the probability distribution is rectangular, then the expected proportions, and thus the expected frequencies, are equal for all categories. If the probability distribution is the binomial, then the expected proportions would be obtained by using probabilities taken from the table of the binomial distribution and converted to expected frequencies by multiplying by N.

For contingency analysis, the null hypothesis of independence generates the expected frequencies. Two events are independent if the probability of their occurring jointly is the product of their separate probabilities. The null hypothesis that sex and handedness are independent is the claim that the expected proportion of left-handed men is the proportion of men multiplied by the proportion of left-handed people. Again, the expected proportion derived from the hypothesis of independence is converted to an expected frequency by multiplying by N.

11.1.2 Fitting a Model and Estimating Parameters

Having formulated a model, the remaining difficulty is that we do not know the values of the various parameters such as μ, or α_i, and we must therefore estimate their values from the data.

For all the linear models we have considered, the estimated parameter values were chosen to provide the best fitting model "in the least squares sense." Least squares estimates are those values that yield the minimum sum of squared residuals. Using this criterion, no other values of the parameters will produce a better fit.

For categorical predictor variables, the least squares estimates of parameters are based on the relevant sample means. For example, the estimate of the overall mean, μ, is the mean of all the observations, $\overline{Y}$, and the estimates of α_i are $a_i = \overline{Y}_i - \overline{Y}$.

For a quantitative predictor variable, fitting the linear regression model involves finding estimates of α and β that minimize the sum of squared residuals. Formulas for these estimates were given in Chapter 9. Thus the fitted model is

$$Y = a + bX + e$$

Although the formulas for estimating α and β may be more complicated than simply calculating means as we did with a categorical predictor variable, the rationale is the same in both cases: Find those estimates that minimize the sum of the squared residuals.

11.1.3 Residuals

Once the parameters have been estimated, the residuals can also be estimated. Recall that

$$\text{data} = \text{model fit} + \text{residuals}$$

so the residual estimates are

$$\text{residual} = \text{data} - \text{model fit}$$

For linear regression, to take just one example,

$$e = Y - (a + bX)$$

The statistic used to describe the magnitude of the residuals is the sum of the squared residuals—the same statistic that the least squares estimation criterion minimized. This sum of squares is symbolized by SS_e. For independent-groups designs (Chapters 6 and 7), SS_e corresponds to the sum of squares within each condition and is therefore often referred to as SS_{within}.

Mean Square of the Residuals, MS_e

Regardless of the model, the sum of squares of the residuals can be converted to a variance by dividing SS_e by the appropriate degrees of freedom. Such variances were called mean squares and denoted by MS_e. For independent-groups designs, the degrees of freedom are $N - k$, where N refers to the total number of observations and k to the number of conditions. If there is an equal number of observations (n) in each condition, then $N - k$ can be written as $k(n - 1)$.

Although formulas for the degrees of freedom differ for the different models, they share a common rationale. In each case, the formula gives the number of *independent* deviations that enter into the residual sum of squares. This value corresponds to the number of independent observations less the number of independent parameters that were estimated in order to calculate the sum of squares.

Consider the independent-groups design as an example. In an experiment with k conditions and a total of N observations, MS_{within} has $N - k$ degrees of freedom because, to calculate the sum of squares, k parameters (the means of the k conditions) needed to be estimated.

For linear regression, the degrees of freedom for MS_e were $N - 2$, because two parameters (α and β) had to be estimated.

For block or within-subjects designs, the degrees of freedom for MS_e are $nk - (k + n - 1)$. There are nk observations in all. The parameters to be estimated consist of k condition means and n block or subject means. However, there are only $k + n - 1$ independent parameters because, as explained in Chapter 8, both condition means and block means share a common overall mean, μ.

11.1.4 Evaluating Models

There are two aspects to evaluating models. One is to provide a measure of the strength of the relationship between the predictor and response variables. The second is to decide whether the data warrant a model more complex than the null model. We will review each of these aspects in turn.

Measuring the Strength of the Relationship Between Predictor and Response Variables

The variance (mean square) of the residuals, MS_e, provides an overall measure of the size of the residuals and enters into many of the formulas for evaluating hypotheses and calculating confidence intervals. However, MS_e is not very useful as a stand-alone measure of how well a model fits. To state that $MS_e = 28.5$ for a particular experiment is not meaningful unless there is something against which to compare it.

A more useful measure is R^2, which provides a descriptive index of the proportion of variance that the model accounts for. A value for R^2 was calculated for all models of data with a quantitative response variable; and in every case, it has the same general form:

$$R^2 = \frac{SS_{model}}{SS_{total}} = \frac{SS_{total} - SS_e}{SS_{total}}$$

For quantitative predictor variables and the fitting of a linear regression model, the square root of R^2 is the product moment correlation coefficient and is denoted by r.

For contingency analysis, the phi coefficient (ϕ) provides a measure of the strength of the relationship between the two bases of classification. The larger the value of ϕ, the better one can predict category membership on one attribute (left- versus right-handedness, for example) from knowledge of category membership on the second attribute (gender, say).

Deciding to Reject or Retain the Null Model

Are the residuals larger than could be expected by chance?

Although R^2 indicates the amount of variance that the model accounts for, investigators usually want to answer a more fundamental question: Do the data demand a model that is any more complicated than the null model? Recall from Chapter 1 that, in the interests of parsimony, the simpler (null) model should be retained unless the data provide evidence that a model with additional parameters is needed, and they establish the case beyond a reasonable doubt. Rejection of the null model implies that the predictor variable accounts for at least some of the variability in the response measure. The claim is that different values of the predictor variable are associated with different values of the response variable. In the case of categorical predictor variables, values of the predictor variable are labels designating different conditions, so rejection of the null hypothesis amounts to the claim that there are differences among the condition means.

Do the data demand a model that is any more complicated than the null model? In answering this question, there is, once again, a rationale common to all the models we have considered, including those for categorical response variables discussed in Chapter 10. The plausibility of the null model is evaluated by fitting the null model and asking whether the resulting residuals are small enough to be attributable to chance—small enough to be considered noise. If so, then the null hypothesis is retained. If, on the other hand, the null model results in so poor a fit that the residuals are larger than could be expected by chance, then the null model is rejected: The data demand a model with additional parameters.

The details of methods for evaluating the residuals under the null model vary, of course, from one model to another. However, you should not allow these differences in detail to conceal the common underlying question: Does the null model provide a sufficiently good fit to remain plausible? Another way of posing this question is to ask whether a model with additional parameters (a full model) provides a significantly better fit than the null model.

For designs with categorical predictor variables, analysis of variance provides the general method of answering this question. With a quantitative predictor variable, the corresponding procedure is referred to as regression analysis. In both cases, the basic logic is to compare two mean squares. One of these mean squares is MS_e, a direct estimate of the variance of the residuals. The second is a mean square that estimates the combined contribution of residual variation *plus* any variability accounted for by the predictor variable. If this contribution is 0 (as claimed by the null model), then this second mean square is also a pure estimate of residual variation—in which case, the two mean squares should differ only by chance. The F-ratio was used to evaluate this null hypothesis of equal mean squares. If the null hypothesis is true, then the expected value of the F-ratio is 1.0.

In the special case of an experiment with just two conditions, a number of simplifications are possible. The basis of these simplifications is that, with two conditions, there is only one difference between pairs of means of the conditions, so the total impact of the predictor variable is captured by a single difference between two conditions. It is therefore possible to test the null hypothesis by evaluating this single difference directly. Chapters 6 and 8 explained how the t-ratio can be used for this purpose. When there are three or more conditions, the impact of the predictor can be reflected in more than one comparison or difference between pairs of means. In this case, we use the variance among the condition means ($MS_{between}$) as a single measure of the total impact of the predictor variable. And we use the F-ratio rather than the t-ratio.

For categorical data, the evaluation of the residuals is even more straightforward. The residuals are the differences between frequencies expected under the null hypothesis and those actually observed. The chi-square statistic provides a direct measure of the magnitude of these residuals.

> With just two conditions, the t-ratio offers a possible simplification compared with analysis of variance.

Significance Levels and Decision Error Rates

The decision to reject or retain a null hypothesis is based on a rationale that is common to all the methods we have considered. Statistics such as the F-ratio, the t-ratio, or chi square all provide an index of the extent to which the data depart from the predictions of the null model. The larger their value, the less plausible the null hypothesis. How large must they be before the null hypothesis is rejected as implausible? The minimum value of the statistic needed to reject the null hypothesis is referred to as the critical value.

Defining the Critical Values of Test Statistics Such as t or F The null hypothesis is rejected if the data are unlikely to have arisen from a situation in which the null hypothesis (or the null model) is true. Five successive heads is an unlikely outcome from five tosses if a coin is fair; so, if five heads *are* obtained in five tosses, then the null hypothesis of a fair coin is rendered implausible and would be rejected. Similarly, if the null hypothesis is true, then large values of F, t, or χ^2 are improbable; and if large values *are* obtained, then the null hypothesis should be rejected. The criterion for sufficiently improbable determines the critical value of the statistic, that is, the minimum value of the statistic needed to reject the null hypothesis. This probability is referred to as the required significance level, or the Type-1 error rate, and is denoted by α. The most commonly used value is a probability of $\alpha = .05$.

Decision Error Rates The term *error rate* reminds us that when the null hypothesis is true, values of F, t, or χ^2 that exceed the critical value, although improbable, are not impossible. If we use $\alpha = .05$ as the criterion, then we concede the fact that, with a probability of .05, the obtained value of F, t, or χ^2 will exceed the critical value despite the fact that the null hypothesis is true. Such a circumstance would lead to the mistaken decision to reject the null hypothesis. That is, even when the null hypothesis is true, rejection occurs with a probability of .05—hence the term *error rate*. The probability associated with rejecting a true null hypothesis is called the Type-1 error rate.

Trade-Off Between Type-1 and Type-2 Error Rates Why not reduce the risk of a Type-1 error by setting an even more stringent criterion such as a probability of .01, .001, or even .0001? Although such criteria are sometimes used, they come with a cost. The cost is an increased risk of failing to reject a false null hypothesis. This mistake of failing to reject a false null hypothesis is referred to as a Type-2 error, and the probability of making it is denoted by β. Suppose you consider five successive heads to be too lenient a criterion for declaring a coin to be biased and demand an even less likely outcome—ten successive heads, say. Now the risk is that a coin that is genuinely biased will fail to satisfy so strict a criterion and will not be declared biased—a Type-2 error.

If the Type-1 error rate is fixed (at $\alpha = .05$, say), then the only way to reduce the risk of a Type-2 error (reduce β) is to improve the precision of the experiment. Chapter 8 described two broad strategies for achieving this goal. One was to increase the number of observations (n, or N); the other was to introduce some form of blocking or matching, a special case of which was within-subjects designs in which the same subject is measured under each condition.

11.1.5 Examining Differences Between Conditions

Although the decision to retain or reject the null model is a frequent concern of the behavioral scientist, there is much more to the interpretation of data than this simple yes/no dichotomy. Either decision leaves the investigator in an ambiguous situation. Rejection of the null hypothesis implies that there is a relationship between predictor and response variables. But how strong is the relationship? What is the magnitude of the effect? How large are the differences among conditions?

The significance level is not a good index of the magnitude of an effect.

Note that the size of the test statistic (the value of F or t, for example) and its associated probability do not provide a good answer to this question. The problem is that the value of these statistics is determined not only by the magnitude of the effect but also by the precision of the experiment. A value of $F = 20.0$ and $p < .001$, for example, may seem like a very strong effect, but it could be a small effect in an experiment with a high degree of precision. The p-value is an index, not of the magnitude of an effect, but of its *reliability,* that is, how likely it is to have arisen by chance and therefore how unlikely it is to be replicated if the experiment were to be done over again.

Of course, other things being equal, larger effects will be detected with greater reliability. In this case, "other things" means the general precision of the data as reflected in the value of MS_e. If different experiments have the same MS_e, then the larger the effect size, the smaller will be the Type-2 error, β. The difficulty is that, in the world of real experiments, other things are usually not equal.

Failure to reject the null hypothesis is similarly ambiguous. Sufficiently noisy data will virtually guarantee retaining the null hypothesis; so the investigator's lingering question becomes whether retaining the null hypothesis was a consequence of the null hypothesis being true (correct decision) or of a false null hypothesis being masked by noisy data (wrong decision).

To resolve this ambiguity, we need to go beyond a simple yes/no decision and address the matter of the strength and the size of effects. Previous chapters described a number of solutions. The value of R^2 gives an overall measure of the strength of the relationship between the predictor variable and the response variable. For categorical response variables and contingency tables, the contingency coefficient based on the value of chi square serves the same function.

Effect Size

With categorical predictor variables, it is usually valuable to provide information that is more specific than an overall index such as R^2. This information consists of estimates of the differences between the means of conditions. One such measure is Cohen's index of effect size, **d**; the other is the confidence interval.

The estimated value of Cohen's **d** for two conditions is the observed mean difference between the two conditions divided by the estimated standard deviation, $\sqrt{MS_e}$. Because it expresses differences in units of the standard deviation, this measure is particularly useful in comparing effect sizes across different experiments. In this regard, it is analogous to z-scores, which, as noted in Chapter 2, can serve as a useful basis for comparing single scores across different distributions.

Confidence Intervals

Confidence intervals provide information about the range of plausible values of a parameter, or of the true difference between two parameters. All the confidence intervals covered in this book have the same general form:

$$CI = \text{point estimate} \pm w$$

where w is the product of two components. One component is a critical value obtained from the table of the relevant theoretical distribution—the t-distribution or the Studentized range (q) distribution, for example. This value will vary with factors such as degrees of freedom and the desired level of confidence. The second component is the relevant standard error—the standard deviation of a sampling distribution. This value is determined by the value of MS_e and the sample size.

In experiments with more than two conditions (and therefore more than one comparison between pairs of means), a distinction was made (in Chapter 7) between simultaneous and individual confidence intervals. With individual confidence intervals, the confidence level refers to each interval considered separately. However, if this confidence level is .95, then the probability that *all* of the intervals will include the true difference is less than .95. The larger the number of intervals, the more chances there are that at least one of them will not include the true difference, just as the more dice you roll, the greater the chance that at least one of them will land six. For this reason, most investigators prefer to calculate simultaneous confidence intervals by using the Studentized range (q) distribution. With these intervals, the level of .95 refers to the probability that all the intervals include the true value.

Table 11.1 lists these components for the various confidence intervals we have considered. Even a cursory examination of the entries is sufficient to indicate the common rationale underlying the calculation of these intervals. All these intervals can be used to make decisions about the plausibility of some hypothesized value of the

Table 11.1 Components of confidence intervals

Confidence interval for	Point estimate	Distribution	df	w
Single mean, μ	$|\overline{Y}|$	t	$n - 1$	$t \times \sqrt{\dfrac{MS_e}{n}}$
Individual difference between pairs, $|\mu_i - \mu_j|$	$|\overline{Y}_i - \overline{Y}_j|$	t	$k(n - 1)$	$t \times \sqrt{\dfrac{2MS_e}{n}}$
Simultaneous difference between pairs, $|\mu_i - \mu_j|$ (Tukey)	$|\overline{Y}_i - \overline{Y}_j|$	q	$k, k(n - 1)$	$q \times \sqrt{\dfrac{MS_e}{n}}$
Regression	b	t	$N - 2$	$t \times \sqrt{\dfrac{MS_e}{SS_X}}$
Proportion	p	z	—	$z \times \sqrt{\dfrac{p(1 - p)}{N}}$

The formulas assume an equal number of participants in each condition. More general formulas are given in the text.

w is the minimum value needed for significance.

parameter or differences between parameters. This hypothesized value is usually the null hypothesis of 0. Using confidence intervals to decide about the null hypothesis is equivalent to a direct test using w as the minimum value needed to be declared significant.

Evaluating the Null Hypothesis The null hypothesis that $|\mu_i - \mu_j| = 0$ can be evaluated by finding whether the confidence interval for $|\mu_i - \mu_j|$ includes the value of 0, retaining the null hypothesis if it does and rejecting it if it does not. The confidence interval will include 0 if the obtained difference is less than w. That is, w is the minimum difference needed to reject the null hypothesis. If the interval is a 95% confidence interval, this decision rule is equivalent to using a significance level (or setting a Type-1 error rate) at .05. The same decision would be reached by calculating a t-ratio (obtained by dividing this difference between the means by the estimated standard error, $\sqrt{2MS_e/n}$) and comparing this ratio with the critical value obtained from the table of the t-distribution.

When there are more than two conditions, a distinction is made between error rates per comparison and error rates per experiment. This distinction parallels that between individual and simultaneous confidence intervals. An error rate per comparison refers to each decision considered separately, whereas an error rate per experiment refers to the set of decisions considered collectively. Thus, using individual 95% confidence intervals is equivalent to setting the error rate per comparison at .05, whereas using simultaneous 95% confidence intervals is equivalent to setting an error rate per experiment at .05. For example, when Tukey's procedure (based on the Studentized range distribution) is used to obtain simultaneous 95% confidence intervals, the value of w is known as the honestly significant difference (HSD). The HSD is the minimum difference needed for significance with an error rate per experiment of .05.

11.1.6   Assumptions

With the exception of Chapter 10, the various methods described in this text have four basic assumptions in common. To the extent that these assumptions are violated, inaccuracies enter into the inferences made on the bases of the analyses. A full discussion of these matters is beyond the scope of an introductory text, but it is important to know the basic assumptions and to recognize the need to examine data (as described in Chapter 2) before analyzing them.

The assumptions are about the conditional distributions. Recall that a conditional distribution is the distribution of observations for a given fixed value of the predictor variable, that is, the distribution of SAT scores for those with an IQ of 110, for example. With categorical predictor variables, values of the variable designate conditions, so a conditional distribution consists of the observations for a specified condition.

The assumptions are best expressed in terms of the residuals. However, for the models considered in this text, the residuals are the differences between the scores and the sum of the constants that make up the components of the model. Thus shape and variance of the distributions of scores and residuals will be the same. The four common assumptions about the conditional distributions of the residuals are

■ Residuals are normally distributed.

■ These normal distributions have the same variance (the assumption of homogeneity of variance).

■ The distributions are independent (uncorrelated).

■ The population mean (of the residuals, note) is 0 (the assumption of no bias).

For block designs and within-subjects designs, there is an additional assumption: The condition effects and the block (subject) effects are additive. For the regression and correlation designs considered in Chapter 9, there is the added assumption of linear regression: The means of the conditional distributions of the scores lie on a straight line.

Nonparametric tests provide an alternative method when these assumptions have been seriously violated. However, such methods are not cost free. They represent a retreat from the quantitative prediction and estimation characteristic of parametric methods into the narrow focus of hypothesis testing. Moreover, violation of assumptions may be indicative of more basic problems with the data that the investigator should address rather than sidestep.

When both the response and predictor variables are categorical (Chapter 10), there are no assumptions about underlying distributions. The only assumption is that the frequencies are independent. Remember also that the chi-square test becomes very insensitive (has low power) if the *expected* frequencies are small—less than five, say—and under these circumstances other methods should be used.

11.2 Extensions

This final section describes some of the immediate extensions to the methods covered in this introductory text. The intent is not to explain how to use these more advanced methods but to demonstrate that they are further variations on the same underlying rationale used throughout the book. When you encounter a reference to these methods in books and journal articles, you may not understand the details of their use, but they will be familiar and their purpose comprehensible. If you enroll in a more advanced course in statistical data analysis, mastering these advanced methods will be greatly facilitated by understanding how they are developed from the principles with which you are already familiar.

11.2.1 Higher Order Factorial Designs

The two-way factorial designs described in Chapter 7 can be extended to three-way or even higher order designs by combining three or more factors. Take as an example a simple extension to the experiment investigating the effect of alcohol and sleep deprivation on reaction time. Suppose we add *driving experience* as a third factor and assume that this factor has three levels: novice, intermediate, and experienced. Recall that, in the original example, there were two levels of alcohol consumption and two levels of sleep deprivation. With the addition of the third factor, the design would be described as a 2×2×3 three-way factorial design.

Analysis of Variance for a Three-Way Design

The conditions of the 2×2×3 could be set out in Table 11.2. The total number of conditions is 12; so 12 groups of participants would be needed. Participants from the three groups would be assigned randomly and independently to the four conditions.

The analysis of this experiment is a straightforward extension of the analysis of the two-way design. For the two-way design, the model and the associated analysis of variance partitioned the condition effects into main effects and their interaction. The same partitioning is done with the three-way design. The only nonobvious feature of the extension is in the number of interactions.

Table 11.2 Three-way factorial design					
		No sleep deprivation		**24 hours sleep deprivation**	
		Zero alcohol	1 ounce alcohol	Zero alcohol	1 ounce alcohol
Driving Experience	Novice	____	____	____	____
	Intermediate	____	____	____	____
	Experienced	____	____	____	____

Higher Order Interactions

For convenience, we will label the factors A (alcohol consumption), B (sleep deprivation), and C (experience). There are three main effects: A, B, and C. There are, however, *four* possible interactions. Three of these are two-way interactions: A×B, A×C, B×C. The fourth is the three-way interaction A×B×C. Higher order interactions such as a three-way interaction are difficult to express verbally, but in essence what they reflect is that one of the two-way interactions—say, the A×B—is different for the various levels of the other (C) factor. In terms of our example, this might mean that the strength of the interaction between alcohol consumption and sleep deprivation depends on experience level. Perhaps there is a strong interaction for novice drivers, but only a small one, or none at all, for experienced drivers.

MS_e for a Three-Way Design

The calculation of MS_e for such higher order designs follows exactly the same procedure as that for smaller between-groups design. The sum of squares is obtained for each condition, added, and divided by the appropriate degrees of freedom. As with previous designs, the degrees of freedom for MS_e is $N - k$, where N is the total number of participants and k is the total number of conditions in the experiment. If there is an equal number of participants in each condition, then the degrees of freedom are $k(n - 1)$. Thus if our example experiment used ten participants in each of the $2 \times 2 \times 3 = 12$ conditions, the degrees of freedom for MS_e would be $df = 12(10 - 1) = 120 - 12 = 108$.

Significance tests for main effects and their interactions in higher order designs are the same as those for one-way and two-way designs. The mean square corresponding to each component of the model is divided by MS_e to form an F-ratio. A significant F-ratio indicates that this component should be retained.

11.2.2 Larger Within-Subjects and Block Designs

The within-subjects and block designs considered in Chapter 8 were all single-factor designs. However, this design can be extended to include factorial arrangements of the conditions. Consider the following example. A study of word perception investigates the role of two factors in the perception of words briefly flashed on a screen. One factor is word frequency, the other is word length. There are three levels of the frequency factor (common, medium frequency, and rare) and two levels of word length (one syllable and two syllables). These levels are arranged in a 3×2 factorial design to give six different word types, as shown in Table 11.3. Participants attempt to recognize a sequence of 120 words, containing 20 words of each type in a random order. Thus all participants contribute to all six conditions.

In this experiment, as with many experiments in the behavioral sciences, the design uses a within-subjects design rather than blocks of independent subjects matched on some attribute. The analysis of variance for such a design would partition the condition effects into the two main effects and their interaction. It would also contain a term (π) corresponding to differences among participants. The mean square for each of these components would be divided by MS_e to form F-ratios and the significance of each evaluated.

Table 11.3 3×2 within-subjects factorial design

		Frequency		
		Common	Medium	Rare
Length	One syllable	_____	_____	_____
	Two syllables	_____	_____	_____

11.2.3 Between–Within Designs

It is common in the behavioral sciences to design experiments that include *both* independent-groups (between-subjects) and within-subjects components. Consider the following example. A drug evaluation experiment has two factors. One is a drug factor with two levels (experimental and a placebo control). This is a between-subjects factor, and the participants are assigned randomly and independently to one of the two groups. The second factor is time. This is a within-subjects factor with three levels: Behavior is measured immediately before starting the experiment, after two weeks, and again after two months.

In this design, there is one between-subjects factor (drug) and one within-subjects factor (time). The analysis of variance for such a design reflects this hybrid quality. The analysis partitions the two factors into a between-subjects sum of squares (drug) and within-subjects sums of squares (time, and the interaction between time and drug). This distinction has an important consequence when forming F-ratios to evaluate these components. The mean squares corresponding to within-subjects factors will have a different MS_e from that used to evaluate the between-subjects components.

We will not enter into the details of such analyses, but there is a feature of these hybrid designs that is important in interpreting the results and in evaluating published experiments. Chapter 8 made the point that a major purpose in using within-subjects designs is to improve precision. It follows that in designs that mix both within and between components, the MS_e for the within-subjects components will usually be smaller than for the between-subjects components.

The important consequence of this fact is that the within-subjects components will be tested with higher precision than will the between-subjects component. In other words, the Type-2 error rate will be higher for the between-subjects component. Care therefore needs to be taken when an experiment fails to reject the null hypothesis for the between-subjects component but rejects it for a within-subjects component. In such cases, it would be important to ask whether this pattern of acceptance and rejection of the null hypothesis might be attributable to one test being more powerful than the other.

11.2.4 Multiple Regression

Suppose our goal is to predict the GPA of students at graduation. Chapter 9 described how this might be done by using a single predictor variable such as IQ. Other variables might also have served as effective predictors. Candidate variables might include final-year high school grades, scholastic aptitude test results (SAT), or a scale measuring relevant motivational factors. If measurements are obtained on these variables, then it is possible to combine the predictive power of each in the form of a single model.

With one predictor variable, the regression model was

$$\hat{Y} = \alpha + \beta X$$

where α is the intercept parameter and β is the regression coefficient. Incorporating additional predictor variables is a matter of extending this model by simply adding variables, each with its own regression coefficient. If we use three predictor variables and denote them as X_1, X_2, X_3, then the model becomes

$$\hat{Y} = \alpha + \beta_1 X_1 + \beta_2 X_2 + \beta_3 X_3$$

For example, X_1 might be IQ; X_2, high school grade; X_3, SAT score. The goal of multiple regression is the same as that for single-variable regression: to find estimates of α, β_1, β_2, etc. that will minimize the sum of the squared residuals. Thus a fitted model would yield a prediction rule

$$\hat{Y} = a + b_1 X_1 + b_2 X_2 + b_3 X_3$$

The formulas for multiple regression coefficients are quite complex, but all standard statistical computer packages will perform the necessary computations. Once the parameter estimates have been calculated, it is possible to obtain a value for R^2. In the context of multiple regression, R^2 is often referred to as the squared multiple correlation coefficient, but in concept it is exactly the same as all other examples of R^2. It is the proportion of variance accounted for by the model. With more than one predictor variable, the square root of R^2 is called the multiple correlation coefficient rather than the Pearson product moment correlation coefficient.

11.2.5 Analysis of Covariance

Analysis of covariance is the continuous variable counterpart of the blocking strategy described in Chapter 8. As with blocking, the purpose is to gain precision (a smaller MS_e) by eliminating some of the within-condition variability. Analysis of covariance achieves this goal by using the logic of regression described in Chapter 9.

Consider as an example an investigation designed to compare three methods of instruction. The investigator wishes to gain precision by eliminating the contribution of differences in scholastic aptitude (as measured by the SAT) to the within-groups sums of squares. One method would be to set up blocks of three participants matched on SAT scores, assigning one to each of the three conditions. This is the standard randomized block design described in Chapter 8. In analysis of covariance, blocks are not formed. Instead, participants are assigned randomly to conditions, and the SAT score for each participant is used to adjust that participant's score on the response measure.

The model for the randomized block design was

$$Y_{ij} = \mu + \alpha_i + \pi_j + e$$

where π_j represents the SAT level for the members of the jth block. In analysis of covariance, the parameter π_j is replaced by $\beta \times$ SAT, where β is the regression coefficient (reflecting the correlation between the SAT scores and the response measure) and SAT is the individual SAT score of that participant. Thus, unlike the randomized block design, which applies the same adjustment to all scores within a block, analysis of covariance adjusts each score individually.

Chapter 11 Exercises

The exercises for Chapter 11 differ from those of earlier chapters in that they draw upon material from the entire book. In the world of real science, the appropriate form of statistical data analysis is not indicated by a conveniently preceding chapter describing the relevant method, nor do the data come with an attached reminder to check for the kinds of anomalies that might invalidate routine analysis.

Answers to these exercises are in two parts. The preliminary part answers the question as to the appropriate method of analysis and will be found at the end of this chapter immediately following the exercises. This section will, when appropriate, give the results of intermediate calculations that are needed to complete that exercise. The second part gives the final answers, and, as with exercises in earlier chapters, these answers are contained in Appendix A.

Exercise 1 Statistical reasoning (based on Lehman and Nisbett, 1990) (Data Set 11.1)

In this investigation of statistical reasoning, college students from four different areas of study were given descriptions of simple experiments such as the following and asked to explain the finding. The areas of study were natural science, humanities, social science, and psychology. Of interest is whether each student's answer shows sensitivity to statistical factors. The students were given a set of such problems in their first year as college students and again in their senior year. The response measure is the percentage of improvement in their scores as seniors relative to their original scores as first-year students. Are there any differences in improvement among the four areas?

A recent study sought to determine whether noise harms plants. In the study, two identical coleus plants were transplanted from the same greenhouse and grown under identical conditions, except that the first plant was exposed to a loud noise—approximately the same as a person would hear while standing by a busy subway platform—while the other plant grew in quiet conditions. After $1\frac{1}{2}$ weeks of continuous exposure, only the sound-treated plant wilted.

In this problem, statistical reasoning would involve acknowledgment of the role of chance because of the small sample.

The data for this experiment are given in Data Set 11.1.

Data Set 11.1   Data for Exercise 1

Natural science major

2	21	31	11	29	3	41	54	45	36
44	56	0	7	11	11	19	35	9	15
4	22	4							

Humanities major

27	− 3	32	33	33	49	36	8	50	16
35	− 5	8	39	47	21	40	34	9	29
16	16	12							

Social science major

79	79	80	79	88	52	81	61	73	72
63	58	65	78	38	30	62	77	66	51
81	34	68							

Psychology major

74	47	49	46	59	49	53	52	44	56
83	66	61	47	38	87	101	78	62	57
65	74	68							

a. Write out full and null models appropriate to the design of this experiment.

b. What method of analysis would you use to (i) obtain simultaneous 95% confidence intervals for the differences between pairs of groups; (ii) evaluate the null hypothesis for each difference between pairs of means with a Type-1 error rate per experiment of .05; (iii) test the overall tenability of the null hypothesis with a Type-1 error rate of .05?

c. Check your answers to the above questions in the results section at the end of the chapter. Then use the basic computations reported in this section to (i) draw a bar chart showing the mean improvement and error bars for each group; (ii) calculate simultaneous confidence intervals for the differences between pairs of means among the four groups; (iii) decide between the full and null models.

Exercise 2   The hospital problem
Participants were given the following problem. You will recognize it as one discussed in Chapter 4.

A town has two hospitals. Hospital A is large and has an average of 45 births per day; Hospital B is smaller and has an average of 15 births per day.

Each hospital recorded the number of days in which, on that day, at least 60% of the babies born were girls. Assuming the overall proportion of girl babies is 50%, which of the two hospitals recorded more such days: (a) Hospital A; (b) Hospital B; (c) both equal?

There were 72 participants and their choices are recorded in the following table. What procedure would you use to evaluate the null hypothesis that participants have a uniform probability of choosing among the three alternatives? Check your answer, then complete the analysis.

Choice	Number
Hospital A	15
Hospital B	17
Both equal	40

Exercise 3   Evaluating ECT (Data Set 11.2)
The effectiveness of electroconvulsive therapy (ECT) in the treatment of depression was evaluated by using a group of 20 patients. The level of depression for each patient was measured before the administration of ECT and again after three ECT treatments.

The hypothetical data for this exercise are based on results from a genuine study by Abrams et al. (1989) and appear in Data Set 11.2. The response measure is a score representing the patient's level of depression.

a. Write out full and null models appropriate to the design of this experiment.

b. What method of analysis would you use to (i) obtain a 95% confidence interval for the difference between the two conditions; (ii) evaluate the null hypothesis using a .05 significance level?

c. Check your answers to the preceding questions in the results section. Then use the basic computations reported in this section to complete the analysis.

Data Set 11.2   Data for Exercise 3

Patient	1	2	3	4	5	6	7	8	9	10
Pre-ECT	15	38	24	44	30	35	9	20	32	21
After ECT	18	31	16	35	19	38	11	12	20	11

Patient	11	12	13	14	15	16	17	18	19	20
Pre-ECT	29	26	13	25	24	34	18	29	29	14
After ECT	15	25	7	18	16	22	5	9	23	8

Exercise 4   A further evaluation of ECT (Data Set 11.3)
The study of ECT effectiveness described in Exercise 3 was repeated with a different group of 15 patients. In this study, depression for each patient was measured before the administration of ECT and again after three ECT treatments, and then again after six treatments.

The hypothetical data for this exercise and Exercise 3 are based on results from a study by Abrams et al. (1989) and appear in Data Set 11.3. The response measure is a score representing the patient's level of depression.

a. Write out full and null models appropriate to the design of this experiment.

b. What method of analysis would you use to (i) obtain simultaneous confidence intervals for the differences between pairs of groups; (ii) evaluate the null hypothesis?

c. Check your answers to the preceding questions in the results section. Then use the basic computations reported in this section to (i) obtain simultaneous confidence intervals for the differences between pairs of means among the three conditions; (ii) decide between the full and null models.

Data Set 11.3   Data for Exercise 4

Patient	1	2	3	4	5	6	7	8
Pre-ECT	18	37	24	11	19	28	16	35
After 3 ECTs	11	28	26	17	8	28	15	26
After 6 ECTs	10	4	11	3	10	14	1	18

Patient	9	10	11	12	13	14	15	Mean
Pre-ECT	40	8	14	31	12	26	11	22.00
After 3 ECTs	23	10	12	17	11	11	3	16.40
After 6 ECTs	24	14	5	9	8	10	4	9.67

Exercise 5   Stress and the common cold

Does stress increase the risk of succumbing to a cold virus? This question is an example of the more general issue of the relationship between stress and the effectiveness of the immune system. In this investigation, participants were divided into two groups (low and high psychological stress) on the basis of a stress index derived from self-reports. There were 44 participants in the low stress group and 35 participants in the high stress group. All participants were then exposed to cold virus. Participants subsequently had blood tests to detect whether or not they had become infected.

The results are shown in the following table. What procedure would you use to evaluate the hypothesis that stress increases the risk of succumbing to a cold virus? Check your answer, then complete the analysis.

	High stress	Low stress
Infected	25	20
Not infected	10	24

Exercise 6 Latent learning (Data Sets 11.4 and 11.5)

In a classic investigation of latent learning, Tolman and Honzik (1930) studied maze learning in three groups of rats over a 17-day period. The following experiment and hypothetical data are modeled on his original experiment.

Rats in group 1 were not rewarded at any point in the 17-day period. Rats in group 2 were not rewarded for correct responses for the first 10 days, but were rewarded for days 11 to 16. Rats in group 3 were rewarded for correct responses throughout the 17-day period. Is reward necessary for learning to occur? The hypothesis of latent learning claims that learning can occur without reward but reward is needed for the learning to reveal itself in actual performance. Without reward, learning remains latent. If this hypothesis is correct, then after 10 days rats in groups 2 and 3 should show poorer performance (more errors) than those in group 3. However, once reward is introduced, the latent learning of rats in group 2 should begin to appear and they should catch up to the performance of rats in group 1.

Data Set 11.4 Number of errors after 10 days of learning (Exercise 6)

Group 1

9	7	6	12	9	14	13	8	11	8
5	3	8	10	13	9	11	9	7	9

Group 2

7	7	9	5	9	7	8	10	4	10
12	12	11	11	13	9	3	4	9	9

Group 3

6	4	6	1	2	5	7	5	9	2
5	8	8	6	4	3	1	7	6	6

a. Data Set 11.4 shows the mean level of performance (number of errors) after 10 days—just prior to the time at which the group 2 rats begin receiving reward. Thus for this measure, groups 1 and 2 have received no reward, whereas group 3 has been rewarded throughout. The response measure is the number of errors. There were 20 animals in each condition.

Describe how you would analyze the data in Data Set 11.4 to obtain the simultaneous confidence interval for the differences between pairs of means among the three groups. Check your answer against that given at the end of the chapter, then use the basic computations provided to obtain simultaneous confidence intervals for the differences between pairs of means among the three groups.

Data Set 11.5   Number of errors after 17 days of learning (Exercise 6)

Group 1

6	8	8	8	7	5	5	11	10	9
10	8	8	7	9	7	4	7	5	8

Group 2

0	1	7	3	6	6	5	5	3	7
5	2	2	4	4	2	3	0	2	4

Group 3

3	1	4	3	9	0	4	2	6	4
4	6	5	6	2	3	6	5	2	5

b. Data Set 11.5 gives mean level of performance after 17 days. Use the results given with the answers at the end of the chapter to obtain simultaneous confidence intervals for the differences between pairs of means among the three groups at day 17.

c. Evaluation of the latent learning hypothesis depends in part on claiming the truth of a null hypothesis of no difference between groups 1 and 2. Why should an investigator therefore be particularly concerned about the precision of the experiment? Evaluate the precision of the experiment as revealed in the second set of data. Use whatever method you judge to be the most appropriate.

Exercise 7   Stability of extroversion (DS11_06.dat in the *ASCII Files*)

One of the major personality traits used by psychologists is extroversion. The data for this exercise investigated the stability over time of this trait for adults aged 30 and older. A 15-point scale measuring extroversion was administered to participants and then readministered to the same participants 4 to 5 years later. How would you evaluate the stability of the extroversion trait? Check your answer and then complete the analysis.

Exercise 8   Modeling aggression (DS11_07.dat in the *ASCII Files*)

The following hypothetical data are from a study of the social learning of aggressive behavior in young boys arising from their observations of the behavior of an adult model playing with an inflatable doll. There were three conditions:

1. a real-life model who behaves aggressively
2. a filmed model who behaves aggressively
3. a no-model control

The response variable is a measure of the child's subsequent aggressive behavior, that is, the number of aggressive responses over a fixed time period. A sample of 75 boys was used; they were assigned randomly to the three conditions, $n = 25$ in each.

Classify the design of this experiment and describe how you would evaluate the pattern of differences among the three conditions. Check your answer against the one given at the end of the chapter, then use the basic computations provided to answer the questions given in this answer section.

Exercise 9   Birth order and radical ideas

Sulloway (1996) investigated whether willingness to embrace radical ideas is related to birth order. In particular, he tested the hypothesis that first-born children tend to be conservative and likely to reject radical new ideas, whereas later-born children tend to be more rebellious and willing to accept new ideas. As a historian, he examined the writings of 179 scientists between 1859 and 1870 and classified them with respect to birth order and whether they accepted or rejected Darwinian theory.

The results are shown in the following table. What procedure would you use to evaluate Sulloway's hypothesis? Check your answer and then complete the analysis.

	First-born	Later-born
Accepted	14	67
Rejected	54	44

Exercise 10   Evaluating amnesia (DS11_08.dat in the *ASCII Files*)

Twenty-four patients in a neuropsychological institution have suffered brain damage from strokes or head injuries. They all show symptoms of amnesia. As part of their clinical assessment, their memory ability was compared with that of a group of 24 normal control participants by using a cued recall task. All participants were shown a list of words; then their memory was tested by showing them the first three letters of each word and asking them to recall the entire previously shown word.

Classify the design of this experiment and describe how you would calculate a 95% confidence interval for the difference in recall between the two groups.

Exercise 11   Implicit memory (DS11_09.dat in the *ASCII Files*)

The 24 brain-damaged patients from Exercise 10 were given a slightly different task. They were again shown a list of words. However, rather than a subsequent cued recall test, they were given a task known as stem completion. They were shown the first three letters of each word in a list and instructed to "complete this three-letter stem with the first word that comes to mind." Half these words were from the previously seen list. The other half were control words, that is, words not shown previ-

CHAPTER 11 EXERCISES ■ 585

ously. However, no mention was made of the words seen previously. The data (DS11_09.dat in the *ASCII Files*) consist of each participant's percentage of correct stem completions for each of the two kinds of words. Superior stem completion performance for previously shown words would be evidence for "priming": the facilitation of the completion of a word stem by its prior presentation. The memory system responsible for this facilitation is commonly referred to as "implicit memory." Do these amnesic patients show priming?

Classify the design of this experiment and describe how you would calculate a 95% confidence interval for the difference in recall between the two types of words. Check your answer and then complete the analysis.

Exercise 12   Priming (DS11_10.dat in the *ASCII Files*)

Amnesic patients, by definition, are impaired in terms of their explicit memory as measured, say, by cued recall. But what of their implicit memory system? For example, do amnesic patients show less priming than normal participants? To answer this question, investigators studied priming in a group of 20 amnesic patients and 20 normal participants. The procedure described in Exercise 11 was followed for both groups. The response variable is a single priming measure for each participant. The measure is the difference in percentage of correct completions between previously presented and control words (words not previously presented). Thus a positive score indicated priming, that is, superior completion for words previously seen.

Classify the design of this experiment and describe how you would calculate a 95% confidence interval for the difference in priming between the two groups. Check your answer and then complete the analysis. Do normal and amnesic participants differ in their levels of priming?

Exercise 13   Age and height (DS11_11.dat in the *ASCII Files*)

A school district would like to be able to predict the height of girls aged 3 to 6 years on the basis of their age. A sample of 50 girls in this age range is selected and their height measured.

Describe how you would use these data to calculate a linear prediction rule for predicting height for any given age in this range. Check your answer to this question and then use the given computational results to construct the rule. Suppose someone asks, "How rapidly do girls grow in this age range?" How would you reply?

Exercise 14   Matching attractiveness (Data Set 11.12)

In most societies, physical attractiveness is a desirable attribute, especially in the domain of social interaction. The study used in this exercise was designed to evaluate the hypothesis that, in seeking partners, people tend to find partners of roughly equal attractiveness. This is the matching hypothesis proposed by Berscheid, Dion, Walster, and Walster (1971).

The hypothetical data consist of separate attractiveness ratings of each member of opposite-sex couples observed at various social events. The ratings, made on a 10-point scale, are shown in Data Set 11.12 for 50 pairs. F indicates the attractiveness rating for the female, M for the male member of the pair.

How would you analyze these data to decide how strongly these results support the matching hypothesis proposed by Berscheid et al.? Check your answer; then use the computations provided to complete the analysis.

Data Set 11.12 Data for the matching hypothesis experiment (Exercise 14)

Pair	1	2	3	4	5	6	7	8	9	10
F	2	7	4	7	8	7	3	3	5	7
M	4	5	5	6	4	6	4	8	4	5

Pair	11	12	13	14	15	16	17	18	19	20
F	3	6	10	7	6	7	1	6	7	2
M	5	4	8	8	3	5	3	5	2	5

Pair	21	22	23	24	25	26	27	28	29	30
F	4	4	4	4	6	6	5	5	9	5
M	4	1	3	6	5	3	6	5	6	5

Pair	31	32	33	34	35	36	37	38	39	40
F	6	5	4	6	8	8	3	5	6	7
M	3	2	6	6	5	7	1	5	7	7

Pair	41	42	43	44	45	46	47	48	49	50
F	1	3	9	5	10	6	8	2	4	6
M	6	2	9	6	9	6	7	4	5	7

Answers to the Preliminary Part of the Exercises

Exercise 1 Statistical reasoning (Based on Lehman and Nisbett, 1990)

a. This is an independent-groups design, so the full model is $Y_i = \mu + \alpha_i + e$. The null hypothesis for that model is that all α_i are 0, so the null model is $Y_i = \mu + e$.

b. The appropriate method of analysis to obtain simultaneous confidence intervals would be to obtain MS_e and use the q-statistic to calculate w. Recall that, in this case, w is also Tukey's HSD and can be used to evaluate the null hypothesis for each difference. The overall test requires performing an analysis of variance and the calculation of an F-ratio.

The sum of squared residuals under the null model is $SS_{total} = 60,406$. The other intermediate results needed to complete the above procedures for $n = 23$ appear in Table 11.4.

Exercise 2 The hospital problem

Use a chi-square test for goodness of fit. The null hypothesis is that of a rectangular distribution.

Exercise 3 Evaluating ECT

a. This is a within-subjects design, so the full model is $Y_{ij} = \mu + \alpha_i + \pi_j + e$. The null hypothesis for that model is that all α_i are 0, so the null model is $Y_{ij} = \mu + \pi_j + e$.

Table 11.4 Intermediate results for Exercise 1

Major	Mean	SS
Natural science	22.17	6757
Humanities	29.30	5549
Social science	65.87	5631
Psychology	61.57	5384

b. The appropriate method of analysis is to calculate the standard error of the difference scores and use the t-distribution to calculate the confidence interval. This interval can be used to retain or reject the null hypothesis; alternatively, a t-ratio for matched pairs could be calculated.

c. The means for the pre- and post-ECT groups are 17.95 and 25.45, respectively. The standard deviation of the 20 difference scores is $s_D = 5.85$.

Exercise 4   A further evaluation of ECT

a. This is a within-subjects or repeated measures design, so the full model is $Y_{ij} = \mu + \alpha_i + \pi_j + e$. The null hypothesis for that model is that all α_i are 0, so the null model is $Y_{ij} = \mu + \pi_j + e$.

b. The appropriate method of analysis to obtain simultaneous confidence intervals would be to obtain MS_e and use the q-statistic to calculate w. Because w is also Tukey's HSD, it can be used to evaluate the null hypothesis for each difference. The overall test requires an analysis of variance and the calculation of an F-ratio.

Use the following sums of squares to complete the analysis: between groups, 1144.0; between patients, 2046.3; residual, 892.6.

Exercise 5   Stress and the common cold

Generate expected cell frequencies under the hypothesis of independence, then use the chi-square statistic to evaluate the residuals. Rejection of the null hypothesis would constitute evidence that stress increases the risk of succumbing to a cold virus.

Exercise 6   Latent learning

a. The experiment uses an independent-groups design. To obtain a simultaneous confidence interval for the differences between pairs of means among the three groups, calculate MS_e (MS_{within}), then use the q-statistic to calculate w, which is the confidence interval half-width and also HSD. For the first set of data, the means (number of errors) and sums of squares for the three groups $n = 20$ are given in Table 11.5.

b. The second set of data shows the mean level of performance (number of errors) and sums of squares after 17 days. The mean (number of errors) and sums of squares for the three groups ($n = 20$) are given in Table 11.6.

Table 11.5 Intermediate results for Exercise 6a		
Group	Mean	SS
1	9.05	147.0
2	8.45	153.0
3	5.05	103.0

Table 11.6 Intermediate results for Exercise 6b		
Group	Mean	SS
1	7.5	65.0
2	3.55	85.0
3	4.00	84.0

Exercise 7   Stability of extroversion

The correlation coefficient would be the commonly used statistic to answer this question. Stability over time (reliability) implies that a person's score is predictable from one occasion to a later occasion. Note that simply comparing the means across the two occasions is inadequate because the overall mean could remain constant while individual scores could be highly variable. Intermediate results are time 1, $SS = 839.0$; time 2, $SS = 1248.6$; $SP = 828.8$.

Exercise 8   Modeling aggression

The experiment uses an independent-groups design. Use the computational results shown in Table 11.7 to set out an analysis of variance summary table. Then, if appropriate, compute Fisher's LSD to evaluate the differences between pairs of means. The between-groups sum of squares is $SS_{between} = 5802.0$; $n = 25$.

Exercise 9   Birth order and radical ideas

Generate expected cell frequencies under the hypothesis of independence, then use the chi-square statistic to evaluate the residuals. Rejection of the null hypothesis would constitute evidence that first-born children tend to reject radical new ideas whereas later-born children tend to be more willing to accept new ideas. Estimate the strength of the contingency between the two classifications.

Exercise 10   Evaluating amnesia

The design is an independent-groups design. The results from this study in Table 11.8 can be used to calculate a 95% confidence interval for the difference in recall between the two groups; $n = 24$.

Table 11.7 Intermediate results for Exercise 8		
Group	Mean	SS
Real life	27.92	463.9
Filmed	23.72	567.1
Control	7.52	362.1

Table 11.8 Intermediate results for Exercise 10		
Group	Mean	SS
Amnesic patients	9.96	406.9
Control	19.71	444.9

Table 11.9 Intermediate results for Exercise 12

Group	Mean	SS
Amnesic patients	3.90	301.9
Control	4.90	279.7

Exercise 11 Implicit memory

The design is a within-subjects design. The results from this study are stated below and can be used to calculate a 95% confidence interval for the difference in recall between the two groups. The appropriate method of analysis is to calculate the standard error of the difference scores and use the t-distribution to calculate the confidence interval. This interval can be used to retain or reject the null hypothesis of no priming.

The means for the new and old words are 13.54 and 17.21, respectively. The standard deviation of the 24 difference scores is $s_D = 4.86$; $n = 24$.

Exercise 12 Priming

The design is an independent-groups design. The results from this study, shown in Table 11.9, can be used to calculate a 95% confidence interval for the difference in priming between the two groups; $n = 20$.

Exercise 13 Age and height

The goal is to estimate the parameters of a linear prediction rule of the form

$$\text{predicted height} = a + (b \times \text{age})$$

Height was measured in inches. Age is recorded in months. SP = 1137 and $SS_e = 396.8$. Other results from the analysis are shown in Table 11.10.

Exercise 14 Matching attractiveness

The appropriate analysis is linear regression/correlation. Results of basic computations are shown in Table 11.11.

SP = 94.68.

Table 11.10 Intermediate results for Exercise 13

Measure	Mean	SS
Age	53.2	5763
Height	41.2	621

Table 11.11 Intermediate results for Exercise 14

Group	$\bar{Y}$	SS
Female	5.44	236.32
Male	5.06	174.82

APPENDIX A

Glossary

accept region   In statistical hypothesis testing, the region of the sampling distribution representing outcomes compatible with the null hypothesis and thus leading to its acceptance.

additivity   In factorial analysis of variance, two effects are additive if there is no interaction between them.

alpha (α)   Probability of a **Type-1 error**. Also used as the parameter for the conditions effect in analysis of variance models and as the intercept parameter in the linear regression model.

analysis of variance   Partitioning (analysis) of the total sum of squares into components corresponding to the terms in a model.

bar chart   Graph of frequencies for a categorical variable.

beta (β)   Probability of a **Type-2 error**.

beta coefficient   Another name for regression coefficient

between-conditions (between-groups) sum of squares ($SS_{between}$)   In a between-groups design, the sum of squared deviations of the condition means from the overall mean.

bias   Systematic tendency for an estimate to be larger or smaller than the parameter being estimated.

bimodal distribution   Distribution with two distinct modes or peaks.

binomial distribution   Discrete probability distribution that gives the probability for the number of times that one of two possible outcomes will occur in n trials (for example, the number of heads in n tosses of a coin).

binomial test   Test of a hypothesis about the value of a proportion based on the binomial distribution.

bivariate normal distribution   Joint probability distribution (density function) of two variables in which the conditional distributions for each variable are normal with equal variances and both regression lines are linear.

block   Set of elements (participants, for example) matched on some variable (see **randomized block design**).

Bonferroni procedure   Method of **planned comparison** testing in which the Type-1 error rate per comparison is set as α/k—the error rate per experiment divided by the number of comparisons being tested.

boxplot (box-and-whisker plot)   Graphical depiction of the range and quartiles of a distribution. The box represents the interquartile range, within which the median is marked with a line or asterisk. "Whiskers" are lines extending as far as the most extreme values excluding outliers.

carryover effect   In a within-subjects design, the unwanted influence of a prior condition on a later one.

categorical variable   Variable whose values are category labels.

cell   Condition defined by the joint values of two (or more) values of predictor variables in a factorial or contingency arrangement.

cell frequency   Number of cases falling into the cell of a frequency table.

cell mean   Mean of the observations within a cell of a factorial design.

central limit theorem   Theorem stating that the distribution formed as the sum of independent observations tends to a normal distribution.

chi square (χ^2)   Probability distribution used (among other things) to test hypotheses about categorical data.

Cohen's d   Measure of the size of an effect. It is the difference between two means divided by the standard deviation of the variables.

comparison   Difference between the means of two conditions in an experiment.

completely randomized design   Design in which subjects are assigned randomly and independently among the conditions.

conditional distribution   Distribution of a response variable for a specified value of the predictor variable.

conditional mean   Mean of a conditional distribution.

confidence interval   Range of values that, with a specified probability (e.g., .95), includes the true value of the parameter being estimated.

confidence level   Probability associated with a confidence interval. The term is also used to refer to the *p*-level.

contingency   Dependency between two categorical variables.

contingency coefficient   Measure of the degree of dependency between two categorical variables. The phi (ϕ) coefficient is the most common example.

continuous variable   Variable for which, within a defined range, any numerical value (and thus infinitely many values) is possible.

control group   Condition that establishes a baseline against which other conditions can be compared.

correlation   General term to describe the strength of relationship (and thus predictability) between two quantitative variables.

correlation coefficient   Numerical index (such as the product moment) that quantifies the strength of the relationship between two quantitative variables. See also **Pearson's r**.

count data   Data that consist of frequencies rather than quantities.

covariance   Average **sum of products**.

Cramér's phi coefficient, ϕ_c   Modified version of the **phi coefficient** for contingency tables larger than 2×2.

decile   One of the nine values of a variable that divides a distribution into ten equal areas.

degrees of freedom (*df*)   Number of independent observations on which an estimate is based.

discrete variable   Variable with a limited number of values. See also **continuous variable**.

effect size   See **Cohen's d**.

elementary events   In probability theory, the set of distinct outcomes or events that are taken to be equiprobable.

error rate per comparison In statistical hypothesis testing, the Type-1 error rate for each comparison considered individually.

error rate per experiment In statistical hypothesis testing, the overall Type-1 error rate for the entire set of comparisons made in a single experiment.

estimated standard error of the mean ($s_{\overline{Y}}$) Estimate of the standard deviation of the sampling distribution of the mean.

expected frequency (f_e) Frequency predicted by a null hypothesis.

experimental control Method of controlling unwanted influences by eliminating them or holding them constant across the conditions of an experiment.

experimental design General term referring to the nature and arrangement of conditions of an experiment and the method of assigning subjects to conditions.

explanatory variable Another name for **predictor variable**.

F-distribution Probability distribution used to test the ratio of two mean squares in analysis of variance and regression analyses.

F-ratio Ratio of two independent mean squares, usually calculated in an analysis of variance.

factor In experimental design a factor is a set of conditions belonging to single category. The conditions within this category are called levels of the factor.

factorial arrangement of conditions Arrangement in which each level of one factor is paired with all levels of a second factor.

Fisher's LSD (least significant difference) A post hoc method for testing differences between means. The method presupposes a significant F-ratio. It is the minimum difference needed to obtain a significant t-ratio.

frequency data Values of a categorical variable consisting of frequency counts (see **count data**).

frequency distribution Table or graph that sets out the frequency with which the values of a variable occurs.

frequency polygon Graph of a frequency distribution formed by connecting the points representing frequencies plotted against the midpoint of the class interval.

full model Model that includes all possible parameters.

general replicability Principle that the same conditions should always produce the same pattern of results but not a numerically identical outcome. See also **strict replicability**.

goodness of fit Measure of the size of the residuals after fitting a model.

grand mean Mean of all the observations in an experiment.

histogram Graph of a frequency distribution formed by representing frequencies as rectangular bars.

homogeneity of variance Assumption that the variances of **conditional distributions** are all equal.

HSD (honestly significant difference) A post hoc method for testing differences between means devised by John Tukey. It uses the studentized range statistic (q) to establish the minimum significant difference for a specified error rate per experiment.

independent events or outcomes Events are independent if the occurrence of one event does not change the probability of another event occurring.

independent groups design Experimental design in which subjects within one condition are selected independently from subjects in any other condition.

independent samples Samples drawn such that occurrence of a selection of the members of sample does not change the probability of selection of potential members of the other sample.

interaction Interaction exists when two factors are nonadditive. The effect of one factor is different for different levels of the other factor.

intercept parameter (α) Point at which the regression line crosses the vertical (y-) axis.

interquartile range *(IQR)* Distance between the first and third quartile ($Q_3 - Q_1$).

interval estimate Estimate of a parameter consisting of a range of values. See **confidence interval**.

law of large numbers Law stating that estimates become less variable (become more stable) the larger the sample size.

leaf Part of a stem-and-leaf plot that sets out the right-hand remaining digits of observations that have that **stem**.

least significant difference Smallest difference needed to achieve statistical significance.

least squares estimate Estimate that satisfies the least squares criterion of yielding the minimum value of the sum of squared residuals.

level Specific value of a predictor variable, used especially in the context of factorial designs, as in "levels of a factor."

linear model Model in which the response variable is the weighted *sum* of parameter values. In regression, the weights are the regression coefficients.

linear regression Prediction rule for a quantitative predictor variable consisting of a **linear model**.

linear transformation Transformation involving the addition and/or multiplication by a constant. Transformation to standard scores is an example.

LSD procedure See **Fisher's LSD**.

main effects In analysis of variance, the differences among the means of the levels of one factor averaged over the levels of the other factor(s).

manipulated predictor variable Variable whose levels can be set and controlled by the experimenter. See also **natural predictor variable**.

marginal distribution In a bivariate distribution, the distribution of each variable collapsed over the values of the second variable.

marginal frequency In a contingency table, the set of row totals or the set of column totals.

matched-pair design Design consisting of a set of paired subjects matched on some variable, with one member of each pair in each condition. Each pair difference is thus uninfluenced by the matching variable.

mean Sum of scores divided by the number of scores.

mean square Sum of squares divided by its degrees of freedom.

MS_e The mean square of the residuals. In an independent-groups design MS_e is also called the within-groups mean square, MS_{within}.

$MS_{between}$ In an independent-groups design, the mean square reflecting the variability among the condition means.

$MS_{regression}$ Mean square reflecting the variability accounted for by the regression line.

MS_{within} In an independent groups design, the mean square reflecting the variability among the scores within a condition. See **MS_e**.

median Value that divides a distribution into two equal halves.

mode Most frequently occurring value of a variable.

model Statement that expresses the value of a response variable in terms of its contributing components or parameters.

mutually exclusive categories Categories such that membership in one precludes membership in the other.

mutually exclusive events or **outcomes**   Two events that cannot occur together.

natural variable   Variable whose values are existing attributes, such as age or sex.

nonparametric tests   Statistical tests that do not involve the estimation of the parameters of a sampling distribution and thus do not depend on assumptions about the form of underlying distributions.

normal distribution   Symmetrical, bell-shaped probability distribution (density function). See also **central limit theorem**.

null hypothesis (H_0)   Hypothesis that there is no relationship between the predictor and response variables. The hypothesis takes different forms depending on the nature of the predictor and response variables.

null model   Model stating that there is no relationship between the predictor and response variables.

observed frequency (f_o)   In a chi-square analysis, the number of cases falling into a category or cell

one-tailed test   In statistical hypothesis testing, the location of the rejection region on one side of the sampling distribution.

outlier   Extreme score that is usually discarded before analysis of the data. Commonly defined as a score more extreme than 1.5 *IQR* units above the third quartile or below the first quartile.

parameter (of a model)   True or population value of the terms in a model.

parameters of a distribution   Constants that define the exact shape of a distribution. For a normal distribution, the parameters are the mean and the standard deviation.

parsimony   Principle stating that models should contain as few parameters as possible — no more than the data demand.

Pearson's chi square   Test statistic used to test contingency hypotheses for frequency data.

Pearson's r   Another name for **product-moment correlation coefficient**.

percentile   One of the ninety-nine values of a variable that divides a distribution into one hundred equal areas.

phi coefficient (ϕ)   Measure of the strength of contingency in a chi-square analysis. See also **Cramér's phi**.

planned comparisons   Differences between pairs of means that have been designated in advance for hypothesis testing. Contrast **post hoc comparisons**.

point estimate   Sample-based estimate of a parameter consisting of a single value. See also **interval estimate**.

population   Entire set of potential observations from which a sample has been taken.

post hoc comparisons   Differences between pairs of means that have not been designated in advance for hypothesis testing. See also **planned comparisons**.

power ($1-\beta$)   Probability of correctly rejecting a false null hypothesis.

precision   Amount of residual variance associated with an estimate. The lower the variance, the higher the precision. The standard error or the width of a confidence interval are indicators of precision.

predictor variable   Variable that serves as the basis for predicting values of the **response variable**. Sometimes called independent variable or explanatory variable.

probability   In this text, long-run relative frequency.

probability density   Concentration of probability at a point in a continuous random variable.

probability distribution   Distribution that specifies probabilities over the values of a random variable.

product-moment correlation coefficient   Index of the strength of linear relationship between two continuous random variables.

***p*-value**   In testing the null hypothesis, the probability of obtaining a test statistic (such as t or F) as large or larger than the one obtained. Also called significance level.

quantitative variable   Variable whose values are numbers representing a quantity. See also **categorical variable**.

quartiles   The three values of a variable that divide the distribution into four equal areas. The second quartile is the median.

quasi-experiments   Experiments that have not used random assignment of participants, usually because the predictor variable is **natural** rather than **manipulated**.

R^2   Proportion of the total variance accounted for by the model.

random sample   Sample chosen in such a way that all samples of a given size have an equal chance of being selected.

random selection   Selection for which all elements have an equal probability of being selected.

random variable   Variable on which a probability distribution has been defined, thus enabling probability statements to be made about its values (discrete random variables) or ranges of values (continuous random variables).

randomization   Method of controlling the potentially biasing effect of unwanted influences in an experiment by use of random assignment.

randomized block designs   Extension of the **matched-pair design** using blocks of subjects matched on a relevant variable with one member of the block being randomly assigned to each condition.

range   Difference between the largest and smallest score of a distribution.

rank-order methods   Nonparametric or distribution-free methods that replace scores with their ranks.

regression analysis   Partitioning of the total sum of squares according to a regression model.

regression coefficient   Slope of the regression line (β or its estimate, b). It is the constant in the regression equation by which the predictor variable is multiplied in predicting the response variable.

regression line   Line representing the prediction rule in a regression model.

regression model   Model for predicting the response variable on the basis of a continuous quantitative predictor variable. A special case is **linear regression**.

regression to the mean   Property of a regression model that implies that predicted values of the response variable will be less extreme than the corresponding values of the predictor variable.

regression weight   Another name for the **regression coefficient**.

reject region   In statistical hypothesis testing, the region of the sampling distribution representing outcomes incompatible with the null hypothesis and thus leading to its rejection.

repeated measures (within-subjects) design   Design in which each subject is measured under more than one condition.

residual   Difference between the value predicted by a model and the value actually observed.

residual plot   Graph that plots values of residuals against some other variable such as values of the predictor variable.

resistant statistics   Estimates that are relatively uninfluenced by aberrant features of a distribution such as outliers and skew. Quartiles are resistant statistics, the mean and variance are not.

response variable   Variable representing the observations to be made or predicted. Also known as the dependent variable. Contrasted with **predictor, explanatory,** or **independent variables**.

restriction of range   Sample-selection process or measuring scale that artificially reduces the variance of a distribution.

sample   Measures actually selected from a **population**.

sampling distribution of the mean   Probability distribution defined on the sample mean considered as a random variable thus enabling probability statements to be made about ranges of values of the sample mean.

scatterplot   Graph of a bivariate frequency distribution in which each pair of observations is represented by a dot in the two-dimensional space defined by the two variables.

significance level   In testing the null hypothesis, the probability of obtaining a test statistic (such as t or F) as large as or larger than the one obtained. Also called the p-value.

simultaneous confidence intervals   In experiments with more than two conditions, confidence intervals for which the confidence level (e.g., 95%) refers to the set of intervals considered collectively.

skew (positive and negative)   Degree of asymmetry of a frequency or probability distribution. With positive skew, the distribution is compressed at the low end with an extended tail at the high end. Negative skew is the reverse.

slope parameter (β)   In linear regression, the slope of the regression line, also known as the **regression coefficient**.

$SS_{between}$ In an independent-groups design, the sum of squares reflecting the differences among the condition means. See SS_{model}.

SS_e Sum of squares of the residuals. In an independent-groups design, SS_e is also called the within-groups sum of squares, SS_{within}.

SS_{model} Sum of squares accounted for by the model. In an independent-groups design, SS_{model} is equivalent to the between-groups sum of squares, $SS_{between}$. In a regression analysis it is equivalent to $SS_{regression}$.

$SS_{regression}$ Sum of squares accounted for by the regression line. See SS_{model}.

SS_{total} Sum of squares corresponding to the null model. It is the sum of the squared deviations of each score from the overall mean.

SS_{within} In an independent-groups design, the sum of squares reflecting the differences among the scores within a condition. See SS_e.

standard deviation   Square root of the **variance**.

standard error of the difference between independent means   Standard deviation of the sampling distribution of the difference between two means.

standard error of estimate   In regression analysis, the square root of the mean square of the residuals. It is the standard deviation of the conditional distributions.

standard error of the mean   Standard deviation of the sampling distribution of the mean.

standard error of a regression coefficient   Standard deviation of the sampling distribution of the regression coefficient.

standard score   Score from a distribution scaled to have a mean of zero and a standard deviation of 1.

standardized regression coefficient Regression coefficient (β or its estimate, b) for variables that have been transformed to **standard scores**.

statistics (a) Discipline concerned with the theory and practice underlying the analysis and interpretation of data. (b) Summary measure such as the mean or variance describing the property of data.

stemplot (stem-and-leaf plot) Graphical representation that displays each score in terms of a stem (the leading digit of the observation) and a **leaf**.

strict replicability Principle that the same conditions should always produce a numerically identical outcome. See also **general replicability**.

studentized range distribution Sampling distribution of the **range** of a set of sample means.

sum of products In a bivariate distribution, the sum of the products of pairs of scores expressed as deviations from their mean.

sum of squares Sum of the squared deviations of scores from their mean.

***t*-distribution** Theoretical probability distribution for the *t*-ratio.

***t*-ratio** Random variable formed by dividing the sample mean or the difference between two sample means by its estimated standard error.

total sum of squares See SS_{total}.

Tukey's HSD See **HSD**.

two-tailed test In statistical hypothesis testing, the location of the rejection region on both sides of the sampling distribution. See also **one-tailed test**.

Type-1 error The mistaken rejection of a true null hypothesis—declaring an effect when none exists; a false alarm.

Type-2 error The mistaken acceptance of a false null hypothesis—declaring no effect when one really exists; a miss.

unbiased An estimate is unbiased if its expected value (its long-run average) equals the true value (parameter) it is estimating—there is no systematic tendency for the estimate to be larger or smaller than the true value.

variable Attribute that can have different values.

variance Average squared deviation from the mean.

width of confidence interval Distance between the low and high end of a confidence interval.

within-groups mean square See MS_e.

within-subjects (repeated measures) design Design in which each subject is measured under more than one condition.

***z*-score** Standard score—a score from a distribution scaled to have a mean of zero and a standard deviation of 1.

Answers to Problems and Exercises

Students using computer software may occasionally obtain answers that differ in the final decimal place from those reported here. This rounding error can arise when a final answer uses the results of intermediate computations that have been rounded for the purpose of reporting their values within the text. Direct computation, of course, performs no such intermediate rounding.

CHAPTER 1 Purpose of Statistical Data Analysis

Section 1.1 Overall Goal of Statistical Data Analysis

Problem 1

	F	M	F	M	M	F	F	F	M	M
Model 1	1	−1	1	0	−1	0	1	2	−1	−2
Model 2	0	0	0	1	0	−1	0	1	0	−1
Model 3	−1	1	−1	2	1	−2	−1	0	1	0

Model 2 provides the best fit.

Problem 2 Experiment 1 is noisier.

Problem 3 Lapses of attention, fatigue, varying eye fixation point, varying foot position, etc.

Problem 4 Most choose webbed feet; we know such features to be less variable than nest size.

Section 1.2 Variables

Problem 1 Variables: a, b, f, h. Constants: c, d, e, g

Problem 2 Manipulated: b, e, f, h. Natural: a, c, d, g, i, j.

Problem 3

		Response Variable	
		Categorical	Quantitative
Manipulated predictor variable	Categorical	Study 7	Study 1
	Quantitative	Study 3	Study 4
Natural predictor variable	Categorical	Study 6	Study 8
	Quantitative	Study 2	Study 5

Exercises

Exercise 1 a. Number of visits. b. Categorical. c. Manipulated. d. One and two visits. e. Compliance. f. Categorical. g. Agree, disagree.

Exercise 2 a. Reward information. b. Categorical. c. Manipulated. d. Some versus none. e. Time spent drawing. f. Quantitative.

Exercise 3 a. Gesture shown to infant. b. Categorical. c. Manipulated. d. Lip protrusion, mouth opening, tongue protrusion, finger movements. e. Response gesture. f. Categorical. g. Lip protrusion, mouth opening, tongue protrusion, finger movements, hand opening, finger protrusion, passive hand. h. The highest frequency in each column is in the row corresponding to a response that is the same as the gesture. That is, the single most frequent response is imitation.

Exercise 4 a. Surface texture of pacifier. b. Categorical. c. Manipulated. d. Smooth and "nubbled." e. Proportion of total looking time the infant spends looking at the tactually familiar object. f. Quantitative. g. The quantity A is the proportion of time above (or below) the chance level of 50% that each infant displays.

Exercise 5 a. Retention interval. b. Quantitative. c. Manipulated. d. 3, 6, 9, 12, 15, and 18 seconds. e. Proportion of items correctly recalled. f. Quantitative. g. A prediction for a retention interval of 10 seconds would be based on a model containing a function (equation) that expresses the proportion of correct items recalled as a continuous function of the retention interval.

Exercise 6 a. Instructions. b. Categorical. c. Manipulated. d. Normal, mnemonic. e. Number of words correctly recalled. f. Quantitative.

Quiz model, natural, quantitative, categorical, explanatory variable, manipulated categorical predictor, quantitative response, model, residual, residual, 2%, parsimonious, general replicability, strict replicability, bias, confounding, randomly, continuous, discrete.

CHAPTER 2 Graphical and Numerical Descriptions of Data

Section 2.1 Displaying Data as Distributions of Frequencies
Problem 1

Code	H	Su	Sa	A	D	F
Frequency	8	20	2	5	4	11

Problem 2 Use the following back-to-back stemplots and frequency counts to check your answer. Your histogram should have the same class intervals as these stemplots.

f	Opposite sex		Same sex	f
1	3	1		
1	5	1		
2	76	1		
4	9998	1		
5	11000	2		
6	322222	2	2	1
3	444	2	5	1
5	76666	2	777	3
3	998	2	8888999	7
		3	0001	4
		3	222233	6
		3	4555	4
		3	677	3
		3	9	1

Problem 3 a. 22 students obtained a mark higher than 81. 14 students obtained a mark lower than 56.

Interval	f
95–99	2
90–94	6
85–89	6
80–84	12
75–79	23
70–74	19
65–69	21
60–64	16
55–59	17
50–54	5
45–49	4
40–44	4

b. Histogram or frequency polygon. The mark of 81 falls into the class interval 80–84. The number of marks falling above this interval is $6 + 6 + 2 = 14$.

Problem 4 (A) Note positive skew. (B) Note three possible outliers (14, 15, 15). (C) The distribution is "healthy." (D) Note negative skew. (E) Note negative skew. (F) The distribution is "healthy." (G) Note positive skew. (H) The distribution is bimodal. (I) The distribution has three possible outliers (5, 5, 7).

Section 2.2 Numerical Descriptions of Frequency Distributions

Problem 1 Mode = C-grade.

Problem 2 Means: 31.0 (same-sex); 22.0 (opposite-sex). Medians: 30.5 (same-sex); 22.0 (opposite-sex).

Problem 3 Same-sex: $-2, -6, 6, 6, 3, -3, -2, 4, 4, -1, -3, 1, -2, -1, -4, 2, 4, -1, -3, 0, -3, -4, -9, 2, 1, 5, 1, -4, 1, 8$. Different-sex: $2, -1, 6, 0, -2, -2, 2, -7, 4, -9, 5, 7, 0, 0, 4, 4, 4, -1, 0, -3, 0, -4, -5, -6, -2, 7, 2, 1, -3, -3$.

Problem 4 The actual means are A 8.6, B 7.7, C 9.9, D 11.4, E 11.4, F 10.1, G 8.2, H 9.6, I 12.2.

Problem 5 Sets 4 and 10 have incorrect means. Both these means should be 37.

Problem 6 $IQR = 111 - 92 = 19$.

Problem 7

Y_A	$Y_A - \bar{Y}_A$	$(Y_A - \bar{Y}_A)^2$	Y_B	$Y_B - \bar{Y}_B$	$(Y_B - \bar{Y}_B)^2$
11	1	1	16	6	36
10	0	0	10	0	0
8	−2	4	7	−3	9
10	0	0	8	−2	4
9	−1	1	13	3	9
10	0	0	5	−5	25
9	−1	1	11	1	1
10	0	0	12	2	4
9	−1	1	10	0	0
10	0	0	7	−3	9
12	2	4	14	4	16
11	1	1	6	−4	16
9	−1	1	11	1	1
11	1	1	9	−1	1
10	0	0	12	2	4
9	−1	1	10	0	0
10	0	0	11	1	1
9	−1	1	9	−1	1
10	0	0	15	5	25
11	1	1	10	0	0
10	0	0	9	−1	1
9	−1	1	12	2	4
12	2	4	7	−3	9
10	0	0	10	0	0
11	1	1	6	−4	16
Sums	0	24	Sums	0	192

Variance of $Y_A = 24/24 = 1.0$, standard deviation $= \sqrt{1.0} = 1.0$.
Variance of $Y_B = 192/24 = 8.0$, standard deviation $= \sqrt{8.0} = 2.83$.

Problem 8 1. Set 5. 2. Set 1. 3. Set 4. 4. Set 1. 5. Set 2. 6. Set 5. 7. Set 7. 8. Set 8. The actual standard deviations: Set 1. 16.5, Set 2. 12.2, Set 3. 4.1, Set 4. 10.4, Set 5. 14.6, Set 6. 2.2, 6.2, Set 7. 8.2.

Problem 9 The actual means and standard deviations for the five data sets: Set 1 48, **8**; Set 2 15, **2**; Set 3 25, 6; Set 4 12, 3; Set 5 **37**, 5. Values in bold type are the correct values for errors in the original table.

Problem 10 a. Set 4 shows bimodality, so both mean and median would be a poor measure of centrality. b. Set 2 and Set 5 have possible high outliers and/or positive skew, so for these distributions the mean should be greater than the median. c. Set 3 shows negative skew, so the median should be greater than the mean for these data.

Problem 11 In Data Set 2, the values 113, 117, and 122 are outliers. In Data Set 3, the value 35 is an outlier. In Data Set 5, the values 156, 169, and 214 are outliers.

Problem 12 The five boxplots are shown in Figure B.1. Sets 2, 3 and 5 have outliers.

Problem 13 Use the median. There are four low-end outliers. Their impact will be greater for the mean. In fact, the mean is 177.4 and the median is 180.5 centimeters.

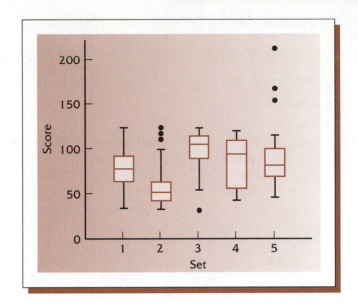

Figure B.1
Boxplots for Section 2.2, Problem 12.

Problem 14 Distributions of house prices are often positively skewed. Positive skew results in a higher mean than median.

Problem 15 Rogers's joke is at the expense of Californians. Whereas those people migrating were below average relative to Oklahomans, they were above average relative to Californians.

Section 2.3   Linear Transformations of Scale and z-scores

Problem 1 (a) and (c) are linear transformations; (b) is not.

Problem 2

Ounces	Grams	Time	Speed	Frequency	Proportion	Area (A)	Circumference (C)
1.7	48.2	1.9	.53	93	.78	55	26.3
1.4	39.7	1.6	.62	104	.87	38	21.8
1.3	36.9	2.8	.36	76	.63	25	17.7
0.9	25.5	0.9	1.11	88	.73	48	24.6
2.1	59.5	2.3	.43	95	.79	45	23.8
0.7	19.8	1.7	.59	80	.67	30	19.4

Note: Your graph for area and circumference may *appear* linear; however, a careful examination of the points will reveal curvature. This curvature would become more apparent with a wider range of area values.

Problem 3 a. $\overline{Y} = 658$ milliseconds; $s_Y = 284$ milliseconds. b. $\overline{Y} = .56$; $s_Y = .166$.

Problem 4

Y	5	8	7	10	9	11	6	10	6	8
z	−1.5	0	−0.5	1.0	0.5	1.5	−1.0	1.0	−1.0	0

Problem 5 a. 2.44; −1.11; −2.00. b. $\overline{Y} = .625$; $s_Y^2 = 0.0127$. c. All transformations are linear.

Problem 6 $z_{math} = -0.29$, $z_{chem} = -0.83$. Math is therefore the better score.

Problem 7

Y	5	8	7	10	9	11	6	10	6	8
T	35	50	45	60	55	65	40	60	40	50

Problem 8 $Y = 60$ gives a z-score of -0.857; this converts to a T-score of 41.43.

Exercises

Exercise 1 a.

	One-visit group	Two-visit group	Totals
Agreed	9	21	30
Refused	31	19	50
Totals	40	40	80

b. You should have plotted a bar chart with two separated bars, one for the one-visit condition, the other for the two-visit condition. Plot "proportion agreeing" on the vertical axis. For the one-visit condition the height should be .225 (9/40), and for the two-visit condition the height should be .525 (21/40). c. In order to gain some sense of whether the results support the prediction of attribution theory you would look for a difference in the proportion of participants agreeing in the two conditions.

Exercise 2 a. payment; categorical; manipulated; $1 versus $100; enjoyment rating; quantitative. b. These data are free of skew, bimodality, and outliers. c. For the $1 condition, $\overline{Y} = 5.0$. For the $100 condition, $\overline{Y} = 6.0$. d. For the $1 condition, the Md = 5.0, Mo = 6. For the $100 condition, Md = 6.0, Mo = 5. e. For the $1 condition, $s^2 = 3.565$. For the $100 condition, $s^2 = 2.522$

Exercise 3 a.

	Reward		No reward
0	0	2	5
1	99	⋮	⋮
2	34	7	5
3	7	8	249
4	7	9	4678
5	225	10	15688
6	05	11	335
7	2889	12	6
8	58	13	8
⋮		⋮	
16	0		

In the reward condition, the score of 16.0 appears to be an outlier. In the no-reward condition, the score of 2.5 appears to be an outlier.

b. Reward: $IQR = 7.8 - 2.4 = 5.4$. no reward: $IQR = 11.3 - 8.9 = 2.4$.

c. In the reward condition, 16.0 is an outlier; in the no-reward condition, 2.5 is an outlier.

d. See Figure B.2.

e. In the reward condition, the variance is 12.75; in the no-reward condition, the variance is 5.5.

f. Reward: $IQR = 7.8 - 2.4 = 5.4$; no reward $IQR = 11.3 - 9.3 = 2.0$.

g. The effect of removing outliers on the standard deviation is greater than its effect on the IQR. This reflects the fact that IQR is a resistant statistic, whereas the standard deviation is strongly influenced by outliers. Similarly, the median is a resistant statistic, whereas the mean is strongly influenced by outliers.

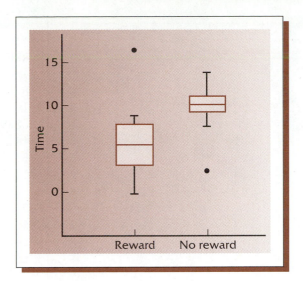

Figure B.2
Boxplots for Chapter 2, Exercise 3d

Exercise 4 a. The figures should be bar graphs (separated bars), with the vertical axis indicating response frequency. The height of each bar indicates the frequency of each of the gestural responses. There should be one graph for each of the four stimulus conditions. b. The statistic you would use to describe the center of these four distributions is the mode. c. These modes support the hypothesis of imitation. (See Chapter 1 analysis of this data set.)

Exercise 5 a.

3	3
3	79
4	124
4	55678
5	3
5	79
6	0233
6	6
7	34
7	57
8	114
8	55677
9	02344
9	5666

The stemplot shows negative skew but no outliers, and although there is a slight suggestion of bimodality, the low-end peak seems more likely to be a consequence of the negative skew.

b. The actual mean and standard deviation are 69.3 and 20.5, respectively.

c. The median is 73.5. This value is greater than the mean, reflecting the negative skew.

d. The standard deviation is 20.5. The impact of the negative skew makes the actual standard deviation greater than it might seem from a casual inspection of the data.

Exercise 6 a. face; categorical; manipulated; mother versus stranger; percentage of time spent looking at mother's face; quantitative.

b.

1	8
2	1
2	889
3	
3	8
4	1
4	6889
5	113
5	556788999
6	1234
6	56778
7	23
7	5668
8	24
8	66779
9	223

c. Md = 61.5; Q_1 = 51; Q_3 = 76

d. IQR = 76 − 51 = 25.

e. See Figure B.3.

Exercise 7 a.

Group 1		Group 2
0	**0**	3
8	**0**	89
331	**1**	2334
986	**1**	6889
32110	**2**	024
865	**2**	56789
421	**3**	34
6	**3**	56
100	**4**	⋮
⋮	**4**	⋮
⋮		⋮
	7	0
9	**7**	

The observations 79 and 70 are outliers.

b. See Figure B.4.

c. Group 1: $\overline{Y}$ = 23.4; Group 2: $\overline{Y}$ = 21.0. These values can be obtained by multiplying the original means by 24 to get the total, subtracting the outlier, and then dividing by 23.

d. Group 1: s^2 = 117.2, s = 10.8; Group 2: s^2 = 85.3, s = 9.2. Including the outliers you should have estimated larger values. In fact, Group 1: s^2 = 240.9, s = 15.5; Group 2: s^2 = 181.8, s = 13.5.

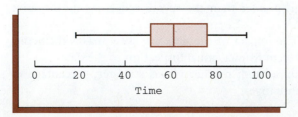

Figure B.3
Boxplot for Chapter 2, Exercise 6e

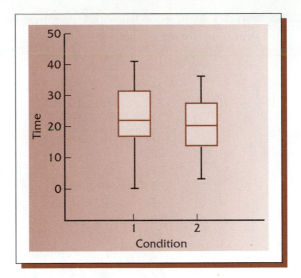

Figure B.4
Boxplots for Chapter 2, Exercise 2b

Exercise 8 a. Class interval width = 5. b. A twins: $IQR = 110 - 91 = 19$. B twins: $IQR = 112 - 90 = 22$. c. Using the $1.5 \times IQR$ criterion, there are no outliers.

Exercise 9 a. Class interval width = 2. b. For verbal $IQR = 35.0 - 28.0 = 7.0$; for performance, $IQR = 33.0 - 26.5 = 6.5$. c. Using the $1.5 \times IQR$ criterion, there are four outliers in each set. For verbal, the outliers are 9, 13, 17, and 17. For performance, the outliers are 61, 64, 66, and 69.

Quiz interquartile range, third quartile, outliers, resistant statistic, mean, positively skewed, linear transformation, linear transformation, mean, standard deviation, standard scores, mean square, sum of squares, degrees of freedom.

CHAPTER 3 Modeling Data and the Estimation of Parameters

Section 3.1 Imperfect Predictions, Models, and Residuals
Problem 1 a. Residuals: -31, 15, -3, -16, 1, -25, 37, 26, 4, -8. $s^2 = 466.9$; $s = 21.6$. b. $Y_4 = 470 = 486 - 16$. c. Trial 5 has the smallest residual, trial 7 the largest.

Section 3.2 Estimating the Parameters of a Model
Problem 2 a. The population is the imaginary (hypothetical) one of an infinitely large number of hypothetical tosses. Assuming the coin to be fair, the population proportion of heads would be .5.

Section 3.3 Fitting Models with Categorical Predictor Variables

Problems 1 and 2 The null model is $H_0: \mu_1 = \mu_2 = \mu$

Y_1	e_{full}	e_{null}	Y_2	e_{full}	e_{null}
29	−2	2.5	24	2	−2.5
25	−6	−1.5	21	−1	−5.5
37	6	10.5	28	6	1.5
37	6	10.5	22	0	−4.5
34	3	7.5	20	−2	−6.5
28	−3	1.5	20	−2	−6.5
29	−2	2.5	24	2	−2.5
35	4	8.5	15	−7	−11.5
35	4	8.5	26	4	−.5
30	−1	3.5	13	−9	−13.5
28	−3	1.5	27	5	.5
32	1	5.5	29	7	2.5
29	−2	2.5	22	0	−4.5
30	−1	3.5	22	0	−4.5
27	−4	.5	26	4	−.5
33	2	6.5	26	4	−.5
35	4	8.5	26	4	−.5
30	−1	3.5	21	−1	−5.5
28	−3	1.5	22	0	−4.5
31	0	4.5	19	−3	−7.5
28	−3	1.5	22	0	−4.5
27	−4	.5	18	−4	−8.5
22	−9	−4.5	17	−5	−9.5
33	2	6.5	16	−6	−10.5
32	1	5.5	20	−2	−6.5
36	5	9.5	29	7	2.5
32	1	5.5	24	2	−2.5
27	−4	.5	23	1	−3.5
32	1	5.5	19	−3	−7.5
39	8	12.5	19	−3	−7.5

Problem 3 a. $MS_e = 930/58 = 16.03$. b. $\hat{d} = 2.25$.

Problem 4 a. Predictor variable: SAT; response variable: GPA; quantitative. b. Predictor variable: treatment; response variable: level of hyperactivity; categorical. c. Predictor variable: age; response variable: vocabulary size; quantitative.

Exercises

Exercise 1 a. $\bar{Y}_1 = 5.0$; $\bar{Y}_2 = 6.0$; $\bar{Y} = 5.5$.

Y_1	$\bar{Y}_1$	e(full)	e(null)	Y_2	$\bar{Y}_2$	e(full)	e(null)
7	5	2	1.5	5	6	−1	−.5
7	5	2	1.5	5	6	−1	−.5
2	5	−3	−3.5	9	6	3	3.5
4	5	−1	−1.5	4	6	−2	−1.5
4	5	−1	−1.5	6	6	0	.5
3	5	−2	−2.5	5	6	−1	−.5
6	5	1	.5	6	6	0	.5
6	5	1	.5	8	6	2	2.5
6	5	1	.5	6	6	0	.5
6	5	1	.5	8	6	2	2.5
5	5	0	−.5	6	6	0	.5
5	5	0	−.5	7	6	1	1.5
7	5	2	1.5	4	6	−2	−1.5
6	5	1	.5	9	6	3	3.5
5	5	0	−.5	4	6	−2	−1.5
4	5	−1	−1.5	7	6	1	1.5
6	5	1	.5	5	6	−1	−.5
5	5	0	−.5	3	6	−3	−2.5
9	5	4	3.5	7	6	1	1.5
3	5	−2	−2.5	7	6	1	1.5
3	5	−2	−2.5	5	6	−1	−.5
7	5	2	1.5	5	6	−1	−.5
3	5	−2	−2.5	7	6	1	1.5
1	5	−4	−4.5	6	6	0	.5

b. $SS_1 = 82.0$; $SS_2 = 58.0$.   d. $SS_e = (82 + 58) = 140$. $MS_e = 140/46 = 3.04$.
e.   The null model: $Y_1 = Y_2 = \mu + e$.   f.   See the table.   g. $SS_{total} = 152.0$.
h. $\hat{d} = -1/1.74 = -0.57$.

Exercise 2 a. For the reward condition, $SS = 6.98 \times 17 = 118.66$; for the no-reward condition, $SS = 2.43 \times 17 = 41.31$. b. $MS_e = 4.705$. This averaging is questionable because the two variances appear to be unequal (6.98 versus 2.43). c. For Exercise 2, $\hat{d} = -5.09/2.17 = -2.35$. For Exercise 1, $\hat{d} = -0.57$. Therefore the experiment in Exercise 2 has the larger estimated effect size.

Exercise 3 a. degree of threat; predictor variable is being treated as categorical; manipulated; mild and severe threat; rated desirability; quantitative. b. Severe threat data show slight negative skew. The hint of bimodality for the severe threat data is not serious: The peak at 6 is created by a single observation that gives a frequency of 4. With a frequency of 3 there would be no peak. There are no outliers. c. Full model: $Y_1 = \mu_1 + e$; $Y_2 = \mu_2 + e$; the estimate of μ_1 is $\bar{Y}_1 = 6.3$; the estimate of μ_2 is $\bar{Y}_2 = 7.8$. d. Null hypothesis model: $Y_1 = Y_2 = \mu + e$. The estimate of μ is $\bar{Y} = 7.05$. e. For a score of 5 in the mild threat condition, $e = -1.3$ (full model) and $e = -2.05$ (null model); for a score of 9 in the severe threat condition $e = 1.2$ (full model) and $e = 1.95$ (null model). f. $MS_e = 2.932$. g. $\hat{d} = -1.5/1.712 = -0.876$. These results appear to support the prediction.

Quiz sample, population, parameters, least squares, point estimates, SS_e, goodness of fit, degrees of freedom, mean square, MS_e, homogeneity of variance, null model, SS_{total}, full model, SS_e, SS_{model}, SS_{total}, R^2.

CHAPTER 4   Probability Distributions

Section 4.1   The Law of Large Numbers and the Meaning of Probability

Problem 1 Because the student knows most of the material, the true outcome would be a passing grade. She therefore wants a small residual. The student should prefer a 50-item test over a 10-item test on the grounds that on the longer test (larger sample of answers) it is less likely that the result will be divergent from the true outcome.

Problem 2 Candidate A. If we assume the opinion poll to be accurate, and that there is no last-minute issue to change the 5% lead for candidate A, the only hope for candidate B is that the actual vote differs from the "true" value. Such a discrepancy is more likely in a small sample (small voter turnout). Candidate A, on the other hand, would like the actual vote to be close to the true value and so would prefer a large voter turnout.

Problem 3 a. Answer this question by rephrasing it: Who is less likely to obtain fewer than 40% heads? Jane. b. Jane's. Because of her larger sample, her residual of 10% is less likely to have arisen from a fair coin.

Problem 4 The scores over this range are not equally probable. There are more elementary outcomes for some totals than others. For example, only one outcome produces 2 (1,1), but four distinct outcomes produce 5 (1,4; 2;3; 4;1; 3;2).

Problem 5 The probability that sports will be the randomly selected area is $1/5 = .2$. A device suitable for TV that would assure the viewing audience that the selection was truly random is one that is commonly used—a wheel of fortune.

Section 4.2   Discrete Probability Distributions

Problem 1 The counselor needs to know the probability that the number of suicides could be as large as 15 "just by chance" when the expected number is 10. A small probability would suggest unusual circumstances rather than normal a fluctuation.

Problem 3 a. .137. b. .076. c. .787.

Section 4.3   Central Limit Theorem and the Normal Distribution

Problem 1 Time is a continuous variable; John should state a range of travel times.

Problem 2 The total weight of people in an elevator. The important properties are that the total be formed by taking the sum of a number of independent elements, such as individual weights.

Problem 3 The mode of this distribution would be 69 inches, assuming the distribution to be symmetrical. The interval 68.0 to 70.0 inches would include the height of the greater number of men. This interval (which surrounds the mean) spans a region of higher probability density.

Section 4.4   Obtaining Probabilities for Normally Distributed Variables

Problem 1 a. $P(z < -1.0) = .1587$; b. $P(z < 0.5) = .6915$; c. $P(z < -1.5) = .0668$; d. $P(z > -0.5) = .6915$; e. $P(z < -0.7) = .2420$; f. $P(z < 1.96) = .9750$; g. $P(-1.5 < z < -0.5) = .2417$; h. $P(-.67 < z < .67) = .4972$; i. $P(-1.65 < z < 1.65) = .9010$; j. $P(-2.0 < z < 2.0) = .9544$; k. $P(-.25 < z < .25) = .1974$; l. $P(-1.96 < z < 1.96) = .9500$.

Problem 2 a. .1587, b. .0228, c. .1587, d. .8413, e. .0548, f. .3085, g. .2119, h. .0250, i. .1587, j. .4448, k. .3830, l. .6826, m. .8764, n. .7154, o. .9500, p. .4972, q. .7994, r. .5704.

Problem 3 The 6th, 8th and 9th deciles correspond to scores of 52, 57, and 60 respectively (rounded to the nearest whole number).

Exercises

Exercise 1 a. Score = 550: $z = .5$; $P(z) = .6915$; percentile rank = 69. Score = 480: $z = -.2$; $P(z) = .4207$; percentile rank = 42. Score = 370: $z = -1.3$; $P(z) = .0968$; percentile rank = 10. Score = 680: $z = 1.8$; $P(z) = .9641$; percentile rank = 96. b. $Q_1 = -.67 \times 100 + 500 = 433$; $Q_3 = .67 \times 100 + 500 = 567$; $IQR = 567 - 433 = 134$. c. $d_1 = 372$, $d_2 = 416$, $d_3 = 448$, $d_4 = 475$ $d_5 = 500$, $d_6 = 525$ $d_7 = 552$, $d_8 = 584$ $d_9 = 628$.

Exercise 2 a. 125 b. $Q_1 = 90$, $Q_3 = 110$, thus $IQR = 20$ c. 50%.

Exercise 3 Differences reflect the fact that estimates based on samples (statistics) will not typically equal their population counterparts.

Quiz 1. discrete random, binomial, law of large numbers, long-run relative frequency, continuous random, normal distribution, parameters, probability density. 2. T, F, F, T, F.

CHAPTER 5 Sampling Distributions and Internal Estimation

Section 5.1 Sampling Distribution of the Mean

Problem 1

Parameter set	a	b	c	d	e	f	g	h	i	j
$\sigma_{\bar{Y}}$	.50	.30	1.33	.50	.56	.63	1.69	.37	.58	.54
Probability	.1587	.8413	.0668	.9772	.0367	.0559	.1190	.9115	.6985	.7704

Parameter set	k	l	m	n	o	p	q	r	s	t
$\sigma_{\bar{Y}}$	.66	.13	.20	1.58	.41	2.01	.59	1.15	.48	2.69
Probability	.8714	.8764	.8664	.9426	.7776	.3830	.9090	.3078	.6911	.4686

Problem 2 a. No. b. The smaller. c. The smaller. d. The larger. e. (i) 22.36 (ii) 14.14; (f) (i) $Q_1 = 485$; $Q_3 = 515$; $IQR = 30$. (ii) For $n = 50$ $Q_1 = 490.5$; $Q_3 = 509.5$; $IQR = 19$. The larger the sample, the closer the sample mean is likely to be to 500. With $n = 50$ the sample means will be more closely packed around 500 than with $n = 20$. Thus, in the former case, a narrower range than would be needed for the more spread-out sample means for $n = 20$ will cover 50% of cases. (g) With $n = 20$, 510 gives $z = 10/22.36 = 0.45$; with $n = 50$, 510 gives $z = 10/14.14 = 0.71$. Using the tables of the normal curve, the corresponding probabilities are .3264 and .2389. With $n = 20$, 485 gives $z = -15/22.36 = -0.67$; with $n = 50$, 485 gives $z = -15/14.14 = -1.06$. The corresponding probabilities are .2514 and .1446. For (d) use the results from (b). With $n = 20$ the probability is .3472. With $n = 50$ the probability is .5222.

Section 5.2 Calculating Confidence Intervals

Problem 1 a. $\mathbf{CI}_{.95} = 6.0 \pm 1.40 \times 2.023 = 6.0 \pm 2.83 = 3.17$ to 8.83. b. (i) The lower bound of the 90% confidence interval would be greater than 3.17. (ii) The upper bound of the 99% confidence interval would be greater than 8.83. (iii) $\mathbf{CI}_{.90} = 6.0 \pm 1.40 \times 1.685 = 3.64$ to 8.36; $\mathbf{CI}_{.99} = 6.0 \pm 1.40 \times 2.708 = 2.21$ to 9.79.

Problem 2 a. $\mathbf{CI}_{.90} = 7.2 \pm 1.596 \times 1.685 = 4.51$ to 9.89. b. The calculation of the boundaries of the confidence interval is based on sample estimates of the mean and the variance. Because these estimates will have different values from one sample to another, so too will the boundaries of the confidence interval.

Section 5.3 Interpreting Confidence Intervals

Problem 1 For population A, $CI_{.95} = 645 \pm 2.59 \times 2.262 = 645 \pm 5.86 = 639.14$ to 650.86. For population B, $CI_{.95} = 551 \pm 35.80 \times 2.262 = 551 \pm 81.0 = 470.0$ to 632.0.

Problem 2 a. The interval must be wider than $CI_{.90}$ but still centered on 7.2. Thus the correct answer is 3.97 to 10.43. b. The correct answer is 2.88 to 11.52. c. Statement 3 is the one that most clearly assigns the sampling variation to the interval itself. d. None of the confidence intervals includes the value zero. In this sense they state that $\mu = 0$ is not a plausible claim. Therefore the data support the existence of the phenomenon.

Exercises

Exercise 1 a and b. Intermodal matching: $s_{\bar{Y}} = 3.246$, $CI_{.95} = 69.27 \pm 2.023 \times 3.246 = 69.27 \pm 6.57 = 62.70$ to 75.84. Face recognition: $s_{\bar{Y}} = 2.771$, $CI_{.95} = 62.00 \pm 2.021 \times 2.771 = 62.00 \pm 5.60 = 56.40$ to 67.60. c. Intermodal matching: $s_{\bar{Y}} = 3.246$, $CI_{.99} = 69.27 \pm 2.708 \times 3.246 = 69.27 \pm 8.79 = 60.48$ to 78.06. Face recognition: $s_{\bar{Y}} = 2.771$, $CI_{.99} = 62.00 \pm 2.704 \times 2.771 = 62.00 \pm 7.49 = 54.51$ to 69.49. (Note: For $df = 47$ in face recognition, the tabled value for $df = 40$ has been used.)

Exercise 2 a.

1	5677
2	3578
3	04567
4	22356778899
5	11233669
6	11147789
7	037889
8	137
9	8

The data show no abnormalities. b. $s_{\bar{Y}} = 2.858$ c. $CI_{.95} = 51.98 \pm 2.021 \times 2.858 = 51.98 \pm 5.78 = 46.20 - 57.76$. (Note: The tabled value for $df = 40$ has been used.)

Exercise 3 The confidence intervals for intermodal matching, and face recognition did not include the 50% value; thus 50% is an "unlikely" value for the true percentage. In these two cases the data indicate that the infant can discriminate. For the role of smell, the confidence interval includes 50% and thus the possibility that the true percentage is 50 (guessing or nondiscrimination) remains plausible.

Quiz 1. random variable, sampling distribution, normal distribution, central limit theorem, standard error, standard deviation, n, standard deviation, z-score, normal distribution, t-ratio, t-distribution. **3.** Narrower. **4.** (iii).

CHAPTER 6 Experiments with Two Independent Groups

Section 6.1 Independent-Groups Design

Problem 1 Assignment of participants to the two conditions is not independent; once one sibling has been assigned to one condition the second sibling must be assigned to the other condition.

Problem 2 The sex comparison is a natural predictor variable and thus a quasi-experiment. Causal interpretation would thus be speculative. There are many other attributes (social influences, for example) correlated with sex roles that would also be possible explanations for any obtained difference.

Section 6.2 Analyzing Data from Independent-Groups Designs with Two Treatments

Problem 1 a. $df = 34$. b. $s_{\bar{Y}_1 - \bar{Y}_2} = 0.626$, $\text{CI}_{.95} = 1.7 \pm 0.626 \times 2.032 = 0.43$ to 2.97, $\text{CI}_{.99} = 1.7 \pm 0.626 \times 2.728 = -0.01$ to 3.41. c. Based on the 95% confidence interval, the results support the claim that an induced facial expression such as frowning can change mood. The 95% confidence interval does not include the value of zero, so in this sense it is unlikely that the data have come from a population in which the true difference is zero. Notice that a different conclusion would be drawn from the 99% confidence interval.

Problem 2 a. $df = 50$. b. $s_{\bar{Y}_1 - \bar{Y}_2} = 0.826$, $\text{CI}_{.95} = 0.5 \pm 0.826 \times 2.009 = -1.16$ to 2.16.b, $\text{CI}_{.90} = 0.5 \pm 0.826 \times 1.676 = -0.88$ to 1.88. c. Based on the 95% confidence interval, the results do not support the claim that intentional and incidental study differ in their effectiveness for subsequent remembering. Because zero lies with the confidence interval, the data are quite compatible with a true difference of zero.

Section 6.3 Deciding Between Models Using the *t*-Distribution Directly

Problem 1 a. $t = 1.7/0.626 = 2.7$. b. $.01 < p < .05$. c. Reject the null hypothesis, using .05 as the criterion for significance. d. The difference of 1.7 between the means has an estimated standard error of 0.626. This gives $t(34) = 2.7$; $p < .05$. The data provide evidence that an increase in anger can be induced through a facial expression.

Problem 2 a. $t = 0.6$. b. $p > .10$. c. Do not reject the null hypothesis. d. The difference between the means of 0.5 has an estimated standard error of 0.826. This gives $t(50) = 0.6$; $p > .1$. The data provide no evidence of a difference between intentional and incidental remembering.

Problem 3 a. $t(42) = 5.6$; $p < .01$, so a full model is required. b. The data provide evidence of a difference between the two forms of incidental remembering.

Section 6.4 Decision Error Rates: The Neyman-Pearson Tradition

Problem 1 Problems 1 and 3 of Comprehension Check 6.3 led to a rejection of the null hypothesis, so a Type-1 error is a logical possibility. Problem 2 did not reject the null hypothesis, so a Type-2 error is a possibility.

Problem 2 a. $H_0: \mu_1 = \mu_2$. b. $H_1: \mu_1 \neq \mu_2$. c. Your sketch should show a rejection region in each tail beyond $t = \pm 2.021$ and an acceptance region in the area between $t = \pm 2.021$. (Note: The critical values of t are based on $df = 40$, the closest tabled value below $df = 44$.) d. $t(44) = (11.7 - 7.2)/1.55 = 2.90$. This value is greater than the critical value of 2.021 and thus falls into the rejection region.

Problem 3 a. Your sketch should show a rejection region in each tail beyond $t = \pm 2.000$ and an acceptance region in the area between $t = \pm 2.000$. b. $t(60) = |13.7 - 17.8|/1.71 = 2.40$. This value is greater than the critical value of 2.000 and thus falls into the rejection region. c. Recall is better under the self-reference incidental orienting task than under intentional instructions.

Section 6.5 Overview and Evaluation

Problem

Experiment	MS_e	$s_{\bar{Y}_1 - \bar{Y}_2}$	df	$t_{.95}$	t	p-value	$|\hat{d}|$	$CI_{.95}$ for $|\mu_1 - \mu_2|$	R^2
Induced happiness	31.21	1.77	38	2.024	2.26	$<.05$	0.72	.42—7.58	.12
Induced anger		3.53	0.63	34	2.032	2.70	$<.05$	0.90	0.42—2.98.	.18
Intentional vs. incidental remembering	8.87	0.83	50	2.009	0.61	$>.10$	0.17	−1.17—2.17	.01
Two levels of incidental remembering	9.68	0.94	42	2.021	5.64	$<.01$	1.70	3.40—7.20	.43
Social interaction	16.03	1.03	58	2.009	8.74	$<.01$	2.25	6.93—11.07	.57

Exercises

Exercise 1 1. H_0: $\mu_1 = \mu_2$; model: $Y_i = \mu + e$. H_1: $\mu_1 \neq \mu_2$; model: $Y_i = \mu_i + e$. 2. $df = 46$; $t_{.95} = 2.021$ (using $df = 40$). 3. a. $\hat{d} = 0.57$ b. $R^2 = .08$ c. $CI_{.95}$: $1.0 \pm .504 \times 2.021 = 1.0 \pm 1.02 = -0.02$ to 2.02. d. $t(46) = 1.98$ (or -1.98); $p > .05$. 4. With $\alpha = .05$, do not reject H_0.

Exercise 2 1. H_0: $\mu_1 = \mu_2$; model: $Y_i = \mu + e$. H_1: $\mu_1 \neq \mu_2$; model: $Y_i = \mu_i + e$. 2. $df = 34$; $t_{.95} = 2.032$. 3. a. $\hat{d} = 2.35$. b. $R^2 = .59$. c. $CI_{.95}$: $5.09 \pm .723 \times 2.032 = 5.09 \pm 1.47 = 3.62$ to 6.56 d. 4. $t(34) = 7.04$. 4. With $\alpha = .05$, reject H_0.

Exercise 3 1. H_0: $\mu_1 = \mu_2$; model: $Y_i = \mu + e$. H_1: $\mu_1 \neq \mu_2$; model: $Y_i = \mu_i + e$. 2. $df = 38$; $t_{.95} = 2.024$. 3. a. $\hat{d} = 0.88$. b. $R^2 = .17$. c. $CI_{.95}$: $1.5 \pm .5415 \times 2.024 = 1.50 \pm 1.10 = 0.40$ to 2.60. d. 4. $t(38) = 2.77$. 4. With $\alpha = .05$, reject H_0.

Exercise 4 1. H_0: $\mu_1 = \mu_2$; model: $Y_i = \mu + e$. H_1: $\mu_1 \neq \mu_2$; model: $Y_i = \mu_i + e$. 2. $df = 44$; $t_{.95} = 2.021$ (using $df = 40$). 3. a. $\hat{d} = 0.24$. b. $R^2 = .015$. c. $CI_{.95}$: $2.43 \pm 2.967 \times 2.021 = 2.43 \pm 6.00 = -3.57$ to 8.43. d. $t(44) = 0.82$. 4. With $\alpha = .05$, do not reject H_0.

Exercise 5 H_0: $\mu_1 = \mu_2$; model: $Y_i = \mu + e$. H_1: $\mu_1 \neq \mu_2$; model: $Y_i = \mu_i + e$. 2. $df = 42$; $t_{.95} = 2.021$ (using $df = 40$). 3. a. $\hat{d} = 0.89$. b. $R^2 = .17$. c. $CI_{.95}$: $17.50 \pm 5.95 \times 2.021 = 17.50 \pm 12.02 = 5.47$ to 29.53. d. $t(42) = 2.94$. 4. With $\alpha = .05$, reject H_0.

Exercise 6

Normal		Imagery
30	1	
98765	1	
433322111	2	4
9877666	2	566666899
4400	3	1123444
776	3	556666778
	4	113
	4	7

See Figure B.5.

1. H_0: $\mu_1 = \mu_2$; model: $Y_i = \mu + e$. H_1: $\mu_1 \neq \mu_2$; model: $Y_i = \mu_i + e$. 2. $df = 58$; $t_{.95} = 2.009$ (using $df = 50$). 3. a. $\hat{d} = 1.33$. b. $R^2 = .31$. c. $CI_{.95}$: $8.6 \pm 1.66 \times 2.009 = 8.6 \pm 3.33 = 5.27$ to 11.93. d. $t(58) = 5.18$. 4. With $\alpha = .05$, reject H_0.

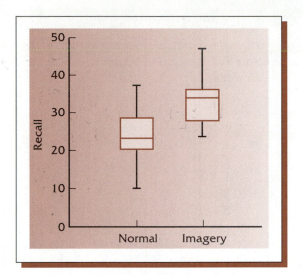

Figure B.5
Boxplots for Chapter 6, Exercise 6

Exercise 7 1. H_0: $\mu_1 = \mu_2$; model: $Y_i = \mu + e$. H_1: $\mu_1 \neq \mu_2$; model: $Y_i = \mu_i + e$. 2. $df = 34$; $t_{.95} = 2.032$. 3. a. $\hat{d} = 1.78$. b. $R^2 = .46$. c. $CI_{.95}$: $4.89 \pm 0.916 \times 2.032 = 4.89 \pm 1.86 = 3.03$ to 6.75. d. $t(34) = 5.34$. 4. With $\alpha = .05$, reject H_0.

Quiz 1. less precise, biased, natural, independent-groups, 28, Cohen's d, $\sqrt{2MS_e}/\sqrt{15}$, estimated standard error of the difference, t-distribution, 28, estimated standard error of the difference, rejected, .05, Type-1, Type-1, Type-2. **2.** F, T, F, T, F, T, F.

CHAPTER 7 Large Experiments with Independent Groups: Analysis of Variance

Section 7.1 Models for Experiments with More Than Two Conditions

Problem 1 a. $MS_e = 0.049$; $q = 3.40$. For $|\mu_1 - \mu_2|$, $CI_{.95} = .194 \pm .151$; for $|\mu_1 - \mu_3|$, $CI_{.95} = .214 \pm .151$; for $|\mu_2 - \mu_3|$, $CI_{.95} = .020 \pm .151$. b. HSD = .151. c. 1 and 2; 1 and 3.

Problem 2 a. $MS_e = 42.16$; $q = 3.40$. For $|\mu_1 - \mu_2|$, $CI_{.95} = 5.0 \pm 4.03$; for $|\mu_1 - \mu_3|$, $CI_{.95} = 4.3 \pm 4.03$; for $|\mu_2 - \mu_3|$, $CI_{.95} = 0.7 \pm 4.03$. b. HSD = 4.03. c. A and B; A and C.

Section 7.2 Evaluating the Null Model: Analysis of Variance

Problem 1 a. $\bar{Y} = .519$; $a_1 = -0.136$; $a_2 = +0.058$; $a_3 = +0.078$.

b.

Source	SS	df	MS
Model: Between conditions	0.699	2	0.350
Residual: Within conditions	3.526	72	0.049
Total	4.225	74	

c. $F = \dfrac{0.349}{0.049} = 7.12$. d. LSD $= 0.0626 \times 1.994 = 0.125$. Groups 1, 2 and 1, 3 differ; groups 2, 3 do not. e. $R^2 = \dfrac{0.699}{4.225} = .165$.

Problem 2 a. $\bar{Y} = 11.5$; $a_1 = +2.2$; $a_2 = +1.1$; $a_3 = -3.3$.

b.

Source	SS	df	MS
Model: Between conditions	360	2	180.0
Residual: Within conditions	512	60	8.5
Total	872	62	

c. $F = \dfrac{180.0}{8.5} = 21.2$. Reject H_0. d. LSD $= 0.9 \times 2.000 = 1.8$; A and C; B and C.

Section 7.3 Analysis of Variance of Factorial Designs

Problem 1 b.

	SS	df	MS	F	$F_{critical}$
Model					
Between conditions	815.4	5			
A	708.9	2	354.4	40.3	3.09
B	104.0	1	104.0	11.8	3.94
A × B	2.5	2	1.25	0.14	3.09
Residual					
Within conditions	843.4	96	8.79		
Total	1658.8	101			

c. $R^2 = 815.4/1658.8 = .49$. d. The interaction term should be dropped from the full model. e. Reject the hypothesis. The absence of an interaction indicates that the fast presentation rate influences all age groups equally.

Exercises

Exercise 1 a. $MS_e = 3.83$; $q = 3.44$; HSD $= 1.74$. The $1 condition differs from the other two, which themselves do not differ. b. $Y_i = \mu + \alpha_i + e$.

c.

Source	SS	df	MS
Model: Between conditions	38.98	2	19.49
Residual: Within conditions	160.93	42	3.83
Total	199.91	44	

$F(2, 42) = 19.49/3.83 = 5.09$; critical $F(2, 42) = 3.22$; hence $p < .05$. (d) $R^2 = .195$

Exercise 2 $Y_i = \mu + \alpha_i + e$.

Source	SS	df	MS
Model: Between conditions	195.52	2	97.76
Residual: Within conditions	364.96	45	8.11
Total	560.48	47	

$F(2, 45) = 97.76/8.11 = 12.05$; $p < .01$. c. LSD $= t(45) \times \sqrt{\dfrac{2MS_e}{n}} = 2.021 \times 1.01 = 2.04$ (using $df = 40$). The reward expected condition differs from the other two, which themselves do not differ. d. $R^2 = .349$.

Exercise 3 b.

	SS	df	MS	F	$F_{critical}$
Model:					
Between conditions:	313.28	5			
A	286.19	2	143.10	27.9	3.14
B	2.72	1	2.72	0.53	3.99
A × B	24.36	2	12.18	2.4	3.14
Residual:					
Within conditions	338.00	66	5.12		
Total	651.28	71			

Thus, the main effect for A should be retained in the model. c. $R^2 = 0.48$

Quiz wider, less, null, MS_{total}, MS_{within}, MS_{model}, $MS_{between}$, 44, 3, $MS_{between}$, MS_{within}, 2.82, factors, levels, between, additive, is not, nonparallel.

CHAPTER 8 Increasing the Precision of an Experiment

Section 8.1 Choosing an Appropriate Value of n in Two-Condition Experiments

Problem 1 a. $d = .66$; $n =$ approximately 30. b. From the table, d is between .90 ($n = 13$) and .95 ($n = 11$) giving a needed difference of somewhere in the range of 13.7 ($.90 \times 15.2$) and 14.5 ($.95 \times 15.2$).

Problem 2 a. $n = 2\mathrm{MS}_e \left(\dfrac{z}{w}\right)^2 = 2 \times 8.865 \times (1.96^2/1.5^2) = 30.27$. Use $n = 31$. b. The power of the t-test to detect a difference of 1.5 ($= w$) is $(1 - \beta) = .5$. c. $d = 1.5/\sqrt{8.865} = .5$; $n = 63$.

Problem 3 a. $d = 2.5/\sqrt{9.667} = .80$; $n = 25$. b. $d = 2.0/\sqrt{9.667} = .64$; $n = 25$; $1 - \beta = .6$.

Section 8.2 Reducing Residuals by Using Matched Pairs

Problem 1 a. (i) 10.46. (ii) -0.75. (iii) -0.96. (iv) $9.5 = 10.46 - 0.75 - 0.06 - 0.15$. b. $\mathbf{CI}_{.99} = 1.51 \pm \dfrac{1.433}{\sqrt{15}} \times t(14) = 1.51 \pm 0.37 \times 2.977 = 1.51 \pm 1.1$. Yes. c. $t = 4.08$. d. $F = t^2 = 16.65$. e. (i)

Source	SS	df	MS
Model	57.737	15	
Between conditions	17.025	1	17.025
Pairs	40.712	14	2.908
Residual	14.375	14	1.027
Total	72.112	29	

(ii) $F = 17.025/1.027 = 16.6$. (iii) critical $F = 8.86$ ($= 2.997^2$). (iv) $s_{\bar{D}} = \sqrt{\dfrac{2\mathrm{MS}_e}{n}} = \sqrt{\dfrac{2.06}{15}} = 0.37$. f. $R^2 = 57.737/72.375 = .80$. With blocking factor removed, R^2 $17.025/72.112 = .24$. g. Use MS_e or $s_{\bar{D}}$. Example 1 achieved greater precision.

Problem 2 $\mathbf{CI}_{.95} = 8.07 \pm 2.16 \times 1.155 = 5.6$ to 10.6. Thus 10 remains a plausible value.

Section 8.3 Matching and Within-Subjects Designs with More Than Two Conditions

Problem 1 a. $\mathrm{HSD} = 3.44 \times \sqrt{\dfrac{0.883}{25}} = 0.65$. For $|\mu_1 - \mu_2|$, $\mathbf{CI}_{.95} = 2.40 \pm 0.65$. For $|\mu_1 - \mu_3|$, $\mathbf{CI}_{.95} = 3.96 \pm 0.65$. For $|\mu_2 - \mu_3|$, $\mathbf{CI}_{.95} = 1.56 \pm 0.65$.

Source	SS	df	MS
Model	403.63	26	
Between conditions	198.96	2	99.48
Participants	204.67	24	8.53
Residuals	42.37	48	.88
Total	446.00	74	

c. $F = 113.05$; for $\alpha = .05$, $F(2,48) = 3.19$.

Problem 2 b. HSD $= 4.04 \times \sqrt{\dfrac{42.4}{12}} = 7.6$. c. The results are a simple demonstration of stimulus generalization in that the response rate drops the farther away from yellow is the condition.

Source	SS	df	MS
Model	6767	15	
Between conditions	3586	4	896.5
Participants	3181	11	289.2
Residuals	1866	44	42.4
Total	8633	59	

Exercises

Exercise 1 a. Within subjects. b. $CI_{.95} = 28.12 \pm 2.120 \times 5.702 = 28.12 \pm 12.09$. c. Yes.

Exercise 2 a. $t = 3.46$; reject H_0. b. $CI_{.95} = 18.5 \pm 2.060 \times 5.332 = 18.5 \pm 11.0$. c. Yes.

Exercise 3 a.

Source	SS	df	MS
Model	6193.6	22	
Between conditions	99.0	1	99.0
Pairs	6094.6	21	290.2
Residuals	2697.0	21	128.4
Total	8890.6	43	

b. For the conditions effect, $F < 1$; there is thus no evidence for a difference between viewing times. c. Estimated $d = 0.63$. From Table 8.4, $(1 - \beta)$ is between .8 and .9.

Exercise 4 a. $t = 6.1$. b. $CI_{.95} = 17.8 \pm 2.080 \times 2.92 = 17.8 \pm 6.07$.

Exercise 5 a.

Source	SS	df	MS
Model	17,482	20	
Between conditions	10,345	2	5,172.5
Blocks	7,137	18	396.5
Residuals	3,393	36	94.25
Total	20,875	56	

b. $F = 54.9$; $F(2,36)$ for $\alpha = .05$ is 3.26. Reject null hypothesis. c. HSD $= 3.49 \times \sqrt{\dfrac{94.25}{19}} = 7.8$ (using $df = 30$).

Quiz smaller, half-width, power, $1 - \beta$, sample size, smaller, an increase, residual, MS_e, blocks, matched, response measure, within, randomized block, conditions, randomly, MS_e, carryover effects, blocks/subjects, conditions, residual.

CHAPTER 9 Models for Quantitative Predictor Variables: Simple Linear Regression and Correlation

Section 9.1 Fundamentals of Regression and Correlation

Problem 1 a. The complete scatterplot is shown in Figure B.6. Check your figure against the plot for dosage = 12. b. -65.1, -1.7. c. a = 44.54, b = -2.24. d. See Figure B.6; -2.58, -3.62. e. Recall declines at the rate of 2.24% of words recalled per

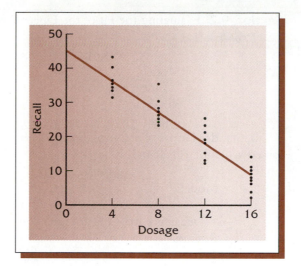

Figure B.6
Scatterplot for Section 9.1, Problem 1

milligrams of THC. f. s_b = 0.118, $t(46)$ = 2.021; **CI$_{.95}$** = −2.24 ± .24. Therefore reject the null hypothesis that β = 0.

Problem 2 a. $\overline{X}$ = 20; a = −2.283, b = 1.303. For X = 12, Y = 13.356; for X = 27, Y = 32.90. b. Over the range of 10 to 30 minutes, the number of words remembered increases by a constant amount (1.3 words) per minute study time.

Problem 3 b = 0.011, s_b = 0.018, $t(98)$ = 1.987; **CI$_{.95}$** = .011 ± .036. The data provide no evidence of a linear relationship between income and happiness.

Problem 4 a. Time = .383 × rating + .16. b. Rating = .726 × time + 11.94. c. See Figure B.7. d. s_b = .089; $t(48)$ = 2.021; **CI$_{.95}$** = .383 ± 2.021 × .089 = .383 ± .180. e. s_b = .169; $t(48)$ = 2.021; **CI$_{.95}$** = .726 ± 2.021 × .169 = .726 ± .342. f. The data support the claim that β is not zero—the claim that mother's looking time *is* influenced by her infant's rated attractiveness.

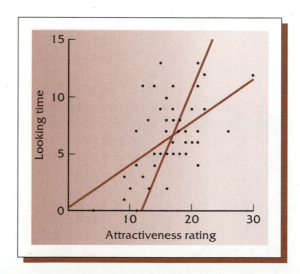

Figure B.7
Scatterplot for Section 9.1, Problem 4c

Section 9.2 Evaluating the Fit of the Linear Regression Model

Problem 1 a.

Source	SS	df	MS
Model:	4815	1	
Linear regression	4815	1	4815
Residual	615	46	13.4
Total	5430	47	

b. Standard error of estimate: 3.656. c. $F = 360.2$ — a value obviously larger than the tabled value for $F(1,46)$. d. $R^2 = .887$.

e.

Source	SS	df	MS
Model	4846	3	
Linear regression	4815	1	4815
Departure from linear regression	31	2	15.5
Residual	584	44	13.3
Total	5430	47	

The F-ratio for departure from linear regression is $15.5/13.3 = 1.17$, which is well below the value needed for significance; $F(2,44) = 3.21$ for $\alpha = .05$. Linear model is therefore appropriate.

Problem 2 a.

Source	SS	df	MS
Model	5157	4	
Linear regression	5096	1	5096
Departure from linear regression	61	3	20.3
Residual	1841	55	33.5
Total	6998	59	

The F-ratio for departure from linear regression is < 1.0. Linear model is therefore appropriate. b. The data support the total time hypothesis.

Problem 3 a.

Source	SS	df	MS
Model: Linear regression	5.3	1	5.3
Residual	1349.4	98	13.77
Total	1354.7	99	

b. The F-ratio for linear regression is < 1.0. The data do not support the hypothesis of a relationship between happiness and income. c. $R^2 = .004$.

Problem 4 a.

Source	SS	df	MS
Model: Linear regression	153.02	1	153.02
Residual	397.30	48	8.28
Total	550.32	49	

b. The F-ratio for linear regression is 18.5. The tabled value for $F(1,48)$ with $\alpha = .05$ is 4.04. Therefore, we reject the null hypothesis of zero effect. c. $R^2 = .278$.

d.

Source	SS	df	MS
Model: Linear regression	289.87	1	289.87
Residual	752.63	48	15.68
Total	1042.50	49	

e. $R^2 = .278$.

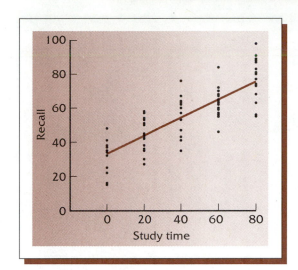

Figure B.8
Scatterplot for Chapter 9, Exercise 1e

Section 9.3 Correlation Coefficient

Problem 1 a. Product-moment correlation coefficient: $r = .527$. b. (i) $r = b \times \sqrt{\dfrac{SS_X}{SS_Y}}$, so $b = r \times \sqrt{\dfrac{SS_Y}{SS_X}} = .527 \times 0.727 = 0.383$. (ii) $r = b \times \sqrt{\dfrac{SS_Y}{SS_X}}$, so that $b = r \times \sqrt{\dfrac{SS_X}{SS_Y}} = .527 \times 1.376 = 0.725$.

Exercises

Exercise 1 a. $a = 33.2$; $b = .533$

b.

Source	SS	df	MS
Model: Linear regression	18,169	1	18,169
Residual	8,533	78	109.4
Total	26,702	79	

c. $s_b = 0.041$, $t(78) = 1.994$ (using $df = 70$); $CI_{.95} = .533 \pm .08$. d. $R^2 = .68$. e. See Figure B.8.

f.

Source	SS	df	MS
Model	18,335	4	
Linear regression	18,169	1	18,169
Departure from linear regression	166	3	55.3
Residual	8,367	75	111.56
Total	26,702	79	

The F-ratio for departure from linear regression is < 1.0. Linear model is therefore appropriate.

Exercise 2 T1: $r = .58$; T2: $r = .69$; T3: $r = .85$.

Exercise 3 a. $a = 17.2$, $b = .55$. b. $a = 11.7$; $b = .97$. c. See Figure B.9. d. $Y = 50.64$; $X = 60.85$.

e.

Source	SS	df	MS
Model: Linear regression	11,569	1	11,569
Residual	10,111	108	93.6
Total	21,680	109	

f. Standard error of estimate: 9.7. g. $F = 123.6$, obviously larger than the tabled value for $F(1,108)$.

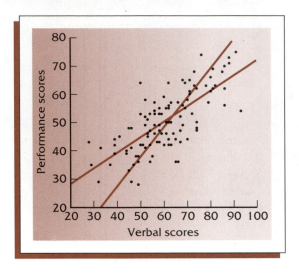

Figure B.9
Scatterplot for Chapter 9, Exercise 3

Source	SS	df	MS
Model: Linear regression	6,543	1	6,543
Residual	5,718	108	52.9
Total	12,261	109	

i. Standard error of estimate: 7.28. j. R^2 = .534, the product-moment correlation coefficient is .73. The assumption of linearity of regression.

Exercise 4 a. Verbal regressed on performance: a = 21.3; b = .32. b. Performance regressed on verbal: a = 23.1, b = .21. c. See Figure B.10.

d.

Source	SS	df	MS
Model: Linear regression	252.7	1	252.7
Residual	3559.5	98	36.3
Total	3812.2	99	

e. Standard error of estimate: 6.03. f. F = 6.96. This value is greater than the tabled value for $F(1,98)$ for α = .05.

g.

Source	SS	df	MS
Model: Linear regression	161.3	1	161.3
Residual	2272.7	98	23.2
Total	2434.0	99	

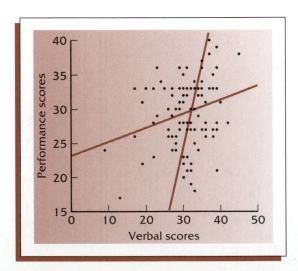

Figure B.10
Scatterplot for Chapter 9, Exercise 4c

h. Standard error of estimate: 4.8. i. $R^2 = .0.066$; the product-moment correlation coefficient is .257. j. Reduce it.

Exercise 5 a. $R^2 = .923$. The product-moment correlation coefficient is .961. b. The different results reflect the effects of different forms of selection: restriction of range (Exercise 4) and the artificial inflation of range (Exercise 5).

Quiz scatterplot, conditional distribution, marginal distribution, linear regression, conditional distributions, means, variances, homogeneity of variance, intercept, regression coefficient, sum of squared residuals, response variable, predictor variable, total, $SS_{regression}$, residuals, standard error of estimate, $MS_{regression}$, MS_e, $N - 2$, $SS_{regression}$, SS_{total}, product-moment correlation coefficient, underestimate, underestimate.

CHAPTER 10   Studies with Categorical Response Variables and Distribution-Free Methods of Analysis

Section 10.1   Count Data with a Single Basis or Classification: Goodness of Fit

Problem 1 $\chi^2 = 6.1$; $\chi^2(5)$ for $\alpha = .05$ is 11.07. Therefore there is no evidence of bias.

Problem 2 $\chi^2 = 3.676$; $\chi^2(3)$ for $\alpha = .05$ is 7.81. Therefore there is no evidence against the hypothesis of uniform distribution.

Problem 3 $\chi^2 = 9.9$; $\chi^2(2)$ for $\alpha = .05$ is 5.99. Therefore the hypothesis of uniform distribution is implausible; a response bias appears to exist.

Problem 4

Litter size after two weeks

	0	1	2	3	4	5	Total
f_0	4	5	13	19	50	9	100
f_e	.4	4.1	16.5	32.9	32.9	13.2	100

$\chi^2 = 49.4$; $\chi^2(5)$ for $\alpha = .05$ is 11.07. Therefore the hypothesis of a binomial distribution is implausible.

Section 10.2   Contingency Analysis: Count Data with Two Bases of Classification

Problem 1 $\chi^2 = 10.977$; $\chi^2(1)$ for $\alpha = .05$ is 3.84. Therefore there appears to be a contingency between gender of voter and candidate preference. $\phi = 0.23$.

Problem 2 $\chi^2 = 0.271$; $\chi^2(1)$ for $\alpha = .05$ is 3.84. Therefore there no evidence incubation.

Problem 3 $\chi^2 = 4.596$; $\phi = .214$. Reject the null hypothesis of independence.

Problem 4 a. $\chi^2 = 12.034$; $\phi = .370$. Reject the null hypothesis of independence. b. The memory training is more effective only if the problem is identical to the one originally learned.

Problem 5 $\chi^2 = 15.194$; $\phi_c = .386$. $\chi^2(2)$ for $\alpha = .05$ is 5.99. Reject the null hypothesis of independence. Yes.

Problem 6 $\chi^2 = 18.339$; $\phi_c = .451$. $\chi^2(2)$ for $\alpha = .05$ is 5.99. Reject the null hypothesis of independence. Yes

Problem 7 $\chi^2 = 10.8$; $\phi_c = .424$. $\chi^2(1)$ for $\alpha = .05$ is 3.84. Reject the null hypothesis of independence. Yes

		Group	
		Memory	Help
	Yes	3	16
Solution?			
	No	27	14

$\chi^2 = 13.017$; $\phi = .466$. $\chi^2(1)$ for $\alpha = .05$ is 3.84. Reject the null hypothesis of independence.

Exercises

Exercise 1 $\chi^2 = 7.68$; $\phi = .31$. $\chi^2(1)$ for $\alpha = .05$ is 3.84. Reject the null hypothesis of independence.

Exercise 2 $\chi^2 = 10.07$; $\phi_c = .305$. $\chi^2(2)$ for $\alpha = .05$ is 5.99. Reject the null hypothesis of independence.

Exercise 3 $\chi^2 = 7.03$; $\phi_c = .255$. $\chi^2(2)$ for $\alpha = .05$ is 5.99. Reject the null hypothesis of independence.

Exercise 4 $\chi^2 = 18.21$; $\phi_c = .436$. $\chi^2(2)$ for $\alpha = .05$ is 5.99. Reject the null hypothesis of independence.

Exercise 5 The assumption of independence has been violated. Each infant contributes to all categories of the predictor variable.

Quiz count, expected frequencies, residuals, observed frequencies, chi square, degrees of freedom, goodness of fit, contingency, phi coefficient, independent, nonparametric tests, ranks, parametric tests

CHAPTER 11 Review

Exercise 1 c. (i) Using the standard error of the mean, the error bars should extend $\sqrt{\dfrac{MS_e}{n}} = \sqrt{\dfrac{265}{23}} = 3.39$ above and below the top of each bar. (ii). $w = HSD = q \times \sqrt{\dfrac{MS_e}{n}} = 3.74 \times 3.39 = 12.7$ (using $df = 60$ as the closest lower value to 88).

Source	SS	df	MS	F-ratio
Between groups	37,085	3	12,361.9	46.6
Within groups	23,321	88	265.0	
Total	60,406	91		

The full model is required.

Exercise 2 The expected frequency is 24 in each cell. $\chi^2 = (15 - 24)^2/24 + (17 - 24)^2/24 + (40 - 24)^2/24 = 16.08$. $\chi^2(2) = 5.99$ for $\alpha = .05$. Thus, reject the null hypothesis.

Exercise 3 $s_{\bar{D}} = \dfrac{5.85}{\sqrt{20}} = 1.31$. $CI_{.95} = 7.5 \pm 1.31 \times 2.093 = 7.5 \pm 2.74 = 4.76$ to 10.24. Because this interval does not include zero, the null hypothesis can be rejected. An alternative method is to calculate a t-ratio. $t = \dfrac{7.5}{1.31} = 5.7$. For $\alpha = .05$, $t(19) = 2.093$, so reject the null hypothesis.

Exercise 4 Use $q(3,25) = 3.52$. $w = HSD = 3.52 \times 1.46 = 5.13$. $MS_{between\ groups} = 1144/2 = 572.0$; $MS_e = 892.6/28 = 31.88$; thus $F = 572.0/31.88 = 17.9$. For $\alpha = .05$, $F(2,28) = 3.34$, so reject the null hypothesis.

Exercise 5 Expected frequencies:

	High Stress	Low Stress
Infected	19.94	25.06
Not infected	15.06	18.94

Pearson chi-square $= 5.365$; $df = 1$. For $\alpha = .05$, $\chi^2(1) = 3.84$, so reject the null hypothesis.

Exercise 6 a. $w = HSD = q \times \sqrt{\dfrac{MS_e}{n}} = 3.44 \times \sqrt{\dfrac{7.07}{20}} = 3.44 \times 0.595 = 2.05$

(using $df = 40$ as the closest lower value to 57). Thus, as predicted, Group 3 differs from both Groups 1 and 2 but there is no evidence for a difference between Groups 1 and 2.

b. $w = HSD = q \times \sqrt{\dfrac{MS_e}{n}} = 3.44 \times \sqrt{\dfrac{4.11}{20}} = 3.44 \times 0.453 = 1.56$ (using $df = 40$ as the closest lower value to 57). Thus, as predicted by latent learning, Group 1 differs from both Groups 2 and 3 but there is no evidence for a difference between Groups 2 and 3.

Exercise 7 $r = \dfrac{SP_{XY}}{\sqrt{SS_X SS_Y}} = \dfrac{828.8}{\sqrt{839.0 \times 1248.6}} = .81$

Exercise 8

Source	SS	df	MS	F-ratio
Between groups	5802.0	2	2901.0	150
Within groups	1393.1	72	19.3	
Total	7195.1	74		

Fisher's $LSD = t(72) \times \sqrt{\dfrac{2MS_e}{n}} = 1.994 \times \sqrt{\dfrac{2 \times 19.3}{25}} = 2.48$. Thus all three groups differ from each other.

Exercise 9 Pearson's chi-square $= 26.9$. For $\alpha = .05$, $\chi^2(1) = 3.84$, so reject the null hypothesis.

Exercise 10 The standard error of the difference is $\sqrt{\dfrac{2MS_e}{n}} = \sqrt{\dfrac{2 \times 18.52}{24}} = 1.24$, giving $CI_{.95} = 9.75 \pm t(46) \times 1.242 = 9.75 \pm 2.021 \times 1.24 = 7.24$ to 12.26.

Exercise 11 $s_{\bar{D}} = \dfrac{4.86}{\sqrt{24}} = 0.99$. $CI_{.95} = 3.67 \pm 0.99 \times 2.069 = 3.67 \pm 2.05 = 1.62 - 5.72$. Because this interval does not include zero, the null hypothesis can be rejected. Amnesics show priming.

Exercise 12 The standard error of the difference is $\sqrt{\dfrac{2MS_e}{n}} = \sqrt{\dfrac{2 \times 15.305}{20}} = 1.24$, giving $CI_{.95} = 1.00 \pm t(38) \times 1.24 = 1.00 \pm 2.024 \times 1.24 = -1.51$ to 3.51.

Exercise 13 $b = \dfrac{SP_{XY}}{SS_X} = \dfrac{1137}{5763} = 0.20.$ $a = \overline{Y} - b\overline{X} = 41.4 - .20 \times 53.2 = 30.8$

Predicted height $= 30.8 + 0.20 \times$ age. Height is increasing at the rate of .2 inches per month, or 2.4 inches per year (point estimate) or between .12 and .27 inches per month (interval estimate).

Exercise 14 $r = \dfrac{SP_{XY}}{\sqrt{SS_X SS_Y}} = \dfrac{94.68}{\sqrt{236.32 \times 174.82}} = .466$

APPENDIX C

Statistical Tables[1]

[1] All tables were computed by the author.

STATISTICAL TABLE 1 Probabilities for the Normal Distribution

The table gives two probabilities for each value of z. The column headed $P(z)$ is the probability to the left of that z-score. The column headed $1 - P(z)$ is the area to the right of that z-score.

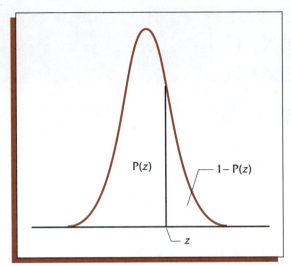

Only probabilities for positive values of z are tabled. Because of symmetry, negative values can be obtained from the same table. To obtain probabilities for negative values of z, simply treat the z-score as positive and reverse the columns. For example, to obtain probabilities for a z-score of -1.2, consult the table for $z = +1.2$, finding $P(z) = .8849$ and $1 - P(z) = .1151$. For $z = -1.2$ $P(z) = .1151$ and $1 - P(z) = .8849$. Remember, if z is positive then $P(z)$ must be greater than .5; if z is negative then $P(z)$ must be smaller than .5.

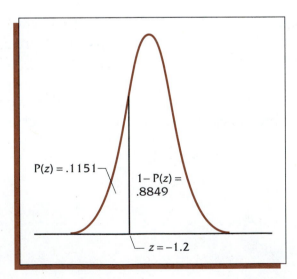

z	P(z)	1 − P(z)	z	P(z)	1 − P(z)	z	P(z)	1 − P(z)
0.00	.5000	.5000	0.50	.6915	.3085	1.00	.8413	.1587
0.01	.5040	.4960	0.51	.6950	.3050	1.01	.8438	.1562
0.02	.5080	.4920	0.52	.6985	.3015	1.02	.8461	.1539
0.03	.5120	.4880	0.53	.7019	.2981	1.03	.8485	.1515
0.04	.5160	.4840	0.54	.7054	.2946	1.04	.8508	.1492
0.05	.5199	.4801	0.55	.7088	.2912	1.05	.8531	.1469
0.06	.5239	.4761	0.56	.7123	.2877	1.06	.8554	.1446
0.07	.5279	.4721	0.57	.7157	.2843	1.07	.8577	.1423
0.08	.5319	.4681	0.58	.7190	.2810	1.08	.8599	.1401
0.09	.5359	.4641	0.59	.7224	.2776	1.09	.8621	.1379
0.10	.5398	.4602	0.60	.7257	.2743	1.10	.8643	.1357
0.11	.5438	.4562	0.61	.7291	.2709	1.11	.8665	.1335
0.12	.5478	.4522	0.62	.7324	.2676	1.12	.8686	.1314
0.13	.5517	.4483	0.63	.7357	.2643	1.13	.8708	.1292
0.14	.5557	.4443	0.64	.7389	.2611	1.14	.8729	.1271
0.15	.5596	.4404	0.65	.7422	.2578	1.15	.8749	.1251
0.16	.5636	.4364	0.66	.7454	.2546	1.16	.8770	.1230
0.17	.5675	.4325	0.67	.7486	.2514	1.17	.8790	.1210
0.18	.5714	.4286	0.68	.7517	.2483	1.18	.8810	.1190
0.19	.5753	.4247	0.69	.7549	.2451	1.19	.8830	.1170
0.20	.5793	.4207	0.70	.7580	.2420	1.20	.8849	.1151
0.21	.5832	.4168	0.71	.7611	.2389	1.21	.8869	.1131
0.22	.5871	.4129	0.72	.7642	.2358	1.22	.8888	.1112
0.23	.5910	.4090	0.73	.7673	.2327	1.23	.8907	.1093
0.24	.5948	.4052	0.74	.7704	.2296	1.24	.8925	.1075
0.25	.5987	.4013	0.75	.7734	.2266	1.25	.8944	.1056
0.26	.6026	.3974	0.76	.7764	.2236	1.26	.8962	.1038
0.27	.6064	.3936	0.77	.7794	.2206	1.27	.8980	.1020
0.28	.6103	.3897	0.78	.7823	.2177	1.28	.8997	.1003
0.29	.6141	.3859	0.79	.7852	.2148	1.29	.9015	.0985
0.30	.6179	.3821	0.80	.7881	.2119	1.30	.9032	.0968
0.31	.6217	.3783	0.81	.7910	.2090	1.31	.9049	.0951
0.32	.6255	.3745	0.82	.7939	.2061	1.32	.9066	.0934
0.33	.6293	.3707	0.83	.7967	.2033	1.33	.9082	.0918
0.34	.6331	.3669	0.84	.7995	.2005	1.34	.9099	.0901
0.35	.6368	.3632	0.85	.8023	.1977	1.35	.9115	.0885
0.36	.6406	.3594	0.86	.8051	.1949	1.36	.9131	.0869
0.37	.6443	.3557	0.87	.8078	.1922	1.37	.9147	.0853
0.38	.6480	.3520	0.88	.8106	.1894	1.38	.9162	.0838
0.39	.6517	.3483	0.89	.8133	.1867	1.39	.9177	.0823
0.40	.6554	.3446	0.90	.8159	.1841	1.40	.9192	.0808
0.41	.6591	.3409	0.91	.8186	.1814	1.41	.9207	.0793
0.42	.6628	.3372	0.92	.8212	.1788	1.42	.9222	.0778
0.43	.6664	.3336	0.93	.8238	.1762	1.43	.9236	.0764
0.44	.6700	.3300	0.94	.8264	.1736	1.44	.9251	.0749
0.45	.6736	.3264	0.95	.8289	.1711	1.45	.9265	.0735
0.46	.6772	.3228	0.96	.8315	.1685	1.46	.9279	.0721
0.47	.6808	.3192	0.97	.8340	.1660	1.47	.9292	.0708
0.48	.6844	.3156	0.98	.8365	.1635	1.48	.9306	.0694
0.49	.6879	.3121	0.99	.8389	.1611	1.49	.9319	.0681

z	P(z)	1 − P(z)	z	P(z)	1 − P(z)	z	P(z)	1 − P(z)
1.50	.9332	.0668	2.00	.9772	.0228	2.50	.9938	.0062
1.51	.9345	.0655	2.01	.9778	.0222	2.51	.9940	.0060
1.52	.9357	.0643	2.02	.9783	.0217	2.52	.9941	.0059
1.53	.9370	.0630	2.03	.9788	.0212	2.53	.9943	.0057
1.54	.9382	.0618	2.04	.9793	.0207	2.54	.9945	.0055
1.55	.9394	.0606	2.05	.9798	.0202	2.55	.9946	.0054
1.56	.9406	.0594	2.06	.9803	.0197	2.56	.9948	.0052
1.57	.9418	.0582	2.07	.9808	.0192	2.57	.9949	.0051
1.58	.9429	.0571	2.08	.9812	.0188	2.58	.9951	.0049
1.59	.9441	.0559	2.09	.9817	.0183	2.59	.9952	.0048
1.60	.9452	.0548	2.10	.9821	.0179	2.60	.9953	.0047
1.61	.9463	.0537	2.11	.9826	.0174	2.61	.9955	.0045
1.62	.9474	.0526	2.12	.9830	.0170	2.62	.9956	.0044
1.63	.9484	.0516	2.13	.9834	.0166	2.63	.9957	.0043
1.64	.9495	.0505	2.14	.9838	.0162	2.64	.9959	.0041
1.65	.9505	.0495	2.15	.9842	.0158	2.65	.9960	.0040
1.66	.9515	.0485	2.16	.9846	.0154	2.66	.9961	.0039
1.67	.9525	.0475	2.17	.9850	.0150	2.67	.9962	.0038
1.68	.9535	.0465	2.18	.9854	.0146	2.68	.9963	.0037
1.69	.9545	.0455	2.19	.9857	.0143	2.69	.9964	.0036
1.70	.9554	.0446	2.20	.9861	.0139	2.70	.9965	.0035
1.71	.9564	.0436	2.21	.9864	.0136	2.71	.9966	.0034
1.72	.9573	.0427	2.22	.9868	.0132	2.72	.9967	.0033
1.73	.9582	.0418	2.23	.9871	.0129	2.73	.9968	.0032
1.74	.9591	.0409	2.24	.9875	.0125	2.74	.9969	.0031
1.75	.9599	.0401	2.25	.9878	.0122	2.75	.9970	.0030
1.76	.9608	.0392	2.26	.9881	.0119	2.76	.9971	.0029
1.77	.9616	.0384	2.27	.9884	.0116	2.77	.9972	.0028
1.78	.9625	.0375	2.28	.9887	.0113	2.78	.9973	.0027
1.79	.9633	.0367	2.29	.9890	.0110	2.79	.9974	.0026
1.80	.9641	.0359	2.30	.9893	.0107	2.80	.9974	.0026
1.81	.9649	.0351	2.31	.9896	.0104	2.81	.9975	.0025
1.82	.9656	.0344	2.32	.9898	.0102	2.82	.9976	.0024
1.83	.9664	.0336	2.33	.9901	.0099	2.83	.9977	.0023
1.84	.9671	.0329	2.34	.9904	.0096	2.84	.9977	.0023
1.85	.9678	.0322	2.35	.9906	.0094	2.85	.9978	.0022
1.86	.9686	.0314	2.36	.9909	.0091	2.86	.9979	.0021
1.87	.9693	.0307	2.37	.9911	.0089	2.87	.9979	.0021
1.88	.9699	.0301	2.38	.9913	.0087	2.88	.9980	.0020
1.89	.9706	.0294	2.39	.9916	.0084	2.89	.9981	.0019
1.90	.9713	.0287	2.40	.9918	.0082	2.90	.9981	.0019
1.91	.9719	.0281	2.41	.9920	.0080	2.91	.9982	.0018
1.92	.9726	.0274	2.42	.9922	.0078	2.92	.9982	.0018
1.93	.9732	.0268	2.43	.9925	.0075	2.93	.9983	.0017
1.94	.9738	.0262	2.44	.9927	.0073	2.94	.9984	.0016
1.95	.9744	.0256	2.45	.9929	.0071	2.95	.9984	.0016
1.96	.9750	.0250	2.46	.9931	.0069	2.96	.9985	.0015
1.97	.9756	.0244	2.47	.9932	.0068	2.97	.9985	.0015
1.98	.9761	.0239	2.48	.9934	.0066	2.98	.9986	.0014
1.99	.9767	.0233	2.49	.9936	.0064	2.99	.9986	.0014

STATISTICAL TABLE 2   Probabilities for the Binomial Distribution

In these tables, p is the probability of the outcome on each trial and r is the number of times this outcome occurs in n trials. For example the tables give probabilities of obtaining r heads from n tosses of a coin which lands heads with a probability of p.

$n = 5$

r	¼	⅓	½	⅔	¾
			p		
0	.237	.132	.031	.004	.001
1	.396	.329	.156	.041	.015
2	.264	.329	.313	.165	.088
3	.088	.165	.313	.329	.264
4	.015	.041	.156	.329	.396
5	.001	.004	.031	.132	.237

$n = 6$

r	¼	⅓	½	⅔	¾
			p		
0	.178	.088	.016	.001	.000
1	.356	.263	.094	.016	.004
2	.297	.329	.234	.082	.033
3	.132	.219	.312	.219	.132
4	.033	.082	.234	.329	.297
5	.004	.016	.094	.263	.356
6	.000	.001	.016	.088	.178

$n = 7$

r	¼	⅓	½	⅔	¾
			p		
0	.133	.059	.008	.000	.000
1	.311	.205	.055	.006	.001
2	.311	.307	.164	.038	.012
3	.173	.256	.273	.128	.058
4	.058	.128	.273	.256	.173
5	.012	.038	.164	.307	.311
6	.001	.006	.055	.205	.311
7	.000	.000	.008	.059	.133

$n = 8$

r	¼	⅓	½	⅔	¾
			p		
0	.100	.039	.004	.000	.000
1	.267	.156	.031	.002	.000
2	.311	.273	.109	.017	.004
3	.208	.273	.219	.068	.023
4	.087	.171	.273	.171	.087
5	.023	.068	.219	.273	.208
6	.004	.017	.109	.273	.311
7	.000	.002	.031	.156	.267
8	.000	.000	.004	.039	.100

$n = 9$

r	¼	⅓	½	⅔	¾
			p		
0	.075	.026	.002	.000	.000
1	.225	.117	.018	.001	.000
2	.300	.234	.070	.007	.001
3	.234	.273	.164	.034	.009
4	.117	.205	.246	.102	.039
5	.039	.102	.246	.205	.117
6	.009	.034	.164	.273	.234
7	.001	.007	.070	.234	.300
8	.000	.001	.018	.117	.225
9	.000	.000	.002	.026	.075

$n = 10$

r	¼	⅓	½	⅔	¾
			p		
0	.056	.017	.001	.000	.000
1	.188	.087	.010	.000	.000
2	.282	.195	.044	.003	.000
3	.250	.260	.117	.016	.003
4	.146	.228	.205	.057	.016
5	.058	.137	.246	.137	.058
6	.016	.057	.205	.228	.146
7	.003	.016	.117	.260	.250
8	.000	.003	.044	.195	.282
9	.000	.000	.010	.087	.188
10	.000	.000	.001	.017	.056

STATISTICAL TABLE 3   Critical Values for the *t*-Distribution

df	PROPORTION IN TWO TAILS		
	0.10	0.05	0.01
1	6.314	12.706	63.657
2	2.920	4.303	9.925
3	2.353	3.182	5.841
4	2.132	2.776	4.604
5	2.015	2.571	4.032
6	1.943	2.447	3.707
7	1.895	2.365	3.499
8	1.860	2.306	3.355
9	1.833	2.262	3.250
10	1.812	2.228	3.169
11	1.796	2.201	3.106
12	1.782	2.179	3.055
13	1.771	2.160	3.012
14	1.761	2.145	2.977
15	1.753	2.131	2.947
16	1.746	2.120	2.921
17	1.740	2.110	2.898
18	1.734	2.101	2.878
19	1.729	2.093	2.861
20	1.725	2.086	2.845
21	1.721	2.080	2.831
22	1.717	2.074	2.819
23	1.714	2.069	2.807
24	1.711	2.064	2.797
25	1.708	2.060	2.787
26	1.706	2.056	2.779
27	1.703	2.052	2.771
28	1.701	2.048	2.763
29	1.699	2.045	2.756
30	1.697	2.042	2.750
31	1.696	2.040	2.744
32	1.694	2.037	2.738
33	1.692	2.035	2.733
34	1.691	2.032	2.728
35	1.690	2.030	2.724
36	1.688	2.028	2.719
37	1.687	2.026	2.715
38	1.686	2.024	2.712
39	1.685	2.023	2.708
40	1.684	2.021	2.704
50	1.676	2.009	2.678
60	1.671	2.000	2.660
70	1.667	1.994	2.648
80	1.664	1.990	2.639
90	1.662	1.987	2.632
100	1.660	1.984	2.626

Note: For *df* > 100 the normal distribution is a satisfactory approximation to the *t*-distribution.

STATISTICAL TABLE 4 Critical Values for the Studentized Range Statistic (q)

Lightface type indicates critical values of q for $\alpha = .05$; boldface indicates values for $\alpha = .01$.

df	k = NUMBER OF TREATMENTS						
	2	3	4	5	6	7	8
6	3.46	4.34	4.90	5.31	5.63	5.90	6.12
	5.27	**6.35**	**7.05**	**7.57**	**7.99**	**8.34**	**8.63**
7	3.35	4.17	4.68	5.06	5.36	5.61	5.82
	4.97	**5.93**	**6.56**	**7.02**	**7.39**	**7.69**	**7.95**
8	3.26	4.04	4.53	4.89	5.17	5.40	5.60
	4.76	**5.65**	**6.22**	**6.64**	**6.97**	**7.25**	**7.49**
9	3.20	3.95	4.42	4.76	5.03	5.25	5.43
	4.61	**5.44**	**5.97**	**6.36**	**6.67**	**6.92**	**7.14**
10	3.15	3.88	4.33	4.66	4.91	5.13	5.31
	4.49	**5.28**	**5.78**	**6.15**	**6.44**	**6.68**	**6.88**
11	3.11	3.82	4.26	4.58	4.82	5.03	5.20
	4.40	**5.16**	**5.63**	**5.98**	**6.25**	**6.48**	**6.68**
12	3.08	3.77	4.20	4.51	4.75	4.95	5.12
	4.33	**5.06**	**5.51**	**5.84**	**6.11**	**6.33**	**6.51**
13	3.06	3.74	4.15	4.45	4.69	4.89	5.05
	4.27	**4.97**	**5.41**	**5.73**	**5.99**	**6.20**	**6.38**
14	3.04	3.70	4.11	4.41	4.64	4.83	4.99
	4.22	**4.90**	**5.33**	**5.64**	**5.89**	**6.09**	**6.27**
15	3.02	3.68	4.08	4.37	4.60	4.78	4.94
	4.18	**4.84**	**5.26**	**5.56**	**5.80**	**6.00**	**6.17**
16	3.00	3.65	4.05	4.33	4.56	4.74	4.90
	4.14	**4.79**	**5.20**	**5.50**	**5.73**	**5.92**	**6.09**
17	2.99	3.63	4.02	4.30	4.52	4.71	4.86
	4.11	**4.75**	**5.15**	**5.44**	**5.66**	**5.85**	**6.01**
18	2.97	3.61	4.00	4.28	4.50	4.67	4.83
	4.08	**4.71**	**5.10**	**5.39**	**5.61**	**5.79**	**5.95**
19	2.96	3.59	3.98	4.25	4.47	4.65	4.80
	4.06	**4.68**	**5.06**	**5.34**	**5.56**	**5.74**	**5.89**
20	2.95	3.58	3.96	4.23	4.45	4.62	4.77
	4.03	**4.65**	**5.02**	**5.30**	**5.52**	**5.69**	**5.84**
25	2.91	3.52	3.89	4.15	4.36	4.53	4.67
	3.95	**4.53**	**4.89**	**5.15**	**5.35**	**5.52**	**5.66**
30	2.89	3.49	3.85	4.10	4.30	4.47	4.60
	3.90	**4.46**	**4.80**	**5.05**	**5.25**	**5.41**	**5.54**
40	2.86	3.44	3.79	4.04	4.23	4.39	4.52
	3.83	**4.37**	**4.70**	**4.94**	**5.12**	**5.27**	**5.40**
60	2.83	3.40	3.74	3.98	4.16	4.31	4.44
	3.77	**4.29**	**4.60**	**4.82**	**5.00**	**5.14**	**5.26**
120	2.80	3.36	3.69	3.92	4.10	4.24	4.36
	3.71	**4.20**	**4.50**	**4.71**	**4.88**	**5.01**	**5.12**

STATISTICAL TABLE 5   Critical Values for the *F*-Distribution

Lightface type indicates critical values for $\alpha = .05$; boldface indicates values for $\alpha = .01$.

df_2	1	2	3	4	5	6	7	8	9	10	11	12
6	5.99	5.14	4.76	4.53	4.39	4.28	4.21	4.15	4.10	4.06	4.03	4.00
	13.75	**10.92**	**9.78**	**9.15**	**8.75**	**8.47**	**8.26**	**8.10**	**7.98**	**7.87**	**7.79**	**7.72**
7	5.59	4.74	4.35	4.12	3.97	3.87	3.79	3.73	3.68	3.64	3.60	3.57
	12.25	**9.55**	**8.45**	**7.85**	**7.46**	**7.19**	**6.99**	**6.84**	**6.72**	**6.62**	**6.54**	**6.47**
8	5.32	4.46	4.07	3.84	3.69	3.58	3.50	3.44	3.39	3.35	3.31	3.28
	11.26	**8.65**	**7.59**	**7.01**	**6.63**	**6.37**	**6.18**	**6.03**	**5.91**	**5.81**	**5.73**	**5.67**
9	5.12	4.26	3.86	3.63	3.48	3.37	3.29	3.23	3.18	3.14	3.10	3.07
	10.56	**8.02**	**6.99**	**6.42**	**6.06**	**5.80**	**5.61**	**5.47**	**5.35**	**5.26**	**5.18**	**5.11**
10	4.96	4.10	3.71	3.48	3.33	3.22	3.14	3.07	3.02	2.98	2.94	2.91
	10.04	**7.56**	**6.55**	**5.99**	**5.64**	**5.39**	**5.20**	**5.06**	**4.94**	**4.85**	**4.77**	**4.71**
11	4.84	3.98	3.59	3.36	3.20	3.09	3.01	2.95	2.90	2.85	2.82	2.79
	9.65	**7.21**	**6.22**	**5.67**	**5.32**	**5.07**	**4.89**	**4.74**	**4.63**	**4.54**	**4.46**	**4.40**
12	4.75	3.89	3.49	3.26	3.11	3.00	2.91	2.85	2.80	2.75	2.72	2.69
	9.33	**6.93**	**5.95**	**5.41**	**5.06**	**4.82**	**4.64**	**4.50**	**4.39**	**4.30**	**4.22**	**4.16**
13	4.67	3.81	3.41	3.18	3.03	2.92	2.83	2.77	2.71	2.67	2.63	2.60
	9.07	**6.70**	**5.74**	**5.21**	**4.86**	**4.62**	**4.44**	**4.30**	**4.19**	**4.10**	**4.02**	**3.96**
14	4.60	3.74	3.34	3.11	2.96	2.85	2.76	2.70	2.65	2.60	2.57	2.53
	8.86	**6.51**	**5.56**	**5.04**	**4.69**	**4.46**	**4.28**	**4.14**	**4.03**	**3.94**	**3.86**	**3.80**
15	4.54	3.68	3.29	3.06	2.90	2.79	2.71	2.64	2.59	2.54	2.51	2.48
	8.68	**6.36**	**5.42**	**4.89**	**4.56**	**4.32**	**4.14**	**4.00**	**3.89**	**3.80**	**3.73**	**3.67**
16	4.49	3.63	3.24	3.01	2.85	2.74	2.66	2.59	2.54	2.49	2.46	2.42
	8.53	**6.23**	**5.29**	**4.77**	**4.44**	**4.20**	**4.03**	**3.89**	**3.78**	**3.69**	**3.62**	**3.55**
17	4.45	3.59	3.20	2.96	2.81	2.70	2.61	2.55	2.49	2.45	2.41	2.38
	8.40	**6.11**	**5.18**	**4.67**	**4.34**	**4.10**	**3.93**	**3.79**	**3.68**	**3.59**	**3.52**	**3.46**
18	4.41	3.55	3.16	2.93	2.77	2.66	2.58	2.51	2.46	2.41	2.37	2.34
	8.29	**6.01**	**5.09**	**4.58**	**4.25**	**4.01**	**3.84**	**3.71**	**3.60**	**3.51**	**3.43**	**3.37**
19	4.38	3.52	3.13	2.90	2.74	2.63	2.54	2.48	2.42	2.38	2.34	2.31
	8.18	**5.93**	**5.01**	**4.50**	**4.17**	**3.94**	**3.77**	**3.63**	**3.52**	**3.43**	**3.36**	**3.30**
20	4.35	3.49	3.10	2.87	2.71	2.60	2.51	2.45	2.39	2.35	2.31	2.28
	8.10	**5.85**	**4.94**	**4.43**	**4.10**	**3.87**	**3.70**	**3.56**	**3.46**	**3.37**	**3.29**	**3.23**
21	4.32	3.47	3.07	2.84	2.68	2.57	2.49	2.42	2.37	2.32	2.28	2.25
	8.02	**5.78**	**4.87**	**4.37**	**4.04**	**3.81**	**3.64**	**3.51**	**3.40**	**3.31**	**3.24**	**3.17**
22	4.30	3.44	3.05	2.82	2.66	2.55	2.46	2.40	2.34	2.30	2.26	2.23
	7.95	**5.72**	**4.82**	**4.31**	**3.99**	**3.76**	**3.59**	**3.45**	**3.35**	**3.26**	**3.18**	**3.12**
23	4.28	3.42	3.03	2.80	2.64	2.53	2.44	2.37	2.32	2.27	2.24	2.20
	7.88	**5.66**	**4.76**	**4.26**	**3.94**	**3.71**	**3.54**	**3.41**	**3.30**	**3.21**	**3.14**	**3.07**
24	4.26	3.40	3.01	2.78	2.62	2.51	2.42	2.36	2.30	2.25	2.22	2.18
	7.82	**5.61**	**4.72**	**4.22**	**3.90**	**3.67**	**3.50**	**3.36**	**3.26**	**3.17**	**3.09**	**3.03**
25	4.24	3.39	2.99	2.76	2.60	2.49	2.40	2.34	2.28	2.24	2.20	2.16
	7.77	**5.57**	**4.68**	**4.18**	**3.85**	**3.63**	**3.46**	**3.32**	**3.22**	**3.13**	**3.06**	**2.99**
26	4.23	3.37	2.98	2.74	2.59	2.47	2.39	2.32	2.27	2.22	2.18	2.15
	7.72	**5.53**	**4.64**	**4.14**	**3.82**	**3.59**	**3.42**	**3.29**	**3.18**	**3.09**	**3.02**	**2.96**

df_2	NUMERATOR DEGREES OF FREEDOM (df_1)											
	1	2	3	4	5	6	7	8	9	10	11	12
27	4.21	3.35	2.96	2.73	2.57	2.46	2.37	2.31	2.25	2.20	2.17	2.13
	7.68	**5.49**	**4.60**	**4.11**	**3.78**	**3.56**	**3.39**	**3.26**	**3.15**	**3.06**	**2.99**	**2.93**
28	4.20	3.34	2.95	2.71	2.56	2.45	2.36	2.29	2.24	2.19	2.15	2.12
	7.64	**5.45**	**4.57**	**4.07**	**3.75**	**3.53**	**3.36**	**3.23**	**3.12**	**3.03**	**2.96**	**2.90**
29	4.18	3.33	2.93	2.70	2.55	2.43	2.35	2.28	2.22	2.18	2.14	2.10
	7.60	**5.42**	**4.54**	**4.04**	**3.73**	**3.50**	**3.33**	**3.20**	**3.09**	**3.00**	**2.93**	**2.87**
30	4.17	3.32	2.92	2.69	2.53	2.42	2.33	2.27	2.21	2.16	2.13	2.09
	7.56	**5.39**	**4.51**	**4.02**	**3.70**	**3.47**	**3.30**	**3.17**	**3.07**	**2.98**	**2.91**	**2.84**
32	4.15	3.29	2.90	2.67	2.51	2.40	2.31	2.24	2.19	2.14	2.10	2.07
	7.50	**5.34**	**4.46**	**3.97**	**3.65**	**3.43**	**3.26**	**3.13**	**3.02**	**2.93**	**2.86**	**2.80**
34	4.13	3.28	2.88	2.65	2.49	2.38	2.29	2.23	2.17	2.12	2.08	2.05
	7.44	**5.29**	**4.42**	**3.93**	**3.61**	**3.39**	**3.22**	**3.09**	**2.98**	**2.89**	**2.82**	**2.76**
36	4.11	3.26	2.87	2.63	2.48	2.36	2.28	2.21	2.15	2.11	2.07	2.03
	7.40	**5.25**	**4.38**	**3.89**	**3.57**	**3.35**	**3.18**	**3.05**	**2.95**	**2.86**	**2.79**	**2.72**
38	4.10	3.24	2.85	2.62	2.46	2.35	2.26	2.19	2.14	2.09	2.05	2.02
	7.35	**5.21**	**4.34**	**3.86**	**3.54**	**3.32**	**3.15**	**3.02**	**2.92**	**2.83**	**2.75**	**2.69**
40	4.08	3.23	2.84	2.61	2.45	2.34	2.25	2.18	2.12	2.08	2.04	2.00
	7.31	**5.18**	**4.31**	**3.83**	**3.51**	**3.29**	**3.12**	**2.99**	**2.89**	**2.80**	**2.73**	**2.66**
42	4.07	3.22	2.83	2.59	2.44	2.32	2.24	2.17	2.11	2.06	2.03	1.99
	7.28	**5.15**	**4.29**	**3.80**	**3.49**	**3.27**	**3.10**	**2.97**	**2.86**	**2.78**	**2.70**	**2.64**
44	4.06	3.21	2.82	2.58	2.43	2.31	2.23	2.16	2.10	2.05	2.01	1.98
	7.25	**5.12**	**4.26**	**3.78**	**3.47**	**3.24**	**3.08**	**2.95**	**2.84**	**2.75**	**2.68**	**2.62**
46	4.05	3.20	2.81	2.57	2.42	2.30	2.22	2.15	2.09	2.04	2.00	1.97
	7.22	**5.10**	**4.24**	**3.76**	**3.44**	**3.22**	**3.06**	**2.93**	**2.82**	**2.73**	**2.66**	**2.60**
48	4.04	3.19	2.80	2.57	2.41	2.29	2.21	2.14	2.08	2.03	1.99	1.96
	7.19	**5.08**	**4.22**	**3.74**	**3.43**	**3.20**	**3.04**	**2.91**	**2.80**	**2.71**	**2.64**	**2.58**
50	4.03	3.18	2.79	2.56	2.40	2.29	2.20	2.13	2.07	2.03	1.99	1.95
	7.17	**5.06**	**4.20**	**3.72**	**3.41**	**3.19**	**3.02**	**2.89**	**2.78**	**2.70**	**2.63**	**2.56**
55	4.02	3.16	2.77	2.54	2.38	2.27	2.18	2.11	2.06	2.01	1.97	1.93
	7.12	**5.01**	**4.16**	**3.68**	**3.37**	**3.15**	**2.98**	**2.85**	**2.75**	**2.66**	**2.59**	**2.53**
60	4.00	3.15	2.76	2.53	2.37	2.25	2.17	2.10	2.04	1.99	1.95	1.92
	7.08	**4.98**	**4.13**	**3.65**	**3.34**	**3.12**	**2.95**	**2.82**	**2.72**	**2.63**	**2.56**	**2.50**
65	3.99	3.14	2.75	2.51	2.36	2.24	2.15	2.08	2.03	1.98	1.94	1.90
	7.04	**4.95**	**4.10**	**3.62**	**3.31**	**3.09**	**2.93**	**2.80**	**2.69**	**2.61**	**2.53**	**2.47**
70	3.98	3.13	2.74	2.50	2.35	2.23	2.14	2.07	2.02	1.97	1.93	1.89
	7.01	**4.92**	**4.07**	**3.60**	**3.29**	**3.07**	**2.91**	**2.78**	**2.67**	**2.59**	**2.51**	**2.45**
75	3.97	3.12	2.73	2.49	2.34	2.22	2.13	2.06	2.01	1.96	1.92	1.88
	6.99	**4.90**	**4.05**	**3.58**	**3.27**	**3.05**	**2.89**	**2.76**	**2.65**	**2.57**	**2.49**	**2.43**
80	3.96	3.11	2.72	2.49	2.33	2.21	2.13	2.06	2.00	1.95	1.91	1.88
	6.96	**4.88**	**4.04**	**3.56**	**3.26**	**3.04**	**2.87**	**2.74**	**2.64**	**2.55**	**2.48**	**2.42**
90	3.95	3.10	2.71	2.47	2.32	2.20	2.11	2.04	1.99	1.94	1.90	1.86
	6.93	**4.85**	**4.01**	**3.53**	**3.23**	**3.01**	**2.84**	**2.72**	**2.61**	**2.52**	**2.45**	**2.39**
100	3.94	3.09	2.70	2.46	2.31	2.19	2.10	2.03	1.97	1.93	1.89	1.85
	6.90	**4.82**	**3.98**	**3.51**	**3.21**	**2.99**	**2.82**	**2.69**	**2.59**	**2.50**	**2.43**	**2.37**

STATISTICAL TABLE 6   Critical Values for χ^2-Distribution

df	PROPORTION IN CRITICAL REGION		
	0.10	0.05	0.01
1	2.71	3.84	6.63
2	4.61	5.99	9.21
3	6.25	7.81	11.34
4	7.78	9.49	13.28
5	9.24	11.07	15.09
6	10.64	12.59	16.81
7	12.02	14.07	18.48
8	13.36	15.51	20.09
9	14.68	16.92	21.67
10	15.99	18.31	23.21
11	17.28	19.68	24.72
12	18.55	21.03	26.22
13	19.81	22.36	27.69
14	21.06	23.68	29.14
15	22.31	25.00	30.58
16	23.54	26.30	32.00
17	24.77	27.59	33.41
18	25.99	28.87	34.81
19	27.20	30.14	36.19
20	28.41	31.41	37.57
21	29.62	32.67	38.93
22	30.81	33.92	40.29
23	32.01	35.17	41.64
24	33.20	36.42	42.98
25	34.38	37.65	44.31
26	35.56	38.89	45.64
27	36.74	40.11	46.96
28	37.92	41.34	48.28
29	39.09	42.56	49.59
30	40.26	43.77	50.89
31	41.42	44.99	52.19
32	42.58	46.19	53.49
33	43.75	47.40	54.78
34	44.90	48.60	56.06
35	46.06	49.80	57.34
36	47.21	51.00	58.62
37	48.36	52.19	59.89
38	49.51	53.38	61.16
39	50.66	54.57	62.43
40	51.81	55.76	63.69
50	63.17	67.50	76.15
60	74.40	79.08	88.38
70	85.53	90.53	100.43
80	96.58	101.88	112.33
90	107.57	113.15	124.12
100	118.50	124.34	135.81
150	172.58	179.58	193.21
200	226.02	233.99	249.45

STATISTICAL TABLE 7 Sample Sizes Needed to Achieve a Specified Power $(1 - \beta)$ for Different Effect Sizes (d) in an Independent-Groups Design with Two Conditions.

EFFECT SIZE	POWER $(1 - \beta)$									
d	.1	.2	.3	.4	.5	.6	.7	.8	.9	.95
.15	41	112	184	259	342	436	549	698	934	1156
.20	24	63	104	146	193	245	309	393	526	650
.25	15	41	66	94	123	157	198	252	337	416
.30	11	28	46	65	86	109	138	175	234	289
.35	8	21	34	48	63	80	101	129	172	213
.40	6	16	26	37	49	62	78	99	132	163
.45	5	13	21	29	38	49	61	78	104	129
.50	4	11	17	24	31	40	50	63	85	104
.55	4	9	14	20	26	33	41	52	70	86
.60	3	7	12	17	22	28	35	44	59	73
.65	3	6	10	14	19	24	30	38	50	62
.70	2	6	9	12	16	20	26	33	43	54
.75	2	5	8	11	14	18	22	28	38	47
.80	2	4	7	10	13	16	20	25	33	41
.85	2	4	6	9	11	14	18	22	30	36
.90	2	4	6	8	10	13	16	20	26	33
.95	2	3	5	7	9	11	14	18	24	29
1.0	1	3	5	6	8	10	13	16	22	26

STATISTICAL TABLE 8 Sample Sizes Needed to Achieve a Specified Power $(1 - \beta)$ for Different Effect Sizes (d) in a Matched-Pair Design.

EFFECT SIZE	POWER $(1 - \beta)$									
d	.1	.2	.3	.4	.5	.6	.7	.8	.9	.95
.15	21	56	92	130	171	218	275	349	467	578
.20	12	32	52	73	97	123	155	197	263	325
.25	8	21	33	47	62	79	99	126	169	208
.30	6	14	23	33	43	55	69	88	117	145
.35	4	11	17	24	32	40	51	65	86	107
.40	3	8	13	19	25	31	39	50	66	82
.45	3	7	11	15	19	25	31	39	52	65
.50	2	6	9	12	16	20	25	32	43	52
.55	2	5	7	10	13	17	21	26	35	43
.60	2	4	6	9	11	14	18	22	30	37
.65	2	3	5	7	10	12	15	19	25	31
.70	1	3	5	6	8	10	13	17	22	27
.75	1	3	4	6	7	9	11	14	19	24
.80	1	2	4	5	7	8	10	13	17	21
.85	1	2	3	5	6	7	9	11	15	18
.90	1	2	3	4	5	7	8	10	13	17
.95	1	2	3	4	5	6	7	9	12	15
1.0	1	2	3	3	4	5	7	8	11	13

REFERENCES

Barrera, M. E., & Maurer, D. (1981a). The perception of facial expressions by the three-month-old. *Child Development, 52,* 203–206.

Barrera, M. E., & Maurer, D. (1981b). Recognition of mother's photographed face by the three-month-old infant. *Child Development, 52,* 714–716.

Berscheid, E., Dion, K., Walster, E., & Walster, G. W. (1971). Physical attractiveness and dating choice. *Journal of Experimental Social Psychology, 7,* 173–189.

Bouchard, T. J., Jr., & McGue, M. (1981). Familial studies of intelligence: A review. *Science, 212,* 1055–1059.

Bushnell, I. W. R., Sai, F., & Mullin, J. T. (1989). Neonatal recognition of the mother's face. *British Journal of Developmental Psychology, 7,* 3–15.

Cohen, J. (1962). The statistical power of abnormal-social psychological research: A review. *Journal of Abnormal and Social Psychology, 65,* 145–153.

Cohen, J. (1988). *Statistical power analysis for the behavioral sciences.* Hillsdale, NJ: Erlbaum.

Cohen, S., Tyrrell, D. A., & Smith, A. P. (1991). Psychological stress and susceptibility to the common cold. *The New England Journal of Medicine, 325,* 606–612.

Craik, F. I. M., & Tulving, E. (1975). Depth of processing and the retention of words in episodic memory. *Journal of Experimental Psychology: General, 1,* 268–294.

David, F. N. (1962). *Games, gods and gambling.* London: Charles Griffin.

Eich, J. E. (1980). The cue-dependent nature of state-dependent retrieval. *Memory & Cognition, 8,* 157–173.

Festinger, L., & Carlsmith, J. M. (1959). Cognitive consequences of forced compliance. *Journal of Abnormal and Social Psychology, 58,* 203–210.

Freedman, J. L., & Fraser, S. (1966). Compliance without pressure: The foot-in-the-door technique. *Journal of Personality and Social Psychology, 4,* 195–202.

Gigerenzer, G., Swijtink, Z., Porter, T., Daston, L., Beatty, J., & Krüger, L. (1989). *The empire of chance.* Cambridge: Cambridge University Press.

Howell, D. C. (1992). *Statistical methods for psychology.* Boston: PWS-Kent.

Jacklin, C. N., & Maccoby, E. E. (1978). Social behavior at 33 months in same-sex and mixed-sex dyads. *Child Development, 49,* 557–569.

Kahle, L. R. (1980). Stimulus condition self-selection by males in the interaction of locus of control and skill-chance situations. *Journal of Personality and Social Psychology, 38,* 50–56.

Kahneman, D., & Tversky, A. (1972). Subjective probability: A judgement of representativeness. *Cognitive Psychology, 3,* 430–454.

Kahneman, D., & Tversky, A. (1973). On the psychology of prediction. *Psychological Review, 80,* 237–251

Katona, G. (1940). *Organizing and memorizing.* New York: Columbia University Press.

Kellman, P. J., & Spelke, E. S. (1983). Perception of partially occluded objects in infancy. *Cognitive Psychology, 15,* 483–524.

Laird, J. D. (1974). Self-attribution and emotion: The effects of expressive behavior on the quality of emotional experience. *Journal of Personality and Social Psychology, 29,* 475–486.

Lehmann, D. R., & Nisbett, R. (1990). A longitudinal study of the effects of undergraduate education on reasoning. *Developmental Psychology, 16,* 592–960.

Lepper, M. R. (1973). Dissonance, self-perception, and honesty in children. *Journal of Personality and Social Psychology, 25,* 65–74.

Lepper, M. R., Greene, D., & Nisbett, R. E. (1973). Undermining children's intrinsic interest with extrinsic reward: A test of the "overjustification" hypothesis. *Journal of Personality and Social Psychology, 28,* 129–137.

Matarazzo, J. D. (1972). *Wechsler's measurement and appraisal of intelligence* (5th ed.). Baltimore, MD: Williams and Wilkins.

Meltzoff, A. N., & Borton, R. W. (1979). Intermodal matching by human neonates. *Nature, 282,* 403–404.

Miller, R. L., Brickman, P., & Bolen, D. (1975). Attribution versus persuasion as a means for modifying behavior. *Journal of Personality and Social Psychology, 31,* 430–441.

Moore, D. S., & McCabe, G. P. (1993). *Introduction to the practice of statistics.* New York: W. H. Freeman.

Nisbett, R., Krantz, D. H., Jepson, C., & Kunda, Z. (1983). The use of statistical heuristics in everyday inductive reasoning. *Psychological Review, 9,* 339–363.

Petty, R. E., Cacioppo, J. T., & Goldman, R. (1981). Personal involvement as a determinant of argument-based persuasion. *Journal of Personality and Social Psychology, 41,* 847–855.

Quattrone, A., & Jones, E. E. (1980). The perception of variability within in-groups and out-groups: Implications for the law of small numbers. *Journal of Personality and Social Psychology, 38,* 141–152.

Rosenblith, J. F. (1992). *In the beginning: Development from conception to age 2.* Newbury Park, CA: Sage.

Sedlmeier, P., & Gigerenzer, G. (1989). Do studies of statistical power have any effect on the power of studies? *Psychological Bulletin, 105,* 309–316.

Shepard, R. N., & Metzler, J. (1971). Mental rotation of three-dimensional objects. *Science, 171,* 701–703.

Stigler, S. M. (1986). *The history of statistics.* Cambridge, MA: Belknap Press.

Sulloway, F. J. (1996). Born to rebel: birth order, family dynamics, and creative lives. New York: Pantheon Books.

Tolman, E. C., & Honzik, C. H. (1930). Degrees of hunger, reward and non-reward, and maze learning in rats. *University of California Publications in Psychology, 4,* 241–256.

Tversky, A., & Kahneman, D. (1971). The belief in the "law of small numbers." *Psychological Bulletin, 76,* 105–110.

INDEX

Important Formulas

Sample statistics

$\text{Mean } \overline{Y} = \dfrac{\Sigma Y}{n}$

Sum of squares $SS = \Sigma(Y - \overline{Y})^2$

Variance $s^2 = \dfrac{SS}{n-1}$ $\qquad$ standard deviation $s = \sqrt{\dfrac{SS}{n-1}}$

Single means

	σ_Y known	σ estimated by s_Y
Standard score	$z = \dfrac{Y - \overline{Y}}{\sigma_Y}$	$z = \dfrac{Y - \overline{Y}}{s_Y}$
Standard error	$\sigma_{\overline{Y}} = \dfrac{\sigma_Y}{\sqrt{n}}$	$s_{\overline{Y}} = \dfrac{s_Y}{\sqrt{n}}$
Confidence interval	$\overline{Y} \pm z \times \sigma_{\overline{Y}}$	$\overline{Y} \pm t \times s_{\overline{Y}} (df = n - 1)$

For two independent conditions

$SS_e = SS_1 + SS_2$ $\qquad\qquad$ $MS_e = \dfrac{SS_e}{df}$

$df = 2(n-1)$ for equal n $\qquad$ $df = (n_1 - 1) + (n_2 - 1) = N - 2$ for unequal n

Effect size $\qquad \hat{d} = \dfrac{\overline{Y}_1 - \overline{Y}_2}{\sqrt{MS_e}}$

Standard error $\qquad s_{\overline{Y}_1 - \overline{Y}_2} = \sqrt{\dfrac{2MS_e}{n}}$ $\qquad t = \dfrac{(\overline{Y}_1 - \overline{Y}_2) - (\mu_1 - \mu_2)}{s_{\overline{Y}_1 - \overline{Y}_2}}$

Confidence interval $\qquad |\overline{Y}_1 - \overline{Y}_2| \pm t \times s_{\overline{Y}_1 - \overline{Y}_2}$ $\qquad$ t-ratio

For an experiment with *k* independent conditions

$SS_e = SS_1 + SS_2 + \ldots SS_k$ $\qquad\qquad$ $MS_e = MS_{within} = \dfrac{SS_e}{df}$

$df = k(n-1)$ for equal n $\qquad\qquad$ $df = N - k$ for unequal n

$SS_{model} = SS_{between} = SS_{total} - SS_e$ $\qquad$ $R^2 = \dfrac{SS_{model}}{SS_{total}}$

Tukey's HSD $= q \times \sqrt{\dfrac{MS_e}{n}}$ $\qquad$ Fisher's LSD $= t \times s_{\overline{Y}_i - \overline{Y}_j} = t \times \sqrt{\dfrac{2MS_e}{n}}$

$MS_{between} = \dfrac{SS_{between}}{(k-1)}$ $\qquad\qquad$ $F = \dfrac{MS_{between}}{MS_{within}}$